Tyndale Old Testament Commentaries

Volume 8

TOTC

1 and 2 Samuel

To Iain and Lynette Provan
in gratitude for many years of companionship,
collaboration, and counsel
'As iron sharpens iron, so one person sharpens another.'
(Proverbs 27:17)

Tyndale Old Testament Commentaries

Volume 8

Series Editor: David G. Firth
Consulting Editor: Tremper Longman III

---

1 and 2 Samuel

An Introduction and Commentary

V. Philips Long

ivp Academic
An imprint of InterVarsity Press
Downers Grove, Illinois

InterVarsity Press, USA
P.O. Box 1400
Downers Grove, IL 60515-1426, USA
ivpress.com
email@ivpress.com

Inter-Varsity Press, England
36 Causton Street
London SW1P 4ST, England
ivpbooks.com
ivp@ivpbooks.com

©2020 by V. Philips Long

V. Philips Long has asserted his right under the Copyright, Designs and Patents Act, 1988, to be identified as Author of this work.

All rights reserved. No part of this publication may be reproduced, stored in a retrieval system, or transmitted, in any form or by any means, electronic, mechanical, photocopying, recording or otherwise, without the prior permission of the publisher or the Copyright Licensing Agency.

InterVarsity Press®, USA, is the book-publishing division of InterVarsity Christian Fellowship/USA® and a member movement of the International Fellowship of Evangelical Students. Website: intervarsity.org.

Inter-Varsity Press, England, originated within the Inter-Varsity Fellowship, now the Universities and Colleges Christian Fellowship, a student movement connecting Christian Unions in universities and colleges throughout Great Britain, and a member movement of the International Fellowship of Evangelical Students. Website: www.uccf.org.uk.

Unless otherwise indicated, Scripture quotations are taken from the Holy Bible, New International Version (Anglicized edition). Copyright © 1979, 1984, 2011 by Biblica (formerly International Bible Society). Used by permission of Hodder & Stoughton Publishers, an Hachette UK company. All rights reserved. 'NIV' is a registered trademark of Biblica (formerly International Bible Society). UK trademark number 1448790.

First published 2020

USA ISBN 978-0-8308-4258-2 (print)
USA ISBN 978-0-8308-4809-6 (digital)

UK ISBN 978-1-78359-950-9 (print)
UK ISBN 978-1-78359-951-6 (digital)

Typeset in Great Britain by CRB Associates, Potterhanworth, Lincolnshire

Printed in the United States of America ∞

InterVarsity Press is committed to ecological stewardship and to the conservation of natural resources in all our operations. This book was printed using sustainably sourced paper.

Library of Congress Cataloging-in-Publication Data
A catalog record for this book is available from the Library of Congress.

British Library Cataloguing in Publication Data
A catalogue record for this book is available from the British Library.

P	21	20	19	18	17	16	15	14	13	12	11	10	9	8	7	6	5	4	3	2	1
Y	37	36	35	34	33	32	31	30	29	28	27	26	25	24	23	22	21	20			

CONTENTS

General preface — vii
Author's preface — ix
Abbreviations — xiii
Select bibliography — xix

Introduction — 1

1. The greatness of the book of Samuel — 1
2. The structure and storyline of the book of Samuel — 6
3. The character of the book of Samuel — 10
4. The characters in the book of Samuel — 13
5. The text — 23
6. Author and date — 25
7. Theological centre — 27

Analysis — 31

Commentary — 35

GENERAL PREFACE

The decision to completely revise the Tyndale Old Testament Commentaries is an indication of the important role that the series has played since its opening volumes were released in the mid-1960s. They represented at that time, and have continued to represent, commentary writing that was committed both to the importance of the text of the Bible as Scripture and a desire to engage with as full a range of interpretative issues as possible without being lost in the minutiae of scholarly debate. The commentaries aimed to explain the biblical text to a generation of readers confronting models of critical scholarship and new discoveries from the Ancient Near East while remembering that the Old Testament is not simply another text from the ancient world. Although no uniform process of exegesis was required, all the original contributors were united in their conviction that the Old Testament remains the word of God for us today. That the original volumes fulfilled this role is evident from the way in which they continue to be used in so many parts of the world.

A crucial element of the original series was that it should offer an up-to-date reading of the text, and it is precisely for this reason that new volumes are required. The questions confronting readers in the first half of the twenty-first century are not necessarily those from the second half of the twentieth. Discoveries from the Ancient Near East continue to shed new light on the Old Testament, whilst emphases in exegesis have changed markedly. Whilst remaining true to the goals of the initial volumes, the need for contemporary study of the text requires that the series as a whole be updated. This updating is not simply a matter of commissioning new volumes to replace the old. We have also taken the opportunity to update the format of the series to reflect a key emphasis from linguistics, which is that texts communicate in larger blocks rather than in shorter segments such as individual verses. Because of this, the treatment of each section of the text includes three segments. First, a short note on *Context* is offered, placing the passage under consideration in its literary setting within the book as well as noting any historical issues crucial to interpretation. The *Comment* segment then follows the traditional structure of the commentary, offering exegesis of the various components of a passage. Finally, a brief comment is made on *Meaning*, by which is meant the message that the passage seeks to communicate within the book, highlighting its key theological themes. This section brings together the detail of the *Comment* to show how the passage under consideration seeks to communicate as a whole.

Our prayer is that these new volumes will continue the rich heritage of the Tyndale Old Testament Commentaries and that they will continue to witness to the God who is made known in the text.

David G. Firth, Series Editor
Tremper Longman III, Consulting Editor

AUTHOR'S PREFACE

Stories are powerful, and true stories all the more so. Of the stories recounted in the Scriptures known to him, the apostle Paul writes: 'These things happened to them as examples and were written down as warnings for us, on whom the culmination of the ages has come' (1 Cor. 10:11); or again, 'everything that was written in the past was written to teach us, so that through the endurance taught in the Scriptures and the encouragement they provide we might have hope' (Rom. 15:4). The Scriptures known to Paul are today sometimes called the Hebrew Bible or the Old Testament. But the fact that the larger testament is called 'Old' must not be taken to suggest that it is somehow obsolete or irrelevant. 'May it never be,' Paul would likely say. Indeed, readers of the New Testament will not fully grasp what they read unless and until they are oriented by the antecedent Scripture that is the Old Testament.

My engagement with the books of Samuel began many decades ago, and with every re-reading, or every course or seminar taught, I see things that I had formerly missed. I learn things about God and about what it means to be human that I had not known so clearly before. Many people have helped further my journey of understanding. Other commentators have, of course, played a major role. Many of their names will appear in footnotes and in the bibliography in this volume. Whenever I remember learning something specific and distinctive from one or the other, I make every effort to credit them with the insight. I have made no attempt, however, to canvas exhaustively everything that others have said about the book of Samuel. I have chiefly sought to engage with the text directly, drawing in whatever secondary literature helps me discover answers to questions the texts raise. To those commentators whose distinctive insights I may have missed, or to those who may have anticipated me in an insight that I arrived at independently, I apologize in advance for failing to mention them.

Others who have played a major role in my own journey of understanding in the texts of Samuel are the students over the years who have done me the honour of engaging in courses or seminars focusing on some aspect of the book of Samuel. They are far too many to mention by name. But occasionally a name will appear in a footnote, as I have made a practice of jotting a note when a student draws my attention to something genuinely interesting in the text that I had not seen before. A particular note of gratitude is due to Teaching Assistants and Research Assistants who over the years have cheerfully and brilliantly completed tasks I assigned them. Alex Breitkopf, Josiah McDermott and Ben Tombs invested countless hours collecting and organizing a sizeable Samuel bibliography. Andrew Krause and Matt Lynch proved excellent researchers in seeking out information when I was writing a background commentary on 1 and 2 Samuel (which appeared in 2009 and to which reference is regularly made in the present work). I had the privilege of serving as advisor for James Rutherford's ThM thesis on the book of Samuel and learned from his keen insights. Others who have contributed in one way or another are Mark Arnold, Joshua Coutts, Sarah Steele and Rachel Wilkowski. A special note of thanks goes to Avery Choi, who in recent months read the entire manuscript thoroughly, checking for accuracy and helping me to avoid not a few mistakes.

The format of the present commentary is explained in the 'General preface', but let me mention a few more specifics. When referring to distances, I speak of miles 'as the crow flies'. Actual travel routes would be longer, sometimes significantly longer. In referring to texts and versions, I use the standard abbreviations, but it is worth noting that 'NIV' indicates the 2011 edition; the 1984 edition is indicated when it is cited. It is the NIV that I have chosen as the base English text for this commentary, though the commentary itself is based on careful study of the original Hebrew and, when needed, of the ancient versions. The Hebrew text of the book of Samuel often involves text-critical questions. Where a textual issue is present, but its resolution is either quite straightforward or exegetically inconsequential, I have chosen for the most part not to comment, as space simply does not allow. Considered as one book, 1 and 2 Samuel is almost the longest book in the Old Testament, eclipsed by only a little more than a thousand words by 1 and 2 Kings. For more detailed discussion of textual issues, the reader may consult the commentaries by, for example, Firth, McCarter, Tsumura and (succinctly) Gordon. Amongst commentators on Samuel, none has instructed and inspired me more than Robert Gordon, not least because it was under his guidance as my doctoral supervisor at Cambridge that my early forays into Samuel scholarship were made. His example of devotion and scholarly excellence continues to inspire me to this day.

As David could not have accomplished what he did without the support of his 'mighty men', so the present work would not have come to be without the support of various women and men. Amongst these are the members of the board of trustees at Regent College, who have granted me several sabbaticals to pursue this project. My colleagues on Regent's faculty have been a particular encouragement, through their numerous conversations, through the inspiration of their own work and through the occasional flyfishing adventure. Simply put, they have been good friends, 'mighty men and women'. My best friend for almost a half-century has been my wife, Polly, and I can no longer even imagine life without her. The grace and blessing that she has brought to our life together cannot begin to be described (especially given my word limit!). Many of my greatest joys are the human beings Polly and I together have the privilege of calling our children, our in-laws and our grandchildren. Their willingness to sacrifice time with Pops, so that he could put in some extra work hours, has not gone unnoticed. Three of our parents are now with the Lord, but to all four we owe a debt of gratitude for the prayers that went up for me as I worked on this project.

I would be remiss not to mention also the expert counsel and unstinting encouragement that I have received from the series editor David Firth and from Philip Duce of Inter-Varsity Press.

Thank you for your patience and understanding and for the efforts and expertise of many at IVP in bringing this book to completion.

Finally, in the life of David we see a deeply flawed man for whom Yahweh was nevertheless central to all of life. My prayer is that through our study of 1 and 2 Samuel, Yahweh will become ever more central in my life and in the lives of all who seek to follow him.

V. Philips Long, PhD Cantab
Professor Emeritus, Regent College

ABBREVIATIONS

ABD	D. N. Freedman et al. (eds.), *The Anchor Bible Dictionary*, 6 vols. (New York: Doubleday, 1992)
ACCS	T. C. Oden (ed.), *The Ancient Christian Commentary on Scripture*, 29 vols. (Downers Grove: IVP Academic, 2014)
ANE	Ancient Near East
ANES	*Ancient Near Eastern Studies*
ANET	James B. Pritchard (ed.), *Ancient Near Eastern Texts Relating to the Old Testament*, 3rd edn (Princeton: Princeton University Press, 1969)
Ant.	Josephus, *Antiquities of the Jews*
ARI	A. K. Grayson, *Assyrian Royal Inscriptions*, 2 vols. (Wiesbaden: Otto Harrassowitz, 1976)
AUSS	*Andrews University Seminary Studies*
BAR	*Biblical Archaeology Review*
BASOR	*Bulletin of the American Schools of Oriental Research*
BBR	*Bulletin for Biblical Research*
BDB	F. Brown, S. R. Driver and C. A. Briggs, *A Hebrew and English Lexicon of the Old Testament* (Oxford: Clarendon, 1906)
BEvT	*Beiträge zur evangelischen Theologie*
Bib	*Biblica*
BibInt	*Biblical Interpretation*
BJRL	*Bulletin of the John Ryland Library*
BJS	Brown Judaic Studies

BRev	*Bible Review*
BT	*The Bible Translator*
BWANT	Beiträge zur Wissenschaft vom Alten und Neuen Testament
CBQ	*Catholic Biblical Quarterly*
ConBOT	Coniectanea Biblica: Old Testament Series
COS	W. W. Hallo and K. L. Younger Jr. (eds.), *The Context of Scripture*, 3 vols. (Leiden: Brill, 1997)
CTAT	D. Barthélemy, *Critique textuelle de l'Ancien Testament*, 5 vols. (Göttingen: Vandenhoeck & Ruprecht, 1982)
CTJ	*Calvin Theological Journal*
DBI	L. Ryken, J. C. Wilhoit and T. Longman III (eds.), *Dictionary of Biblical Imagery: An Encyclopedic Exploration of the Images, Symbols, Motifs, Metaphors, Figures of Speech and Literary Patterns of the Bible* (Downers Grove: InterVarsity Press; Leicester: Inter-Varsity Press, 1998)
DCH	D. J. A. Clines (ed.), *Dictionary of Classical Hebrew*, 8 vols. (Sheffield: Sheffield Phoenix, 1993–2011)
DJD	Discoveries in the Judaean Desert
EA	El-Amarna tablets
EBC	The Expositor's Bible Commentary
ECC	The Eerdmans Critical Commentary
ExpTim	*Expository Times*
GKC	F. Gesenius, E. Kautzsch and A. E. Cowley, *Gesenius' Hebrew Grammar*, 2nd revised English edn (Oxford: Clarendon Press, 1910)
HALOT	L. Koehler et al., *The Hebrew and Aramaic Lexicon of the Old Testament*, trans. and ed. M. E. J. Richardson, 2 vols. (Leiden: Brill 2011)
HS	*Hebrew Studies*
HSM	Harvard Semitic Monographs
IBS	*Irish Biblical Studies*
IMAJ	*Israel Medical Association Journal*
Int	*Interpretation*
JANES	*Journal of the Ancient Near Eastern Society*
JBL	*Journal of Biblical Literature*

JET	*Jahrbuch für Evangelische Theologie*
JETS	*Journal of the Evangelical Theological Society*
JHS	*Journal of Hebrew Scriptures*
JNES	*Journal of Near Eastern Studies*
JSOT	*Journal for the Study of the Old Testament*
JSOTS	Journal for the Study of the Old Testament Supplement
KAI	*Kanaanäische und aramäische Inschriften*, 3 vols. (Wiesbaden: O. Harrassowitz, 1962–4)
KAT	Kommentar zum Alten Testament
KHC	Kürzer Hand-Commentar
KM	John R. Kohlenberger III and William D. Mounce (eds.), *Kohlenberger/Mounce Concise Hebrew–Aramaic Dictionary of the Old Testament*, Accordance edn, version 3.1 (OakTree Software, Inc., 2012)
LEH	J. Lust, E. Eynikel and K. Hauspie (eds.), *A Greek–English Lexicon of the Septuagint* (Stuttgart: Deutsche Bibelgesellschaft, 2003)
LHBOTS	Library of Hebrew Bible/Old Testament Studies
NAC	New American Commentary
NEA	*Near Eastern Archaeology*
NIB	The New Interpreter's Bible
NICOT	New International Commentary on the Old Testament
NIDOTTE	Willem A. VanGemeren (ed.), *New International Dictionary of Old Testament Theology and Exegesis*, 5 vols. (Grand Rapids: Zondervan; Carlisle: Paternoster, 1997)
NPNF 1	P. Schaff (ed.), *Nicene and Post-Nicene Fathers*, Series 1 (Edinburgh: T&T Clark, n.d.)
OBO	Orbis biblicus et orientalis
OTE	*Old Testament Essays*
OTL	Old Testament Library
OtSt	Oudtestamentische Studiën
PaVi	*Parole di Vita*
RIMB	The Royal Inscriptions of Mesopotamia, Babylonian Periods
SAAS	State Archives of Assyria Studies

SBET	*Scottish Bulletin of Evangelical Theology*
SBLDS	Society of Biblical Literature Dissertation Series
ScrB	*Scripture Bulletin*
SJOT	*Scandinavian Journal of the Old Testament*
SOTSM	Society for Old Testament Study Monographs
TDOT	G. Johannes Botterweck and Helmer Ringgren (eds.), *Theological Dictionary of the Old Testament*, trans. John T. Willis et al., 8 vols. (Grand Rapids: Eerdmans, 1974–2006)
TLOT	E. Jenni (ed.), with assistance from C. Westermann, *Theological Lexicon of the Old Testament*, trans. M. E. Biddle, 3 vols. (Peabody: Hendrickson, 1997)
TOTC	Tyndale Old Testament Commentaries
TWOT	R. L. Harris, G. L. Archer and B. K. Waltke (eds.), *Theological Wordbook of the Old Testament* (Chicago: Moody, 1980)
TynBul	*Tyndale Bulletin*
VT	*Vetus Testamentum*
VTSup	Vetus Testamentum Supplements
WBC	Word Biblical Commentary
ZABR	*Zeitschrift für altorientalische und biblische Rechtsgeschichte*
ZAW	*Zeitschrift für die alttestamentliche Wissenschaft*

Texts and versions

4QSam[a]	Texts of Samuel from Qumran Cave 4
ESV	The ESV Bible (The Holy Bible, English Standard Version), copyright © 2001 by Crossway, a publishing ministry of Good News Publishers. Used by permission. All rights reserved.
JPS	Jewish Publication Society Tanakh (1985)
KJV	The Authorized Version of the Bible (The King James Bible), the rights in which are vested in the Crown, reproduced by permission of the Crown's Patentee, Cambridge University Press.
LXX	The Septuagint

ABBREVIATIONS

MSG	***THE MESSAGE.*** Copyright © by Eugene H. Peterson 1993, 1994, 1995, 1996, 2000, 2001, 2002. Used by permission of NavPress Publishing Group.
MT	The Masoretic Text
NASB	THE NEW AMERICAN STANDARD BIBLE®, Copyright © 1960, 1962, 1963, 1968, 1971, 1972, 1973, 1975, 1977, 1995 by The Lockman Foundation. Used by permission.
NET	The NET Bible, New English Translation, copyright © 1996 by Biblical Studies Press, LLC. NET Bible is a registered trademark.
NETS	A New English Translation of the Septuagint, © 2007 by the International Organization for Septuagint and Cognate Studies, Inc. Used by permission of Oxford University Press. All rights reserved.
NIV	The Holy Bible, New International Version (Anglicized edition). Copyright © 1979, 1984, 2011 by Biblica. Used by permission of Hodder & Stoughton Ltd, an Hachette UK company. All rights reserved. 'NIV' is a registered trademark of Biblica. UK trademark number 1448790.
NIV 1984	The HOLY BIBLE, NEW INTERNATIONAL VERSION. Copyright © 1973, 1978, 1984 by International Bible Society. Used by permission of Hodder & Stoughton Publishers, a member of the Hachette UK Group. All rights reserved. 'NIV' is a registered trademark of International Bible Society. UK trademark number 1448790.
NKJV	The New King James Version. Copyright © 1982 by Thomas Nelson, Inc. Used by permission. All rights reserved.
NLT	The *Holy Bible*, New Living Translation, copyright © 1996. Used by permission of Tyndale House Publishers, Inc., Carol Stream, Illinois 60189, USA. All rights reserved.
NRSV	The New Revised Standard Version of the Bible, Anglicized Edition, copyright © 1989, 1995 by the

	Division of Christian Education of the National Council of the Churches of Christ in the USA. Used by permission. All rights reserved.
RSV	The Revised Standard Version of the Bible, copyright © 1946, 1952 and 1971 by the Division of Christian Education of the National Council of the Churches of Christ in the USA. Used by permission. All rights reserved.
Syr.	Syriac
Targ.	Targum
Vulg.	Vulgate

SELECT BIBLIOGRAPHY

Ackroyd, P. R. (1971), *The First Book of Samuel*, Cambridge Bible Commentary on the New English Bible (Cambridge: Cambridge University Press).
—— (1977), *The Second Book of Samuel*, Cambridge Bible Commentary on the New English Bible (Cambridge: Cambridge University Press).
Adams, D. L. (2010), 'Between Socoh and Azekah: The Role of the Elah Valley in Biblical History and the Identification of Khirbet Qeiyafa', in Y. Garfinkel and S. Ganor (eds.), *Khirbet Qeiyafa*, vol. 1: *Excavation Report for 2007–2008* (Jerusalem: Israel Exploration Society), pp. 47–66.
Aharoni, Y. (1979), *The Land of the Bible: A Historical Geography*, trans. A. F. Rainey (rev. and enlarged edn; Philadelphia: Westminster).
Alonso Schökel, L. (1985), 'Of Methods and Models', *VTSup* 36: 3–13.
Alter, R. (1981), *The Art of Biblical Narrative* (London: George Allen & Unwin; New York: Basic Books).
—— (1991), *The World of Biblical Literature* (New York: Basic Books).
—— (1999), *The David Story: A Translation and Commentary of 1 and 2 Samuel* (New York/London: W. W. Norton and Co.).
Althan, R. (1981), '1 Sam 13,1: A Poetic Couplet', *Biblica* 62: 241–246.
Anderson, A. A. (1989), *2 Samuel*, WBC 11 (Grand Rapids: Zondervan).

Armerding, C. E. (1975), 'Were David's Sons Really Priests?', in G. F. Hawthorne (ed.), *Current Issues in Biblical and Patristic Interpretation: Studies in Honor of Merrill C. Tenney Presented by His Former Students* (Grand Rapids: Eerdmans), pp. 75–86.

Arnold, P. M., S.J. (1990), *Gibeah: The Search for a Biblical City* (Sheffield: JSOT).

Asmussen, H. (1938), *Das erste Samuelisbuch* (Munich: Kaiser).

Aster, S. Z. (2003), 'What Was Doeg the Edomite's Title? Textual Emendation versus a Comparative Approach to 1 Samuel 21:8', *JBL* 122 (2): 353–361.

Auld, A. G. (2006), 'Exegetical Notes on I Samuel 2:18–20, 26: "Now Samuel Continued to Grow"', *ExpTim* 118: 87–88.

Aurelius, E. (2002), 'Wie David ursprünglich zu Saul kam (1 Sam 17)', in C. Bultmann, W. Dietrich and C. Levin (eds.), *Vergegenwärtigung des Alten Testaments* (Göttingen: Vandenhoeck & Ruprecht), pp. 44–68.

Avioz, M. (2005), 'Could Saul Rule Forever? A New Look at 1 Samuel 13:13–14', *JHS* 5: 1–9 (online numbering).

—— (2011), 'The Names Mephibosheth and Ishbosheth Reconsidered', *JANES* 32: 11–20.

—— (2013), 'The Literary Structure of the Books of Samuel: Setting the Stage for a Coherent Reading', *Currents in Biblical Research* 16 (1): 8–33.

Bailey, R. C. (1990), *David in Love and War: The Pursuit of Power in 2 Samuel 10–12* (Sheffield: Sheffield Academic Press).

Baldwin, J. G. (1988), *1 & 2 Samuel: An Introduction and Commentary*, TOTC (Leicester: Inter-Varsity Press).

Bar-Efrat, S. (1989), *Narrative Art in the Bible,* trans. D. Shefer-Vanson (Sheffield: Almond).

—— (1996), *1 and 2 Samuel: With Introduction and Commentary* (in Hebrew) (Tel Aviv: Am Oved).

Barnett, R. D. (1990), 'Six Fingers and Toes: Polydactylism in the Ancient World', *BAR* 16 (May/June): 46–51.

Barr, J. (1969), 'The Symbolism of Names in the Old Testament', *BJRL* 52: 11–29.

Barthélemy, D. (1982), *Critique textuelle de l'Ancien Testament*, 5 vols., OBO 50/1 (Göttingen: Vandenhoeck & Ruprecht).

SELECT BIBLIOGRAPHY

Barthélemy, D., D. W. Gooding, J. Lust and E. Tov (1986), *The Story of David and Goliath: Textual and Literary Criticism: Papers of a Joint Research Venture*, OBO 73 (Fribourg: Éditions Universitaires).

Begg, C. T. (1999), 'King Saul's First Sin According to Josephus', *Antonianum* 74: 685–696.

—— (2005), *Judean Antiquities Books 5–7*, vol. 4 of *Flavius Josephus: Translation and Commentary*, ed. S. Mason (Leiden: Brill).

Beitzel, B. J. (1985), *The Moody Atlas of Bible Lands* (Chicago: Moody).

Ben-Barak, Z. (1981), 'Meribaal and the System of Land Grants in Ancient Israel', *Bib* 62 (1): 73–91.

Bergen, R. D. (1996), *1, 2 Samuel*, NAC (Nashville: Broadman & Holman).

Berginer, V. M. (2000), 'Neurological Aspects of the David–Goliath Battle: Restriction in the Giant's Visual Field', *IMAJ* 2: 725–727.

Berlin, A. (1983), *Poetics and Interpretation of Biblical Narrative* (Sheffield: Almond Press).

Beuken, W. A. M. (1978), '1 Samuel 28: The Prophet as "Hammer of Witches"', *JSOT* 6: 3–17.

Beyerlin, W. (ed.) (1978), *Near Eastern Religious Texts Relating to the Old Testament*, OTL (London: SCM).

Birch, B. C. (1975), 'The Choosing of Saul at Mizpah', *CBQ* 37: 447–457.

—— (1976), *The Rise of the Israelite Monarchy: The Growth and Development of I Samuel 7–15*, SBLDS 27 (Missoula: Scholars Press).

—— (1998), 'The First and Second Books of Samuel', in L. E. Keck (ed.), *The New Interpreter's Bible*, vol. 2 (Nashville: Abingdon), pp. 949–1383.

Blenkinsopp, J. (1964), 'Jonathan's Sacrilege, 1 Sam 14,1–46: A Study in Literary History', *CBQ* 26: 423–449.

Block, D. I. (2009), 'Judges', in J. H. Walton (ed.), *Zondervan Illustrated Bible Backgrounds Commentary: Old Testament*, vol. 2 (Grand Rapids: Zondervan), pp. 94–241.

Bodner, K. (2004), *Power Play: A Primer on the Second Book of Samuel* (Toronto: Clements).

―― (2008), *1 Samuel: A Narrative Commentary* (Sheffield: Sheffield Phoenix Press).

Bodner, K., and E. White (2014), 'Some Advantages of Recycling: The Jacob Cycle in a Later Environment', *BibInt* 22: 20–33.

Bosworth, D. A. (2011), 'Faith and Resilience: King David's Reaction to the Death of Bathsheba's Firstborn', *CBQ* 73: 691–701.

Botterweck, G. J., H. Ringgren and H.-J. Fabry (eds.) (1974), *Theological Dictionary of the Old Testament* (Grand Rapids/Cambridge: Eerdmans).

Braun, R. L. (1997), '1 Chronicles 1–9 and the Reconstruction of the History of Israel: Thoughts on the Use of Genealogical Data in Chronicles in the Reconstruction of the History of Israel', in M. P. Graham, K. G. Hoglund and S. L. McKenzie (eds.), *The Chronicler as Historian* (Sheffield: JSOT Press), pp. 92–105.

Brettler, M. Z. (1997), 'The Composition of 1 Samuel 1–2', *JBL* 116: 601–612.

Bright, J. (2000), *A History of Israel*, 4th edn, with an Introduction and Appendix by William P. Brown (Louisville: Westminster John Knox Press).

Brueggemann, W. (1990), *First and Second Samuel*, Interpretation (Louisville: John Knox).

Buber, M. (1956), 'Die Erzählung von Sauls Königswahl', *VT* 6: 113–173.

Budde, K. D. (1902), *Die Bücher Samuel*, KHC 8 (Tübingen: J. C. B. Mohr).

Cahill, J. (2004), 'Jerusalem in David and Solomon's Time', *BAR* 30 (6): 20–31, 62.

Carlson, R. A. (1964), *David, the Chosen King: A Traditio-Historical Approach to the Second Book of Samuel* (Stockholm: Almqvist och Wiksell).

Chavalas, M. (2018), 'Did Abraham Ride a Camel?', *BAR* 44 (6): 52, 64–65.

Childs, B. S. (1979), *Introduction to the Old Testament as Scripture* (Philadelphia: Fortress).

Cohen, C., and V. M. Berginer (2006), 'The Nature of Goliath's Visual Disorder and the Actual Role of His Personal Bodyguard: [*nōśē' haṣṣinnâ*] (1 Sam 17:7, 41)', *ANES* 43: 27–44.

Cohen, M. (ed.) (1995), *Samuel 1 & 2*, Mikra'ot Gedolot Haketer (Ramat Gan: Bar Ilan University Press).

Cole, R. (2015), 'Food and Wine as Seductress to Doom, Even If the Sleeping Is with One's Own Wife! A Translation Note on 2 Samuel 11:8b', *BT* 66 (1): 106–110.

Collins, C. J. (2000), *'Miqreh* in 1 Samuel 6:9: "Chance" or "Event"?', *BT* 51 (1): 144–147.

The Committee on Translations of the United Bible Societies (1972), *Fauna and Flora of the Bible* (London: United Bible Societies).

Corti, G. (2001), 'L'unzione di David (1 Am 16, 1–13)', *PaVi* 46: 16–20.

Cross, F. M. (1973), *Canaanite Myth and Hebrew Epic* (Cambridge: Harvard University Press).

Cross, F. M., D. W. Parry, R. J. Saley and E. Ulrich (2005), *Qumran Cave 4.XII (1–2 Samuel)*, DJD 17 (Oxford: Clarendon Press).

Dalley, S. (2000), 'Ancient Mesopotamian Military Organization,' in J. M. Sasson (ed.), *Civilizations of the Ancient Near East* (Peabody: Hendrickson), pp. 413–422.

Davidson, R. M. (2007), *Flame of Yahweh: Sexuality in the Old Testament* (Peabody: Hendrickson).

de Vaux, R. (1959), 'Les combats singuliers dans l'Ancien Testament', *Bib* 40: 495–508.

—— (1961), *Ancient Israel*, 2 vols. (New York: McGraw-Hill).

—— (1972), 'Single Combat in the Old Testament', in *The Bible and the Ancient Near East* (London: Darton, Longman & Todd), pp. 122–135.

Deem, A. (1978), '". . . And the Stone Sank into His Forehead": A Note on 1 Samuel XVII 49', *VT* 28: 349–351.

DeRouchie, J. S. (2014), 'The Heart of YHWH and His Chosen One in 1 Samuel 13:14', *BBR* 24 (4): 467–489.

Dever, W. G. (1997), 'Ashdod', in E. M. Meyers (ed.), *The Oxford Encyclopedia of Archaeology in the Near East*, vol. 1 (Oxford/New York: Oxford University Press), pp. 219–220.

Dhorme, E. (1910), *Les Livres de Samuel* (Paris: J. Gabalda).

Dietrich, W. (2007), *The Early Monarchy in Israel: The Tenth Century B.C.E.*, trans. J. Vette (Atlanta: Society of Biblical Literature).

Dillard, R. (1985), 'David's Census: Perspectives on 2 Samuel 24 and 1 Chronicles 21', in W. R. Godfrey and J. L. Boyd (eds.), *Through Christ's Word: A Festschrift for Dr. Philip E. Hughes* (Phillipsburg: Presbyterian & Reformed), pp. 94–107.

Dorsey, D. A. (1991), *The Roads and Highways of Ancient Israel*, ASOR Library of Biblical and Near Eastern Archaeology (Baltimore/London: Johns Hopkins University Press).

Driver, S. R. (1960), *Notes on the Hebrew Text and Topography of the Books of Samuel*, 2nd edn (orig. 1913; Oxford: Clarendon).

Eberhart, C. (2002), 'Beobachtungen zum Verbrennungsritus bei Schlachtopfer und Gemeinshafts-Schlactopfer', *Bib* 83: 88–96.

Edelman, D. V. (1984), 'Saul's Rescue of Jabesh-Gilead (1 Sam 11:1–11): Sorting Story from History', *ZAW* 96: 195–209.

—— (1991), *King Saul in the Historiography of Judah* (Sheffield: JSOT Press).

—— (1992a), 'Abinadab (Person)', *ABD* 1: 22–23.

—— (1992b), 'Jabesh-Gilead (Place)', *ABD* 3: 594–595.

Elgavish, D. (2002), 'The Division of the Spoils of War in the Bible and in the Ancient Near East', *ZABR* 8: 242–273.

Eph'al, I. (1983), 'On Warfare and Military Control in the Ancient Near Eastern Empires: A Research Outline', in H. Tadmor and M. Weinfeld (eds.), *History, Historiography and Interpretation: Studies in Biblical and Cuneiform Literature* (Jerusalem: Magnes), 88–106.

Eslinger, L. M. (1985), *Kingship of God in Crisis: A Closer Reading of 1 Samuel 1–12* (Sheffield: JSOT).

Firth, D. G. (2008), 'David and Uriah (With an Occasional Appearance by Uriah's Wife): Reading and Re-reading 2 Samuel 11', *OTE* 21: 310–328.

—— (2009), *1 & 2 Samuel*, Apollos Old Testament Commentary 8 (Nottingham: Apollos; Downers Grove: InterVarsity Press).

—— (2013), *1 and 2 Samuel: A Kingdom Comes*, Phoenix Guides to the Old Testament 9 (Sheffield: Sheffield Phoenix Press).

Fishbane, M. (1982), 'I Samuel 3: Historical Narrative and Narrative Poetics,' in K. R. R. Gros Louis and J. S. Ackerman (eds.), *Literary Interpretations of Biblical Narratives*, vol. 2 (Nashville: Abingdon), pp. 191–203.

Fokkelman, J. P. (1981–93), *Narrative Art and Poetry in the Books of Samuel: A Full Interpretation Based on Stylistic and Structural Analyses*, 4 vols. (Assen: Van Gorcum).
—— (1999), *Reading Biblical Narrative: An Introductory Guide*, trans. I. Smit (Louisville: Westminster John Knox).
Fontaine, C. R. (2007), '"Be Men, O Philistines" (1 Samuel 4:9): Iconographic Representations and Reflections on Female Gender as Disability in the Ancient World', in H. Avalos, J. Melcher and J. Schipper (eds.), *This Abled Body* (Atlanta: Society of Biblical Literature), pp. 61–72.
Foster, B. R. (2005), *Before the Muses: An Anthology of Akkadian Literature*, 3rd edn (Bethesda: CDL Press).
Frame, G. (1995), *Rulers of Babylonia: From the Second Dynasty of Isin to the End of Assyrian Domination (1157–612 BC)*, RIMB 2 (Toronto: University of Toronto).
Friedman, R. E. (1992), 'Tabernacle', *ABD* 6: 292–300.
Frisch, A. (2004), '"And David Perceived" (2 Samuel 5,12): A Direct Insight into David's Soul and Its Meaning in Context', *SJOT* 18: 77–92.
Frolov, S. (2007), 'The Semiotics of Covert Action in 1 Samuel 9:1 – 10:16', *JSOT* 31: 429–450.
—— (2011), '1 Samuel 1–8: The Prophet as Agent Provocateur', in L. L. Grabbe and M. Nissinen (eds.), *Constructs of Prophecy in the Former and Latter Prophets and Other Texts* (Atlanta: SBL), pp. 77–85.
Garsiel, M. (1980), 'The Battle of Michmash: An Historical-Literary Study (1 Sam. 13–14) [Hebrew]', in M. Goshen-Gottstein and U. Simon (eds.), *Studies in Bible and Exegesis: Arie Toeg in Memoriam* (Ramat-Gan: Bar-Ilan University Press), pp. 15–50.
—— (1991), *Biblical Names: A Literary Study of Midrashic Derivations and Puns*, trans. P. Hackett (Ramat Gan: Bar-Ilan University).
—— (1993), 'The Story of David and Bathsheba: A Different Approach', *CBQ* 55: 244–262.
—— (2000), 'David's Warfare against the Philistines in the Vicinity of Jerusalem (2 Sam 5,17–25; 1 Chron 14,8–16)', in G. Galil and M. Weinfeld (eds.), *Studies in Historical Geography and Biblical Historiography* (Leiden: Brill), pp. 150–164.

—— (2010), 'The Book of Samuel: Its Composition, Structure and Significance as a Historical Source', *The Journal of Hebrew Scriptures* 10 (5): 2–42.

—— (2011), 'David's Elite Warriors and Their Exploits in the Books of Samuel and Chronicles', *JHS* 11: 2–28 (online numbering).

George, M. (2002), 'Yahweh's Own Heart', *CBQ* 64: 442–459.

Ginzberg, L. (1956), *Legends of the Jews*, 7 vols. (Philadelphia: Jewish Publication Society).

Golani, S. J. (2015), 'Three Oppressors and Four Saviors: The Three-Four Pattern and the List of Saviors in 1 Sam 12,9–11', *ZAW* 127 (2): 294–303.

Gooding, D. W. (1982), 'The Composition of the Book of Judges', *Eretz-Israel* 16: 70–79.

Gordon, R. P. (1980), 'David's Rise and Saul's Demise: Narrative Analogy in 1 Samuel 24-26', *TynBul* 31: 37–64.

—— (1984), *1 & 2 Samuel*, Old Testament Guides, ed. R. N. Whybray (Sheffield: JSOT Press).

—— (1986), *I & II Samuel: A Commentary*, Library of Biblical Interpretation (Grand Rapids: Regency Reference Library).

—— (1988), 'Simplicity of the Highest Cunning: Narrative Art in the Old Testament', *SBET* 6: 69–80.

—— (1994), 'Who Made the Kingmaker? Reflections on Samuel and the Institution of the Monarchy', in A. R. Millard, J. K. Hoffmeier and D. W. Baker (eds.), *Faith, Tradition and History* (Winona Lake: Eisenbrauns), pp. 255–269.

—— (2006), *Hebrew Bible and Ancient Versions: Selected Essays of Robert P. Gordon,* SOTSM (Farnham: Ashgate).

Graham, M. P., K. G. Hoglund and S. L. McKenzie (eds.) (1997), *The Chronicler as Historian*, JSOTS 238 (Sheffield: JSOT Press).

Grayson, A. K. (1976), *Assyrian Royal Inscriptions*, 2 vols. (Wiesbaden: Otto Harrassowitz).

Green, A. R. W. (2003), *The Storm-God in the Ancient Near East* (Winona Lake: Eisenbrauns).

Greenwood, K. R. (2010), 'Labor Pains: The Relationship between David's Census and Corvée Labor', *BBR* 20 (4): 467–478.

Gruber, M. I. (2000), 'Private Life in Canaan and Ancient Israel', in J. M. Sasson (ed.), *Civilizations of the Ancient Near East* (Peabody: Hendrickson), 633–648.

Guggenheimer, H. W. (2005), *Seder Olam Rabbah: The Rabbinic View of Biblical Chronology* (Lanham: Rowman & Littlefield).

Gunn, D. M. (1978), *The Story of King David: Genre and Interpretation* (Sheffield: JSOT Press).

—— (1980), *The Fate of King Saul: An Interpretation of a Biblical Story*, JSOTS 14 (Sheffield: JSOT Press).

Gutbrod, K. (1956), *Das Buch vom König: Das erste Buch Samuel* (Stuttgart: Calwer Verlag).

Hahn, C. (2011), 'The Understanding of the Nazirite Vow', in G. J. Wenham, A. Lo and J. A. Grant (eds.), *A God of Faithfulness: Essays in Honour of J. Gordon McConville on His 60th Birthday* (New York/London: T&T Clark), pp. 46–60.

Halpern, B. (1981a), 'The Uneasy Compromise: Israel between League and Monarchy', in B. Halpern and J. D. Levenson (eds.), *Traditions in Transformation: Turning Points in Biblical Faith* (Winona Lake: Eisenbrauns), pp. 59–96.

—— (1981b), *The Constitution of the Monarchy in Israel*, HSM 25 (Chico: Scholars Press).

—— (2001), *David's Secret Demons: Messiah, Murderer, Traitor, King* (Grand Rapids: Eerdmans).

—— (2010), '"Paths of Glory", Shame and Guilt: The Uriah Story as the Hinge of Fate', in C. Schäfer-Lichtenberger (ed.), *Die Samuelbücher und die Deuteronomisten* (Stuttgart: Kohlhammer), pp. 76–91.

Hamilton, J. M. (1992), 'Kiriath-Jearim (Place)', *ABD* 4: 84–85.

Hamori, E. J. (2010), 'The Spirit of Falsehood', *CBQ* 17: 15–30.

Hertzberg, H. W. (1964), *I & II Samuel*, OTL (Philadelphia: Westminster).

Herzog, C., and M. Gichon (1997), *Battles of the Bible*, 2nd edn (New York: Random House).

Hilber, J. W. (2009), 'Psalms', in J. H. Walton (ed.), *Zondervan Illustrated Bible Backgrounds Commentary: Old Testament*, vol. 5 (Grand Rapids: Zondervan), pp. 316–463.

Hill, A. (1987), 'A Jonadab Connection in the Absalom Conspiracy?', *JETS* 30 (4): 387–390.

—— (2006), 'On David's "Taking" and "Leaving" Concubines (2 Samuel 5:13; 15:16)', *JBL* 125 (1): 129–139.

Hoffmeier, J. K. (2011), 'David's Triumph over Goliath: 1 Samuel 17:54 and Ancient Near Eastern Analogues', in S. Bar (ed.), *Egypt, Canaan and Israel* (Boston: Brill), pp. 87–113.

Hoffner, H. A., Jr. (1968), 'A Hittite Analogue to the David and Goliath Contest of Champions', *CBQ* 30: 220–225.

Holloway, S. W. (1987), 'Distaff, Crutch or Chain Gang: The Curse of the House of Joab in 2 Samuel III 29', *VT* 37 (3): 370–375.

Honeyman, A. M. (1948), 'The Evidence for Regnal Names among the Hebrews', *JBL* 67 (1): 13–25.

Horner, T. (1978), *Jonathan Loved David: Homosexuality in Biblical Times* (Philadelphia: Westminster).

Humphreys, C. J. (1998), 'The Number of People in the Exodus from Egypt: Decoding Mathematically the Very Large Numbers in Numbers I and XXVI', *VT* 48 (2): 196–213.

Humphreys, W. L. (1978), 'The Tragedy of King Saul: A Study of the Structure of 1 Samuel 9–31', *JSOT* 6: 18–27.

Hurvitz, A. (1982), 'The History of a Legal Formula: כֹּל אֲשֶׁר־חָפֵץ עָשָׂה (Psalm 115:3; 135:6)', *VT* 32: 257–267.

Ishida, T. (1977), *The Royal Dynasties in Ancient Israel: A Study on the Formation and Development of Royal-Dynastic Ideology* (Berlin: Walter de Gruyter).

Jackson, F., and K. Lake (1933), *The Beginnings of Christianity*, vol. 4 (London: Macmillan).

Janzen, D. (2012), 'The Condemnation of David's "Taking" in 2 Samuel 12:1–14', *JBL* 131: 209–220.

Jastrow, M. (1903), *A Dictionary of the Targumim, the Talmud Babli and Yerushalmi, and the Midrashic Literature* (New York: Pardes).

Jenni, E. (1968), *Das hebräische Pi'el: Syntaktisch-semasiologische Untersuchung einer Verbalform im Alten Testament* (Zurich: EVZ-Verlag).

Jenni, E., and C. Westermann (eds.) (1997), *Theological Lexicon of the Old Testament*, 3 vols. (Peabody: Hendrickson).

Jobling, D. (1976), 'Saul's Fall and Jonathan's Rise: Tradition and Redaction in 1 Sam 14:1–46', *JBL* 95: 367–376.

Johnson, B. J. M. (2012a), 'Reconsidering 4QSam^a and the Textual Support for the Long and Short Versions of the David and Goliath Story', *VT* 52: 534–549.

—— (2012b), 'The Heart of YHWH's Chosen One in 1 Samuel', *JBL* 131: 455–466.

—— (2013), 'Did David Bring a Gun to a Knife Fight? Literary and Historical Considerations in Interpreting David's Victory over Goliath', *ExpTim* 124 (11): 530–537.

Johnston, S. I. (ed.) (2004), *Religions of the Ancient World: A Guide* (Cambridge: Belknap Press of the Harvard University Press).

Joo, S. (2010), '"Trembled Like Him": Reassessment of 1 Sam 13,7b', *Bib* 91: 433–440.

Joüon, P., and T. Muraoka (1996), *A Grammar of Biblical Hebrew*, Subsidia Biblica 14/1–14/2 (Rome: Pontificio Istituto Biblico).

Keil, C. F., and F. Delitzsch (1996), *Commentary on the Old Testament*, 10 vols. (Peabody: Hendrickson).

Kellermann, D. (1990), 'Die Geschichte von David und Goliath im Lichte der Endokrinologie', *ZAW* 102: 344–357.

Kiel, Y. (1981), ספר שמואל (שמואל א). Jerusalem: Mosad Hrav Kook.

Kim, H. C. P., and M. F. Nyengele (2003), 'Murder S/he Wrote? A Cultural and Psychological Reading of 2 Samuel 11–12', in C. A. Kirk-Dugan (ed.), *Pregnant Passion* (Atlanta: Society of Biblical Literature), pp. 95–116.

King, P. J., and L. E. Stager (2001), *Life in Biblical Israel*, Library of Ancient Israel, ed. D. A. Knight (Louisville: Westminster John Knox).

Kirkpatrick, A. F. (1886), *The Second Book of Samuel, with Maps, Notes and Introduction* (Cambridge: Cambridge University Press).

—— (1919), *The First Book of Samuel, with Map, Notes and Introduction* (Cambridge: Cambridge University Press).

Kitchen, K. A. (1977), *The Bible in Its World: The Bible and Archaeology Today* (Exeter: Paternoster).

—— (2003), *Ramesside Inscriptions,* vol. 4: *Merenptah and the Late Nineteenth Dynasty* (Oxford: Blackwell).

Klein, J. (2010), 'Für und Wider das Königtum (1 Sam 8–15): Figurenperspektiven und Erzählsystem', in E. Eynikel and A. G. Auld (eds.), *For and Against David* (Walpole: Peeters), pp. 91–112.

Klein, R. W. (1983), *1 Samuel*, WBC 10 (Waco: Word).
Klement, H. H. (2000a), 'David und "Hiram von Tyrus": Zum Unterschied von literarischer und chronologischer Sequenz in biblischer Historiographie', *JET* 14: 5–33.
—— (2000b), *II Samuel 21–24: Context, Structure and Meaning in the Samuel Conclusion* (Frankfurt: Peter Lang).
Kleven, T. (1994), 'The Use of *SNR* in Ugaritic and 2 Samuel V 8; Hebrew Usage and Comparative Philology', *VT* 44 (2): 195–204.
Kotter, W. R. (1992), 'Gilgal (Place)', *ABD* 2: 1022–1024.
Kramer, S. N. (1963), *The Sumerians: Their History, Culture, and Character* (Chicago: University of Chicago Press).
Kraus, H.-J. (1988), *Psalms 1–59*, trans. H. C. Oswald (Minneapolis: Augsburg).
Kwakkel, G. (2002), *According to My Righteousness: Upright Behaviour as Grounds for Deliverance in Psalms 7, 17, 18, 26 and 44*, OtSt 46 (Leiden: Brill).
Lambert, W. G. (1965), 'Nebuchadnezzar King of Justice', *Iraq* 27 (1): 1–11.
Landy, F. (2010), 'David and Ittai', in T. Beal, C. Camp and T. Linafelt (eds.), *The Fate of King David* (New York: T&T Clark), pp. 19–37.
Leithart, P. J. (2001), 'Nabal and His Wine', *JBL* 120: 525–527.
—— (2002), 'David's Threat to Nabal: How a Little Vulgarity Got the Point Across', *BRev* 18: 18–23, 59.
Leshem, Y. (2004), 'Shir ha-nitsahon: 'hikkāh Shā'ûl ba-'ălāfāv ve-Dāvid be-rivvōtāv' (Shmu'el ', yh 7) ke-bavu'ah le-nefes Sa'ul', *Beth Mikra* 180: 32–42.
Levenson, J. D. (1978), '1 Samuel 25 as Literature and History', *CBQ* 40: 11–28.
Levenson, J. D., and B. Halpern (1980), 'The Political Import of David's Marriages', *JBL* 99 (4): 507–518.
Levin, Y. (2013), 'Whose God Did Goliath Curse and Where Did David Take His Head: Comments on 1 Samuel 14 [in Hebrew]', *Beth Mikra* 58 (2): 83–99.
Long, V. P. (1989), *The Reign and Rejection of King Saul: A Case for Literary and Theological Coherence*, SBLDS 118 (Atlanta: Scholars Press).

—— (1994), *The Art of Biblical History*, vol. 5, Foundations of Contemporary Interpretation, ed. M. Silva (Grand Rapids: Zondervan).

—— (2003), 'Introduction and Commentary to 1 and 2 Samuel', in R. L. Pratt (ed.), *NIV Spirit of the Reformation Study Bible* (Grand Rapids: Zondervan), pp. 389–490.

—— (2009a), '1 Samuel', in J. H. Walton, *Zondervan Illustrated Bible Backgrounds Commentary: Old Testament*, vol. 2 (Grand Rapids: Zondervan), pp. 266–411.

—— (2009b), '2 Samuel', in J. H. Walton (ed.), *Zondervan Illustrated Bible Backgrounds Commentary: Old Testament*, vol. 2 (Grand Rapids: Zondervan), pp. 412–491.

—— (2018), 'Abraham: Friend of God, Father of the Faithful', in J. M. Houston and J. Zimmermann (eds.), *Sources of the Christian Self: A Cultural History of Christian Identity* (Grand Rapids: Eerdmans), pp. 3–20.

Longman, T., III (1987), *Literary Approaches to Biblical Interpretation*, vol. 3 of *Foundations of Contemporary Interpretation*, ed. M. Silva (Grand Rapids: Zondervan).

Lust, J., E. Eynikel and K. Hauspie (eds.) (2003), *A Greek–English Lexicon of the Septuagint* (Stuttgart: Deutsche Bibelgesellschaft).

McCann, J. C., Jr. (1994), *A Theological Introduction to the Book of Psalms: The Psalms as Torah* (Nashville: Abingdon).

McCarter, P. K. (1980), *I Samuel: A New Translation with Introduction and Commentary*, Anchor Bible (Garden City: Doubleday).

—— (1984), *II Samuel: A New Translation with Introduction and Commentary*, Anchor Bible (Garden City: Doubleday).

Macintosh, A. A. (2012), 'Proverbs 30:32 and the Root נבל', in I. Provan and M. J. Boda (eds.), *Let Us Go Up to Zion: Essays in Honour of H. G. M. Williamson on the Occasion of His Sixty-Fifth Birthday* (Leiden: Brill), pp. 79–93.

McKenzie, S. L. (2000), *King David: A Biography* (Oxford: Oxford University Press).

Malamat, A. (1955), 'Doctrines of Causality in Hittite and Biblical Historiography: A Parallel', *VT* 5: 1–12.

—— (1963), 'Aspects of the Foreign Policies of David and Solomon', *JNES* 11: 1–17.

—— (1982), 'How Inferior Israelite Forces Conquered Fortified Canaanite Cities', *BAR* 8 (2): 24–35.

Malul, M. (2010), 'Absalom's Chariot and Fifty Runners (II Sam 15,1) and Hittite Laws §198: Legal Proceedings in the Ancient Near East', *ZAW* 122: 44–52.

Mare, W. H. (1992), 'Zion (Place)', *ABD* 6: 1096–1097.

Mastéy, E. (2011), 'A Linguistic Inquiry Solves an Ancient Crime: Re-examination of 2 Samuel 4:6', *VT* 61: 82–103.

Mattila, R. (2000), *The King's Magnates: A Study of the Highest Officials of the Neo-Assyrian Empire*, SAAS 11 (Helsinki: University of Helsinki).

Matzal, S. C. (2012), 'A Word Play in 2 Samuel 4', *VT* 62: 462–464.

Mazar, B. (1993), 'Jerusalem', in E. Stern (ed.), *The New Encyclopedia of Archaeological Excavations in the Holy Land* (New York: Simon and Schuster), 698–701.

Mazar, E. (2006), 'Did I Find King David's Palace?', *BAR* 32 (1): 16–27, 70.

—— (2009), *The Palace of King David: Excavations at the Summit of the City of David; Preliminary Report of Seasons 2005–2007*, trans. B. Gordon (Jerusalem: Shoham Academic Research and Publication).

Mendelsohn, I. (1956), 'Samuel's Denunciation of the Kingship in the Light of Akkadian Documents from Ugarit', *BASOR* 143: 17–32.

Mendenhall, G. E. (1958), 'The Census Lists of Numbers 1 and 26', *JBL* 77: 52–66.

Mettinger, T. N. D. M. (1971), *Solomonic State Officials: A Study of the Civil Government Officials of the Israelite Monarchy*, Coniectanea Biblica 5 (Lund: CWK Gleerup).

Michael, M. (2013), 'The Achan/Achor Traditions: The Parody of Saul as "Achan" in 1 Samuel 14:24 – 15:35', *OTE* 26 (3): 730–760.

Middleton, J. R. (2013), 'Samuel Agonistes: A Conflicted Prophet's Resistance to God and Contribution to the Failure of Israel's First King', in M. J. Boda and L. M. W. Beal, *Prophets, Prophecy, and Ancient Israelite Historiography* (Winona Lake: Eisenbrauns), pp. 69–91.

Milikowsky, C. (2013), *Seder Olam: Critical Edition, Commentary, and Introduction*, 2 vols. (Jerusalem: Yad Ben-Zvi).

Millard, A. R. (1978), 'Saul's Shield Not Anointed with Oil', *BASOR* 230: 70.

—— (2009), 'The Armor of Goliath', in J. D. Schloen (ed.), *Exploring the Longue Durée: Essays in Honor of Lawrence E. Stager* (Winona Lake: Eisenbrauns), pp. 337–343.

Miller, P. D., and J. J. M. Roberts, Jr. (1977), *The Hand of the Lord: A Reassessment of the 'Ark Narrative' of 1 Samuel* (Baltimore: Johns Hopkins University Press).

Moran, W. L. (1963), 'The Ancient Near Eastern Background of the Love of God in Deuteronomy', *CBQ* 25: 77–87.

—— (1992), *The Amarna Letters* (Baltimore/London: Johns Hopkins University Press).

Mulzac, K. D. (2002), 'Hannah: The Receiver and Giver of a Great Gift', *AUSS* 40: 207–217.

Na'aman, N. (2008), 'In Search of the Ancient Name of Khirbet Qeiyafa', *JHS* 8: 2–8.

Negev, A., and S. Gibson (eds.) (2003), *Archaeological Encyclopedia of the Holy Land* (New York/London: Continuum).

Neiderhiser, E. A. (1979), 'One More Proposal for 1 Samuel 13:1', *HS* 20/21: 44–46.

Newkirk, M. (2015), *Just Deceivers: An Exploration of the Motif of Deception in the Books of Samuel* (Eugene: Pickwick).

Noth, M. (1983), *The History of Israel*, 2nd edn (London: SCM).

Oswald, W. (2008), 'Is There a Prohibition to Build the Temple in 2 Samuel 7?', in M. Augustin and H. M. Niemann (eds.), *Thinking Towards New Horizons* (New York: Peter Lang), pp. 85–89.

Park, S.-M. S. (2009), 'The Frustration of Wisdom: Wisdom, Counsel, and Divine Will in 2 Samuel 17:1–23', *JBL* 128: 453–467.

Parpola, S. (1995), 'The Assyrian Cabinet', in M. Dietrich and O. Lorenz (eds.), *Vom Alten Orient zum Alten Testament: Festschrift für Wolfram Freiheim Von Soden zum 85. Geburtstag am 19. Juni 1993* (Neukirchen-Vluyn: Neukirchener), pp. 379–401.

Peterson, E. H. (1999), *First and Second Samuel*, Westminster Bible Companion, ed. P. D. Miller, Jr., and D. L. Bartlett (Louisville: Westminster John Knox).

Petter, D. (2004), 'Foregrounding of the Designation *'ēšet 'ûriyyâ haḥittî* in II Samuel XI-XII', *VT* 54 (3): 352–372.

Pisano, S. (1984), *Additions or Omissions in the Books of Samuel: The Significant Pluses and Minuses in the Massoretic, LXX and Qumran Texts*, OBO 57 (Göttingen: Vandenhoeck & Ruprecht).

Polzin, R. (1989), *Samuel and the Deuteronomist: A Literary Study of the Deuteronomistic History*, vol. 2: *1 Samuel* (New York: Seabury).

—— (1993), *David and the Deuteronomist: A Literary Study of the Deuteronomistic History*, vol. 3: *2 Samuel* (New York: Seabury).

Postgate, J. N. (1992), *Early Mesopotamia: Society and Economy at the Dawn of History* (London/New York: Routledge).

Preminger, A., and E. L. Greenstein (eds.) (1986), *The Hebrew Bible in Literary Criticism* (New York: Ungar).

Pritchard, J. B. (ed.) (1969), *Ancient Near Eastern Texts Relating to the Old Testament* (Princeton: Princeton University Press).

Provan, I. (2000), 'On "Seeing" the Trees While Missing the Forest: The Wisdom of Characters and Readers in 2 Samuel and 1 Kings', in E. Ball (ed.), *In Search of True Wisdom: Essays in Old Testament Interpretation in Honour of Ronald E. Clements* (Sheffield: Sheffield Academic Press), 153–173.

Provan, I., and M. J. Boda (eds.) (2012), *Let Us Go Up to Zion: Essays in Honour of H. G. M. Williamson on the Occasion of His Sixty-Fifth Birthday*, VTSup 153 (Leiden: Brill).

Provan, I., V. P. Long and T. Longman III (2015), *A Biblical History of Israel*, 2nd edn (Louisville: Westminster/John Knox).

Rappaport, S. (1930), *Agada und Exegese bei Falvius Josephus* (Vienna: Alexander Kohut Memorial Foundation).

Reed, S. A. (1992), 'Jebus', *ABD* 3: 652–653.

Reich, R., and E. Shukron (2004), 'The History of the Gihon Spring in Jerusalem', *Levant* 36: 211–223.

Reis, P. T. (1994), 'Collusion at Nob: A New Reading of 1 Samuel 21–22', *JSOT* 61: 59–73.

Rendsburg, G. A. (2002), 'Some False Leads in the Identification of Late Biblical Hebrew Texts: The Cases of Genesis 24 and 1 Samuel 2:27–36', *JBL* 121: 23–46.

Reviv, H. (1989), *The Elders in Ancient Israel: A Study of a Biblical Institution*, trans. L. Plitmann (Jerusalem: Magnes Press).

Richardson, H. N. (1971), 'Last Words of David: Some Notes on 2 Samuel 23:1–7', *JBL* 90 (3): 257–266.

Ridout, G. (1974), 'The Rape of Tamar: A Rhetorical Analysis of 2 Sam 13:1–22', in J. J. Jackson and M. Kessler (eds.), *Rhetorical Criticism: Essays in Honor of James Muilenburg* (Pittsburgh: Pickwick), pp. 75–84.

Rollston, C. A. (2013), 'Ad Nomen Argumenta: Personal Names as Pejorative Puns in Ancient Texts', in A. F. Botta (ed.), *In the Shadow of Bezalel: Aramaic, Biblical, and Ancient Near Eastern Studies in Honor of Bezalel Porten* (Leiden: Brill), pp. 367–386.

Rosenberg, A. J. (1980), *Samuel 1: A New English Translation of the Text and Rashi, With a Commentary Digest* (New York: Judaica Press).

—— (1986), *Samuel 2: A New English Translation of the Text and Rashi, With a Commentary Digest* (New York: Judaica Press).

Rost, L. (1926), *Die Überlieferung von der Thronnachfolge Davids*, BWANT 3/6 (Stuttgart: W. Kohlhammer).

Rowe, J. Y. (2011), *Michal's Moral Dilemma: A Literary, Anthropological and Ethical Interpretation*, LHBOTS 533 (New York: T&T Clark).

—— (2012), *Sons or Lovers: An Interpretation of David and Jonathan's Friendship*, Library of Biblical Studies (New York/London: T&T Clark).

Rudman, D. (2000a), 'David's Lament for Abner (2 Samuel 3:33–34)', *IBS* 22: 91–94.

—— (2000b), 'The Commissioning Stories of Saul and David as Theological Allegory', *VT* 50: 519–530.

—— (2001), 'Why Was Saul Rejected? A Reassessment of 1 Samuel 9–15', *ScrB* 31: 101–107.

Rutherford, J. A. (2019), *God's Kingdom through His Priest-King: An Analysis of the Book of Samuel in Light of the Davidic Covenant*, Teleioteti Technical Studies (Vancouver: Teleioteti).

Ryken, L. (1984), *How to Read the Bible as Literature* (Grand Rapids: Academie Books).

—— (1987), *Words of Delight: A Literary Introduction to the Bible* (Grand Rapids: Baker).

Ryken, L., and T. Longman III (eds.) (1993), *A Complete Literary Guide to the Bible* (Grand Rapids: Zondervan).

Ryken, L., J. C. Wilhoit and T. Longman III (eds.) (1998), *Dictionary of Biblical Imagery: An Encyclopedic Exploration of the Images, Symbols, Motifs, Metaphors, Figures of Speech and Literary Patterns of the Bible* (Downers Grove: InterVarsity Press; Leicester: Inter-Varsity Press).

Ska, J. L., S.J. (1990), *'Our Fathers Have Told Us': Introduction to the Analysis of Hebrew Narratives*, Subsidia Biblica 13 (Rome: Editrice Pontifico Istituto Biblico).

Smelik, K. A. D. (1977), *Saul, de voorstelling van Israels eerste Konig in de Masoretische tekst van het Oude Testament* (Amsterdam: Drukkerij en Uitgeverij P. E. T.).

Smith, J. P. (1903), *A Compendious Syriac Dictionary: Founded upon the Thesaurus Syriacus of R. Payne Smith, D. D.* (Oxford: Oxford University Press).

Smith, R. G. (2009), *The Fate of Justice and Righteousness During David's Reign*, Library of Biblical Studies (New York/London: T&T Clark).

Sonnet, J.-P. (2010), 'God's Repentance and "False Starts" in Biblical History (Genesis 6–9; Exodus 32–34; 1 Samuel 15 and 2 Samuel 7)', in A. Lemaire (ed.), *Congress Volume Ljubljana 2007* (Boston: Brill), pp. 469–494.

Stager, L. E. (1998), 'Forging an Identity: The Emergence of Ancient Israel', in M. D. Coogan (ed.), *The Oxford History of the Biblical World* (New York/Oxford: Oxford University Press), pp. 123–175.

Stern, P. D. (1991), *The Biblical ḤEREM: A Window on Israel's Religious Experience*, BJS 211 (Atlanta: Scholars).

Sternberg, M. (1985), *The Poetics of Biblical Narrative: Ideological Literature and the Drama of Reading* (Bloomington: Indiana University Press).

Stirrup, A. (2000), '"Why Has Yahweh Defeated Us Today Before the Philistines?": The Question of the Ark Narrative', *TynBul* 51: 81–100.

Stoebe, H. J. (1973), *Das erste Buch Samuelis*, KAT 7/1 (Gütersloh: Gerd Mohn).

Süring, M. L. (1980), *The Horn-Motif: In the Hebrew Bible and Related Ancient Near Eastern Literature and Iconography* (Berrien Springs: Andrews University Press).

Taggar-Cohen, A. (2005), 'Political Loyalty in the Biblical Account of 1 Samuel XX–XXII in the Light of Hittite Texts', *VT* 55 (2): 251–268.

Talmon, S. (1986), '"The Rule of the King": 1 Samuel 8:4–22', in S. Talmon (ed.), *King, Cult and Calendar in Ancient Israel* (Jerusalem: Magnes), pp. 53–67.

Terrien, S. (2003), *The Psalms: Strophic Structure and Theological Commentary*, ECC, ed. D. N. Freedman (Grand Rapids: Eerdmans).

Thompson, H. O. (1992), 'Helam (Place)', *ABD* 3: 116–117.

Tsevat, M. (1987), 'Die Namengebung Samuels und die Substitutionstheorie', *ZAW* 99: 250–254.

Tsumura, D. T. (2001), 'List and Narrative in 1 Samuel 6, 17–18a in the Light of Ugaritic Economic Texts', *ZAW* 113: 353–369.

—— (2007), *The First Book of Samuel*, NICOT (Grand Rapids: Eerdmans).

Vannoy, J. R. (1978), *Covenant Renewal at Gilgal: A Study of I Samuel 11:14 – 12:25* (Cherry Hill: Mack).

—— (2009), *1–2 Samuel*, Cornerstone Biblical Commentary (Carol Stream: Tyndale House).

Viberg, Å. (1992), *Symbols of Law: A Contextual Analysis of Legal Symbolic Acts in the Old Testament*, ConBOT 34 (Stockholm: Almqvist & Wiksell International).

Wagner, V. (2013), 'Plante Absalom eine Reform der Gerichtsordnung in Israel? (2 Sam 15:2–4)', *VT* 63 (1): 159–165.

Walters, S. D. (2002), 'Reading Samuel to Hear God', *CTJ* 37: 62–81.

Waltke, Bruce K., and M. O'Connor (1990), *An Introduction to Biblical Hebrew Syntax* (Winona Lake: Eisenbrauns).

Walton, J. H. (2015), 'A King Like the Nations: 1 Samuel 8 in Its Cultural Context', *Bib* 96: 179–200.

Walton, J. H. (ed.) (2009), *Zondervan Illustrated Bible Backgrounds Commentary: Old Testament*, 5 vols. (Grand Rapids: Zondervan).

Weinfeld, M. (2000), *Social Justice in Ancient Israel and in the Ancient Near East*, 2nd edn (Minneapolis: Fortress).

Wenham, G. J. (1975), 'Were David's Sons Priests?', *ZAW* 87: 79–82.

Wentz, H. S. (1970–1), 'The Monarchy of Saul: Antecedents, "Deuteronomic" Interpretations and Ideology' (PhD diss., University of Exeter).

Wesselius, J.-W. (2009), 'A New View on the Relation between Septuagint and Masoretic Text in the Story of David and Goliath', in C. D. Evans and D. H. Zacharias (eds.), *Early Christian Literature and Intertextuality*, vol. 2: *Exegetical Studies* (New York: T&T Clark), pp. 5–26.

Westermann, C. (1960), *Grundformen prophetischer Rede*, BEvT (Munich: Christian Kaiser Verlag).

—— (1991), *Basic Forms of Prophetic Speech*, trans. H. C. White, Foreword and ed. by G. M. Tucker (Louisville: Westminster/John Knox).

White, M. C. (2006), 'Saul and Jonathan in 1 Samuel 1 and 14', in M. C. White and C. Ehrlich (eds.), *Saul in Story and Tradition* (Tübingen: Mohr Siebeck), pp. 119–138.

Williams, C. (1939), *The Descent of the Dove: A Short History of the Holy Spirit in the Church* (London: Longmans, Green).

Williams, R. J. (2007), *Williams' Hebrew Syntax*, 3rd edn (Toronto: University of Toronto Press).

Wong, G. T. K. (2010), 'Goliath's Death and the Testament of Judah', *Bib* 91: 425–432.

—— (2013), 'A Farewell to Arms: Goliath's Death as Rhetoric against Faith in Arms', *BBR* 23 (1): 43–55.

Woodhouse, J. (2008), *1 Samuel: Looking for a Leader*, Preaching the Word, ed. R. K. Hughes (Wheaton: Crossway).

Yadin, Y. (1955), 'Some Aspects of the Strategy of Ahab and David', *Bib* 36: 332–351.

—— (1963), *The Art of Warfare in Biblical Lands in Light of Archaeological Study*, 2 vols. (New York: n.p.).

Yahalom-Mack, N., N. Panitz-Cohen and R. Mullins (2018), 'From a Fortified Canaanite City-State to "a City and a Mother" in Israel: Five Seasons of Excavation at Tel Abel Beth Maacah', *NEA* 81 (2): 145–156.

Yee, G. A. (1988), '"Fraught with Background": Literary Ambiguity in II Samuel 11', *Int* 42: 240–253.

Youngblood, R. F. (1992), 'Elkanah (Person)', *ABD* 2: 475–476.

—— (2009), *1 and 2 Samuel*, EBC 3, rev. edn (Grand Rapids: Zondervan).

Zahavi-Ely, N. (2012), '"Turn Right or Left": Literary Use of Dialect in 2 Samuel 14:19', *HS* 53: 43–53.

Zakovitch, Y. (1980), 'A Study of Precise and Partial Derivations in Biblical Etymology', *JSOT* 15: 31–50.

Zevit, Z. (2001), *The Religions of Ancient Israel: A Synthesis of Parallactic Approaches* (London: Continuum).

INTRODUCTION

1. The greatness of the book of Samuel

> It would be hard to find anywhere a greater narrative. Eli, Samuel, Saul, David, Goliath, the witch of Endor, around whom is written one of the best stories of the supernatural, Jonathan the true friend, Joab, Uriah, Bathsheba, Nathan, Absalom and other characters are depicted and played up against each other with a sureness of touch, technique, and fidelity never surpassed. Scenes and events are handled with the utmost sincerity and with graphic power. And here, as is generally the case in the Bible, all this is accomplished with the fewest words.
> (Hilary G. Richardson)[1]

With the exception of the book of Genesis, no major narrative book in the Old Testament has attracted more attention than the

---

1. Hilary G. Richardson, *Life and the Book* (New York: Macmillan, 1929), p. 210. Cited in Preminger and Greenstein (1986: 557).

book of Samuel.² Reasons for this popularity are not difficult to discover. But before we consider some of these reasons, a few words on the name of the book are in order.

First and Second Samuel can be referred to in several different ways. One may speak of 'the book' (singular) of Samuel, because what we now refer to as 1 and 2 Samuel was originally one book (or, more properly, one scroll). That the book was so regarded by its early transmitters (the 'Masoretes') is evident from the fact that the statistical information they typically appended to the end of discrete books comes at the end of 2 Samuel and takes into account both 1 and 2 Samuel.³ Early Jewish and Christian sources also refer to a single book of Samuel.⁴ It makes sense, therefore, to refer to 'the book' of Samuel. But it also makes sense to refer to 'the books' (plural) of Samuel, as this usage also has ancient precedent and is common practice today. When the consonants-only (and thus compact) Hebrew text of Samuel was translated into consonants-and-vowels Greek (sometime in the second century BC), two scrolls were required to accommodate the greater length that the addition of vowels caused. These two scrolls were called 1 and 2 'Reigns' (or 'Kingdoms') in the Greek tradition.⁵ The present commentary speaks sometimes of the book of Samuel, sometimes of the books of Samuel, sometimes of 1 and 2 Samuel and sometimes simply of Samuel (in contexts where it is clear that the person Samuel is not meant).

Whether naming the book after the prophet Samuel was the best titular choice is another question. Samuel was not the author of the book, which is formally anonymous, though it is not

---

2. There are *poetical* books of equal or greater popularity than the book of Samuel – the book of Psalms, for instance, or Isaiah – but the focus here is on predominantly *narrative* literature.

3. Among various bits of information included, the Masoretic notation cites 1 Sam. 28:24 as the mid-point of the composition.

4. E.g. Alter (1999: x) cites the Jewish Talmud, while Gordon (1986: 19) mentions the 'third-century Christian scholar Origen' (as noted in Eusebius, *Ecclesiastical History*, 6.25).

5. For more details, see Gordon (1986: 20).

impossible that he could have played some part in retaining a written memory of events prior to his death (noted in 1 Sam. 25:1 and 28:3). In Jewish tradition, the Hebrew canon is divided into three large sections: the Torah (*tôrâ*), the Prophets (*nĕbî'îm*) and the Writings (*kĕtûbîm*). The second division is further subdivided into Former Prophets (the 'historical books' in the English canon) and Latter Prophets (the 'writing prophets', so called because they not only proclaimed God's word to their contemporaries but also left behind written prophecies bearing their names). If the Latter Prophets were both speakers and writers, might not the Former have been both as well? Might not Samuel, for instance, who is portrayed as an authorized messenger of Yahweh to his contemporaries, also have retained some written record of contemporary events as seen from a prophetic perspective? This speculation finds some encouragement in 1 Chronicles 29:29's reference to the *events [dibrê] of King David's reign . . . written in the records [dibrê] of Samuel the seer [rō'eh], the records [dibrê] of Nathan the prophet [nabi'] and the records [dibrê] of Gad the seer [ḥōzeh]*.[6]

That said, Samuel could not have been the main writer of the book that bears his name, nor is he its main character (we have noted already that he dies well before 2 Samuel even begins). There is nevertheless a certain appropriateness in naming the book after Samuel. The book as a whole is about the institution of kingship in Israel, and Samuel was the prophet whom Yahweh commissioned to anoint Israel's first two kings. These kings, Saul and David, are the other main characters in the book of Samuel. Even after his death, Samuel's shadow is cast over the book. He reappears posthumously to Saul on the eve of Saul's death (1 Sam. 28). And of greatest import, it is Samuel whom Yahweh uses to set forth the

---

6. Samuel, Nathan and Gad are referred to using three common Heb. synonyms for 'prophet'. The rendering of Hebrew *dibrê* first as 'events' and then three times as 'records' highlights the range of meaning of the Hebrew noun *dābār* ('word, thing, affair'). Interestingly, the English word 'history' has a similar range of meaning; 'history' can refer to 'events' of the past, as well as to written 'accounts' of past events (Long 1994: 58–63).

kind of king that Israel should have (see, e.g., commentary on
1 Sam. 8:19–20). In sum, naming the book(s) of Samuel after the
prophet so instrumental in the establishment of monarchy in Israel
is perhaps more appropriate than might at first appear.

Returning to the question of the popularity of the book of
Samuel, we may note three reasons for this, and there are doubtless
more. The first is the fact that the book describes a very significant
change in ancient Israel's political and religious life – the transition
from a loose tribal confederation to a united monarchy. This makes
the book inherently interesting to historians – at least to historians
who understand that written testimony is one of the main ways we
learn about the past.[7] As the book opens, the period of the judges
is winding down and monarchy is about to emerge. Israel is experiencing both external and internal pressures (cf. Birch 1998: 949).
Chief among Israel's adversaries in this period are the Philistines
to the south-west, whose monopoly on arms manufacture (1 Sam.
13:19–21) gave them a distinct military advantage. The Ammonites,
one of Israel's eastern neighbours, are also making trouble, at least
some of the time (1 Sam. 11:1). Internally, the religious establishment under the leadership of Eli is in a degenerate state (1 Sam.
2:12–17, 22–25, 29–30). Something needs to change. And Yahweh's
chosen change agent turns out to be Samuel. Given its subject
matter, the book of Samuel is of interest to historians of ancient
Israel.

A second and perhaps even more important reason why the book
of Samuel has proven irresistible to readers has to do with the characters it presents. The stories of Hannah, Samuel, Saul, David,
Jonathan, Abigail, Joab, Amnon, Absalom and many, many more
make riveting reading. These characters are portrayed with a power
and telling complexity unsurpassed in world literature – in
antiquity, without doubt, but arguably in any era down to the
present. Robert Alter (1999: ix) describes the story of David as
'probably the greatest single narrative representation in antiquity of
a human life evolving by slow stages through time, shaped and

---

7. For discussion of this view, see Long (1994: 74); Provan, Long and
Longman (2015: 45–58).

altered by the pressures of political life, public institutions, family, the impulses of body and spirit, the eventual sad decay of the flesh'. Thus, the book of Samuel is popular by virtue of its literary sophistication and the brilliant human portraits it presents.

Alter's comment above may remind us of a third reason for the popularity of the book of Samuel, even if it does so not so much by what it says as by what it does not say. Of David's deep religious faith Alter's comment says nothing, unless the mention of 'impulses of . . . spirit' is a nod in that direction. And yet neither David nor Saul nor Samuel nor Jonathan nor any other of the characters can be rightly comprehended if the role of religious faith (or its absence) in their lives is neglected. Religious faith is itself a historical datum. The theological profundity of the book of Samuel has been an unmistakable draw to countless generations of readers. Through its finely wrought narrations of the lives and circumstances of its characters, the book of Samuel establishes what we might call a kind of baseline theology. At the heart of the book we find not just human protagonists and antagonists, but God himself. Whether in the text God engages directly in the action or remains behind the scenes, the divine presence inevitably raises crucial theological questions. What does living in the world in relationship to one's creator look like? What does it mean to be a person *after [God's] own heart* or, as the phrase can also be rendered, a person 'of God's own choosing'? What does it take for a leader to succeed? How is a failed leader to respond when deposed from office? Why was Saul rejected as king, while David was not, even after the latter committed adultery and murder? Questions such as these have engaged and perplexed communities of faith for millennia.

In sum, the book of Samuel is of great importance in at least these three respects: it covers a strategic transition in Israel's history, it is powerful literature and it grounds theological verities in actual lives and circumstances.[8] Literature, history and theology

---

8. We shall have more to say below on the literary, historical and theological character not just of the book of Samuel but of biblical narrative generally.

combine in the book of Samuel to make it great. Careful literary reading is necessary to any effort to discover the historical or theological import of the book, so in the next section we turn our attention to the larger literary shape of the book.

2. The structure and storyline of the book of Samuel

Determining the structure of a book as long and sophisticated as the book of Samuel is difficult. We might liken this challenge to that faced by art critics seeking to describe the compositional decisions underlying the visual masterpieces of great painters. No two critics are likely to agree entirely in their descriptions. But amongst competent and fair-minded critics, at least some overlap of opinion and analysis will likely emerge. This is as true in respect of the compositional shaping of Samuel as it is of any other work of high art. Thus, while no two scholars describe the literary shape of Samuel in precisely the same ways, there does appear to be 'a developing scholarly consensus about the major segments into which the narrative falls' (Birch 1998: 959).

A convenient survey of structural analyses of Samuel from the beginning of the twentieth century to circa 2013 is provided by Michael Avioz (2013). Certain approaches, such as that of Herbert Klement (2000b), are particularly promising. But the present writer is not yet sufficiently convinced of any particular analysis to make it an interpretive key in the commentary to follow. The present work seeks simply to follow the story as it unfolds, generally observing the given chapter divisions for the sake of convenience and only departing from them where necessary. The story tends to unfold in a basically chronological sequence, as stories generally do, though there are instances of minor dischronologization, such as flashbacks, and of major ones, as in the so-called Samuel 'appendix' (or, better, 'conclusion') comprising 2 Samuel 21 – 24.[9]

---

9. See, in addition to the commentary itself, Firth's (2013: 67–79) discussion of 'achronologized' and 'dischronologized' narration as features of Samuel's literary art.

The inclusion of an 'Analysis' at the end of this introduction, to say nothing of the commentary itself, makes detailed description of content at this juncture unnecessary. But a very broad-brush overview may be useful.

1 Samuel 1 – 7. As noted earlier, the story begins near the end of the period of the judges, with the prospect of kingship hanging in the air (the song of Hannah, for instance, makes reference to the Lord's *king* in 2:10). Taken together, the first seven chapters of 1 Samuel describe the demise of the priestly house of Eli and the rise of God's new representative, Samuel. Raised as a priest in the house of Eli (chs. 1–2), Samuel is established as a prophet by Yahweh (ch. 3) and, upon reaching maturity, leads Israel (in judge-like fashion) in a great victory over Israel's arch-enemy, the Philistines (ch. 7). The intervening chapters describing the capture of the ark of the covenant by the Philistines (chs. 4–6) demonstrate not Yahweh's defeat but, rather, his unmatched power. The so-called 'ark narrative' demonstrates that it is folly for anyone, whether Israelite or Philistine, to try to manage or manipulate the ark (6:20). In chapter 7, Yahweh's power to save his people is manifested through the leadership of his new agent, Samuel, now grown. Samuel's declaration after successfully leading Israel to victory – *Thus far the* LORD *has helped us* (7:12) – provides the backdrop for what comes next.

1 Samuel 8 – 12. Despite the Lord's provision of leaders *Thus far*, the elders come to Samuel in chapter 8 and request *a king to lead us* [lit. 'to judge us'], *such as all the other nations have* (8:5). This request meets with disapproval and warnings, not so much because human kingship itself is a bad idea but because having a king *of the sort that other nations have* is a bad idea. Even when warned of the abuses that such a king will inflict, the elders persist, and Yahweh eventually instructs Samuel to appoint 'for them' (*lahem*) a king (8:22; contrast 16:1, where Yahweh speaks of espying a king 'for myself' [*lî*]). The people's king turns out to be Saul, a man of impressive physical proportions but less than impressive in other respects. Saul's rise is recounted in a complex and – I will argue – *coherent* sequence of events that eventually lands him on the throne.[10] Immediately before Saul's enthronement, Samuel offers one final warning about the importance of both king and people following the Lord faithfully (12:14–15, 24–25).

1 Samuel 13 – 15. The story of Saul's reign and rejection has perplexed readers for centuries. Many find Samuel's treatment of Saul to be both inexplicable and inexcusable. Saul, according to these readers, is a victim of an irascible prophet seeking to maintain his grasp on power by reducing Saul to a puppet king. The more thorough-going of these types of readings bring serious charges not just against Samuel but against Samuel's God. The approach taken in the present commentary is very different. The readings just described, I shall argue, arise from serious misunderstandings of certain key elements in the story of Saul's rise, reign and rejection. To name but one example, many readers misunderstand the nature of Saul's first charge, issued at the time of his anointing (see 1 Sam. 10:7–8), and they consequently misunderstand also Samuel's indictment of Saul in 1 Samuel 13:13. (We shall look further at these and other questions below in our discussion of the characters Samuel and Saul.) Saul is definitively rejected in 1 Samuel 15 and thus no longer rightful king in God's eyes.

1 Samuel 16 – 31. Unlike the deposed priest, Eli, who accepted his rejection from office by recognizing the rightness of God's judgment (3:18), Saul, though no longer rightful king in God's eyes, refuses to step aside. Chapters 16–31 trace Saul's progressive decline and eventual demise, while at the same time focusing on the increasing prominence and popularity of David. Saul repeatedly seeks to take David's life and, having failed in that, in the end takes his own life on Mount Gilboa (ch. 31). David's years as a fugitive in the wilderness are some of his better years, inasmuch as dangerous and desperate times call for trust in Yahweh, who is repeatedly said to be *with* David (16:18; 2 Sam. 7:9; etc.).

2 Samuel 1:1 – 5:5. As 2 Samuel opens, Saul is dead and David is in a position to ascend the throne without raising his hand against *the*

---

10. See, in addition to the commentary, the discussion of Saul in the 'Characters in the book of Samuel' section below.

LORD's anointed – something he steadfastly refused to do when given opportunity in 1 Samuel 24 and 26. His rule over Judah is established without incident, but blood is spilt before the way is clear for him to become king also over the northern tribes. Some recent writers have suggested that David somehow orchestrated the deaths of Abner (Saul's former general) and Ish-Bosheth (Saul's surviving son), to name but two. But the biblical narrators are at pains to show that David was as innocent in these deaths as he was in the deaths of Saul and his son Jonathan. We shall return to this question in our discussion below of David's character.

2 Samuel 5:6 – 10:19. With David now enthroned over a united Israel, the remainder of chapters 5–10 records the transactions, both political and theological, by which David's rule is secured. Chapters 5–6 describe his acquisition of Jerusalem as his capital city, his resounding defeat of the Philistines and his transfer of the ark of God to Jerusalem. Chapter 7, whose significance cannot be overstated, tells of the so-called 'Davidic promise', or 'dynastic oracle', in which the Lord, having refused David's offer to build him a *house* (temple), promises instead to build David a *house* (dynasty) that will endure for ever. This promise to David marks the continuation and specification of the divine promise of blessing to the patriarchs (beginning in Gen. 12:1–3) and is a major new development in the messianic hope that finds its ultimate fulfilment in Christ. Little wonder that 2 Samuel 7 is sometimes referred to as the pinnacle of the Old Testament. Chapters 8–10 summarize some of David's major achievements, both military and personal.

2 Samuel 11 – 20. The 'Davidic promise' of chapter 7 establishes that the purposes of God for the house of David are sure. But this does not mean that David or his descendants may not forfeit some of the temporal benefits of their privileged position if they fall into sin. Chapters 11–20 describe the domestic and political chaos that follows in the wake of David's sins of adultery and murder (ch. 11). In response to David's lapse, God in chapter 12 graciously sends the prophet Nathan to confront him. David repents genuinely, and God forgives him. But sin is never without cost. And the replication within David's own household of sins involving sex and violence proves to be almost more than the disoriented David can bear. Only after he has experienced two rebellions, by his own son Absalom and by Sheba son of Bikri, does David begin to regain his balance and, at the urging of Joab, reassume his royal responsibilities.

2 Samuel 21 – 24. The book of Samuel concludes with what is sometimes called an appendix but which might more properly be called an epilogue or conclusion. At the heart of the symmetrically structured unit (ABCC'B'A') are two Davidic poems (22:1–51; 23:1–7) celebrating the two fundamental reasons for David's success: the Lord has (1) delivered him (22:2, 44 and *passim*) and (2) made an *everlasting covenant* with him (23:5). David's success is fundamentally a result of the fact that the Lord was with him. But David's human supporters also play a role. Framing the two central poems are two lists of David's champions, the human agents of his success (21:15–22; 23:8–39). And framing all this are two accounts of royal sin, consequent disaster and eventual resolution. It is Saul's sin that is emphasized in 21:1–14 and David's in 24:1–25. This sets up a telling comparison and raises an important question. Why does Saul's sin bring him down, while David's does not? The answer lies in the heart of Saul and of David. The sins themselves are but symptoms of something much deeper. The position that will be developed in this commentary is that David, though a deeply flawed and indeed sinful human being, was nevertheless a man of genuine faith in Yahweh. Saul was not (cf. 1 Chr. 10:13–14).

3. The character of the book of Samuel

Unless we understand the character of what we are reading, we are likely to misread it. In his magnum opus *The Poetics of Biblical Narrative*, Meir Sternberg convincingly argues that biblical narratives are 'regulated by a set of three principles: ideological, historiographic, and aesthetic' (1985: 41). Couched in our preferred terms, biblical narratives are concerned with theology, history and literature (as we have suggested already above). Occasionally one reads statements such as, 'The Bible is a work of literature, not history', or it is 'a work of theology, not history', and so forth. But such dichotomies are to be avoided. The Bible is concerned not *just* with literature, nor *just* with history nor *just* with theology, but with all three in complex relationship.

'*In the abstract*,' as Sternberg notes, these principles 'form natural rivals' (1985: 44). The ideological (or theological) principle would seem to drive towards a kind of 'transparent representation' in order to 'establish a world view', a 'doctrinal pattern', if you will. Historiography, again in the abstract, would concern itself with the past and with getting 'the facts' of the past right, even if this meant 'marching across all artistic and ideological design'. For literature (Sternberg's 'aesthetics'), 'the play's the thing, ideally (as in abstract painting or the fantastic) with no strings attached to what is, was, or should be'. 'Given free rein, therefore, each [principle] would pull in a different direction and either win the tug of war or tear the work apart' (ibid.).[11] Remarkably, this is not what happens in biblical narrative. Rather, 'Biblical narrative emerges as a complex, because multifunctional, discourse' (ibid.: 41). That is to say, the three seemingly rival principles 'are manipulated into operating as a system, a three-in-one, a unity in variety'. The Bible is not only the 'first and most ambitious of large-scale coordinators', it is 'also the greatest' (ibid.: 44).

A sense of how literary-artistic, historical-referential and theological-perspectival interests can be combined in a single work may be gained by considering the analogy of a portrait painting. A portrait is undeniably a work of art, but it is not art for art's sake. It is a work of art designed and executed to capture a true likeness of its historical subject, as viewed from a certain perspective and in a certain light. The narratives of Samuel, similarly, are literary works of art designed to capture telling likenesses of their historical subjects, as viewed in the light of certain theological perspectives.[12] The purpose of such literature is not merely to entertain, nor even

---

11. As an aside, it may be noted that biblical scholarship has at times itself been pulled in different directions, with the result that scholars find themselves segregated into what Alonso Schökel (1985) describes as 'sound-proof rooms', scholars pursuing their interest in one of the three principles in splendid isolation from much concern for, to say nothing of dialogue with, the other two.
12. For fuller discussion, see Long (1994: 58–87, 106–107); Provan, Long and Longman (2015: 114–118, 217–218).

to inform, but to persuade. The books of Samuel seek to convey and inculcate certain perspectives and convictions on matters of fundamental importance.

Given the book of Samuel's complex character, our task as readers is to do justice to all the text's truth claims, literary, historical and theological. Perhaps a better way to say this is that competent *literary* reading of the book of Samuel is the gateway to better understandings of whatever *historical* and *theological* truth claims the text makes. Of course, reading sophisticated literature competently is not an easy task. And the task is even harder when one is dealing with literature from long ago and far away. Given the challenges involved, some might think that the book of Samuel is best left to literary scholars, biblical experts, historians and theologians. But this is not the case. Every reader has much to gain. Samuel's stories can be read with as much or as little literary sophistication as the reader can bring. Even rather simple readers can grasp the main points. But because the book of Samuel consists of sophisticated narrative, far richer readings are available to those who bend the effort to develop as much 'ancient literary competence' as time and opportunity afford them.[13]

All readers should be asking the kinds of questions that they would ask of any well-written story. Who are the main characters? What is the point of tension that drives the story forward? How is the tension ultimately resolved, or does it spill over into the next scene? What is revealed about the characters from the way they are presented and play off of each other? If one can read a good short story or novel, or watch a film, and then discuss it in terms of plot development, characterization, narrative pacing, dialogue, and so forth, then one can get somewhere reading biblical narratives with these concerns in mind. The book of Samuel is, of course, neither short story nor novel, but it does make use of the kinds of literary techniques typical of those genres. There are, moreover, some distinctively Hebrew storytelling techniques (or literary devices) that should be borne in mind: the significant use of repetition (either

---

13. On what is meant by 'ancient literary competence', see Long (1994: 33–35, 42–43), and the literature cited there.

verbatim or with telling variation), comparative and contrastive characterizations, dramatic irony, wordplays, the intentional withholding of information in order to pique the reader's curiosity (a technique called 'gapping'), the telling of similar stories in such a way as to cause the reader to read the one in the light of the other ('narrative analogy'), and so forth. A number of fine discussions of the 'poetics of biblical narrative' have appeared in recent decades, and these will richly reward those who become conversant with them.[14] One goal of the present commentary is to bring some of the best in recent literary theory to bear in our reading of the book of Samuel. This will be done not so much by engaging in theoretical discussion as by reading the texts themselves in the light of improved understanding of their character and literary 'poetics'.

4. The characters in the book of Samuel

We turn now from the character of the book to the characters in the book. '*The role of personality* in Israel's story of this period is central. Samuel, Saul, and David loom over the story in overlapping domination of the narrative landscape' (Birch 1998: 957–958). Philosophers of history often distinguish between *nomothetic* and *ideographic* forces as drivers of historical change. A 'nomothetic' (law-giving) approach focuses on large-scale matters such as economic and demographic conditions, social structures, class conflict, environmental factors, and the like. An 'ideographic' approach (sometimes referred to as the 'great person' view of history) focuses more on individuals and on their decisions and actions as drivers of history. A balanced approach to history recognizes the importance of both nomothetic and ideographic influences.[15] While the

---

14. Influential early works include Alter (1981); Berlin (1983); Fokkelman (1981–1993); Longman (1987); Polzin (1989; 1993); Ryken (1984; 1987); Ryken and Longman (1993); Ska (1990); and Sternberg (1985). That the book of Samuel often figures prominently in these treatments of the 'workings' of biblical narrative is a testimony to its importance and popularity.
15. For discussion, see Long (1994: 135–149); Provan, Long and Longman

biblical narratives make some room for nomothetic considerations, the primary focus of biblical historiography is on individuals and the power of their decisions to change things. These individuals, moreover, are not just the powerful or politically significant. The book of Samuel begins with Hannah, an ordinary woman in a difficult situation. As it turns out, this ordinary woman proves to be extraordinarily important. Not only is it through the faithfulness of Hannah that Samuel is born, but her prayer in 1 Samuel 2:1–10 provides the opening frame for all that follows in the book, setting forth 'foundational theology' that is mirrored in King David's own framing poems near the end of the book (2 Sam. 22:1–51 and 23:1–7).

It is right then that we focus on the characters in Samuel and what is revealed through them. Literary theorists distinguish 'plots of resolution' and 'plots of revelation' (Ska 1990: 18). In Samuel we have both. The points of tension arising in the stories press towards *resolution*, but along the way the inner lives and motives of the characters are *revealed* to greater or lesser extent. The main characters in the book of Samuel are three – Samuel, Saul and David – or four, if Yahweh can be spoken of as a character in the story without wrongful reduction. Beyond David and the principals are many others who figure significantly in the stories. In fact, as Birch (1998: 958) notes, 'No segment of the Old Testament is filled with a richer cast of characters.' Many of these are discussed in the commentary as they appear. But a few character sketches at this juncture seem in order, not least because some recent interpreters paint these characters rather differently from what earlier readers – to say nothing of the biblical writers themselves – would have anticipated or countenanced. Given space constraints, we shall focus below on Samuel, Saul and David, while other characters will be discussed in the commentary proper as they appear in the narrative.

Samuel provides a good first example. Though established in 1 Samuel 3:19–20 as Yahweh's authoritative prophet and recognized as such by *all Israel from Dan to Beersheba*, Samuel is portrayed in some recent writings as a rather nasty character: a 'resentful,

---

(2015: 104–107).

crotchety old man' (Middleton 2013: 88); a power-protecting political animal who sets Saul up for failure and will be content 'only with a puppet king' (Alter 1999: 73); a 'petulant', 'peevish' prophet who 'plays a daring, brutal game with Saul's faith, Saul's career, and eventually Saul's sanity', prompting the reader to wonder 'about Samuel (who appears to be unprincipled) and about Yahweh' (Brueggemann 1990: 101). In the light of these recent characterizations of Samuel, the objections of earlier writers that Samuel seems to combine in his person too many roles (priest, prophet, judge) pale into insignificance.[16]

But are these revisionist readings justified? The position taken in the present commentary is that they are not and that they create more problems than they solve. For instance, Middleton (2013), like various other interpreters today, regards Samuel as so concerned to protect his own position of power[17] that he is not above issuing prophecies of his own making.[18] Middleton acknowledges, though, that in various places Yahweh seems to endorse Samuel's words as his own. Middleton summarizes (87):

> I have argued that God did not initiate a decision to find someone to replace Saul (chap. 13); the reference to someone after God's heart was an extemporaneous utterance by the prophet, made in anger.

---

16. For reasoned defences of the biblical portrayal of Samuel as a multifaceted transitional figure at a critical juncture in Israel's history, see Gordon (1984: 27); cf. Gordon (1994); Provan, Long and Longman (2015: 274).
17. In brief summary, Middleton argues that Samuel is so worried that 'his unique and privileged position of leadership in Israel will now be threatened' by the anointing of a king (2013: 72) that he 'drags out the installation of Saul into three stages' in an attempt to 'keep Saul under his thumb' (73). Resentful of 'God's decision to give the people a king', Samuel 'seems determined to jerk Saul around and so psychologically sabotage his leadership potential' (74).
18. Middleton sees 'Samuel's misuse of prophetic authority (which has been intensifying since chap. 9)' as culminating 'in chap. 15 with his instructions to Saul to eradicate the Amalekites' (2013: 79; cf. 78).

Nor did God give a command through Samuel for Saul to destroy the Amalekites (chap. 15); that was Samuel's own invention. However, God clearly ends up backing Samuel on both counts.

To resolve this conundrum, Middleton (87–88) contends that Yahweh is essentially forced to endorse Samuel's words by virtue of the fact that he had committed himself in 1 Samuel 3:19 to *let none of Samuel's words fall to the ground*. To the present writer, Middleton's solution seems quite forced. Are we to understand that Yahweh is presented in Samuel as having placed himself in a bind? Moreover, were it the case that some of Samuel's prophetic pronouncements were of his own invention and not the word of Yahweh, would this not make Samuel a 'false prophet' (cf. Deut. 18:20)? Granted, Samuel can get things wrong, just like other characters in the book. For instance, his assumption, based on appearance, that Eliab must be the son of Jesse destined to be the next king after Saul is mistaken (1 Sam. 16:6). Another prophet, Nathan, also gets it wrong when he approves David's proposal to build Yahweh a *house* (2 Sam. 7:3). But in both these instances – and this is an important point – Yahweh immediately corrects the prophet (Samuel in 1 Sam. 16:7; Nathan in 2 Sam. 7:3–16). A further example is Samuel's misreading of the elders' request in 1 Samuel 8 as a rejection of him as judge; and again, Yahweh quickly corrects Samuel's misjudgment, pointing out that the offence is far graver (see 1 Sam. 8:6–7).

Before moving on to discuss other characters, it is worth reflecting on how and why revisionist readings may have arisen. Answers are doubtless many, but let me mention three possible contributing factors that occur to me. First, and rather ironically, these rather harsh and accusatory readings of Samuel may have something to do with the move in recent decades towards a greater appreciation of the *literary character* of the book of Samuel. High literature invites readers not simply to read what is made explicit 'in the lines' of a text but also to search out what is implicit 'between the lines'. As Sternberg (1985: 52) remarks, 'if the biblical truth is explicit, then the whole truth is implicit; and the more you bring to this art of implication, the more secrets and prizes it yields'. Having learned the art of implicit reading, some recent interpreters

INTRODUCTION

(of varying theological stripe) have begun to read not so much 'between the lines' as, rather, 'outside the lines'. That is, either they fail to take with sufficient seriousness what is explicitly stated 'in the lines' of the texts themselves or they simply choose to read against the grain of the text.

Second, the characters in the book of Samuel are often read in largely political terms, to the neglect of the theological issues involved. For instance, Alter's contention that Samuel wants to reduce Saul to a 'puppet king' can be seen rather differently when the question is not 'What does Samuel want?' but 'What does Yahweh want?' The key theological question is this: 'How can Israel have a human king, while Yahweh remains the Great King?' In other words, what kind of human king is suitable within a theocracy? God is willing, even desirous, to give Israel a king of the right sort (1 Sam. 16:1; see esp. commentary at 1 Sam. 2:10b). But this king must be a vassal king, or vice-regent, submissive to the initiatives and directives of the Great King. Sometimes Yahweh's instructions are communicated through one of his authorized messengers (prophets): Samuel, Nathan, Gad, and so forth. Other times he makes his will known in response to oracular enquiry, prayer, and so on. But the key point is that Samuel's instructions to Saul are not designed to keep Saul under Samuel's thumb as a 'puppet' but to test Saul's willingness to assume an appropriately subordinate posture as a 'vassal' of Yahweh.

Third, at the heart of revisionist readings not just of Samuel but also of Saul is a crucial exegetical misunderstanding. There is widespread confusion regarding the *command*, or 'charge', of the Lord which Samuel (in 1 Sam. 13:13) accuses Saul of not keeping. Of Samuel's accusation, Brueggemann (1990: 100) writes: 'This is a remarkable statement because Samuel cites no commandment that has been broken, nor can we construe one' (cited approvingly by Middleton 2013: 76). My own position, developed in several studies including the present commentary, is that we can indeed construe the 'commandment' to which Samuel refers.[19] It is the first

---

19. See, e.g., the commentary on 1 Sam. 10:7–8 and the bibliography mentioned in the next footnote.

'commandment' or 'charge' that Saul received on the occasion of his anointing by Samuel, at Yahweh's behest (see at 1 Sam. 10:7–8; 9:16–17, respectively). Understanding the nature of Saul's first charge as a test of his suitability to reign as king in Israel is of utmost importance to a right understanding of the book as a whole. It is to Saul, then, that we now turn.

Saul is one of the most perplexing characters in all of Scripture, or at least he has been perceived as such in the history of interpretation. He is chosen by Yahweh in response to the people's request for a king, and yet he is soon rejected as king for what seem to many interpreters to be very minor infractions, if infractions at all. He seems to mean well, at least at first, and he seems at times clueless in the face of Samuel's disappointment with his actions. One cannot but have some sympathy for Saul, who seems very much out of his depth. He is, of course, responsible for his own actions, or inactions, and it is worth noting that whatever 'good faith' Saul seems to demonstrate early in the story soon gives way to 'bad faith' as he learns more of what is expected of him. This bad faith is evidenced in various ways: in his declining interest in hearing from Yahweh (see at 1 Sam. 14:36); in his rather self-serving confession in 1 Samuel 15 (contrast vv. 24–25 with v. 30); in his relentless pursuit of David (19:1 and *passim*), 'the man of God's own choosing' (13:14), one better than Saul (15:28), whom Saul himself recognizes as the one to replace him on the throne (18:8; 20:31); in his slaughter of the priests of Nob (22:6–19); and so on. But for all this, one cannot avoid the sense that Saul is, to some degree at least, a victim of the circumstances in which he finds himself. He did not put himself forward to become king. Quite the contrary.

But if Saul is in some respects a victim, who is the villain? In his influential book entitled *The Fate of King Saul*, David Gunn concludes that Saul was 'essentially an innocent victim of God' (Gunn 1980: 123). Gunn, and the many who have followed his lead, focus on the wording of Saul's *rejection* in 1 Samuel 13 in coming to this conclusion. My contention, by contrast, is that one will never understand Saul's rejection if one does not first come to a clear understanding of his *election*. Unless and until Saul's 'first charge' (1 Sam. 10:7–8) is rightly understood as setting a test of his suitability to rule as

Yahweh's vassal, the nature and necessity of his rejection will remain a mystery. Moreover, to the extent that Saul is a victim, he is a victim not of Samuel nor of Yahweh, but of the people, who persist in asking for a king such as other nations have. Saul is 'the people's king'. Their request for such a king is consistently regarded as a sinful rejection – because it is a reductive redefinition – of the kingship of Yahweh (see commentary at 1 Sam. 8:19–20; 10:17–27; 12:19).

The difficulty of reading Saul correctly is exacerbated by the widespread (if mistaken) view that the story of Saul's rise to power, recorded in 1 Samuel 9 – 13, simply cannot be read as a coherent story. Tomoo Ishida (1977: 26), for instance, refers to the literary analysis and historical evaluation of the 'Samuel–Saul complex' as 'among the most vexed questions in biblical studies' and asserts that 'it is futile from the outset to attempt a reconstruction of a continuous history from all the narratives' (ibid.: 42). Here, too, the present commentary demurs and builds an argument for the literary and theological coherence of the Saul narratives.[20] An important key to understanding Saul's rise is to recognize that leaders in the Bible and in the ANE often progressed through three stages in their rise to power; we refer to these stages as *designation*, *demonstration* and *confirmation*.[21]

---

20. Our interpretation of Saul's rise and rejection was first and most fully presented in Long (1989) and developed more succinctly in several subsequent works, including Long (1994: 201–223) and, most recently, Provan, Long and Longman (2015: 276–285). In the latter two, a case is made also for the historical plausibility of the narrative sequence.
21. Halpern provides the seminal discussions of this process in a monograph and a lengthy article (both published in 1981); cf. also Edelman (1984). The three-part accession process for the king-designate informs our reading of the rise of Saul in numerous places (see, e.g., at 1 Sam. 9:15–17; the 'Meaning' sections to 1 Sam. 9:1 – 10:16 and to 10:17–27; 1 Sam. 11:14–15; the 'Meaning' section to 1 Sam. 12; 1 Sam. 13:1; 'Meaning' section to 1 Sam. 17; and *passim*).

In the briefest possible terms, Saul's anointing was his *designation*. On the occasion of this designation, Saul received a two-part charge. He was first to do what his hand found to do (10:7); I read this as a reference to the Philistine garrison mentioned in 10:5 and suggest that Saul's first action should have been to attack that garrison and thus provoke the Philistines, from whom Saul was meant to deliver Israel (9:16). The second part of his first charge was that he should then repair to Gilgal to await further instructions from Yahweh's prophet Samuel. Had Saul completed both parts of this first charge, he would have demonstrated his ability to lead in obedience to Yahweh's instruction. He would have shown himself to be a suitable vassal to the Great King. This would have led, in turn, to his confirmation as Israel's king. In the event, however, Saul does not attack the garrison. He does not demonstrate the ability to lead, and so he is not confirmed.

The three-stage rise to the throne is thus derailed by Saul's inaction. It becomes necessary, therefore, for Samuel to bring Saul to public attention in some other way. This he does by arranging a lot-casting in Mizpah (10:17–27). The lot falls on Saul, who is found hiding behind some baggage. The lot-casting constitutes a second *designation* of sorts. At this point in the story, Saul has still not done anything to *demonstrate* his ability to lead (e.g. he has not attacked the Philistine garrison of 10:5). This prompts certain naysayers to ask, *How can this fellow save us?* (10:27).

Soon enough, Saul has an opportunity to lead in battle against the Ammonites, and his victory on that occasion is a *demonstration* sufficient to silence the naysayers, please the people and get the kingship process back on track (ch. 11). In the aftermath of the defeat of the Ammonites, Saul and all the people hold a great celebration (11:15). Samuel, however, is not mentioned as one of the celebrants. Instead, he addresses the people in chapter 12 to the effect that kingship and the new king may succeed or fail, depending on whether both people and king *fear the* LORD *and serve him faithfully with all your heart* (12:24). The point is this: a test remains to be stood. Samuel's reticence to celebrate has to do with the fact that Saul has still not fulfilled his first charge (10:7–8), a charge specifically designed to test Saul's suitability to rule as a vassal king willing to take his orders from the Great King.

With Jonathan's attack on the Philistine garrison in 13:3, Saul's first charge comes back into play (cf. 10:5, 7). Saul repairs to Gilgal (13:4) to wait for Samuel, in accordance with the second stage of his charge (cf. 10:8). The test is on, and Saul fails (see at ch. 13 in the commentary for discussion). Saul will be given further chances to succeed, but, in the end, he is rejected as king, because he has *rejected the word of the* LORD (15:23). Saul proves, in the end, to be the kind of king the people desired, but not the kind of king the Lord desired for them (see 16:1 and commentary).

David has not been regarded as quite so difficult to understand as Saul, but it remains the case that David is regularly misunderstood. Some regard him as virtually flawless up to his sudden catastrophic fall into adultery (with Bathsheba) and murder (of Bathsheba's husband Uriah) in 2 Samuel 11. Such a view of David betrays a lack of attention to various details in the texts. Other interpreters regard David as a rather unsavoury, to say nothing of unsafe, character – someone you would not wish to invite for dinner. Both Halpern (2001: 73–103) and McKenzie (2000: 32–34) cast David as a 'serial killer' ultimately responsible for deaths which the writers of Samuel explicitly ascribe to others. To be sure, some of David's enemies (e.g. the Benjaminite Shimei in 2 Sam. 16) regarded David as a 'man of blood'. But it is not clear why modern readers should side with Shimei rather than with the biblical writers. The contention of the present commentary is that they should not.[22] A close reading of the story of David reveals a talented, if deeply flawed, man, and yet a man with a genuine heart for God. From the life of David we learn many lessons: the faithfulness of God to his people *in extremis*; the proper orientation to leadership (raised up by God for the sake of the people, 2 Sam. 5:12); the sad consequences of laxity and abuse of power; the ripple effects of sin in families and communities; the interconnectedness of private and public life; and so on.

Yahweh. Revisionist readings of Samuel's main characters, such as we have described above, cannot but lead on to revisionist readings of Yahweh's own character and actions. One of the earliest

---

22. For full discussion, see Provan, Long and Longman (2015: 288–293).

examples is also one of the most extreme. Gunn (1980: 128–129) writes:

> At the level of the reader's 'overview', questions about the moral basis of Yahweh's actions are inescapable. If we are to condemn Saul for his jealous persecution of David, how much more is Yahweh to be condemned for his jealous persecution of Saul! And the question is one that lies before us in the story not only in our puzzlement (not to speak of Saul's) at the judgement scenes but repeatedly, from then on, in the striking disparity of treatment between Saul and David. Yahweh manipulates Saul mercilessly, and he does so for what, on most men's terms, must count as less than honourable motives. He is insulted, feels jealous, is anxious to justify himself. It is tempting to say that this is the human face of God – but to say that is perhaps to denigrate man, and that is not something this Old Testament story does; rather we might say that here we see the dark side of God.

The present commentary sees things very differently. While it has no interest in simply repeating traditional understandings of Samuel, Saul or David, neither does it wish to engage in revisionist readings which seem unwarranted by the texts themselves. As I have suggested above, the key to better readings begins with a better understanding of Saul's first charge and of his failure in respect of it. This in turn leads to a better understanding of the prophet Samuel[23] and of Yahweh himself. It also contributes to a clearer understanding of what is needed if human kingship is to function appropriately in what remains fundamentally a theocracy, where God is king. All this provides the necessary background for understanding why Saul was rejected and David was not.

So, again, the goal of the present commentary is not to present traditional understandings of the characters of Samuel simply because they are traditional. And in fact, some readings presented in the commentary will not seem very traditional at all. The goal, simply, is to read the texts well, attending to both their explicit and

---

23. It is worth noting that Samuel is regarded favourably in other parts of Scripture (e.g. Ps. 99:6; Jer. 15:1).

implicit messages, and seeking to read appropriately 'between the lines' and 'with the grain' of the text. Reading in this way can be challenging, not least because of the interplay of literary, historical and theological concerns in the book of Samuel, and because of the characteristic reticence of the writer(s) to spell out the 'moral of the story'. For readers able to read the text in Hebrew, or in one or more of the ancient languages into which it was translated (e.g. the Greek Septuagint, the Aramaic Targums, the Syriac Peshitta, the Latin Vulgate, and so forth), the interpretive task is both harder and, at the same time, more rewarding. It is more rewarding because one can better appreciate subtleties not always apparent in English: wordplays, dramatic ironies, double meanings (double entendres – though not necessarily of the risqué sort), and so forth. It is more challenging, however, simply because of the state of the Hebrew text that has come down to us.

5. The text

The Masoretic Hebrew text (MT) of 1 and 2 Samuel appears to 'have suffered more in the process of transmission than perhaps any other part of the Old Testament' (Gordon 1986: 57). There is no certainty as to why this is, though one suggestion is that the very popularity of the Samuel scroll may have caused it to suffer more wear and tear between copyings than other biblical books. A worn manuscript could lead to inadvertent scribal errors. Whatever the reason or reasons, Samuel exhibits a fair number of places where material appears to have been lost through 'haplography'. Haplography occurs when a scribe's eye inadvertently skips from a word or phrase in the text to the same word or phrase elsewhere in the text and thereby leaves out some intervening material (see, e.g., the commentary at 1 Sam. 10:27 – 11:1a; 13:15).[24] Conversely,

---

24. It is, of course, possible that some longer readings, say, in LXX, which are generally regarded as preserving a reading lost in the MT by haplography, may in fact involve scribal expansions employing 'resumptive repetition' where a word or phrase just prior to the insertion is repeated at the end of the insertion to signal that the

possible instances of 'dittography', double writing, also occur. For instance, the Amalekite king Agag's improbably hopeful statement in MT 1 Samuel 15:32 – *Surely the bitterness of death is past* – may have arisen from a scribe's mistakenly writing the word 'bitter' (*mar*) a second time as 'is past' (*sār*); the initial consonants look similar in Hebrew. The circa second-century-BC Greek translation of the Old Testament (LXX) has Agag simply asking, 'Is death as bitter as this?' The Aramaic Targum, on the other hand, reads, 'Please my master, death is bitter.' The Targum may attest the double occurrence of *mar*, with the Targumist taking one of the occurrences as *mar* IV, meaning 'master', and the second as *mar* II, 'bitter' (Jastrow 1903: 834).

In addition to the versional witnesses to the Old Testament text, the discovery of the Dead Sea Scrolls in the middle of the twentieth century brought to light additional ancient Hebrew witnesses to the book of Samuel (or at least to parts of it). The most important of the Qumran discoveries with respect to Samuel was found in Cave 4 and is referred to as 4QSam[a]. In text-critical decision-making, LXX and 4QSam[a] are often considered alongside MT as major witnesses. Some English translations put particular store by these witnesses, especially when LXX and 4QSam[a] agree against MT. NRSV, for instance, includes many longer readings from LXX (1 Sam. 13:15 offers a case in point).

The recensional history of the various witnesses has been much discussed and debated and need not be further discussed here. For convenient summaries of the strengths and weaknesses of various theories, see, for example, Gordon (1986: 57–62); Firth (2009: 39–40); and Vannoy (2009: 10–14). When all is said and done, and with our present state of knowledge, 'it seems best to approach each textual problem in an unprejudiced way, evaluating any differing readings in the Qumran materials or the Septuagint on their own merits and on a case-by-case basis' (Vannoy 2009: 13). The present commentary begins with the MT, but with an eye to how other witnesses may on occasion help us. Text-critical decisions are reached on the basis of both external and internal

---

insertion is complete (cf. in some respects Pisano 1984).

criteria. The former have to do with the weight of the manuscript evidence (e.g. agreement of LXX and 4QSam^a against MT carries some weight). The internal evidence, however, is equally important, and here standard text-critical protocols come into play. All things being equal, a briefer reading (*lectio brevior*) or more difficult reading (*lectio difficilior*) may be given the edge, based on the assumption that scribes tend to expand/elaborate or to improve/smooth out difficult readings. The overriding question in the end is this: which reading best explains how the others could have arisen? Put differently, the best reading is the one by which the emergence of the other readings can be explained. At the end of the day, text-critical decisions involve a host of considerations, including one's overall understanding of the passage in which the difficult text sits. As Alter (1999: xxvi) remarks, 'Ultimately, such decisions depend on the interpreter's discretion.' The present commentary makes no attempt to address every significant textual variant. Rather, those are considered when a question of exegetical significance is involved.

Before leaving the issues of text and text-critical decisions, it is worth mentioning that in writing this commentary I was occasionally struck by the potential of double entendres in texts that are regularly regarded as textually corrupt (see, e.g., at 1 Sam. 14:18–19 ['ark' or 'ephod']; 14:47 ['inflict punishment' or 'make oneself guilty' or 'be delivered']). Other instances of possible double meanings not necessarily involving text-critical issues include 1 Samuel 2:29; 8:6; 9:17, 20; 10:27; 18:9, 15; 23:26, 28; 25:2; 31:3; 2 Samuel 1:19, 21; 6:6; 9:4–5 [17:27]; 11:8, 24; 12:24; 13:20; 15:27; 16:15–19; 17:20.

6. Author and date

Who wrote the book of Samuel, and when? As has been noted already, the book itself does not tell us. Ancient Jewish tradition (e.g. Babylonian Talmud tractate *Baba Bathra* 14b–15) ascribes some of the book to Samuel and the rest to Gad and Nathan. Medieval Jewish commentator Isaac Abrabanel (1437–1508) suggests that Jeremiah may have been responsible for incorporating the earlier work of these prophets into what is now considered the book of

Samuel, though he also mentions that Ezra may have played some part in the final editing (see Garsiel 2010: 4). Attempts to name specific authors of the book are highly speculative, and a more fruitful approach is to focus on the question of the date of the book's composition. The book may well have come together in stages, but the question is when the text essentially as we now have it might have been formed.[25] It comes as no surprise that opinions on this question vary widely. Still, there seem to be good reasons to assume that the bulk of the book was composed early, perhaps during the reign of David's son Solomon in the tenth century (see, e.g., Halpern 2001: 57–72, 224–227; Garsiel 2010). The following is but a sampling of some of the considerations that Garsiel mentions (in some cases anticipated by Halpern): the book of Samuel makes no reference to the major powers, Assyria and Babylonia, that begin to dominate in the ninth century (12); Samuel's description of kingship in 1 Samuel 8 is appropriate to its setting but not to later periods when monarchy was more developed (12); geographic details and war strategies are accurately described (15); 'one cannot find in the book any significant influence of the Aramaic language that later became an international means of correspondence' (18); literacy seems to be widespread, especially amongst scribes, military commanders and priests (29–31); the Philistine monopoly on 'metal weaponry and agricultural tools' mentioned in 1 Samuel 13:19–23 existed only in the eleventh century BC, after which Israel had such items (33); references in 1 Samuel 27 to settlements in the Negev wealthy enough to yield spoils of war make little sense after the tenth century, as they were destroyed during Shishak's campaign in 926 BC, after which the Negev hills 'remained desolate until the Persian Period' (34). These and other considerations lead Garsiel to conclude (34) that

> In the light of the above literary, historical and archaeological considerations, it seems to me that there is no possibility other than to attribute most of the significant composition of the book of Samuel to the tenth century BCE, though small changes took place

---

25. For more detailed discussion, see Firth (2013: 41–54).

much later.

Having earlier blazed a similar trail, Halpern (2001: 226) writes, 'Overall, the implication of the preceding chapters is that large parts of our information on the United Monarchy stem from roughly contemporary sources.'

Certainty in matters of authorship and dating is not possible, inasmuch as the text makes no *explicit* statements, but neither is certainty in such matters crucial to our understanding the book and its central messages. We turn now finally, and briefly, to what may be regarded as central theological concerns of the book.

7. Theological centre

Given the richness and size of the book of Samuel, any attempt to describe its theology under but a few rubrics is bound to be deficient. The discussion below will be conducted under but three headings, but the book itself has much more to offer, as shall become apparent in the reading of the biblical text and the commentary thereto. Nevertheless, it seems that certain theological verities are quite central to the book of Samuel, and it is to these that the following three sections are dedicated.

a. The weight of God

At the risk of stating the obvious, the theological centre of the book of Samuel is God himself. More specifically, the central conviction of the book is that Yahweh carries ultimate weight in all things, including the affairs of men and women, religion and politics, leadership and society. And this 'weight' (*kabôd*) is to be 'honoured' (the Heb. root *kbd* includes notions of weight, honour, glory and the ascribing of such). Failure to recognize God's weight/glory brings disaster, much as failure to recognize the force of gravity brings disaster. The weight of God's sovereignty is signalled from the very beginning of the book: in the explanation of Hannah's infertility as resulting from the fact that *the LORD had closed her womb* (1:5), in Hannah's serious engagement with the Lord with respect to her pain (rather than having recourse to coping strategies such as avoidance or aggression) and in her prayer celebrating the Lord's elevation of the humble and abasement of the proud (2:1–10). The most direct, early references to the importance of giving God honour/weight come in the judgment pronounced against Eli by the man of God in 2:29–30. This passage serves programmatically to establish the basis for success and failure in the book of Samuel. Those who 'underweight' God (fail to honour him) will themselves be lightly esteemed, while those who give him weight will themselves carry weight in God's eyes. This explicit theologizing in the context of Eli's rejection from the priestly office is programmatic in the sense that it elucidates the grounds of Saul's later rejection from the kingly office. By the same token, Eli's acceptance of the divine will in removing him from office (3:18) stands in stark contrast to Saul's refusal to accept the divine will. The grounds of Saul's rejection become less mysterious when seen in the light of the earlier, more clearly explained rejection of Eli. Throughout the book of Samuel, the question is always whether Yahweh is the centre of gravity in the characters' lives and actions. Despite his severe lapses, David sought to honour Yahweh and found in him the centre of his being, even in confession: 'Against you, you only, have I sinned' (Ps. 51:4). Saul sought to keep to religious protocol up to a point, but ultimately he showed more concern for his own honour than for that of Yahweh: he *set up a monument in his own honour* (15:12) and appealed to Samuel to *honour me before the elders of my people and before Israel* (15:30).

b. The weight of the prophetic word

Derivative of the weight of the Lord's glory is the weight of the prophetic word. Old Testament prophets were regarded as messengers of Yahweh. Their prophecies were not of their own making. Indeed, any prophet presenting as a prophetic pronouncement a message of his own design was liable to death. In a classic passage found in Deuteronomy 18, Yahweh says to Moses:

> I will raise up for them a prophet like you from among their fellow Israelites, and I will put my words in his mouth. He will tell them everything I command him. I myself will call to account anyone who does not listen to my words that the prophet speaks in my name. But a prophet who presumes to speak in my name anything I have not

commanded, or a prophet who speaks in the name of other gods,
is to be put to death.
(Deut. 18:18–20)

If the theological centre of the book of Samuel is God himself, then his prophetic spokespersons are also very close to the centre, as it is through them that Yahweh speaks, raising up kings or removing them, calling the people to repentance and rescuing them. As we noted earlier, the prophets were human beings capable of being wrong, but the pattern of the book suggests that, at least when the prophets were functioning in their messenger role, any mistaken judgments were quickly corrected (we noted 1 Sam. 8:6–7; 16:7; 2 Sam. 7:3–16; see discussion of Samuel in the section on characters in Samuel). Fraudulent prophecies would be met with the strictest of sanctions.

c. The character of kingship

Once we recognize that God as Israel's king and the prophets as God's messengers stand at the centre of the book of Samuel, we can begin to solve some of the riddles of the book. Pre-eminent among these is the matter of Saul's rejection and David's restoration, despite the sins of each. We touched upon this matter earlier in the discussion of Saul as a perplexing character in the book, and we shall return to it repeatedly in the commentary. As we read Saul's story leading up to his enthronement, his divine rejection and his resistance to removal from office, we see repeated signs of his 'underweighting' God. In our reading of David's life, with all its good and bad moments, we discover that in the grand scheme of things God is at the centre of David's world (notwithstanding David's egregious and costly sins). The difference between Israel's first two kings is as simple as this: Saul occasionally bowed the knee to Yahweh (1 Sam. 15:30), while David not only assumed the posture of worship, he worshipped (2 Sam. 7:18–29).

ANALYSIS

1. BEFORE THE MONARCHY: GOD RULES AND RESCUES HIS PEOPLE (1 SAMUEL 1:1 – 7:17)
   A. God's prophet: Hannah, Samuel and the priestly house of Eli (1:1 – 4:1a)
      i. Hannah's problem (1:1–28)
      ii. Hannah's prayer (2:1–10)
      iii. Eli, his boys and the boy Samuel (2:11–26)
      iv. Rejection of the priestly house of Eli (2:27–36)
      v. Establishment of Samuel as a prophet (3:1 – 4:1a)
   B. God's power: the ark of God at large in Philistia (4:1b – 7:1)
      i. The ark's 'capture' by the Philistines (4:1b–22)
      ii. The ark's victory tour of Philistia (5:1–12)
      iii. The ark's return from Philistia (6:1 – 7:1)
   C. God's power at work in God's prophet: 'Thus far the Lord has helped us' (7:2–17)

2. THE BEGINNING OF MONARCHY: THE RISE OF ISRAEL'S KING (1 SAMUEL 8:1 – 12:25)
   A. Israel asks for a king 'such as all the other nations have' (8:1–22)

B. The rise of Saul: 'and Saul and all the Israelites held a great celebration' (9:1 – 11:15)
      i. Saul anointed and charged (9:1 – 10:16)
      ii. Saul chosen by lot (10:17–27)
      iii. Saul's victory over the Ammonites (11:1–15)
   C. Samuel's instructions and warnings about kingship (12:1–25)

3. THE PEOPLE'S KING: THE REIGN AND REJECTION OF KING SAUL (1 SAMUEL 13:1 – 15:35)
   A. Saul versus the Philistines: Saul's first rejection (13:1 – 14:52)
      i. Jonathan's first initiative and Saul's response (13:1–23)
      ii. Jonathan's second initiative and Saul's response (14:1–52)
   B. Saul versus the Amalekites: Saul's second rejection (15:1–35)

4. GOD'S KING: THE RISE OF DAVID AND FALL OF SAUL (1 SAMUEL 16:1 – 31:13)
   A. David's rise delights all but Saul (16:1 – 18:30)
      i. David is anointed by Samuel and enters Saul's court (16:1–23)
      ii. David defeats Goliath and routs the Philistines (17:1–58)
      iii. David finds favour with the house of Saul, but is feared by Saul himself (18:1–30)
   B. Saul seeks David's life (19:1 – 23:29)
      i. Saul's attempts to kill David are thwarted by Jonathan, Michal, Samuel and God himself (19:1–24)
      ii. Jonathan aids and encourages David (20:1–42)
      iii. David deceives Ahimelech and escapes to Gath (21:1–15)
      iv. David continues his flight; Saul massacres the priests at Nob (22:1–23)
      v. David delivers and is delivered (23:1–29)
   C. David protects Saul's life and avoids blood-guilt (24:1 – 26:25)
      i. David spares Saul's life in the cave (24:1–22)

ANALYSIS

      ii. Abigail saves David from incurring blood-guilt (25:1–44)
      iii. David spares Saul's life in the camp (26:1–25)
   D. Desperate times for David and for Saul (27:1 – 31:13)
      i. David flees to the Philistines (27:1–12)
      ii. Saul goes to the witch at Endor (28:1–25)
      iii. David escapes a tight spot and rescues his own city of Ziklag (29:1 – 30:31)
      iv. Saul takes his own life in a losing battle with the Philistines (31:1–13)

5. GOD'S KING REIGNS (2 SAMUEL 1:1 – 5:5)

   A. David's reaction to news of Saul's death (1:1–27)
      i. David's interrogation and execution of the Amalekite messenger (1:1–16)
      ii. David's lament over Saul and Jonathan (1:17–27)
   B. David becomes king over Judah, and the war between the houses of David and Saul continues (2:1 – 4:12)
   C. David becomes king over all Israel (5:1–5)

6. DAVID'S REIGN BLESSED BY GOD (2 SAMUEL 5:6 – 10:19)

   A. David secures his rule (5:6–25)
      i. David conquers Jerusalem and makes it his capital (5:6–16)
      ii. David conquers Israel's arch-enemy, the Philistines (5:17–25)
   B. David brings the ark to Jerusalem (6:1–23)
   C. The dynastic promise to David: on the building of houses (7:1–29)
   D. David's successes and his officials (8:1–18)
   E. David's kindness received by Mephibosheth (9:1–13)
   F. David's kindness rebuffed by Hanun (10:1–19)

7. DAVID'S SIN AND ITS CONSEQUENCES (2 SAMUEL 11:1 – 20:26)

   A. Sin and reconciliation (11:1 – 12:31)
      i. David's sin (11:1–27)

    ii. David's repentance (12:1–31)
  B. Sin and incomplete reconciliation (13:1 – 14:33)
    i. Sexual abuse and murder within the household of David (13:1–39)
    ii. The return of Absalom to Jerusalem (14:1–33)
  C. Absalom's revolt and death (15:1 – 19:43)
    i. Absalom's revolt, David's flight (15:1 – 16:14)
    ii. Absalom's folly, David's escape (16:15 – 17:29)
    iii. Absalom's death, David's grief and Joab's ultimatum (18:1 – 19:43)
      a. Absalom's death (18:1–18)
      b. David's grief (18:19 – 19:8a)
      c. David's return to Jerusalem (19:8b–43)
  D. Sheba's revolt and death (20:1–26)

8. CONCLUSION: LAST WORDS ABOUT DAVID AND HIS REIGN (2 SAMUEL 21:1 – 24:25)
  A. Royal sin and its resolution (21:1–14)
  B. Short list of David's champions (21:15–22)
  C. Long poetic composition: David's song of praise (22:1–51)
  D. Short poetic composition: David's last words (23:1–7)
  E. Long list of David's champions (23:8–39)
  F. Royal sin and its resolution (24:1–25)

COMMENTARY

1. BEFORE THE MONARCHY: GOD RULES AND RESCUES HIS PEOPLE (1 SAMUEL 1:1 – 7:17)

A. God's prophet: Hannah, Samuel and the priestly house of Eli (1:1 – 4:1a)

Context

How a story begins is important. As the book of Samuel opens, we find ourselves at the end of the period of the judges. But kingship is in the air. The book will in due course recount the lives of powerful men and far-reaching political changes. But it begins with the story of a woman in pain. With all its human interest, Hannah's story serves a much larger purpose in the book of Samuel.

i. Hannah's problem (1:1–28)
Comment
1–3. Master storytellers can say a lot in just a few lines. The first three verses of the opening scene to the book of Samuel introduce the main characters, locate them and suggest the point of tension that will propel the story along. In verse 1 we meet *a certain man*

named *Elkanah*. The manner of his introduction,[1] along with his ample genealogy and the mention of his *two wives*, *Hannah* and *Peninnah* (v. 2), suggests that Elkanah was a man of some importance.

Whenever the names of characters are expressly mentioned in biblical narratives, it is worth asking whether the meanings of the names bear some significance beyond their function as labels. With respect to the present narrative, and in answer to the question '*sunt nomina omina*' (lit. 'are names omens?'), Walter Dietrich (2007: 317–318) writes:

> 'El-kanah' means 'God created', and 'Hannah' means 'He (God) was merciful' (probably a shortened form of Ḥani-El). God emerges from the period of the judges – not in person, but through this man and this woman. Elkanah will prove himself to be a mild and loving (yet not especially helpful) husband, very different from the men who were the subject during the end of Judges (Judg 19–21). Hannah is a strong and determined woman, not merely the victim of male action and violence, like so many women during the end of the period of the judges.

In a sense, then, the book of Samuel opens not just with the story of Elkanah, Hannah and Peninnah, but with the story of God's response to 'the desperate hopelessness of Israel. God makes a new beginning possible by giving Elkanah and Hannah to Israel, Samuel to Elkanah and Hannah, and Saul through Samuel to Israel' (Dietrich 2007: 318).

What are we to make of Elkanah's two wives? Polygyny (having more than one wife) was practised by 'kings' in this period, but seldom by commoners.[2] Elkanah was a commoner, even if a prominent one, and so the question arises as to what may have prompted him to take two wives. The text does not tell us directly. But if Hannah was Elkanah's first wife, as may be suggested by the fact

---

1. Cf. similar introductions at Josh. 1:1; Judg. 13:2; 1 Sam. 9:1.
2. On polygamous practices in the ancient world, see Long (2009a: 271–272). And for a full discussion, see Davidson (2007).

that she is named first before Peninnah in verse 2, then perhaps it was her childlessness that led Elkanah to take a second wife. If so, then neither childless Hannah nor second-wife, baby-producing Peninnah (whose name may suggest something like 'fruitful' or 'fecund') can have been very happy. Such a familial arrangement would have been a formula for conflict.[3] And conflict there was, not least when Elkanah would take his family *Year after year . . . to worship and sacrifice to the* LORD *Almighty*[4] *at Shiloh*[5] (v. 3). Religious festivals were a regular feature of ancient life, and not just in Israel. Ancient Egyptians may have celebrated as many as fifty or sixty festivals annually (Kitchen 1977: 86). The Pentateuch stipulates three, named in Deuteronomy 16:1–16 (cf. also Exod. 23:14–17; 34:18–23). The present passage may have in view 'the annual festival of the LORD in Shiloh' referenced in Judges 21:19 or perhaps a family ceremony in Shiloh such as the one in Bethlehem presupposed in 1 Samuel 20:6.

Three more characters are mentioned in verse 3: *Eli* ('exalted one'?) and his two sons, *Hophni* ('tadpole'?) and *Phinehas* ('black

---

3. On the generally negative depiction of polygyny in the OT, Davidson remarks: 'In the narratives containing the practice of polygamy or concubinage, invariably the divinely inspired narrators include their tacit condemnation of these practices' (2007: 211 and *passim*).

4. 'LORD Almighty' (*yhwh ṣĕbā'ôt*) occurs here for the first time in the OT, and will be repeated nine more times in Samuel. The title, which is a favourite among the writing prophets (esp. Isaiah, Jeremiah, Haggai, Zechariah, Malachi), combines the personal covenant name of God with the word 'hosts' (according to the traditional understanding). Depending on the context, the hosts in view might be the hosts of Israel (as in 1 Sam. 17:45), the celestial hosts, sun, moon and stars (Deut. 4:19), or the angelic hosts (Josh. 5:14). The combination 'Yahweh of Hosts', then, is expressive of Yahweh's sovereignty over all heavenly and earthly powers, which leads naturally to the rendering 'LORD Almighty'.

5. Shiloh (modern Khirbet Seilun) lies midway between Jerusalem and Shechem to the north. Its first mention in the Bible is in Josh. 18:1, where it is associated with the 'tent of meeting'.

one'?), who were *priests of the LORD* in Shiloh.[6] They will not figure in the story, however, until later. So the story begins with the introduction of Elkanah, a *man from Ramathaim* ('Twin heights'?), a *Zuphite from the hill country of Ephraim*.[7] But the story is chiefly about Hannah, a woman of faith and a woman in pain.

4–7. In verse 4 the action gets underway, signalled in the Hebrew text by the discourse marker *wayĕhî* ('and it happened'). Though difficult to capture with precision in English translation, the Hebrew syntax suggests that verses 4–7 make up one lengthy sentence, with a digression in the middle. The sentence begins with the statement that on a particular day Elkanah sacrificed (v. 4a) and concludes with the statement that (on that day) Hannah *wept and would not eat* (v. 7b). In the middle is the digression explaining the cause of Hannah's misery. *Year after year* (v. 7), at festival time, Elkanah *would give portions* to Peninnah, to each of her children and to Hannah. Just what kind of portion Elkanah gave to Hannah – 'double' (ESV, NASB, NIV, NRSV), 'worthy' (KJV), 'one portion only' (JPS), 'only one choice portion' (NLT), and so on – is the subject of debate, as the Hebrew phrase *mānāh 'aḥat 'appāyim* is difficult.[8] Whatever the precise nature of Hannah's portion, Elkanah's motivation is clear enough (as his words in v. 8 reinforce). He hopes to soothe Hannah's wounded spirit, *because . . . the LORD had closed her womb* (v. 5). Not so Peninnah, Hannah's *rival* (v. 6). Her every inclination, especially at festival times, is to rub as much salt into Hannah's wound as possible. (Peninnah's own pain may have been

---

6. These name meanings are by no means assured, but are mooted by some lexica.

7. *Zuphite* may refer to Elkanah's Levitical ancestor Zuph (1 Chr. 6:26, 35; Samuel is mentioned in 6:27–28, 33) or to a district of Ephraim (see *district of Zuph* in 1 Sam. 9:5), or perhaps to both, if the district derived its name from the individual. That Elkanah was resident in Ephraim, though of the tribe of Levi, is commensurate with the stipulation in Josh. 21 that the Levites were to live in towns scattered throughout the other tribes (on Ephraim, see Josh. 21:5, 20–21).

8. For discussion of the various options, see Firth (2009: 51); McCarter (1980: 51–52); Tsumura (2007: 113).

considerable if, as suggested above, she became Elkanah's wife mostly for reproductive purposes.) And so, on the day, *Hannah wept and would not eat*.[9]

8. *Don't I mean more to you than ten sons?* Elkanah matches his well-intended actions with well-intended words, but both prove ineffectual. In fact, Elkanah's attempt to 'fix' Hannah's problem through sublimation may have only deepened her despair. Her rival doesn't care, and even her loving husband doesn't understand. In her pain, several courses of action are open to her. Given her favoured status with Elkanah, Hannah could meet Peninnah's fire with fire: 'You have children, *I* have *our* husband's love,' she might say. Or she could follow Elkanah's implicit suggestion and flee the pain through sublimation. As the next section reveals, however, she responds with neither fight nor flight, but takes her pain to God.

9–11. *Once they had finished eating and drinking in Shiloh, Hannah stood up* (v. 9). The pronoun *they* is supplied by LXX. MT lacks it and reads literally: 'Hannah arose, after eating and drinking in Shiloh.' It is possible that Hannah agreed to eat in deference to Elkanah's concern. But it seems more likely – especially in view of the later notice in verse 18 that Hannah *ate something* – that the reference is to the generalized eating and drinking of those gathered, at the conclusion of which Hannah exited. *In Shiloh* has seemed redundant to some commentators, and various alternative readings of the Hebrew have been suggested. Gordon (1986: 74) lists the chief contenders as including 'boiled flesh' (Wellhausen), 'in the dining hall' (Kittel) or 'privately' (McCarter), all of which make some sense of the Hebrew consonants in MT and of the general context. He notes, nevertheless, that 'the versional support for MT is very strong', and we might add that it is not out of keeping with Hebrew narrative technique to recall by way of repetition something mentioned earlier in the text (viz., Shiloh in v. 3).

Before we are given any further information on what Hannah arose to do, the narrator digresses to recall another individual mentioned in passing in verse 3, namely, Eli. He is described as *the priest*,

---

9. Refusal to eat because of deep anguish features at various key points in Samuel (e.g. 1 Sam. 1:7–9, 18; 20:34; 28:20–25; 2 Sam. 3:35; 12:17–21).

by which we should understand that he was 'chief priest' at this time (Gordon 1986: 74). He is *sitting on his chair* [or 'throne', Heb. *kissē*'] *by the doorpost of the* LORD's *house* [Heb. *hêkal*, 'temple' or 'palace']. 'Throne' and 'palace' may hint at the trajectory of the book of Samuel towards kingship – and there will be further linguistic hints – but the more mundane understanding of Eli's passive posture and cultic location is appropriate to the present context. Reference to the Lord's 'temple' (v. 9) at this juncture in Israel's story might seem anachronistic, as indeed might the earlier reference to the *house of the* LORD (v. 7). But the reference is almost certainly to the tabernacle.[10]

Weeping and praying (v. 10), Hannah makes a vow (v. 11). The modern reader may find Hannah's vow surprising in a couple of respects. First, as Tsumura (2007: 118) notes, 'a woman who had suffered so from not having a child would not [normally] give him up once he was born'. Second, Hannah's *if you . . . then I* proposition might sound like crass bargaining with God. But the ancient writer would not likely have seen things this way. The making of vows was a regular feature in petitionary prayers (cf. the 'lament psalms'), and Fokkelman is on the right track when he suggests that 'Hannah's case', like Abraham's willingness to sacrifice Isaac in Genesis 22, 'is also about a total relinquishing in the context of a living relationship with God' (Fokkelman 1993: 4.38). Abraham's action was commanded by God, as a kind of test (Gen. 22:2). What can be said of Hannah's vow? We can deduce from the long-term nature of Hannah's distress that her prayers will likely have been habitual. In one of his homilies on Ephesians, Chrysostom makes the following remark about Hannah: 'Where tears are, there is always affliction also; where affliction is, there is great wisdom and attentiveness . . . Truly here was a daughter of Abraham. He gave when it was demanded of him. She offers even before it is demanded' (*NPNF 1* 13: 17; cited in *ACCS* 4: 197). Was Hannah's offer solely her idea? Perhaps. But if we may be permitted to speculate, long-term engagement with God in prayer may have led to a

---

10. See Long (2009a: 274); and, more thoroughly, Friedman (1992: 292–300).

growing conviction that, should God give her a son, God would also have very special plans for that son. If there is any truth in this speculation, then Hannah's words may seem less indicative of bargaining than of submission to the divine will.

Hannah promises further that *no razor will ever be used on his head* (v. 11). According to Numbers 6:1–22, 'Nazirites' (those consecrated by a vow to God) were to signify their consecration by abstaining from three things: drinking the fruit of the vine, cutting the hair and touching a dead body. The MT of the present verse mentions only the second of these two requirements. LXX and 4QSam[a] present a longer text and *may* contain the word *nāzîr* (from which 'Nazirite' derives), though the fact that the former is in Greek and the latter is quite fragmentary makes this uncertain. LXX (followed by NRSV) explicitly includes in verse 11 the first two of the three restrictions. Whether Hannah was dedicating Samuel as a Nazirite remains a point of debate, but it is clear that she is dedicating him for lifelong service to God.[11]

12–14. So far, Eli has been named (v. 3) and located sitting at the entrance to the 'temple' (v. 9). Now, for the first time, he speaks. And he doesn't make a very good first impression, whether with respect to his powers of observation or to his appraisal of the situation. Having observed Hannah's mouth moving without making any sound, Eli assumes that she is drunk. Perhaps his failing eyesight (3:2; 4:15) is to blame, or perhaps fervent prayer, like the word of the Lord (3:1), is a rare phenomenon at the end of the period of the judges over which Eli presides. The introduction of Eli's sons, beginning in 2:12, will make it clear that cultic laxity and abuse are widespread in Eli's world. Whatever the case, Hannah is quick to correct Eli's misperception.

15–18. *Not so, my lord . . . I am a woman who is deeply troubled . . . I have not been drinking wine or beer* – the only thing being poured out is *my soul to the LORD*. Hannah in verse 16 is particularly concerned that Eli not misjudge her as a *wicked woman* (lit. 'daughter of belial'; to be *bĕliyyāʿal* is to be worthless, wicked, good-for-nothing).

---

11. For a brief discussion, see Tsumura (2007: 118–119); more fully, Youngblood (2009: 47–48); Hahn (2011: 56–60).

Ironically, while Hannah does not deserve such an epithet, Eli's own sons very much do and are explicitly branded as *bĕnê-bĕliyyā'al* ('sons of belial') when we meet them in 2:12. Eli may be obtuse, but he is not unkind to Hannah: *Go in peace, and may the God of Israel grant you what you have asked of him* (v. 17). Hannah responds deferentially to Eli and then departs and eats something, *and her face was no longer downcast*. Nothing has yet materially changed in Hannah's circumstances, but she appears both comforted for having poured out her heart to God and encouraged by Eli's blessing.

19–20. Hannah's confidence is well founded. In due course the Lord, who had closed her womb (vv. 5–6), remembers her, and she conceives. She bears a son and names him *Samuel*, explaining that she *asked the* LORD *for him*. Intriguingly, Hannah's explanation of Samuel's name employs the verb *š'l* ('ask'), which verbal root underlies the name Saul (*šā'ûl*). The same root occurs seven times in 1 Samuel 1 in wordplays surrounding the birth and dedication of Samuel (vv. 17 [2x], 20, 27 [2x], 28 [2x]) and twice more in Eli's blessing of Elkanah and Hannah in 2:20. English translations unavoidably mask these repetitions, but they are quite apparent in Hebrew, and their presence has prompted some scholars to speculate that the birth narrative of Samuel may actually be a reworking of an original Saul birth narrative.[12] Despite its supporters, the theory is best rejected, for a number of reasons.[13] First, it is unnecessary. Biblical naming is very often *not* based on strict word derivation, or etymology. A loose association of the name with the explanatory gloss is sufficient. As Garsiel (1991) has documented in detail, biblical narrators seem more interested in exploiting the sound potential of a name than in offering a precise etymological explanation.[14] In the case before us, the *š'l* root shares three of the

---

12. According to White (2006: 121), the theory was first proposed in the nineteenth century and has been widely adopted since that time (e.g. McCarter 1980: 65–66).
13. For thorough rebuttals, see Tsevat (1987: 250–254); Gordon (1994: 263–269); White (2006: 120–128).
14. On this general point, cf. also Zakovitch (1980), cited by White (2006: 123–124).

four consonants of the name Samuel (*šmʾl*), and there are a number of plausible suggestions as to how Hannah's 'asking' might relate to the meaning of the name Samuel, which has been variously explained as 'heard by God' (so NIV text note), 'name of God', and so on. Thus, the name Samuel is perfectly sensible as the culmination of Hannah's words.

Why then seven occurrences of the root from which the name Saul derives? White (2006: 125) notes that there are also precisely seven occurrences in chapter 1 of the root from which the name Jonathan derives ('Jonathan' being a combination of Yahweh, represented by 'Jo', and the verb *nātan*, 'gave' – thus Jonathan means 'Yahweh gave'). The word *nātan* is found in verse 4 (Elkanah would *give* portions); verse 5 (but to Hannah Elkanah *gave*); verse 11 (Hannah prays *if you will . . . but* give *. . . a son, then I will* give *him*); verse 16 (Hannah protests to Eli, 'don't *give* [=set, assign] your servant as a wicked woman'); verse 17 (Eli responds, 'may the God of Israel *give* [=*grant*] your request [=your asking]); and finally verse 27 (Hannah declares, 'the Lord has *given* the asking I asked). The final occurrence does not spell out the name Jonathan, but it carries the same meaning. Unless the double seven-fold pattern is mere coincidence, it may represent a narratorial hint of the importance of Saul and Jonathan in the narrative to come. Perhaps the righteous 'asking' of Hannah, in answer to which Samuel is given, foreshadows by way of contrast the sinful 'asking' of the elders in 1 Samuel 8, in answer to which Saul ('asked for') is given.[15] Perhaps there is even an echo of Deuteronomy 18:16, where Moses reminds the people of their 'asking' not to hear the word of the Lord directly, in response to which the Lord promised to 'raise up for them a prophet like' Moses who would 'tell them everything I command him' (Deut. 18:18) (cf. Walters 2002: 71–72). Samuel was to become such a prophet.

---

15. White (2006) construes matters rather differently, suggesting that Saul's behaviour in 1 Sam. 14 mirrors Hannah's piety, thus enclosing an original history of Saul that legitimated his kingship. My reading of Saul's behaviour in 1 Sam. 14 is much more negative.

21–28. Hannah's story is not complete until her obedience to her vow is recorded. When next Elkanah *went up with all his family to offer the annual sacrifice* (v. 21), *Hannah did not go*, citing as grounds her desire to wean the child first (v. 22). In the Ancient Near East, children were typically weaned at about three years of age[16] and, as Abraham's 'great feast' at the time of Isaac's weaning suggests (Gen. 21:8), such occasions were celebrated.

'Do what seems best to you,' her husband Elkanah told her (v. 23). Elkanah's response to Hannah may suggest some growth in his appreciation of her situation. In contrast to his 'shortsighted, helpless, and imperceptive' response in verse 8, here he adopts a more supportive stance (Mulzac 2002: 216). Somewhat difficult is MT's *only may the LORD make good his word*. It is unclear what 'word' of the Lord is in view, unless Walters is correct in suggesting an allusion back to the promise to raise up a prophet like Moses (Walters 2002: 71–72). Other key witnesses, however, attest 'your word' (LXX, 4QSam^a, Peshitta), thus Hannah's word. Gordon (1986: 77) draws attention to the fact that the first two of these key witnesses employ wording that corresponds to Numbers 30:2 (Heb. v. 3): 'that which has gone out of your mouth'. Numbers 30 deals with the making and keeping of vows and uses the Hebrew verb *qûm* (in the hip'il) when speaking of the husband's 'confirming' (establishing, making good) a vow made by his wife (see, e.g., 30:13[Heb. 14]). Use of the same verb (*qûm* hip'il) here in 1 Samuel 1:23 may suggest that Elkanah is both approving his wife's vow and invoking the Lord's help for Hannah in *mak[ing] good* on it (cf. NLT: 'and may the LORD help you keep your promise').

After he was weaned, she took the boy with her . . . and brought him to the house of the LORD at Shiloh (v. 24). The account of Hannah's fulfilment of her vow raises various small questions: did she bring three bulls (KJV, JPS, NET, following MT) or, as seems more likely, a three-year-old bull (NRSV, NIV and most modern translations, following LXX, 4QSam^a)? Who is the *he* who is said to worship the Lord in

---

16. See, e.g., the Egyptian Instruction of Any ('her breast was in your mouth three years'; *COS* 1.46:113); 2 Maccabees 7:27 ('I carried you nine months in the womb, suckled you three years').

the final line of the story (v. 28b)? Elkanah? Samuel? Or should we follow 4QSam[a] in reading that 'she' (Hannah) worshipped? Or perhaps MT should be read as a 'shortened form' of a third masculine plural, thus 'they worshipped' (cf. Tsumura 2007: 134). On the noteworthy four-fold repetition of the *š'l* root in verses 27–28, concluding with Hannah's statement that *For his whole life he shall be given over* [*šā'ûl*] *to the* LORD, see the comment on verses 19–20 above. Whatever the uncertainties with respect to details, the text clearly means us to understand that Hannah fulfilled her vow and entrusted Samuel to Eli for the service of the Lord.

Meaning
If how stories begin is an important indication of where they intend to go, then beginning the grand story of Israel's transition from tribal confederacy to monarchical society with the story of an everyday woman's personal pain may seem an unnecessary delay in getting on with what is truly important. But to think this would be quite wrong, for the story of Hannah provides essential orientation to the dynamics of the book of Samuel as a whole. First, her story signals that individual actors and individual actions are significant, often well beyond the lifetime of the individual. Second, in giving weight to God in the midst of troubled circumstances, Hannah anticipates a central theme that will emerge as the story continues (see, e.g., 2:29–30). Provoked by a rival wife, misunderstood by a well-meaning but hapless husband, misjudged by her religious leader, Hannah models how God-fearers are to respond under pressure. She resists fighting her rival. She resists fleeing to the empty comfort Elkanah offers. She even resists taking offence at the obtuseness of Eli. Instead, she takes her burden to God, implying that she understands that he alone carries enough weight to meet her need. What Hannah's actions have signalled, her prayer will spell out, and to that we turn in 1 Samuel 2:1–10.

ii. Hannah's prayer (2:1–10)
Context
Hannah's story began in the context of pain. Pain led to prayer. And her story now culminates in celebration. Explicitly intro-

duced as her 'prayer', Hannah's song, as it is often called, seems to combine two types of psalms (and perhaps even a third, if the 'wisdom' flavour of v. 9b is taken into account): it begins like a *song of thanksgiving*, expressing gratitude for a specific act of divine deliverance (esp. v. 1), and then, like a *hymn*, extols in more general terms God's character and actions: his holiness and uniqueness (v. 2); his judgment of the proud (v. 3); his reversal of human fortunes by which the privileged are brought low and the weak are compensated (vv. 4–5); his sovereignty over life and death, wealth and poverty, honour and dishonour, and indeed over the whole world whose 'pillars' he has set in place (vv. 6–8); and his care for his 'faithful ones' and condemnation of the wicked (v. 9a). As Hannah brings her prayer/poem towards its close, she draws out the implications of these grand truths, here approximating the style of Israel's *wisdom* teachers: 'for not by might does one prevail' (v. 9b, NRSV). In verse 10b, Hannah returns to the specific circumstances in which she finds herself, anticipating that the Lord *will give strength to his king, and exalt the horn of his anointed*. Thus, she anticipates key themes that will underlie the unfolding story of the birth of monarchy in Israel.

Apart from its beginning (v. 1) and ending (v. 10b), the prayer is cast in rather general terms, as is typical for poetic compositions intended for wider use beyond the occasioning circumstance. Whether the song represents Hannah's own composition or an existing composition adopted by her remains an open question. In view of the concluding references to the Lord's *king* and *anointed*, some commentators speculate that the song must have been composed after the rise of monarchy in Israel. But this speculation is neither necessary nor helpful to our understanding of the book. Kingship was 'in the air' in the time of Hannah, and that she should anticipate its soon arrival does not seem unreasonable.[17]

---

17. The Targum, which is quite expansionist in its rendering of Hannah's prayer, states explicitly that 'Hannah prayed in the spirit of prophecy'.

Comment
1. *My heart . . . my horn . . . My mouth.* The first-person possessive pronouns call attention to Hannah's specific experience of deliverance. Hannah addresses the Lord directly: *I delight in your deliverance.*

My horn is sometimes rendered 'my strength' (e.g. NRSV), but it is best to retain the ancient metaphor, as NRSV does when David uses the image in 2 Samuel 22:3: 'my shield and the horn of my salvation'. Hebrew *qeren* was a general term for the horns, antlers or even tusks of animals. Horns served as 'weapons' and lent a regal appearance to animals sporting them. The image of the raised horn evokes a majestic picture of an animal victorious over its foe or prey. It is suggestive of virility and, in some contexts, progeny (McCarter 1980: 71–72), which makes its metaphorical usage in Hannah's circumstances, now that she has a son, all the more apt. Given its capacity to symbolize strength, regal appearance and even progeny, it is not surprising that 'horn' is a frequently used metaphor in biblical and extra-biblical literatures and in extra-biblical iconography, where kings and deities are sometimes depicted with horns.[18] It is the Lord, as Hannah well understands, who cuts off the horns of the wicked, but exalts the horns of the righteous (Ps. 75:10). The song will return in verse 10 to the Lord's exalting the *horn* of his anointed.[19]

2. *No Rock like our God.* Hebrew *ṣûr* ('rock' or 'mountain') occurs in biblical and extra-biblical literature both in theophoric names (names that include a divine appellation) and as a metaphor suggesting stability, security and safety (cf. David's words in 2 Sam. 22:3). Here Hannah's *our God* intimates a contrast to false gods, also occasionally referred to (mockingly) as 'rocks' (e.g. Deut. 32:31, 'their rock is not like our Rock'; Deut. 32:37, 'where are their gods, the rock they took refuge in . . . ?'). The true God who is a

---

18. Michelangelo's 'horned Moses' is of a different order and reflects the Vulgate's misreading of *qāran* ('to shine') as *qeren* ('horn') in Exod. 34:29–30, 35, where the reference is actually to the skin of Moses' face shining after his descent from the holy mountain.
19. For further discussion, see Long (2009a: 277); *DBI* 400; and for a thorough treatment, see Süring (1980).

'sanctuary' to those who fear him becomes a 'rock of offence' to those who don't (Isa. 8:13–14). The metaphor is applied to Christ in both senses in the New Testament (Rom. 9:33; 1 Pet. 2:8).

3. *Do not keep talking so proudly . . . for the* LORD *is a God who knows.* In view of the God just described, the proud are well advised to fall silent (cf. also v. 9). God's 'knowledge' implies more than cognitive awareness. In this context – as in various others – God's 'knowing' implies active concern for and care of someone (e.g. 2 Sam. 7:20; 1 Chr. 17:18; Ps. 144:3; Hos. 13:5; Nah. 1:7), or even the choosing of someone (Gen. 18:19; Jer. 1:5; Amos 3:2).[20] He is the one by whom *deeds are weighed*, and by whom wrongs are righted and human fortunes reversed, as the following verses illustrate.

4–5. These verses describe reversals in three key areas of human experience: power and weakness; plenty and want; shame (barrenness) and honour. Commentators occasionally stumble over verse 5b's statement that *She who was barren has borne seven children*, worrying over the fact that Hannah in the course of time bore only six (v. 21). But several considerations lessen this worry: (1) the number 'seven' is the Hebrew 'poetic ideal' (Gordon 1986: 80) symbolizing completeness; (2) as noted earlier, biblical poems often trade in generalizations in the interest of applicability to analogous situations, rather than focusing on the specifics of a particular situation; and (3) in the narrative flow, Hannah has at this point borne only one child, in any case, making the eventual sum a moot point.

6–9a. If verses 4 and 5 describe reversals in three key areas, verses 6–8 explain who it is that makes the adjustments in each. *The* LORD *brings death*[21] *and makes alive . . . sends poverty and wealth . . . lifts the needy . . .* [*to*] *inherit a throne of honour.* The notion that the gods held human destinies in their hands was widespread in the Ancient Near Eastern world.[22] More distinctive in the biblical corpus is the

---

20. See *HALOT*, *ydʿ* I, esp. definition 7.
21. This clause is paralleled in the next line by *he brings down to the grave* (Sheol). Though its etymology is uncertain, 'Sheol' refers to the grave, or the 'realm of the dead' (*TLOT* 3: 1279–1282, which see for bibliography on OT views of the afterlife).
22. E.g. the god Marduk is credited with the ability to 'raise or bring low'

notion that God's adjusting of the balances is an expression of his concern for *his faithful servants* (v. 9a). The final couplet of verse 8 explains why the Lord can make these adjustments of power, property and prestige: quite simply, the world is his because he made it.

9b–10a. *It is not by strength that one prevails; those who oppose the* LORD *will be broken.*[23] Given the content of Hannah's song, the logic of these twin assertions is obvious. Beyond mere logic, these theological tenets are also demonstrated in the events of the book of Samuel, often events involving conflicts with the Philistines (e.g. in the ark narrative of chs. 4–6, in the Samuel-led victory of ch. 7, in David's defeat of the Philistine giant in ch. 17, and so forth). More negatively, they are demonstrated in the life of Saul, where his physical prowess is unable to offset his spiritual weakness (more on this in due course). The Lord does indeed 'break', or 'shatter', those who oppose him, much as gravity, if ignored, can result in breakage.

The Most High[24] *will thunder from heaven* (v. 10). The ancients regarded thundering in the heavens as mighty signs of the presence and perhaps displeasure of the gods. Biblical writers adopted this imagery and may on occasion have taken over pagan compositions and transformed them to express the supremacy of Yahweh over the false gods; an oft-cited example is Psalm 29, with its emphasis

---

(*ANET* 66), while in the Egyptian Instruction of Amenemope, the deity 'tears down and builds up every day' (Beyerlin 1978: 61); for fuller discussion, see Long (2009a: 277–278).

23. 4QSam[a] and LXX both make the Lord the subject of the verb 'break', but the syntax of the MT is quite acceptable as it stands; 'The LORD' is in emphatic initial position as a *casus pendens*, or 'rhetorical absolute' (Joüon and Muraoka 1996: §156; R. J. Williams 2007: §35). NRSV nicely captures the force of the syntax: 'The LORD! His adversaries shall be shattered.'

24. 'Most High' assumes a conjectural emendation of MT's *'ālāw* ('against them') either to *'elyôn*, as in 2 Sam. 22:14 (*The LORD thundered from heaven; the voice of the Most High resounded*), or perhaps to the simpler *'ēlî* (a divine epithet meaning 'Exalted One'). See discussion in Gordon (1986: 81).

on the mighty 'voice' of Yahweh (Kraus 1988: 347; Green 2003). The book of Samuel records several instances of the Lord thundering against adversaries. In 1 Samuel 7:10, the Lord thunders 'with a mighty voice . . . against the Philistines' (NRSV), and David celebrates the Lord's thundering in 2 Samuel 22:14. These are the only three occurrences of Hebrew *rʿm* I ('to thunder') in Samuel, but one wonders if Hannah's use of the word in 2:10 may not involve an ironic echo of the homonymous *rʿm* II ('to humiliate') in the description in 1:6 of Peninnah's provocation of Hannah.

10b. *He will give strength to his king.* This conclusion to Hannah's song, more than any other feature, has led some to assume that the song must be a late interpolation into the text of Samuel, at least as late as the inception of kingship in Israel. It should be noted, however, that kingship was well known in the Ancient Near East and, indeed, among Israel's closest neighbours, long before it was established in Israel. Furthermore, the Pentateuch anticipates a time when Israel would have a king (Gen. 17:6; 49:10; Num. 24:7, 17–19; Deut. 17:14–17; 28:36). The book of Judges flirts with kingship, or something very like it, on a couple of occasions (i.e. the offer of dynastic 'rule' [*mšl*] to Gideon in Judg. 8:22; and Abimelek's abortive bid for power in Judg. 9, in which anointing a king is specifically mentioned [9:8, 15]). And even the doleful refrain at the end of the book of Judges – 'In those days Israel had no king' (Judg. 17:6; 18:1; 19:1; 21:25) – anticipates a time when there would be a king. It does not require great imagination, therefore, to assume that in the time of Hannah kingship was on people's minds. Importantly, her reference to *his king*, that is, the Lord's king, establishes at the outset of the book of Samuel that kingship, or monarchy, at least of a certain sort, is in keeping with the divine purpose for Israel.[25]

---

25. It is, of course, Hannah's perspective that is here expressed. But as we note elsewhere, the early chapters of 1 Samuel, and in particular the song of Hannah, establish the theological and thematic baseline for the book.

Concluding as it began, the song stresses that the Lord will *exalt the horn of his anointed*. Whereas in verse 1 it was Hannah's horn that was exalted, here it is the horn of the Lord's *anointed*. Anointing with oil was widely practised in the Ancient Near East. When applied to persons, it conferred a special, even sacrosanct, status. The recipient was anointed by someone to fulfil a particular role or to accomplish a task. Typically, the greater party (e.g. a Hittite suzerain, himself anointed with the 'holy oil of kingship') would anoint the lesser to serve as a vassal ruler of the Great King. According to the fourteenth-century Amarna Letters, Egyptian rulers would sometimes have Palestinian local-kings anointed as a symbol of their vassal status.[26] To be noted in the present context is that the king to whom the Lord will give strength will be *his anointed*, thus his appointed 'vassal'. The greater party, the Great King, will *exalt the horn* of his human representative.

Meaning

As Alter (1999: 9) notes in his introductory comment on Hannah's song, 'the larger thematic assertion in the poem of God's power to reverse fortunes, plunging the high to the depths and exalting the lowly, is a fitting introduction to the whole Saul–David history'. Saul's career, as it develops, will bear out the truth of Hannah's declaration that *those who oppose the LORD will be broken* (v. 10a). By contrast and despite his quite obvious failings, David's story will bear out the truth of verse 10b: *He* [*the LORD*] *will give strength to his king and exalt the horn of his anointed*. In these and other ways, Hannah's song, along with her entire story, sets the theological tone and establishes the thematic trajectory for the book of Samuel. David will return to many of these same themes in his own bookending poetic compositions in 2 Samuel 22:1 – 23:7. Beyond the borders of Samuel, the entire Old Testament supports Hannah's fundamental assertions regarding God's holiness, uniqueness, knowledge and concern, his readiness to adjust the balances of human fortune, his right over life and death, his care for the humble and the needy, his ownership of all the earth, his righteous

---

26. See further Long (2009a: 278–279) and the literature cited there.

judgment of the wicked, his care for his people, and his will to provide and empower godly leadership. Looking to the New Testament, Hannah's song finds echoes in Mary's 'Magnificat' in Luke 1:46–55.

iii. Eli, his boys and the boy Samuel (2:11–26)
Context
Though Eli's sons have been mentioned in the preceding story (1:3), and Eli has figured in some of the action so far (1:12–17, 25–28), the focus has clearly been on Hannah and the birth of her long-awaited son Samuel. The focus now shifts. The house of Eli will be the subject of the remainder of chapter 2, though the boy Samuel will serve as a foil to the boys of Eli (i.e. in 2:11, 18–21, 26). In contrast to Eli's worthless sons, Samuel continues to *grow in stature and in favour with the* LORD *and with people* (v. 26). Eli himself does not make a favourable impression; recall his earlier misapprehension of Hannah's fervent prayer as drunkenness (1:12–14). In the present episode, the cultic abuse taking place under his watch is sketched in lurid detail. At least with respect to Eli's sons, this was indeed a time when 'everyone did as he pleased' (Judg. 21:25, JPS).

Comment
11. *Then Elkanah went home to Ramah.* Verse 11 is transitional. Looking backwards, it provides a tidy conclusion to the account of the birth and dedication of Samuel which began with the introduction of Elkanah in 1:1. Looking forwards, it sets the stage for the sad tale of Eli's misbehaving boys by mentioning, by way of contrast, that *the boy* [*Samuel*] *ministered before the* LORD *under Eli the priest*. The latter statement might be better rendered 'the boy served the LORD in the presence of Eli the priest'; the phrase *'et-pĕnê* occurs three other times in the book of Samuel (1 Sam. 1:22; 2:17; 22:4), and in none of these instances does 'under' make sense. See further comment at 3:1.

12. The first thing we learn of *Eli's sons* is that they were *scoundrels*, or 'sons of Belial' (KJV). 'Belial' is a transliteration of the Hebrew *bĕlîya'al*, which as a noun connotes 'uselessness, wickedness' and as an adjective speaks of that which is 'good for nothing' (*HALOT*; cf. at 1:16). This term of opprobrium is applied to a variety of troublemakers in the Old Testament, including idolaters (Deut.

13:13), the sexually immoral (Judg. 19:22), insurrectionists (1 Sam. 10:27; 2 Sam. 16:7; 20:1) and liars (1 Kgs 21:10, 13). In 1:16 Hannah was concerned that Eli might falsely take her to be a 'daughter of belial' (*a wicked woman*, NIV). Given that biblical narratives tend to do more 'showing' than 'telling', the fact that the narrator here offers an explicit evaluative statement regarding Eli's sons carries particular weight.

The sons' wickedness stemmed from the fact that *they had no regard for the* LORD (which can also be rendered 'did not know the LORD'). 'No regard' renders the Hebrew verb *yd*ᵏ ('to know, acknowledge, recognize', etc.), which will recur in an ironic contrast in 3:7, where it is stated that *Samuel did not yet know the* LORD.

13–17. *Now it was the practice of the priests.* Whether the priests' 'pot luck' procedure (vv. 13–14) itself is to be understood as abusive or whether the abuse only begins with their demand for uncooked meat (v. 15) continues to be debated among interpreters.[27] The Hebrew noun *mišpāṭ*, here rendered *practice*, has a generally positive semantic range around the idea of justice, judgment, and so on. This might suggest that the priests' wielding of the three-pronged fork is justified, despite the variance with the sacrificial procedures stipulated, for instance, in Leviticus 7:28–36 and Deuteronomy 18:3. NRSV assumes a positive understanding of *mišpāṭ* as 'duties' and, changing MT's sentence division, reads verses 12b–13a thus: 'they had no regard for the LORD or for the duties of the priests to the people'. This still leaves unanswered the question whether the remainder of verses 13–14 describes proper duties neglected or abuses resulting from such neglect. Furthermore, *mišpāṭ* can simply connote 'manner, custom' (*DCH*, s.v., def. 4) or 'claim' (*HALOT*, s.v., def. 3b), leaving open the possibility of good or bad customary behaviour. Favouring the latter interpretation is the description of the priest's servant plunging his trident into *pan or kettle or cauldron or pot* (v. 14). Such a level of descriptive detail is unusual in biblical narrative, leading Alter (1999: 12) to suggest a 'satiric purpose: Eli's

---

27. E.g. Eberhart (2002: 88–96) defends the practice described in vv. 13–14 as legitimate.

sons are represented in a kind of frenzy of gluttony poking their three-pronged forks into every imaginable sort of pot and pan'.

The priests were taking meat *even before the fat was burned* (v. 15). The verse begins with an emphatic *gam* ('also, even'), which further supports the view that the behaviours of verses 13–14 are part and parcel of the Elides' *treating the* LORD'*s offering with contempt* (v. 17). Certainly, to demand uncooked meat with the fat still in it was, by Old Testament and even some ANE standards, flagrantly abusive (Long 2009a: 279–280). Witness the shocked protest of the rank-and-file sacrificer in verse 16 and the threat with which his pious caution is met. According to Pentateuch law, the fat of sacrifices was not to be eaten, and abuse carried the heavy penalty of being 'cut off from [one's] people' (Lev. 7:25–27).

18–21. *But Samuel was ministering before the* LORD – *a boy.* The insertion of boy-Samuel material into the story of Eli's sons is part of a literary strategy to juxtapose brief notices of the *boy* (*naʿar*) Samuel with the longer tale of Eli's 'boys' (NIV's *young men* in v. 17 renders the same word, *naʿar*, though in the plural, *nĕʿārîm*). The effect of this strategy is to paint the misdeeds of Eli's 'boys' in even darker tones by virtue of their contrast with the faithful service of the 'boy' Samuel. The pattern of interleaving notices about Samuel with notices about Eli's sons begins in 2:11 and continues until 2:26.

The *linen ephod* that the boy Samuel is wearing is a simple priestly garment (cf. 22:18; 2 Sam. 6:14)[28] and is indicative of his early induction into priestly service. As Gordon notes (1986: 82), 'there is no talk of lower age-limits for priestly service in this story where grown men have failed (*cf.* Nu. 8:24–26; 1 Ch. 23:24–32)'.

Each year his mother made him a little robe (v. 19). This homely notice of a mother lovingly sewing a little robe (*mĕʿîl*) and offering it up annually to her growing son, from whom she must be away most

---

28. The term 'ephod' can also be used (1) for elaborately constructed garments, such as the ornate ephod worn by the high priest (see descriptions in Exod. 28 and 39); (2) for the high-priestly breastplate containing the oracular Urim and Thummin (see at 14:3, 18–19); and (3) possibly for an ornately clothed idol; cf. Block's brief discussion of Gideon's ephod in Judg. 8:27 (2009: 166).

of the year, portends more than a surface reading might suggest. Robes in the ancient world often carried symbolic and/or social value, and robes will prove to be significant not only in the life of Samuel but in the book of Samuel in general. It will be Saul's tearing of the adult Samuel's robe that will become a sign of the tearing of the kingdom from him (15:27–28); Jonathan will signify his willing surrender of royal prerogatives to David by the surrender of his princely robe (18:4); David's conscience will smite him for surreptitiously carving off a corner of Saul's robe (24:4), though he will still use the remnant in his attempt to convince Saul that he wishes him no harm (24:11); at Endor the necromancer's mere description of *an old man wearing a robe* will suffice to alert Saul to the fact that he is encountering Samuel (28:14); and in 2 Samuel 13, Tamar will signify the disgrace she has suffered by tearing her *ornate robe ... the kind of garment the virgin daughters of the king wore* (v. 18). At this point in the narrative, Samuel's robe, like his ephod, may suggest a priestly role, but he will soon become *a prophet of the* LORD (3:20). In these roles, Samuel will be instrumental in the Lord's election and rejection of kings, and his robe, as we have just seen, will figure in his commerce with them.

Eli would bless Elkanah and his wife (v. 20). Eli here appears in a considerably more favourable light than his sons, whose modus operandi was not to bless but to abuse those who came to sacrifice. Nevertheless, as Auld (2006: 87) notes, 'the narrator is beginning to distance Samuel from him, and to hint at the lad's separate development'. For instance, in this brief section, Eli is absent from the opening and closing notices of Samuel's service and growth in the presence of the Lord (vv. 18 and 21); contrast the mention of Eli in 2:11.

22–25. *Now Eli ... heard.* The focus shifts back to Eli and his sons. Eli is described as *very old* (v. 22) – 4QSam[a] puts him at ninety(-eight?) – and this might seem to suggest an excuse for his apparent obliviousness and inaction. The verbal syntax in the MT of verse 22 may suggest, however, that Eli is not hearing for the first time of his sons' abuses; rather, he 'kept hearing' (so ESV; cf. MSG, 'He kept getting reports').[29] Whatever the case, the sons are

---

29. Verse 22's *wěšāmaʿ* can be read as a waw-consecutive perfect indicating

engaged in continuing abuses against *all Israel*. The reference to their sleeping with *the women who served at the entrance to the tent of meeting* is textually uncertain (as it is lacking in 4QSam[a] and in LXX[B]).[30] Tsumura (2007: 160) remarks that 'this less-than-flattering information is more likely to have been deleted than to have been added', but it is best to leave the question open. If we assume for the moment that MT's reading is correct, what can we say about it? Whether the women's sleeping with the priests was consensual or not is left unstated. It might be supposed that the women were involved in some kind of cultic prostitution,[31] but the notice that the women *served* (*ṣābā'*) is more suggestive of the fulfilment of appropriate duties; the same verb is used of Levites in pursuit of their proper duties in Numbers 4:23 and 8:24, and it parallels *'ābad*, 'serve', in Numbers 8:26. In Exodus 38:8, women are explicitly mentioned as serving at the 'entrance to the tent of meeting'. Unless, then, the tight verbal similarity between the present verse and Exodus 38:8 is designed as a kind of ironic contrast, we should assume that the women's assigned duties were approved. Their involvement with the sons of Eli would certainly not have been.

Eventually, Eli confronts his sons (v. 23), pointing out to them just how unwise their behaviour is (v. 25). In cases of strife amongst humans, God (*'elōhîm*, which might also connote 'judges' [e.g. Exod. 21:6; 22:8]) can arbitrate (*pll* in the pi'el), but if the affront is against the Lord himself, who is there to intercede (*pll* in the hitpa'el)? As Exodus 32:7–14 illustrates, God may choose to be forbearing in judgment, but this is not something to be presumed upon. Eli's logic is unimpeachable. But it falls on deaf ears, *for it was the LORD's will to put them to death* (v. 25). As in the classic case of the hardening

---

repeated action. Alternatively, it could be read as a simple waw-conjunctive followed by the perfect, which would suggest past but not necessarily repeated action. 4QSam[a] attests *wayyišma'*, the standard narrative tense, 'and he heard', and may find support in LXX's aorist *ēkousen*.

30. See discussion in McCarter (1980: 81).
31. Cultic prostitution appears to have been practised among the Canaanites (cf. 1 Kgs 14:23–24; 15:12; 2 Kgs 23:7; Hos. 4:14).

of Pharaoh's heart in Exodus, so in this instance, persistence in sin over time results in the inability to do otherwise (cf. Josh. 11:20; Rom. 1:24–28). In Exodus, both the Lord and Pharaoh are credited with hardening the latter's heart.[32] The phrase *for it was the LORD's will* utilizes a verb, *ḥāpēṣ*, which can be suggestive of 'delighting' in something. But that is not the implication here. Rather, the expression should be understood in a judicial sense: the Lord has rendered a verdict (cf. Hurvitz 1982). The biblical writers in both Old and New Testaments show no difficulty in holding together God's sovereignty over all things with humans' accountability for their own actions.

26. *And the boy Samuel continued to grow in stature and in favour with the LORD and with people.* The effrontery of Eli's sons with respect to both God and people is again set in contrast to the boy Samuel, who is growing not only bigger but better. While the degeneracy of Eli's sons seals their doom, Samuel's growth in more than merely physical proportions portends great things. In some senses, the outward–inward (or physical–spiritual) dynamic suggested in Samuel's growth adumbrates an eventual contrast between the tall and outwardly impressive Saul and the smaller but inwardly impressive David (see at 9:2).

Interestingly, Eli is not named among those with whom Samuel finds favour (Auld 2006: 87). If this omission is meant to say anything, then it is less likely to be that Samuel is out of Eli's favour than that Eli is out of favour with God and man. The events that immediately follow drive home this point.

Meaning
The manner in which the boy Samuel and the boys of Eli are repeatedly contrasted in this section makes several things clear. First, Eli's house must go. The main focus is on the abuses of Eli's sons, but there are already hints that Eli himself is in some serious respects culpable for the sad state of affairs under his rule. Samuel, by contrast, is growing up in both 'size and sanctity' (Peterson

---

32. Pharaoh is said to harden his heart in Exod. 8:15, 32; 9:34, while the Lord does the hardening in 4:21; 7:3; 9:12; 10:20, 27; 11:10; 14:4, 8, 17.

1999: 35). Peterson links this kind of growth to what it means to be truly human: 'There is no true growth that does not embrace both human and God relationships.' Many centuries later it will be said of Jesus' forerunner, John, that 'the child grew and became strong in spirit' (Luke 1:80). Of Jesus himself it will be written that 'the child grew and became strong; he was filled with wisdom, and the grace of God was on him' (Luke 2:40). Most strikingly of all, in an almost verbatim repetition of 1 Samuel 2:26, it will be said that Jesus 'grew in wisdom and stature, and in favour with God and man' (Luke 2:52). Samuel is in good company! He has more growing to do, but God is already at work, preparing a new leader whom he will use to introduce a new polity in Israel.

iv. Rejection of the priestly house of Eli (2:27–36)
Context

This section, verses 27–36, takes the form of a prophetic judgment speech, whose basic shape is widely recognized to comprise two main parts: an Accusation, followed by an Announcement of Judgment.[33] The Accusation itself may involve a simple declarative statement or an accusing question, or both. The Accusation is typically introduced with the 'messenger formula', 'This is what the LORD says', or similar, and often includes a description of the Lord's prior beneficence towards the accused. The Announcement of Judgment may be preceded by another reminder that what follows is an utterance of the Lord and thus carries authority. The pronouncement of judgment itself is introduced by 'Therefore' (*lākēn*) or 'but now' (*wĕʻattâ*) and often involves what Westermann calls a 'correspondence motif' – namely, a statement showing that the punishment is appropriate to the offence. A prophetic sign is sometimes included to confirm what has been announced. In the prophetic corpus, 'oracles of judgment' are regularly accompanied by a word of hope, an 'oracle of salvation', and the same is true here: though Eli is rejected, the Lord will not leave Israel without a faithful priest. The several elements of the judgment against the house of Eli may be charted as follows:

---

33. For a seminal discussion, see Westermann (1991).

ACCUSATION (vv. 27–29)
This is what the LORD says (v. 27a)
    The Lord's beneficence to the house of Eli (vv. 27–28)
    Accusing questions (v. 29)
ANNOUNCEMENT OF JUDGMENT (vv. 30–36)
Therefore the LORD, the God of Israel, declares (v. 30a)
    Past beneficence reiterated (v. 30a)
But now the LORD declares (v. 30b)
    The judgment itself (vv. 30b–33)
        including the correspondence motif (v. 30b)
    Sign of confirmation (v. 34)
    Word of hope (v. 35)
    Final word of judgment (v. 36)

Like Hannah's song in 2:1–10, the present section drives important thematic stakes into the ground. Both centre on the importance of giving weight to God more than to any other person, circumstance or consideration. These key passages frame the alternating and contrastive portraits in 2:11–26 of the boy Samuel (destined to rise) and the boys of Eli (doomed to fall). Taken together, the whole of chapter 2 provides vital interpretive lenses that will facilitate understanding of the sometimes perplexing events that follow.

Comment

27–29. The new scene opens with the arrival of *a man of God*[34] to speak Yahweh's words to Eli. This is the first time that Yahweh speaks in Samuel, and 'his message is one of judgment' (Firth 2009: 70). The house of Eli has been privileged to serve as Yahweh's priests, serving at the altar and wearing *an ephod* (v. 28). The man of God's reference to the Lord's revealing himself to Eli's *ancestor's family* [lit. 'father's house'] *when they were in Egypt under Pharaoh* (v. 27) raises the question of Eli's ancestry, and of its relationship to what came to be known as the Zadokite priestly line. Piecing together the biblical evidence, we arrive at the following plausible genealogy. According

---

34. 'Man of God' is sometimes used in the OT in parallel with 'prophet' (1 Sam. 9:8–11; 2 Kgs 5:8; 6:10–12).

to 1 Chronicles 24:1b–2, Aaron had four sons, two of whom died early – namely, Nadab and Abihu (cf. Lev. 10:1–2). This left only the other two sons, Eleazar and Ithamar (cf. Lev. 10:6). First Chronicles 24:3 states that David worked with both priestly families, the house of Eleazar in the person of Zadok and the house of Ithamar in the person of Ahimelek. Of Ahimelek we learn in 1 Samuel 22:20 that he was a son of Ahitub and the father of Abiathar, the latter being the sole survivor of Saul's massacre of the priests of Nob. Of Ahitub, we learn in 1 Samuel 14:3 that he was the son of Phinehas, the son of Eli. Thus, we arrive at the following genealogy for Eli, making allowance of course for generational gaps:[35] Aaron – Ithamar – Eli – Phinehas – Ahitub – Ahimelek – Abiathar.[36]

Eli's *ephod* mentioned in verse 28 is not like Samuel's 'ephod' mentioned in verse 18 but, almost certainly, the high-priestly ephod described in detail in Exodus 28:4–30. Affixed to the ephod was a 'breastpiece for making decisions' containing the Urim and Thummim (Exod. 28:15). These were oracular devices by which divine guidance could be sought (Exod. 28:30). The statement that *I also gave your father's house all the offerings made with fire by the Israelites*[37] may contain a subtle reminder of the abuses of Eli's sons, who demanded *raw* meat (2:15). Further abuse of the Lord's 'sacrifice and offering' will be mentioned in the next verse.

In bringing the Accusation to a close (v. 29), the man of God poses one final accusing question: *Why do you honour your sons more than me by fattening yourselves* on my offerings? Eli is guilty of giving more 'weight' (*honour*) to his sons than to God. And the evidence of this is that they have actually fattened themselves. The manner in which 'weight', 'honour' and 'glory' are all related in the semantic range of the Hebrew root *kbd* can be illustrated from English usage: to accord people social weight, or to speak of their *gravitas*, or to consider their opinions as 'weighty', is to honour them. A

---

35. 'Son of' sometimes means 'descendant of'.
36. For Josephus's explanation of how priestly rule toggled between the descendants of Aaron's two sons Eleazar and Ithamar, see *Ant.* 5.361–362.
37. So NIV 1984 and most English translations; NIV 2011 unnecessarily reads 'food offerings' instead of 'fire offerings'.

similar dynamic obtains in Hebrew. The first use of the Hebrew root *kbd* in Samuel came in Hannah's celebration of the God who elevates the poor and needy to a *throne of honour* (2:8). Introduced a second time in the present context, the root *kbd* will function as a *Leitwort* (a recurring keyword) as the narrative continues (e.g. in 4:18, 21; 5:6; 6:5, 6). The accusing questions addressed to Eli in verse 29 indicate that he himself, and not just his sons, is guilty of 'making himself heavy' (physically and otherwise) on sacrificial meat illicitly commandeered. The original hearers would likely have detected the dramatic irony in this charge: God is underweighted, even while Eli and his sons have become overweight.

30–33. The Announcement of Judgment that begins with *Therefore* (*lākēn*) in verse 30 drives home a truth of fundamental importance for understanding not just the story of Eli but also the stories of Saul and David. The truth is this: *Those who honour me I will honour, but those who despise me will be disdained.* Those who give 'weight' (*honour*) to God will receive 'weight' from him. Conversely, those who underweight, or *despise* (*bzh*), God can expect to be *disdained*, that is, to carry little weight (*qll*) with him.[38] There is a correspondence between attitude and outcome.

The consequences of Eli's slighting Yahweh will not be trivial. The Hebrew of verses 31–33 is difficult in several places, as the variations amongst the versions and in the English translations indicate. But none of the difficulties affects the basic sense of the pronouncement. The doom of the house of Eli is sure. Few, if any, in his house will reach old age. Any who do so will know only grief and tears.

34–36. The judgment speech nears its end in typical prophetic fashion, with *a sign* (v. 34), a word of grace (v. 35) and a final word of judgment (v. 36). The sign will be the deaths of Eli's two sons, Hophni and Phinehas, both *on the same day*. The fulfilment of this sign is recorded in 4:11 and is followed shortly by the death of Eli himself (4:18). In due course almost the entirety of Eli's priestly house is massacred at Nob (22:17–19). The final blow will be dealt by Solomon,

---

38. Heb. *bzh* means to despise in the sense of thinking lightly of (cf. *NIDOTTE*, *bzh*), while *qll* suggests that which is small or insignificant.

however, when he removes the surviving Elide, Abiathar, from the priesthood (1 Kgs 2:26–27; for Abiathar's offence, see 1 Kgs 1:7).

Judgment is not the end of the story. *I will raise up for myself a faithful priest* (v. 35). Even in the midst of judgment, the Lord lays plans to provide for his people. The word *ne'ĕmān,* rendered *faithful,* connotes firmness, reliability, faithfulness, and so on. The word is used a second time in this same verse to describe the 'firm/faithful house' that the Lord will build for his 'firm/faithful' priest. In the rest of Samuel, the word is used to describe Samuel's being *attested* [con-*firm*ed] *as a prophet of the LORD* (3:20), to describe the loyalty of David (22:14), to describe the *lasting dynasty* (firm house) the Lord will build for David (25:28) and to describe David's enduring house and kingdom (2 Sam. 7:16).

The new priest that the Lord will provide *will do according to what is in my heart and mind* and *will minister before my anointed one* (v. 35). The first clause spells out what it means to be *faithful,* while the second recalls Hannah's earlier reference to the Lord's *anointed* (see at v. 10). Kingship is indeed in the air.

The final words of the man of God contain a fine irony. Any who survive of the house of Eli – that wrongly 'fattened' household (v. 29) – will do so only to beg a *loaf of bread* from the faithful priest (v. 36). The correspondence of crime and punishment is again evident (cf. at v. 30b).

Meaning

At various points above we have noted themes that the song of Hannah (2:1–10) and the judgment speech of the man of God (2:27–36) have in common. Both make reference to the Lord's anointed who is coming, and both stress the indispensable necessity of honouring (giving weight to) God. In between the song and the speech, we have the alternating portrayals of the boy Samuel and the boys of Eli (vv. 11–26). Thus, both in principle and in practice, these three sections present a compelling picture of what honouring and dishonouring God look like. God at the centre is the bedrock tenet not just of the story so far but of the story as it continues. And on this rock, many will rise and fall.

v. Establishment of Samuel as a prophet (3:1 – 4:1a)

Context

Just as Eli was involved in the events leading up to Samuel's birth, so now in chapter 3 Samuel is involved in predicting Eli's demise. The shape of the chapter can be analysed chiastically:[39]

- A. Samuel's youth, Eli's dim-sightedness and the rarity of the word of Yahweh (vv. 1–3)
  - B. Samuel is called three times and goes to Eli for information (vv. 4–9)
    - C. Samuel is called a fourth time, responds and receives a vision (vv. 10–14)
  - B'. Eli goes to Samuel for information about the vision (vv. 15–18)
- A'. Samuel's growth and establishment as a prophet, and the return of the word of Yahweh (vv. 19–21 and 4:1a)

Comment

1. Given the time period – the end of the period of the judges, when 'everyone did as they saw fit' (Judg. 17:6) – and the infirmity and inattentiveness of its presiding high priest, it is no wonder that *the word of the LORD was rare*. While the comment that *there were not many visions* might seem to suggest that there were few divine 'appearances', the Hebrew term *ḥāzôn* often has more to do with the revelatory word (cf. *DCH*; *HALOT*) and thus with an auditory experience.[40] Implicit in this lack of 'visions' is divine displeasure (see, e.g., 14:37; Ps. 74:9; Lam. 2:9; Amos 8:11–12). But there is also hope, for *the boy Samuel* is ministering before the Lord. As Samuel was God's response to 'the barrenness of Hannah's womb', so too will he be God's answer to 'the barrenness of the spiritual life at Shiloh' (Peterson 1999: 37).

2–3. *Eli . . . lying down in his usual place . . . Samuel . . . lying down in the house of the LORD.* Just as physical features are sometimes mentioned

---

[39]. Cf. the somewhat different description of the chiasm by Fishbane (1982: 193).

[40]. See further comment on 3:10.

to suggest spiritual conditions (see immediately below), so the sleeping locations of Eli and Samuel suggest the contrast between them. Eli is in his *usual place*, while Samuel is not only *lying down in the house of the LORD* but is in some way near to the *ark of God*.[41] The ark's mention here is the first in the book of Samuel, and it anticipates the so-called 'ark narrative' that will unfold in the next three chapters. References to the ark occur some 203 times in the Old Testament, and fully sixty-one times in the book of Samuel alone. As the ark was a visible symbol of the Lord's presence and power, its frequent mention in Samuel, a book recounting the rise of kingship in Israel, underscores the importance of remembering Israel's true King.

The notices that Eli's *eyes were becoming so weak that he could barely see* (v. 2) and that *the lamp of God had not yet gone out* (v. 3) might be construed as mere physical facts, the former suggesting Eli's aged infirmity and the latter what time of night it is – that is, 'just before dawn'.[42] But these notices also carry thematic significance. Eli's diminished physical eyesight is quite likely meant to suggest his diminished spiritual eyesight (see comment on v. 13). As for the reference to the *lamp of God*, it is worth noting that 'lamp' is often used metaphorically in Scripture to suggest hope, or the one in whom hope resides: for example, 'for David's sake the LORD his God gave him a lamp in Jerusalem by raising up a son to succeed him and by making Jerusalem strong' (1 Kgs 15:4; cf. also 2 Sam. 21:17; 22:29; 1 Kgs 11:36; 2 Kgs 8:19; 2 Chr. 21:7; Job 18:5; Ps. 132:17; Prov. 13:9). Of the present passage, Alter (1999: 16) writes: 'though vision has become rare, God's lamp has not yet gone out, and the

---

41. The ark (sometimes called the ark of the testimony or the ark of the covenant) was first built in the time of Moses. Instructions for its construction are recorded in Exod. 25:10–22. Made of acacia wood overlaid with gold, the ark was a relatively small chest (*c.*45 in. by 27 in. (note 41 *cont.*) by 27 in.) fitted with carrying poles. Portable chests of similar size and construction were found in the tomb of Pharaoh Tutankhamun (*c.*AD 1336–1327) when the undisturbed tomb was discovered in 1922.

42. McCarter (1980: 3), citing Exod. 27:20–21.

young ministrant will be the one to make it burn bright again'. For Alter, Eli is 'immersed in permanent darkness', but 'God's lamp' remains alive in the young Samuel. Fishbane (1982: 199) takes a different tack, associating the *not yet* extinguished *lamp of God* with Eli himself and contrasting Samuel's 'not yet' illuminated state with 'Eli's flickering but as yet not totally undiminished [*sic*; read 'diminished'] spiritual vision'. There is truth in both readings, as shall become apparent as we continue.

4–9. *Then the LORD called Samuel* (v. 4). Samuel famously mistakes the Lord's voice for Eli's, and runs to Eli, who is at first confused and sends Samuel to lie back down again. Eli's reference to Samuel as *My son* in verse 6 (cf. also v. 16), if not merely formulaic,[43] may suggest a 'fondness of the blind and doomed Eli for his young assistant' (Alter 1999: 17). Beyond this, however, and against the backdrop of his rather miserable experience with his own 'sons', Eli's address may be a first hint of a realignment not only of his affections but of his allegiances (see further at v. 18 and 4:13).

For his part, *Samuel did not yet know the LORD* (v. 7a). While often lost in translation, the Hebrew sentence is identical with what was said of Eli's sons in 2:12, save for the replacement of 'not' with 'not yet'. Lest it be thought that Samuel's 'not knowing' is the same as the 'not knowing' of Eli's sons,[44] the narrator immediately states the basis of Samuel's not knowing: *the word of the LORD had not yet been revealed to him* (v. 7b). Thus, the verbal overlap between 2:12 and 3:7 continues the comparison-in-order-to-contrast pattern developed in chapter 2.

When Samuel runs to Eli a third time, Eli finally *realised that the LORD was calling* (v. 8). Excuses might be made for Eli's slowness to grasp what is going on. After all, Eli is old (2:22), it is the middle of the night and a vision is the last thing he's expecting, visions being so rare in his day. Nevertheless, Eli's dullness here joins with earlier impressions of misperception (1:12–13) and obliviousness (2:22) to reinforce the point that Eli's dim-sightedness is not just physical,

---

43. As it may be in 4:16.

44. I.e. a culpable refusal to know, acknowledge, recognize (see at 2:12).

but spiritual. Now that Eli has grasped what is actually happening, he sends Samuel back to his place with instructions to respond to the next call with *Speak, Lord, for your servant is listening* (v. 9). The narrative description of the Lord's repeated calling is suggestive of increasing intensity. Verse 4 states simply that *the Lord called Samuel*. In verses 6 and 8, the Lord directly addresses Samuel by name: *Samuel!* And the fourth time he calls, the Lord repeats the name twice: *Samuel! Samuel!* (v. 10).

10–14. The fourth and final call to Samuel begins with the statement that *The Lord came and stood there* (v. 10). Some interpret this statement to mean that Samuel's theophany was not only auditory but visionary as well (e.g. Baldwin 1988). At least three considerations tell against this notion. First, the Hebrew term rendered *stood there* means to 'take one's stand' in the sense of positioning oneself to do something, and thus may not necessarily connote a visible appearance (note that *there* is lacking in the Hebrew text). Second, the Lord 'calls' rather than 'speaks' to Samuel, which is suggestive of an auditory rather than a visionary experience. And third, the Lord is said to be calling *as at the other times*, which would seem to exclude a visible appearance, for otherwise Samuel would have had no reason to run to Eli on the earlier occasions.

Now aware that it is not Eli but the Lord who is calling, Samuel answers, *Speak, for your servant is listening* (v. 10b). Conspicuous by its absence is the vocative 'Lord', which Eli had instructed Samuel to include in his response to the divine address. Perhaps Alter (1999: 17; following Bar-Efrat 1996) is correct in suggesting that Samuel's omission reflects 'diffidence about addressing God'. But there may also be a subtle hint of Samuel's distancing himself from Eli, whom he has been observing for some time now and whom he might regard as not entirely reliable.[45]

Verses 11–14 report the Lord's message to Samuel. The judgment against Eli and his house is unavoidable for two reasons: *his*

---

45. All this assumes that 'Lord' is part of Eli's instruction in v. 9, but note Gordon's cautionary remark that 'part of the LXX tradition omits the word in verse 9' (1986: 89).

sons uttered blasphemies against God, and he failed to restrain them (v. 13). NIV 1984 follows MT and reads that Eli's sons 'made themselves contemptible', but NIV 2011 is almost certainly correct in following LXX and reading uttered *blasphemies against [cursed] God*. The difference in the two readings in the consonantal Hebrew text would be a matter of only one letter; the loss of the first letter of the word God, *'lhm* ('Elohim'), leaves *lhm* ('themselves'). While the loss could be accidental, it is generally regarded as an instance of an intentional scribal correction (MT attests eighteen such *tiqqûnê sôperîm*) effected to avoid juxtaposing 'curse' and 'God'.[46]

If the first charge is that Eli's sons blasphemed God, the second is that Eli *failed to restrain them* (v. 13). Some English translations charge Eli with failing to 'rebuke' his sons (e.g. JPS, NASB). But this would not be true (see at 2:22–25). NIV and most English translations are correct in reading *restrain*.[47] In the light of Eli's position as high priest, his dealings with his miscreant sons should have involved more than mere words – he could have removed them from office. On the level of language, a clever link is drawn between the weakness of Eli's physical (and spiritual) eyes (v. 2) and the weakness of his dealing with his sons: his eyes were *weak* (restrained; *khh* I) and he didn't *restrain* (weaken; *khh* II) his sons. Whether one root or two, this word occurs only eighteen times in the Old Testament, and just these two times in the whole book of Samuel. The significance of this double occurrence is not to be overlooked.

---

46. The juxtaposition is not avoided in Exod. 22:28 and Lev. 24:15, but this may be explained by the fact that the former expresses a prohibition and the second a sanction.

47. The verb in question, *khh* II, occurs only once in the OT, so its precise definition is uncertain. Some lexica translate simply 'rebuke' (*HALOT*, BDB). But Jenni (1968: 247) contends that *khh* II carries a stronger meaning than Heb. *g'r* ('rebuke, scold'). In contrast to the latter, Jenni writes that the goal in view for *khh* II is its 'result' (*'Ergebnis'*). Various lexica grasp this important point: e.g. *khh* II has 'a stronger meaning than rebuke, something like "restrain, prevent"' (*NIDOTTE*); 'to rebuke, set (someone) right, with an implication that future bad behavior is curtailed' (*KM*; cf. also DCH).

The verdict on the house of Eli is final; it shall *never be atoned for* (v. 14). The focus is not on atonement for sin generally but on the *guilt of Eli's house* and the fact that the rejection of Eli's house from the priestly office cannot be reversed *by sacrifice or offering*. While Old Testament law made provision for unintentional priestly sins to be atoned for (Lev. 4:1–12), no such provision was made for the 'high-handed' sin of blasphemy which 'despised the LORD's word' (Num. 15:30–31). Moreover, inasmuch as the offence of the Elides was in respect of the sacrifices and offerings, which were the normal means of atonement, their doom was doubly assured.

15–18. The notice that Samuel *opened the doors of the house of the LORD* (v. 15) may seem unimportant. But given the rarity of extraneous physical description in biblical narrative, Fishbane (1982: 201) may be justified in linking this and other features in 1 Samuel 3 with a 'thematic shift from human blindness and divine absence to human insight and divine presence'; both literally and metaphorically, the doors of the house of the Lord are opened by Samuel.

Having run to Eli so readily in the night, Samuel is now hesitant, for he *was afraid to tell Eli the vision* (v. 15). Eli, however, having three times denied calling Samuel in the night, now in the morning explicitly calls him, and for the fifth time, Samuel says, *Here I am* (*hinnēnî*; v. 16).

May God deal with you . . . if you hide from me anything he told you (v. 17). Formulaic in expression, Eli's insistence that Samuel disclose fully what God has said tells us something about Eli. He must have known, in the aftermath of the judgment speech delivered by the man of God in 2:27–36, that the news would not be good. But Eli nevertheless is intent on hearing what the Lord has said. He even uses an oath to make sure Samuel hides nothing.

He is the LORD; let him do what is good in his eyes (v. 18). Having dragged from the reluctant Samuel a report of what the Lord said to him during the night, Eli responds admirably and submissively, recognizing that the divine judge is in the right.[48] With this

---

48. Gutbrod (1956: 35) remarks that the text depicts Eli not only as 'yielded to God' ('Gottergebenen') but as 'believing in the divine justice' ('im Gericht Glaubenden').

response Eli sets a standard by which later responses to divine judgment in the book of Samuel may be measured. For instance, Saul's stubborn refusal to accept his rejection as king (1 Sam. 20:30–31 and *passim*) may be contrasted with both Eli's and David's submission to the divine will (for the latter, see 2 Sam. 15:25–26, where David uses the same expression: 'what is good in his eyes').[49]

3:19 – 4:1a. *The L*ORD *was with Samuel.* Having rejected the priestly house of Eli, the Lord does not leave Israel without help. As promised in 2:35, he raises up a *faithful priest, who will do according to what is in my heart and mind.*[50] The simplicity of the statement that *The L*ORD *was with Samuel* must not be allowed to mask its importance. In the book of Samuel, the presence of the Lord with someone makes all the difference. What we might call the divine accompaniment formula is applied to Samuel here at the beginning of his prophetic ministry, and the result is that *he [the L*ORD*] let none of Samuel's words fall to the ground* (v. 19).[51] The formula is applied repeatedly to David (16:18; 17:37; 18:12, 14, 28; 20:13; 2 Sam. 7:3). And it is never said of Saul, except in Jonathan's tacit transfer of rule from his father to David: *May the L*ORD *be with you as he has been with my father* (20:13).

*Dan to Beersheba . . . Samuel was attested as a prophet of the L*ORD (v. 20). Throughout the land, from Dan in the far north to Beersheba in the south,[52] Samuel's reputation spreads. As Samuel matures, his roles

---

49. Eslinger's appraisal of Eli's reaction as cynical (1985: 154–155) does not do justice to the text.
50. The longer-term fulfilment of this prophecy is found in Solomon's elevation of the Zadokites (1 Kgs 2:26–27), but in the short term the focus is on Samuel himself.
51. The Hebrew text has simply 'his words', but the tendency of most translations to assume that it is Samuel's (and not just the Lord's) words that are in view is probably correct; though, once stated like that, it becomes apparent that this may be a distinction without a difference, given Samuel's confirmation as a prophet, i.e. one who speaks the word of the Lord. In any case, Samuel's impeccable record establishes him as a true prophet according to Deut. 18:17–22.
52. For this conventional description of the entirety of the land of Israel, see Judg. 20:1; 2 Sam. 3:10; 1 Kgs 4:25; and many others.

increase. Raised as a priest, he is now confirmed as a prophet and will soon be functioning as a judge-deliverer (7:15–17). The final line of this section (4:1a) adds that the word of Yahweh was revealed not just to Samuel but through Samuel *to all Israel*.

Meaning
Bringing the first major section of the book of Samuel to its close, 1 Samuel 3:1 – 4:1a is a narrative of change. Eli and Samuel change places, in a sense. The old priest's impending rejection is confirmed, and the boy priest's future prominence is indicated. Not only is Samuel to fill the role, at least initially, of the *faithful priest* promised in 2:35, but he is established also as a prophet. In this latter capacity, he will be used, as he grows, to effect further changes, pre-eminent among them the transition to monarchy. In the present context, the key change is the resolution to the problem highlighted in the opening 'exposition', namely, the rarity of the *word of the LORD* (3:1). By the chapter's end, in its 'denouement' (3:20 – 4:1a), the Lord's word is being regularly revealed to Samuel and through him to all Israel. These final verses constitute a proleptic summary; after all, in chapter 3 Samuel is still young and growing (v. 19). The heart of the chapter is its centre, where a change in the boy Samuel is described; the young Samuel for the first time hears and learns to recognize the voice of the Lord. It can be argued that a change in Eli, or at least its beginning, is also evident. Though Eli remains as dim-sighted as ever physically, there are hints that his spiritual senses may be quickening. Slow to grasp that the Lord is calling Samuel, Eli does eventually sort out what is happening. More importantly, Eli insists on hearing the word of the Lord spoken to Samuel in his night vision and responds with acceptance and submission to the rejection of his house. These hints of Eli's reorientation to God will be reinforced in the next chapter, first, by the statement that the blind old priest is *watching, because his heart feared for the ark* (4:13) and, second, by the fact that it is the loss of the ark, even more than the loss of his sons, that bowls him over (4:18).

B. God's power: the ark of God at large in Philistia (4:1b – 7:1)

Context

Since Leonard Rost (1926: 4–47) first gave prominence to the notion of an independent 'ark narrative' secondarily inserted into the text of Samuel, much ink has been spilt seeking to define and delimit this unit. Rost argued that the ark narrative, which he takes to be most of 1 Samuel 4 – 6 as well as 2 Samuel 6, proves itself on the basis of vocabulary and style to be a unit independent of its surrounding context and complete in its structure (Rost 1926: 47). More recent discussions have undermined these claims, noting for instance that without at least some parts of 1 Samuel 1 – 3, the ark narrative is lacking in information vital to its understanding (Miller and Roberts 1977: 70). It is of course likely that events as dramatic as the loss of the ark and the death of the high priest would have been much talked about in the immediate aftermath of their occurrence, but there is little to commend the view that the present position of the ark narrative interrupts the flow of the Samuel narrative. Quite the opposite; without the earlier chapters, the reader would know nothing of the Elides or of the grounds of their rejection and loss.

One feature of the text sometimes cited in support of the notion that an 'ark narrative' does not quite fit its current textual context is the fact that Samuel, despite his prominence in the preceding chapters, makes no appearance at all in 1 Samuel 4:1b – 7:1. But this line of reasoning overlooks an important chronological feature. At the assumed time of the loss of the ark and fall of the Elides, Samuel was but a boy and thus hardly likely to take the field in battle. The summary of 3:19 – 4:1a underscores what Samuel *eventually became*. When Samuel next appears (i.e. in 1 Sam. 7), he is a grown man and leader of the people, and the text is explicit about *twenty years* having elapsed (7:2).

The three chapters recounting the ark's adventures in enemy territory may be succinctly characterized as follows: the ark's capture by Philistines (4:1b–22); the ark's victory tour in Philistia (5:1–12); the ark's return from Philistia (6:1 – 7:1). First Samuel 4 comprises three sections: the ark leaves (vv. 1b–11); Eli dies (vv. 12–18); Ichabod is born (vv. 19–22).

i. The ark's 'capture' by the Philistines (4:1b–22)
Comment

1b–3. Israel's initial defeat by the Philistines is described quickly. Responsibility for starting the conflict is not assigned, but for several reasons it seems likely that the Philistines were the aggressors: (1) Aphek[53] was captured by Israel in the time of Joshua (Josh. 12:18); (2) the Philistines were generally associated with their five key cities farther to the south-west, namely, Ashdod, Ashkelon, Ekron, Gath and Gaza (1 Sam. 6:17; cf. Josh. 13:3), but in the pre- and early-monarchical periods clearly had expansionist ambitions. As Peterson (1999: 42) notes, the Philistines were one of the 'Big Three Enemies in Israel's History', bracketed on either side by 'the earlier Egyptian oppression and the later Babylonian exile'. *Philistines* are mentioned several times in the Pentateuch,[54] briefly in the book of Joshua where they are listed amongst the territories yet to be 'taken over' (Josh. 13:1–3), and then frequently in the period of the judges, most famously in their conflicts with Samson (Judg. 13 – 16). They are regularly referred to as the 'uncircumcised' (e.g. 1 Sam. 14:6; 17:26, 36; 31:4)[55] and in the Bible are held in contempt, not for lacking culture – their material culture was in many respects richer than Israel's in this period – but for their inexorable opposition to the people and purposes of God. That the Philistines represented the quintessential foreign adversary may be suggested by LXX's common rendering of the word 'Philistine' as *allophylos*, 'foreigner, Gentile, heathen, pagan'.

The magnitude of Israel's first defeat in the present passage – *about four thousand* (v. 2) – is made uncertain by questions surrounding the proper reading of Hebrew '*elep*, 'thousand' or (military) 'unit'.[56] Regardless of whether the defeat cost Israel four thousand

---

53. Tel Ras el-'Ain, located at the southern end of the plain of Sharon, some 9 miles inland from the Mediterranean near the sources of the Yarkon River.
54. Gen. 10:14; 21:32, 34; 26:1, 8, 14, 18; Exod. 13:17; 23:31.
55. Many of Israel's other neighbours were in fact circumcised, but for different reasons from those in Israel; see Long (2009a: 286).
56. The seminal discussion is in Mendenhall (1958: 52–66). C. J.

soldiers or four military units comprising perhaps as few as forty soldiers, the mere fact of a loss was sufficient to cause consternation amongst Israel's elders: *Why did the LORD bring defeat upon us today before the Philistines?* (v. 3). The theological understanding underlying this question is appropriate (cf. 17:47). Lamentably, the elders do not pursue an answer to their question (there is no mention of prayer or oracular enquiry, for instance)[17] but proceed immediately to propose a plan of their own: *Let us bring the ark of the LORD's covenant from Shiloh* (v. 3). On the character and significance of the ark, see comment at 3:3 and also below.

4–5. The people waste no time in bringing from Shiloh the *ark of the covenant of the LORD Almighty, who is enthroned between the cherubim* (cf. Exod. 25:17–22; Num. 7:89). The ark carried powerful associations. At a much later period, Hebrews 9:4 states that the ark contained 'the gold jar of manna, Aaron's staff that had budded, and the stone tablets of the covenant'. While the contents of the ark are not listed so succinctly in the Old Testament, the writer of Hebrews likely drew on texts indicating that at some point all three items were deposited in the ark: see Exodus 25:16 and *passim* for the deposit of the tablets; Exodus 16:32–34 for the manna; and Numbers 17:10 for Aaron's staff. The contents of the ark are suggestive of three aspects of the Lord's care for his people: that he instructs them in godly living (the tablets), that he provides for their physical needs (the manna) and that he sanctions godly leaders positively and impostors negatively (Aaron's staff; see the broader context of Num. 16 – 17).

Lest the reader be tempted to join *all Israel* in their unrestrained enthusiasm (*great shout*) as the *ark of the LORD* is brought *into the camp* (v. 5), the narrator notes at the end of verse 4 that the ark is attended

---

Humphreys (1998: 211) avers that a 'unit' may have contained about ten persons. For further discussion and bibliography, see Tsumura (2007: 189–190).

57. Bodner (2008: 45) remarks: 'One may have expected the elders to seek "the word of the LORD" from Shiloh, since 3:21 refers to the ubiquity of the divine word at Shiloh through the prophet . . . Instead, the elders choose the ark.'

by *Eli's two sons, Hophni and Phinehas*. This brief notice is ominous, given what the foregoing narratives have described of the shameful behaviour of these two and the judgment certain to befall them.

6–11. The *great shout* in the Israelite camp not only shook the ground (v. 5) but alerted the nearby Philistines that something momentous must have occurred in the Hebrew camp (v. 6). That the Philistines refer to the *Hebrew* camp is noteworthy. At one level, of course, the name Hebrew may simply be derived from Abraham's Shemite ancestor Eber, mentioned various times in Old Testament genealogies (e.g. Gen. 10:21, 24; 11:14–17) as well as in Luke 3:35. But ever since the discovery in 1888–1889 of hundreds of letters in a royal archive at the Egyptian site of el-Amarna (ancient Akhetaten), scholars have puzzled over how the 'Habiru' (spelled *'apiru*) mentioned in some sixteen of the Amarna letters might be related, if at all, to the biblical 'Hebrews'. Despite initial attempts to equate the two groups, it soon became clear that this was impossible, as further archaeological discoveries showed the Habiru to be far too widespread across the Ancient Near East for all of them to be Hebrews. This does not mean, however, that the Hebrews might not have been viewed by their adversaries as belonging to that class of displaced, potentially troublesome migrants known as 'Habiru'. It is noteworthy, for instance, that references to biblical 'Hebrews' are most often found on the lips of or in the presence of non-Israelites.[58] Even the biblical writers sometimes make a distinction between Israelites and Hebrews (see 1 Sam. 14:21).[59]

A god has come into the camp . . . They are the gods who struck the Egyptians with all kinds of plagues in the wilderness (vv. 7–8). The Philistines do not appear to be very precise theologians (god or gods?) or historians (plagues in the wilderness?). But they do know enough to exclaim, *Oh no!* (lit. 'Woe to us!', v. 7). The import

---

58. E.g. Potiphar's spurned wife calls Joseph a 'Hebrew' in Gen. 39:14, 17; Pharaoh's daughter calls Moses a 'Hebrew' in Exod. 2:6.

59. For bibliography and more nuanced discussion of the Habiru/Hebrew question, see Long (2009a: 289); Provan, Long and Longman (2015: 227–231, 255–256).

of Israel's divinely arranged departure from Egypt is not lost on the Philistines (see also 6:6), nor was it on some of the earlier inhabitants of Canaan, such as Rahab (Josh. 2:9–11). But whereas at other times 'hearts melted in fear' (Josh. 2:11, margin), the Philistines choose to fight, steeling one another with the call to *Be strong . . . ! Be men . . . !* (v. 9).[60] In the short term, at least, the Philistines seem to have made the right decision, and *Israel lost thirty thousand foot soldiers* (v. 10).[61] More shocking, the ark of God was captured (v. 11)! Clearly, the elders' plan (v. 3) has proved disastrous. Whatever their initial plan, whether to wield the ark as a kind of cultic power object or, as seems more likely, to force the Lord's hand by bringing the symbol of his presence onto the field of battle, it has failed dramatically. While the ark's 'capture' might seem to constitute a theological crisis, the collateral notice regarding Hophni and Phinehas may hint at the fact that the Lord has not lost control of the situation; after all, that they should die together on the same day is precisely in fulfilment of the *sign* announced by the *man of God* in 2:34.

12–18. Eli dies. The shocking ('ear-tingling', 3:11) news of Israel's catastrophic defeat is brought speedily to Shiloh, where Eli is stationed, *watching* [!], *because his heart feared for the ark of God* (v. 13). While Eli's *watching* might simply be a case of 'sighted language' in reference to a blind old man, several considerations suggest otherwise: (1) as noted earlier, the narrator's regular references to Eli's dim-sightedness seem intended to connote not just a physical malady but a spiritual dim-sightedness as well (see at 3:2, 13); (2) the explicit focus of Eli's fear – not for Israel nor even for his own sons but *for the ark of God* – suggests a refocusing of his affections and allegiances (see at 3:6); (3) despite all the bad news of the day, including the deaths of his two sons, it was only when the Benjaminite messenger *mentioned the ark of God* that Eli *fell backwards off his chair by the side of the gate* (v. 18). Taken together, these features paint a picture of an old priest who has been slumbering but is

---

60. For discussion of this ancient martial formula, see Fontaine (2007: 61–72).
61. On large numbers and uncertainties regarding 'thousand(s)', see at v. 2.

beginning to wake up. Eli is beginning to regain his balance, to find again his centre of gravity. Sadly, whatever encouragements the text may contain regarding Eli's spiritual rehabilitation, the dire news of the day causes him to lose his physical balance and fall. Now an *old man* and *heavy* (*kbd*!) – recall the honour/weight (*kbd*) language of 2:29–30 – Eli dies under his own weight. We shall have more to say on Eli in the 'Meaning' section below.

He had led Israel for forty years. With this notice the story of Eli comes to an end. He is presented as both priest and judge; the verb rendered *led* (*šāpaṭ*) might as easily be translated 'judged' (cf. the use of the nominal form, *šōpēṭ*, to designate the string of leader-judges from the death of Joshua to the birth of monarchy). The combination of priestly and judge-type roles is not without biblical precedent.[62]

19–22. Ichabod is born. Three deaths in the family of Eli have already been recorded in 1 Samuel 4, and there is to be one more – plus a birth. The pregnant *daughter-in-law* of Eli, hearing the calamitous news of the day, goes into premature labour and gives birth to a son.[63] As she dies, she names him *Ichabod* (v. 21). This naming marks yet another use of the *kbd* root, first introduced into the Eli story in 2:29–30. The name Ichabod may mean 'no glory' or 'where is the glory?'[64] The point is much the same in either case. Josephus (*Ant.* 5.360) relates the name to the 'ignominy that befell the army', but the dying woman ties it directly to the loss of the ark: *The Glory has departed from Israel, for the ark of God has been captured* (v. 22).

Meaning
The events of 1 Samuel 4 conclude the story of the decline and fall of Eli and his sons. Eli will be referred to again in 14:3, and his

---

62. See, e.g., Num. 25:5–8; Deut. 17:8–12; 19:17; 1 Chr. 23:2–4; 2 Chr. 19:8; Ezek. 44:24.
63. Josephus (*Ant.* 5.360) makes the birth two-months premature, but this is based on tradition not found in the biblical text.
64. For a compact discussion of the linguistic details, see Youngblood (2009: 76, note on 1 Sam. 4:21).

remaining descendants will be massacred by Saul in chapter 22, but the dramatic events of chapter 4 lead to the deaths of the key Elide players in the preceding chapters. Eli's sons were wildly off balance. Eli was less dramatically tilting, but he, too, had lost his centre of gravity. We noted the 'weight/honour/glory' language introduced in the judgment announced by the man of God in 2:29–30: 'Those who give me weight will receive weight ... why are you fattening yourselves?' The continued occurrence of the *Leitwort* (keyword stem) *kbd* (weight, honour, glory) into chapter 4 and beyond is another indication of the fitted-ness of the 'ark narrative' in its current textual context. Occurrences of *kbd* continue in the account of the ark's travels in and return from Philistia (1 Sam. 5 – 6), thus stitching the whole story neatly together.

As suggested before, the early chapters of 1 Samuel are in various respects programmatic for the rest of the book. We noted the important theological lenses provided by the story of Hannah and her song (1:1 – 2:10). She recognized God's weight and gave him weight in her words and actions. By contrast, Eli and his sons slighted God (underweighted him), thus losing their balance and eventually their lives. In all this, it becomes very clear that the word of God (e.g. through the man of God in 2:27–36 and to Samuel in ch. 3) carries weight and must be respected.

Chapter 4 underscores another key theme in the book of Samuel, namely, the importance of waiting for the word of the Lord and the danger of failing to do so. After the initial defeat by the Philistines, the elders are sufficiently astute theologically to wonder aloud why the Lord has brought defeat. But they do not in fact enquire of the Lord and wait for an answer. They immediately go about planning their own rescue, thinking to manipulate the ark almost as a tool in their own hands. The results are predictably disastrous, and the ark departs.

ii. The ark's victory tour of Philistia (5:1–12)
Context
Thinking themselves to have the ark and the situation well in hand, the Philistines soon begin to discover just how very difficult handling the cult symbol of the Lord's presence can be. As the episode develops, it becomes obvious that the ark has lost none of

its 'weight' in travelling from Israel to Philistia. The heavy hand of the Lord soon begins to make itself felt, first on the chief god of the Philistine pantheon (vv. 1–5) and then on the Philistines themselves (vv. 6–12). The Philistines do not immediately associate their trials with their 'capture' of the ark of God – other, more 'natural' explanations of their difficulties must first be tested. But soon the results of their experiments seem sufficiently clear that other Philistine cities resist continued experimentation in their own precincts.

Comment

1–5. After chapter 4's focus on the disastrous results of Israel's attempts to take the ark in hand and bring it into battle, 1 Samuel 5 turns to consider the Philistines. Now it is the Philistines' turn to 'handle' the ark. Twice we read that the Philistines 'took the ark . . . and brought it' (my lit. translation),[65] first to the coastal city of Ashdod (v. 1) and then right into the temple of their chief God, Dagon (v. 2).

Ashdod (NT Azotus; Acts 8:40), though assigned to Judah in the time of Joshua (Josh. 15:47), apparently fell into Philistine hands at the time of their arrival with other 'Sea Peoples' (Dever 1997: 219). By the time of Samuel, Ashdod was well established as one of the Philistines' five key cities. Today, due to natural shoreline accretion, the ancient site of Ashdod lies several miles inland from the coast of the Mediterranean Sea, but in biblical times it was a major seaport. This fact will help us to understand the Philistines' several attempts to relocate the ark (see below). Nine seasons of excavation between 1962 and 1972 uncovered various Philistine cult installations, but the temple of Dagon itself is yet to be found.[66]

In 'taking' and 'bringing' the ark into the temple of Dagon, the Philistines were behaving as most of their Ancient Near Eastern neighbours at the time. It was customary for opposing armies to bring their own 'gods' (in the form of images or idols) into battle

---

65. This repetition is lost in NIV and various other English translations.
66. For more detail, see Long (2009a: 290–291).

with them in the belief that success in battle was as dependent on the gods as on the human combatants. The gods of the winning side were considered the stronger, and the defeated deities were typically 'captured' and brought home as trophies of war, where they would be deposited in the sacred precinct of the 'superior' deities. Such behaviours are widely attested in the literature and iconography of the ANE across a long span. The following boast of the Assyrian king Tiglath-pileser I (1115–1076) provides a typical example (from some decades before the events of our present passage):

> With the mighty power of the god Ashur, my lord, I marched to the land of Sugu of the land of Habhu, [people] insubmissive to the god Ashur my lord ... I conquered the entire land of Sugu. I brought 25 of their gods, their booty, their possessions, [and] their property ... At that time I donated the 25 gods of those lands, my own booty which I had taken, to adorn the temple of the goddess Ninlil, beloved chief spouse of the god Ashur, my lord, [the temple of] the gods An [and] Adad, [the temple of] the Assyrian Ishtar, the temples of my city, Ashur, and the goddesses of my land.[67]

Dagon appears to have been the chief god of the Philistines (cf. Judg. 16:23; 1 Chr. 10:10). Just what kind of deity Dagon/Dagan[68] was remains a matter of debate. In the fourth century, Jerome (followed in the nineteenth by Wellhausen) favoured the view that Dagon was a fish god, noting the similarity between the name and the Hebrew word for 'fish', *dāg*. A more recent theory is that Dagon should be related to the west-semitic word *dāgān*, 'grain', making him an agricultural deity. A third theory, going back to W. F. Albright, proposes that Dagon was a storm god, citing the similarity of the name to the Arabic root *dajana*, 'to be gloomy, cloudy', and the fact that Dagan is often positioned in the polytheistic hierarchy as the father of Baal, god of storm. Whatever

---

67. *ARI* 2.28:11–12. For further bibliography and discussion, see Long (2009a: 295).
68. The latter spelling is preferred in extra-biblical references to the deity.

uncertainties remain regarding the significance of Dagon's name and status, his prominence in ANE religious culture is not in doubt; worship of Dagon is attested over some two thousand years from late third-millennium BC Ebla to the Maccabean period (1 Macc. 10:83–85).[69]

If the Philistines were encouraged by their victory over the Israelites to assume that Dagon was more powerful than Yahweh, they were quickly disabused of this assumption. Arising early the day after depositing the ark *beside Dagon*, they discover Dagon *fallen on his face on the ground before the ark of the LORD!* (vv. 2–3). This spectacle does not immediately bring the Philistines to their knees, however. They doubtless knew from experience what today's seismologists also know, namely, that shaking ground in their region was not unusual.[70] So they 'take' Dagon – the dramatic irony of this third occurrence of the verb 'take' in these few verses should not be missed (recall their 'taking' of the ark) – and return him to his place. Next morning, the Philistines rise early and again find Dagon *fallen on his face on the ground before the ark of the LORD!* This time, however, *His head and hands had been broken off and were lying on the threshold* (v. 4). Dagon's 'belittlement' (Vannoy 2009: 72) is telling. Removal of head, hands or other body parts was standard treatment of enemy dead in the martial cultures of the ANE, including Israel (Judg. 7:25; 8:6; 1 Sam. 17:54; 31:9; 2 Sam. 4:12). The Philistines had thought their god to have the upper hand over Israel's, but they now find him both headless and handless. And they themselves will soon be feeling in their own bodies the 'heavy hand' of Yahweh (see at v. 6).

Before proceeding to recount the further adventures of the ark (vv. 6–12), the narrator breaks frame to describe a customary behaviour that continued to his own day: *to this day neither the priests of Dagon nor any others* entering the temple at Ashdod *step on the*

---

69. For more thorough discussion, see Long (2009a: 292–293).
70. The Jordan Rift Valley is part of the so-called Afro-Arabian fault line, which stretches some four thousand miles from Turkey to Tanzania and is described as 'one of the longest, deepest, and widest fissures in the earth's surface' (Beitzel 1985: 37).

threshold (v. 5). Whether this notice is meant to convey information regarding the origin of a Philistine practice or, as seems more likely, to associate an existing practice with a humiliating defeat remains an open question.[71]

6–12. The humiliation of the god Dagon now complete, attention turns to the Philistines themselves. *The LORD's hand* is *heavy* (Heb. *kbd*) *on the people of Ashdod and its vicinity* (v. 6), and the painful evidence is an outbreak of *tumours*. The precise nature of these *tumours* is unclear. The Hebrew consonantal text calls them simply *'opālîm*, a word meaning in the first instance 'hills, mounds', which by extension came to refer to 'hill-shape growths' and thus swellings, tumours, boils, haemorrhoids, or the like.[72] While bacillary dysentery was suggested as early as Josephus (*Ant.* 6.3), the more likely cause of the tumours was bubonic plague. Several references to rodents in the next chapter (6:4, 11, 18) lend support to the bubonic plague view, as rodents are known carriers of plague. It is worth noting that LXX mentions rodents also here in 5:6: 'And the hand of the Lord was heavy upon Azotus and brought trouble on them, and it broke out upon them into the ships, and in the midst of its territory mice grew up, and there was great confusion of death in the city' (NETS). A port city such as Ashdod would have been all too familiar with the arrival of pestilence via ships.

The people of Ashdod quickly conclude that they cannot keep *the ark of the God of Israel* in their city, because both they and their god, Dagon, are feeling the weight of his hand. Instead of the now familiar Hebrew root *kbd*, the Philistines use the synonym *qšh*, which adds the nuance of being 'hard' or 'harsh' (v. 7). They are no more capable of manipulating the ark to their advantage than were the Israelites in the preceding chapter. In fact, its mere presence amongst them is crushing them. While the Israelites had 'sent' (*šlḥ*) to Shiloh for the ark (4:4), the Philistines now 'send' (*šlḥ*) to the *rulers of the Philistines* – probably the five rulers of the so-called

---

71. On the avoidance of thresholds, cf. Zeph. 1:9.
72. The Qere indicates the Heb. word *ṭĕḥōrîm*, 'tumours' in a 'more straightforward sense' (Tsumura 2007: 208).

Philistine pentapolis (cf. 6:16) – to plan how to be rid of the ark (5:8). The plan suggested, either by the rulers themselves or by the people of Gath (LXX assumes the latter; MT has simply 'they'), is that the ark should be moved to Gath. This plan suggests that the Philistines are not yet fully convinced as to the cause of their several difficulties. Gath (Tel Zafit/tell es-Safi) lay some 11 miles east-south-east of Ashdod. By removing the ark from the port city of Ashdod to a more inland location, the Philistines may have hoped to test the theory that their woes had nothing to do with the ark they had 'captured' but, rather, with the fact that pestilence often breaks out in port cities. In the next chapter, we see further evidence of the Philistines' empiricist inclination to test whether the disaster they are suffering is the Lord's doing or merely *happened to us by chance* (6:9).

Moving the ark to Gath soon demonstrates that it is indeed the LORD's *hand* that is *against that city*, and the city is thrown into a *great panic* (v. 9). No longer so concerned to test their 'natural-explanation' hypothesis, the Gittites simply want to be rid of the ark, and they send it to Ekron (v. 10), some 5 miles north of Gath. The discovery in 1996 at Tel Miqne of a royal dedicatory inscription by the 'ruler of Ekron' confirms that ancient city's location. The inscription reads:

> The temple [house] that Akhayus, son of Padi, son of Ysd, son of Ada, son of Ya'ir, ruler of Ekron, built for PTGYH, his lady. May she bless him, and prote[ct] him, and prolong his days, and may she bless his [l]and.[73]

The people of Ekron have been paying attention to events in Ashdod and Gath, and the arrival of the ark induces immediate panic. For a second time the *rulers of the Philistines* are sent for (*šlḥ*; see at 5:8), but this time it is not to request counsel but to issue a directive: *Send the ark of the god of Israel away; let it go back to its own place, or it* [*he?*] *will kill us and our people* (v. 11). The weight of God's hand is mentioned yet again in verse 11 (as in 5:6, 7, 9); but here the

---

73. *COS* 2.42:164. For discussion, see Long (2009a: 297–298).

intensifier *very* (*mĕ'ōd*) is added: *God's hand was very heavy* (*kābĕdāh mĕ'ōd*) *against Ekron*. Not surprisingly, 'deadly panic' or 'panic of death' is the result; the Hebrew phrase *mĕhûmat-māwet* can be understood as 'panic, confusion, dismay' either caused by the dying all around or characterized as 'deadly' earnest (cf. *HALOT*'s 'fatal dismay'). The *outcry of the city*, that is, of those who, though afflicted with tumours, had not died, *went up to heaven* (v. 12). This final statement of chapter 5 'balances on the edge of ambiguity', as Alter (1999: 29) observes. Since *heaven*, or 'the heavens' (*haššāmāyim*), 'can simply mean the sky or the abode of God', the question is whether God, who has been

> present in the story through His acts, His heavy hand – but not, as it were, in person – is listening to the anguished cries of the Philistines, or is this merely an image of the shrieks of the afflicted Philistines echoing under the silent vault of the heavens?
> (Ibid.)

With respect to Alter's question, it is worth noting that the combination of the noun *šaw'â* ('call for help, scream, cry'; *HALOT*) and the verb *'ālāh* ('go up, ascend') occurs only here and one other time in the Old Testament – namely, in Exodus 2:23, where it is the cry of the Israelites in slavery in Egypt that goes up 'to God'.

Meaning
The dramatic irony of the events of 1 Samuel 5 is hard to miss. If the Philistines thought at the end of the battle of chapter 4 that Israel's loss was their gain, they were soon to learn a very bitter lesson. Far from being their captive, the ark of God quickly and relentlessly began bringing them to their knees (if not their graves). It was not the ark, of course, that had this effect, for if 1 Samuel 4 and 5 teach anything about the ark, it is that it is not the object itself that is the source of power but, rather, the God whom the ark represents. It is the Lord's *hand* that weighs heavily upon the citizens of Ashdod and Gath, and *very* heavily upon Ekron. It is his power that puts Dagon on his face, depriving him in the second round of both head and hands. If it was customary for conquerors to go on a victory tour of their newly conquered cities, it is hard to see the

travels of the ark as anything less.[74] Hannah had warned that *those who oppose the LORD will be broken* (2:10a). She had extolled the Lord as the God who reverses human fortunes, humbling the proud and exalting the humble (2:4–8). In 1 Samuel 4 and 5, both the Israelites and the Philistines encounter a God of reversals, a God whom they cannot control. He can neither be manipulated by those who confess him (ch. 4) nor managed by those who defy him (ch. 5). How will it all end? The story reaches its climax in the next chapter.

iii. The ark's return from Philistia (6:1 – 7:1)
Context
Having departed from presumptuous, superstitious Israel in 1 Samuel 4, and having induced a deadly panic amongst empiricist Philistia in 1 Samuel 5, the ark in 1 Samuel 6 makes its return journey to the land whence it came. But if the departure of the ark brings some relief for the Philistines, its return to Israel, though initially greeted with joy,[75] has the opposite effect in the border town of Beth Shemesh. Clearly, Israel still has much to learn about what it takes to *stand in the presence of the LORD, this holy God* (6:20). The chapter divides broadly into two scenes – the departure of the ark from the Philistines (6:1–12) and the arrival of the ark in Beth Shemesh (6:13–20) – with a concluding description of how the ark ultimately found its way to Kiriath Jearim (6:21 – 7:1).

Comment
1–6. The ark leaves the Philistines. Though the crisp narrative of 1 Samuel 5 appropriately conveys the sense that panic spread quickly amongst the Philistines, the actual course of events took several months, perhaps *seven months* (v. 1). The number 'seven' is frequently used in Scripture to indicate fullness or completeness, so the literal sense need not be pressed here, though it is certainly possible. It is worth noting in passing that the first plague in Egypt was said to last for seven days (Exod. 7:25).

---

74. See Gordon (1986: 100), who speaks of 'a parody of a victory tour, in which the roles of victor and vanquished are reversed'.
75. On the complexities of this reading, see at 6:13.

Whatever the precise time frame, the Philistines have clearly had enough, and they call for *the priests and the diviners* (v. 2). In the preceding chapter, it was *all the rulers of the Philistines* who were twice summoned (5:8, 11); here it is the religious personnel. Apparently, the events of chapter 5 convinced the Philistines that resolving their current crisis would require more than political solutions. All Ancient Near Eastern peoples had *priests*, and some of Israel's neighbours, in addition to the Philistines, also accepted *diviners*. The leaders of Moab and Midian, for instance, in their attempt to hire Balaam to curse the Israelites, brought a 'fee for divination' with them (Num. 22:7). In Ezekiel 21:21 (Heb. v. 26), the king of Babylon is described as standing 'at the parting of the way, at the fork in the two roads, to use divination; he shakes the arrows, he consults the teraphim, he inspects the liver' (NRSV). Amongst the Israelites, however, divination was explicitly and repeatedly forbidden (e.g. Deut. 18:10, 14; Jer. 27:9; Ezek. 13:23).

The two-fold advice given by the Philistine priests and diviners is in this instance sound. First, *do not send it [the ark] back to him without a gift; by all means send a guilt offering to him* (v. 3). The *guilt offering* (*'āšām*) in contexts such as the present one carries the idea of a sacrifice that propitiates or compensates for an offence. It is an offering that makes restitution in the hope of the rehabilitation and, as verse 3 makes clear, the healing of the offender: *Then you will be healed, and you will know why his hand has not been lifted from you.*[76] The specific form suggested for the guilt offering reflects the nature of the Philistines' distress and the number of their rulers: *Five gold tumours and five gold rats* (v. 4). As these objects symbolize both the Philistines' physical distress and its evident cause, they suggest an apotropaic function – that is, a 'carrying away' function – not unlike the scapegoat ritual described in Leviticus, where the scapegoat was to 'carry on itself all their sins to a remote place'

---

76. For a full discussion of the word *'āšām*, see Averbeck, *NIDOTTE*, s.v.; see also Jenni and Westermann (1997: s.v.). The combination of the verb *šûb* ('return', here rendered *send* in NIV) and the noun *'āšām* (*guilt offering*) occurs also in Num. 5:7–8, where the context clearly indicates that restitution is being made.

(Lev. 16:22).[77] The guilt offering was apparently meant to bring relief by bearing away the Philistines' guilt and its repercussions and by making restitution.

The aspect of restitution, or compensation, brings us to the second aspect of the priests' and diviners' counsel: *give glory to Israel's god* (v. 5). *Glory* renders the Hebrew noun *kābôd*, the root of which we have encountered many times in the book of Samuel so far, quintessentially in 2:29–30 in the accusation that Eli was honouring (giving weight to) his sons more than God. The semantic range of the root *kbd* includes 'weight, honour, glory', so the common rendering of 6:5 as *give glory* is accurate semantically. Literally, though, it would be preferable – and equally accurate – to render it as 'give weight' or 'give honour' to Israel's God. The advantage of rendering the *kbd* group (whether noun, verb or adjective) as uniformly as possible is that the English reader can better follow this keyword in its various occurrences in Samuel.[78] Of course, it is not always possible to indicate in English translation that the same Hebrew root is involved. This is evident in verse 6, where the *kbd* root occurs twice more: *Why do you harden [tĕkabbĕdû] your hearts as the Egyptians and Pharaoh did* [lit. 'hardened their hearts', *kibbĕdû . . . 'et-libbām*]?

What we have, then, is an elaborate use of a keyword – beginning with the rejection of Eli – in order to underscore the importance of giving weight, honour or glory to Israel's God. We noted earlier, at 4:7–8, that the Philistines were deficient as both theologians and historians, but they seem to understand at least enough of the exodus story and its God to realize that he must be given weight. Even the Philistine priests and diviners seem to grasp this essential point. Will the Israelites do as well? As the Egyptians and Pharaoh eventually came to the conclusion that the Israelites themselves had

---

77. For discussion of apotropaic rituals in the ANE, see Long (2009a: 299–300). And on the number of gold objects, whether ten or five, see Tsumura (2001: 353–369), who favours five (on 365).

78. English translations choosing to use 'honour' instead of 'glory' in 6:5 include JPS, NET, NIV 1984, NLT.

to be sent *on their way* (v. 6), so the Philistines conclude that the ark must be sent on its way.

7–12. But how is the ark to be returned? The Philistine priests and diviners suggest a procedure involving a *new cart* and *two cows that have calved and have never been yoked* (v. 7). The newness of the cart and the inexperience of the cows with the yoke may be intended to ensure the ritual purity of the conveyance. That the cows *have never been yoked* will, of course, make hitching them to the cart more difficult, to say nothing of the fact that they have recently calved and their calves are to be taken from them and penned up. Under such conditions, if the cows, against all natural instincts, proceed towards Beth Shemesh (a border town between Israel and Philistia),[79] this will be a sign that *the LORD has brought this great disaster on us* (v. 9). So strong is the instinct for cows to stay with their calves that, as depicted in Egyptian reliefs, a calf was sometimes used to draw reticent cattle across a river (see Long 2009a: 300). Ever the good empiricists,[80] the Philistines still apparently entertain the outside possibility that all their woes are not due to *his hand that struck us but that it happened to us by chance* (v. 9).

Once hitched to the cart, the cows proceed directly towards Israelite territory, not happy – *lowing all the way* – but not veering in the slightest; *keeping on the road . . . they did not turn to the right or to the left* (v. 12). The unusual amount of descriptive detail underscores the exceptional and, indeed, miraculous behaviour of the cows. All the while the *rulers of the Philistines followed* at a distance, observing as instructed in verse 9, until they reach *the border of Beth Shemesh* (v. 12). There will be one further notice regarding

---

79. Identified with Tell er-Rumeilah since the investigations of Edward Robinson in 1838. Beth Shemesh ('house of the sun') lay over 7 miles east of Ekron in a strategic position in the Sorek Valley, along an ancient route from the coastal plain into the central hill country near Jerusalem. As a border town, it was frequently contested by the Philistines and Israelites, as is evidenced both by 2 Chr. 28:18 and by the discovery of Philistine wares at the site prior to a massive destruction near the beginning of the eleventh century BC.

80. Cf. Collins (2000: 144–147).

the rulers of the Philistines in verse 16, but apart from that we hear nothing more of them. Lesson learned, they return to Ekron (v. 16).

13–16. The ark at Beth Shemesh. The focus now switches from the Philistines to the Israelites, and specifically the people of Beth Shemesh.[81] In the valley harvesting wheat (which would make it about May or June), *the people of Beth Shemesh* see the ark approaching, and *they rejoiced at the sight* (v. 13). *Joshua of Beth Shemesh* is mentioned again in verse 18, but otherwise nowhere else in the Old Testament. His significance lies in the fact that the *large rock* (vv. 14, 15, 18) in his field not only figures prominently in the events surrounding the ark's arrival but remained a *witness* to the events up to the time of the biblical narrator's day (v. 18). The *cart* and *cows* provide ready means for the sacrifice of a *burnt offering to the* LORD (v. 14) and the *large rock* offers a resting place for both the *ark of the* LORD *and the chest containing the gold objects*, both removed from the cart by *the Levites* (v. 15). That Levites should be present is not surprising, as Beth Shemesh was one of the levitical cities assigned to the descendants of Aaron in Joshua 21:16. The *five rulers of the Philistines*, who have been following the ark's relentless march towards home (v. 12), *saw all this and then returned that same day to Ekron* (v. 16).

The procedure followed by the Philistines finds loose analogies in other Ancient Near Eastern apotropaic rituals, as noted above. One Hittite text,[82] for instance, describes the return of an apotropaic representative, clothed with adornments of sufficient value to pacify the offended deity, and accompanied by 'all the lords'. Distinctive in the text before us, however, is the Philistines' focus on providing 'guilt offerings' (v. 3) and giving 'honour to Israel's god' (v. 5).[83] The return of the ark to Israel and the return of the Philistine rulers to Philistia might suggest that the episode is ended, but this is unfortunately not the case.

17–18. Though these verses may strike English readers as odd, with their seemingly pedantic rehearsal of *the gold tumours . . . one each*

---

81. On this border town, see note at v. 9.
82. 'Pulisa's Ritual against Plague', trans. B. J. Collins (*COS* 1.62:161).
83. For citation of texts and discussion, see Long (2009a: 299).

for Ashdod, Gaza, Ashkelon, Gath and Ekron (v. 17), they would likely not have seemed odd to an ancient audience familiar with the inclusion of such lists in narrative contexts (see Tsumura 2001; 2007: 222–223). Tsumura cites, inter alia, Genesis 2:4 and 2 Samuel 6:19 as heading similar lists. In combination with the summary remark of verse 18 that the *large rock . . . in the field of Joshua of Beth Shemesh* remains *a witness to this day*, these two verses again suggest an appropriate ending for the episode, but as just noted, this is not to be the case.

19–20. *God struck down . . . seventy . . . because they looked into the ark of the* LORD (v. 19). This sentence would make good, if tragic, sense, were it not for a couple of textual issues pertaining first to the number struck down and, second, to the nature of the offence. Regarding the first issue, MT and all the major extant witnesses add 'fifty thousand' to the 'seventy', arriving at an impossibly high number for the village of Beth Shemesh as we know it. Large numbers are notoriously difficult in the Old Testament, especially when involving the Hebrew word *'lp* (see at 4:2, 10). The 'fifty thousand' may be an early(?) gloss, though it stands rather awkwardly after 'seventy' in the Hebrew text, lacking even 'and' to connect the two numerals.[84] Josephus is content with 'seventy' and makes no reference to 'fifty thousand' (*Ant.* 6.16).

The second issue, pertaining to the nature of the offence, is not apparent in most English translations, which read that the *inhabitants of Beth Shemesh . . . looked into the ark of the* LORD (v. 19). But the Hebrew does not indicate precisely that they looked 'into' the ark but only that they looked 'on' (prep. *bĕ*) the ark. Perhaps something in the manner of the looking was offensive (e.g. 'gaze at' [BDB, citing this verse]; 'gloat over' [in a negative sense, Ps. 22:17; Obad. 12; cf. *HALOT* s.v. 7.a.iii.]). Or perhaps the quite different reading of LXX, followed by NRSV, should be followed: 'The descendants of Jeconiah did not rejoice with the people of Beth-shemesh when they greeted the ark of the LORD; and he killed seventy men of them.'[85] It may be observed in favour of the

---

84. A few Heb. manuscripts add 'and'.
85. Driver (1960: 59) notes that the Greek word rendered 'did not rejoice'

traditional understanding that it is difficult to discover just how the notion of seeing, looking or peering into something would be expressed in Hebrew, if not with an expression such as we have here. It is well recognized that the preposition *bĕ* is used with verbs of motion to mean 'into', and one might suppose that the same preposition could plausibly be employed with a verb of 'seeing', or directing one's vision.[86] The traditional rendering might find some support in texts such as Exodus 19:21 ('warn the people so they do not force their way through to see the LORD and many of them perish') and Numbers 4:20 ('the Kohathites must not go in to look at the holy things, even for a moment, or they will die'). Both of these passages involve a kind of seeing/looking (*r'h*) that can cause offence.[87] On present knowledge, it seems impossible to determine just what went wrong at Beth Shemesh. But if the offence did involve looking *into* the ark, this raises the question of what motivated such a daring move. Perhaps the valuable contents of the small chest returned by the Philistines tempted its recipients to wonder what the larger chest might contain?

Whatever the precise nature of the offence, it proved costly! And it elicited the quite sensible question: *Who can stand in the presence of the LORD, this holy God?* (v. 20).

6:21 – 7:1. The ark goes to Kiriath Jearim. The people of Beth Shemesh were afraid to keep the ark or, apparently, even to transport it, so *they sent messengers to the people of Kiriath Jearim*, some 9 miles east-north-east of Beth Shemesh, requesting that they come and *take it up to your town* (6:21). Kiriath Jearim is called Baalah Judah

---

occurs nowhere else in the LXX, leaving its meaning uncertain; as an alternative to rejoicing, he suggests reading 'And the sons of Jechoniah *came not off guiltless* . . . because they gazed at the ark of Yahweh.' McCarter's conjectural emendation of 'sons of Jeconiah' (*bny yknyhw*) to 'sons of the priests' (*bny hkhnym*) offers yet another option (McCarter 1980: 131).

86. First Sam. 16:7 could offer some indication of how 'looking into' might be expressed, but see the comment there.
87. Cf. Gordon (1986: 337 n. 52).

in 2 Samuel 6:2,[88] suggesting a possible cultic association with the Canaanite god Baal; the name change to Kiriath Jearim may have been intended to overcome this association. The fact that the ark is not returned to Shiloh, from which it had been taken, is one of several indications that Shiloh must have been destroyed in the aftermath of the Philistine victory recounted in 1 Samuel 4 (cf. Ps. 78:60–61; Jer. 7:12; 26:9).[89]

So the men of Kiriath Jearim came and took up the ark and *brought it to Abinadab's house on the hill and consecrated Eleazar his son to guard the ark* (7:1). *Abinadab* ('Father has proved himself generous'; *HALOT*) is a common name in Samuel,[90] and the name *Eleazar* ('God's help') recalls the much earlier son of Aaron (Exod. 6:23; Josh. 24:33). It seems unlikely, however, that the Eleazar consecrated in Kiriath Jearim was of levitical ancestry, unless we assume a link with the nearby levitical city of Gibeon (Josh. 21:17; note that Kiriath Jearim is associated with Gibeon in Josh. 9:17 as one of four Hivite cities).[91]

Meaning

With the ark under the careful guard of Eleazar, the story of the ark's departure from Israel (ch. 4), its devastation of the land of its presumed 'captors' (ch. 5) and its eventual return to Israel (6:1 – 7:1) is at an end – at least until 2 Samuel 6. In the course of the so-called ark narrative, both the Philistines and the Israelites have learned hard lessons under the heavy hand of Yahweh. The Philistines not only saw their chief god decapitated but felt in their own bodies the price of trifling with Yahweh. The Philistines' own words show their awareness that they are dealing with a powerful, personal deity and not simply a cultic object

---

88. Cf. other designations of the site as Baalah (Josh. 15:9) and Kiriath Baal (Josh. 15:60; 18:14).
89. On the fortunes of the tabernacle, see Vannoy (2009: 82 n. 1), who considers how the tabernacle might have been relocated to Gibeon (see 1 Kgs 3:4; 1 Chr. 21:29; 2 Chr. 1:2–6).
90. Jesse and Saul both had a son named Abinadab: 1 Sam. 16:8 and 31:2.
91. For more on the cultic associations of Kiriath Jearim, see Edelman (1992a: 22–23); Hamilton (1992: 84–85).

(6:3–9). The Philistines learned the necessity of giving weight (honour) to this powerful, personal God and of not weighing down (hardening) their hearts. The Israelites, too, learned the folly of trifling with the ark, and thus with Yahweh (6:19–20). The entire account of 1 Samuel 4:1 – 7:1 underscores the fact established already in 1 Samuel 1 – 3 that the Lord carries weight and must be accorded weight. As David will learn in a later episode involving the ark (2 Sam. 6:1–11), honouring God involves more than simply meaning well; it involves attending carefully and obediently to what he says.

C. God's power at work in God's prophet: 'Thus far the Lord has helped us' (7:2–17)

Context
Much has changed since the beginning of the book of Samuel. The aged, neglectful and in some quarters scandalous priestly house of Eli has been rejected in favour of God's new leader, Samuel, the boy-priest and growing prophet (1 Sam. 1 – 3). The key to these changes was in several respects Hannah, an everyday woman profoundly convinced that God was big enough to bear her sorrows. She believed that her Rock was a God who reversed human fortunes and who would effect change not only on the personal level but on the political as well; she sensed that the Lord would 'give strength to his king' (2:10).

Beginning with the story of Hannah, 1 Samuel 1 – 3 detailed the rise of God's new priest-prophet, while the so-called ark narrative of 1 Samuel 4:1 – 7:1 displayed the independence and power of God himself. Now, in the present episode, God's power is exhibited through his priest-prophet to bring deliverance to his people (7:2–17). Thus, Samuel proves to be not only priest and prophet but judge-deliverer as well. The main action is recounted in 7:2–13a. The remaining verses describe the long-term effects of Samuel's divinely empowered leadership (vv. 13b–14) and conclude by detailing the route that Samuel's lifelong service as 'circuit judge' took (vv. 15–17).

Comment

2–4. There is debate about whether the *long time – twenty years in all* – that the ark *remained at Kiriath Jearim* (v. 2) refers to the total length of the ark's sojourn up to David's retrieval of it in 2 Samuel 6 or, as seems almost certainly the case, to the length of time that elapsed between the ark's deposit in the house of Abinadab (7:1) and the events recounted in the rest of this chapter. Twenty years is clearly too short a time period for all of the events leading up to 2 Samuel 6, namely, the maturing, ministry and death of Samuel,[92] the reign, rejection and death of Saul, the establishment of David as king of all Israel and David's capture of Jerusalem. Therefore, the *twenty years* of verse 2a is best understood as setting the scene for the present episode.[93]

Variation in how verse 2b is translated – *turned back to* (NIV), 'mourned and sought after' (NIV 1984), 'lamented after' (NRSV), 'yearned after' (JPS) – reflects the rarity of the underlying Hebrew verb and consequent uncertainty regarding its precise nuance.[94] The basic sense, in any case, is clear. The people are wanting to return to the Lord.

Samuel, now fully grown after twenty years, challenges the people that *returning to the* LORD *with all your hearts* must entail rejection and removal of *foreign gods and the Ashtoreths* (v. 3). To the Ashtoreths,[95] verse 4 adds the *Baals*. Baal was the Canaanite god of fertility and storm, while Ashtoreth (Astarte) was his consort and goddess of fertility and war. The allure of fertility religion in a land as dependent on weather and seasonal rainfall as Canaan is

---

92. Note that the description of Samuel as *old* in 8:1 precludes the possibility that he died young.
93. Further support may be the discourse initial *wayĕhî* that begins v. 2.
94. *DCH* lists three homonyms and cites the present verse under each, in combination with 'after' (*'ahărê*): nhh I 'lament' after; II 'follow' after; III 'turn' after.
95. On the mocking mongrelization of the name Astarte by insertion of the vowel sounds of the Heb. word for 'shame', *bōšet*, see Long (2009a: 302, at 1 Sam. 7:4) and the further examples and literature listed there. See also below, at 2 Sam. 2:8.

understandable. In Egypt, by contrast, the annual inundation of the Nile brought fertility to the land and could generally be relied upon. But given Israel's dependence on rain to produce crops, the pull to embrace fertility rituals could be strong, as the frequent warnings against religious syncretism attest (e.g. Deut. 32:16; Josh. 24:19–23; and pervasively in the Former and Latter Prophets). In the present passage, the Israelites add action to their words and *put away their Baals and Ashtoreths, and served the* LORD *only* (v. 4; contrast the words-only response in Josh. 24:24). The link between wholehearted dependence on the Lord and deliverance *out of the hand of the Philistines* (v. 3) will be demonstrated positively in the lives of Jonathan (14:6–15 etc.) and David (17:45–51 and *passim*) and negatively in the life of Saul (13:13–14; 14:52; 31:1–4; etc.).

5–6. Israel's return to the Lord does not immediately solve their problems but, on the contrary, seems to make them worse. In verse 5 Samuel summons the people to Mizpah (meaning 'watchtower', 'lookout'). Mizpah appears to have been the site of Israelite assemblies on various occasions (for instance, later in the narrative Mizpah will be the place of Saul's selection by lot in 1 Sam. 10:17–27).[96] Samuel's stated purpose is to pray to the Lord for the people. Their actions (fasting and confession) suggest a kind of covenant renewal ceremony. They also *drew water and poured it out before the* LORD (v. 6). While water libations are known from the ANE (Long 2009a: 303–304), the present instance is the only Old Testament example of a ritual water-pouring. Figurative expressions such as Hannah's *pouring out my soul to the* LORD (1:15) or pouring out one's 'heart like water' (Lam. 2:19; cf. Ps. 62:8) may suggest something of what the ritual symbolized. David's pouring out of the water brought to him

---

[96]. The name (or designation) Mizpah (*mispāh*) is related to the Heb. root *sph*, 'to keep watch, (be a) lookout' and is a name for various sites on both sides of the Jordan River. The Mizpah of the present passage is not to be confused with the Mizpahs of Gen. 31:44–49; Josh. 11:3; 15:38–39; Judg. 11:11, 29, 34; or 1 Sam. 22:3. It is, rather, a Benjaminite site some 8 miles north-east of Kiriath Jearim and 8 miles north of Jerusalem, probably to be identified with Tell en-Naṣbeh. This site figured earlier in the judges period (Judg. 20:1; 21:1–24).

by courageous supporters in 2 Samuel 23:16 is of a different order and its significance is explained by David in 23:17.

Samuel was serving as leader of Israel at Mizpah (v. 6). Many translations render the Hebrew literally, 'and Samuel judged [root *špṭ*] Israel at Mizpah' (e.g. NRSV, ESV). But since Israel's judges (*šōpĕṭîm*) served as 'leader-delivers', NIV's rendering is equally appropriate (cf. JPS: 'Samuel acted as chieftain of the Israelites at Mizpah').[97] So far, then, and in keeping with the transitional period in which he served, Samuel is described as a 'multitasking' leader: priest, prophet and judge-deliverer.[98]

7–9. The assembly at Mizpah, as necessary as it was for Israel's visible recommitment to Yahweh, does not go unnoticed by the Philistines. Whether suspecting that Israel is mustering for war – a procedure that in the ANE typically involved gathering for pre-battle sacrifices – or merely taking the opportunity of an Israelite assembly to deal a decisive blow *en masse*, the *Philistines came up to attack them*. Quite naturally, the people *were afraid because of the Philistines* (v. 7). In keeping with their right behaviours so far in the chapter, the people look to the Lord for rescue, beseeching Samuel to keep *crying out to the* L ORD *our God for us* (v. 8). Earlier in the book, both Israel and the Philistines cried out in distress, but not to the Lord (4:13; 5:10). This time, Samuel as intermediary sacrifices a *suckling lamb* and cries out *to the* L ORD *on Israel's behalf, and the* L ORD *answered him* (v. 9). Brueggemann (1990: 51) writes:

> In the pattern of cry–answer, we are at the core of biblical faith . . .
> To cry to Yahweh is to acknowledge trust in and release in Yahweh . . .
> The 'cry' of Samuel at the behest of Israel is an act of repentance, an act of acknowledgment, and therefore an act of rightly relating to God. Samuel guides Israel into the act of faith that is necessary to Israel's well-being in the world.

---

97. This understanding of the 'judge' as serving more than judicial functions is supported by cognate ANE usage. At Mari, for example, 'a provincial or district ruler or administrator' was called a *šāpiṭum* (Long 2009a: 304).

98. On Samuel's varied roles, see Provan, Long and Longman (2015: 274).

10–11. That Samuel continues *sacrificing the burnt offering* even as the Philistines are drawing near *to engage Israel in battle* is a mark of Samuel's courage, highlighting his conviction that the outcome of battles is in Yahweh's hands (cf. later Jonathan in 14:6 and David in 17:45–47). In answer to Samuel, *the* LORD *thundered with loud thunder against the Philistines* (v. 10), a dramatic manifestation that recalls Hannah's words of 2:10: *those who oppose the* LORD *will be broken. / The Most High will thunder from heaven* (cf. 2 Sam. 22:14).

The effect of the divine thundering on the Philistines is dramatic: it *threw them into such a panic that they were routed before the Israelites* (v. 10). The Philistines are routed both psychologically (suggested by the verb *hmm*, which connotes being confused and panicked) and physically (*ngp* speaks of being struck down). Earlier, when Israel thought that they could manipulate Yahweh simply by bringing the ark into battle, it was Israel that was 'routed [*ngp*] before the Philistines' (4:2, 10). The tables are now turned, and Israel pursues the Philistines *to a point below Beth Kar* (v. 11). Beth Kar is not mentioned elsewhere in the Old Testament, so the extent of the pursuit is unknown, unless Beth Kar is a corruption of Beth Horon (located some 6 miles west of Mizpah).

12. In order to mark the divinely wrought victory, *Samuel took a stone and set it up between Mizpah and Shen.*[99] Victory stele and boundary stones were both quite prevalent in the ANE (see Long 2009a: 306). That Samuel names the stone *Ebenezer* (which sounds like 'stone of help') and proclaims, *Thus far the* LORD *has helped us* invites several comments. First, it was at a different Ebenezer (see 4:1 and 5:1) that Israel was roundly defeated by the Philistines on the occasion of the 'capture' of the ark. Now at a new Ebenezer, the situation is reversed. Second, the name and its explanation suggest the extent of the victory not only geographically but also temporally; as Israel's king, Yahweh has proved faithful *thus far*. This recognition provides the backdrop against which the elders'

---

99. 'Shen' means 'tooth' (of rock) and may indicate a prominent landmark (cf. 14:4–5, where NIV reads *cliff*). Alternatively, 'Shen' may be a truncation of a place name 'Jeshanah' (so NRSV, NLT; supported by LXX, Syr.), on the location of which see McCarter (1980: 146).

insistence in the next chapter on having a *king to lead us, such as all the other nations have* (8:5) should be judged (cf. Gordon 1986: 107–108).

13–14. The statement that the Philistines *stopped invading Israel's territory* is not to be taken in an absolute sense, as if the Philistine wars were permanently ended. Hostilities certainly continue during the reign of Saul, leading up to his death in 1 Samuel 31, and on into the reign of David (2 Sam. 8:1). The reference, rather, is to the immediate situation. One may compare 2 Kings 6:23–24 in which the writer follows the statement that 'the bands from Aram stopped raiding Israel's territory' (v. 23) with the notice that subsequently the 'king of Aram mobilised his entire army and marched up and laid siege to Samaria' (v. 24).[100] The more general statement is that *Throughout Samuel's lifetime, the hand of the LORD was against the Philistines*. The Hebrew reads 'all the days of Samuel', which some have taken to mean Samuel's tenure as Israel's leader prior to the installation of a king. But even if Samuel's full lifetime is intended, it is true that Israel generally fared well in the Philistine wars (e.g. through Jonathan in chs. 13–14 and through David in ch. 17), though the fighting was at times bitter (14:52). Only after Samuel's death, noted in 1 Samuel 25:1 and 28:3, does Israel suffer a major defeat by the Philistines, in chapter 31.

In the aftermath of the victory of 1 Samuel 7, the contested border towns *from Ekron to Gath* are *restored to Israel*, and Israel experiences peaceful coexistence with *the Amorites*, a term often used for the pre-Israelite, particularly hill-country inhabitants of Canaan.

15–17. *Samuel continued as Israel's leader* [or 'judge'; see on v. 6 above] *all the days of his life* (v. 15). This summary statement signals that a major section is coming to a close and a new section is about to begin. The description of Samuel's approximately 30-mile circuit (v. 16) from Bethel (modern Beitin?) down into the Jordan Valley to Gilgal,[101] then back to Mizpah, and finally to Samuel's home town in Ramah (cf. 1:19; 2:11), reflects the rather local activity of

---

100. A similar dynamic obtains in 2 Sam. 2:28 and 3:1.
101. The precise locations of ancient Bethel and Gilgal continue to be debated; on the latter, see Kotter (1992: 1023).

Israel's judges and in some ways prepares the reader for the more expansive leadership that kingship will provide. The final notice, that in his home town Samuel *built an altar . . . to the LORD* (v. 17), also reminds the reader of what is to anchor leadership in Israel, whatever specific polity is involved.[102]

Meaning

The first seven chapters of 1 Samuel have established the background for the major political shift Israel is about to experience. The story of Hannah demonstrated how God can work through everyday faithfulness to accomplish great things. Her song anticipated that one of these great things would be the introduction of *his king* (2:10). The story of Eli underscored the necessity of godly leaders giving full weight (honour) to God himself and showed what happens when God is 'underweighted'. Eli's story also provided key insights for understanding the lives of Saul and David, with respect to both why leaders fail and how they should respond when disciplined or deposed. In chapter 7 itself, godly leadership and faithful response came together. The people longed for God and in response to Samuel's instructions got rid of their false gods. When these actions precipitated a circumstantial crisis, the people continued to look to God and to Samuel to pray for them. God ultimately rescued them, and a marker was established: *Thus far the LORD has helped us* (v. 12). A period of relative peace and prosperity was established under Samuel's leadership, all centred on the worship of Yahweh.

---

102. Prior to David's capture of Jerusalem and its establishment as the central sanctuary, other sites served as centres of worship. Shiloh was such a centre during the period of the judges but was likely destroyed in the aftermath of the loss to the Philistines in 1 Sam. 4. Deuteronomy 12 did not forbid local altars per se but, rather, Canaanite cultic practices.

2. THE BEGINNING OF MONARCHY: THE RISE OF ISRAEL'S KING (1 SAMUEL 8:1 – 12:25)

A. Israel asks for a king 'such as all the other nations have' (8:1–22)

Context

Against the backdrop of the first seven chapters of the book, and especially of the demonstration in chapter 7 that Yahweh is fully capable of delivering his people through his chosen leaders, the elders' insistence in the present chapter on having a king like the kings of other nations comes as a surprise. But they have their reasons. Samuel is old and his sons are ne'er-do-wells. Upon hearing their request, Samuel is at first affronted, as if their concern were with his own leadership as judge. But Yahweh is quick to correct him, noting that the heart of the matter is Israel's rejection of his own rule over them as king. As we shall see, the issue is not kingship per se but, rather, the kind of king the elders desire.

The chapter can be subdivided as follows: narratorial introduction (vv. 1–3); the elders' request, Samuel's initial response, Yahweh's clarification of the nature of the problem and his instruction to Samuel to warn them of what the king they want will do (vv. 4–9); Samuel's description to the elders of what the king they are choosing will do (vv. 10–18); the elders' insistence notwithstanding (vv. 19–20); and the Lord's instruction to Samuel to give them their king (vv. 21–22).

Comment

1–3. How much time has passed since the great victory of chapter 7 is not specified, but as chapter 8 opens, Samuel has grown old (v. 1). Also not specified is the thinking behind the aged Samuel's appointing *his sons as Israel's leaders* (*šōpĕṭîm*, 'judges'). Hereditary succession of judges was without precedent in ancient Israel, and Gideon, for instance, explicitly rejected the offer to establish dynastic rule (Judg. 8:22–23). Hereditary succession had not fared well in the house of Eli (2:12, 25), and Samuel's sons resemble Eli's sons more than they resemble their father. Whatever hopes Samuel may have entertained in giving his two sons pious names, *Joel* (essentially 'Yahweh is God') and *Abijah* ('Yahweh is my father'), they *did not follow his ways* but *turned aside* [*nṭh* qal] *after dishonest gain and accepted bribes and perverted* [*nṭh* hipʻil] *justice* (vv. 2–3). In other words, they were workers of violence (cf. Tsumura 2007: 246). Such behaviour was condemned not just in Israel but generally in the ANE. In a Hittite text addressing the duties of 'border governors', 'Arnuwanda the great king' warns against any perversion of justice: 'Let no one take a bribe. He is not to make the stronger case the weaker, or the weaker the stronger one. Do what [is] just.'[1] Perhaps by stationing his sons in the far south at Beersheba[2] Samuel hoped to minimize their influence, while still retaining a leadership role for the house of Samuel. Attempts to infer from the misdeeds of his sons that Samuel was deficient as a father are weak, especially in the book of Samuel, where bad

---

1. *COS* 1.84:221–25 [§37].

2. On the location and relative insignificance of Beersheba in Samuel's day, see Long (2009a: 307–308).

fathers can have laudable sons (e.g. Saul and Jonathan) and vice versa.[3]

4–9. In view of the authoritative narratorial voice in verses 1–3, the claim of *all the elders of Israel* that Samuel's age and his sons' malfeasance present a leadership crisis cannot be denied. But the elders come not just to state the problem but also to state what is in their view the solution: *now appoint a king to lead us, such as all the other nations have* (v. 5). Samuel's displeasure at this importunity may have been triggered by its wording: *Give us a king to lead* [*špṭ*, 'judge'] *us* (v. 6). As Israel's 'judge', Samuel may have felt the sting of personal rejection. But Yahweh cautions Samuel to listen more carefully *to all that the people are saying*. He then spells out the real issue: *it is not you they have rejected, but they have rejected me as their king* (v. 7). Such behaviour, tantamount to *forsaking* [*God*] *and serving other gods*, does also affect Samuel – *so they are doing to you* (v. 8) – in his role as God's appointed leader and prophetic spokesman, but the main affront is to God himself. Nevertheless, Yahweh again instructs Samuel to *listen to them*, this time in the sense of granting their request (v. 9). But first Samuel must *warn them solemnly* regarding the manner (*mišpaṭ*) of *the king who will reign over them* (v. 9).

What Samuel describes in the following verses regarding the manner of the king is largely negative. But this does not mean that Israel's having a human king is in and of itself a bad thing (see, e.g., at 2:10). The instructions of Deuteronomy 17:14–20 speak of a future king who must be chosen by Yahweh, a fellow Israelite, not given to the trappings of imperial kingship nor trusting in chariots, harems or material wealth, and one who is studious in the divine instruction (*tôrâ*) and learns to revere and obey Yahweh his God. To such a one and his descendants is promised a long and prosperous reign. Samuel's oral and written description of the *mišpaṭ hammĕlukâ* (*rights and duties of kingship*) in 10:25 quite likely reflected these perspectives. This understanding of royal power

---

[3]. On a more broadly theological note, one would not ascribe parental deficiency to God the Father from the fact that his 'children' are often less than upstanding in their behaviour (thanks are due to John Stackhouse for suggesting this point).

does *not* entail rejection of the kingship of Yahweh, and so this cannot be the kind of kingship that the elders have in mind. Their insistence is repeatedly portrayed as a grave sin (10:19; 12:17, 19, 25).[4] For discussion of the precise nature of the elders' offence, see below at verses 19–20.

10–18. Samuel's solemn warning constitutes not his own thoughts but *the words of the LORD* (v. 10). The elders' complaint is that Samuel's sons take (*lqḥ*) bribes (v. 3). Ironically, the king they want will take and take and take and take. The four-fold repetition of the verb *lqḥ* (vv. 11, 13, 14, 16) constitutes the highest density of its usage in the entire book of Samuel. The king will *take your sons* and assign them to ceremonial, military and agricultural duties (vv. 11–12). *He will take your daughters* to serve in house and kitchen (v. 13). *He will take the best of your* cultivated lands and *give them to his attendants* (v. 14) and still exact *a tenth* of whatever grain and wine you manage to produce and *give it to his officials and attendants* (v. 15). Nothing will escape his grasp, neither *male* or *female servants* nor *the best* of the livestock.[5] All *he will take for his own use* (v. 16). As with the fields, so with the livestock: he will take the best and tax the rest (v. 17). Whether the royal 'tithe' is to be thought of as encroaching on what is due to the Lord himself (cf. Lev. 27:30–32; Deut. 14:22, 28) or as creating an added tax burden is not made clear. Admittedly, the notion that sons and daughters would become associated with the royal house may not have sounded too bad to the people. 'Running at the wheel' of a royal chariot might even be considered an honour, as a couple of eighth-century Aramaic texts indicate.[6] But as the warnings

---

4. Cf. Hos. 13:10–11, which may refer obliquely to 1 Sam. 8 but more directly to 1 Kgs 12:16–20.

5. While MT attests *baḥûrêkem* ('your young men') in v. 16 (and is so rendered in NKJV, NASB, ESV), NIV assumes *bĕqārêkem* (*your cattle*) following LXX and in keeping with the logic of the text – young men would be covered by *sons* in v. 11 – and ANE usage, where slaves, cattle and donkeys are sometimes mentioned together (see Gordon 1986: 117).

6. *COS* 2.37:159 [lines 11b–19a] and *COS* 2.38:161 [lines 7b–15]). For discussion, see Long (2009a: 310).

continue, the abusive requirements of a king like the kings of all the nations become ever more apparent. In the end, *you yourselves will become his slaves* (v. 17) and will *cry out for relief from the king you have chosen*, but on that day it will be too late, and *the* LORD *will not answer* (v. 18).[7] How different the situation will be from that in 1 Samuel 7 where, at the people's behest, Samuel *cried out to the* LORD . . . *and the* LORD *answered him* (7:9). Now is the time to heed the warning, but the people remain insistent.[8]

A commonplace in the older commentary tradition was to assume that Samuel's warnings betray a later perspective reflecting the exploitative practices of Solomon's reign. But a seminal essay by Isaac Mendelsohn effectively demonstrated from texts from Alalakh and Ugarit that

> Samuel's warnings about the costs of a standing army with chariot forces, royal expropriation of land, taxation including the royal tithe, and corvée labor all reflect an accurate understanding of 'the semi-feudal Canaanite society as it existed prior to and during the time of Samuel'.
>
> (Long 2009a: 310, citing Mendelsohn 1956; cf. also Talmon 1986)

Samuel's mention of chariots in verse 11 is also appropriate to his day, as Israel's neighbours were using chariots from the time of Israel's entry into Canaan (see Josh. 11 and 17). Whether Saul acquired chariots is not stated, though David certainly captured (and destroyed?) chariots (2 Sam. 8:4; 10:18). Both Absalom and Adonijah staged their bids for the throne by mounting chariots and having men run ahead of them (2 Sam. 15:1; 1 Kgs 1:5).

19–20. Refusing to heed the Lord's warnings as delivered by Samuel (recall v. 10), the people persist in their demand for *a king over us* (v. 19), because they want to *be like all the other nations, with a king to lead us and to go out before us and fight our battles* (v. 20). It is often

---

7. Divine silence can be a sign of divine judgment (14:37; 28:6; 2 Sam. 22:42; Mic. 3:4), though it is not invariably so (Job 30:20; Ps. 22:2).
8. While it was the elders who came to Samuel, it is clear from vv. 7, 10, 19 and 21 that they represented the people.

assumed that in this demand the people are rejecting the theocratic ideal. After all, does not Yahweh himself say that *they have rejected me as their king* (v. 7)? Another view is that they are rejecting what we might call the charismatic ideal, namely, rule by judges whom God raises up as needed and bestows on them the 'charism' (gifting) to lead in times of crisis. After all, the 'judge' Samuel feels rejected (v. 6). What the elders explicitly say is that they want to be like their neighbours (*kĕkol-haggôyim*, 'like the nations', is stressed in vv. 5 and 20). Jonathan Walton (2015: 179–200) explores what lies at the heart of the elders' request. Central to Walton's proposal is the issue of how the kings of the nations surrounding Israel related to their gods. These kings were hardly 'secular' in their thinking, but they related to their gods very differently from what was expected of Israel in its relationship to Yahweh. The kings of the nations were responsible for seeing to the needs of their gods and, having done so, could expect the gods to back them when they (the kings) took initiatives – military operations and the like. 'While the king derives his power from the gods and is compelled to care for and obey them, his position also allows him leverage to negotiate with them' (Walton 2015: 199–200).

At issue in the Israelite elders' sinful request for a king is not the introduction of kingship per se (which, as we have seen, was long anticipated; see discussion at vv. 4–9 above), nor the rejection of Samuel as judge, nor even the rejection of Yahweh as king in favour of some other deity. At issue, rather, is the redefinition of how Yahweh as king is to be handled by a 'king like that of all the nations'. The nations' gods were in a sense passive and co-dependent, needing to be properly tended by the king (with temples, regular sacrificial feedings, etc.). Having been so served, they were then obligated to come to the aid of the king in his initiatives: 'when the king calls the gods out to battle, the gods comply' (Walton 2015: 200). Israel's elders had on an earlier occasion attempted to drag Yahweh into battle with them by fetching the ark. The result was disastrous (1 Sam. 4)! Walton argues that the elders' offence in the present context is the same. They want to gain some measure of control over Yahweh so they can be assured of his aid when needed. Yahweh had come to Samuel's aid when he prayed in 1 Samuel 7, but Samuel is ageing and his sons are singularly unpromising. And so the elders seek a 'king like the kings of the nations', and this entails the reduction of Yahweh to 'a god like the gods of the nations'. But this is precisely what Yahweh is not – passive and co-dependent! 'And this is exactly what Yahweh means when he says, "They have rejected me"' (Walton 2015: 199). To seek to reduce Yahweh by redefinition is tantamount to the idolatry that Yahweh charges the people with engaging in *from the day I brought them up out of Egypt* (v. 8).

21–22. Earlier in the present chapter, Yahweh twice instructed Samuel to *listen* to the people. In verse 7 the focus was on Samuel's listening carefully to the precise content of what the elders were asking for, while in verse 9 Yahweh instructed Samuel to 'listen' in the sense of granting their request, but only after issuing solemn warnings. Now that the elders have *refused to listen to Samuel* (v. 19), Yahweh tells Samuel one more time to *Listen to them and give them a king* (v. 22). The pressing question is what kind of king this will be: a king of the standard ANE variety or a king in keeping with the standards of Deuteronomy 17:14–20? That Samuel's response to this divine directive is to say to the Israelites *Everyone go back to your own town* (v. 22) is sometimes interpreted as reticence on Samuel's part to obey Yahweh, because he is jealous to protect his own power. Given the magnitude of the task to be undertaken, however, and indeed the question of what kind of king Israel is to be given, it seems far more likely that Samuel simply needs time to receive further, more specific instructions from Yahweh, which indeed he receives in the next chapter (9:15–16), and to prepare for the big event (see, for instance, 9:22–24).[9]

Meaning

The people of Israel in 1 Samuel 8 find themselves at a critical turning point. They had grounds for concern. Not only was Samuel ageing and his sons corrupt, but political pressures threatened left and right (Philistines on the west, Ammonites on the east). Though Yahweh had proved himself capable of delivering through judge-deliverers raised up as occasion required, living in dependence on

---

9. For a similar understanding of Samuel's actions, see Josephus, *Ant.* 6.44.

Yahweh required a kind of day-to-day trust. And the elders desired something more stable, more constant. The judge-deliverers of Israel's past (including now Samuel) generally operated on a rather local and ad hoc basis. How much better to have a king like other nations have! Kingship, after all, was not an alien idea. As we have seen, kingship was anticipated in multiple ways in the Torah, as well as by Hannah, Samuel's own mother. It was the *kind of king* that the elders wanted that was the problem. The problem with the kings of other nations was not only that they served false gods but the manner in which they related to them – feed and house the god and then expect the god's aid in support of royal initiatives. Yahweh was not like one of the gods of the nations, nor could Israel's king relate to him as if he were.

There is ever a tendency in the human heart to seek security and safety in individual leaders, social institutions, financial instruments, ecclesial structures or political parties, rather than in God himself and *his* king. There is, as Paul notes, ever the danger of being conformed in our thinking and living to the world around us (Rom. 12:2). Birch (1998: 1031) states the 'ultimate issue raised by 1 Samuel 8' this way:

> To what degree have we let our trust in human authority overshadow our trust in God? . . . In 1 Samuel 8, God gives Israel the freedom to choose a king, but God does not give up the claim of divine sovereignty . . . human power is only subordinate to divine power.

B. The rise of Saul: 'and Saul and all the Israelites held a great celebration' (9:1 – 11:15)

i. Saul anointed and charged (9:1 – 10:16)
Context
The way in which 1 Samuel 9 begins is similar to the way the book as a whole began. An important individual is introduced and his genealogy given, followed by the introduction of the person who will become a key character in the ensuing narrative. In 1 Samuel 1, the important man was Elkanah and the key character Hannah. In the present chapter, the important man is Kish and the key character Saul. Moreover, as the seemingly everyday story of Hannah

would eventually lead to a major change in Israel's leadership, so too the seemingly mundane account of Saul's search for some lost livestock will lead to a major change in Israel's polity. By a series of seeming 'coincidences', Saul comes into contact with Samuel, whom Yahweh has prepared to fulfil the mandate of 1 Samuel 8:22: *give them a king*.

Comment

1–2. In several respects Saul is a good candidate to become the king that the people 'asked for' (root *šʾl*) in the preceding chapter (8:10). Even his name is fitting – Saul (root *šʾl*) sounds like 'one asked for'. His home in the relatively insignificant tribal territory of Benjamin (v. 1) is advantageous, because his tribal affiliation will be unlikely to provoke rivalry between the more powerful tribes of Ephraim to the north and Judah to the south. His impressive physical appearance is also an asset by ANE standards: Tukulti-Ninurta of Assyria is lauded as 'godly in his limbs . . . cast sublimely from the womb of the gods' (Foster 2005: 301); Nebuchadnezzar I is described as a 'valiant male whose strength is directed towards doing battle' (Frame 1995: 34); and the legendary Gilgamesh is praised as two-thirds deity, 'fearful like a wild ox, lofty' (*ANET* 73). Saul is *as handsome a young man as could be found anywhere in Israel, and he was a head taller than anyone else* (v. 2). The adjective *handsome* renders Hebrew *ṭôb* ('good'), and *young* renders Hebrew *bāḥûr*, a term that in some contexts can mean 'young' but can also simply mean 'choice' or 'prime' – Saul is, after all, a head taller than his fellows and so not necessarily particularly young (see Long 1989: 204–205). The significance of this point will become clear as the narrative unfolds.

Most notable in Saul's introduction is its lack of any mention of qualities beyond the physical.[10] Traits and abilities are not noted,

---

10. Even Saul's description as *gābōah* (big and tall; cf. also 10:23) is disconcerting, as the term can be suggestive of pride, and in its only other occurrences in Samuel it is not used positively: see Hannah's charge to the haughty to cease talking *so proudly* (*gěbōhâ gěbōhâ*, 2:3), Yahweh's rejection of Eliab despite his *height* (*gěbōah qômātô*, 16:7) and the extreme *height* (*gobhô*) of the doomed Goliath (17:4). I am

and the comment 'Yahweh was with him', a common feature in the introductions of godly characters such as David (16:18) and Joseph (Gen. 39:2–3), is lacking in Saul's introduction. The closest analogy to Saul's introduction is the description of Absalom in 2 Samuel 14:25–26, where again the focus is on physical qualities and little else. This lends a 'discordant subtone' to Saul's introduction (W. L. Humphreys 1978: 20). Some early Jewish interpreters understood both Saul and Absalom as possessing 'beauty of body but not of soul' (Ginzberg 1956: 6.238 n. 80). Perhaps sensing that something is missing, Josephus invents for Saul 'a spirit and mind surpassing these outward advantages' (*Ant.* 6:45).

3–10. The route of Saul's travels in search of his father's lost donkeys is difficult to determine, as the sites mentioned in verse 4 are of uncertain location. We are told that he *passed through the hill country of Ephraim* (to the north) before returning to *the territory of Benjamin*, but all to no avail. When Saul and the servant he had taken along with him, in accordance with his father's instructions (v. 3), reach *the district of Zuph*, Saul is ready to abandon the quest and return home, more worried about his father than about his father's livestock (v. 5). The servant, however, knows that *in this* [unnamed] *town there is* [an unnamed] *man of God*. Lack of specificity at this point in the narrative has led some to speculate that a tale of an obscure village seer has been co-opted to create a story about Samuel, who is first named in verse 14. It seems more likely, however, that the seer's identity is purposely withheld in order to allow the reader to share in Saul's process of discovery. Long before Saul sorts things out, the attentive reader will be suspecting that the *man of God* in question is in fact Samuel. After all, Saul finds himself in the *district of Zuph* (v. 5), and Samuel is son of a Zuphite (see 1:1).[11] This man of God is *highly respected* (has gravitas, *nikbād*) and is reliable; *everything he says comes true* (v. 6). The reader knows already that Samuel is highly respected – recognized *from Dan to*

(note 10 *cont.*) indebted for this insight to my student James Rutherford, who develops the thought more fully in his ThM dissertation (published 2019).

11. Targ. replaces *district of Zuph* with 'the land in which was the prophet'.

Beersheba . . . as a prophet of the LORD (3:20) – and is reliable: the Lord *let none of Samuel's words fall to the ground* (3:19). In answer to Saul's concern that they *have no gift to take to the man of God* (v. 7), the servant offers to finance the enquiry with a *quarter of a shekel* (v. 8).[12] The narrator's aside in verse 9 reminds the reader that *seer* and *prophet* are synonymous titles, thus further tightening the association of the 'seer' with the 'prophet' Samuel.[13] Saul's initial hesitancy is soon overcome by the servant's initiatives, and he agrees to *set out for the town* of the *man of God*, which the reader will now guess must be the town of Ramah (1:19).

11–14. Verse 11 does not specify whether it is Saul or his servant (or both) who asks the *young women coming out to draw water* regarding the seer's whereabouts. But the young women respond excitedly in verses 12–13. Encountering a tall and handsome stranger at the well, a typical venue for betrothals (Alter 1981: 51–62), the women become animated, and their words sometimes lack syntactical correctness in their rush to help Saul (the awkward syntax in Hebrew is largely masked in English translations). Their first words suggest multiple speakers interrupting each other: 'There is / Look, before you / Hurry / Now / Because today he has come to the city' (v. 12).[14] Their last words convey the same sense of excitement. Verse 13 contains an awkward doubling of the direct object 'him' (*'ōtô*), yielding 'for him just now – you will find him' (so Driver 1960: 72). The women tell Saul that the seer has just arrived to preside over *a sacrifice at the high place* (v. 12).[15] They also tell him

---

12. Josephus (*Ant.* 6.48) attributes Saul and his servant's concern about payment to 'their ignorance that the prophet accepted no reward'. On the issue, see Long (2009a: 312).
13. The association is further reinforced by wordplays in the immediate context; e.g. the question 'what can we give/bring?' (*nābî'*) and the word for prophet (i.e. *nābî'*) are spelled the same in Hebrew.
14. Neither MT nor the versions has *to our town* but simply 'to the town', quite likely Samuel's home town. The fact that he is just arriving may recall his regular circuit (7:15–17).
15. Given the association of 'high places' with Canaanite worship practices, Israelite worship at any high place (*bāmâ*) was broadly

where and when he will meet Samuel: *As soon as you enter the town, you will find him* (v. 13). And as Saul and his servant enter the city, *there was Samuel, coming towards them* (v. 14). What the reader has likely already concluded from the various clues earlier in the narrative (vv. 5, 6, 9) is now explicitly confirmed: the *man of God*, the *seer*, the *prophet*, is indeed Samuel. How will Saul respond when he meets him (see at v. 18)?

15–17. Before recounting Saul's response to meeting Samuel, the narrator digresses to provide necessary background information.[16] Clearly, Saul's travels have to do with more than lost donkeys. The day before Saul's arrival, *the LORD had revealed*[17] to Samuel that he was sending *a man from the land of Benjamin* whom Samuel was to anoint as *ruler [nāgîd] over my people Israel*. The title *nāgîd* can be used of officials generally, but when relating to kingship it seems to mean something like 'king-designate' (see *NIDOTTE* 3: 20–21; McCarter 1980: 178–179). As Martin Buber noted in a discussion of *Leitwortstil* (keyword style) in the Saul narratives (1956: 126), the narrator draws attention to the title *nāgîd* by surrounding it with several instances of the verbal root *ngd* ('to tell'; 9:6, 8, 18, 19).[18] The task of the 'king-designate' whom

---

(note 15 *cont.*) discouraged (Num. 33:52; Deut. 12:2–3; cf. Jer. 2:20 where *gibʻat gĕbōhâ* is used). The practice became especially problematical during the divided monarchy, such that destruction of the 'high places' became a priority in the reform movements of Hezekiah (2 Kgs 18:4) and Josiah (2 Kgs 23:5). In the time between the destruction of the Israelite sanctuary at Shiloh and the building of the Jerusalem temple, however, worship at high places seems to have been condoned, provided it did not involve idolatrous practices. (For fuller discussion, see King and Stager 2001: 320.) Targ. replaces *high place* in 9:12 and 9:25 with 'house of dining', thus betraying later sensitivities.

16. The word order in the Heb. of v. 15 indicates a shift from the main storyline to background information.
17. On possible modes of divine revelation, see 28:6.
18. The verb will also occur four times in Saul's interrogation by his uncle in 10:15–16.

Samuel is to anoint will be to deliver the people *from the hand of the Philistines* (v. 16).

As Samuel the 'seer' (*rō'eh*, v. 18) 'sees' (*rā'āh*) Saul, Yahweh confirms to Samuel that Saul is the one who *will govern my people* (v. 17). The word rendered *govern* (*'āṣar*) is not one of the common words for ruling (e.g. *mālak*, *māšal*). The word *'āṣar* normally has connotations of restraining, holding back, hindering, and so on. Thus, its sense in the present context is ambiguous. Positive readings are possible. Perhaps Saul's task is to 'rein in' the people (cf. Rudman 2000b; 2001), or to muster them in order to fight the Philistines (so McCarter 1980: 179), or to 'restrain' Israel from becoming 'like the nations' (Woodhouse 2008: 163). But negative readings are also possible. Might there be a hint that Saul will, for a time, 'hinder' Israel from realizing the kind of kingship they need, the kind that will eventually come under David? Whatever positive or negative nuances echo in the use of the word *govern*, Saul will not in fact 'reign' (*mālak*) until he ascends the throne in chapter 13.

18–20. The first meeting between Saul and Samuel does not mark an auspicious beginning. Saul's servant has had to take the lead (vv. 6, 8) to get Saul this far. Moreover, having been explicitly told by the young women at the well where and when to expect to meet Samuel (*As soon as you enter the town*, v. 13), Saul nevertheless fails to deduce that the man before him *in the gateway* is Samuel and instead asks if he knows *where the seer's house is* (v. 18). Saul's ability to listen and understand is called into question (perhaps adumbrating subsequent, more serious failures to listen, as in 1 Sam. 15).

Samuel's *I am the seer* (v. 19) is followed immediately by instructions that show that Saul has been expected. Samuel's credibility as a prophet is confirmed by his knowledge not only of Saul's quest for lost donkeys but also of their successful recovery (v. 20). Livestock worries aside, Samuel turns to a more important issue: *And to whom is all the desire of Israel turned, if not to you . . . ?* (v. 20). The ambiguity of the phrase *all the desire of Israel* is evident in the comparison of NRSV ('And on whom is all Israel's desire fixed . . . ?') and ESV ('And for whom is all that is desirable in Israel?'). NIV reflects the first understanding, namely, you are the kind of leader all Israel desires (cf. 8:5, 20).[19] The *desire* (*ḥemdâ*) in view shares the same root as the verb 'to covet' (*ḥāmad*), which often, though not always, carries a negative connotation (e.g. Exod. 20:17; Josh. 7:21).

21–24. Saul's protestations of smallness – not only *from the smallest tribe of Israel* but from *the least of all* its *clans* (v. 21) – are met not with words but actions. Samuel seats Saul and his servant at the head of a prearranged meal (v. 22) and has a prearranged special portion of meat set before Saul (vv. 23–24). The rather full description of Samuel's preparations (vv. 23–24) is testimony to the momentousness and providential ordering of the *occasion*.[20] The events of the day may have come as a surprise to Saul, but not to Samuel nor, one might imagine, to those who had presented Israel's request for a king *such as all the other nations have* (8:5). How best to understand *the thigh with what was on it* is debated (cf. Tsumura 2007: 279), but at the very least the honour suggests that Saul's status is about to change. *And Saul dined with Samuel that day* (v. 24). Throughout the story so far, Saul has voiced misgivings and hesitations. The story has moved forward by the servant's initiatives, then Samuel's, and behind it all is the divine providence.

25–27. While the flat-roofed architecture of houses in the period makes it possible that, when Samuel and Saul had returned to town from the high place, *Samuel talked with Saul on the roof of his house* (so MT), a different reading is suggested by LXX: 'a bed was spread for Saul on the roof' (so NRSV, ESV). MT of verse 25 does not explicitly name 'Samuel' but reads simply *wydbr*, 'and he spoke'. LXX seems to reflect a Hebrew text reading *wyrbdw*, 'and they prepared (a bed)'. Thus, MT may have confused the relatively rare verb *rbd* ('to prepare [a bed]') with the very common *dbr* ('to speak') – the two verbs contain the same consonants but in reverse order, and the first and last letters are easily confused in Hebrew script. Of course,

---

19. On the syntactical possibility of reading 'the longing of all Israel', see Tsumura (2007: 277). Stoebe (1973: 191) suggests that Samuel's words may carry a double sense.

20. *Occasion* renders the Heb. *mô'ēḏ*, a word connoting a meeting to take place at a set time and place; the next mention of a *mô'ēḏ* set by Samuel will come in 13:8.

it is reasonable to assume that Saul and Samuel will have needed to talk after the events of the day, and this may also have encouraged MT's reading. A further textual variation occurs in verse 26a: MT has *wyškmw*, 'and they rose early', whereas LXX assumes *wyškb*, 'and he slept'. The latter makes best sense in view of what comes next: Samuel called to Saul on the roof (v. 26). If Samuel and Saul had already risen *about daybreak*, as MT would have it, then there would have been no reason for Samuel to call to Saul.[21]

Whatever unrecorded conversations may or may not have taken place between Samuel and Saul the night before, the time has come for Samuel to deliver *a message from God* to Saul, but only after the servant has been sent on *ahead* (v. 27). The purpose of this secrecy is not stated explicitly. Frolov (2007: 444–445) attributes the 'covert mode of Saul's anointing' to 'Philistine military occupation' at the time, necessitating a 'narrow circle of confidants', lest the Philistines catch wind of the changes and 'prevent Israel from constituting itself as a polity and thereby making a step towards independence'. There may be something in this suggestion, especially as Saul's assignment was to *deliver [Israel] from the hand of the Philistines* (9:16). The dismissal of the servant, however, suggests a different, or perhaps additional, reason for the anointing being conducted in private. Given the servant's proactive role in the preceding story, where it was he, not Saul, who tended to initiate forward progress, Samuel's concern may be to test Saul's (not the servant's) suitability to step into a leadership role. Will he respond appropriately, even without the help of his servant?

10:1. *Then Samuel took a flask [pak] of olive oil and poured it on Saul's head* (v. 1). Samuel's using a *flask*, or 'vial', rather than the more customary 'horn' used in the royal anointings of David (16:1, 13) and Solomon (1 Kgs 1:39) may be vaguely unsettling (so Edelman 1991: 52), but it may also relate to the covert nature of Saul's anointing; compare the similarly covert anointing of Jehu, also with a 'flask' (*pak*) of oil, in 2 Kings 9:1–3. *Has not the LORD anointed*

---

21. It is possible, however, that 'they rose early' offers a summary before the event is then spelled out in more detail (cf. *CTAT* 1: 162). For a recent defence of MT, see Frolov 2007: 436.

you ruler over his inheritance? (v. 1). Though God is willing, in response to the elders' insistence in 1 Samuel 8, to give his people a king, they remain nevertheless his people, *his inheritance* (cf. 2 Sam. 20:19; Deut. 32:9; *my people* in 9:16). The role of an Israelite king is, therefore, to be vice-regent to the Great King Yahweh. As the story of Saul's anointing unfolds, including especially the two-part charge accompanying it (vv. 7–8), we discover how this subordinate relationship to Yahweh is to be worked out practically and structurally.

2–6. Before issuing Saul's first charge, Samuel describes in verses 2–6 three encounters that Saul will have *When you leave me today* (v. 2). While MT does not use the word *sign*[*s*] to describe these encounters until verse 7, the longer reading of verse 1 in LXX does, and this is the implicit sense of MT.[22] If original, the additional words in LXX represent a reprise of Yahweh's words to Samuel in 9:16–17 (Birch 1976: 37), which are now passed on to Saul by Samuel in his role as prophetic mediator of Saul's commissioning.

The precise significance of the three signs is debated. Tsumura (2007: 283–284) points out that the verbal syntax in verses 2–6 indicates 'predictive discourse' and then charts the three encounters as follows:

You will meet		*THEN*
2	two men	they will say to you:
3–4	three men	they will give you two loaves of bread
5–6	a band of prophets	the spirit of the Lord will rush upon you

---

22. 10:1b in LXX reads as follows: 'Is it not the case that the LORD has anointed you to be *nāgîd* (king-designate) over *his people, over Israel? And you shall reign over the people of the LORD and you shall save them from the hand of their enemies all around. And this shall be the sign to you that the LORD has anointed you to be* nāgîd *over* his heritage' (my reading of LXX and the underlying Hebrew it seems to reflect; italics indicate the LXX plus). The additional words in LXX of v. 1 might have been lost through haplography, when a copyist's eye skipped from the first 'the Lord has anointed you . . . over' to the second, leaving out what was in between.

The first encounter (v. 2) confirms the veracity of Samuel's words in 9:20 (*the donkeys . . . have been found*) and thus effectively establishes the trustworthiness of Samuel's other words to Saul (cf. also the assurances of 3:19–20; 9:6). It will be important for Saul, going forwards, that he trust Samuel's words. The second encounter (vv. 3–4) may be intended to underscore to Saul that his status has changed and that at least some (perhaps especially God-worshippers) are able to recognize this. Gordon (1986: 117) discovers 'a hint at the sacral character of Saul's appointment as the anointed ruler of Israel'. The final encounter (vv. 5–6) in which Saul is to join a *procession of prophets* seems designed to demonstrate that the Spirit[23] of God is available to Saul and can, at least on occasion, come upon him powerfully.[24] In sum, then, Samuel's words are reliable, Saul's status is changing, and God's Spirit is available to empower Saul.

7–8. Now that Saul has been anointed (v. 1) and the signs that will confirm his new status have been predicted (vv. 2–6), we come to one of the most important – and most misunderstood – parts of Saul's commissioning, namely, his first charge in verses 7–8. The understanding of these verses proposed below unlocks much of what follows in the narrative of Saul's rise.[25] Reviewing and correcting misunderstandings of these two verses is one way to proceed.

One misunderstanding is to assume that Samuel's charge to *do whatever your hand finds to do* relates to Saul's prophesying with the procession of prophets he will meet. Saul's prophesying is part of the third sign itself, however, and Samuel's charge to Saul is about what he is to do afterwards, *Once these signs are fulfilled* (v. 7).

A second misunderstanding is apparent in NIV's rendering of verse 7b as *do whatever your hand finds to do, for God is with you*. The

---

23. Translators differ as to whether to use upper or lower case with 'spirit'. JPS joins NRSV in preferring 'spirit'. NIV prefers 'Spirit', as do ESV, NASB, NLT, etc.
24. On prophecy and prophetic bands in the period, see Long (2009a: 317).
25. The reading proposed here was first worked out in Long (1989) and further developed in subsequent publications.

Hebrew text does not say 'do whatever' (which would be *ʿśh kl ʾšr*) but, rather, 'do what' (*ʿśh lk ʾšr*). Perhaps 'do whatever' is influenced by LXX, which does say 'do all, whatever your hand finds to do' (*poiei panta, hosa ean heurē hē cheir sou*). But LXX may itself reflect a misunderstanding of Saul's first charge, either resulting from or encouraging a transposition of Hebrew *lk* ('for yourself') to *kl* ('all'). MT is correct as it stands, displaying what grammarians call a 'dativus commodi', whereby a preposition with pronominal suffix (here *lk*, 'for yourself') follows an imperative (here 'do'), in order to emphasize 'the significance of the occurrence in question *for* a particular subject' (GKC 119s; cf. Joüon and Muraoka 1996: 133d). Thus, Samuel's first charge to Saul should read, 'Once these signs are fulfilled, do *what* your hand finds to do, for God is with you' (v. 7).

This of course raises the question as to what, specifically, Samuel has in mind for Saul to do. The answer is found back in verse 5. The third sign will take place at *Gibeah of God, where there is a Philistine outpost*. Saul will be on his home turf and hardly in need of topographic orientation, so why does Samuel mention these specific details? Quite likely the mention of 'God's hill'[26] and a Philistine outpost in the same breath is meant to underscore the inappropriateness of the situation. When the third and final sign is fulfilled, Saul will be on or near this hill of God, and so 'what his hand should find to do' is fairly obvious: he should attack the Philistine outpost, as various commentators have recognized.[27] The fact that Saul does not in fact attack the Philistine outpost when the signs are fulfilled may have caused some readers to miss the significance of verse 5,[28] but we shall have more to say on this shortly.

---

26. Gibeah is the word 'hill' in Hebrew.
27. See Long (1989: 51–54) for a discussion of some of these, including, among modern commentators, Stoebe, Halpern, Kittel, Lods, Goslinga and Smelik, as well as the medieval rabbinic commentator David Kimchi, who explains 10:5 as Samuel's providing a 'hint' to Saul 'that he should remove them [the Philistines] from there and save Israel out of their hands' (my translation of Kimchi's Hebrew: *rmz lw ky hwʾ yṣyrym mšm wywšyʿ yśrʾl mydm*).
28. E.g. McCarter (1980: 182) dismisses v. 5a as 'immaterial at this point in the narrative and probably secondary'.

A third misunderstanding of Saul's first charge has to do with the fact that verse 8 – *Go down ahead of me to Gilgal* and *wait seven days until I come to you and tell you what you are to do* – seems to countermand the permission given in verse 7. This has led scholars over many decades to assume that verse 8 must be a secondary 'prophetic correction', an interpolation by a later prophetic circle worried that Samuel in verse 7 gives Saul far too much latitude. But the perceived difficulty is based on a misunderstanding of verse 7. Saul is not given carte blanche permission in verse 7 to do 'whatever' he sees fit to do. As we have seen, Samuel authorizes not 'whatever' but a very specific 'what' that Saul's hand should find to do. The significance of verse 8 becomes clear when we consider what attacking the Philistine outpost would have accomplished. It would hardly have defeated the Philistines, but it would surely have provoked them and quite likely would have precipitated armed retaliation. In such a situation, it would be vitally important that Saul rendezvous with Samuel to ritually consecrate the ensuing battle and to receive further instructions from the prophet about how Yahweh, the Great King, would have the war conducted (v. 8). Such an understanding of verses 7–8 shows that the two verses are not in tension with one another but, rather, constitute a two-part, or two-stage, charge to Saul. The enactment of stage two only becomes appropriate after stage one has been enacted. Saul's rendezvous with Samuel in Gilgal to receive further instructions will become necessary only after the gauntlet has been thrown down to the Philistines by an attack on their garrison in Gibeah.

9–12. *As Saul turned to leave Samuel, God changed Saul's heart* (v. 9). Samuel had in verse 6 predicted that, as part of the third sign, the *Spirit of the* LORD would come powerfully (verb *ṣlḥ*)[29] upon Saul and change him into *a different person*. Here in verse 9, we hear that *God*

---

29. The same verb is used to describe the activity of the Spirit on Samson in Judg. 14:6, 19; 15:14 and on Saul in 10:10; 11:6. It is worth noting that in the two instances involving Saul – and despite Samuel's reference to the *Spirit of the* LORD [*yhwh*] in 10:6 – the terminology is shifted to the *Spirit of God* [*'ĕlōhîm*]. Is the narrator avoiding associating the covenantal name of God (i.e. Yahweh) with Saul? See also at 11:6.

changed Saul's heart, and all these signs were fulfilled that day. Though modern readers may hear echoes of New Testament 'regeneration' language (*different person, changed . . . heart*), the present passage is not to be understood in such terms. Hertzberg (1964: 86) remarks that 'we should not . . . think of a conversion in the spiritual sense, but merely of a readiness in Saul for the intervention of the Lord'. What is described is a divinely empowered (temporary) change in Saul, in order that the signs can be fulfilled as predicted. The fulfilment of the first two signs is not described but is to be assumed. The fulfilment of the third is described in full (v. 10).

When all those who had formerly known him saw him prophesying with the prophets (in fulfilment of the third sign), they were astonished and asked what could have happened *to the son of Kish* (v. 11). Clearly, Saul is acting out of character, as if a different person, and this is the likely sense of the saying, *Is Saul also*[30] *among the prophets?* (v. 11). The same saying will be repeated, with considerable irony, in 19:24.

To the question elicited by Saul's unexpected behaviour, *A man who lived there answered, 'And who is their father?'* (v. 12). Much ink has been spilt seeking to explain the significance of the man's remark. Perhaps he is simply asking what heredity has to do with prophetic activity; so what if Saul is a son of Kish and of a family with little connection to prophetic circles (recall that it was not Saul but his servant in 9:6 who knew of the man of God)? Or perhaps he is asking who the leader of this particular band of prophets is; leaders of such bands were sometimes referred to as 'father' (2 Kgs 2:12; 6:21; 13:14). If the onlookers themselves held prophecy in high esteem, then the question may relate to the quality of this particular band's leader; how could he admit a man like Saul to the group? Or if their attitude towards prophetic bands was more negative, then they might be wondering how a son of an upstanding family could

---

30. Heb. *gam* can also mean 'even', yielding 'Is even Saul among the prophets?' Of the five occurrences of *gam* with an interrogative particle in the OT, four favour reading *gam* as 'even', or 'really' (Gen. 16:13; 1 Kgs 17:20; Esth. 7:8; Job 41:1 [Eng. 41:9]), while the fifth (Ps. 78:20) is ambiguous.

be associating with 'madmen' (cf. 2 Kgs 9:11). Perhaps Saul is himself leader/father of the band? There can be little doubt that in the book of Samuel true prophecy is esteemed, and so whatever the specific sense of the man's question about *their father*, the consternation that Saul should be involved casts a somewhat negative light on him.

13–16. *After Saul stopped prophesying, he went to the high place* (v. 13). NRSV reads the last clause as 'he went home', perhaps assuming the last word in Hebrew to be *hbyth* ('to home') in place of MT's *hbmh* ('to the high place'). In favour of NRSV's reading is the fact that one normally 'goes up' (*'lh*) to high places, whereas the verb in verse 13 is simply 'to come (or go)' (*bw'*). If there was in fact a shift from an original 'home' to 'high place', this shift could have been triggered by a sense that after the wondrous events of the day Saul should not simply go home but should do something important; and the earlier mention of the procession of prophets *coming down from the high place* (v. 5) could have suggested what this might be (worship?). Though the reading 'he went home' is without support from the ancient versions, Josephus (*Ant.* 6.58) does write of Saul 'enter[ing] his house'. In the end, the sense is much the same either way. Whether Saul went to a high-place shrine or up a hill (his home was on a hill), or simply came home, there is no mention of worship or any other response to the events of the day. Instead, he finds himself in conversation with his *uncle* (v. 14). In response to his uncle's keen interest in his encounter with Samuel (v. 15), Saul mentions Samuel's words of assurance regarding the lost donkeys but tells him nothing of *what Samuel had said about the kingship* (v. 16). On the sense of this curious scene at the end of an eventful day, see the 'Meaning' section below.

Meaning
Inasmuch as Saul's more blatant lapses are recounted in 1 Samuel 13 and 15, many commentators have regarded the earlier chapters of the Saul narrative, namely, chapters 9–11, as largely positive towards Saul. Our reading of the account of events leading up to and including Saul's anointing (9:1 – 10:16) calls this view into question. Various elements in the portrayal of Saul as we first meet him are unsettling.

When Saul is initially introduced, the focus is exclusively on his commanding physique, with no mention of qualities of character and no reference to the Lord being 'with' him. In the search for the lost donkeys, Saul appears rather indecisive and ready to give up the quest, while his servant is the one who knows of the man of God who might help and who overcomes Saul's objection about payment (which may not even have been expected by Samuel). When Saul comes face-to-face with Samuel, he fails to recognize him, despite the rather elaborate briefing he received from the women at the well – how well does Saul listen? The reader, in contrast to Saul, has long since deduced from the topography and other clues mentioned in the text that the *seer* and Samuel are one and the same. When Samuel's words and actions single out Saul as the one Israel desires (an allusion to the elders' demand in 1 Sam. 8?), Saul protests his inadequacy.

Saul is nevertheless anointed and commissioned to *do [what] your hand finds to do* (which, in the light of 10:5, we understood to be an attack on the Philistine outpost at Gibeah of God). This action is to be taken as soon as the three signs confirming Samuel's words to Saul come to pass. In order for the third sign, which involves prophesying, to take place, Saul is changed into a different man, and he joins with the prophets, much to the consternation of those who have known him before. With the completion of the third sign at Gibeah Elohim, where there is a Philistine outpost, the time and place are right for Saul to do what lies at hand. Saul is the *nāgîd*, the king-designate. Now is the time for him to demonstrate that he is the one chosen by Yahweh to deliver God's people from the Philistines. But he simply returns home (or to the high place), and when questioned by his uncle, says nothing of the kingship.

Why Saul's silence? Some see it as a matter of military necessity – he dare not provoke the Philistines. According to our reading, however, provoking the Philistines is precisely what he is meant to do. And having done so, he is to rendezvous with Samuel in Gilgal to receive further instructions from Yahweh about what he is to do next. Saul's two-part first charge – namely, to do what lies at hand, then go and await further instructions from Yahweh – is designed to establish an authority structure whereby Israel can have a human king, a vice-regent, while Yahweh remains their true king.[31] Others explain Saul's silence regarding the kingship as exhibiting laudable humility, but in the light of all that has gone before (and all that follows), the far likelier explanation is that Saul is fearful, obtuse, or both, and is shrinking back from doing what lies at hand (cf. 10:22).

Once Saul's faltering is grasped by the reader, the episodes leading up to 1 Samuel 13, where Saul finally ascends the throne but fails in respect of his first charge, can be understood as forming a coherent, sequential narrative of Saul's rise to the throne, as we shall see below.

ii. Saul chosen by lot (10:17–27)
Context
Saul's failure to carry out part one of his two-part charge, namely, *to do [what his] hand finds to do* (10:7), or even to mention the matter of the kingship to his uncle (10:16), means that he does not come to public attention. If invited guests at the special meal of 9:22–24 suspected that the special treatment afforded to Saul singled him out as in some way God's answer to the request for a king in 1 Samuel 8, they have yet to see an opportunity to fall in behind Saul. In other words, there has so far been no *public* indication that Saul is the king-designate and no demonstration on Saul's part that he is empowered to lead. A successful attack on the Philistine outpost mentioned in 10:5 could have demonstrated Saul's calling and readiness to lead, but no such action is recorded. Samuel, therefore, must find another way to bring Saul to public attention and to move the accession process along (on this accession process, see the discussion of Saul in the Introduction). So he summons the people to Mizpah. As the scene opens, Samuel does not seem happy. In fact, he begins as if delivering a judgment speech (McCarter 1980: 195).

---

[31]. This reading is far more in keeping with the theological perspectives of the book of Samuel than are readings that indict Samuel as simply trying to protect his own personal power by reducing Saul to a 'puppet' king, with Samuel pulling the strings.

Comment

17–19. *Samuel summoned the people of Israel to the* LORD *at Mizpah* (v. 17). Mizpah was one of the regular stops in Samuel's circuit (7:16) and has been plausibly identified with Tell en-Naṣbeh some 8 miles north of Jerusalem (see comment at 7:5–6). Mizpah was the site of a great victory in response to Samuel's prayer in 1 Samuel 7, and it was near Mizpah that Samuel had raised up the stone *Ebenezer* and proclaimed, *Thus far the* LORD *has helped us* (7:12). It is not without irony, therefore, that this is the site chosen for the public selection of the one given in response to the people's demand for a king (ch. 8), a demand interpreted by Yahweh as a rejection of his own kingship (8:7).

This is what the LORD, *the God of Israel, says: 'I brought Israel up out of Egypt, and I delivered you . . . But you have now rejected your God . . . So now present yourselves* (vv. 17–19). Samuel's words bear hallmarks of a prophetic judgment speech. There is, for instance, a 'messenger formula' (*kōh-'āmar yhwh*, lit. 'thus says Yahweh'), a 'contrast motif' citing God's past beneficence as opposed to Israel's current behaviour, an 'accusation' of wrong-doing, and a 'so now' (*wĕ'attâ*) formula where one might expect an 'announcement' of judgment.[32] Instead of the expected announcement of judgment, however, Samuel says, *So now present yourselves before the* LORD *by your tribes and clans* (v. 19). With these words, he initiates a lot-casting procedure. Numerous scholars have noted the similarities between this episode and two other passages involving lot-casting: Joshua 7 and 1 Samuel 14:38–44. The purpose of the lot-casting in the latter two passages is to discover a guilty party (Achan and Jonathan, respectively). What of Saul in the present episode? Is he already guilty of something? McCarter (1980: 196) hesitates to conclude that 'Saul is guilty of something', noting that 'that will come later', but he does detect 'a clear but subtle implication that he is an offending party

---

32. Cf. Judg. 6:7–10, where the cry of the people, already suffering judgment, is answered by a prophetic pronouncement that shares many of these same features. Cf. also Birch (1975: 452–454; 1976: 48–51). On Westermann's seminal analysis of the judgment speech form (1960; Eng. 1991), see Long (1989: 85–86).

by virtue of the election itself'. In the light of our understanding of Saul's failure to take action against the Philistine outpost as instructed (cf. our reading of 10:7 in the light of 10:5), it seems fair to say that Saul is indeed already 'guilty of something'.

20–22. With the sinfulness of the people's behaviour duly noted (v. 19), Samuel proceeds with the lot-casting. Samuel has *all Israel come forward by tribes* (v. 20). Logic and logistical considerations suggest that *all Israel* could not come forward *en masse* but, rather, in the form of representatives. After several sortitions, *Saul son of Kish was taken* (v. 21). He is nowhere to be found, however, and so further divine enquiry is required to discover that *he has hidden himself among the supplies* (v. 22).[33] Josephus (*Ant.* 6.63) construes Saul's hiding as exhibiting 'restraint and modesty': 'the young man promptly took himself away, not wishing, I imagine, to appear eager to take the sovereignty'. Various modern commentators take a similar view, but this view must be questioned. Given all that has happened so far in the narrative (or not happened!), a more negative reading of Saul's hiding seems warranted. Not humility, but something else (fear? incomprehension?) lands Saul *among the supplies* (v. 22).

23–24. *They ran and brought him out*, and *he was a head taller than any of the others* (v. 23). A certain comic irony attends this scene – Israel's biggest man found crouching amongst the supplies and then unfolded for public viewing. The description of Saul's stature repeats virtually verbatim his introduction in 9:2, which focused, as we noted, exclusively on Saul's outward, not inward, qualities. While outwardly as impressive as ever, his internal smallness may be beginning to show.

Samuel's declaration, now that Saul is found, is difficult to interpret with certainty: *Do you see the man the LORD has chosen? There is no one like him among all the people* (v. 24). That Saul is chosen of Yahweh

---

33. Commentators have fretted over how Saul, though in hiding, could be chosen. But as noted, it is likely that only representatives would need to be physically present for the lot-casting. The representative of the final grouping chosen (a family?) would then name the possible candidates for selection within the group, and then one of the names would be indicated by lot.

is not to be gainsaid, but the background of that choice in 1 Samuel 8 must not be forgotten (especially 8:19–22). Samuel's no-one-like-him praise of Saul again recalls Saul's first introduction in the narrative: 'There was not a man among the people of Israel more handsome than he' (9:2, NRSV). And again, the focus is on outward qualities. It may be worth noting in this context that Samuel will later need to be cautioned not to judge by outward appearance or height (16:6–7). Given Samuel's experience of Saul so far, there may also be a touch of irony in his pronouncement. But at the very least it underscores that Yahweh has conceded to the people's request and given them what they asked for. *Long live the king!* (v. 24): the people seem delighted, or at least most of them do (see at vv. 26–27).

25. Before the people are dismissed to return home, *Samuel explained to the people the rights and duties of kingship.* NIV's *the rights and duties of kingship* renders *mišpaṭ hammĕlukâ* (lit. 'the manner of the kingship), which sounds very much like *mišpaṭ hammelek* (lit. 'the manner of the king'), a phrase that occurs twice in 1 Samuel 8 (vv. 9 and 11). Despite the terminological similarity, however, two very different things are in view. First Samuel 8 describes the abusive 'manner of the king' which the people can expect from the kind of king they want.[34] By contrast, the 'manner of the kingship' that Samuel describes here in verse 25, and indeed prescribes by writing it *on a scroll and deposit[ing] it before the* LORD, represents – we can only assume, because we are not told – the kind of king Yahweh wants. Vannoy (1978: 231) explains:

> In this action Samuel takes the first step in resolving the tension which existed between Israel's improper desire for a king, as well as their misconceived notion of what the role and function of this king should be, on the one hand, and the stated fact that it was Yahweh's intent to give them a king on the other . . . This constitutional-legal description of the duties and prerogatives of the king in Israel would clearly distinguish the Israelite kingship from that known to the Israelites in surrounding nations. In Israel, the king's role was to be strictly compatible with the continued sovereignty of Yahweh over the nation.

---

34. Cf. the abusive 'manner [*mišpaṭ*] of the priests' in 2:13.

26–27. Samuel having *dismissed the people to go to their own homes* (v. 25), *Saul also went to his home in Gibeah* (v. 26a). He does not go alone, however, for he is *accompanied by valiant men whose hearts God had touched* (v. 26b). *Valiant men* renders *haḥayil* (roughly 'the powerful', as the noun *ḥayil* can connote wealth, standing, ability, power or even army; perhaps compare English expressions such as military 'powers' or 'forces'). Both 4QSam^a and LXX have 'sons of' before *ḥḥyl*. The Targum offers an expansionist interpretation: these are 'men who feared sin'. NIV's *valiant men* is suitably general, as also is JPS's 'upstanding men'. The key point is that these are people *whose hearts God had touched* (v. 26). As far as possible, God supports Saul, surrounding him with good people. But there are also *some scoundrels* (*bĕnê bĕliyyaʻal*; a term applied to Eli's sons in 2:12) who refuse to support Saul, asking instead, *How can this fellow save us?* (v. 27). Although clearly wrong to question Yahweh's selection of Saul, these scoundrels do have grounds for their scepticism. Saul, so far, has done nothing to demonstrate leadership qualities; the outpost at Gibeah Elohim is still standing (see at 10:7), and the people's first encounter with Saul involved dragging him out of hiding (v. 22). Saul's response to all this, according to MT, is to keep silent. But here we arrive at one of the more famous and difficult textual cruxes in Samuel.[35] This textual crux merits a brief excursus.

Excursus on the text of 1 Samuel 10:27 – 11:1a
An initial glimpse of the nature of the issues involved can be gained by comparing NIV's rendering of 10:27b – 11:1a with that of NRSV. Picking up with the last line of verse 27 in MT, NRSV includes a number of additional lines attested in 4QSam^a (displayed here in italics):

> But he held his peace.
> *Now Nahash, king of the Ammonites, had been grievously oppressing the Gadites and the Reubenites. He would gouge out the right eye of each of them and would not grant Israel a deliverer. No one was left of the Israelites across the Jordan whose*

---

35. Barthélemy (1982: 166–172) takes some five tightly packed pages just to summarize the state of the question.

right eye Nahash, king of the Ammonites, had not gouged out. But there were seven thousand men who had escaped from the Ammonites and had entered Jabesh-gilead.

About a month later, Nahash the Ammonite went up and beseiged Jabesh-gilead; . . .

NRSV is a composite of the ancient witnesses; no extant witness attests NRSV's reading in its entirety. The first line is derived from MT. 'But he held his peace' (NIV *But Saul kept silent*) renders MT's *wyhy kmḥryš*. The remaining lines in italics are from 4QSam[a], with 'about a month later' (11:1) being supported also by LXX. Josephus (*Ant.* 6.68) includes much of the information found in 4QSam[a], but he places 'about a month later' at the beginning of his account of Nahash's grievous oppression of 'the Jews who had settled beyond the river Jordan', rather than at its end, as in 4QSam[a]. This prompts Cross (2005: 66) to speculate that MT may originally have had two instances of 'about a month later', one at the beginning of the longer reading and one at its end, and to further speculate that the intervening lines may have been lost in MT when a copyist's eye skipped from the first to the second occurrence of 'about a month later'. This phrase in 4QSam[a] is written *wyhy kmw ḥdš*. It should be noted that this Hebrew phrase is not very different from the Hebrew of 'but he kept silent', *wyhy kmḥryš*. The visual similarity of the two phrases is even closer if both phrases are stripped of optional elements such as *matres lectionis* (consonants used to represent vowels); this yields virtually identical phrases, *wyhy kmḥrš* and *wyhy kmḥdš*.[36] The only difference involves the letters *resh* (*r*) and *dalet* (*d*), often confused in Hebrew in both the paleo- and the square-scripts. We arrive then at a variation on the suggestion of Cross. A scribe's eye may have skipped from 'and he held his peace' to the nearly identical 'about a month later', inadvertently omitting the lines in between. The situation is of course complex, solutions are debated and full discussion is not possible here. But some such reasoning may lie behind NRSV's decision to combine

---

36. On the latter construction, cf. Gen. 38:24, where the temporal clause 'About three months later' begins *wyhy km* (the *km* being a combination of the prepositions *kĕ* and *min*).

MT and 4QSam³ as it does. When all is said and done, 'the wise course for the present', as Gordon (1986: 64) notes, 'is to reserve judgment on the status of these additional lines in 4QSam³'. Should the longer reading be accepted, it would help explain what motivated Nahash's siege of Jabesh Gilead. Escapees from Nahash's other aggressions had fled to Jabesh Gilead, and Nahash came after them.

Whatever we make of the text-critical issue at the juncture between chapters 10 and 11, it is best to retain MT's final comment on Saul: *But Saul kept silent* (v. 27). What are we to make of it? Formally, as Firth (2013: 37) notes, Saul's silence 'balances Samuel's cry at 1 Sam. 10.17 with which [the passage] opens'. But how is Saul's silence to be evaluated? In 2 Samuel 19:9–10 (Heb. vv. 10–11), the tribes of Israel fault each other for keeping silent ('sit[ting] idle', according to JPS) instead of bringing David back after Absalom's failed revolt. The same Hebrew expression that was used to describe Saul's silence (*kĕmaḥărîš*) is used to describe the 'silence/idling' (*maḥărîšîm*) of the Israelite tribes. In addition, while 10:27 employs the verb *ḥrš* II, the homonymous verb *ḥrš* I is used to describe Saul's 'plotting evil' (*maḥărîš hārā'â*) against David in 1 Samuel 23:9. Too much should not be made of subtleties, but they may add to the general sense of the story so far that Saul's inaction (going home and remaining silent/idling) in the aftermath not only of his anointing but also of his selection by lot is not to be praised.

Meaning
Contrary to some traditional interpretations that view the portrayal of Saul as largely positive up to 1 Samuel 13, our own reading discovers a portrayal that is, at best, ambivalent. Twice Saul has been designated as leader of Israel, first by anointing in private and then by sortition in a public assembly at Mizpah, and in both instances he has failed to do anything that would have rallied support and resulted in his confirmation by the people. After his anointing, he did not do what lay at hand (10:7; cf. 10:5), nor even mention to his uncle the matter of his designation as king (10:16). When his inaction made a second designation necessary, Saul responded to his public election by simply falling silent in the face

of those who questioned his ability to save (10:27). Did he share their misgivings? Saul's failures to this point, if we can call them that, involve reluctance to assume the responsibilities to which he has been called. But this reluctance hints at an anaemic faith in Yahweh, who has designated him as leader and surrounded him with supporters (10:26). And this, in turn, raises the question whether Saul will prove suitable to be king in Israel, or will prove to be a king such as all the nations have.

iii. *Saul's victory over the Ammonites (11:1–15)*
Context
The nagging question of 10:27, *How can this fellow save us?*, is answered in 1 Samuel 11 by Saul's dramatic deliverance of Jabesh Gilead from the threat of King Nahash of the Ammonites. His success both in mustering his forces and in defeating Nahash is a demonstration of leadership capabilities sufficient to silence his earlier detractors. The episode is nevertheless unsettling in a couple of respects. First, the description both of Saul's spirit-empowerment and of the manner by which he gains the attention of his countrymen and mobilizes them to action is reminiscent of aspects of the period of the judges, recalling especially the Levite of Judges 19 – 20 whose time period is described as one when 'Israel had no king' (Judg. 17:6; 21:25). Second, Saul's victory is against the Ammonites, not the Philistines, which leaves the foes central to Saul's anointing and first charge unaffected.

Comment
1–3. *Nahash the Ammonite went up and besieged Jabesh Gilead* (v. 1).[37] While the Philistines threatened Israel's heartland from the west, the Ammonites, though sometimes on friendly terms with Israel (cf. 2 Sam. 10:2), were often a threatening force on the east (cf. Judg. 3:13; 11:4–32). Their territory was in Transjordan, south of the Jabbok River, and their capital was at Rabbath Ammon (modern Amman, Jordan). The Amman Citadel Inscription (*COS* 2.24:139) confirms the close linguistic affinity between Ammonite and

---

37. On the text-critical issue involving 11:1, see the excursus at 10:27.

Hebrew.³⁸ Genesis 19:38 and Deuteronomy 2:19 trace the ancestry of the Ammonites to Abraham's nephew Lot. *Jabesh Gilead*'s ancient location is still debated, but the likeliest suggestion is Tell Maqlub, a site along the Wadi el-Yabis (cf. Jabesh) in northern Gilead, within the tribal territory of Gad.³⁹ As noted in the discussion of the text of 1 Samuel 10:27, 4QSamᵃ (cf. Josephus) situates the siege of Jabesh Gilead in the context of a larger offensive by Nahash.

In response to the plea by *all the men of Jabesh* for treaty terms (v. 1), Nahash agrees on the condition *that I gouge out the right eye of every one of you* (v. 2). Nahash's stated purpose is to *bring disgrace on all Israel*, but blinding the right eye would also, as Josephus explains (*Ant.* 6.70), render the men of Jabesh 'utterly unserviceable' in war. Right-handed fighters (the majority) would have to lower their shields or literally stick their necks out in order to see around the shields in their left hands. Such mass blinding of defeated enemies was common practice in the Ancient Near East.⁴⁰

Give us seven days (v. 3). The elders' ostensible reason is to have time to send messengers *throughout Israel* in search of a *môšîaʿ* ('deliverer, saviour'). Should none be found, then *we will surrender to you* (lit. 'we will go out to you'). There is ambiguity in the elders' offer of surrender, as the verb used (*yṣʾ*) can also connote 'going out' to do battle (for the hostile sense, see 8:20; 18:30; 2 Sam. 18:2–4, 6; and for surrender, see 2 Kgs 24:12; Isa. 36:16; Jer. 38:17). But Nahash seems oblivious to the ambiguity, or perhaps too confident to care.

4–5. *When the messengers came to Gibeah of Saul* (v. 4). A straightforward reading of the Hebrew text has *the messengers* coming directly to Gibeah of Saul, which seems to betray an awareness that Saul is the one who has been designated leader of Israel. (LXX has the messengers come not just to Gibeah but 'to Saul' himself.) It seems unlikely, simply in terms of logistics and timing, that a general search for a deliverer throughout Israelite territory took

---

38. For a photograph of the inscription, see Long (2009a: 321).
39. For arguments in favour of this site identification, see Edelman (1992b: 594–595) and the brief summary in Long (2009a: 321).
40. See Postgate (1992: 255); Long (2009a: 321–322).

place. In verse 7, Saul will send the messengers *throughout Israel* to order a general muster. One seven-day period hardly seems enough time to allow for the messengers to go throughout Israel twice, first in search of a saviour and then to call up the troops.[41] Hearing the news of Nahash's aggression, *the people . . . all wept aloud* (v. 4). Their reaction is not explained, but in view of the fact that Saul has apparently returned to farming (v. 5), they perhaps despair of effective rescue. So far, Saul has done nothing to answer his detractors' question, *How can this fellow save us?* (10:27). But that is about to change.

6–8. *When Saul heard their words, the Spirit of God came powerfully upon him, and he burned with anger* (v. 6). The description of the Spirit falling powerfully on Saul (*ṣlḥ*, 'rush upon') recalls the activity of the Spirit on the judge Samson (Judg. 14:6, 19; 15:14), though in Samson's case it was invariably the Spirit of 'Yahweh', whereas here it is the Spirit of *God*. The same deity is of course in view, but 'Yahweh' is the more personal, relational name, while 'God' is the more general term. In 10:6, Samuel predicted that Saul would be endued with the Spirit of Yahweh, but in the event it was the Spirit of God (10:10). The narrator's choice of words is vaguely unsettling.[42] Less subtle is the obvious similarity between what Saul does next (v. 7) and the gruesome dismemberment and distribution of body parts by the Levite in Judges 19:29; 20:6. In the entire Old Testament, the verb *ntḥ* ('cut up') and the verb *šlḥ* ('send') are combined only in the story of the Levite in Judges and in this story of Saul. Saul's butchering of oxen and sending around of bovine remains is less ghastly than the Levite's similar treatment of his concubine, but Saul's action still recalls – ironically in view of his king-designate status – a very dark period in Israel's

---

41. As argued by Stoebe (1973: 226); Long (1989: 220–224).
42. See Beuken (1978: 5); Wentz (1970–1: 216–217); Long (1989: 228); Firth (2009: 138–139). Cf. also the Balaam story (Num. 22 – 24) where a similar avoidance strategy may be in place; while Balaam refers regularly to Yahweh, it is the Spirit of 'God' that comes upon him (Num. 24:2), and Balaam's long-term effect on the people of Israel is negative (Num. 31:16).

history when there was no king in Israel (cf. Judg. 17:6; 18:1; 19:1; 21:25).

This is what will be done to the oxen of anyone who does not follow Saul and Samuel (v. 7). Notably, it is *the terror of the* LORD that falls on the people, and they muster *en masse* at *Bezek*, a site to the west of the Jordan and some 17 miles away from Jabesh Gilead.[43] Having gathered at Bezek, *the men of Israel numbered three hundred thousand and those of Judah thirty thousand*. On large numbers in the Old Testament, see at 4:2 and 6:19; Hebrew *'elep*, 'thousand', can indicate a 'unit' such as a 'clan' (as in 10:19) or a military unit of perhaps as few as ten soldiers. That Israel and Judah are mentioned separately reflects the fact that even before the division of the kingdom in the time of Solomon's son Rehoboam (1 Kgs 12) a sense of distinction between northern and southern tribes was felt.[44]

9–11. Having received promise of rescue (v. 9), the communiqué of the men of Jabesh Gilead to the Ammonites is rich in dramatic irony: *Tomorrow we will surrender to you* (v. 10), literally, 'tomorrow we will come out [*yṣ'*] to you'. As noted at verse 3, this expression can as easily suggest coming out to fight as to surrender. Saul's military strategy in verse 11 is conventional and effective. By dividing his forces into three divisions,[45] Saul can surround and attack the enemy from several sides, and by launching the attack very early (*during the last watch of the night*), he benefits from the element of surprise.[46] So successful is his victory over the Ammonites that by *the heat of the day . . . no two of them were left together* (v. 11).

---

43. Two possible site identifications have been suggested (Khirbet Ibziq or Khirbet Salhab); see Long (2009a: 323).
44. Cf. Josh. 11:21; 1 Sam. 17:52; 18:16; 2 Sam. 2:10; 3:10; 5:5; 11:11; 12:8; 19:11, 40–43; 20:2; 21:2; 24:1, 9.
45. Cf. 1 Sam. 13:17 (the Philistines); Judg. 7:16 (Gideon); 9:43 (Abimelech); 2 Sam. 18:2 (David).
46. NIV's *last watch* renders 'morning watch' in Heb. In contrast to the NT period, when the night was divided into four watches, in the OT period there seem to have been three (note the 'middle watch' of Judg. 7:19), and so the third watch would likely have involved the early morning hours from about 2 am onwards. See Gordon (1986: 124, 341 n. 71).

12–15. In the flush of Saul's commanding victory, which Josephus (*Ant.* 6.80) creatively enhances by crediting Saul with the subjugation and sacking of Ammon more broadly, returning 'in glory to his own land', the people demand that Saul's earlier detractors (10:27) be turned over *that we may put them to death* (v. 12). Their enthusiasm is curbed, however, by Saul (or is it Samuel?), who responds that *No one will be put to death today, for this day the* LORD *has rescued Israel* (v. 13). McCarter (1980: 201) follows some LXX manuscripts in making Samuel the speaker of these words. Given that the people addressed Samuel in verse 12, it may have been more appropriate for Samuel to respond than Saul. But this very sense of propriety may have influenced LXX's preference of Samuel over Saul as the speaker.[47] Assuming the response to be Saul's, we arrive at a somewhat mixed review. Crediting the victory of the day to Yahweh is a theological high-point for Saul, but wresting the right of decision from Samuel may betoken things to come.

Then Samuel said... 'let us go to Gilgal and there renew the kingship' (v. 14). Some scholars sense a tension between the reference to renewing the kingship and the notice in the next verse that *all the people... made Saul king in the presence of the* LORD (v. 15). How can the kingship be renewed if Saul is only made king in verse 15? The difficulty can be resolved, however, in the light of a three-part accession process involving designation, demonstration and confirmation.[48] In the lengthy episode 9:1 – 10:16, Saul is designated in private by anointing but then fails to demonstrate his king-designate status by attacking the Philistine outpost explicitly mentioned in 10:5. To bring Saul to public attention, Samuel finds it necessary to conduct a public designation in 10:17–27, but the lack of demonstration by the hiding giant leaves some doubting (10:27). Even after the public selection, Saul apparently returns to farming. Finally, the victory against the Ammonites in the present chapter provides a demonstration that can move the accession process

---

47. Some LXX manuscripts agree with MT in reading 'Saul', as do Targ., Syr., Josephus, etc.
48. See discussion of Saul in the Introduction.

towards the confirmation stage. Now that Saul has actually done something, the 'kingship' (namely, the rise-to-kingship process) can be 'renewed' (put back on track); the Hebrew verb *ḥdš* pi'el has to do with the renewal or restoration of something that already exists but is in need of repair.[49] And so, with the dissenters now satisfied, all the people make Saul king, and *Saul and all the Israelites held a great celebration* (v. 15).[50]

Meaning
The events of chapter 11 bring to completion, in some respects at least, a long and faltering process. Saul has finally moved from *designation* (twice) to a *demonstration* of his ability to lead (albeit against the Ammonites, not the Philistines), to *confirmation* by the people. But what of confirmation by Yahweh? And why is Samuel not listed among the celebrants at the end of the chapter? As the story continues into the next chapter, Samuel's sobering words to the people and to Saul underscore the fact that kingship can succeed (and thus Saul can succeed) only if both king and people respond appropriately to the continuing rule of the Great King.

---

49. Cf. Vannoy (1978: 62–64, 126); Long (1989: 224–228).
50. Vannoy (1978: 87) notes that 'to make someone king' (*mlk* hip'il) is to invest him formally 'with the prerogatives and responsibilities of his office'. Vannoy argues that, since Saul is only now made king in v. 15, the renewal of v. 14 must have to do not with Saul but, rather, with the kingship of Yahweh. But while the continuing rule of Yahweh as Israel's Great King is arguably *the* central concern throughout the book of Samuel, the focus in the present context is on Saul's faltering rise and the fact that the twice-designated Saul, having finally demonstrated his capabilities, can be formally installed as king. A choice need not be made between the kingship of Yahweh and the kingship of Saul (cf. Fokkelmann 1993: 4.491). As the prophet Samuel makes crystal clear in the next chapter, the latter can only succeed if it is subordinated to the former.

C. Samuel's instructions and warnings about kingship (12:1–25)

Context

Saul's great victory in 1 Samuel 11 silenced his critics and led to his full confirmation by the people. As far as they are concerned, the king-designate is now the king proper. His reign can begin. They have their king, and this is a cause of great rejoicing for Saul and for all the people (11:15). Samuel, though a key player in the Gilgal ceremony (11:12–15) and implicitly in the earlier events of the chapter (11:7), is not mentioned as joining the celebration. Does he still harbour misgivings about the people's king? First Samuel 12 opens with Samuel addressing the people, and what he has to say indicates that the fate of the people's king still hangs in the balance and is dependent on how successfully a human king can be incorporated into an authority structure whereby the divine king continues to rule.

Comment

1–5. The preponderance of first-person pronouns in verses 1–5 is not surprising; Samuel wishes to defend his own record as Israel's leader before instructing both people and king about how the new leader can succeed. *I have listened to everything you said to me and have set a king over you* (v. 1). Fundamentally, of course, Samuel has listened to the voice of Yahweh (8:7, 22), but it must be remembered that Yahweh's instructions to Samuel came in response to the people's persistent demand for a king like those of the nations (1 Sam. 8). *Now you have a king as your leader. As for me . . . I have been your leader from my youth* (v. 2). The parallelism in Samuel's words – in Hebrew 'a king to walk before you . . . I walked before you' – effectively contrasts the new polity of kingship with the old one under Samuel (himself a judge, prophet and priest). *Here I stand. Testify against me in the presence of the* LORD *and his anointed* (v. 3). As the first stage in a three-pronged argument designed to impress on the people the gravity of the current moment, Samuel looks to the immediate past, putting his own leadership record on trial. He presents his case by posing a series of questions: *Whose ox have I* taken? Whose donkey . . . ?, and so on (v. 3).[51] The people return the verdict of 'innocent': *You have not cheated or oppressed us* (v. 4), and Samuel evokes God as witness (v. 5). He has already mentioned in passing his agedness and even his sons, who *are here with you* (v. 2), but he gives these factors little if any weight in evaluating the elders' insistence on having a king (1 Sam. 8).

6–8. Having taken the stand and successfully elicited from the people a verdict of 'innocent' (vv. 4–5), Samuel turns from defence to prosecution, and to the second stage of his argument. Not only in the recent past, but from the beginning, Yahweh has provided capable leaders like *Moses and Aaron* (vv. 6, 8). *Now then, stand here* (v. 7). The Hebrew particle *'attâ* ('now') and verb *yṣb* (hitpaʻel 'take your stand') occur in combination only three times in the Old Testament. The first occurrence was in 10:19, on the occasion of Saul's selection by lot. The second is here in verse 7, and the third comes in verse 16. In each case, the people are challenged to present themselves and, in essence, to pay attention to something that Yahweh is about to do or say. In the present instance, it is Yahweh's prophet, the judge Samuel, who proposes to *confront* the people *before the* LORD. *Confront* renders the verb *špṭ* from which, not inappropriately, the noun *šōpēṭ* ('judge') is derived. Samuel has not yet retired. The verb *špṭ* in the nipʻal, as here, is broadly reciprocal, as the translations demonstrate: 'enter into judgment with' (NRSV); 'plead with' (ESV); 'cite against' (JPS); 'reason with' (NKJV). There is, in fact, room for each of these nuances in Samuel's confrontation as it plays out in the chapter. The basic point is that Yahweh has ever proved responsive to his people, providing timely leaders to rescue them – for example, *out of Egypt* (v. 6) – and to provide for them – *settled them in this place* (v. 8).

9–11. *But they forgot the* LORD *their God* (v. 9). As Samuel turns to the third stage in his argument (namely, that even in the face of Israel's unfaithfulness Yahweh has responded with correction and rescue), he continues his brief history lesson, moving on to the period of the judges. Because of Israel's forgetfulness, *the* LORD *their*

---

51. The tenth commandment forbidding covetousness explicitly mentions ox and donkey (Exod. 20:17; Deut. 5:21).

God . . . sold them into the hands of . . . Hazor in the north, and *into the hands of the Philistines* in the south-west and of *the king of Moab* in the south-east (v. 9). Embattled on all sides, Israel *cried out to the LORD* (v. 10). The progression Samuel describes is very much along the lines of the well-known pattern from the book of Judges involving sin, subjugation, supplication and salvation. The basic elements of supplication (v. 10) are that it is directed towards Yahweh, entails confession of specific sin – *we have forsaken the LORD and served the Baals and the Ashtoreths* – and is followed by a plea for deliverance and a promise of redirected worship: *we will serve you*. In response to such supplication in Israel's earlier history, Yahweh raised up judge-deliverers, four of whom Samuel names in verse 11 (including himself in final position): *Jerub-Baal* [i.e. Gideon; Judg. 6:32; 7:1], *Barak*,[52] *Jephthah and Samuel*. Samuel's limiting the list to four names may be in the interest of capitalizing on the well-known 'three–four pattern' in Hebrew, three enemies in verse 9 followed by four deliverers in verse 11 (cf. Golani 2015). The names included in Samuel's list of judges seem related to what has gone before. In verse 9 he named three enemies surrounding Israel. Barak (along with Deborah, whom Syr. adds to the list) dealt with the enemy in the north at Hazor (see Judg. 5:1 and Judg. 4 – 5 *passim*). But Barak is not mentioned first in the list; Jerub-Baal (Gideon) is.[53] The mention of Baals and Ashtoreths in verse 10 may have called Gideon to mind, as he was the judge who destroyed Baal's altar (Judg. 6:25–32). Additionally, Gideon may head the list due to his prominence as the central and pivotal judge in the book of Judges (cf. Gooding 1982). Samson finds his way onto the list in some ancient witnesses; the Targum replaces MT's Bedan with Samson, while the Syriac replaces Samuel himself with Samson. Mention of the Philistines in verse 9 may have seemed to call for Samson, who 'led Israel for twenty years in the days of the Philistines' (Judg. 15:20) and

---

52. MT has 'Bedan' (so also Vulg.), which is either a corruption of 'Barak' (the letters *r* and *d* being easily confused in Hebrew) or an otherwise unknown deliverer. 'Barak' is attested in LXX and Syr.
53. Except in Syr., which reorders the list to have Gideon follow Deborah and Barak.

who 'killed many more [Philistines] when he died than while he lived' (Judg. 16:30). But Samuel, too, routed the Philistines rather decisively and rather recently (7:13). Retaining MT's list of four (though substituting Barak for Bedan), we arrive at a logical listing that begins with the judge who took dramatic action against idols inimical to faith (Gideon), followed by three who delivered Israel from foes to the north (Barak), to the east in Transjordan (Jephthah) and in the south-west (Samuel). The Lord, through a series of judges, had indeed rescued Israel from enemies *all around you* (v. 11).

12–15. *But when you saw . . . Nahash . . . you said to me, 'No, we want a king to rule over us'* – *even though the LORD your God was your king* (v. 12). In tone, Samuel's words recall his earlier speech in 10:17–19 and, also like that speech, build to a *wĕʿattâ* ('so now') with hints of judgment to follow. *Now here is the king you have chosen, the one you asked for* (v. 13). There can be no question that Saul is the people's king, the one they wanted (8:10, 18; cf. 16:1), but there can also be no question that Yahweh remains in control: it is he who *has set a king over you* (v. 13). Of questionable beginning, the kingship can nevertheless succeed, because Yahweh remains involved. *If you fear the LORD and serve and obey him . . . and if both you and the king who reigns over you follow the LORD your God – good!* (v. 14). *Good* is not in the Hebrew text but is supplied to provide an apodosis ('then' clause) after the double protasis ('if' clause). It is possible, however, to read the second clause not as a second protasis but as an apodosis, yielding 'then both you and the king who rules over you will be following the LORD your God' (cf. Tsumura 2007: 321, 324). The second clause in verse 14 is syntactically similar to the second in verse 15 – both begin with a *wĕqāṭal* of the verb *hyh* – and the latter is clearly to be read as an apodosis. Understood in this way, verse 14 is describing what fearing, serving and obeying Yahweh must look like, not just for the people but for the king, if kingship is to succeed. From the beginning, whether in Moses' day (Deut. 6:2, 24; 10:12; 31:12–13) or Joshua's (Josh. 4:24; 24:14), or in the new era of the monarchy, 'fearing the LORD' was the fundamental requirement for rightly relating to Yahweh.[54] To *fear the*

---

54. It is, as Israel's wisdom tradition underscores, the beginning of wisdom (e.g. Job 28:28; Ps. 111:10; Prov. 1:7).

LORD is to give him weight (honour), and to commit to serving him and to obeying him. Whatever the intricacies of the Hebrew text, the general sense of verses 14–15 is clear. Human kingship that continues to honour Yahweh as the Great King can succeed, but *if you rebel against his commands, his hand will be against you, as it was against your ancestors* (v. 15). LXX has 'against your king' instead of 'against your ancestors' and is followed by, for instance, NRSV and ESV. Focus on both people and king nicely parallels verse 14 and anticipates also verse 25.[55]

16–19. For a second time in the chapter, Samuel challenges the people to stand up and take notice (see at v. 7), this time in order to witness *this great thing the LORD is about to do before your eyes!* Prophetic utterances were frequently accompanied by a sign of some sort (e.g. 2:34; 10:7, 9; 15:27–28).[56] *I will call on the LORD to send thunder and rain* (v. 17). That Yahweh responds (v. 18) both confirms Samuel's authority as Yahweh's prophet and subjects the people to a mild punishment for the *evil thing you did in the eyes of the LORD when you asked for a king* (v. 17). Rain at harvest time is never welcome, potentially causing pre-harvest sprouting and a reduced yield, and the additional threat of thunder recalls both Hannah's warnings in 2:10 of *thunder from heaven* against *those who oppose the LORD* and Yahweh's thundering in 7:10 *with loud thunder against the Philistines*. The force of the sign is not lost on the people, who stand *in awe of the LORD and of Samuel* (v. 18) and plead with Samuel to pray to *your God* on behalf of *your servants* lest they die. When last the people had asked Samuel to pray ('cry out') for them, it was for *rescue . . . from the hand of the Philistines*, and the prayer was directed to *the LORD our God* (7:8). Now their prayer is for clemency from the Lord himself, *so that we will not die, for we have added to all our other sins the evil of asking for a king'* (v. 19).

20–25. In the face of genuine repentance, Samuel offers genuine comfort – *Do not be afraid* – and challenges the people to renewed

---

55. Driver (1960: 94–95) favours LXX's 'against your king' and attributes 'ancestors' (lit. 'fathers') in MT to a slip of the scribal pen, 'perhaps due to a reminiscence of vv. 6–8'. For further discussion, see Barthélemy (1982: 174–175).
56. See, e.g., 1 Kgs 11:30–32; 13:3, 5; 2 Kgs 19:29; 20:8–9.

commitment: *serve the* LORD *with all your heart* (v. 20). Twice he enjoins the people not to turn away from Yahweh (vv. 20–21). Twice he enjoins them to serve Yahweh *with all your heart* (*běkol-lěbabkem*, vv. 20, 24). Idols (*tōhû*, empty nothings) *can do you no good, nor can they rescue you* (v. 21). In contradistinction to the counterfeit gods, Yahweh offers solid hope, hope as sure as his name and his sovereign freedom: *For the sake of his great name the* LORD *will not reject his people, because the* LORD *was pleased to make you his own* (v. 22). Samuel, too, commits to doing his part, to pray and to *teach you the way that is good and right*. He is emphatic in his commitment – *As for me, far be it from me . . .* – for to fail to do these things would be to *sin against the* LORD (v. 23). Samuel is not retiring from public life, but his leadership role is changing. After one final encouragement to *consider what great things he has done for you* (v. 24), Samuel concludes with a sober warning: *if you persist in doing evil, both you and your king will perish* (v. 25).

Meaning

Long and halting has been Saul's rise to the throne, from his initial anointing (9:1 – 10:16), to his public selection by lot met by mixed reviews (10:17–27), to his eventual dramatic victory and winning of solid public support (11:1–15). By the end of 1 Samuel 11, Saul and all the people are celebrating the inauguration of his kingship. No longer merely king-designate (*nāgîd*), Saul is fully king (*melek*), at least in the eyes of the people. But what about in the eyes of Yahweh and his prophet Samuel? The long 'covenant renewal ceremony' recounted in 1 Samuel 12 reminds the people of several things: Samuel's unimpeachable record (vv. 1–5); Yahweh's provision of good leaders from the beginning of Israel's history as a people (vv. 6–8); and Yahweh's continued provision of good leaders even in the troubled period of the judges (vv. 9–11). Against this backdrop, the people's insistence on a human king 'such as other nations have' is shown to be a faithless act of rebellion, nothing less than a rejection of Yahweh as king (v. 12; cf. 8:7). Nevertheless, Yahweh has acquiesced to their request. And so kingship can flourish, but it cannot be 'kingship as usual', kingship as practised among the nations. Israel's king can flourish only if he assumes the posture of a vice-regent and remains attentive and obedient to the continuing rule of Yahweh (vv. 13–15). Prophetic word and sign (vv. 16–18) have the desired effect on the people (v. 19), so the assembly ends with words of comfort and encouragement (vv. 20–24). The account notes the people's response here and there but says nothing of Saul's response. Is he still 'as one keeping silent' (10:27)? Samuel's final words underscore the fact that the ultimate fate of the people and their king still hangs in the balance (v. 25).

3. THE PEOPLE'S KING: THE REIGN AND REJECTION OF KING SAUL (1 SAMUEL 13:1 – 15:35)

A. Saul versus the Philistines: Saul's first rejection (13:1 – 14:52)

Context

The ceremony of 1 Samuel 12 brought the period of the judges to an end and established in no uncertain terms what it would take for a king in Israel to succeed. At each point in Samuel's speeches, the people responded appropriately. They confessed the gravity of their sin in demanding a king of the kind that other nations had. They grasped the significance of the prophetic sign of rain at harvest time and turned to the prophet to pray to Yahweh on their behalf. The people appear to be in the right state of mind. Of Saul's response, however, nothing was said. And this raises a question. Will Saul prove a suitable king for Israel? Will he adopt an appropriate posture as vice-regent, subordinate to the continuing rule of Yahweh?

Not unexpectedly, the drama that will answer these questions is played out in the context of Saul's Philistine wars – we recall that the Philistines were to be the focus of Saul's acts of deliverance, according to 9:16. Moreover, as has been argued above, Saul's first act of daring (his 'demonstration' that he was chosen to lead) should have been an assault on the Philistine presence in Gibeah of God (10:5, 7). Chapters 13 and 14 comprise a single story involving several sequential scenes. The narrative is formally delimited by an opening regnal formula in 13:1 and a closing regnal summary in 14:47–52 and is further bound together by a consistency of characters and setting, thematic continuity, verbal and material links, and a progressive unfolding of plot (see Long 1989: 69–70). The prominence of Saul's son Jonathan in chapter 14 is striking. We shall discover that Saul's words and actions in this crucial section are best understood in the light of the words and actions of his son Jonathan.

Comment
i. Jonathan's first initiative and Saul's response (13:1–23)
1. *Saul was thirty years old when he became king, and he reigned over Israel for forty-two years.* This seemingly simple verse has in fact baffled interpreters both ancient and modern. As the NIV text notes indicate, the numbers *thirty* and *forty* are not actually in the MT. A few late LXX manuscripts supply 'thirty', while 'forty' is surmised by some modern translators on the basis of Acts 13:21, though it is possible that the 'forty' of Acts 13:21 refers to the tenures of both Samuel and Saul combined.[1]

To approach the question properly, then, we must start with what MT actually says: 'Saul was a year old when he became king, and two years he reigned over Israel.' A fairly wide modern consensus assumes that MT is simply defective, having lost or never had the numbers (though the number 'two' is present). NRSV reflects this view, supplying ellipses where the numbers are thought to be missing: 'Saul was . . . years old when he began to reign; and he reigned . . . and two years over Israel.' Among those ancient versions that do not follow MT, LXX simply omits the verse, apart

---

1. See Provan, Long and Longman (2015: 267–268); cf. also Long (1989: 71–75); Long (2009a: 325–326).

from the few late manuscripts mentioned above. The Targum makes Saul like a 'one year old in whom is no sin'. Another correct way to read the first clause, although awkward in English translation, is 'Saul was a son of a year in his becoming king [*bĕmolkô*]' or, more smoothly, 'when he began to reign' (NRSV). The prepositional phrase *bĕmolkô* occurs thirty-nine times in the Old Testament: three times in Samuel (the case before us and 2 Sam. 2:10; 5:4) and the remainder in Kings and Chronicles. Often conjoined to the age of the king at accession, the focus is on the official commencement of the king's reign. For instance, while David is anointed to replace Saul some years before Saul's death, he does not begin to reign as king until he is thirty years old (2 Sam. 5:4). Neiderhiser (1979: 45) glosses *bĕmolkô* as 'in his beginning to function as king'.

While the broad consensus among modern scholars that MT is defective may well be correct, a case can also be made for accepting MT as it stands. Clearly, Saul could not have been a one-year-old in biological terms when he began to reign. But might it not be the case that a year has elapsed since his anointing in chapter 10, when he was radically, if only temporally, changed (10:6, 9)? It was on that occasion that Saul's faltering rise to kingship began. Saul's failure, after his anointing as king-designate (*nāgîd*), to proceed immediately to a public demonstration of his valour slowed the pace of his rise. This necessitated further efforts by Samuel to bring Saul to public attention (as we saw above at 10:17–27). Eventually, Saul did demonstrate his ability to deliver in battle (ch. 11), after which he was confirmed by the people. Now, following Samuel's final exhortations, Saul ascends the throne. Another way to put this is that Saul became king *de jure* at the time of his anointing in 10:1 but not king *de facto* until 13:1. Perhaps Saul was a year old as king *de jure* before becoming king *de facto*.[2]

The second half of 13:1 could then refer to the length of Saul's official reign as king until his definitive rejection in 15:28. After his rejection in chapter 15, Saul refuses to step down, and so remains

---

2. For more extended discussion, see Long (1989: 71–75); Provan, Long and Longman (2015: 266–268).

king *de facto*. But the rightful king, in God's eyes (the king *de jure*), becomes David when he is anointed in 16:1–13. The reading suggested here was arrived at on the basis of the logic of the preceding context. But there is also, as it turns out, considerable precedent in early Jewish interpretation for adopting this kind of reading, stretching all the way back to the second-century Seder Olam Rabbah.[3] Medieval commentator Isaac Abravanel (1437–1508) proffered a reading quite similar to the one proposed here (Long 1989: 75 n. 30).

2. The purpose of Saul's deployment of troops is not stated. His son Jonathan is mentioned here for the first time, and without introduction, suggesting that he would have been well known to readers. That Saul and Jonathan are both in charge of troops sets up a comparison (or contrast) that will be developed throughout 1 Samuel 13 – 14 and, indeed, throughout the Saul story until their deaths in chapter 31. *Michmash* (mod. Mukhmas) is a hilltop village some 7 miles north-east of Jerusalem, while Geba/*Gibeah* (mod. Jeba) lies just a couple of miles south-west of Michmash. Between the two towns runs the Wadi Suweinit, whose valley provides a route for travel between the Jordan Valley and the central hill country.

3–4. *Jonathan attacked the Philistine outpost at Geba* (v. 3). Whether Jonathan is acting on orders from his father or, as later (14:1), on his own initiative is not made clear. Either way, it is noteworthy that he does what, according to our interpretation, Saul should have done at the time of his anointing (cf. 10:7 in view of 10:5). *Then Saul had the trumpet blown throughout the land* (v. 3). The trumpet was a standard signalling device in times of war (cf. 2 Sam. 2:28; 18:16; 20:1, 22). *Let the Hebrews hear!* (v. 3).[4] Saul has the message disseminated that *Saul has attacked the Philistine outpost* (v. 4), which is

---

3. Accessible in English translation in Guggenheimer (2005: 131–132); critical text in Milikowsky (2013: 260 [Hebrew]).
4. On the textual uncertainties surrounding this phrase – i.e. whether it is what the Philistines heard or the Israelites, and whether it should be read 'the servants [reading '*bdym* instead of '*brym*] have revolted' (following LXX) – see Long (1989: 79–81); Tsumura (2007: 336–338).

true at best in an indirect sense (was Jonathan acting under orders?). The result of Jonathan's defiant act is as anticipated – the Philistines are provoked – and so Saul repairs to Gilgal to rendezvous with Samuel (in keeping with the second stage of his initial charge; see 10:8). There he summons the people to join him. It is occasionally suggested that Saul's abandoning the hill country to descend into the Jordan Valley makes no sense militarily, but this is not true. Gilgal provides a safe location for an assembly and general muster beyond immediate threat from the Philistines. It is worth noting that the Philistines themselves in verse 5 first assemble to fight Israel (presumably in some safe location) and only then go up and camp at Michmash. Gilgal, moreover, with its deep significance in Israel's earlier history (Josh. 4:19–20; 5:10; 9:6; 10:6–15, 43; 1 Sam. 7:16; 11:14), is a very fitting place for Saul's suitability as king to be put to the test.

5–7a. The Philistines respond to the Israelite affront by mustering chariots, charioteers and *soldiers as numerous as the sand on the seashore* (v. 5).[5] NIV's *three thousand chariots* (following LXX and Syr.) is a tenth the size of MT's 'thirty thousand chariots'. Both numbers seem large by comparative standards.[6] It may be that 'thousands' should be rendered 'units' (Tsumura 2007: 338–339).[7] The key point is that the Philistine response is overwhelming, and the Israelites are indeed overwhelmed. *When the Israelites saw . . . that their army was hard pressed [niggaś], they hid* in every available hiding place, natural or man-made (v. 6). *Some Hebrews [ʿibrîm] even crossed [ʿāberû] the Jordan* (v. 7a). The designation *Hebrews* is usually found in the mouths of Israel's adversaries, but the narrator's use here may be in the interest of punning on the root *ʿbr*, 'cross over' (cf. Alter 1999: 71).

7b–12. *Saul remained at Gilgal* (v. 7b), to which he had repaired (v. 4) immediately following Jonathan's throwing down the gauntlet to the Philistines (v. 3). His troops are still with him, but *quaking*

---

5. For this hyperbolic expression, see Gen. 22:17; Josh. 11:4; 1 Kgs 4:29.
6. Long (2009a: 327–328), which see for a discussion of the use of chariotry in hill-country environments.
7. On this point, see at 4:2; 6:19.

with fear.[8] Saul is waiting for Samuel to arrive, according to *the time set by Samuel* (v. 8). NIV's *time* renders Hebrew *môʿēd*, which in a context such as this refers to an 'appointment' (or 'meeting'), which naturally involves a set time and place. Recalling Saul's first charge at the time of his anointing, we find in 10:8 the 'appointment' to which reference is here made. Once the provocative act of attacking the Philistine garrison was accomplished (i.e. the command of 10:7 fulfilled by Jonathan in 13:3), Saul's next move was to go to Gilgal, where he was to wait seven days until Samuel should arrive, as stipulated in 10:8. The reason for this appointed meeting with Samuel was to consecrate the forthcoming battle with sacrifices and to provide Saul with further instructions.[9]

When Samuel is late arriving and the pressures are mounting, Saul calls for the *burnt offering and the fellowship offerings* (v. 9) and begins the sacrifice without Samuel, who arrives just as Saul has completed the first set of sacrifices (v. 10). To Samuel's dismayed *What have you done?* (v. 11), Saul is ready with answers: Saul's men were *scattering*, Samuel was late in arriving and pressure from the Philistines *assembling at Michmash* was mounting. In the light of these factors, Saul continues, *I felt compelled to offer the burnt offering* (v. 12). Saul is not here admitting to having 'forced' himself against his conscience (as many translations seem to assume; e.g. NRSV, ESV, JPS) but, rather, is claiming to have pulled himself together in the face of great pressure and to have done what had to be done.[10]

13–14. Despite the prima facie plausibility of Saul's explanation of his actions, Samuel responds, *You have done a foolish thing* (v. 13).

---

8. Joo (2010) argues on grammatical grounds that the people were 'like Saul' in their fear of the Philistines.

9. Attempts to loosen the link between 10:8 and 13:8 (cf. Tsumura 2007: 343–344) are unnecessary, once the pattern of provocation followed by convocation is recognized and the Philistine focus of Saul's first charge is recalled.

10. Apart from the present instance, each of the other six occurrences of the hitpaʿel of the verb *'pk* in the OT suggests an act of self-restraint. For defence of this understanding also in the present passage, see Long (1989: 89–90).

Folly always entails a degree of culpability, but the focus here is on Saul's lack of perception regarding his responsibilities as king. Some have suggested that Saul's error was in arrogating to himself the duties of a priest.[11] But this does not square well with the fact that kings elsewhere offer sacrifices without censure (14:33–35; 2 Sam. 6:13, 17; 1 Kgs 8:62–63). In any case, Samuel's explicit censure of Saul lies elsewhere: *You have not kept the command the LORD your God gave you* (v. 13). This statement has baffled commentators, who suggest that the nature of this *command* is unknown and unknowable.[12] The view argued in the present commentary, however, is that the *command*, or 'charge' (*miṣwâ*), is precisely the charge given Saul at the time of his anointing (i.e. 10:7–8). This charge was specifically designed to test Saul's suitability as a vassal king who would rule in submission to Yahweh. The point of 10:8 – the second half of Saul's two-part charge – was not simply that he should wait seven days but that he should wait until Yahweh's prophet arrived and provided further instructions. Samuel's late arrival, whether intentional on Samuel's part or simply providentially arranged, put Saul to the test, and he failed.

The result of Saul's failure is that his *kingdom will not endure* (v. 14). Kingship in the Ancient Near East was typically dynastic, and this certainly seems to be the expectation in ancient Israel; Deuteronomy 17:20 underscores obedience to the divine command as assuring both the king and his descendants of a long rule over Israel (cf. Avioz 2005: 5–6). Saul certainly assumes that Jonathan should succeed him (20:30–31). But Saul's folly means that this will not be the case: *the LORD has sought out a man after his own heart* (v. 14). McCarter (1980: 229) is correct in asserting that *after his own heart* means 'of his own choosing', but he overstates the case when he insists that 1 Samuel 13:14b 'has nothing to do with any great fondness of Yahweh's for David or any special quality of David, to

---

11. Cf. Josephus, *Ant.* 6.102; for discussion, see Begg (1999: 695).
12. E.g. Brueggemann (1990: 100) characterizes Samuel's indictment of Saul for not having 'kept the commandment of the LORD your God' as 'a remarkable statement because Samuel cites no commandment that has been broken, nor can we construe one'.

whom it patently refers'. Despite his evident flaws, David will be portrayed as in sync with the divine will and purpose in a way that Saul never is. And this will play some part in his being appointed as Israel's new *ruler* (*nāgîd*) and, in due course, in his becoming Yahweh's anointed. As 16:7 famously states, *People look at the outward appearance, but the* LORD *looks at the heart*.[13]

Verse 14 ends where verse 13 began, with an emphasis on Saul's failure to keep Yahweh's *command*/'charge'. Though not apparent in English translation, the four occurrences of the root *ṣwh* in verses 13–14 underscore the gravity of this failure: your not keeping the 'charge' (*miṣwâ*) with which the Lord 'charged you' (*ṣiwwāk*) means that he has 'charged' another (*wayĕṣawwēhû*), because you did not keep that with which Yahweh 'charged you' (*ṣiwwĕkā*).

15. *Then Samuel left Gilgal and went up to Gibeah in Benjamin.* So reads MT, but in verse 16 it is Saul, not Samuel, who is in Gibeah with Jonathan. A few have argued that the grammatical subject of verse 15 should be Saul, not Samuel, but there is no manuscript support for this speculation (see Barthélemy 1982: 180). LXX offers an attractive, longer reading that is adopted by NRSV and a number of other translations and commentators: 'And Samuel left and went on his way from Gilgal. The rest of the people followed Saul to join the army; they went up from Gilgal toward Gibeah of Benjamin' (similarly ESV, NLT). MT may have lost the longer reading when a copyist's eye skipped from the first occurrence of 'from Gilgal' to the second, inadvertently omitting the intervening words (for full discussion, see Long 1989: 94–95). Whether the *six hundred* men remaining in Saul's company are a remnant of the original three thousand deployed in 13:2 or the meagre result of the general muster in Gilgal (v. 4b), the day has not gone well, and Saul is sorely overmatched.

16–23. Just how dire Saul's predicament is is made clear in the remainder of 1 Samuel 13. Saul has lost control of Michmash, which

---

13. On 13:14 as implying *both* Yahweh's sovereign choice and something about the state of David's heart, see Long (2009a: 329); cf. George (2002); Johnson (2012b); DeRouchie (2014). And compare also the similar phrase used by Jonathan's armour-bearer in 14:7.

has now been occupied by the Philistines (v. 16). The latter are on the offensive, sending out three *raiding parties* designed either to put pressure on Saul's camp in Gilgal by creating a 'pincer movement' (so Garsiel 1980) or to control passes into the hill country, or both (Long 2009a: 329–330).[14] Not only are the Israelites outnumbered, they are also 'outgunned', as the Philistines have banned blacksmiths from operating in Israel, lest *the Hebrews . . . make swords or spears* (v. 19). Even to have farm implements sharpened, the Israelites are forced to pay exorbitant prices (v. 21). The hapax legomenon *pym* baffled interpreters until archaeologists in the twentieth century began discovering stone weights inscribed with *pym* and weighing *two-thirds of a shekel* (0.268 oz.).[15] The final two verses of the section set up the dramatic events of chapter 14. Only Saul and Jonathan are properly armed (v. 22), so the focus is on king and crown prince. How will they respond to the Philistine menace, most recently underscored by the advance of *a detachment of Philistines . . . to the pass at Michmash* (v. 23)?[16]

ii. Jonathan's second initiative and Saul's response (14:1–52)

1. Not surprisingly in view of his performance in the preceding chapter, *Jonathan* is the one who takes bold action against the Philistines in the present chapter as well. Any glory that might accrue to Saul by virtue of the epithet *son of Saul* attached to Jonathan's name is dimmed by the notice that Jonathan *did not tell his father* of his daring plan. Jonathan's reason for keeping his intentions secret from his father is not stated, but in view of Saul's recent failures, Jonathan's decision not to involve his father may imply a vote of no confidence similar to that evident in Abigail's decision not to tell her husband of her own daring plan in 25:19.

2–5. Verses 2–5 pause to set the scene. Saul is *on the outskirts of Gibeah under a pomegranate tree in Migron* (v. 2). The Hebrew text lacks

---

14. Division of troops into three units was a common ancient practice (cf. Judg. 7:16; 9:43; 1 Sam. 11:11; 2 Sam. 18:2).
15. On Philistine metallurgical superiority, see Youngblood (2009: 140); Long (2009a: 330 and bibliographic footnotes).
16. On this pass, see at 14:4–5.

the word *tree*, and a good case has been made (Arnold 1990) that Saul was in fact in a cave located on the south wall of the Wadi Suweinit (the Migron) that separated Gibeah to the south from Michmash to the north. The cave can still be seen, and its rounded, pitted interior, which resembles an open pomegranate. This may have earned it the name Rimmon (Heb. for 'pomegranate'). Judges 20:47 speaks of six hundred Benjaminites fleeing to the rock of Rimmon, perhaps the cave in question. If Saul and his men are 'in the pomegranate cave at Migron' (so ESV), rather than on a hilltop under a tree, this makes sense of the need for lookouts to report Philistine movements to Saul (14:16). Furthermore, there may be something vaguely unsettling in the reminder of Judges 20, not the most illustrious episode in Benjaminite history.

Also unsettling is the curious description of the priest accompanying Saul. That *Ahijah . . . was wearing an ephod* (v. 3) is in one sense encouraging. The priestly ephod was used in divine enquiry (see on 2:28).[17] Its presence in Saul's camp, therefore, might inspire hope that Saul will yet hear from Yahweh, despite the recent breach with Samuel. But Ahijah's genealogy in verse 3 is curious. It goes out of its way to mention an uncle, namely, *Ichabod* ('no glory'; see on 4:21), and to associate Ahijah with the rejected house of Eli (2:30). This subtly reminds the reader of Saul's own diminished glory in the aftermath of chapter 13 (cf. Jobling 1976: 368).

Verses 4 and 5 dramatize the challenge faced by Jonathan and his armour-bearer in crossing over to the Philistine outpost. A *cliff* (or 'rocky crag'; lit. 'tooth of rock') was on each side of the wadi which the two wished to cross. The meanings of the names of the two teeth of rock, Bozez and Seneh, are uncertain, but the suggestion that Bozez means 'slippery' and Seneh 'thorny' (cf. Stoebe 1973: 258–259) could help explain the narrator's purpose in including these details (v. 4). In the autumn of 1983, the present writer made two visits to the area and was able to confirm that the fissured rock cliffs make the description of Jonathan and his armour-bearer climbing up undetected entirely plausible.[18]

---

17. Cf. David's use of the ephod for divine enquiry in 23:9–12; 30:7–8.
18. For more detailed description of the area, see Long (1989: 106–107).

6–7. After the digression of verses 2–5, the narrative returns to Jonathan's bold proposal of verse 1, which is repeated with the variation that the Philistines are this time referred to as *those uncircumcised men* (v. 6). This is a common term of disparagement for those who stand outside God's covenant (cf. Gen. 17:14; Exod. 12:48; Judg. 14:3; 15:18). Elsewhere in Samuel it is used in the context of David's confidence in the face of Goliath – *Who is this uncircumcised Philistine that he should defy the armies of the living God?* (17:26, cf. 36) – and in Saul's fearful request that he be killed by his armour-bearer rather than fall into the hands of *these uncircumcised fellows* (31:4). In contrast to his father, Jonathan is confident that *Nothing can hinder the LORD from saving, whether by many or by few* (v. 6), and he makes a very different proposition to his armour-bearer, who responds enthusiastically, *I am with you heart and soul* (lit. 'according to your heart', *kilĕbābekā*).[19] By his statement that numbers don't matter when Yahweh determines to save, Jonathan perhaps inadvertently undermines at least one of his father's earlier excuses for not waiting for Samuel, namely, that his troops were deserting (13:11).[20]

8–12a. In yet another contrast to his father (see on 10:8; 13:13–14), Jonathan is intent on discovering Yahweh's will in respect of the anticipated conflict and suggests an ad hoc means of discovery: *if they say, 'Come up to us,' . . . that will be our sign that the LORD has given them into our hands* (v. 10). During the passage across the wadi, Jonathan and his armour-bearer *showed themselves to the Philistine outpost*, and the Philistines mock them as *Hebrews . . . crawling out of the holes they were hiding in* (v. 11; cf. 13:6) and invite them to come up and take a lesson (v. 12), thus unwittingly confirming the sign Jonathan had set (vv. 9–10).

12b–17. Emboldened by the favourable sign (v. 12b), Jonathan ascends *using his hands and feet*, which is to say, he climbs up one of the craggy fissures, *with his armour-bearer right behind him* (v. 13). Probably capitalizing on the element of surprise – Jospehus (*Ant.* 6.113) even imagines the Philistines asleep – Jonathan and his armour-bearer are able to kill *some twenty men in an area of about half*

---

19. For discussion of this expression, see on 13:14.
20. Cf. also Samuel's steadiness under Philistine pressure in 7:10.

an acre (v. 14). The precise sense of the Hebrew of the last phrase is unclear, but the general sense is that 'the Philistines were killed in a brief time and a short distance' (so Youngblood 2009: 142, who suggests that the Hebrew connotes a '"furrowed area" . . . of a field small enough to be ploughed by a yoke of oxen in half a day'). The effect on the remaining Philistines is *panic* throughout *the whole army*. Three times the root *ḥrd* appears in verse 15 (connoting 'trembling', or, as we might say, 'quaking' in fear). Even *the ground shook*, or 'quaked' (different root, *rgz*), and all together this created *a panic sent by God* (or 'a terrible panic', as in NIV note). That the panic is attributed to divine agency is appropriate in this context, though reference to divinity can also serve as an intensifier, as in English expressions such as 'that meal was simply divine'. Perhaps both notions are implied here – magnitude and divine causation (McCarter 1980: 240).

The disturbance in the enemy camp does not go unnoticed by *Saul's lookouts at Gibeah in Benjamin* (v. 16; on the locations of Gibeah and of Saul, see on 13:2 and 14:2). That Saul must muster the troops to discover that Jonathan and his armour-bearer are missing (v. 17) is a reminder of Jonathan's decision not to share his plans with his father (v. 1).

18–19. Saul's response to all the commotion raises a question. Did he order Ahijah to bring *the ark of God* or the 'ephod'? MT attests 'ark' (*'ărôn*) and is followed by a majority of modern translations. LXX has 'ephod' (which in Heb. is *'ēpôd*). Josephus (*Ant.* 6:115) speaks of the garments of the high priesthood, thus implying the ephod. The Targum has Saul call for the 'ark' in verse 18 and the 'ephod' in verse 19.[21] The two words look fairly similar in Hebrew, and thus could be confused. Contextual logic supports reading 'ephod': Ahijah is in possession of the ephod (not ark) in 14:3; comparing 7:1 and 2 Samuel 6:3 suggests that the ark was not in play during Saul's reign (a point made explicitly in 1 Chr. 13:3); the verb rendered *Bring* (*ngš* hip'il) is used in combination with

---

21. The rabbis attempted to devise scenarios whereby both ark and ephod were present (Rosenberg 1980: 108–109). On the possibility that both ephod and ark were on the scene, see also Tsumura (2007: 366).

'ephod' in 23:9 and 30:7, where David calls for the ephod in order to enquire of God; and Saul's ordering Ahijah to *Withdraw your hand* in verse 19 makes far better sense in relation to the sacred lots (Urim and Thummin) contained in the breastpiece of the priestly ephod (de Vaux 1961: 2.351) than in relation to the ark. The strong contextual evidence favouring 'ephod' means, of course, that MT presents the more difficult reading (*lectio difficilior*) and for that reason is retained by some commentators. Perhaps the text is engaging in a kind of sophisticated word association. The narrative effect of Saul's calling for the 'ark' would be to recall the earlier disastrous episode in 4:3, when the elders of Israel did in fact call for the ark.

Whichever reading is adopted, it is clear that Saul has in mind to enquire of God regarding his next move. The increasing *tumult in the Philistine camp*, however, prompts Saul to abort the procedure – *Withdraw your hand* (v. 19). And this reflects poorly on Saul. While he had waited seven days in chapter 13 for Samuel to arrive (though falling short when Samuel was late and the pressures were mounting), in the present context he succumbs to circumstantial pressure much sooner (see also 14:36 and comment).

20–24. As *Saul and all his men* enter the fray, they find the Philistines *in total confusion* (v. 20). This is the *panic sent by God* mentioned in verse 15. Such is the Philistines' disorientation (*mĕhûmâ*, a different word for panic from the 'trembling' of v. 15) that they are fighting one another. Israel's army is only gaining in strength, reversing the trend in chapter 13, with *Hebrews* returning to Israel (v. 21; see 13:7) and formerly frightened Israelites coming out of hiding to join the rout of the Philistines (v. 22). *So on that day the* LORD *saved Israel* (v. 23). Despite the heroism of Jonathan and his armourbearer, the focus of the narrative remains firmly theological.[22]

Saul, for his part, continues to disappoint. Verse 24 presents some interpretational challenges. LXX, for instance, says nothing of the Israelites being *in distress that day*, but asserts, rather, that Saul

---

22. Israel's battles are consistently regarded in Samuel as the battles of Yahweh, and it will be chiefly David who fights them (25:28; cf. 17:45; 18:17; 30:26).

committed a great folly (lit. 'was ignorant with a great ignorance', *ēgnoēsen agnoian megalēn*). Among modern translations, NRSV follows LXX: 'Now Saul committed a very rash act on that day.' Most modern translations, however, stick with MT and read something like *Now the Israelites were in distress that day* (NIV; similarly, JPS, NASB, etc.). *In distress* renders Hebrew *niggaś* ('hard pressed'). The key question is what caused the distress. Most interpretations assume that the distress was caused by Saul's binding the people *under an oath* not to eat anything *before evening comes, before I have avenged myself on my enemies* (v. 24). But this common understanding (reflected in NIV, JPS, NASB, NKJV, NLT, to name a few) is out of accord with normal Hebrew grammar. The second clause of verse 24 begins with a *wayyiqtōl* verbal form, the normal sense of which is to express 'actions, events, or states, which are to be regarded as the temporal or logical sequel of actions, events, or states mentioned immediately before' (GKC §111a). In other words, Saul's oath is *in response to* the distress of the people, *not its cause*.[23] Verse 24 is best read as a flashback to earlier in the day, before the Philistine rout was in full swing. Apart from its occurrence in 14:24, the verb *niggaś* occurs only one other time in Samuel, namely, in 13:6. There Jonathan's provocation of the Philistines in 13:3 placed the Israelites in serious jeopardy and prompted many to hide or flee. Discovery that Jonathan is again out making mischief (14:1, 16–17) will have done little to calm Israelite nerves, and Saul's truncation of the divine enquiry (vv. 18–19) can only have made matters worse. Saul's imposition of an oath, then, was apparently designed to force frightened troops to prosecute the battle by threatening them with a curse if they didn't. This understanding of verse 24 is now followed by various commentators (e.g. Gordon 1986: 138–139; Vannoy 2009: 130) and is reflected in the ESV:

> And the men of Israel had been hard pressed that day, so Saul had laid an oath on the people, saying, 'Cursed be the man who eats food until it is evening and I am avenged on my enemies.' So none of the people had tasted food.

---

23. For detailed discussion, see Long (1989: 114–117).

As becomes clear as the narrative continues, Saul's oath has the opposite of its desired effect.

25–30. Having already slipped away with his armour-bearer prior to Saul's placing the people under oath (see above), Jonathan has *not heard that his father had bound the people with an oath* (v. 27). And so he does not hesitate to refresh himself with some honey he fortuitously encounters in the woods (vv. 25–26). Immediately informed of his father's *strict oath* by *one of the soldiers* (v. 28), Jonathan responds that *My father has made trouble for the country* (v. 29). Specifically, the magnitude of the victory over the Philistines is less than it might otherwise have been (v. 30). Saul's denial of nourishment along the way is *why the men are faint* (v. 28).

The significance of this short section is reinforced by several instances of literary artifice – namely, the nearly homonymous *ya'ar* (*woods*) of verses 25–26 and *ya'rat* (*honeycomb*) of verse 27, and the consonantal reversals in *ṭā'amtî mĕ'aṭ* (*I tasted a little*) of verse 29. There are also six occurrences in verses 24–29 of significant words involving the Hebrew consonants Aleph (') and Resh (*r*): fear (*yr'*), curse (*'rr* 2x), brightening (*'wr* 2x) of the eyes and see (*r'h*) (Long 1989: 120). Even the unusual choice of the verb *nśg* in verse 26 to describe each soldier's refusal to *put his hand to his mouth* may offer a subtle reminder of the distress, *ngś*, in which Saul's forces found themselves that day (v. 24; cf. 13:6). All this literary crafting underscores the importance of the section.

31–35. Eventually, very exhausted from the 20-mile pursuit from the area of *Michmash to Aijalon* in the west (v. 31; cf. v. 28), the Israelites pounce on the plunder, butcher some livestock and begin to eat them, *together with the blood* (v. 32). Whether they are prompted by Jonathan's example or because evening has fallen and the oath is no longer in force,[24] the people's consuming meat with the blood still in it was contrary to pervasive biblical law (e.g. Gen. 9:4; Lev. 3:17; 7:26–27; 17:10, 12; Deut. 15:23; Ezek. 33:25).[25] When told

---

24. Cf. Gordon (1986: 140) who draws attention to the reference to *night* in v. 36.
25. On the grounds for this prohibition in the OT and throughout the ANE, see Long (2009a: 336).

what the people are doing, Saul charges them with having *broken faith* (v. 33), organizes an impromptu mode of slaughtering the animals more properly and charges the people not to *sin against the* LORD *by eating meat with blood still in it* (v. 34). It is hard to know how to read Saul's behaviour here. It may be sincerely intended. But, given his responsibility for the way the day has unfolded, his actions are hardly above reproach. Nor will his actions be above reproach in the next chapter, where Saul himself will be charged with pouncing upon the spoil (cf. 15:19 with 14:32; in both instances the rare verb '*yt*, 'to fly upon, swoop upon', is used).[26]

Then Saul built an altar to the LORD; *it was the first time he had done this* (v. 35). This action is also difficult to assess. No further altars built by Saul are ever mentioned, and it is quite possible that the Hebrew should be read, 'Then Saul built an altar to the LORD; that is, he began to build it, an altar to the LORD' (but didn't finish it).[27]

36–46. *Let us go down and pursue the Philistines by night* (v. 36). Saul's enthusiasm to continue the pursuit and plundering of the Philistines is understandable, and the people are in agreement: *Do whatever seems best to you*. The priest intervenes, however: *Let us enquire of God here* (v. 36). Some think the text must be confused at this point. Budde (1902: 100–101; cf. Hertzberg 1964: 116), for instance, proposes emending the text to have Saul instruct the priest, which he regards as more appropriate. But this misses the point the narrator seems to be making. Saul's commitment to hearing from Yahweh has been tested and found wanting in the past: in 13:8–11 he waited seven days but not until Samuel arrived; in 14:18–19 he called for the ephod but aborted the enquiry midstream. Now he doesn't even think to enquire and must be reminded by the priest. The trajectory suggests a declining commitment on Saul's part to submitting his rule to the divine will.

---

26. Cf. Smelik (1977: 128); Gordon (1984: 58); Long (1989: 121).
27. Targ. and LXX lend some support to this reading. See further Long (1989: 121–123). This basic approach was taken also by Isaac Abrabanel (cited in Rosenberg 1980: 114–115) and has been adopted by various recent commentators, e.g. Bodner (2008: 142); Woodhouse (2008: 592 n. 4); Vannoy (2009: 135).

Once reminded, Saul enquires of God but receives no answer (v. 37). Divine silence can indicate judgment (cf. Samuel's warning of the people in 8:18), and on the only other occasion when Saul is said to enquire of God (28:6) the correlation of silence and judgment is evident. Here Saul assumes that cultic infraction must be responsible for the divine silence, and so he determines to discover by lot who the culprit is (v. 38). He insists that *even if the guilt lies with my son Jonathan, he must die*. Though the people are sometimes quite happy to go along with Saul (cf. *Do whatever seems best to you* in v. 36 and again in v. 40), here *not one of them said a word* (v. 39). The description of Saul's prayer in MT verse 41 is quite cryptic, *hābâ tāmîm*, yielding something like 'give a perfect [lot?]' (cf. NASB, NKJV). LXX offers a much longer reading:

> And Saoul [Saul] said, 'O Lord God of Israel, why is it that you have not answered your slave today? If this guilt is in me or in my son Ionathan [Jonathan], O Lord God of Israel, give clear ones, and if this is what you say, "In your people Israel," give, now, holiness.' And Ionathan and Saoul were indicated by the lot, and the people were cleared. (NETS)

Despite the evident uncertainty about how to render Urim and Thummim ('clear ones' and 'holiness', respectively),[28] LXX may suggest the more original reading. The longer reading attested by LXX may have been lost in MT via homoeoteleuton when a copyist's eye skipped from the first occurrence of 'Israel' to the third. The longer reading is reflected in the NIV, NRSV, ESV, and so on.

Ultimately the lot falls on Jonathan (v. 42), and in answer to Saul's interrogation, Jonathan responds, *ṭā'ōm ṭā'amtî . . . mĕ'aṭ . . . 'āmût*, 'I surely tasted . . . a little . . . I must die' (v. 43). The use of assonance in Jonathan's reply draws attention to the link between crime and punishment (and indeed to its disproportionality). The last word might also be rendered, 'must I die?' Saul is convinced that Jonathan must and swears an oath to that effect (v. 44). The

---

28. LXX shows similar uncertainty in other references to the Urim and Thummim (Exod. 28:30; Lev. 8:8; Deut. 33:8; Ezra 2:63; Neh. 7:65).

people, who often enough go along with Saul (vv. 36, 40), move from their earlier silence at the mention of Jonathan (v. 39) now to open defiance of Saul: *Never! As surely as the* LORD *lives, not a hair of his head shall fall to the ground, for he did this today with God's help* (v. 45). Jonathan, not Saul, is the one leading as God directs. Saul's initiatives, as Jonathan earlier noted, have only *made trouble for the country* (v. 29).[29] As the account of the battle of Michmash draws to a close, we find Saul estranged not just from Samuel, but also from Jonathan, and even from his own troops. He will be given second chances, however, by his troops, his son (e.g. 20:2) and even by Samuel (ch. 15).

Then Saul stopped pursuing the Philistines (v. 46). From the start, the chief focus of Saul's delivering of Israel was to be the Philistines (cf. 9:16). They are the first to be mentioned after Saul's ascent to the throne. But despite its dramatic beginning, catalysed by two bold ventures by Jonathan (13:3; 14:6, etc.), the battle of Michmash ends rather weakly. It will remain for David ultimately to deal with the Philistines.

47–52. *After Saul had assumed rule over Israel, he fought against their enemies on every side* (v. 47). That a proleptic summary of Saul's accomplishments, family and chief military officer is offered so early in the account of his reign is perhaps a signal that the focus will not long remain on him, though he will remain on the throne for a number of years. Already in chapter 13, notice was given of a man of Yahweh's own choosing, *a man after his own heart* (13:14). And in chapter 15, the reader will be cued to begin looking for Saul's replacement, one of Saul's *neighbours* who is better than he (15:28). In the present summary, the listing of Israel's *enemies on every side* offers no surprises. More intriguing is the Hebrew describing Saul's treatment of them: *Wherever he turned, he inflicted punishment on them* (Heb. *yaršîaʿ*). The Hebrew term is unusual in such contexts,

---

29. Links between the present account and the story of Achan, the quintessential troubler of Israel in Josh. 7, are frequently noted by commentators, as indeed are the links with Saul's own selection by lot in 10:17–27. See, e.g., Blenkinsopp (1964: 428–429); Long (1989: 119–120, 216); and most recently, Michael (2013).

prompting many to follow LXX in reading a *waw* (*w*) in place of *resh* (*r*) and revocalizing as *yiwwāšēaʿ* (Gk *esōzeto*, 'he was being saved').³⁰ Others retain the Hebrew and understand it as a 'declarative' hipʿil: 'pronounce guilty', 'cause to be condemned' (cf. *HALOT* s.v.). Alternatively, the hipʿil may be understood as 'internally transitive': 'make oneself guilty' (ibid.). Given the rather negative portrayal of Saul in chapters 13–14, the ambiguity of what is said of Saul's performance is at least worth noting: wherever he turned, was Saul inflicting punishment, being saved or making himself guilty? Also worrying is the fact that, unlike the summary of David's victories and officers in 2 Samuel 8, there is here no mention of Yahweh giving victory (contrast *The LORD gave David victory wherever he went* in both 2 Sam. 8:6 and 8:14; cf. 1 Sam. 18:12, 14, 28).³¹

Picking up on the inconclusive results reported in verse 46, the final verse of the chapter notes that *All the days of Saul there was bitter war with the Philistines*, though Saul continues to add worthy soldiers to his service (v. 52).

Meaning
The story of Saul's Philistine war, framed as it is by an introductory regnal formula and a concluding summary of Saul's deeds, signals in many respects why Saul will not succeed as king in Israel. His evident weaknesses are made all the more obvious by the contrasting actions of his son Jonathan. As noted in our discussion of Samuel's speech to people and king in chapter 12, Israel can thrive under a human king only if both people and king continue to follow the Lord. In this respect, Jonathan in 13:3 not only does what Saul should have done in response to his original commission in 10:7, but in 14:6–10 goes out of his way to discover whether the Lord would have him and his armour-bearer venture forth against the Philistines. Saul, by contrast, shows a declining commitment to hearing from the Lord (see at 14:36). Pressured circumstances regularly trump his concern for divine guidance. With respect to

---

30. For further attempted solutions involving emendations, see Tsumura (2007: 382–383 n. 108).
31. See further at 2 Sam. 8:6.

Samuel's role in the rise and fall of King Saul, it has often been observed that, despite pre-monarchic precursors, the prophetic office came into its own with the establishment of kingship in Israel (e.g. Westermann 1960: 70; Cross 1973: 223; Long 1989: 61–65). In some recent writing on the book of Samuel, the prophet Samuel has been criticized as an uncaring, power-preserving political animal. But this approach is misguided. Samuel's dealings with Saul in the episode just completed and in the one that follows in chapter 15 are not to be read as self-serving but as God-serving.

B. Saul versus the Amalekites: Saul's second rejection (15:1–35)

Context
Things have not gone well for Saul in the earliest recorded events following his enthronement, or even since his anointing. We have noted his faltering in the aftermath of his anointing and commission in chapter 10. We have seen his failure in chapter 13 to wait for Samuel to arrive. This failure signalled a lack of seriousness about hearing from God's appointed spokesman. Numerous writers characterize Saul's failures in chapter 13 as trivial, but we have seen that this is far from the case, provided we understand the nature of Saul's first charge given at the time of his anointing. Samuel's reaction to Saul's failure is sometimes regarded as peevish and petulant. But again, this is wide of the mark. As God's appointed messenger, the prophet Samuel was called to fulfil not only pleasant but sometimes unpleasant duties. He was used to designate leaders but also to pronounce their rejection when necessary. After Saul's failure in chapter 13, it is clear that he will not establish a dynasty (13:13–14), but Saul himself is not yet deposed. As chapter 15 opens, Samuel's hope that Saul might yet succeed is evident in his emphatic plea that Saul even now listen to the voice of the Lord.

Comment
1–3. *I am the one the* LORD *sent to anoint you king over his people Israel* (v. 1a). Samuel's words are even more emphatic in Hebrew than in English translation, as indeed is his instruction to *listen now to the*

message from the LORD (v. 1b). Verse 1 piles more than enough words together, literally 'listen to the sound of the words of the LORD'. Samuel's intensity, akin to 'read my lips', comes as no surprise, since Saul has proved inattentive in the past. The combination of the verb *šāmaʿ* ('listen, hear, heed') with the object *qôl* ('sound, voice') recurs significantly in chapter 15 in several senses (vv. 1, 14, 19, 20, 22, 24) and underscores the central theme of 'obedience' to the Lord's instructions.

This is what the LORD *Almighty says: 'I will punish the Amalekites for what they did to Israel'* (v. 2). If the Philistines came to represent the chief opponents of God's people once 'in' the land of promise, the Amalekites occupied a similar position in the early history of God's people when they were en route from Egypt 'to' the land of promise. For their aggression, the Amalekites fell under God's curse (see Exod. 17:8–16; Num. 24:20; Deut. 25:19). *Now go, attack the Amalekites and totally destroy [ḥrm* hipʿil *] all that belongs to them* (v. 3). Treatment of defeated foes varied in the ancient world, and indeed in the book of Samuel, but placing particularly dangerous or unrelenting enemies under the 'ban' (or *ḥērem*) was not unknown[32] and would not have elicited the same visceral reaction as it does amongst modern peoples. Saul's orders are that he should act as Yahweh's agent of judgment against this 'archetypal implacable enemy of Israel' (Alter 1999: 87). 'The severity of the treatment of the Amalekites commanded by Yahweh here must be seen in the light of their initial and ongoing opposition to Israel (see, e.g., Judg. 3:13; 6:3–5, 33; 7:12; 10:12)' (Long 2009a: 337).[33]

4–6. Whether *ʾelep* should be read as 'thousands' or as 'units' in verse 4, the twenty-to-one ratio of northerners to southerners may reflect the heart of Saul's power base and may also suggest an attempt to curry favour with the south, as the Amalekites were

---

32. So far, the only known extra-biblical reference to *ḥrm* occurs in line 17 of the Mesha Inscription (ninth century BC).

33. For the rationale for and nature of *ḥērem* warfare, see Deut. 7:1–6; 20:16–17. And on the heinousness of the Amalekites' aggression that earned them the status of 'enemies of YHWH', see Stern (1991: 173–174 and *passim*).

largely a southern problem (cf. Firth 2009: 173). That Saul alerts the Kenites of what he is about to do, explaining that *you showed kindness to all the Israelites when they came up out of Egypt* (v. 6),[34] shows that he understands why he is being sent against the Amalekites. This makes his laxity in following orders (see below) all the more inexcusable. The Kenites seem to have been a semi-nomadic people associated with metal-smithing and attested predominantly in southern parts of Palestine. Though associated with the Amalekites (e.g. Num. 24:20–21), the Kenites were quite unlike the Amalekites, in that they were friendly towards the Israelites.

7–9. Saul's prosecution of the battle against the Amalekites *from Havilah to Shur* (v. 7) indicates an extensive campaign in the Negeb, even if specific site identifications are uncertain. Though the Amalekites were roundly defeated, *Saul and the army spared Agag and the best of the sheep and cattle*, and so on (v. 9). Only what was *despised and weak* did they destroy (v. 9). Saul will later try to blame the people for sparing the livestock (see vv. 15, 24), but the narrator in verse 8 makes Saul solely responsible for sparing King Agag. *Agag* was either a personal name or a title (cf. the usage of 'Pharaoh' for Egyptian kings). An earlier Agag is mentioned in Numbers 24:7, and in a much later time, the infamous Haman of the book of Esther is described as an 'Agagite' (Esth. 3:1, 10 and *passim*). Josephus (*Ant.* 11.209) assumes Haman to be an Amalekite descendant of Agag. In the story of Esther, this Haman is bent on utterly destroying the Jews, but in a fitting irony it is another son of Kish, the Jew Mordecai (Esth. 2:5), who turns the tables on him.

10–11. Saul's motivation for sparing Agag and the best of the livestock is not explained (though Saul will later make his excuses). Perhaps greed played a part (as in Joshua 7 in the case of Achan, who coveted 'banned' spoil), or pride, Saul wishing to parade Agag as a trophy of war, or even politics (cf. Ahab's sparing of Ben-Hadad in 1 Kgs 20:32–34). Whatever motivated Saul's disobedience, the Lord is not pleased: *I regret [nḥm nipʻal] that I have made Saul king, because he has turned away from me and has not carried out my instructions*

---

34. A reference perhaps to the kindness of Moses' Kenite father-in-law as described in Exod. 18 (see also Judg. 1:16).

(v. 11). Whatever Saul may yet have to say in an attempt to justify his actions, the divine verdict has already been rendered: Saul has turned away from Yahweh and disobeyed him, a damning indictment in view of the requirements of a successful reign as stipulated in 12:14–15.

Samuel's response is anger and outcry *to the* LORD *all that night*. The nature of Samuel's anger and the content of his outcry are, as Alter (1999: 89) puts it, 'wonderfully unspecified'. This being so, it is best to hold our speculations lightly. At the end of chapter 15 and again at the beginning of chapter 16, we find Samuel mourning for Saul. This lends support to the speculation that Samuel's anger may have been with the entire state of affairs – Saul has failed and God regrets having made him king. His outcry may contain a hint of exasperation for all the efforts expended futilely, it seems. Or it may contain a plea that the situation yet be rescued. But we are not told.[35]

12. Samuel's rising early, especially after a largely sleepless night, suggests his resolute determination to set about the task that fell to him as God's prophet, even if it be an unpleasant one (cf. Abraham's rising early in Gen. 22:3). On his way *to meet Saul*, Samuel is informed of what Saul had been doing, before eventually going *on down to Gilgal*. At *Carmel*, a town not to be confused with Mount Carmel but, rather, the Carmel associated with the churlish Nabal in 25:2, Saul had apparently busied himself erecting *a monument* [*yād*] *in his own honour* (lit. 'to himself'). Although common enough amongst Israel's neighbours, the erection of victory stelae in one's own honour does not appear to have been an approved practice in Israel; the reason is obvious in a conceptual environment where it was understood that victory belonged to the Lord. The nearest parallel to Saul's action here is Absalom's setting up a pillar 'to/for himself' in *the King's Valley* in 2 Samuel 18:18. Indications are that the imminent encounter between Samuel and Saul will be no less fraught than the one in chapter 13 was.

13–16. On the occasion of Saul's failure in chapter 13, it was not entirely clear whether his foolish behaviour was witting or

---

35. For a survey of speculations, see, e.g., Bodner (2008: 153–154).

unwitting. In the present context, the same uncertainty obtains. Is Saul's claim to have *carried out the* LORD's *instructions* (v. 13) brazen dissimulation or the mark of a man who seems incapable of grasping what it means to 'listen [*šmʿ*] to the sound [*qôl*] of the words of the LORD' (15:1)? Either way, Samuel's response, citing the bleating (*qôl*) and lowing (*qôl*) that he is hearing (*šmʿ*), underscores the disparity between claim and performance (v. 14). Saul defends his actions first by shifting the blame – *The soldiers brought them* – and then by suggesting that the underlying motivations were honourable in the first place: *they spared the best of the sheep and cattle to sacrifice to the* LORD *your God*. Saul's use of pronouns is worth noting. It is *they* (the soldiers) whose actions are in question, and it is *your* God to whom they ostensibly plan to sacrifice. *We*, however, *totally destroyed the rest* (v. 15).

Given what the reader already knows (including the clear divine pronouncement of Saul's guilt in vv. 10–11), Saul's protestations have a rather hollow ring. *Enough!* (*ḥerep*, 'stop it, desist'). Samuel has heard enough of Saul's evasions and proposes to tell him *what the* LORD *said to me last night*. Unfazed, or momentarily at a loss for words, Saul's reply is a simple *Tell me* (v. 16).

17–19. Samuel's response dismantles Saul's excuses. Whatever Saul's sense of impotence – *small in your own eyes* (v. 17) – his status as *head of the tribes of Israel*, as the Lord's anointed *king over Israel* (v. 17), disallows blame-shifting. It was he who received the order to *completely destroy* [*ḥrm*] *those wicked people, the Amalekites* . . . *until you have wiped them out* (v. 18), and so failure in these regards must be laid at his feet. Some recent commentators have questioned the legitimacy of Samuel's charge and indeed his reliability, noting that his words differ from Yahweh's words in verse 11 (see Bodner 2008: 158, who cites Green and Edelman). But when Yahweh's charge in verse 11 that Saul *has not carried out my instructions* is correlated with the words of instruction themselves in verses 2–3, we discover that Samuel's words are neither more nor less than a fair summary of those instructions. Most significant is the accusing question of verse 19, *Why did you not obey* [*šāmaʿ* plus *qôl*] *the* LORD?, as obedience (*šmʿ* plus *qôl*) was the first and foremost responsibility pressed upon Saul at the very start of the episode (v. 1). A second accusing question, *Why did you pounce on the plunder* . . . ? (v. 19), recalls the identically worded transgression of the people in 14:32, for which Saul accused them of having *broken faith* (14:33).

20–23. *But I did obey* [*šmʿ* plus *qôl*] *the* LORD (v. 20). Not yet willing to concede his guilt, Saul reiterates his excuses forcefully, taking care to sandwich the delicate issue of Agag's survival between two assertions of obedience. NIV unnecessarily reverses the order of the last two clauses; the Hebrew order of all Saul's claims in verse 20 is as follows: I obeyed, went on a mission, brought back Agag, completely destroyed the Amalekites. Saul continues to ascribe responsibility for sparing livestock to the soldiers and to claim that the best were spared *in order to sacrifice them to the* LORD *your God at Gilgal* (v. 21). But this is out of accord with the narrator's description of events in verses 8–9, where both Saul and the army spare Agag and, indeed, *everything that was good*, not just enough for sacrifice.

In reply, Samuel does not contest the veracity of Saul's claims about sacrifice, though he hardly believes them (cf. v. 19). Instead he makes a more fundamental point: *To obey is better than sacrifice* (v. 22). The repugnance to God of ritual performance in the absence of a right heart is a consistent theme in Scripture.[36] The elevated diction of verses 22–23 sets them apart as of particular significance. Verse 23 spells out the gravity of Saul's offences: *rebellion, arrogance* and rejection of *the word of the* LORD. All three, just like divination and idolatry, mark a refusal to bow the knee to Yahweh. Thus, the verdict must fall: *Because you have rejected* [*m's*] *the word of the* LORD, *he has rejected* [*m's*] *you as king* (v. 23).

24–31. The final exchange between Saul and Samuel displays features that have led some commentators to wonder if parts of it have been secondarily inserted. Chief among purportedly problematic features are the following: Saul offers not one but two confessions; Samuel responds not once but twice (and reverses himself); and Samuel's pronouncement in verse 29 that *the Glory of Israel does not lie or change his mind* (*nḥm*, 'repent') seems to contradict verses 11 and 35, where it is expressly stated that Yahweh *regretted* [*nḥm*, 'repent'] *that he had made Saul king* (v. 35). Careful reading of

---

36. See, e.g., Ps. 51:16–17 [Heb. vv. 18–19]; Prov. 15:8; 21:3, 27; Isa. 1:10–17; Jer. 6:19–20; 7:21–26; Hos. 6:6; Amos 5:21–24; Mic. 6:6–8.

these features in context, however, discovers not only that they are coherent as they stand but also that this final exchange is the climax of the episode.

To begin, comparing Saul's first and second confessions is instructive. The first is rather full and fine sounding, though there is also something damning in Saul's admission that he *was afraid of the men and so . . . gave in to them* (v. 24). Still, Saul's plea, *I beg you, forgive my sin and come back with me, so that I may worship the* LORD (v. 25), sounds good on the face of it. So why does Samuel refuse his request to go back with him and, instead, reiterate Saul's rejection (v. 26)? The answer lies in Saul's second confession: *I have sinned. But please honour me before the elders of my people and before Israel; come back with me, so that I may worship the* LORD *your God* (v. 30). We note that a number of things have changed since the first confession. Saul's admission of sin is reduced to one word in Hebrew (*ḥāṭā'tî*), after which the rhetoric turns to Saul's desire to receive honour; this is a shocking request in a book in which honouring God is of paramount importance (cf. 2:30). Again, the pronouns speak volumes: *please honour me before the elders of my people . . . come back with me, so that I may worship* [the Hebrew can mean simply 'bow to'] *the* LORD *your God* (v. 30). The true character of Saul's 'confession' is thus revealed. It is designed to strike a deal that serves Saul's political and Samuel's religious interests. Samuel's initial refusal to return with Saul is indicative of his (correct, it now seems) judgment that Saul's first confession was not sincere. Now that Saul's cards are on the table, Samuel is free to return with (or after) Saul.[37] Samuel must deal with Agag, and he can now do so without giving the impression that Saul's confession somehow mitigates his sentence.

This brings us to the final perplexing feature in the section, namely, Samuel's insistence that God does not *change his mind* (*nḥm*), when in fact *nḥm* appears in verses 11 and 35 with the Lord as subject. The context of each statement is key. Samuel's statement comes in the midst of the dramatic scene in which he, having just reiterated Saul's rejection (v. 26), turns to leave, only to have Saul catch hold of the hem of his robe (v. 27; the Hebrew uses only the

---

37. The Hebrew literally says that Samuel returned 'after Saul' (*'aḥărê šā'ûl*).

pronoun 'he', but Saul is the likeliest agent). Whether intended as an act of submission or of aggression, Saul's catching hold of Samuel's robe causes it to tear, and this tearing is interpreted as a prophetic sign: *Samuel said to him: 'The LORD has torn the kingdom of Israel from you today and has given it to one of your neighbours – to one better than you'* (v. 28). It is at this point that Samuel underscores the irrevocable nature of Saul's rejection as king: *He who is the Glory of Israel does not lie or change his mind; for he is not a human being, that he should change his mind* (v. 29). Neither fine-sounding but insincere confessions nor submissive or (as seems more likely) aggressive physical actions can succeed in 'managing' the Glory of Israel, for he is not subject to manipulation as humans are. It is in this respect that Yahweh does not change his mind. The verdict stands.

In other contexts, sincere petitions can be effective; one thinks, for instance, of Abraham in Genesis 18:20–33, and especially of Moses in Exodus 32:9–14, where *nḥm* is used in verse 14. God's actions are not unchanging, just ever consistent with his character.[38] That he in verses 11 and 35 expresses his repentance/regret for having made Saul king is entirely understandable, now that Saul has demonstrated that he is indeed much like the kings of other nations. As such, he is unfit to rule under Yahweh, because he is unwilling to 'heed his voice'.[39]

32–35. The chapter ends with hapless Agag quite mistaken, if we follow MT, about his fate: *'Surely the bitterness of death is past'* . . . *And Samuel put Agag to death before the LORD at Gilgal* (vv. 32–33). Complexities in how to read MT and some variation in the versions (e.g. LXX lacks *is past*) make certainty about Agag's mood elusive,[40] but, in any case, it was short-lived. Samuel and Saul depart to their respective homes (v. 34) and have no further official encounters

---

38. The OT is replete with instances when Yahweh does or does not *nḥm* ('repent, relent'), depending on circumstances: he does in Judg. 2:18; 2 Sam. 24:16 (par. 1 Chr. 21:15); Jer. 26:13, 19; Joel 2:13–14; Amos 7:3, 6; Jon. 3:9–10; 4:2; he does not in Ezek. 24:14; Amos 1:3, 6, 9, 11, 13; 2:1, 4, 6.
39. On Yahweh's 'repentance' as a kind of 'course correction', see Sonnet (2010).
40. Cf. the translations and, e.g., Tsumura (2007: 409–410).

(the likely sense of v. 35a; Saul and Samuel do find themselves in the same place in ch. 19).

Meaning
Chapter 15 represents a second chance for Saul to prove himself suitable as a king in Israel, but again he fails. The heart of his failure is his neglect of the word of Yahweh. Saul obeys up to a point, but that is the problem. He obeys only up to the point at which other concerns begin to carry more weight. As we have learned in reading the book of Samuel so far, those who give God weight will themselves carry weight, but those who make light of him will themselves be lightweights (cf. 2:30, of which this is a paraphrase). Since ascending the throne, Saul has demonstrated his unsuitability twice, in the battle against the Philistines and in the battle against the Amalekites. On both occasions, Saul makes some effort to obey God – but only up to a point. And over time, that point seems to be reached with increasing speed and ease. In chapter 13 Saul forfeited any possibility of founding a dynasty. In chapter 15 he disqualified himself from *legitimately* continuing to rule. He does, in fact, remain on the throne for many more years, but only by dint of his stubborn determination and defiance of the divine will. He remains king *de facto* after chapter 15, but he is no longer king *de jure*. Yahweh has turned his attention to another, a neighbour who is better suited than Saul.

4. GOD'S KING: THE RISE OF DAVID AND FALL OF SAUL (1 SAMUEL 16:1 – 31:13)

Context

With Saul having shown himself unsuitable to be king in Israel and having been definitively rejected, the narrative now turns its attention to his replacement. The rise of David to the throne will take a long time, not least because Saul refuses to accept his divine rejection and step aside. Unlike the deposed priest Eli, who did not resist his replacement by Samuel, Saul never gives any indication of submitting to the divine will. The words *He is the LORD; let him do what is good in his eyes* (so Eli in 3:18) never pass Saul's lips. Instead, after initially receiving David favourably into his court (16:21–22), Saul soon comes to fear him (18:12, 15, 28–29) and to seek his death (e.g. 18:17, 24–25; 19:1). David, for his part, though occasionally faltering (e.g. 27:1), is overall able to entrust himself to Yahweh during his years on the run from Saul. Even when he is given opportunities to take Saul's life, David refuses to do so (chs. 24 and 26). Only after Saul has taken his own life (31:4) and only after enquiring of the Lord does David begin moving towards the throne (2 Sam. 2:1 and following).

A. David's rise delights all but Saul (16:1 – 18:30)

i. David is anointed by Samuel and enters Saul's court (16:1–23)
Comment

1–3. There is no joy in Saul's failure and rejection, least of all on the part of Samuel, who continues to mourn for him (v. 1; cf. 15:35). But Saul has proven unsuitable, and so Yahweh has chosen for himself (lit. 'seen for me') another to replace him (v. 1).[1] The prepositional phrase 'for me' is not translated by NIV, but in the Hebrew it sets up a nice contrast with the 'for them' designation of Israel's first king (8:22).[2] Saul was the kind of king the people wanted; David is Yahweh's king. It now falls to Samuel to go and anoint David. So Yahweh instructs Samuel, *Fill your horn* [Heb. *qeren*] *. . . and be on your way* (v. 1). The use of *horn* here and in verse 13, rather than *flask* (*pak*), as had been used in Saul's anointing (10:1), resonates with the song of Hannah, where *horn* (*qeren*) is used twice in the sense of 'strength' (2:1, 10). The only other occurrence of *qeren* in 1 and 2 Samuel is in 2 Samuel 22:3, where David echoes themes from the song of Hannah.[3]

If Saul hears about it, he will kill me (v. 2). Samuel's fear of physical violence may tip the scales in the direction of reading the torn robe incident of 15:27 as involving physical aggression on Saul's part. Yahweh offers a cover: *Take a heifer with you and say, 'I have come to sacrifice to the LORD'* (v. 2). Samuel will in fact offer a sacrifice, but his primary purpose is to anoint Saul's replacement. As the words Samuel is to say are a half-truth at best, this divinely commended stratagem raises ethical eyebrows. But perhaps God's remark that Samuel should mention *sacrifice* is meant to give Saul a bit of his

---

1. As Alter (1999: 95) points out, 'to see' (*rā'â*) is a 'thematically weighted word' in the present chapter, 'just as the previous episode turned on "to listen"'.
2. Cf. 'out of you will come *for me* one who will be ruler of Israel' (Mic. 5:2, emphasis added).
3. I am indebted to my ThM student James Rutherford for drawing my attention to the significance of Samuel's *horn* of oil in recalling these earlier and later contexts.

own medicine, as in the preceding chapter Saul claimed *sacrifice* as his reason for sparing livestock that the Lord had told him to destroy (15:15, 21; cf. Gordon 1986: 150; 2006: 30–31).[4] In the event, Samuel apparently does not encounter Saul on his way to Bethlehem (v. 1). Lying some 6 miles south-west of Jerusalem, Bethlehem figures prominently throughout the Bible: Rachel was buried nearby (Gen. 35:19); Ruth married Boaz there and became an ancestress of David (Ruth 4:11); and Jesus was born in Bethlehem (Matt. 2:5–6; John 7:42) in fulfilment of prophecy (e.g. Mic. 5:2).

4–7. Given the role of the elders in initiating the now apparently failed experiment of kingship (see ch. 8), it comes as no surprise that, upon Samuel's arrival in Bethlehem, *the elders of the town trembled* (v. 4). A visitation from a prophet was not always pleasant (recall the judgment speech to Eli by the man of God in 2:27–34). But judgment was characteristically followed by an act of grace (cf. the promise in 2:35 that the Lord would raise up *a faithful priest, who will do according to what is in my heart and mind*). In the present circumstance, Samuel comes in peace (v. 5) to sacrifice and, as the reader already knows, to anoint a more faithful king. This is an act of grace. The new king will be Yahweh's choice, *a man after his own heart* (13:14; see comment).

Not yet knowing which of Jesse's sons he is to anoint, Samuel is impressed with the eldest, Eliab (v. 6), but *the LORD said to Samuel, 'Do not consider his appearance or his height, for I have rejected him'* (v. 7a). *Rejected* is a strong word for someone who has not yet been chosen, but in combination with the emphasis on Eliab's appearance and height the words are meant to recall Saul and his rejection. The problem in the elders' earlier request for a king like those of the nations, and now even in Samuel's own sizing up of kingly qualities, is that *People look at the outward appearance, but the LORD looks at the*

---

4. For a thorough discussion of divine deception in the book of Samuel, see Newkirk (2015). Other instances of deception in Samuel include 1 Sam. 19:14; 20:6; 21:2; 27:10; 2 Sam. 16:17–19. Each must be judged in terms of its particular circumstances, motivations and outcomes.

heart (v. 7b).[5] As Hannah's story and especially her song powerfully illustrated at the beginning of the book of Samuel, Yahweh is a God who reverses expectations, abases the proud and exalts the humble. In the present episode, he rejects the big and impressive and chooses the small and seemingly insignificant (see below; and on this consistent aspect of the character of God, see 1 Cor. 1:26–31).

8–12. When none of Jesse's seven sons are chosen, Samuel enquires and learns that *There is still the youngest . . . He is tending the sheep* (v. 11). This would make David Jesse's eighth son, which stands in tension with 1 Chronicles 2:13–15, where David is the seventh. The number seven is special in Hebrew thinking, however, connoting completeness or perfection. Thus, seven in the present passage may be meant to say that a full complement of sons is passed before Samuel before David is summoned (after all, only three sons are explicitly named). Alternatively, the Chronicler may have abbreviated the list to allow David the favoured seventh position. In any case, David is described as *haqqāṭān, the youngest*, which can also be translated 'the smallest'. What counts with God is not physical stature or any other external quality but, rather, internal character. God looks at the heart. The heart in the Hebrew understanding is more than the seat of the emotions. It is the core of the person's being, the centre of 'intellectual, ethical, moral, and religious consciousness' (Long 2009a: 342). As in Egypt, so in Israel, the heart was 'the center of the entire personality and its relationship to God' (*TDOT* 7: 401–403).

Having learned of one more son, Samuel insists that *we will not sit down* [assumedly at the sacrificial meal; recall the auspicious meal

---

5. The sentence might also be rendered, 'People see with the eyes, but Yahweh sees with the heart' (cf. Alter 1999: 96). But Ps. 64:5 (Heb. v. 6) confirms that *rā'â lĕ* can mean 'to look at'. And *'ayin* ('eye') can apparently mean 'appearance' (e.g. Lev. 13:55; Num. 11:7). So the traditional understanding of Yahweh's words to Samuel can stand. But even if one adopts Alter's reading, the sense is much the same. Humans look with the eyes and perceive only the outward appearance, while Yahweh looks with his heart and thus perceives the heart of a person.

on the eve of Saul's anointing, 9:22–24] *until he arrives* (v. 11). Somewhat curiously, David's arrival is accompanied by a description of his outward appearance: *glowing with health . . . fine appearance . . . handsome features* (v. 12). The Hebrew description of David's appearance is patient of various translations, as modern versions amply demonstrate. To mention but one instance, the Hebrew *'admônî*, which seems to mean 'reddish', is variously interpreted as referring to David's complexion (ruddy), hair colour or even state of health (so NIV's *glowing with health*). Perhaps there is even a hint of David's youthfulness, as in JPS's 'ruddy-cheeked, bright-eyed, and handsome' (cf. 17:42). The point is that David is attractive, even if not impressively tall or even full grown. But why, in a context where the emphasis is on the heart, would David's appearance be mentioned? And, more broadly, why does the Old Testament elsewhere often mention the comeliness of major characters: Moses in Exodus 2:2, for instance, or Abigail in 1 Samuel 25:3? That Moses was a handsome (*ṭôb*) baby may have played a part in his rescue. Abigail's intelligence and beauty may have been mentioned to contrast with the foolishness of her churlish husband. Perhaps David's appearance is mentioned to prevent the reader from drawing the conclusion that good looks are necessarily a detriment to one's usefulness to God. That would be a mistaken conclusion. They can, in God's economy, serve God's purpose, as can any other of the attributes one possesses. But good looks, in and of themselves, are not what counts most. God looks at the heart.

13–14. No sooner is he anointed than 'the spirit[6] of the LORD came mightily upon David from that day forward' (v. 13, NRSV). David's permanent enduement with the Spirit of Yahweh contrasts with, for instance, the intermittent coming of the Spirit on Samson (Judg. 14:6, 19; 15:14) or on Saul (1 Sam. 10:10; 11:6, where the terminology is *Spirit of God*, despite Samuel's anticipation in 10:6 of the *Spirit of the LORD*). The sporadic falling of the Spirit on Samson or Saul was to empower for a particular occasion or sometimes to overpower (see 19:23–24). David's enduement with the Spirit is of

---

6. As noted at 10:6, translators differ as to whether to use upper- or lowercase 's' with 'spirit'. NIV prefers 'Spirit', as do ESV, NASB, NLT, etc.

a different order, marking a new beginning in Israel's history (cf. Corti 2001).

Now the Spirit of the LORD had departed from Saul (v. 14). Hebrew syntax is rightly reflected in NIV's pluperfect *had departed*, as the Spirit's departure from Saul preceded the reception of the Spirit by David. The validating and empowering presence of God's Spirit must have left Saul no later than the time of his final rejection in 15:26–29 (cf. also 16:1). The *evil spirit from the LORD* that now 'torments' (or 'terrifies') Saul has been the subject of much discussion. The range of meaning of the Hebrew adjective *ra'* includes not only that which is evil or wicked but also that which is harmful, injurious or calamitous. Thus, many translations opt for the more mundane sense, that Saul became troubled in his spirit, and this troubled spirit is traced back to divine action (as was typically the perspective of the biblical writers).[7] Others draw attention to the parallel with the beneficent spirit of Yahweh, which seems to be more personal in nature (as with angelic beings), and contend that the personal character of this evil or troubling spirit from Yahweh should not be downplayed. The most obvious example of a troubling (or deceiving) spirit being deployed by Yahweh is in 1 Kings 22:21–23. Hamori (2010) argues that the 'spirit of falsehood' is more widely attested in the Old Testament than is generally recognized. Examining eight key contexts,[8] he concludes that

> The picture throughout is consistent with the divine court context of 1 Kings 22, in which Yahwh [*sic*] uses the רוח [*rûaḥ*, 'spirit'] as a subversive messenger to bring destructive justice through deception to those who are already in the wrong.
> (Hamori 2010: 29)

15–23. The departure of Yahweh's spirit from Saul (v. 14) becomes the catalyst for the introduction of David to Saul's court. Noting

---

7. Alter (1999: 98) speaks of the 'theopsychology of ancient Israel'.
8. He considers these passages in the following order: 1 Kgs 22:19–23; 1 Sam. 16:14–23; 18:10–12; 19:9–10; Judg. 9:23–24; 2 Kgs 19:7; Isa. 19:13–14; Isa. 29:9–10; Job 4:12–21; and Hos. 4:12; 5:4; 9:7; 12:2.

their master's tormented mental state, *Saul's attendants* propose music therapy (vv. 15–16). Saul is agreeable to the suggestion and instructs them to *Find someone who plays well and bring him to me* (v. 17). As it happens, a general search is not necessary, because *one of the servants* already has someone in mind (v. 18). Does the immediate mention of David reflect knowledge of his recent anointing, or is it just coincidental? Either way, this *son of Jesse of Bethlehem* comes with impressive qualifications. To begin with, he *knows how to play the lyre* (the key requirement for the job of music therapist), and he is also *a brave man and a warrior* (v. 18). This description seems in some tension with the description of David by Saul in 17:33 as but a boy (*naʿar*). The tension is lessened when we note that Saul in that same verse goes on to describe *this Philistine* (Goliath) as *a warrior from his youth* (also drawing on the root *nʿr*). Apparently one can be considered a warrior already in one's youth. The tension is lessened further when we note that apparently no-one thought it odd that David was still *with the sheep* (16:19), despite the accolades of verse 18. Perhaps job recommendations in antiquity were as prone to hyperbole and to over-realized potential as are their modern counterparts.[9] Continuing his recommendation of David, the servant notes that he *speaks well* (*nĕbôn dābār*, 'is prudent in speech') and *is a fine-looking man*. Ultimately, though, what sets David apart is the last thing the servant mentions: *the LORD is with him* (v. 18; cf. 2 Sam. 7:9).[10] Saul will soon enough come to realize that Yahweh is indeed with David, but as Saul is in no mood to abdicate in favour of one better than he, this realization will only heighten his mental torment (17:37; 18:12–16, 28–29; 20:13).

At present, though, Saul is keen to acquire David's services and so sends *messengers to Jesse* to fetch him (v. 19). Jesse's response involves loading a *donkey* with *bread, a skin of wine and a young goat* (v. 20), each of which echoes in some respect the circumstances

---

9. For the argument that the text exhibits what Russian literary theorist Mikhail Bakhtin calls 'double-voiced' discourse, see Johnson (2013).
10. As noted earlier, no such statement of divine accompaniment is made at the time of Saul's introduction in 9:2.

surrounding Saul's own anointing (cf. 10:2–4), to which may even be added the focus on the playing of lyres (10:5; 16:18). For now, as David enters his service, he (presumably Saul; the Hebrew does not specify) loves/likes (Heb. *'āhab*) him very much (vv. 21–22). That will soon change, but, for now, the music therapy provides Saul with some relief (v. 23).

Meaning
Dramatic irony abounds in this episode. At the suggestion of one of his servants, Saul brings David into his court to help ease his troubled mind. But soon enough the effect is the reverse. As the narrative continues in the following chapters, Saul becomes increasingly paranoid and afraid of David. In one respect, though, Saul is correct: David is the one to succeed him on the throne of Israel. As we shall see, however, this realization is not enough to cause Saul to step aside willingly.

ii. David defeats Goliath and routs the Philistines (17:1–58)
Context
Commensurate with the three-stage accession process involving *designation, demonstration* and *confirmation*,[11] it comes as no surprise that David's designation by anointing and his introduction into Saul's court in chapter 16 are followed in chapter 17 by a dramatic demonstration that God's hand is upon him. One of the most famous stories in the book of Samuel, and indeed in the Bible, the story of David's defeat of Goliath is nevertheless controversial in several respects. For one, MT and LXX[B] tell somewhat different stories, the latter being much shorter than the former (17:12–31, 41, 48b, 50 and 55–58 are lacking in LXX[B]).[12] Interestingly, these lacking sections are amongst the more problematic portions when chapter 17 is viewed in its larger context. That is to say, on the basis of their

---

11. For discussion, see at 11:14–15 and the section on Saul in the Introduction.
12. It is not only ch. 17 that evidences fewer verses in LXX when compared to MT. LXX of 1 Sam. 18, for instance, lacks vv. 1–5, 8b, 10–11, 12b, 17–19 and 30.

contents, these portions strike many modern interpreters as difficult to square with the larger context.[13] This suggests that LXX may well have omitted the problematic portions in the interest of presenting a less complex text.[14] On balance, the longer text (MT) is to be preferred on internal grounds and also on the basis of other criteria, such as the likelihood that 4QSam^a attests the longer reading (Johnson 2012a, though recognizing that the evidence is very partial).[15]

A second major point of controversy is over the question whether it was David, in fact, who killed Goliath, or someone else (see at 2 Sam. 21:19). However these controversies are settled, at the end of the eventful day in the Valley of Elah David has earned the respect of the people, the loyalty of Jonathan (see 18:1–4) and the vexation of Saul (18:6–9).

Comment
1–3. *They pitched camp at Ephes Dammim, between Sokoh and Azekah* (v. 1). The notices in verses 1–3 map well onto the known topography of the Elah Valley (Wadi es-Sant), which lies some 12 miles west of Bethlehem. The Elah Valley was a major corridor descending from the Judean hill country westwards towards Philistine territory along the coast and was of great strategic importance. *Sokoh* lies to the south of the Elah Valley, almost 15 miles west of Bethlehem, while *Azekah* is 3 miles north-west of Sokoh. Gath (Goliath's home town; v. 4) is 5 miles west of Azekah (for details, see Long 2009a: 345). *Ephes Dammim* may not be the name of a town; after a thorough review of interpretive possibilities, Adams (2010: 53–56) makes a cogent case for understanding it to mean something like 'border of bloodshed' or 'bloody border', referring

---

13. See the insightful discussion in Gordon (1986: 64–66).
14. So Gooding, in Barthélemy et al. (1986: *passim*). Cf. also Gordon's concluding comment on the subject: 'Some of the "omissions", it must be said, seem to indicate a caviling and unimaginative approach to the business of story-telling' (1986: 66).
15. Other recent writers preferring the longer text, though for reasons of varying cogency, include Aurelius (2002); Wesselius (2009).

to the contested boundary between Philistine and Israelite territory. *The Philistines occupied one hill and the Israelites another* (v. 3). With the Philistines south of the valley at Sokoh, the Israelites may well have been north of the valley at the recently excavated Khirbet Qeiyafa (see at v. 20).

4–11. Israel is formidably challenged by a Philistine *champion named Goliath* (v. 4). The Hebrew rendered *champion* is *'îš-habbēnayim*, literally 'the man between two (armies)'. The role of this man in the middle was to engage a champion from the opposing army in single combat, with the understanding that the outcome would decide the fate of the respective armies. The outcome was deemed to represent the will of the gods. In an important essay on such contests by champions, Hoffner (1968: 222) cites the example of the Hittite king Hattusili III, who boasts of personally slaying 'the man who was the *piran ḫuyanza* [one who runs/marches in front]', after which '(the rest of) the enemy fled' (cf. also the seminal essay by de Vaux 1959; Eng. 1972).

If Goliath is known for anything, it is for his incredible size. MT makes him over 9 ft tall, while LXX, 4QSam[a] and Josephus (*Ant.* 6:171) have him top out at about 6 ft 6 in. – still gigantic by ancient standards (v. 4). Goliath is also extremely well armed, which seems to be the point of the unusually detailed description in verses 5–7 of his military gear.[16] The weight of Goliath's *scale armour of bronze* (v. 5) has been estimated at 126 lb and the point of his spear (v. 7) at 15 lb (R. W. Klein 1983: 175).

Goliath lays out terms of engagement in verses 8–9, ending with a resounding *This day I defy the armies of Israel! Give me a man and let us fight each other* (v. 10). The logical man to face Goliath would seem to be Israel's own impressively tall Saul, but *On hearing the Philistine's words, Saul and all the Israelites were dismayed and terrified* (v. 11). The question that begs to be asked, but seldom is, is where is Jonathan in all this? Is he, too, dismayed and terrified (see at 18:1)?

---

16. On the appropriateness of Goliath's armour to his late eleventh-century setting, see Millard (2009). And for further discussion on Goliath's role, size and armour, see Long (2009a: 347).

12–15. *Now David was the son of an Ephrathite named Jesse* (v. 12). Apart from the additional identifier of David as an *Ephrathite*,[17] this information is already known to the reader from 16:1–13, 18. Its inclusion here may reflect a time when the story of David's triumph over Goliath circulated independently, prior to its inclusion in the larger history. The current function of this notice, including the listing of *Jesse's three eldest sons* (v. 13) and the comments that *David was the youngest* (v. 14) and that he *went back and forth from Saul* (v. 15), may be to remind the reader of 1 Samuel 16, where the same information is given. The effect of this link to 1 Samuel 16 is to remind the reader of David's status as Yahweh's anointed and to heighten expectations of what is about to happen. The reader is also prompted to read Eliab's peevish exchange with David in verse 28 against this backdrop.

16–31. *For forty days the Philistine came forward* (v. 16). As in the early chapters of 1 Samuel, where there was a toggling back and forth between the boy Samuel and the boys of Eli (see at 2:18–26), so also here the scene toggles back and forth between the boy David and the giant Goliath. *Forty days* not only underscores Goliath's persistence in taunting Israel but, as Bodner (2008: 180) notes, also hints at the momentousness of what is about to take place: 'remarkable things tend to happen in the Bible after such a length of time'. Whether it is the words of Jesse (so NIV) or the narrator (so NRSV), the comment in verse 19 that *Saul and all the men of Israel* are *fighting against the Philistines* only serves to underscore the irony of the situation in which fear, not fighting, characterizes Saul and his men (see v. 11). Once loaded with goods, David's mission is to *See how your brothers are and bring back some assurance* [*'arubbātām*] *from them* (v. 18). How best to render Hebrew *'arubbātām* is unclear.

---

17. Not to be confused with someone from Ephraim. Though the two terms do sometimes seem synonymous (e.g. *HALOT* cites Judg. 12:5; 1 Sam. 1:1; 1 Kgs 11:26), the present context has in view a tribal group associated with Bethlehem (cf. Gen. 35:19; 48:7; Ruth 1:2; 4:11; 1 Chr. 4:4). 'Bethlehem Ephrathah' in the justly famous Mic. 5:2 is in Judah, while another Bethlehem is attested in the tribe of Zebulun (Josh. 19:15).

It may refer to an *assurance* of the brothers' welfare (NIV), or a 'token' (NRSV, JPS) confirming David's successful delivery of supplies, or a 'token' proving that Jesse has fulfilled the common duty of local populations to supply troops, which in turn would entitle David's brothers to their rations. Or perhaps this *'arubbātām* is a 'pledge' that would entitle Jesse to 'a certain portion of plunder that might be taken from the Philistines in the event of an Israelite victory' (Bergen 1996: 191–192; on these options, see Long 2009a: 348).

Early in the morning [see on 15:12] *David left the flock in the care of a shepherd* (v. 20). Upon arriving at the 'camp',[18] *David left his things with the keeper of supplies* before running to the battle lines to check on his brothers (v. 22). These notices provide background for evaluating Eliab's angry words to David just a bit later: *Why have you come down here? And with whom did you leave those few sheep in the wilderness? I know how conceited you are and how wicked your heart is* (v. 28). The reader knows that David has acted responsibly in his duties (vv. 20, 22). Eliab's anger may well be that of a 'big' brother cowed by Goliath's challenge and resentful of his 'little' brother proving to be his better. His accusations of negligence are groundless, and as a kind of Saul figure (see on 16:7), his misjudgment of David's heart is a foreshadowing of Saul's later behaviour. Eliab also knows that David, not he, has been chosen by Yahweh and anointed by Samuel (16:13). Not for the first time is an older brother resentful of harbingers of greatness in respect of a younger brother; Joseph, for instance, also received indications of future greatness (Gen. 37:2–11), was sent by his father to check on older brothers and was abused by them (Gen. 37:12–19).

---

18. Elsewhere in 1 Sam. 17, *camp* renders the rather common word *maḥăneh*. Here the rare word *ma'gāl* is used (it appears elsewhere only in 26:5, 7). Heb. *ma'gāl* suggests something circular or ring-shaped (cf. 'the circle of the camp', NASB; Firth [2009: 191] translates 'secured area'). Perhaps the reference is to Khirbet Qeiyafa (excavated between 2007 and 2013), a site sitting atop a hill north of the Elah Valley (Levin 2013). The site is circular in shape, and may well have served as Saul's headquarters in the current episode (Adams 2010: 65).

Whatever bravado may be suggested by the army's *shouting the war cry* (v. 20), the mere sight and sound of Goliath, shouting *his usual defiance*, is sufficient to send them fleeing *from him in great fear* (vv. 23–24). Saul, also terrified (v. 11) but ever proactive in trying to get more out of his troops (cf. 14:24), makes rich promises to the man who will kill Goliath: both social advancement – *his daughter in marriage* – and material increase – *great wealth . . . exempt his family from taxes in Israel* (v. 25).[19] But Saul's words have little effect until David arrives. David's question *What will be done for the man who kills this Philistine . . . ?* (v. 26) might appear to be self-serving. But according to the narrative, David is chiefly motivated by righteous indignation: *Who is this uncircumcised Philistine that he should defy the armies of the living God?* (v. 26). Whether intended to do so or not, David's repeated counter-defiance of Goliath (v. 30) eventually brings him to Saul's attention (v. 31).

32–40. The first recorded words in David's meeting with Saul are David's: *Let no one lose heart . . . your servant will go and fight* (v. 32). LXX reads 'Let not my lord lose heart'. And this reading may be original.[20] Saul is quick to object on the basis of David's youth, though in the same breath he admits that Goliath *has been a warrior from his youth* (v. 33; see on 16:18). David famously counters that Yahweh *who rescued me from the paw of the lion and the paw of the bear will rescue me from the hand of this Philistine* (v. 37a). While the possibility of encountering a lion or a bear in the land of Israel is unlikely in the extreme today, this was not the case in David's day. Lions were attested in Israel until the thirteenth century AD and bears until the first half of the twentieth century. Archaeologists excavating

---

19. The Hebrew does not explicitly mention taxes but speaks of making the victor and his father's house 'free' (*ḥopšî*) in Israel. Suggested understandings of this freedom are several (see Long 2009a: 350), but freedom from obligation to the king (in the form of taxes or otherwise) is probably implied. Gordon (1986: 156) adds the possibility that the victor's family might even live 'as pensioners of the royal house'.
20. Greek *kardia tou kyriou* reflects consonantal Hebrew *lb-'dny*, 'heart of my lord', which may have been misread as the similar-looking and more deferential *lb-'dm*, 'heart of a man'.

Iron Age levels in Palestine (i.e. the period of the settlement and early monarchy) have uncovered remains of both lions and bears.[21] Apparently persuaded by David, Saul replies, *Go, and the* LORD *be with you* (v. 37b), thereby invoking on David that which most distinguishes him from Saul – Yahweh is with him (see on 16:18).

Whether Saul's attempt to dress David up in his own kit (vv. 38–39) is meant to better David's chances or to bolster Saul's own reputation (a reminder perhaps of his taking credit in 13:4 for Jonathan's daring deed in 13:3) is unclear. Though David tries it on, it proves unsuitable for him and is, in any case, beside the point in the light of David's confidence in Yahweh as the one who will give victory. Nevertheless, the irony of Saul's words and actions in verses 37–38 is not to be missed. Unwittingly, he both blesses and dresses as a king the one who has already been anointed to replace him. David's preferred fighting tools, however, are those of a shepherd, *his staff in his hand, five smooth stones . . . in his shepherd's bag and . . . his sling*. It is with these that Yahweh had delivered him from fearsome beasts, and with these David *approached the Philistine* (v. 40).

41–44. The approach of *the Philistine* to David is curious in several respects. He has a *shield-bearer* (v. 43; also v. 7), the presence of whom in a *mano a mano* contest of champions is difficult to explain or justify. As Goliath comes closer to David, he rightly perceives him to be *little more than a boy, glowing with health and handsome* (a description that reminds the reader of 16:12 and thus also of David's anointed and divinely empowered status). But Goliath misperceives what David is carrying. He sees *sticks* (*maqlôt*), whereas it was but one stick/staff (*maqlô*) that David took up in verse 40. Is Goliath mistaking David's shepherd's sling (hanging limp at his side) as another stick? It has long been supposed that Goliath may have suffered from a visual disorder, a kind of tunnel vision associated with acromegalic gigantism (cf. Kellermann 1990; Berginer 2000; Cohen and Berginer 2006). Had Goliath seen the sling, he might have known that such a simple device could prove a

---

21. For more on the ecosystems and flora and fauna of Israel in the biblical period, see Long (2009a: 350–351) and bibliography cited there.

dangerous long-range weapon in the hand of a practised shepherd, even if only a boy.[22] If Goliath's vision was not good, this might also explain the presence of an assistant, euphemistically called a *shield bearer* but serving actually as Goliath's guide to the visually impaired (a view defended thoroughly by Cohen and Berginer 2006).

Goliath's eyesight may not be great, but his voice seems perfectly fine – perhaps made all the more thunderous as a result of his gigantism. Engaging in the ancient practice of 'flyting', a kind of 'trash-talking' or 'verbal contest' designed to shame and ridicule an opponent,[23] Goliath *curse[s] David by his gods* (v. 43)[24] and threatens to give David's *flesh to the birds and the wild animals* (v. 44), 'a horrendous thought to any Israelite contemplating death' (Gordon 1986: 157, citing Jer. 8:1–2; 16:6).

45–47. Uncowed, David's 'flyting' turns in a decidedly theological direction. In sync with Jonathan's earlier confession of confidence in Yahweh's ability to save, *whether by many or by few* (14:6), David famously pronounces, *You come against me with sword and spear and javelin, but I come against you in the name of the* LORD *Almighty . . . whom you have defied* (v. 45). 'How dare you? You don't stand a chance.' In the Hebrew mind, a name is more than a label; it connotes the very character of the one who bears it. David comes in the power of Yahweh himself. The victory is assured and the defeat will be more expansive than just Goliath's defeat. Not only Goliath's flesh, but *the carcasses of the Philistine army* will become carrion *to the birds and the wild animals* (v. 46). The weight of Yahweh is about to be felt, *and the whole world will know* several things: *that there is a God in Israel, that it is not by sword or spear that the* LORD *saves* and that *the battle is the* LORD's (vv. 46b–47).

---

22. Cf. Johnson (2013) who recognizes the effectiveness of slings in certain situations but rightly stresses that the text highlights David's reliance on Yahweh as the ultimate key to his success.
23. See Long (2009a: 351–352) for discussion and bibliography.
24. Whether the reference is to the gods of the Philistines or to the one true God of David is debated. Hebrew *'ĕlōhîm* is plural in form but is used in Hebrew to designate either 'gods' or 'God'.

48–51a. After such a theological crescendo, the actual engagement is almost anti-climactic, recounted in but four verses (vv. 48–51). There are a couple of puzzles worth pondering, however. Where did David's well-aimed stone strike Goliath (v. 49): on the 'forehead' (*mēṣaḥ*) or at the bronze greave (*misḥâ*) covering Goliath's shin (v. 6)? 'Forehead' is the traditional understanding, but 'greave' has been argued, given how similar the two words are in Hebrew (Deem 1978). Fokkelman (1986: 2.186) follows Deem in assuming that the stone entered just above the greave in the space necessary for walking and lodged between the greave and the shin, causing Goliath to fall forwards (v. 49) not backwards, as would likely have been the effect of a stone to the forehead. He remarks that 'the Achilles' heel in the Bible must in future be *Goliath's knee*' (further support for the view is in Wong 2010; 2013). At the very least, the word choice would underscore the uselessness of Goliath's armour in the face of Yahweh's agent.

A second puzzle has to do with Goliath's death itself. Was it the sling-stone that killed him, or was it Goliath's sword? NIV's rendering of verses 50–51 eases the tension somewhat, but NRSV sticks closer to the Hebrew syntax:

> So David prevailed over the Philistine with a sling and a stone, striking down the Philistine and killing him; there was no sword in David's hand. Then David ran and stood over the Philistine; he grasped his sword, drew it out of its sheath, and killed him; then he cut off his head with it.

In view of Hebrew narrative style, where a summary statement is often followed by a more detailed description, the problem is more apparent than real. The Philistine landed face down on the ground in verse 49, his heavy armour then becoming more of a liability than an asset. Verse 50 reiterates David's triumph with sling not sword, rendering the Philistine's death certain. It is worth noting that two different verbal stems of the root *mût* ('to kill') are used in verses 50–51: a hipʻil in verse 50 and a polel in verse 51; the former is more general, and the latter perhaps describes the *coup de grâce* (cf. *HALOT*, 'make a full end of, deliver the death blow', citing, in addition to 1 Sam. 17:51, Judg. 9:54; 1 Sam. 14:13; 2 Sam. 1:9–10, 16).

51b–54. The decisive outcome of the contest of champions has a predictable effect. The Philistines *turned and ran* (v. 51b), and *the men of Israel and Judah* are emboldened and ultimately enriched. They pursue the Philistines right out of Israelite territory up to the Philistine cities of Gath and Ekron (v. 52) and then return and plunder the Philistine camp (v. 53). David, meanwhile, *took the Philistine's head and brought it to Jerusalem* (v. 54a). Some regard this notice as anachronistic, as Jerusalem will not be conquered by David until 2 Samuel 5:6–10. But perhaps David already has Jerusalem in his sights as a suitable future capital and is putting the Jebusite inhabitants of Jerusalem on notice. Numerous examples in ANE texts and iconography of analogous actions by individuals following their victories lend credence to this view (Hoffmeier 2011: 103–109). Not only did David retain Goliath's head, but he also *put the Philistine's weapons in his own tent* (v. 54b). Most assume that it was David's personal tent into which Goliath's weapons were deposited, but Hoffmeier (2011: 97–103) contends, in the light of both verse 53's reference to plundering the Philistine camp and the ancient practice of 'seizing the tent of one's opponent in battle', that David may in fact have taken 'Goliath's tent (back to Bethlehem?), along with his weapons' (ibid.: 102–103).

55–58. At verse 55, the focus of the narrative returns to Saul and to much earlier in the day, when David was *going out to meet the Philistine*. To Saul's question *whose son is that young man?*, Abner has no answer. This exchange has perplexed interpreters, as by this point in the narrative David should be known to Saul. If narrative sequence is taken to indicate chronological sequence, then David has already entered Saul's service as a music therapist and armour-bearer (16:21–23). If a satisfactory answer is to be found, it must begin by our paying close attention to what Saul is actually asking. He does not ask 'Who is that young man?' but, rather, *whose son is that young man?* (v. 55; cf. vv. 56, 58). As Gooding (in Barthélemy et al. 1986: 55–86) remarks,

> Any but the slowest of readers would surely get the point: it is David's father, not David, that Saul is wanting to inform himself about. And that is hardly surprising [as] Saul . . . has promised, that if any man can defeat the champion, he (Saul) will make his father's house free in Israel (17,25). (Ibid.: 60)

In point of fact, though Saul has heard Jesse's name at least once (16:18), his communications with him involved intermediaries (16:19, 22), and so his knowledge of Jesse may have been minimal. His concern in any case would not have been simply to know Jesse's name but, in view of the promises of social and material advancement he had made (17:25, 27), to know as much as possible about the status of the house of Jesse. What will be the cost in revenue? And who is this who could become my son-in-law? Even Saul's awareness of David may have been less extensive than one might assume. Though David had been made *one of [Saul's] armour-bearers* (16:21) – which implies that there were others (Tsumura 2007:432) – David's services as music therapist would have been most required when Saul was in a disturbed state of mind (16:23). Saul may not have learned much about David himself during these encounters. Add the fact that Saul has been told that his kingdom will be given to one better than he (15:28), and Saul's concern to learn all he can of this intrepid youth going out to face the giant is quite understandable. 'If all this begins to sound a bit complex, consider that "a full, real-life story is often more complicated and difficult to understand than abridged stories make out"' (Provan, Long and Longman 2015: 296; citing Gooding in Barthélemy et al. 1986: 101).

Meaning
To this point in the book of Samuel, two individuals have been designated by anointing as Israel's king. Saul's anointing was in 10:1 and David's in 16:12–13. These anointings established Saul and David, each in his own time, as *nāgîd*, 'designee', but did not place them immediately on the throne. As we have come to see, designation was to be followed by some demonstration of the designee's ability to lead. In this respect, Saul was slow and faltering, requiring further efforts on Samuel's part even to bring him to public attention (see at 10:17–27). In David's case, by contrast, his defeat of Goliath in the name of the Lord places him very much in the public eye and demonstrates that the Lord is with him. Though many will soon be praising David in such exalted terms that Saul will become angry (ch. 18) and eventually murderous (ch. 19 until his death in ch. 31), David's confirmation as king (his ascent to the

throne) will be delayed by Saul's tenacious refusal to step down to make way for the neighbour better than he (15:28).

iii. *David finds favour with the house of Saul, but is feared by Saul himself (18:1–30)*
Context
Saul was definitively rejected in chapter 15 for his disobedience to the word of the Lord. In chapters 16–17 we witnessed the rise of the 'neighbour' who is better than Saul. Now in chapter 18 we observe how David is received. At first, everyone loves David: Saul's son Jonathan, Saul's daughter Michal, and all Israel and Judah. Even Saul sees David's potential and gives him a high rank in his army. But soon Saul's attitude towards David begins to sour. David's popularity and success evoke in Saul first jealousy, then aggression, and ultimately fear, *because the* LORD *was with David but had departed from Saul* (v. 12). Saul's every attempt to marginalize David has the opposite effect. And the chapter that began with joy in the aftermath of David's defeat of Goliath and of Israel's victory over the Philistines ends with Saul becoming David's lifelong enemy (v. 29).

Comment
1–4. *After David had finished talking with Saul, Jonathan became one in spirit with David* (v. 1). The temporal clause that opens chapter 18 links the events of this chapter to what has preceded.[25] Jonathan, though unmentioned throughout chapter 17, has apparently been on site to witness some (perhaps all) of David's words and actions in the face of Goliath's threat and eventual defeat. Jonathan's failure to face Goliath himself is unlikely to have resulted from fear (cf. 13:3; 14:6) or even parental control (cf. 14:1). Rather, he will almost certainly have been aware of Saul's earlier failures and of the prophetic pronouncements they elicited – namely, that there would be no Saulide dynasty (13:13–14) and that Saul himself would be replaced by a neighbour (*rēaʻ*, not a son, *bēn*) better than he (15:28).

---

25. Alter (1999: 112) remarks that 'This is a clear instance in which the (late medieval) chapter division actually interrupts the narrative unit.'

And so it is reasonable to assume that Jonathan's inaction in the face of the Philistine may have been in the hope that Saul's replacement would show himself. In David, Jonathan sees courage born of faith like his own, and so he *became one in spirit with David* (v. 1); the Hebrew more literally means his *nepeš* (soul, life, person) became 'bound up' (*qšr* nip'al) with David's *nepeš*. The closest verbal analogue to this statement in the Bible is the description of Jacob's attachment to his son Benjamin (Gen. 44:30; 'his life is bound up in the boy's life', NRSV).

Twice in the opening verses, it is stated that Jonathan *loved him [David] as himself* (vv. 1, 3). While some recent writers have sought to cast Jonathan's love of David in homoerotic terms (e.g. Horner 1978), such attempts overlook or dismiss the use of 'love language' (including the Hebrew verb used here, *'hb*)[26] in covenantal and treaty contexts. First Kings 5:1 offers a clear instance of the more political sense of love; King Hiram is said always to have 'loved' (*'hb*) David (so ESV).[27] See also on 2 Samuel 1:26.

From that day Saul kept David with him (v. 2). In a chapter that is generally quite clear about Saul's motivations, the present verse is an exception. Perhaps Saul still regards David favourably (cf. 16:21) and takes him *into his* [full-time] *service*, as was his custom whenever he *saw a mighty or brave man* (14:52). In any case, David will no longer be going *back and forth from Saul to tend his father's sheep at Bethlehem* (17:15).

Jonathan wastes no time in making *a covenant with David because he loved him as himself* (v. 3). He also transfers to David the rights and regalia of crown prince: his robe, tunic, sword, bow and belt (v. 4). These actions carried both symbolic and legal significance. Viberg (1992: 131) speaks of 'a deliberate and free transference of the right to the throne by Jonathan to David'. Jonathan appears already to

---

26. Lev. 19:18, 34 support also a non-technical use of *'hb*. God's people are to 'love' both neighbours and foreigners residing amongst them as they love themselves.

27. Modern translations agree on the basic sense, rendering variously 'been a friend' (NRSV, JPS), 'been on friendly terms' (NIV), 'been a loyal friend' (NLT).

know what he later will expressly state: David is Yahweh's choice to replace Saul (cf. 20:14–15; 23:17).

5–9. Once in Saul's military service David proves *so successful* (*śkl* hip'il, a root suggesting insight, prudence and thus success) that *Saul gave him a high rank in the army* (v. 5), perhaps the highest rank, as the Hebrew says simply that Saul put him over the men of battle (cf. JPS, 'put him in command of all the soldiers'). The troops are pleased, as are even Saul's officers, who might have viewed David as a rival. Saul's own feelings have remained hidden, but that is about to change. Verse 6 introduces a brief flashback to the time of David's return from killing Goliath. On that occasion, *the women* who *came out from all the towns of Israel to meet King Saul* sang,

Saul has slain his thousands,
    and David his tens of thousands.
(v. 7)

It is characteristic of Hebrew parallelism to 'step up' one or more terms in the second half of a poetic couplet (or bicolon). So the shift from a thousand to ten thousand is not surprising (the identical intensification occurs in Deut. 32:30; Pss 91:7; 144:13; Mic. 6:7). It has been suggested that Saul's anger (v. 8) is misguided and that in his troubled state of mind he has failed to take account of the nature of Hebrew songs and poetry (e.g. Leshem 2004), but this does not quite do justice to the situation (Fokkelman 1986: 2.220). While it may be true that poetic convention should not be pressed in too literal a direction, and also true that the women were surely not keen to insult Saul, it remains the case the Hebrew poetry typically involves 'intensification' of some sort, and so by placing David in the second line, the women not only elevate David to royal status but place him in the climactic position. *What more can he get but the kingdom?* exclaims an angry Saul in verse 8b. Does Saul sense – as Jonathan seemed to recognize – that David is the 'neighbour' who is to replace him (see 15:28)? If so, he is galled by the prospect, and he *kept a close eye on David* (v. 9). The Targum and many early rabbinic commentators understand Saul to be looking for an opportunity to kill David. If so, he doesn't have to wait long.

10–11. *The next day an evil spirit from God came forcefully on Saul* (v. 10; see on 16:14). Saul's *prophesying in his house* recalls his earlier prophesying in public (10:6, 10). The same verb (*nbʾ* hitpaʿel) is used on both occasions and will recur several times in 19:20–24. Many translations speak of Saul 'raving' in the present context (a sense of *nbʾ* also attested, e.g., in 1 Kgs 18:29). While David is making music with his hand (*bĕyad*), Saul readies the spear in his hand (*bĕyad*) to try to *pin* [lit. 'strike'] *David to the wall* (v. 11). David, however, is able to elude him twice. As Bodner (2008: 196) remarks:

> David of Judah says 'I will strike' (נכה) in 17.35 and hits the mark,
> Saul of Benjamin says 'I will strike' (נכה) but does not hit the mark.
> Consequently, there is damage to the wall of Saul's house, and further indentations will be made before long (19.10).

12–16. Having rejected the word of Yahweh (see on 15:23), Saul's every action seems counterproductive. Refusing to accept his rejection from office, Saul puts himself in opposition to Yahweh (contrast Eli's acceptance in 3:18 of his own rejection from office). The result is fear of David, *because the* LORD *was with David but had departed* [*sûr* qal] *from* [*mēʿim*] *Saul* (v. 12). *So he sent David away* [*sûr* hipʿil] *from him* [*mēʿimmô*] and put him in command, not of all the men of battle (as in v. 5), but of only *a thousand men*. Saul may have hoped that, by sending David away accompanied by a smaller fighting force, he would increase David's chances of dying in battle and at the same time diminish David's prominence and popularity with the people. The effect of his demoting David, however, was in fact the reverse. David's going out and returning before the people (so literally the last clause of v. 13) actually brought him into closer contact with the general populace, and *all Israel and Judah loved David* (v. 16). Verse 14 captures the heart of the matter: *In everything he did he had great success* [see v. 5 on what kind of success], *because the* LORD *was with him* (see on 16:18).

17–19. *Saul said to David, 'Here is my elder daughter Merab. I will give her to you in marriage'* (v. 17). Given David's growing prominence and popularity, Saul must make good on the promise of 17:25, to which he now adds a further condition: *only serve me bravely and fight the battles of the* LORD. That Saul's offer of his elder daughter Merab to

David is not well meant is made expressly clear by a glimpse into what he is thinking: *I will not raise a hand against him. Let the Philistines do that!* (v. 17b). It seems not to have dawned on Saul that the God who gave David victory over 'the Philistine' in chapter 17 is hardly likely to let him down in relation to lesser Philistines. David demurs, as was appropriate in such circumstances, protesting his family circumstances (and perhaps reckoning on the difficulty of coming up with a 'royal' bride-price). Saul, perhaps assuming that his promise has been discharged by his having made the offer, in due course gives Merab to Adriel of Meholah (v. 19).

20–27. Having so far failed to rid himself of David by his own hand (vv. 10–11) or by the hand of the Philistines (v. 17), Saul sees another opportunity in the fact that his second daughter, Michal, is *in love with David* (v. 20). Again, the narrative is crystal clear regarding Saul's motives in offering Michal to David as wife: *so that she may be a snare to him and so that the hand of the Philistines may be against him* (v. 21). Saul sets a bride-price that is not monetarily costly but is extremely risky: *a hundred Philistine foreskins* (v. 25). Saul's terms are not without precedent in the ancient world. As evidenced by both texts and reliefs, body parts were often brought back as evidence of enemy dead (heads, hands, etc.).[28] Saul's choice of foreskins may have been designed to prove that the slain were in fact Philistines, as most other peoples surrounding Israel practised circumcision, though not for the same reasons as Israel (see on 14:6). David wastes no time in meeting Saul's challenge twice over, returning with evidence of not just one hundred but two hundred Philistine dead (v. 27). For Saul's part, he appears to have learned little since chapter 15. Despite his challenge to David in 18:17 to *fight the battles of the* LORD (the proper role of an Israelite king), Saul's concern is still to *take revenge on his enemies* (v. 25; cf. comment on pronoun usage at 15:30).

28–30. All of Saul's efforts to diminish David, or indeed to destroy him, have accomplished precisely the opposite. Saul is more

---

28. E.g. the Great Libyan War Inscription of Merenptah at Karnak in Egypt mentions 'phalli with foreskins' obtained from enemy dead (Kitchen 2003: 6–7).

convinced than ever that *the LORD is with David*, while his own daughter Michal continues to love him (v. 28). And so Saul fears him more than ever and is hardened in his enmity towards him: *he remained his enemy for the rest of his days* (v. 29). David's reputation continues to grow, as he continues to meet *with more success [śkl]*[29] *than the rest of Saul's officers* (v. 30).

Meaning
First Samuel 18 tells the story of David's growing success and popularity and of Saul's growing dismay and rapid decline. Both Jonathan and Saul seem to sense that David is Yahweh's choice to replace Saul as king (vv. 1 and 8, respectively), but their reactions are polar opposites. Jonathan willingly and visibly defers to David (vv. 1–4), while Saul is angry (v. 8), aggressive (v. 11), ever more fearful (vv. 12, 15, 29) and in the end David's lifelong enemy (v. 29). That Yahweh is with David (v. 14) is not lost on Saul (vv. 12, 28). But having determined to resist to the death his own deposition from the kingly office, Saul finds himself in every respect out of sync with Yahweh's will and purposes. Being at odds with Yahweh puts him at odds not just with David, but also with virtually everyone else in the chapter. Framing the chapter are Saul's son Jonathan (v. 1) and his daughter Michal (v. 28), both of whom 'love' David. Even Saul's own troops and officers are pleased by David's success and promotion (v. 5). In the summative midpoint of the chapter, we learn that *all Israel and Judah loved David* (v. 16).

B. Saul seeks David's life (19:1 – 23:29)

i. Saul's attempts to kill David are thwarted by Jonathan, Michal, Samuel and God himself (19:1–24)
Context
Although chapter 19 marks a turning point, as Saul's intention to destroy David becomes blatant, a number of features nevertheless

---

29. Used for the fourth time in the chapter to describe David's wise and effective leadership (see vv. 5, 14, 15).

tie chapters 18 and 19 together, as Firth (2009: 214–215) explains. Chapter 18 begins and chapter 19 ends with divestments of royal clothing. In 18:1–4 Jonathan voluntary divests himself of and transfers to David the clothing and arms that mark him as crown prince. In 19:24 Saul is involuntarily divested of his royal robe when overcome by the Spirit of God. Saul's son Jonathan and daughter Michal figure prominently in both chapters, as do the Philistine wars and the calamitous spirit of Yahweh. Firth offers the following chart comparing the contents of chapters 18 and 19:

David and Jonathan	18:1–5	19:1–7
Philistine war	18:6–9	19:8
The grievous spirit	18:10–11	19:9–10
David and Saul's daughters	18:17–30	19:11–16

There is also movement between the chapters. As noted above, Saul's covert scheming to orchestrate David's death in chapter 18 gives way to overt orders in chapter 19 that he must be killed. The hardening of Saul's position pushes Jonathan and Michal to decide where their loyalties lie, and they both side with David.

Comment

1–7. More subtle approaches having failed, *Saul told his son Jonathan and all the attendants to kill David* (v. 1a). Jonathan, however, like his father at an earlier stage, *had taken a great liking to David* (v. 1b). In 16:21–22 Saul was said to 'like/love' (root *'ḥb*) David, and David is said to have found favour in Saul's eyes. In the present context, Jonathan is said to *ḥāpēṣ* ('take pleasure in, delight in') David, recalling the recent assurance of Saul's servants to David that *the king likes you* (*ḥāpēṣ*, 18:22). Such assurances now ring rather hollow, however, as Saul is quite clear about his desire to see David dead. Saul's command that David be killed sparks two conversations, the first between Jonathan and David (vv. 2–3) and the second between Jonathan and Saul (vv. 4–5). The former proposes a plan whereby David will be kept safe until Jonathan can have a word with his father. The latter recounts Jonathan's persuasive words to Saul. To his credit, *Saul listened to Jonathan*.[30] And he even swore that *As surely as the* LORD *lives, David will not be put to death* (v. 6). Saul's record of oath-keeping, however, is not impressive (e.g. 14:24, 39, 44–45), and within four short verses we see him attempting to break this one (v. 10).

8–10. Mention of a Philistine war and David's success in prosecuting it (v. 8) may at first blush seem out of place in the present context, but if we recall how David's earlier successes had affected Saul (18:6–9) we can see how this notice sets up what happens next. In this light, it is best to begin verse 9 not with an adversative *But* (so NIV) but, rather, with 'Then' (so NRSV, ESV, JPS) or some other conjunction that presents 19:9 as logically and consequentially related to verse 8.[31] David's earlier successes had evoked jealousy in Saul and caused him to keep *a close* [and malevolent?] *eye on David* (18:8–9). The response in the present situation is similar, albeit more violent – jealousy followed by an attempt to pin David to the wall (v. 10). As in 18:11, however, David manages to evade the point of the spear. On the earlier occasion, Saul demoted David and *sent David away from him* (18:13). This time, David does not wait for Saul to act but *made good his escape* that very night (19:10). Ironically, the same two verbs used of David's 'striking' (*nkh*) the Philistines and causing them to 'flee' (*nws*) are now used of Saul's attempt to pin/strike (*nkh*) David to the wall, requiring David to flee (*nws*; cf. Alter 1999: 119). Henceforth, and until Saul's death in chapter 31, David will be on the run from Saul.

11–17. Escaping from Saul's presence is not enough to ensure David's safety, as *Saul sent men to David's house to watch it and to kill him in the morning* (v. 11). *Michal, David's wife*, whom Saul had hoped would cost David his life (18:21), in fact acts swiftly to save David's life, first warning him (v. 11), then letting him down through a

---

30. Surely a good thing, though the phrase *šmʿ bqwl* offers a faint reminder of Saul's earlier listening not to the voice of Yahweh but rather to the voice of the people (15:24).

31. According to Hebrew syntax, a clause introduced by a *wayyiqṭōl* verbal form normally introduces the logical or temporal consequence of what has just been mentioned.

window (v. 12) – Saul's men were doubtless watching the doors. For David to make his escape, Michal needs to buy time, so she takes an object (NIV reads *idol*) which in combination with *some goats' hair at the head* (v. 13) is able to fool Saul's emissaries into believing Michal's claim that David is ill (v. 14). The Hebrew name for the object(s) Michal uses is *tĕrāpîm*, the precise nature of which is still debated. Apparently variable in size,[32] teraphim appear from their fifteen occurrences in the Bible to be 'household gods', or perhaps 'ancestor statues', or even protective figurines of some sort (relating teraphim to the Hebrew root *rp'* 'to heal').[33] Michal may have placed the teraphim at or beside the bed, rather than under covers on the bed, and the goat hair may have been placed on the bed's headrest. The sight of protective teraphim by David's bed would have contributed to the illusion that he was ill in bed. While the use of teraphim by David's wife raises its own questions, the mention of teraphim in this chapter serves also to recall the only other occurrence of the term in Samuel (1 Sam. 15:23) and thus to remind readers of Saul's rejected status (cf. Rowe 2011: 198).

From a modern perspective, Michal's loyalty to her husband rather than her father is unremarkable. But ancient readers would likely have regarded loyalty to one's father as more important even than loyalty to one's spouse (cf. Rowe 2011: 145–175). Indeed, 'both Michal's choice of David in preference to Saul and the author's endorsement of her choice would have been startlingly unexpected' (ibid.: 204). That Michal's decision to deceive her father is so 'startlingly unexpected' in terms of the social expectations of her day may help to explain Saul's readiness to believe her (v. 17). On the other hand, Saul has on other occasions shown himself to be rather obtuse (see on 9:18 and 19:19, 22 below).

18. A further reminder of Saul's rejected status is the fact that, while Saul no longer enjoys official audiences with Samuel (15:35), Samuel is the first person to whom David flees. Finding Samuel in

---

32. Gen. 31:34–35 describes Rachel's having hidden Laban's teraphim in the saddle of the camel she is riding.

33. See Gordon (1986: 164) for a quick summary of theories; see also the thorough discussion in Zevit (2001: 267–276).

his home town at Ramah – the very site where Saul had years before been anointed as king – David tells Samuel *all that Saul had done to him*. Together the two relocate to Naioth. Whether *Naioth* is the name of a town or a common noun meaning 'camps' (cf. Heb. *nāweh*, pasturage, camp) is uncertain. Possibly it refers to the location of a 'prophetic commune' (Gordon 1986: 164–165). Naioth is mentioned only in 1 Samuel 19 – 20 and always in tandem with Ramah.

19–22. When word of David's whereabouts reaches Saul (v. 19), he wastes no time before sending men (*mal'ākîm*, 'messengers')[34] to capture ('take') David (v. 20). Seeing *a group of prophets prophesying, with Samuel standing there as their leader*, Saul's agents fall under the sway of *the Spirit of God* and begin themselves to prophesy (v. 20).[35] Twice more, Saul sends his men to capture David, and the result is each time the same (v. 21). Finally, Saul determines to take matters into his own hands and sets out for Ramah, arriving at *the great cistern at Seku* (v. 22a). Seku may be a place name, perhaps to be identified with Khirbet Shuweikeh, a few miles north of Ramah, but an attractive alternative reading has been suggested which has Saul arriving at 'the cistern of the threshing floor on the bare height'.[36] Here, at a water source on the outskirts of Ramah, Saul

---

34. 'These human messengers are fully equated with their senders' (*NIDOTTE* 2: 932).
35. The Hebrew root *nb'* in its verbal and nominal forms is used to describe the activity of both true and false prophets and can range in meaning from uttering divinely inspired messages, to (ecstatic) worship, to raving. While on a few occasions true prophets are referred to by characters in the biblical narratives as madmen (2 Kgs 9:11; Jer. 29:26; Hos. 9:7), the authoritative narrator never endorses such a view. '[W]here prophecy devolves into erratic behavior the focus tends not to be on true worshipers of Yahweh but on those at odds with him (e.g., Saul in 1 Sam. 18:10; the prophets of Baal in 1 Kings 18:29)' (Long 2009a: 317, which see for fuller discussion and bibliography).
36. This reading is based on LXX (which encourages a slight emendation of MT's *baśśekû*, 'at Seku', to *baśśēpî*, 'on the bare height') and requires a minor emendation of *bôr haggādôl* ('the great cistern'; which if correct

asks a surprising question: *Where are Samuel and David?* (v. 22b). The question is disconcerting because Saul has already been told precisely where David is (v. 19). One is reminded of the earlier occasion when Saul, at a water source on the outskirts of Ramah, was expressly told where he would meet Samuel (9:13) and yet a few verses later, face to face with Samuel himself in the predicted location, asks, *Would you please tell me where the seer's house is?* (9:18).

23–24. Despite his firm resolve to kill David, Saul is no more able to resist the overpowering *Spirit of God* than were his agents (vv. 20–21). The Spirit comes *even on him* while he is still on his way to Naioth, so that *he walked along prophesying* (v. 23); clearly, it was not some kind of mob psychology that affected Saul, as he had not yet reached Naioth. Thwarted in his homicidal quest, Saul *stripped off [pšṭ] his garments, and he too prophesied in Samuel's presence* (v. 24a). Saul's garments would presumably include his royal robe. So Saul's 'nakedness'[37] signifies more than his vulnerability and loss of control; it signifies his loss of the kingdom. The same verb as here was used to describe Jonathan's earlier removal (*pšṭ*) of the symbols of his royal status and voluntary presentation of them to David (18:4). Now Saul is involuntarily divested of his own royal garments. The kingdom is no longer rightfully his. The next time the verb *pšṭ* occurs in relation to Saul, it will describe the Philistines' stripping his corpse of his armour (31:9).

This is why people say, 'Is Saul also among the prophets?' (v. 24b). Not for the first time do people find Saul's behaviour out of character. Especially surprising is his engaging in prophecy. In 10:11, those familiar with Saul were surprised to see Saul prophesying and asked, 'Is even Saul among the prophets?' At that point in the narrative, this was still an open question. Perhaps Saul was indeed among the prophets. By the present point in the narrative, however,

---

should read *habbôr haggādôl*) to the grammatically correct *bôr haggōren* ('the cistern of the threshing floor'); cf. Gordon (1986: 165 n. 46); McCarter (1980: 328–329).

37. It is not clear that Saul was completely naked, though he may have been. The word *'ārôm* is variously used to describe one who is naked, lightly dressed or lacking in resources (cf. *HALOT, NIDOTTE, TWOT*).

the question has a more cynical ring to it. Saul's breach with Samuel is final, and Saul is only *among the prophets* when overwhelmed against his will by divine power. Appearances can be deceiving.

Meaning
In several respects, 1 Samuel 19 marks a turning point in the narrative. Saul drops any attempt at subtlety in his determination to kill David. David surrenders any hope of being at peace with Saul and begins the life of a fugitive. Saul's son and daughter face their own crises of allegiance. The breach between Samuel and Saul had become certain at the end of 1 Samuel 15, and in that same chapter, Saul had been rejected by Yahweh for his own rejecting of the word (and hence the rule) of Yahweh. Forced to decide, both Jonathan and Michal decide to choose David and in their own ways demonstrate their loyalty to him. Saul's intransigence in the face of the divine will that he step aside for one better than he means that he is increasingly isolated from those in sync with the divine purposes.

Structurally, the framing of chapters 18–19 by two royal divestments was noted already in the introduction to chapter 19. A further structure involving a larger stretch of text is also worth noting. Taking the two occurrences of the saying *Is Saul also among the prophets?* (10:11 and 19:24) as framing the materials in between, we discover that in the very centre of this stretch of the text are verses describing the definitive rejection of Saul. One way to delimit this central section would be to begin it with 15:11 (*I regret that I have made Saul king*) and conclude it with 15:28 (*The LORD has torn the kingdom of Israel from you today*). Between these two signal passages regarding the fate of King Saul is also his formal rejection in the famous 15:22–23. It may be no more than coincidence, but from the first occurrence of the saying (10:11) to 15:11 there are 143 verses. And from 15:28 to the second occurrence of the saying (19:24) there are also 143 verses.[38]

---

38. Such an observation must be held lightly, as there are numerous variables. The numbers of words either side of the central section differ by only 4%, but text-critical issues make precision in word counting unachievable at present.

Various similarities between the events recounted in 1 Samuel 19 and the Jacob stories of Genesis are sometimes noted: younger daughters (Rachel and Michal) engaging with teraphim while outwitting deceptive fathers (Laban and Saul), husbands (Jacob and David) fleeing their fathers-in-law, and so forth. The effect of these intertextual allusions may be to underscore the 'strength of the divine promise despite continual threat to the fruition of that promise' (Bodner and White 2014: 33). Moreover, the inclusion of echoes of the experience of the patriarchs in the story of David begins to prepare the reader for the refocusing of the patriarchal promise precisely on David and his descendants in 2 Samuel 7.

ii. Jonathan aids and encourages David (20:1–42)
Context
From his first introduction in 1 Samuel 13, Jonathan has served as a foil to his father, Saul. In contrast to Saul's fearful faltering, based on a lack of trust in Yahweh, Jonathan has shown himself to be a man of great faith. The contrasts continue in the present chapter. While Saul set himself to kill David in the preceding chapter, Jonathan sets himself in this chapter to save him, but only after he sees with his own eyes that Saul does indeed mean to kill David. The alienation of Saul even from his own family continues. In the preceding chapter Saul's daughter Michal was forced to choose between obeying her father and protecting David, and she chose the latter. Now it is Jonathan who must choose whether to thwart his father by helping David escape.

Comment
1–11. Not surprisingly, Saul's arrival at Naioth (19:23) causes David to take flight yet again (cf. 19:10, 12). Finding Jonathan, David asks a series of rhetorical questions that amount to an oath of innocence in the face of Saul's attempts to kill him (v. 1). Jonathan's immediate response is *Never!* (v. 2). The Hebrew interjection *ḥālîlâ* lacks a precise English synonym. Similar to Latin *absit*, it means something like 'may that never be' or 'may that be far from you' (cf. JPS 'Heaven forbid!'; NRSV 'Far from it'; NKJV 'By no means!'; NLT 'That's not true!'). The interjection has occurred three times already in 1 Samuel, each time indicating a distancing from some

action (2:30, Yahweh distancing himself from his prior word to the house of Eli; 12:23, Samuel distancing himself from the notion that he might cease to pray for and instruct the people; and 14:45, a particularly interesting reference as it is in the context of Saul's threatening to kill his own son, to which the people respond with a definitive *ḥālîlâ!*).

Jonathan is equally definitive in his response to David, insisting that his father is not seeking to kill David. Jonathan's insistence seems curious in view of Saul's explicit instructions in 19:1 that David must be killed. On that earlier occasion, however, Jonathan was able to reason with his father, and Saul had even sworn an oath that *David will not be put to death* (19:6). Perhaps recalling that oath, and also confident that his father would not attempt anything *without letting me know* (v. 2), Jonathan assumes that David must be mistaken. But David explains that Saul is keeping Jonathan in the dark, because he *knows very well that I have found favour in your eyes* (v. 3a). Finally convinced, Jonathan responds in verse 4, *Whatever you[39] want me to do, I'll do for you*.

David is ready with a plan involving *the New Moon feast* the next day (vv. 5–8). Celebrated on or just before the new moon each month, the feast was a time of rejoicing (Num. 10:10), likely regulated in ways similar to the sabbath (Amos 8:5), with which it is sometimes mentioned (e.g. 2 Kgs 4:23). New moon festivals were celebrated on into the post-exilic period and are mentioned in Colossians 2:16. The king and his court had responsibilities at such times (Ezek. 45:17), and so David's absence may have had political consequences.[40] The fact that David's plan involves deception may or may not raise ethical questions. One recalls Yahweh's instructions in 16:2 that Samuel should tell Saul, if necessary, a half-truth. David's outright deception here may be in some respects justified by the fact that Saul has made himself David's sworn enemy. But as the narrative unfolds it will become evident that others of David's deceptions cost him or others dearly (see, e.g., 21:2 and 22:22).

---

39. Lit. 'your soul' (*napšĕkā*), which neatly echoes David's reference in v. 3 to Jonathan's life, lit. 'your soul' (*napšekā*). Cf. 18:1, 3.
40. For fuller discussion and bibliography, see Long (2009a: 355).

David concludes his plan deferentially and humbly, referring to himself as Jonathan's *servant* and reminding Jonathan of the *covenant* that Jonathan initiated with him (v. 8). David concludes his plea by putting himself at Jonathan's mercy: *If I am guilty, then kill me yourself!* Jonathan responds with a second resounding *Never!* (*ḥālîlâ*, v. 9; cf. v. 2). The two then depart to the field to arrange how Jonathan will be able to get word to David (vv. 10–11).

12–17. Once in the field (v. 11), Jonathan agrees to go along with David's plan and even swears an oath to that effect (vv. 12–13a). Before turning to ask for *unfailing kindness* (*ḥesed*)[41] for himself and his family (vv. 14–15),[42] Jonathan blesses David with these words: *May the* LORD *be with you as he has been with my father* (v. 13b). We have elsewhere noted that Yahweh is not said to be 'with Saul', in contradistinction to the many times he is said to be 'with David'. The apparent exception here must be viewed in its proper context. Jonathan is not suggesting that Yahweh was ever 'with Saul' in any vital or relational sense but, rather, he is invoking upon David the enabling divine presence without which one cannot properly rule as king in Israel. Jonathan is in no doubt of Yahweh's designs for David (cf. 18:4; 23:17). That Saul ruled for a time as Israel's king implies at least a degree of divine enabling, but Saul repeatedly ignored or resisted the word of Yahweh, and so the enabling spirit of God departed from him (16:14).

Having pledged his loyalty to David, Jonathan is wise to seek a reassurance from David of the covenant existing between them (vv. 14–17; cf. 18:1). Descendants of a dethroned king tended not to fare well at the hands of the successful new king (e.g. 2 Kgs 10:11). Whether Jonathan in verse 16 calls upon Yahweh to hold David himself to account or merely David's enemies is not entirely clear in this context, but it seems likely that *enemies* represents a

---

41. This term lacks a precise English equivalent, prompting combinations such as 'lovingkindness'; central to its range of meaning is the notion of covenant loyalty.
42. For David's faithfulness to his affirmative response to Jonathan, see 2 Sam. 9:1–8; 21:7.

euphemism.[43] Whatever the case, covenantal 'love language' is strong in verse 17.[44]

18–23. David's plan to discover Saul's attitude towards him was explained to Jonathan in verses 5–7, but David's question in verse 10 about how the results will be reported to him is still unanswered. Picking up on that issue (v. 18), Jonathan proposes that *The day after tomorrow, towards evening*, David should *go to the place where you hid when this trouble began* (v. 19; the reference must be to David's hiding in 19:2–7). The Hebrew of 20:19 poses difficulties, as the various modern translations attest.[45] The basic sense is clear enough, though. David is to go into hiding and *wait by the stone Ezel* (v. 19). Otherwise unattested in MT as a proper name, *Ezel* (if related to the Hebrew root *'zl*, 'go away, disappear')[46] may designate a well-known

---

43. Clearer examples of the euphemistic inclusion of *enemies* are 1 Sam. 25:22 and 2 Sam. 12:14 (see NIV text notes to both verses; cf. Gordon 1986: 167).

44. The use of personal pronouns in v. 17 leaves some question as to whether it is Jonathan's love for David or David's love for Jonathan that is in focus at the end of the verse. Brueggemann (1990: 149) and Birch (1998: 1135–1136), for instance, lean towards the latter, while most translators and commentators assume the former. If it is David's love for Jonathan that is in view, 'this is noteworthy', as Firth (2009: 226) remarks, 'because elsewhere we hear of others who love David, not of David's love for them'.

45. Is David to 'go a long way down' (NRSV; cf. JPS 'go down all the way'), or is he to 'go down quickly' (ESV), or is he to go down 'towards evening' (NIV)? ESV makes best sense of MT as it stands, fits the context and may find support in Jer. 2:36, where a verb of motion is followed by *mě'ōd* in the sense of moving 'quickly' (Barthélemy 1982: 198–199). Tsumura (2007: 511–514) retains MT and proposes a new reading of v. 19 as follows: 'And you shall wait three days and come after dark on the working day to the place where you hid yourself and stay near the stone Ezel.' Apart from 'after dark', this understanding is very much like that of eleventh-century French rabbi Rashi (Rosenberg 1980: 171).

46. For the verb, see Deut. 32:36; 1 Sam. 9:7; Prov. 20:14; and in Aramaic, Dan. 2:17; Ezra 5:15.

landmark, perhaps connoting something like the 'departure stone' (a prominent stone on the way out of town?) or even the 'hiding stone' (a place to make oneself disappear?).[47] For other potential examples of landmarks bearing descriptive names, see 19:22; 2 Samuel 15:17; 20:8.

Jonathan's plan to shoot three arrows and then shout messages to the *boy* (*na'ar*, 'boy, young man, servant') brought along to retrieve them is both clever and effective (vv. 20–22), disguising his signalling as shooting practice and making it easy to encode a come-or-go message to the hiding David. The boy would also serve as a witness that Jonathan's activities in the field were innocent. In verse 22, the 'boy' is referred to as an *'elem* ('youth, young man'). Why this word choice? The word appears only one other time in the Old Testament, namely, in 17:56, in Saul's reference to David. Moreover, the first of several homonymous verbs of the root *'lm* speaks of that which is hidden, or concealed. A term with such resonances seems particularly fitting in the present episode.

With the plan laid out, Jonathan returns one more time to *the matter you and I discussed*, namely, the covenant of *unfailing kindness* (*ḥesed*) guaranteeing the safety of Jonathan's immediate family (vv. 14–15). In terms reminiscent of the parting between Jacob and Laban (Gen. 31:49–53), Jonathan emphasizes to David that *the LORD is witness between you and me for ever* (v. 23). Great power can be dangerous even in the most capable hands.

24–34. *Saul said to Jonathan, 'Why hasn't the son of Jesse come to the meal, either yesterday or today?'* (v. 27). The scene unfolds as David had anticipated (vv. 5–8). Saul, with his military commander Abner[48] at his side and Jonathan sitting opposite, does not at first react to David's absence from the feast, reckoning that he must be *unclean – surely he is unclean* (v. 26). NIV is justified in adding *ceremonially*, as the focus is on ritual or religious cleanness.[49] Saul's repetition suggests

---

47. Cf. Rashi, who suggests 'travelers' stone' (Rosenberg 1980: 172).
48. Known already from 14:50–51 and 17:55–57.
49. While ritual cleanliness is mentioned throughout the Pentateuch (Gen. 7:2; Lev. 5:2; Num. 5:2; Deut. 14:3–21; etc.), the topic is most fully treated in Lev. 11 – 15; on the present circumstance, see Lev. 7:19–21.

that he is trying to convince himself that nothing more than coincidence and ceremonial protocol is involved in David's absence. When David is absent a second day, however, Saul is unable to quiet his suspicion, and so he asks Jonathan the direct question cited above (v. 27).

Jonathan's answer is according to plan, though in verses 28–29 he embellishes David's basic instructions with believable details (cf. v. 6). Some of Jonathan's embellishments seem unwise and counter-productive, such as his placing in David's mouth the request *let me go* (v. 29; *mlṭ* nipʻal normally speaks of escaping, fleeing, slipping away). But Saul is not buying Jonathan's story in any case, and he unleashes a no-holds-barred attack on Jonathan, first with words (v. 30) and then with his weapon (v. 33). Sandwiched between these attacks is a verbal exchange that shows how great is the divide between Saul and Jonathan when it comes to David. After calling Jonathan a *son of a perverse and rebellious woman*,[50] Saul says, *As long as the son of Jesse lives on this earth, neither you nor your kingdom will be established* (v. 31). Clearly, Saul has not accepted the verdict of 13:14 – that no Saulide dynasty is any longer possible – to say nothing of the verdict of 15:28; had he accepted the latter, he would no longer be acting as king. Jonathan, for his part, defends David: *What has he done?* (v. 32). To this Saul answers with a spear, seeking to *kill* (lit. 'strike', *nkh* hipʻil) Jonathan, as he had sought to kill David in 18:11 and 19:10 (where in both contexts the same verb is used). Like David, however, Jonathan manages to escape unharmed, now fully convinced *that his father intended to kill David* (v. 33). As Polzin (1989: 192) remarks, the point of the whole elaborate exercise is 'to enable Jonathan, not David, to discover that Saul still harbors murderous

---

(note 49 *cont*.) The boundary between physical uncleanness and ritual uncleanness should not be drawn too sharply (on the topic of sin, pollution and purity in the ANE, see Johnston 2004: 496–513).

50. A slur meant to shame Jonathan more than his mother, perhaps not unlike a modern slur such as 'you son of a bitch'; see Youngblood (2009: 204) for further such translational options, but note also Gordon's (1986: 168) commendation of restraint from 'the dysphemisms of some of the more carefree modern versions'.

intentions' towards David. Now fully convinced, *Jonathan got up from the table in fierce anger* and *did not eat*. He is *grieved* (*ṣb* nipʻal). This was precisely what, according to David, Saul had hoped to avoid by keeping Jonathan in the dark (v. 3, where the same verb is used).[51] In keeping with his character, Jonathan is grieved not so much by his father's aggression towards him as by his *shameful treatment of David* (v. 34).

35–42. *In the morning*, probably as soon as possible without raising suspicion, *Jonathan went out to the field for his meeting with David* (v. 35). The sign with bow and arrows is effected as planned, with the addition of words of urgency, ostensibly to the boy fetching the arrows but clearly intended for David: *Hurry! Go quickly! Don't stop!* (v. 38). The boy, for the first time qualified as a *small boy* in verse 35, knows nothing of the true significance of the exercise – *only Jonathan and David knew* (v. 39). Thus, the boy can return to town, carrying Jonathan's weapons (v. 40) and providing a perfect alibi and, if necessary, a trusted witness to the innocence of Jonathan's activities. Sophisticated subterfuge would be unlikely on the lips of a small boy.

Once the boy has gone, David arises from his hiding place[52] and bows face-to-the-ground three times before Jonathan (v. 41). Such repeated bowing was a sign of deference in the ANE (see on 24:8). *Then they kissed each other*, expressing their sworn friendship. A similar exchange is recounted in the Gilgamesh Epic, where Gilgamesh and his friend Enkidu 'kissed each other and formed a friendship' just prior to Gilgamesh's embarking on a dangerous venture (*ANET* 79a).[53] Jonathan and David *wept together – but David*

---

51. The only other time *ṣb* nipʻal is used in Samuel is to describe David's grieving over Absalom (2 Sam. 19:2; Heb. v. 3).
52. Uncertainty in how to understand just where David emerged (*from the south side of the stone*, NIV; 'from beside the stone heap', NRSV; 'from his concealment at the Negeb', JPS; etc.) does not materially affect the scene.
53. In the Bible, as in the ANE generally (and indeed in many cultures today), a kiss can connote many things: friendship, affection, obeisance, etc. In addition to the present context, instances of kissing in 1 and 2 Sam. include the kiss of honour by Samuel at the time of

wept the most, or perhaps, 'until David gained control of himself' (v. 41).⁵⁴

The last words are Jonathan's, pronouncing a blessing on David – *Go in peace* – and reminding him one last time of their sworn friendship *in the name of the* LORD, who will stand as *witness between you and me, and between your descendants and my descendants for ever* (v. 42). Jonathan and David will meet but one more time, in 23:16–18, where Jonathan will help David *find strength in God* and will assure him that he will *be king over Israel*. Jonathan will die with his father on Mount Gilboa in a battle against the Philistines (31:2).

The final sentence of verse 42 is regarded in MT and the ancient versions (with the exception of Vulg.) as the first verse of chapter 21. The sentence, literally 'Then he [David] arose and went, while Jonathan entered the city', is transitional, both concluding chapter 20 by recording the departure of its two main characters and also introducing the commencement in chapter 21 of David's years on the run in the wilderness.

Meaning
There is great poignancy in the parting of David and Jonathan. They will meet again, in a time of great danger for David, and Jonathan will help David *find strength in God* (23:16). Jonathan is the model of a true, faithful and godly friend. His relationship of loyalty to David seems to reflect and be made possible by his relationship to Yahweh. Without a sense of the Lord's providential ordering of events, it seems unlikely that Jonathan would have so freely

---

(note 53 *cont.*) Saul's anointing (1 Sam. 10:1), David's kiss of friendship when parting from Barzillai in 2 Sam. 19:39 and Joab's treacherous kiss of Amasa in 2 Sam. 20:9. In 2 Sam. 14:33, David's kiss of Absalom effectively avoids the needed conversation that might have satisfied Absalom's desire for justice and is soon followed by Absalom's wooing the people with promises of justice and his stealing their affections with a kiss (2 Sam. 15:5–6).

54. The Hebrew, *'ad-dāwid higdîl*, is cryptic and difficult. The notion of David's gaining control of his emotions is reflected, e.g., in the German Schlachter version (1951): 'bis David sich meistern konnte'.

supported David and given up his own rights as crown prince. For some, 'it is simply beyond belief that the crown prince would surrender his right to the throne in deference to David' (McKenzie 2000: 84–85). But such selfless action is not beyond belief for those whose loyalties to God put matters of personal advancement in proper perspective. Noteworthy is the fact that Jonathan did not choose to escape with David but remained behind. Caught in a terrible bind between his loyalty to David, as God's new designee, and his duty to his father, the rejected king unwilling to abdicate, Jonathan courageously sought to do justice to both.

iii. David deceives Ahimelech and escapes to Gath (21:1–15)
Context
With David and Jonathan's parting of the ways, though not of loyalties, David's wilderness years begin. He is on his own, alone. Heretofore he has had supporters – Samuel who anointed him, and Michal and Jonathan who each helped him escape. And he has had admirers – the dancing singers of 18:7, *all the people*, and even Saul's own officers (18:5). The problem is Saul, whose initial liking of David (16:21) quickly turned to jealousy and anger (18:8–9), then fear (18:12), then animosity (18:29), then to a myopic focus on killing David (19:1). So David has to run, or at least so it seems to him. But where will he go, and how will he run? The present chapter describes two encounters, one with Ahimelech, priest of Nob (vv. 1–9), and a second with Achish king of Gath (vv. 10–15).[55]

Comment
1–6. David's first stop is at Nob, described in 22:19 as the *town of the priests*. After the destruction of Shiloh (see at 6:21), Nob appears to have served as a (or the) key cultic centre. Nob has not been definitively located, though several sites within a few miles of Jerusalem make good candidates. The remark in Isaiah 10:32 that invaders will stop at Nob and shake their fist at Jerusalem confirms the nearness of Nob to Jerusalem.

---

55. Regarding versification, it should be noted that the English verse numbers lag one behind the Hebrew; see on 20:42 above.

The priest Ahimelek *trembled when he met him* (v. 1), as indeed the elders had trembled when Samuel arrived in Bethlehem in 16:4 (the verb *ḥrd* is used on both occasions). The cause of Ahimelek's trembling is not specified. One possibility is that Ahimelek is made uneasy by the fact that David comes alone. By this point David is a well-established commander of troops, and Ahimelek quite likely has encountered him often at the head of troops taking to or returning from the field. Another possibility is that Ahimelek's anxiousness stems from his knowledge that an officer of Saul named Doeg the Edomite is on-site to witness whatever transpires between Ahimelek and David (cf. Reis 1994; Bodner 2008: 225). The reader will not learn of Doeg until verse 7. Ahimelek's repetition of essentially the same question to David, *Why are you alone? Why is no one with you?* (v. 1), may simply indicate nervousness, or it may be an ingenious attempt to 'inform David that Ahimelech [himself] is not alone' (Reis 1994: 64).

According to the first and more common view, David's answers to Ahimelek's questions are meant to fool him (or at least to provide him with plausible deniability of any wrongdoing should Saul question him – David claimed to be on a mission for the king). According to the second view, David quickly discerns the situation and begins playing along with Ahimelek's charade to fool Doeg. In either case, his answer that *The king sent me on a mission* (v. 2) artfully avoids naming Saul, though that is the surface implication. Perhaps a veiled reference to Israel's true king, Yahweh, hides below the surface? The conversation turns to David's need for bread for himself and ostensibly for his men, the urgency of the mission having precluded the making of adequate preparations (v. 3). With no *ordinary bread to hand*, Ahimelek offers *consecrated bread . . . provided the men have kept themselves from women* (v. 4).[56] David answers in the

---

56. As Baldwin (1988: 147) observes, this strict discipline 'was based, not on any ascetic view of marriage, which is totally alien to the Bible, but on united and total commitment to the cause of the Lord, in whose name the battle was being fought'. Such abstention related to ritual purity (cf. Lev. 15, esp. v. 18) and could also be required prior to auspicious occasions other than battles (e.g. Exod. 19:15).

affirmative, including himself – *women have been kept from us* – and emphasizing that this is always the case, even on missions less holy than the present one (v. 5). The narrator confirms in verse 6 that there was in fact *no bread there except the bread of the Presence.*[57] On that score at least, Ahimelek is not bluffing.

7. The conversation between David and Ahimelek is briefly interrupted to report that *Doeg the Edomite, Saul's chief shepherd*, was there that day. This new information heightens the tension in the scene and prompts the reader to reconsider what is going on between Ahimelek and David. Are they speaking in veiled language, because one of Saul's men is present? Or, as discussed above, is David genuinely deceiving Ahimelek? The answer is not obvious, but perhaps that is the point.

That Saul's court should require the services of a 'chief of the shepherds' (*'abbîr hārō'îm*) may offer a hint that the acquisitive royal behaviour warned about in Samuel's speech in 1 Samuel 8 (see esp. v. 17) has begun already under Israel's first king. Alternatively, given the fact that in 22:17–18 Doeg is associated with Saul's *rāṣîm* (lit. 'runners', rendered *guards* in NIV), some have suggested that *rō'îm* in the present verse is a misreading of very similar-looking *rāṣîm* (on both possibilities, see Gordon 1986: 171; for a thorough defence of MT based on Assyrian and Hittite military titles, see Aster 2003). If Doeg held a military post in Saul's court, whether as 'chief of the runners/guards' or 'chief of the shepherds', this would explain both David's immediate request in 21:8 for *a spear or sword* – Doeg would have been an experienced fighter. This fact is amply demonstrated in 22:18–19, where Doeg strikes down not only eighty-five priests but pretty much every other living thing in Nob.

8–9. In response to David's request for *a spear or sword* (v. 8), the priest mentions the *sword of Goliath the Philistine, whom you killed in the Valley of Elah* (v. 9). David will hardly have been in need of a history lesson, and so Ahimelek's detailing of the Goliath incident may have been for Doeg's benefit. Perhaps it served to remind Doeg of David's service to Saul, or to remind him that David, even

---

57. On *bread of the Presence*, see Lev. 24:5–9; and for Jesus' comment on David's taking of the consecrated bread, see Matt. 12:1–8.

without standard-issue military equipment, is not to be underestimated. The reader also learns that *there is no sword here but that one*, which may help explain how Doeg later could slaughter so many in Nob with little mention of resistance. David commends the sword and takes it (v. 9), and perhaps breathes a bit more easily in the presence of a potential enemy.

How Goliath's sword ended up wrapped and stowed *behind the ephod* (v. 9) is not explained, but it may reflect the common practice of depositing the spoils of war, including the symbols of defeated 'gods', in the sacred precinct of the victor (see at 5:1–5). On the variety of things the term *ephod* can designate, see at 2:18–21.

10–15. *That day David fled from Saul and went to Achish king of Gath* (v. 10). David has fled Saul's presence before (19:10, 12) but remained each time in Israelite territory (19:18; 20:1; 21:1). This time he chooses to cross a border into Philistine territory. Perhaps he hopes that pursuers will be hesitant to follow and calculates that the risk of suffering harm at Philistine hands is less than that of staying within Saul's reach. Arriving in Gath, a border town between Philistia and Israel that sometimes changed hands (cf. 7:14),[58] David soon discovers that he may have miscalculated. His presence is immediately noted and reported by *the servants of Achish*, who identify him as *the king of the land* about whom the dancers sang (v. 11; cf. 18:7). Their knowledge of the lyric indicates their knowledge of Saul and makes their identification of David as the king of the land all the more telling. David's successes in the field may have alerted them to his rising fortunes. Might they also have heard of Saul's rejection – that he is no longer rightful king, at least in the eyes of Yahweh's prophetic spokesman? At the very least, as Bodner notes (2008: 229), 'their statement has an (unintentionally) prophetic resonance in light of the larger storyline'.

David took these words to heart and was very much afraid of Achish king of Gath (v. 12). David's fear might seem incongruous, given his fearlessness during the earlier showdown with a much more menacing

---

58. Gath is identified with modern Tel Zafit (Tell es-Safi), a site lying some 5 miles west of the famous Valley of Elah (for more, see Long 2009a: 296–297).

Philistine from Gath (ch. 17), but perhaps the difference is that on the earlier occasion David could say with confidence, *You come against me with sword and spear and javelin, but I come against you in the name of the LORD Almighty, the God of the armies of Israel, whom you have defied* (17:45). This time, David has a sword – the sword of Goliath of Gath no less![59] But does he have the Lord's commission? Was it faith or fear that sent the young man westwards into Philistine territory? We are not told. Adding to David's anxiety might be memory of his 'surgical exploits in Philistine territory'[60] whereby David collected a bride-price for Michal (18:27). His bravado in doubling the requested amount will have earned him no friends among the Philistines. And so David is indeed *very much afraid*. But he has the wit to act as if he has lost his wits. There is a certain comic irony in Achish's response: *Am I so short of madmen that you have to bring this fellow here . . . ?* (v. 15). Despite his self-assured air, Achish is clearly duped. Were his servants, whom he slights by his reference to *madmen*, equally outwitted? Perhaps not, but they are not in charge. This will not be the last time that Achish is duped by David (see 28:2).

Meaning
Fear is a harsh master. It can drive one to say and do things that one otherwise would not consider. David's first two recorded experiences of life on the run involve him in deception. In the first, at least according to the traditional understanding, he deceives an ally, Ahimelek priest of Nob. In the second, David's deception involves the Philistine king Achish. That David should run to one of the cities of Israel's perennial enemy seems an odd move. But desperate times call for desperate measures. And David seems desperate. Should he have been? Saul is certainly a danger, and one from whom some safe distance should be gained. But one is prompted to ask whether David in this chapter is following divine directives or is simply fleeing for his life. On various occasions, reference is made to David's enquiring of the Lord with respect to

---

59. Unless he had the wit to conceal or stash it before entering Gath.
60. As Bodner (2008: 229) adroitly puts it.

where he should go and what he should do (e.g. 23:2, 4; 30:8; 2 Sam. 2:1; 5:19, 23). No such reference is recorded in the present chapter. What will come of all this?

iv. David continues his flight; Saul massacres the priests at Nob (22:1–23)

Context

David's flight from Saul began in the preceding chapter with two encounters, the first with an ally, Ahimelek, and the second with an enemy, Achish of Gath. David narrowly escapes Gath and must continue his flight. The present chapter recounts David's initial movements, first to the cave of Adullam and then, directed by the prophet Gad, into the heartland of Judah (vv. 1–5). The bulk of the chapter, however, focuses on the massacre of the priests at Nob at the hands of Saul through his henchman Doeg (vv. 6–19). The final verses of the chapter return to the camp of David and to David's admission of responsibility to Abiathar, the sole survivor from Nob (vv. 20–23).

Comment

1–4. The Philistine city of Gath proved more dangerous than anticipated. So David crosses back into Judahite territory, escaping (*mlṭ* nipʿal) to the *cave of Adullam* (v. 1). In biblical times, as today in parts of the world, caves sometimes provided refuge for those on the run (cf. 13:6).[61] *Adullam* (modern Khirbet esh-Sheikh Madhkur) lies roughly 9 miles east-south-east of Gath, between Sokoh and Keilah, and about midway between Gath and Bethlehem.[62] David's *brothers and his father's household* are not blind to the fact that their own lives are endangered by Saul's animosity towards David. After all, Saul has not hesitated to hurl a spear even at his own son (20:33). And so they join David at Adullam (v. 1), as do others *in distress or in debt or discontented* (*mar-nepeš*; JPS has 'desperate').

---

[61]. The name Adullam may reflect an east Semitic root suggesting a 'closed-in place' (*HALOT*) and so mean something like refuge or retreat.

[62]. See also Adullam in 2 Sam 23:13 and the titles to Pss 57 and 142.

By the end of verse 2 some *four hundred men* have placed themselves under David's command. These disfranchised men form the core of David's wilderness band. But David has also to think about his parents, who are unlikely to fare well as fugitives in the desert. Seeking out the *king of Moab* at *Mizpah*,[63] David requests that his *father and mother* be allowed to stay with the Moabite king until David has learned *what God will do for me* (v. 3). This might seem an odd move but for two considerations. First, having a common enemy sometimes makes for unlikely friends, and neither David nor Moab has fared well at Saul's hand (on the latter, see 14:47). Second, David has a family connection with Moab through his great-grandmother Ruth the Moabitess (Ruth 4:13–17).

So he left them with the king of Moab (v. 4). As on earlier occasions, we see David acting responsibly with respect to his duties (see at 17:28). Also as on other occasions (cf. 2 Sam. 15:25–26), David takes whatever measures seem practical but ultimately entrusts himself to the sovereign will of God (v. 3b).

5. Appearing for the first time and without further introduction (as is sometimes the case with persons assumed to be well known to the ancient audience), *the prophet Gad* instructs David to leave *the stronghold* and to *Go into the land of Judah*. The reasoning behind Gad's instruction is not stated, but perhaps he knew that Saul would hear of David's whereabouts and of his band of four hundred (cf. 22:6), making it best for David not to remain too long in one place. Gad's directive that David should *Go into the land of Judah* seems to indicate that *the stronghold* was somewhere in Moabite territory, in which case the sojourn of David's parents with the king of Moab would have been brief, since verse 4 states that David's parents stayed with the king of Moab *as long as David was in the stronghold* (cf. Firth 2009: 237). The phrase, however, may be a shorthand way of referring to David's 'wilderness years' when he was on the run, being pursued by Saul and frequenting *wilderness strongholds* (23:14). If 'the' stronghold in view in the present verse is Adullam or perhaps Masada,

---

63. Not to be confused with Benjaminite Mizpah (1 Sam. 7:7, 11, 16; 10:17); two sites south-west of Madaba in Transjordan have been conjectured as possible locations for Moabite Mizpah (*ABD* 4: 880).

which according to Aharoni (1979: 290) was near the best ford across the Jordan River between Judah and Moab, then the sense of Gad's instruction may be that David should go deeper into Judahite territory and not remain too long in any one stronghold. David responds by repairing to the *forest of Hereth*, mentioned only here in the Bible. If McCarter (1980: 357) is correct in finding an echo of the name *Hereth* in the modern village of 'Kharas', located near modern 'Khirbet Qîlā' (biblical Keilah), then the forest would be in the vicinity of Adullam (see at 22:1).

6–8. Saul's seat *under the tamarisk tree on the hill at Gibeah, with all his officials standing at his side* (v. 6), suggests that he is holding court in typical Ancient Near Eastern style (cf. *ANET* 151a; Judg. 4:5). But his words, upon hearing *that David and his men had been discovered*, indicate that he is beginning to feel very much alone. It is no surprise, therefore, that he holds his *spear in hand* (v. 6). This small detail reminds the attentive reader of the fact that Saul's spear has recently been wielded not only against David but against Jonathan as well (18:10–11; 19:10; 20:33). And it sets the stage for Saul's violent behaviour in the current episode. Saul's address to the *men of Benjamin*, his own tribe, recalls the kind of royal acquisition and redistribution warned of in 1 Samuel 8:10–18. His point is that this *son of Jesse* (from Judah) is hardly likely to show the kind of favouritism that Saul has apparently shown or promised (v. 7). And yet, in a rhetorical flourish, Saul maintains that nothing short of such benefits can account for the fact that *you have all conspired against me*. Saul is correct that his son has made a covenant with the son of Jesse, but he is grossly mistaken (even paranoid) in assuming that *my son has incited my servant to lie in wait for me* (v. 8). The situation is, in fact, the reverse. It is Saul who, since 19:1, has expressly been seeking David's life.

9–10. Of all those attending Saul, only Doeg the Edomite (see at 21:7) speaks up in response to Saul's complaint that no-one tells him anything. Oddly, Saul does not castigate Doeg for only now mentioning what he had witnessed at Nob, but perhaps that is because what Doeg reports is of sufficient note to capture Saul's attention. Doeg's report differs from the event as recounted in chapter 21 in two key respects. He makes no mention of David's claim that he was on a mission for Saul, and he himself claims that

Ahimelek enquired of the LORD for *the son of Jesse* (Doeg adopts Saul's dismissive reference to David not by name but by patronage). In omitting David's claim about the nature of his mission and adding his own claim that Ahimelek enquired of Yahweh for David, Doeg bolsters the case against Ahimelek, and it is to Ahimelek that Saul's attention now turns.

11–16. Saul wastes no time in sending for *the priest Ahimelek son of Ahitub and all the men of his family* (v. 11). As when referring to the *son of Jesse*, so also with Ahimelek, Saul does not honour him by using his name but calls him simply *son of Ahitub*. Ahimelek's response is nevertheless respectful: *Yes, my lord* (lit. 'Here am I, my lord'; v. 12). Fuelled by Doeg's report and his own paranoia, Saul charges Ahimelek with conspiring with *the son of Jesse, giving him bread and a sword and enquiring of God for him*. He even adds the charge he had earlier levelled against his own men (v. 8): Ahimelek is accused of encouraging David in his rebellion such that he now *lies in wait for me* (v. 13). This charge is as unjustified as it was earlier; David is not seeking Saul's life, and this will shortly be demonstrated twice over (chs. 24 and 26).

To Saul's false charges, Ahimelek offers a truthful response that amounts to a telling defence of David: *loyal* (more than *all your servants*), related (*the king's son-in-law*), useful and trusted (*captain of your bodyguard*) and *respected* [*nikbād*] *in your household* (v. 14). Ahimelek makes no mention of providing bread and a sword, which he tacitly admits, but he does address the matter of enquiring of God for David: *Was that day the first time I enquired of God for him? Of course not!* (v. 15a). Most modern translations and commentators assume that Ahimelek is admitting to having enquired of God for David, but this is by no means certain. First, the account of David's encounter with Ahimelek in chapter 21 makes no mention of any such enquiry. Second, it is difficult to imagine what the nature of such an enquiry would have been. If David was deceiving Ahimelek about the true nature of his mission, what kind of enquiry might he have requested, and how would Yahweh have responded? Alternatively, if Ahimelek was aware of David's true situation and was playing along so as to deceive the watchful Doeg, the same question arises: what kind of enquiry would he have conducted? Would the enquiry have been just for show? What would have been the point of that, and would Yahweh have played along? Third, it was only Doeg who introduced the notion of a divine enquiry in the first place, while omitting other pertinent information; he is hardly to be trusted. But what then of Ahimelek's words in verse 15a? The Hebrew text is ambiguous. While the kind of translation adopted by NIV and most modern translations cannot be excluded, a different reading commends itself: 'Did I begin that day to enquire of God for him [David]? Far be it from me [*ḥālîlâ lî*]' to do such a thing. Ahimelek's claim would be that he was emphatically not in the habit of conducting divine enquiries for David and he did not begin to do so *that day* (cf. Alter 1999: 138; Taggar-Cohen 2005: 262, which see for discussion).

Ahimelek's defence of himself and his family (v. 15b) falls on deaf ears. As Josephus (*Ant.* 6.259) writes, 'These words of the high priest did not persuade Saul, for fear is strong enough to disbelieve even a truthful plea.' Without further discussion, Saul pronounces judgment, referring to Ahimelek for the first and only time by his name: *You shall surely die, Ahimelek, you and your whole family* (v. 16).

17–19. *Then the king ordered the guards at his side* to *Turn and kill* [*mût* hipʿil]⁶⁴ *the priests of the* LORD, citing his belief that they knew that David was fleeing from Saul but chose not to inform the king. Despite their subservient status, *the king's officials were unwilling to raise a hand to strike the priests of the* LORD (v. 17).⁶⁵ Their refusal underscores the enormity of Saul's crime. *Doeg the Edomite* shows no such compunction and, at the king's command, kills that day *eighty-five men who wore the linen ephod* (v. 18). Two other times in the books of Samuel the priestly *linen ephod* is mentioned, once being worn by the boy Samuel (2:18) and once being worn by King David (2 Sam. 6:14). Both Samuel and David, each in his own way, proved to be a nemesis of Saul. As Saul distances himself ever further from Yahweh, his animosity towards those aligned with Yahweh only intensifies.

---

64. The same verbal expression is used, e.g., in 2 Sam. 14:7 in a juridical context.
65. One is reminded of the popular opposition to Saul on the occasion of his attempt to have his own son killed (14:45).

Not satisfied with the extirpation of the priests of Nob, Doeg also puts to the sword *the town . . . , with its men and women, its children and infants, and its cattle, donkeys and sheep* (v. 19). Save for the omission of 'camels', the list is virtually identical to the instruction given Saul in 15:3 with respect to the Amalekites.[66] The irony of Saul's failing to obey Yahweh in utterly destroying the Amalekites but then doing precisely that to the priests of Yahweh and to their town of Nob is extremely damaging to his reputation. Recent studies, setting Saul's massacre at Nob in the context of ANE (especially Hittite) legislation regarding the duties of priests to the king, have described Saul's action as the standard 'way to punish treacherous and disloyal servants' (Taggar-Cohen 2005: 266). While it is true that offences against an ANE king or god often brought disaster not just on the offender but on all associated with him, the situation in Israel was different. For one thing, the first allegiance of priests and prophets in Israel was to be to Yahweh, not the king. Further, in the present context, the unwillingness of Saul's own men to slaughter the priests of Nob shows that they, too, found the thought of slaughtering Yahweh's priests repugnant. Indeed, as Taggar-Cohen (2005: 265) notes, 'the biblical author views the fulfillment of the punishment as illegal'.

On the larger canvas of the book of Samuel, the destruction of the priests of Nob must be seen as fulfilling the judgment pronounced upon the house of Eli in 2:30–33. That Saul's wicked action ultimately accomplishes a providential end does not justify it. Acts 2:23 offers a quintessential biblical example of wicked means being made to serve providentially ordered ends: 'This man was handed over to you by God's deliberate plan and foreknowledge; and you, with the help of wicked men, put him to death by nailing him to the cross.'

20–23. *But one son of Ahimelek son of Ahitub, named Abiathar, escaped and fled to join David* (v. 20). For a second time in the chapter, 'escape'

---

66. Camels are appropriately mentioned in respect of the nomadic Amalekites but would not likely have been among the livestock of the citizens of Nob (cf. Judg. 6:5; 7:12; 8:21, 26). For discussion, see Long (2009a: 385–386); Chavalas (2018).

is mentioned. In verse 1 David *escaped to the cave of Adullam*; now Abiathar escapes to join David. Saul's every effort at self-preservation is driving people from him. By contrast, support for David is growing. At the beginning of chapter 22 he was joined by four hundred men who made him their commander (v. 2). The prophet Gad also appeared to advise David in verse 5. Here at the end of the chapter, David is joined by Abiathar, the surviving priest of Nob. So his entourage now includes not only a loyal band of men but also a prophet and a priest. And, as we shall learn in 23:6, along with the priest comes the oracular ephod, by which David can enquire regarding the will of Yahweh (e.g. 23:9; 30:7). At 14:18–19 we witnessed Saul's truncation of an oracular enquiry involving the ephod. In chapters 13 and 15 we saw Saul's failure to prioritize the word of Yahweh through the prophet. And in the present chapter, we witnessed his massacre of Yahweh's priests. What Saul by his unfaith has lost – loyalty of followers, access to ephod and access to prophet and to priest – David has gained.

I am responsible for the death of your whole family (v. 22). David's ready acceptance of responsibility for what happened at Nob reveals something of his honest and non-defensive demeanour. It also may lend support to the view that David did in fact deceive Ahimelek in the presence of Doeg. For if David had been forthright with Ahimelek, the priest would at least have had the option of defecting to David, as Abiathar is now doing. On the other hand, if Ahimelek was already aware of the breach between David and Saul and was simply keeping up appearances before Doeg, he might have counted on being able to offer a reasonable defence to Saul. David, however, will have known from experience that expecting a reasoned response from Saul was expecting too much, and so he might have given Ahimelek more explicit warning.

Meaning
The contrasting portraits of Saul and David become more and more pronounced in the events of chapter 22. For Saul's part, the 'hard truth', as Birch observes, is that he

> has become an evil man. He was not inherently so or destined to be so. He is not devoid of qualities even now that arouse our sympathy.

But he has become evil in the obsessive desire to maintain his hold on power.
(1998: 1149)

David, for his part, has been involved in some misadventures in his desperate flight from Saul. Lives have been lost. But having begun his flight alone, David is quickly surrounded by supporters (v. 2), including now a prophet (v. 5) and a priest (vv. 20–23). Something of the character of David is beginning to show, both in his handling of family duties (vv. 3–4) and in his willingness to accept responsibility for actions that brought harm to others (v. 22). Life in the wilderness is challenging, and David's initial moves may leave something to be desired. But as his story continues, David's willing dependence on Yahweh becomes ever more evident.

v. David delivers and is delivered (23:1–29)
Context
Despite the extremity of David's own personal situation, we saw him in the preceding chapter caring for others (namely, for the four hundred desperate men who sought him out to be their leader, for his own family and for Abiathar). David showed the capacity to look outwards, beyond his own circumstances, to the concerns of others. This leadership quality is further evidenced in the present chapter, as David rescues the border town of Keilah from the aggression of the Philistines. David's assumption of the risks involved in such a rescue operation does not appear to be motivated mainly by political ambition. For the fact is that the citizens of Keilah show little gratitude to David and, when Saul takes notice, are willing to betray him. Of greatest moment in the present chapter, beyond David's ability to look outwards, is his ability to look upwards. Repeatedly David enquires of the Lord as to how he should proceed. And repeatedly the Lord guides and delivers David from the hand of Saul.

Comment
1–5. *David was told, '. . . the Philistines are fighting against Keilah'* (v. 1). Keilah was located in the western foothills of Judah (Josh. 15:33, 44) some 3 miles south of Adullam (22:1), near Philistine

territory. It is probably to be identified with a site called Qiltu mentioned in the fourteenth-century Amarna Letters.[67] Keilah's fortifications (v. 7) attest to the fact that, as a border town, it was particularly vulnerable to hostile incursions. On this particular occasion, the Philistines are *looting the threshing-floors* (v. 1). One effective means of weakening an enemy was to disrupt agricultural activity (cf. Judg. 6:3–6, 11). Particularly damaging was the looting of threshing floors, since much agricultural effort would have been expended by the time grain got to the threshing floor.

When David hears of the Philistines' aggression, his immediate reaction is to enquire of Yahweh: *Shall I go and attack these Philistines?* (v. 2). David's desire to rescue the city of Keilah stands in stark contrast to Saul's destruction of an Israelite city in the immediately preceding chapter. A further contrast between David and Saul is in their commitment (or lack thereof) to receiving guidance from the Lord (on David, see further at vv. 4, 9–12; 30:7; 2 Sam. 2:1; 5:19; and on Saul, see at 14:18–19, 36–42; 28:3–25). Yahweh answers David's query in the affirmative: *Go, attack the Philistines and save Keilah* (v. 2), but David's men are hesitant. Afraid even in Judah's heartland, they confess that they will be even more so if they go *against the Philistine forces* in a border town like Keilah (v. 3). Tacitly acknowledging their fear, David does not try to force his men, as Saul had done in 14:24. Instead, he seeks to reassure them by making a second enquiry. Again, the Lord responds positively: *Go down to Keilah, for I am going to give the Philistines into your hand* (v. 4). With little fanfare, verse 5 reports that *David and his men* succeeded in rescuing Keilah, while inflicting *heavy losses on the Philistines*. David's actions in this pressured situation evidence his sensitivity as a leader in respect of both Yahweh and his men.

6–8. A brief aside in verse 6 informs the reader that *Abiathar son of Ahimelek had brought the ephod down with him when he fled to David at Keilah*. The phrase *at Keilah* introduces some uncertainty as to when and where Abiathar joined David, but this poses no major difficulty

---

67. See EA 279, 280, 289, 290. Letter 290 names Qiltu along with Gazru (biblical Gezer) and Gimtu (biblical Gath). English translations of all these letters are available in Moran (1992).

for understanding David's deliverance of the city.[68] Whether the ephod or some other means of divine enquiry[69] was employed in the enquiries of verses 2 and 4 is not stated, but the point of mentioning the ephod at this juncture is to prepare for what will occur in verse 9. Saul is pleased to learn of David's whereabouts, imagining that *David has imprisoned himself by entering a town with gates and bars* (v. 7), and so he sets out in force *to besiege David and his men* (v. 8). Unsurprisingly, Saul's theologizing of the situation – *God has delivered him into my hands* (v. 7) – is grossly mistaken, as verse 14 makes clear: *God did not give David into his hands*.

9–14. If Saul has informants – who tell him of David's movements (v. 7) – so too does David (see on v. 10). Thus, he knows that Saul is 'plotting evil' (*maḥărîš hārā'āh*) against him (v. 9).[70] Unlike Saul in verse 7, however, David does not presume to know the mind of God but calls for *Abiathar the priest* to *Bring the ephod* (v. 9). David twice addresses God by his covenant name Yahweh (LORD), three times refers to himself as *your servant* (vv. 10–11) and poses two questions. Having *heard definitely* – thus informants? – *that Saul plans to come to Keilah and destroy the town on account of me* (v. 10), David wants to know if what he has heard is true. His first question, though, is *Will the citizens of Keilah surrender me to him?* Only after

---

68. See Tsumura (2007: 552–553) for a summary of possible solutions.
69. 1 Sam. 28:6 mentions dreams, Urim – implying also the Thummim, both together constituting the lots contained in the priestly ephod – and prophets.
70. It may simply be a coincidence, but the word used to describe Saul's plotting (*maḥărîš*) sounds the same as the word used in 10:27 to describe Saul's keeping silent (*maḥărîš*). Lexicographers cite the hipʻil of the verbal root *ḥrš* II in 10:27 and the hipʻil of the homonymous verbal root *ḥrš* I here in 23:9. While Saul's description as *maḥărîš* ('keeping silent') in 10:27 is difficult to evaluate, his *maḥărîš* ('plotting') in the present context introduces a sinister shading. The lexical root *ḥrš* occurs four more times in ch. 23 in the place name Horesh (vv. 15–16, 18–19; see comment at v. 15). Whether coincidental or not, this concentration (five of thirteen occurrences in 1 and 2 Samuel occur in 1 Sam. 23) draws attention to the root.

posing that question does he ask, *Will Saul come down, as your servant has heard?* (v. 11). The seemingly odd order of these questions may reflect the fact that at the end of verse 10 David admits that the threat to Keilah is *on account of me*, and so his first concern is how they will respond should Saul come down. Yahweh's answers are brief. He answers David's second question first: *He will* (v. 11). David then reiterates his first question, and Yahweh's response is *They will* (v. 12).

Having heard from the Lord, *David and his men*, now *about six hundred in number* (up 50% from the four hundred of 22:2), leave Keilah and keep *moving from place to place*.[71] Saul is told of David's escape and doesn't bother going to Keilah (v. 13). David relocates to the *Desert of Ziph*, where he stays *in the wilderness strongholds and the hills*. Tell Zif, a site some 13 miles south-east of Keilah and 5 miles south-east of Hebron, overlooks the wilderness of Judah and likely represents the site of the ancient town of Ziph.[72] Despite Saul's daily efforts to apprehend David, and contrary to Saul's assumption in verse 7, *God did not give David into his hands* (v. 14).

15–18. The Hebrew of verse 15 begins with the main clause of the compound sentence, which literally reads 'David saw' *that Saul had come out to take his life*. The consonants of the verb rendered *saw* (root *r'h*) could be revocalized to read 'feared' (root *yr'*), which would put David in a mental state similar to that of his men in verse 3. RSV does in fact read 'David was afraid', but this rendering is abandoned by NRSV and most other modern translations, which prefer to read 'saw' or *learned* (as in NIV). Following the main clause in the Hebrew, a subordinate clause describes David's location. He is *at Horesh in the Desert of Ziph*. Horesh (Heb. *ḥōreš*) can mean 'forest' and is translated as 'forest' in Ezekiel 31:3 and 'wooded areas' in

---

71. By a very rough measure, David covers well over 150 miles moving from place to place, from his initial flight in ch. 19 to the end of ch. 23. He will cover an additional 50 miles before arriving a second time in Gath in ch. 27.

72. The town is referenced several times on late eighth-century *lmlk* ('for the king') jar handles (for discussion and bibliography, see Long 2009a: 364).

2 Chronicles 27:4. KJV, NKJV and various (especially older) foreign language translations make the same choice in the present verse. But given David's location in a desert, it is more likely that Horesh is the name of a town, possibly to be identified with modern Khirbet Khoreisa, which lies some 2 miles south of Ziph.

At this crucial juncture, *Saul's son Jonathan went to David at Horesh and helped him to find strength in God* (v. 16). As a true friend, Jonathan does not minimize David's plight but points in the direction of the source of true strength in trial. Apart from the recorded words of Jonathan, the text does not spell out just how he helped David find strength in God, but this exercise will prove valuable on a later occasion when David is once again under great pressure and again is able to find strength in God (30:6).

Jonathan's first words, *Don't be afraid* (v. 17), may support the revocalization mentioned above at verse 15, or Jonathan may simply be assuming that David must be tempted to fear. Jonathan is not entirely correct about how the future will unfold. For instance, he will not live to become David's *second* (see 31:2). But he has no doubt that David will *be king over Israel*. And his declaration that *Even my father Saul knows this* (cf. 20:30–31) leaves Saul without excuse in his desperate attempt to stay on the throne by eliminating his divinely chosen replacement (see also 15:23). *The two of them made a covenant before the* LORD (v. 18). How different from Saul is Jonathan in his ready acceptance of and covenanted loyalty to David (cf. 18:4; 20:13). In this, as in other respects, Jonathan functions as a foil to Saul, a point underscored literarily by the repeated relational epithets: *Saul's son Jonathan* (v. 16); *my father Saul* (v. 17 twice). Moreover, as we have noted before, the behaviour of the old priest Eli near the beginning of 1 Samuel set a standard to which Saul fails to live up. When deposed from his priestly office for his own misdeeds, Eli bows to the divine will (3:18) and does nothing to undermine his replacement, Samuel. How very different is Saul's response to his own rejection from office and to his replacement.

19–23. Despite his misalignment with the purposes of Yahweh, Saul is not without supporters. Some *Ziphites* travel well over 20 miles to *Saul at Gibeah* in order to bring him precise information regarding David's whereabouts: he is *at Horesh, on the hill of Hakilah, south of Jeshimon* (v. 19). On Horesh, see at verse 15. The *hill of Hakilah* is mentioned again in 26:1, 3, but apart from its association with *Jeshimon* is of unknown location. *Jeshimon* sometimes simply connotes a desert, occurring in parallel with *midbār* (wilderness, desert). At other times, Jeshimon seems to function as a proper noun indicating a particular desert. The latter seems to be the case here. What motivated the Ziphites to go to so much trouble is not specified. Was it 'love' for Saul (in the political sense of loyalty)? Or was it fear of him? The recent massacre at Nob (ch. 22) will not have gone unnoticed.

Whatever the Ziphites' motivation, Saul is both grateful – *The LORD bless you for your concern for me* (v. 21) – and wary: *Go and get more information*. He has logged enough experiences futilely pursuing David to have learned that *he is very crafty* (v. 22). Once Saul receives *definite information* of all David's *hiding places*, he will *track him down among all the clans of Judah* (v. 23).

24–29. The Ziphites comply with Saul's instructions and, after returning to Ziph, apparently report to Saul that David is in the *Desert of Maon, in the Arabah south of Jeshimon* (v. 24). *Maon* has been identified with Khirbet el-Maʻin, a site some 5 miles south of Ziph; David continues to try to put distance between himself and Saul. The name Maon may mean something like 'den, haunt, refuge, dwelling' (*NIDOTTE* 2: 1013), a name appropriate both to the remote and rugged terrain of the general area and to the dwellings of the herdsmen who frequented the area. Having been informed of David's location, Saul and his men begin their search in earnest (v. 25).

David, however, is not without his own informants, and so he goes down to *the rock* (*hassela*ʻ), evidently a known landmark in *the Desert of Maon* (v. 25) and quite possibly the rock called Sela Hammahlekoth in verse 28 (the narrator reserving the name until it can fulfil its narrative function). The scene is one of high tension. Saul is in hot pursuit, *going along one side of the mountain*, with David and his men on the other side, *hurrying to get away from Saul*. The *mountain* in question is unnamed and may simply be a 'hill', as Hebrew *har* can describe low hills as well as high mountains. With Saul and his men *closing in* [*ʻōṭĕrîm*] *on David* (v. 26), David is in grave danger. McCarter (1980: 378–379) suggests that 'Saul is advancing toward David around the mountain from both directions in a kind of pincer movement.' McCarter's tactical observation is appropriate in view of the unusual verb (*ʻṭr*) used to describe the movement of

Saul's troops – after all, several other, more common verbs meaning 'surround' or 'encircle' could have been used (*sbb*, *nqp* II, etc.). The verb *ʿṭr* occurs only seven times in the entire Old Testament, and only once in Samuel. In the qal stem, which occurs in the present verse and in Psalm 5:13 (Eng. v. 12), the basic sense is 'to surround' someone or something, or to 'encircle' them. In the five other occurrences of Hebrew *ʿṭr* in the Old Testament (four in piʿel and one in hipʿil), the sense is 'to crown' or 'to encircle with a wreath'. The noun *ʿăṭārâ*, derived from the root *ʿṭr*, means 'crown', or 'that which surrounds' (*NIDOTTE* 3: 382). Rashi, cited by Kiel (1981: 240), speaks of Saul's troops 'encircling and surrounding from side to side like a crown that encircles the head'. Though certainty in such matters is impossible, one wonders if the biblical narrator might not intend a subtle double entendre in his description of Saul's aggression towards David. Saul's attempt to 'encircle' David only drives him closer to the time his head will be encircled with the crown. If we may borrow from colloquial English to illustrate the general idea, Saul's every effort to 'crown' David with a battleaxe simply moves David closer to the 'crown'.

Before Saul can close the noose, news that *Philistines are raiding the land* (v. 27) forces Saul to break off the pursuit and return to *meet the Philistines* (v. 28). By virtue of its timing, this interruption hints at the hand of providence at work. But it also recalls Saul's earlier failures in respect of the Philistines (see, e.g., 14:30, 46, 52). The place where *Saul broke off his pursuit of David* was called *Sela Hammahlekoth* (v. 28). The narrator mentions the name because of its appropriateness to the situation. *Hammahlekoth* involves a root *ḥlq*, which occurs in several homonymous verbal forms, the two more common connoting either 'to be smooth, slippery' (*HALOT*, *ḥlq* I) or 'to divide' (*HALOT*, *ḥlq* II). While the rock in question might have been called something like 'Slippery Rock' (cf. McCarter 1980: 379) even before the current situation, the narrator exploits the name's potential to memorialize the physical division between Saul and David that took place at this spot, thus 'Rock of Division'.[73] If we dare

---

73. On the nature of biblical etymologies, see at 1:19–20; 2 Sam. 15:32–37; and the full treatment in Garsiel (1991).

another colloquial English analogue, we might say that it was at 'slippery rock' that David gave Saul 'the slip'.

The crisis averted, *David went up from there and lived in the strongholds of En Gedi* (v. 29), an oasis some 15 miles farther to the east, in a cavernous region above the western shore of the Dead Sea (on En Gedi, see also at 24:1). This relocation closes the account of David's narrow escape, but it also sets the stage for the events of chapter 24, as the Hebrew chapter division indicates (23:29 is 24:1 in the Hebrew text).

Meaning
First Samuel 23 is packed with action: David rescuing, the rescued betraying (or ready to betray), Saul pursuing, Jonathan encouraging and David escaping. Of key interest are the multiple references to David's enquiring of Yahweh. For it is Yahweh's guidance and providential care of David in the wilderness that most characterizes this chapter. The superscription of Psalm 63 speaks of a time when David was 'in the Desert of Judah'. In that psalm, David gives full voice to his confidence in God:

> Because you are my help,
>   I sing in the shadow of your wings.
> I cling to you;
>   your right hand upholds me.
>
> Those who want to kill me will be destroyed;
>   they will go down to the depths of the earth.
> (Ps. 63:7–9)

C. David protects Saul's life and avoids blood-guilt (24:1 – 26:25)

i. David spares Saul's life in the cave (24:1–22)
Context
The present chapter begins with back references to the events of chapter 23, where Saul was forced to break off his pursuit of David to deal with a Philistine incursion. David, having thus narrowly escaped falling into Saul's hands, repaired to *the strongholds of En Gedi*, where we find him as chapter 24 opens. In this chapter David

will have a golden opportunity to kill the one intent on killing him. Verses 1–7 describe Saul's narrow escape when he goes to relieve himself in a cave in which David and his men are hiding. Verses 8–15 record David's words of defence to Saul, after Saul has exited the cave. And verses 16–22 recount Saul's remarkable acknowledgment of David's righteousness and his destiny to be king, before concluding with Saul's plea that David spare his descendants, to which David agrees on oath.

Comment

1–7. *After Saul returned from pursuing the Philistines* (v. 1) – assumedly successfully, though we are not told – he gathers *three thousand able young men from all Israel* and sets out again to hunt David down. David, with his six hundred men, is clearly outnumbered, and Saul's intelligence operatives are still performing well; Saul knows where to search for David, *near the Crags of the Wild Goats* (v. 2). The name *En Gedi* means 'spring of the young goat', while the region designated *the Crags of the Wild Goats* employs the Hebrew term *yāʿēl*, which designates a species of ibex (*capra ibex nubiana*) that is still found in the region today (see Long 2009a: 366). Coming to *the sheepfolds along the way*, Saul enters a cave – of which there are many in the area – *to relieve himself* (lit. 'to cover his feet', a euphemism for defecating). As Tsumura (2007: 565) remarks, 'Nobody, even his personal bodyguard, would accompany him into the cave for this purpose.' As it happens, *David and his men were far back* in the very same cave (v. 3). That Saul is very vulnerable is not lost on David's men, who urge David to deal with his *enemy . . . as you wish*, even citing an otherwise unattested divine anticipation of this opportunity: *This is the day the* LORD *spoke of . . .* (v. 4). Gordon (1986: 179) rightly notes that searching for the purported oracle is unwarranted, as David's men are most likely simply 'fabricating an oracle to drive home their point'.

Then David crept up unnoticed and cut off a corner of Saul's robe (v. 4). In view of the urging of his troops and of the other uses to which David's sword could have been put in the situation, the fact that he merely cut off a corner of Saul's robe may seem an act of little consequence. *Afterwards*, however, *David was conscience-stricken for having cut off a corner of his robe* (v. 5). As we have seen several times already in Samuel, clothing often carries symbolic significance: Samuel is associated with his robes (from the little ones of 2:19 that his mother would make for him each year, to the robe torn by Saul in 15:27, to the robe by which Samuel will be recognized in 28:14); Jonathan's transferral to David of *the robe he was wearing* in 18:4 symbolized his transferral of the rights of crown prince; and even Saul's divestment by divine overpowering in 19:24 was of symbolic significance. David's stricken conscience in the present circumstance likely arises from the fact that, though he has not physically harmed Saul, he has by his own hand symbolically carved off a portion of Saul's kingdom from *the LORD's anointed* (v. 6). David will be aware that he, too, is now *anointed of the LORD* (see at 16:1–13), and he doubtless knows of Saul's faithless behaviours that have led to his rejection (e.g. 13:13–14 and 15:24–30 in context), but he nevertheless grasps that it is not his place to *lay my hand on him* (v. 6). It is solely the Lord's prerogative to remove from office the one whom he has anointed. *With these words David sharply rebuked [wayĕšassaʿ]*[74] *his men and did not allow them to attack Saul*. So Saul departs unharmed (v. 7), none the wiser, until he hears a familiar voice calling after him.

8–15. Once Saul has left the cave, David too exits the cave and calls out while Saul is still in earshot, *My lord the king!* Turning, Saul sees *David bow[ing] down and prostrat[ing] himself with his face to the ground* (v. 8). The double description of David's 'body language' underscores the deference of his spoken address. David's first concern is to convince Saul that accusations by others that he is *bent on harming Saul* (v. 9) are utterly false. Whatever David's misgivings about having carved off a corner of Saul's robe, he now finds the remnant to be a useful piece of material evidence in making his defence. The truth should be obvious to Saul: *This day you have seen with your own eyes* (v. 10). What Saul must surely be able to see is that *the LORD gave you into my hands in the cave*, and yet, despite the urging of his men,

---

74. The root *šsʿ* occurs only three times in the piʿel (Lev. 1:17 and Judg 14:6 both suggesting the tearing apart of an animal). The third occurrence is here in 1 Sam. 24:7, where the meaning is uncertain, suggestions ranging from 'persuade' to 'restrain' to 'reprimand sharply' (see discussion in *HALOT*).

David refused to *lay my hand on my lord, because he is the* LORD's *anointed* (v. 10). Saul was in David's hands, but David refused to lay a hand upon him, and the proof – *this piece of your robe* – is in his hand. In sum, *there is nothing in my hand to indicate that I am guilty of wrongdoing or rebellion*. Verse 11 ends the case for the defence with a succinct summary: *I have not wronged you* [not sinned against you], *but you are hunting me down to take my life.*

Having stated his case before Saul (and before the reader of the narrative), David turns to the judge to make his appeal: *May the* LORD *judge between you and me*. As in cases of serious injustices suffered, David is disinclined simply to forgive and forget. He has suffered genuine wrong, and so he appeals to Yahweh: *may the* LORD *avenge the wrongs you have done to me, but my hand will not touch you* (v. 12). This reflex is comparable to what one encounters in the so-called imprecatory psalms, where the psalmist doesn't minimize wrongs suffered nor his emotional response to them but, nevertheless, entrusts his grievances to Yahweh and lets them go (treats them as out of his hands).[75]

At this point, David quotes an *old saying (měšal haqqadmōnî)*: *From evildoers come evil deeds* (v. 13). Not unlike its New Testament counterpart, 'By their fruit you will recognise them' (Matt. 7:16), the saying in this context is double-edged, at once indicting Saul as an evildoer and vindicating David as innocent of wrong. For a second time in as many verses, David insists, *my hand will not touch you* (v. 13). Indeed, it is noteworthy how often references to David's hands are made in his defence before Saul: verses 4, 6, 10 (2x), 11 (2x), 12, 13.[76]

In stereotypical language of self-abasement, David continues, *Against whom has the king of Israel come out? Who* [sic; read 'whom'] *are you pursuing? A dead dog? A flea?* (v. 14; cf. the similar language in 2 Sam. 9:8; 16:9). In the ANE, dogs were hardly regarded as 'man's best friend', so to be called a *dog* was insulting. To call oneself a *dead dog* was self-abasing in the extreme. To be a *flea* on that dog

---

75. Psalms including imprecatory material include psalms 5, 6, 11, 12, 35, 37, 40, 52, 54, 56, 58, 69, 79, 83, 109, 137, 139 and 143.

76. References to hands occur with greater frequency in 1 Sam. 24 than in any other chapter in 1 and 2 Samuel.

(Heb. reads a 'single flea') was to be almost nothing at all, at least nothing of concern to the king. Notwithstanding David's desire to assure Saul that he personally is not seeking to harm him, and despite his use of hyperbolic figurative language to make the point, it is hardly true that David is no more than a flea, a virtual nothing. In fact, he is Yahweh's anointed, and he knows this. Moreover, so long as Saul resists the will of Yahweh respecting his replacement on the throne (of whom by now Saul is well aware),[77] he is right to fear the 'neighbour' who is better than he (cf. 15:28). David's dead dog/single flea imagery may, then, operate on more than one level. As regards any malicious intent towards Saul, David is as harmless as a single flea. He will not lift his hand against Saul. But as regards Saul's future, he is hardly a flea. He is destined to found a royal line that will lead ultimately to 'the Lion of the tribe of Judah' (Rev. 5:5).

As David draws his speech to Saul to a close – a speech conducted as if in a court of law – he appeals for the second time in four verses to Yahweh to be judge (*dayyān*) and to judge (*šāpaṭ*) between him and Saul: *May the LORD be our judge and decide between us* (v. 15; cf. v. 12). Moreover, *May he consider my cause and uphold it*. David's invocation, twice using the root *rîb* (a term of juridical advocacy), could be rendered more literally: 'may he see and argue my case'. David closes with a highly compressed final appeal, comprising only two words in Hebrew: *wĕyišpĕṭēnî miyyādekā*, literally, 'may he judge/vindicate me from your hand'. NIV captures the sense more smoothly. Reference to Saul's hand, from which David desires to be delivered, recalls the many references earlier to the innocence of David's own hand(s).[78]

16–22. *When David finished saying this*, the defence rests, and it is Saul's turn to respond. His first words – *Is that your voice, David my son?* – seem curious, as everything in David's speech just ended makes it clear who is talking, and Saul has even been challenged to *look at this piece of your robe in my* [*David's*] *hand* (v. 11). Saul is evidently overcome with emotion: *And he wept aloud* (v. 16). This has suggested to some that his vision may have been clouded by tears, but this

---

77. See, e.g., 18:28–29; 20:31; 23:17.
78. See comment at v. 13.

explanation fails to account for the fact that Saul's tears would have come only near the end of David's speech. The likeliest explanation of Saul's strange question, then, is that he is simply overcome with emotion[79] and at a loss as to how to begin his response to David. In such circumstances, the first words out of one's mouth are not always particularly coherent.

More coherent, if patently obvious, are Saul's next words: *You are more righteous than I* (v. 17). After endorsing, by repeating, David's description of how he has treated Saul well (vv. 17–18), Saul marvels: *When a man finds his enemy, does he let him get away unharmed?* (v. 19). Though Saul has long known (23:17) what others around him have known (e.g. Jonathan, even Achish), namely, that the future of the kingdom is with David, he here for the first time explicitly states, *I know that you will surely be king* (v. 20). Continuing the 'in-someone's-hands' phrasing so prevalent in David's speech, Saul connects the dots: *the LORD gave me into your hands, but you did not kill me* (v. 18), and I know *that the kingdom of Israel will be established in your hands* (v. 20). It was precisely the establishment of the kingdom, that is, the founding of a dynasty, that Saul's failure at Gilgal had cost him (see 13:14). What more could possibly be said or done to legitimate David's right to the throne than for Saul, the rejected but still sitting king, to pronounce these words over the one divinely chosen to replace him?

Saul continues. Well aware of the mortal danger faced by descendants of a deposed king, Saul solicits from David an oath *by the LORD that you will not kill off my descendants or wipe out my name from my father's family* (v. 21). David has already sworn as much to Saul's son Jonathan (20:14–17), but here he gives *his oath to Saul* directly (v. 22). David keeps his oath to Jonathan in the sparing of Mephibosheth (2 Sam. 9) and in so doing also does not *wipe out* Saul's name. This oath to Saul will not be mentioned again, and in fact later events do result in the deaths of Saulide descendants

---

79. We note that he refers to David as *my son*, just as David had earlier referred to Saul as *my father*. On possible allusions to the Gen. 27 story of the duping of Isaac by Jacob, see Brueggemann (1990: 171); Bodner (2008: 254–255).

(2 Sam. 21:1–14). David is neither the cause nor the immediate agent of those later killings, and so he is technically not in breach of his oath to Saul (but see the comment on 2 Sam. 21:2–3).

As cathartic as the mouth-of-the-cave encounter between David and Saul appears to be, and notwithstanding the swearing of oaths, both Saul and David seem to understand that no ultimate resolution has been achieved. Words are one thing, actions another. Saul simply returns home, where he will live to pursue David another day, and *David and his men* return to *the stronghold* (probably Adullam; see at 22:5) where, for the time being at least, they are safe.

Meaning

The close encounter in the cave tested David's resolve to avoid lifting a hand against the LORD's *anointed* and to leave his own safety in God's hands. Recognizing his close call, Saul responds with emotion and, indeed, momentary clarity regarding David. In this episode David entrusts his well-being to God, but he wisely does not entrust it to the mercurial Saul. At the end of the day, Saul and David part ways, Saul returning to his home and David to the stronghold. A very similar test of David's restraint will take place in chapter 26. But first there is an episode in which David very nearly bloodies his hands in respect of the churlish Nabal.

ii. Abigail saves David from incurring blood-guilt (25:1–44)
Context

At first blush, this episode involving David, the boorish Nabal and his perceptive and proactive wife Abigail may seem to interrupt the flow of the Saul–David narrative. But as Gordon (1980, repub. 2006) has convincingly shown, Nabal in this chapter serves as a kind of surrogate Saul. And the chapter as a whole serves as part of David's training in non-retaliation.

Comment

1. *Now Samuel died*. Samuel's death will be mentioned a second time in 28:3 (cf. the double mention of the death of Joshua in Judg. 1:1; 2:8). The prophet's death signals the end of the period of the judges and raises the question of how things will go now that Samuel is off the scene. In chapter 28, Samuel will appear to Saul

from the grave, and so the death notice early in *that* chapter prepares for what follows. Mentioning Samuel's death in the *present* chapter establishes the approximate timing of Samuel's death but also raises the question of how David will behave now that he is no longer supported by Samuel and is left to his own devices.[80] That *all Israel assembled and mourned* for Samuel attests to his prominence as a leader.[81] The assembly concludes with the burial of Samuel *at his home in Ramah* (cf. 1:1, 19; 2:11; 7:17; etc.).

Then David moved down into the Desert of Paran. While MT and a majority of ancient witnesses attest *Paran*, a wilderness area probably to be located in the north-eastern Sinai Penninsula, LXX attests Maon (*maan*), which fits the ensuing context much better, unless the point is that David is attempting to get as far as possible from Saul's reach (cf. Bodner 2008: 259–260).

2–3. Verses 2 and 3 introduce new characters and thus a new episode in David's wilderness period. *A certain man in Maon, who had property there at Carmel, was very wealthy* (v. 2). On Maon, see at 23:24, and on Carmel – the site where Saul erected a monument in his own honour – see at 15:12. If the identification of Carmel with the modern Khirbet el-Kirmil is correct, then the site lay some 8 miles south-east of Hebron (see Long 2009a: 368–369).[82]

Nabal is a very wealthy man (v. 2), but *surly and mean* [lit. 'hard and evil'] *in his dealings* (v. 3). His wife, Abigail, by contrast is *an intelligent and beautiful woman*.[83] The name *Abigail* sounds something

---

80. Bodner (2008: 259) notes further regarding the timing of the notice that, with Saul's admission at the end of ch. 24 that David will surely be king, Samuel's work is done. Thus, *'immediately* after Saul's confession, Samuel gives up the ghost'.
81. Cf. the mourning accompanying the deaths of Jacob (Gen. 49:33 – 50:3, 10), Aaron (Num. 20:29); and Moses (Deut. 34:8).
82. This Carmel is not the same as the famous Mount Carmel of 1 Kgs 18, where Elijah confronted the prophets of Baal.
83. Cf. the description of David in 16:18, where *ṭô'ar* ('goodly' in form or 'beautiful' in appearance', cf. *DCH*) is also used. Cf. also the descriptions of Rachel (Gen. 29:17) and Joseph (Gen. 39:6), which suggest that *ṭô'ar* may refer especially to one's figure or physical build.

like 'my father rejoices', while *Nabal* sounds like several words relating to folly, or that which is morally and intellectually foolish or godless. In verse 25 Abigail will plead with David to pay no attention to Nabal, 'this worthless man' (*'îš habbĕliyya'al hazzeh*), explaining that his name sounds like 'fool' and he lives up to his name. It seems unlikely, of course, that Nabal's parents would have intentionally saddled him with such a negative moniker, so something more favourable may have been in view; suggested possibilities include 'noble' or 'adept' (see *HALOT*, *nābāl* II).[84] As is so often the case in the Old Testament, however, the suggestive potential of the sound of the name is exploited to reinforce a character trait – often by the narrator, and in verse 25 by Abigail herself (for further exploitation of the name, see at v. 37).

Finally, Nabal is described as *a Calebite* (v. 3). The well-known spy Caleb enjoyed an impeccable reputation in the accounts of wilderness wanderings and the conquest.[85] He received Hebron and its environs as 'his inheritance' (Josh. 14:13–14). Thus, to be called a Calebite could be an honour. But another Hebrew word shares the same consonants – the word 'dog' (*keleb*). Perhaps the narrator is engaging in yet another pejorative wordplay. While David referred to himself rhetorically as a *dead dog* (*keleb mēt*) in 24:14, Nabal will literally be a dead Calebite by 25:37–38. LXX renders 'Calebite' as 'dog-like' (*kunikos*). Nabal behaves like a brute beast.

4–9. With the dramatis personae in place (vv. 2–3), the action begins. David hears that Nabal is shearing sheep (v. 4). If, as King and Stager (2001: 147) remark, 'The economies of the biblical world were, to a large extent, based on wool', then Nabal, with his three thousand sheep (v. 2), was a very wealthy man indeed.[86] Shearing

---

84. For further possibilities, see Barr (1969: 25–27) and Macintosh (2012: 79–93), who suggests that in Edomite and Arabic, the root *nbl* connotes 'sagacity' and then suggests that Abigail may have been making a bilingual pun on Nabal's name. For full discussion, see Rollston (2013: 383–386).
85. For a sampling of references, see Num. 13:30; 14:24, 38; 32:12; Deut. 1:36.
86. Based on ancient standards – i.e. 2 lb of wool per sheep – one shearing of Nabal's sheep would have yielded 3 tons of wool.

times were joyous occasions and provided opportunities for generosity. David hopes that Nabal will be generously inclined and sends *ten young men* in his own name (v. 5) to wish Nabal well – thrice invoking the *good health* (*šālôm*) of Nabal, his household and everything that is his (v. 6). The burden of David's message comes in verses 7–8. In essence it is this: my [David's] men were good to your men when they were in the field – *Ask your own servants and they will tell you* (did David anticipate a negative response from Nabal?) – so now will you be good to us at this festive time? Having delivered their message, David's men wait for an answer (v. 9). Some interpreters have suggested that David may be practising a kind of protection racket, and his sending ten men has been cited as evidence that he means to issue a kind of threat to Nabal. Nothing in the text suggests such motivation on David's part, and ten men (instead of just one or two) may have been sent in the hope and expectation that they would return carrying goods and supplies provided by Nabal. Compare the quantity of goods amassed by Abigail in verses 18–19.

10–13. Nabal's response begins by pretending that David is of no account – *Who is this David? Who is this son of Jesse?* – and is no different from the many *servants . . . breaking away from their masters these days* (v. 10). Elsewhere in Samuel, it is Saul who most regularly refers to David disparagingly as *the son of Jesse, ben-yišay* (20:27, 30; 22:7–9, 13), though Doeg does so once as well (22:9). Nabal here joins in the derision, but it must not be forgotten that it was Yahweh himself who chose *one of his [Jesse's] sons to be king* (16:1), and that he was *with him*, as even one of Saul's own servants early recognized (16:18). Nabal is in dangerous territory here, adopting Saul's rhetoric without enjoying Saul's protected status as the Lord's anointed.

Returning to David, the men *reported every word* (v. 12), and David's immediate response is to take up the sword (*ḥereb*), which is mentioned three times in verse 13, ironically paralleling the three-fold reference to *šālôm* (*good health* or 'peace') in verse 6. David's ire has been raised, and he takes *four hundred men* to deal with Nabal, *while two hundred stayed with the supplies* (v. 13). If it takes two hundred men to guard *the supplies*, one may be tempted to ask why David should be seeking more from Nabal. But *supplies* renders *kēlîm* ('goods', 'belongings', etc.), not food or wool. The sense of the

Hebrew is captured reasonably well by NLT: '200 remained behind to guard their equipment'. David is not already well supplied with food and acting greedily in seeking more from Nabal. He and his men have their equipment but nevertheless could use some of the abundance available at shearing time (note the items brought by Abigail in v. 18).

14–17. With David on the warpath, Nabal and his family are in grave danger and, as David will later confess (vv. 32–34), would not have survived the night had Abigail not intervened. She is informed by *one of the servants* about David's message and Nabal's insults (v. 14). The servant's description of the behaviour of David's men, who *were very good to us* and *were a wall around us the whole time we were herding our sheep near them* (vv. 15–16), undercuts the 'protection racket' theory (see at vv. 4–9), at least as far as the narrative is concerned. Those caught in such situations are aware that their 'protectors' are not 'good'. The servant does not venture to suggest to Abigail what she should do – he is after all dealing with an intelligent woman (cf. v. 3) – but encourages her to *think it over and see what you can do* (v. 17). It's no use talking to Nabal, the servant avers, because he is *such a wicked man [ben-bĕliyya'al] that no one can talk to him* (v. 17). Like Eli's sons, themselves *bĕnê-bĕliyya'al*, Nabal is incorrigible (cf. Eli's sons' refusal in 2:25 to listen to their father's rebuke). The result in the case of Eli's sons was that Yahweh put them to death. The same fate awaits Nabal (v. 38).

18–19. *Abigail acted quickly* (v. 18). Once informed of the situation, Abigail wastes no time in preparing literally donkey-loads of supplies (food and drink) for David and his men.[87] Significantly, *she did not tell her husband Nabal* (v. 19). It is not difficult to detect a 'vote of no confidence' in this withholding of information; one is reminded of Jonathan's similar withholding of information from his father Saul in 14:1.[88]

20–22. Not for the first time in the book of Samuel, a meeting of two parties (v. 20) suggests the hand of providence at work.

---

87. For a discussion of these provisions in the light of ANE analogues, see Tsumura (2007: 583–584).

88. The two phrases are syntactically identical in Hebrew.

David would know where to find Nabal (he had just sent messengers to him), but Abigail would not necessarily know David's precise whereabouts. Verse 21 digresses to recount what David has *just said*, whether to his men or to himself: *It's been useless – all this watching over this fellow's property*. *Useless* (or 'in vain', as in many translations) is perhaps not a strong enough rendering of *laššeqer*, as the noun *šeqer* usually has to do with lying, deception or false dealing. Perhaps David felt that there was an at least tacit agreement that his protection of Nabal's herds should be rewarded in some way. Nabal's derisive response to David's request, then, would involve more than simply a lack of generosity; it would involve reneging on a deal. At the very least, *He has paid me back evil for good* (v. 21). Yet again, Nabal reminds us of Saul, who himself admitted that he had treated David badly (lit. 'repaid you with evil'), though David had repaid him with good (24:17). In the case of Nabal, David is not so restrained as he was with Saul, and he swears an oath of self-malediction *if by morning I leave alive one male of all who belong to him!* (v. 22). *One male* renders *maštîn bĕqîr*, literally 'one who urinates against the wall', likely a standard formula for males. The suggestion that the expression is especially crude, 'wall-pisser' or the like,[89] while not unlikely for David in his current state, is undercut by the fact that the formula is used several times by Yahweh (1 Kgs 14:10; 21:21; 2 Kgs 9:8), as well as at least once by the biblical narrator (1 Kgs 16:11).

23–31. When Abigail sees David (v. 23), her immediate actions and words are as humble and deferential as her husband's had been proud and derisive. Falling before David *with her face to the ground* (v. 23), she implores David – whom she repeatedly addresses as *my lord* (vv. 24, 25, 26 [2x], 27, 28, 29, 30, 31 [2x]) – to pardon her and allow her to speak (v. 24). *Pardon your servant* renders a Hebrew phrase that literally reads 'on me, my lord, [be] the iniquity'. This may seem confusing, as the iniquity was clearly on her husband's

---

89. See, e.g., Leithhart (2002). Leithart's comments on word usage in this chapter relating to 'wall', 'pissing against the wall', wine going out of Nabal (as connoting urination), the Calebites as dogs pissing against the wall, etc., are ingenious but not entirely convincing.

part, as she will shortly explain. But, as McCarter (1980: 398) proposes, this manner of speech may simply be the way a person of inferior position might initiate a conversation with a superior. Comparing 2 Samuel 14:9, McCarter captures the gist of Abigail's words as follows: 'Let any burden of blame that might arise from our conversation rest upon me and not you!'

Having gained permission to speak, Abigail is quick to confirm what David has already discovered about Nabal. He is a *wicked man* and a *Fool*, as the sound of his name suggests (see at vv. 2–3 above). For her part, she knew nothing of *the men my lord sent* (v. 25). Abigail is burdened not simply to protect the lives of her family but, as verses 26 and 28 make clear, also to protect David – as Yahweh has already been doing – *from bloodshed and from avenging yourself with your own hands* (v. 26). Her expressed desire that David's *enemies and all who are intent on harming my lord be like Nabal* (v. 26) is at first blush confusing, as nothing yet has happened to Nabal.[90] In the immediate context of Abigail's words to David, however, it is clear that she understands something of the purposes of God for David: for example, *The LORD your God will certainly make a lasting dynasty for my lord, because you fight the LORD's battles* (v. 28). Might she not similarly have insight into the fate of a fool like Nabal and wish the same on all who intend David harm? For her part, Abigail does what she can to make amends for Nabal's rebuff of David's messengers. She brings a *gift* (*bĕrākâ*) to be given *to the men who follow you* (v. 27), even while continuing to ask forgiveness for *your servant's presumption* (v. 28). The Hebrew (*'ămātekā*) makes it clear that the *servant* in question is Abigail, not Nabal. *Presumption* is in this context a reasonable gloss for Hebrew *peša'*, which literally means 'sin' or 'transgression'.

Abigail's brilliant speech to David proves her to be not only an intelligent woman (v. 3) but also one astute in matters spiritual and political. To underscore the certainty of Yahweh's design for David (stated in v. 28), she employs two telling metaphorical wordplays in verse 29: whatever the threat, David *will be bound securely in the bundle*

---

90. Some commentators even suggest relocating this sentence between vv. 41 and 42 (so McCarter 1980: 394).

of the living by the LORD *your God* (employing verb and noun of the root *ṣrr*, bind/bundle), while David's enemies God *will hurl away* [or 'sling away'] *as from the pocket of a sling* (employing verb and noun of the root *qlʿ*, sling out/sling). The heart of her concern for David is that *When the* LORD *has fulfilled for my lord every good thing he promised*, including making David *ruler over Israel* (v. 30), David's conscience will not be saddled with *the staggering burden of needless bloodshed or of having avenged himself* (v. 31).

To this point in her plea to David, Abigail's references to herself as *your servant* have been mainly to ask for pardon (v. 24) or forgiveness (v. 28), to request a hearing (v. 24) and to offer her gift (v. 27). Now, in conclusion, she makes a positive request: *when the* LORD *your God has brought my lord success, remember your servant* (v. 31). Abigail is not simply asking that David bring her to mind but that he remember her favourably. LXX makes this intent explicit: 'remember your slave [*doulēs*] to do good to her'. This sense of 'remember' is illustrated quite clearly in the story of Hannah (1:11, 19).[91]

32–35. Abigail's mission succeeds. David recognizes her as an emissary of Yahweh and praises him for having sent her (v. 32). He blesses Abigail both for her *good judgment* (or 'discernment', *ṭaʿam*) and for her intervening to prevent him from doing what he would later have regretted (v. 33). He acknowledges that it was Yahweh himself who sent her and protected her from harm at David's hand. David makes no effort to hide the fact that he was bent on vengeance when she intercepted him: *if you had not come quickly to meet me, not one male* [*maštîn bĕqîr*; see at v. 22] . . . *would have been left alive by daybreak* (v. 34). Abigail is repeatedly characterized as acting *quickly* (vv. 18, 23, 34, 42), suggesting not only the urgency of the situation

---

91. Some interpret Abigail's speech in terms of power politics, its main objective being to better Abigail's position. But this may be an overinterpretation of the evidence, as Abigail's actions and her request are fully explicable in terms of the situation in which Nabal's folly has placed her and her family. His fate is sure. But this raises the question of what will become of Abigail and her family, once she is widowed. Thus, her request may have more to do with securing a future than with aspiring to greater power.

in which she finds herself but perhaps also the sureness with which she proceeds to rescue what she can of the situation.[92]

Like Abigail, David matches his words with actions, and so he accepts the gift she has brought him and says to her, *Go home in peace. I have heard your words and granted your request* (v. 35). *Granted your request* is literally in Hebrew 'lifted up your face', an expression used also in Genesis 32:20, when Jacob is fearfully anticipating meeting Esau and sends gifts ahead in the hope that Esau 'will receive me' (lit. 'lift up my face'). As is occasionally noted, Abigail's preparations to encounter David recall in several respects Jacob's preparations to encounter Esau. For instance, both involve the fearful party sending gifts ahead and then following behind (Abigail in v. 19), hoping to be 'received' (have their 'face lifted').

36–39a. A day which could have proved disastrous for either David or Abigail is turning out better than might have been expected. Even Nabal will survive the day untroubled, but only just, and only because he is drunk. *When Abigail went to Nabal, he was in the house holding a banquet like that of a king* (v. 36). The kingly simile is the most explicit of a wide range of features in chapter 25 that depict Nabal as a kind of surrogate Saul (see Gordon 1980, repub. 2006). In the best of times, Nabal was hard to talk to (cf. v. 17). How much more so when he is *in high spirits and very drunk*. So Abigail wisely decides to tell him *nothing at all until daybreak* (v. 36). The sobering tale she has to convey must wait until he is in fact sober. *Then in the morning, when Nabal was sober, his wife told him all these things* (v. 37). Leithart (2001) finds in the phrase *běṣē't ḥayyayin minnābāl* (lit. 'when the wine was going/or had gone out of Nabal') a reference to Nabal's morning-after urination. Thus, Abigail would be bringing the bad news when Nabal was, as it were, indisposed. Less uncertain is the suggestion (see Gordon 1980: 51; 2006: 14) that the expression refers simply to Nabal's soberness but does so by making another disparaging pun on the name Nabal, which shares the same consonants with a Hebrew word for a 'leather bottle' or 'wine skin' (cf. *nēbel yayin*, 'skin of wine', in 1:24):

---

92. We may perhaps compare the sureness with which *David ran quickly towards the battle line* to meet and defeat Goliath (17:48).

thus, 'when the wine had gone out of the wine skin [Nabal]'. Once morning comes and Nabal is sober, he should be in a better disposition to digest what Abigail has to say. As it happens, however, Nabal does not digest the news well at all. 'Soberness and sober facts are too great a shock for his system, which promptly seizes up' (Gordon 1986: 186). *His heart failed him and he became like a stone* (v. 37). Nabal's subsequent death is attributed to divine action: *About ten days later, the LORD struck Nabal and he died* (v. 38).[93]

Through his encounter with Abigail, David learns a very important lesson in God-reliance and non-retaliation. He learns, as the imprecatory psalms regularly stress, that Yahweh can be trusted to avenge wrongs suffered – *Praise be to the LORD, who has upheld my cause against Nabal* (v. 39) – so that his servants need not and should not do wrong by seeking personal vengeance themselves.

39b–44. *Then David sent word to Abigail, asking her to become his wife* (v. 39b). While David will prove himself to be susceptible to the allure of a beautiful woman (2 Sam. 11:2), it is unclear in the present circumstance how much love and desire figure in his marriage to Abigail. In the ancient world, marriage was often, as Kramer (1963: 250) explains, 'a practical arrangement in which the carefully weighed shekel counted more than love's hot desire'. Abigail's self-effacing (v. 41) but swift[94] and affirmative response (v. 42) also may have had as much to do with securing her future, now that she is a widow, as with any personal feelings towards David, whom she has met only briefly. David's marriage to the widow of the wealthy Nabal would surely have strengthened his position in the south country around Hebron.

David's prior marriage to *Ahinoam of Jezreel* (mentioned in v. 43 for the first time) would have had a similar effect, as Jezreel (not to be confused with the Jezreel Valley) was a town somewhere in the vicinity of Maon, Carmel and Ziph (cf. Josh. 15:55–56) in the hill country of Judah. That Saul's wife was also called Ahinoam (14:50),

---

93. Elsewhere in Samuel, the Hebrew phrase *wayyiggōp yhwh* ('Yahweh struck') occurs only in 2 Sam. 12:15, in respect of *the child that Uriah's wife had borne to David*.

94. Note *quickly* again; see at v. 34.

the only other person of that name in the Old Testament, has caused some (e.g. Levenson 1978; Levenson and Halpern 1980) to wonder if David might have taken Saul's wife as his own, especially in view of Nathan's remark to David in 2 Samuel 12:8 that the Lord had given *your master's wives into your arms*. This seems hardly likely, however, for at least a couple of reasons: first, as Edelman (*ABD* 1: 118) points out, 'such a presumption would require David to have run off with the queen mother while Saul was still on the throne'; and second, the *of Jezreel* addition to *Ahinoam* in the present passage could well be meant to distinguish her from the other woman called *Ahinoam daughter of Ahimaaz* in 14:50.

While on the topic of David's marriages, the narrator notes that *Saul had given his daughter Michal, David's wife, to Paltiel son of Laish, who was from Gallim* (v. 44). Saul's motivation for taking David's wife and giving her to another man may have been to distance David from the Saulide royal family. Whatever the case, David will take the first opportunity to regain what was his, much to Paltiel's sorrow (2 Sam. 3:14–16). Though no specific site has been identified for *Gallim*, the town is mentioned in Isaiah 10:30 along with Anathoth (a town some 3 miles north-east of Jerusalem) and a town called Laishah, which seems to echo the patronym of Paltiel, to whom Michal has been given.

Meaning
The story of Nabal's ill-treatment of David, of David's enraged reaction and of Abigail's timely intervention serves several purposes in the narrative frame. First, while the narrative is sufficiently decorous not to call Saul a fool explicitly,[95] the wide variety of hints that Nabal is his mirror image, his surrogate, does contribute to the negative characterization of Saul that has been building especially since he ascended the throne, but to some extent already before that event. Second, David is shown to be a fully human, flawed individual, as capable as any of falling into a fit of rage when insulted and slighted. But, as the narrative repeatedly reminds us, the Lord is with David, and it is the Lord,

---

95. Though Saul will admit to his own folly in 26:21.

through the agency of Abigail, who rescues David from his own baser instinct to exact personal revenge. Thus, this chapter that began with David wronged and enraged ends with David vindicated by the Lord and praising him.

iii. David spares Saul's life in the camp (26:1–25)
Context
Lessons seldom have to be learned but once, and in chapter 26 Saul again finds himself vulnerable to David, as in chapter 24. David is again urged by his men to kill Saul, and again he refuses.

Comment
1–6. *The Ziphites went to Saul at Gibeah* to betray David's whereabouts, as they had done before (23:19; cf. also the superscription to Ps. 54). This time Saul asks no further questions but arises, gathers his *three thousand select Israelite troops ('îš bĕḥûrê yiśrā'ēl)* and goes down to *the Desert of Ziph* (v. 2). There he pitches camp *beside the road on the hill of Hakilah facing Jeshimon* (v. 3; on these locations, see 23:19). David, meanwhile, sends scouts to confirm that Saul has arrived (v. 3–4). Once the desired reconnaissance has been conducted, David goes to the place where Saul is camped and finds *Saul and Abner son of Ner* asleep, *with the army camped around him* (v. 5). Unlike the chance encounter in the cave of chapter 24, where Saul was utterly alone and utterly vulnerable, here in chapter 26 Saul is literally surrounded on all sides by his select troops. In the face of this situation, David asks a surprising question: *Who will go down into the camp with me to Saul?* (v. 6). While 'ask' is the appropriate sense in context, verse 6 literally reads, 'David answered and said'. To what is David answering? Perhaps to the situation spread out before him, or to the implicit question, 'What now?' *Ahimelek the Hittite* and *Abishai son of Zeruiah, Joab's brother*, both hear David's bold proposal, and Abishai answers with equal boldness, *I'll go with you* (v. 6).

Ahimelek the Hittite will not figure again in the book of Samuel – or anywhere else in Scripture, for that matter. Perhaps he is mentioned simply to keep the record straight, or perhaps to indicate that Abishai was not cornered into volunteering by virtue of there being no-one else. It is worth noting, however, that the word *Hittite* occurs here for the first time in the book of Samuel, and elsewhere it will be exclusively associated with Uriah the Hittite (seven times in 2 Sam. 11 – 12 and once more in 2 Sam. 23:39, where Uriah appears as the final entry in the list of David's thirty select warriors). Might there be a subtle anticipation, even in this section describing David's training in non-violence, of the fact that David will not always prove himself immune to temptations to do wrong?[96]

While *Abishai son of Zeruiah*, like Ahimelek the Hittite, is mentioned for the first time in verse 6, he (unlike Ahimelek) will be quite prominent in the chapters that follow, though not nearly so prominent as his brother Joab, also mentioned for the first time here.[97]

7–12. Entering Saul's camp by night, David and Abishai discover Saul *lying asleep inside the camp with his spear stuck in the ground near his head*. All Saul's select soldiers, including Abner, are asleep, and remarkably – though see verse 12 – none awake to discover the two intrepid interlopers (v. 7). Both the hand of God and the action to be taken seem obvious to Abishai: *Today God has given your enemy into your hands. Now let me pin* [*nkh*, 'strike'] *him to the ground with one thrust of the spear* (v. 8). The same spear with which Saul has attempted to pin both David (18:10–11; 19:9–10) and Jonathan (20:33) to the wall is now threateningly poised to cost him his own life. The first words of a character in a story can be particularly revelatory, and this is certainly true of Abishai. In his later appearances, Abishai will prove ever ready to strike someone to the ground (e.g. 2 Sam. 3:30; 16:9; 19:21; 21:17; 23:18). In the present instance, however, David restrains him: *Don't destroy him! Who can lay a hand on the* LORD's *anointed and be guiltless?* (v. 9). Sandwiched between this and David's second reference to the sacrosanct status of Yahweh's

---

96. One might also ask – though this is highly speculative – if mention of the name Ahimelek evokes the other Ahimelek, priest at Nob, whose assistance of David cost him his life at the hands of Saul (chs. 21–22). (The only other Ahimelek in Samuel is the son of Abiathar mentioned in 2 Sam. 8:17.)

97. Abishai is mentioned a total of twenty times in Samuel, Joab over a hundred times.

anointed (v. 11)[98] are words demonstrating that David has well learned the lesson of chapter 25, namely, that it is not for David to take matters into his own hands, even when dealing with a fool (Nabal). Rather, *the LORD himself will strike him, or his time will come and he will die, or he will go into battle and perish* (v. 10).

David does not leave empty handed, however, but instructs Abishai to retrieve *the spear and water jug that are near his head* (v. 11). The fact that David himself in verse 12 is said to take the spear and the water jug may suggest that David had second thoughts about trusting Abishai with sharp implements in tempting situations. It is worth noting that Abishai's brother, Joab, will much later prove himself more opportunist than obedient servant in the matter of 'dealing gently' with Absalom (see at 2 Sam. 18:10–14). But perhaps David's words are simply suggesting the appropriate course of action, not singling out its agent. We might compare the words 'don't go that way, go this way', where the intended meaning is 'let's not go that way, but this'.

Despite David and Abishai's encroachment into the camp and their verbal exchanges, *No one saw or knew about it, nor did anyone wake up* (v. 12). While stealth may have played its part, the text foregrounds a theological explanation that reinforces Yahweh's hand in protecting David: *They were all sleeping, because the LORD had put them into a deep sleep* (v. 12). Instances of a deep sleep accompanying Yahweh's special activities recur in the Old Testament, for instance during his removal of a rib from the man's side in Genesis 2:21 and during his covenant-making with Abraham in Genesis 15:12–21. In the present passage, the 'dead sleep from Yahweh' (*tardēmâ yhwh*), if not simply employing the divine epithet as a superlative ('a very deep sleep'), underscores Yahweh's direct action on David's behalf.

13–16. The story is not yet at its end, and Saul and his men are not allowed to continue in their slumbers. Taking up a position *on top of the hill some distance away* with *a wide space between them* (v. 13), David calls out not to Saul, but *to the army and to Abner son of Ner.* David's cry, *Aren't you going to answer me, Abner?*, may suggest

---

98. See the discussion at 24:6, 10.

that Abner was in a very deep sleep indeed. Abner's return question, *Who are you who calls to the king?* (v. 14), is ironic in a couple of respects: first, he doesn't recognize David as the caller; and, second, he assumes that it is the king being called, when in fact David's question is directed explicitly to Abner. Of course, Abner may simply be showing deference to the greater person present, the king, but David continues to address Abner. His address takes the form of an interrogation, beginning with rhetorical and accusing questions – *You're a man, aren't you? . . . Why didn't you guard your lord the king?* (v. 15) – and moving to indicative description – *Someone came to destroy your lord the king* (v. 15) – and concluding with condemnation – *you and your men must die* [or 'deserve to die'],[99] *because you did not guard your master, the LORD's anointed* (v. 16). To prove the veracity of his charge, as well as the severity of Abner's failure, David adds, *Look around you. Where are the king's spear and water jug that were near his head?* (v. 16). The absence of spear and jug proves that David has been very near the king's slumbering (and unguarded!) head, with an instrument of death to hand. That he made no use of the spear proves his innocence, while his removal of Saul's water jug underscores Saul's vulnerability. Whether at a loss for words or because Saul speaks first, Abner renders no response to David's charges.

17–20. Unlike his general, *Saul recognised David's voice and said, 'Is that your voice, David my son?'* (v. 17). Twice more in this chapter Saul will refer to David as *my son* (vv. 21 and 25). David, by contrast, and unlike his one reference to Saul as *my father* in 24:11, does not engage in familial terminology but refers to Saul as *my lord the king* (v. 17) and to himself as the king's *servant* (vv. 18, 19). He never refers to himself as Saul's son, though such figurative language would have been possible (cf. David's messengers' appeal to Nabal on behalf of *your son David*, 25:8). Both physically (v. 13) and rhetorically, David keeps his distance from the erratic Saul. *Now let my lord the king listen to his servant's words* (v. 19). The burden of David's speech in this encounter, as it had been in chapter 24, is not simply

---

99. So NRSV, ESV, JPS, NLT, etc. The Hebrew is literally, 'you are sons of death' (*běnê-māwet 'attem*).

to declare his innocence of wrongdoing towards Saul but also to demonstrate it with material evidence (see at v. 22).

With respect to what can account for Saul's aggression towards David, David sees two possibilities, with accompanying solutions. The first may point the finger at Saul. *If the LORD has incited you against me, then may he accept an offering* (v. 19). The verb 'to incite' (*sŵt*) occurs elsewhere in Samuel only in 2 Samuel 24:1, a chapter in which David admits to wrongdoing (vv. 10, 17) and offers sacrifices (v. 25). Thus, the suggestion here may be that Saul should be the one to offer sacrifices acceptable to the Lord. A second possibility is that the *people have done it* (i.e. *incited you against me*), in which case David would simply have them be cursed (v. 19).

David concludes with a plea that he not be driven *from the presence of the LORD* (v. 20; see also at 27:1). Returning to the image of himself as but a single flea (cf. 24:14), David adds a second image, a *partridge*. David's choice of *partridge* as a self-description is particularly apt, as the Hebrew word for partridge is literally 'caller' (*qōrē'*), and David in verse 14 stood at a distance and *called out* (*wayyiqrā'*), both expressions from the same root, *qr'*. But David may be doing more than making clever wordplays. The sand partridge (*Ammoperdix heyi*) is known as 'a great runner' that 'speeds along the ground when it is chased'[100] and thus is difficult to hunt down. With both metaphors, then, flea and partridge, David may be hinting at the extreme difficulty if not futility of Saul's pursuit of one so hard to discover and capture.

21. It is difficult to gauge the sincerity of Saul's confession (*I have sinned*) and his invitation to David (*Come back*). Saul has said these precise words before, namely, on the occasion of his definitive rejection by Yahweh through Samuel in 1 Samuel 15. On that earlier occasion, Saul twice admitted, *I have sinned* (*ḥāṭā'ti*, 15:24, 30). And two times he enjoined Samuel to *come back* with him (*šûb*, 15:25, 30). Samuel refused to 'come back' until after Saul's second, more candid confession, when it was crystal clear that Saul's chief concern was his own honour (on why Samuel returned with, or

---

100. Youngblood (2009: 259); citing The Committee on Translations of the United Bible Societies (1972).

'after', Saul, see at 15:30). Saul's description of his own actions – *Surely I have acted like a fool [hiskaltî] and have been terribly wrong* – and of David's – *you considered my life precious today* – is accurate enough. And it certainly doesn't hurt David's cause to have these admissions from Saul himself. Saul's admission of folly reinforces the parallels between himself and the fool Nabal of the preceding chapter, and his statement of David's benevolent treatment of him shows that David's behaviour is above reproach. Saul's further claim, however, that *I will not try to harm you again*, cannot be trusted. His tears and conciliatory words in 24:16–21, at the end of the earlier encounter in which David spared Saul's life, did not prevent him from coming out again in pursuit of David (26:1–2). Words are one thing, actions another. And David has had enough experience of Saul's mercurial temperament not to be drawn in.

22–25. Rejecting Saul's invitation – *Come back, David my son* (v. 21) – David answers by again mentioning *the king's spear* and enjoining Saul to *Let one of your young men come over and get it* (v. 22). David is of no mind to lessen the distance between himself and Saul (quite the contrary, as the next chapter will show). No mention is made of Saul's water jug. Perhaps it is deemed unnecessary if Saul is truly going to break off his wilderness pursuit of David and return home. Or perhaps it would have been received with suspicion after having been in David's hands. Or perhaps its inclusion with the spear is simply assumed. The singling out of Saul's spear in David's retort is, as Gordon (1986: 190) remarks, 'crushing'. In response to Saul's tearful, if not to be trusted, words of conciliation, David's reference to Saul's spear, a weapon that more than once has been hurled in his direction (18:10–11; 19:9–10), stings.

Having drawn attention to the material evidence supporting his defence, David summarizes the case: *The LORD gave you into my hands today, but I would not lay a hand on the LORD's anointed* (v. 23). Premised on his conviction that Yahweh *rewards everyone for their righteousness and faithfulness* (v. 23), David expresses his hope that Yahweh will *value my life and deliver me from all trouble* (v. 24). He does not remark on Saul's future, though the implication for one who has been neither righteous nor faithful but has, rather, played the fool is evident.

Still in a conciliatory mood, Saul pronounces on David a blessing and a prediction: *May you be blessed, David my son; you will do great things and surely triumph* (v. 25). No further mention is made of Saul pursuing David, though he might well have done, had David not fled to Gath (27:4). The chapter ends with David going on his way and Saul returning home. David will yet succumb to his fear of Saul (ch. 27), but other concerns than David will occupy Saul's attention until his death in chapter 31.

Meaning
By now the relationship of the three chapters just completed should be evident. Chapters 24 and 26 recount two incidents when David might have been tempted to take matters into his own hands and rid himself of Saul, who seems to think of little else than taking David's life. That David was capable of such violence is evident from his fury in chapter 25, where he had every intention of killing not just Nabal but every male in his family. Only the timely intervention of Abigail, in whom David recognized the hand of the Lord at work, prevented David from bloodying his hands. We see some growth in David through these events. In chapter 24 he refused to lift his hand against *the LORD's anointed* (24:6, 10), but he did carve away a bit of Saul's robe, an act he later regretted. In chapter 26 he similarly upheld the sanctity of *the LORD's anointed* (26:9, 11, 23) but in addition committed no act for which his conscience would later accuse him. Perhaps it was his experience with Nabal in chapter 25 that buttressed his confidence that he could trust the Lord to deal with his adversaries (25:38). The pervasive teaching of Scripture is that 'vengeance' (i.e. the establishment of lawful justice) belongs to the Lord alone (Deut. 32:35; cited in Rom. 12:19 and Heb. 10:30). If the experiences of chapters 24–26 taught David anything, it was that he should 'wait for the LORD, and he will avenge' (Prov. 20:22). But waiting in precarious circumstances can prove difficult, as the next episode illustrates.

D. Desperate times for David and for Saul (27:1 – 31:13)

Context
David and Saul's paths part after chapter 26, and they do not encounter one another again, so far as the text tells us. The main focus in this stretch of text toggles back and forth between what

David is doing (chs. 27, 29–30) and what Saul is doing (chs. 28, 31). The situation in which David finds himself in chapter 29 builds tension in the narrative, as it appears that David may indeed have to encounter Saul on the battlefield, but this in fact does not prove to be the case. As the final episodes in the parallel careers of David and Saul open in chapter 27, David flees to Philistine territory, fearful that at some point he will fall into Saul's hands if he remains in Israelite territory.

i. David flees to the Philistines (27:1–12)
Comment

1–4. *But David thought to himself* (v. 1). This English rendering of the opening statement in chapter 27 captures the sense of the Hebrew, which literally reads 'then David said to his heart'. David's thoughts betray a kind of emotional exhaustion after his two most recent encounters with Saul. While David has had the advantage and has escaped unharmed from close encounters with Saul in a cave (ch. 24) and in Saul's camp (ch. 26), the aggressiveness of Saul's pursuit of David cannot be overlooked. Given Saul's psychological instability, David is savvy enough not to trust either Saul's invitation – *Come back, David my son* (26:21) – or his words of blessing and assurance – *May you be blessed, David my son; you will do great things and surely triumph* (26:25). So David proposes to himself, and perhaps to his men,[101] that *The best thing I can do is to escape to the land of the Philistines* (27:1). David's flight in the aftermath of episodes of high drama and deliverance reminds one of the later Elijah, who, having seen Yahweh triumph over the prophets of Baal on Mount Carmel (1 Kgs 18), nevertheless succumbs to fear in the face of threats from the intrepid Jezebel and flees (1 Kgs 19:1–5). If there is irony in David's fearful thoughts in the aftermath of Yahweh's evident protection, there is irony also in his decision to flee *to the land of the Philistines* (v. 1) and specifically to *Achish son of Maok king of Gath* (v. 2).[102] Once

---

101. On the possibility of 'inner thoughts' becoming 'public knowledge', see Bodner (2008: 284).
102. In 1 Kgs 2:39, at the start of Solomon's reign, two slaves of Shimei (see 2 Sam. 16 and 19) escape to Achish of Gath, whose father is named

before, David had fled to Gath, where he was immediately recognized by the Gittites and reported to Achish, their king (1 Sam. 21). His cover blown, David on that occasion took the words of the Gittites very much *to heart and was very much afraid of Achish king of Gath* (21:12). Only by playing the 'madman' did he manage his escape. Is it not madness again to think of escaping to Achish in Gath?

Perhaps the fact that David is accompanied by *six hundred men* (v. 2) emboldens him, as he can approach Achish from a position of strength (unlike the first time, when David was alone). The fact that his men are accompanied by their families and he by his two wives (v. 3) may also have played a role, as life on the run in the wilderness is not very conducive to family life. David's two wives are named, and the second, Abigail of Carmel, is called *'ēšet-nābāl*, 'the wife of Nabal'. She is, of course, technically *the widow of Nabal*, as NIV renders the phrase, but the explicit Hebrew expression for widow, *'iššâ-'almānâ* (as in 2 Sam. 14:5), is not used, not only here but also in subsequent references to Abigail (30:5; 2 Sam. 2:2; 3:3). Is the attentive reader to hear a faint anticipation of David's later taking of another man's wife (not yet a widow), namely, the *wife of Uriah* (2 Sam. 11:3; 12:9–10; etc.)?[103]

Whatever its motivations, David's decision to flee to Philistine Gath has the desired effect on Saul, who, hearing of David's flight, *no longer searched for him* (v. 4).

5–7. David's first words to Achish begin with a conditional clause, *If I have found favour in your eyes* (v. 5). How he might have found favour with Achish is unspecified, but perhaps his arrival at the head of six hundred men suggested that he could be useful to Achish as a mercenary force (see Achish's words to David in 28:1). David will later have Pelethites (Philistines?) among his personal fighting forces.[104] David's request of Achish is that *a place be assigned*

    Maakah (which has the same consonants as Maok in the present context).

103. Too much should not be made of this usage, however, as Ruth 4:10 refers to Ruth as the 'wife of Mahlon', though she is clearly already his widow.

104. On the Pelethites, always in combination with the Kerethites (e.g. 2 Sam. 8:18; 20:23), see Ehrlich, *ABD* 5: 219.

to me in one of the country towns. He justifies his request by implying that his living *in the royal city with you* might prove burdensome. In fact, his motivation may have been to be out from under Achish's immediate gaze. Achish, who grants the request by assigning him the village of Ziklag (v. 6), may himself have been motivated by self-interest. As Postgate (1992: 87) notes, commenting on ancient Mesopotamian life generally, 'It has always proved politic for a state to secure the continued attachment of its fighting men by finding plots of land for them.' While the site of *Ziklag* has not been definitively identified, the chief contenders[105] all lie well over 20 miles south of Gath, offering David the distance from scrutiny he may have desired. Ziklag had been assigned to the tribe of Simeon in the time of Joshua (Josh. 19:5) and in the period of the judges was counted as belonging to the tribe of Judah (Josh. 15:31). As a border town, it had by the time of David fallen under Philistine control. After Achish's assignment of Ziklag to David, it *belonged to the kings of Judah ever since* (v. 6).[106] David's sojourn in Ziklag lasted *a year*[107] *and four months* (v. 7).

8–12. Once settled in Ziklag, *David and his men went up and raided the Geshurites, the Girzites and the Amalekites* (v. 8). The *Geshurites* in view here are not the Transjordanian people of the same name. Joshua 13 mentions two groups of Geshurites, one group west of the Jordan River (13:2, 'all the regions of the Philistines and Geshurites') and one east of the Jordan (13:11, 'the territory of the people of Geshur and Maakah'). David's raids were against the western Geshurites. The second people mentioned are the *Girzites*. As this people group is mentioned nowhere else in biblical or extra-biblical sources, some scholars have suggested that the name is a corruption of an original 'Gizrites' (i.e. inhabitants of Gezer), but the town of Gezer is too far north and perhaps too near Gath to

---

105. On which, see Long (2009a: 376–377).
106. As Alter (1999: 169) observes, 'this seemingly technical geopolitical notice' foreshadows the fact that David 'is destined to found a lasting dynasty' of 'kings of Judah'.
107. Heb. *yāmîm*, lit. 'days', is used to connote 'year[ly]' in 1 Sam. 1:21; 2:19; 20:6; 2 Sam. 14:26; etc.

lend plausibility to this suggestion (see Long 2009a: 376–377). Perhaps McCarter (1980: 413) is correct in following the shorter reading of LXX^B,[108] which makes no mention of 'Gizrites' but *only* of 'Geshurites' and 'Amalekites'. The *Amalekites*, known already from 1 Samuel 15:1–3, were to be found *in the land extending to Shur and Egypt* (v. 8). *Shur* seems to designate a desert region in the northern Sinai Peninsula, south of Canaanite territories near the eastern border of Egypt (Gen. 25:18). On the perpetual hostility of the Amalekites towards the people of God, see on 1 Samuel 15:1–3.

Whenever David attacked an area, he did not leave a man or woman alive, but took livestock and plunder (v. 9). His execution of both men and women raises questions in the reader's mind, especially as the flight to Philistine territory seems to have been David's own idea (v. 1) and not necessarily in response to a divine directive. Some justification for David's behaviour might be sought in the consistently hostile stance taken by the Amalekites vis-à-vis the Israelites and the resultant divine judgment that rested upon them (cf. Exod. 17:14). The text, however, offers no hint of such a motivation. When David's return from raids with goods and livestock raises questions in Achish's mind, David lies (v. 10), and the narrator explains that David's total destruction of defeated populations was, in fact, to prevent his actual exploits from being reported to Achish. Thus, an episode that began with David thinking to himself (v. 1) concludes with his again thinking to himself of what might happen: *They might inform on us* (v. 11). For his part, Achish is fully duped (v. 12), as will be further demonstrated in the next chapter.

Meaning
With Samuel dead (cf. 25:1), David found himself still on the run from Saul. And though he experienced the protective hand of providence in preventing him from incurring blood-guilt with respect to Saul and Nabal, David's ability to trust seemed to falter in chapter 27. Thinking to himself that he would one day fall into the hand of Saul, David abandoned Israelite territory to seek refuge

---

108. I.e. Codex Vaticanus, one of the major manuscripts of the Septuagint.

in the neighbouring Philistine town of Gath. That David's faith could falter comes as no surprise. Not even Abraham, the so-called father of the faithful, was immune to such lapses (see Long 2018). When faith falters, dubious actions often follow. As in the case of Abraham (e.g. Gen. 12:10–20; 16:1–16; 20:1–18), so also does faith falter in the case of David amongst the Philistines in chapter 27 (see above at vv. 9–12).

ii. Saul goes to the witch at Endor (28:1–25)
Context
As chapter 28 opens, the dramatis personae are the same as in the preceding chapter: David and the Philistine ruler Achish. Having been duped by David in chapter 27, Achish entertained the hope that David would become *my servant for life* (27:12). In the present chapter, Achish promises to make David *my bodyguard for life* (28:2). Clearly, Achish has plans for David. But to see what actually happens we have to wait for chapter 29, because chapter 28 is not mainly about David but about Saul. If chapter 25 tested David's character and actions after the death of Samuel, the present chapter does the same thing in respect of Saul. The narrator's desire to compare and contrast David and Saul, once Samuel is no longer alive, may help to explain why Samuel's death is mentioned twice (25:1; 28:3).

Comment
1–2. *In those days the Philistines gathered their forces to fight against Israel* (v. 1). David had thought that by escaping to the Philistines he would be able to avoid Saul (27:1), but in a not too surprising twist of fate the Philistines with whom he has taken refuge decide to take the fight to Israel, which of course will bring them into direct conflict with Saul. David's success in duping Achish into thinking that he would be his *servant for life* (27:12) now places David in a most precarious situation. Will he have to face Saul on the battlefield? If so, what will he do? Will he lift his hand against Yahweh's anointed, or will he turn on his Philistine host? Or will he, as some early rabbinic commentators suggested, seek a middle course, protecting Achish's person but refusing to take offensive action against Israel? For his part, Achish is in no doubt what David must do. His charge

to David is emphatic, reading literally 'surely you must know[109] that with me you shall go forth in the army,[110] you and your men'. David's evasive response in verse 2, *Then you will see* [lit. 'know', echoing Achish's words to David] *for yourself what your servant can do*, is entirely non-committal and may have earned a wry smile from an ancient audience. Achish's next words would also evoke smiles if not outright laughter: *Very well, I will make you my bodyguard for life*; the humour lies in the fact that *bodyguard* is literally 'keeper of my head', and, of course, David has already collected one famous Gittite head (Goliath's, in ch. 17). Is Achish unwittingly offering to be the second? Despite the humour in the telling, the predicament in which David finds himself is serious. It will not be until chapter 29, however, that we discover how David fares, for the focus of the narrative for the remainder of chapter 28 shifts to Saul and his own predicament.

3. As the narrative turns to Saul's response to the Philistine offensive, one hears for a second time that Samuel is dead (see at 25:1, where the notice is almost identically worded). One hears also that *Saul had expelled the mediums and spiritists from the land*. Both of these notices set the stage for the story to follow. While curiosity regarding Saul's motivations for expelling *mediums and spiritists* from the land is understandable, the text offers no explanation. Occult practices were explicitly forbidden in Israel and their practitioners were deserving of death (e.g. Lev. 19:31; 20:27; Deut. 18:9–13), but whether Saul's expulsion of mediums and spiritists was religiously motivated is unstated and perhaps not of interest to the narrator (for fuller discussion, see Long 2009a: 378).

4–7. *The Philistines assembled*[111] and *set up camp at Shunem* (v. 4). *Shunem* (modern Solem) lay at the eastern end of the Valley of Jezreel on the south-western slope of the Hill of Moreh, within about 16 miles of the Sea of Galilee to the north-east. *Gilboa*, where Saul and all Israel set up camp, probably refers not to the town

---

109. Cf. Solomon's identically worded charge to Shimei in 1 Kgs 2:37, 42.
110. Or perhaps 'go forth to battle' (so LXX; cf. Qumran, which adds 'at Jezreel').
111. At Aphek (see at 29:1).

Gilboa, some 11 miles south of Shunem, but to the mountain range of the same name extending southwards along the eastern side of the Jezreel plain. From there, according to 29:1, Saul's troops encamped *by the spring of Jezreel*, bringing them within 4 miles of the Philistines.

Not for the first time, Saul is terrified by the Philistine challenge (v. 5; cf. 17:11). In desperation, he seeks the divine guidance he had formerly neglected (see 13:8–11; 14:18–19, 36–46), but to no avail. Motivated more by panic than piety, Saul receives no answer, whether *by dreams or Urim or prophets* (v. 6). The three oracular means mentioned here have each played a role in the preceding narrative. One thinks of Samuel's dream theophany in 1 Samuel 3, of the use of the Urim and Thummim in 14:41 (see comment there) and of course of Samuel's prophetic role in Saul's life (e.g. chs. 13 and 15). But Samuel is dead, and the oracular Urim and Thummim are no longer with Saul. They are with David, having been brought to him by Abiathar (23:6), the sole survivor of Saul's massacre of the *priests of the LORD* in Nob (22:17–19). Effectively, Saul has destroyed or distanced himself from the normal means of gaining divine instruction. Moreover, the divine silence is reminiscent of the warning issued to Israel's elders in 8:18, to the effect that those who refuse to heed Yahweh's guidance may one day discover that their cries for relief receive no answer.

Find me a woman who is a medium (v. 7). In Hebrew the term is literally 'ghostwife' or 'ghostmistress', with 'ghost' referring to a spirit of the dead, called up by the necromancer's art. Despite Saul's ostensible purging of the land of mediums and spiritists (v. 3), he seems in no doubt that one can still be found, and he does not hesitate to instruct his attendants accordingly. *There is one in Endor* is their immediate response. *Endor* lay less than 5 miles north-east of Shunem, and so about 10 miles from Saul's encampment. But Saul will have to go behind enemy lines to get there. In Joshua 17:11–13, Endor is named amongst the cities from which the Manassites failed to drive out the Canaanites completely.

8–10. To aid his passage to Endor, which will take him perilously close to the Philistine camp at Shunem, Saul disguises himself in *other clothes* (necessarily non-royal attire), takes two men with him and goes *at night*. Reaching the woman, he gets straight to the point:

Consult a spirit for me (v. 8). Having been warned by Samuel that *rebellion is like the sin of divination* [*qesem*] (15:23), Saul shows no hesitation in asking the woman to 'divine [*qosŏmî*] for me by a ghost' (so JPS). 'Ghost' renders Hebrew *'ôb*, a term used to describe the spirit of the dead supposedly brought up by necromancy. In answer to the disguised Saul's request that she *bring up for me the one I name* (v. 8), the woman protests by citing Saul's expulsion of occult practitioners from the land and asking why her visitor would seek to trap her and cost her her life (v. 9). To calm her fears – but to the consternation of readers familiar with Yahweh's proscription of all occult practices (see v. 3) – Saul utters an oath in Yahweh's name: *As surely as the LORD lives, you will not be punished for this* (v. 10). The tragic irony of Saul's behaviour here is colourfully captured by the Midrash: 'Whom did Saul resemble at that moment? A woman who is with her lover and swears by the life of her husband.'[112]

11–14. Reassured by her visitor's oath, the woman asks, *Whom shall I bring up for you?* Saul names *Samuel*, but without further description; perhaps Samuel's fame (see v. 3) made further description unnecessary, though it is worth noting that in response to Saul's queries in verses 13 and 14, the woman responds not with a name but with descriptions. Modern readers may be curious about the necromancer's procedures, but the text shows no such interest, perhaps avoiding any description of a practice that was banned in Israel.[113] It is also possible that Samuel simply appears before the woman begins her enquiry; the text moves directly from Saul's request that Samuel be brought up to the woman's startled reaction (vv. 11–12). When she sees Samuel, *she cried out at the top of her voice* (*wattizʿaq běqôl gādôl*). The woman immediately recognizes that her night visitor is none other than Saul himself: *Why have you deceived me? You are Saul!* (v. 12). Why the woman is startled, and how Samuel's appearance reveals to her the true identity of her visitor, invites speculation. Perhaps her fright is occasioned by the fact that it is not one of her 'familiar spirits' (cf. *hayyiddĕʿōnîm* of v. 3) that

---

112. *Yalkut Shimoni* 2.247:139; cited by Alter (1999: 173).
113. For a review of such occult practices in the ANE, see Long (2009a: 381–382).

appears but, rather, the great Samuel. Her recognition of Saul, though in disguise, may result from her sudden realization that something momentous, and very *unfamiliar*, is afoot (cf. Alter 1999: 174).

Saul, called *the king* for the only time in chapter 28, is quick to reassure the woman: *Don't be afraid*. Royal duties aside, his immediate concern is for information: *What do you see?* The woman's first response is that she sees *a ghostly figure* [*ʾĕlōhîm*] *coming up out of the earth* (v. 13). The meaning of the word *ʾĕlōhîm* ranges from God to gods to important human beings, such as judges.[114] Here the woman is probably referring to Samuel's arresting appearance. When she describes the figure as *an old man wearing a robe*, Saul knows without doubt that it is Samuel, and he prostrates himself *with his face to the ground* (v. 14). The mere mention of Samuel's robe evokes a flood of memories, from the little robes his mother would make for him each year as he grew up in Eli's house (2:19) to the prophetic robe that was torn on the occasion of Saul's definitive rejection in 1 Samuel 15 (see at 15:27–28). Saul had once before found himself on his face before Samuel, prophesying (see 19:23–24). On that earlier occasion, his initial intent had been to take David's life but in the end he was divested of his own robe. Now, a second time, he finds himself on his face before Samuel, not prophesying but paralysed with fear. His own life is in mortal danger.

15–19. *Samuel said to Saul* (v. 15). Opinions are divided as to whether *Samuel* is the real Samuel or an apparition. While NIV's *ghostly figure* in verse 13 might seem to support the latter option, the Hebrew is *ʾĕlōhîm* (as noted above), which nowhere else in the Old Testament suggests such an apparition.[115] It seems likely that the real Samuel is in view, for the following reasons: the necromancer's fright at the appearance of Samuel suggests that he is not what she is expecting (see v. 12 and comment); the narrator refers to the

---

114. The NIV text note mentions 'spirits' or 'gods' as alternatives to 'ghostly figure'. See further Firth (2009: 293).
115. The ancient versions do not shed much light on the question. Most render the Hebrew rather literally as 'gods': e.g. LXX (*theous*), Syr. (ʾlh) and Vulg. (*deos*). The Targ. reads 'angel of the Lord' (*mlʾkʾ dyy*). Most modern translations follow suit, reading 'a divine being' or 'a god'.

figure simply as Samuel, without qualification (vv. 12, 15, 16, 20); Saul is said to know that it is Samuel (v. 14); Samuel speaks directly to Saul (v. 15 etc.), which is a 'divergence from the usual necromantic procedure' (Alter 1999: 175); the words spoken by Samuel are fully commensurate with his earlier words of judgment on Saul (vv. 17–18); and the further predictions in verse 19 that *tomorrow you and your sons will be with me* (i.e. in the grave) and that *The LORD will also give the army of Israel into the hands of the Philistines* both come to pass. That one's predictions come to pass is a necessary condition of true prophecy (Deut. 18:21–22), though not a sufficient one (Deut. 13:1–3). It seems, then, that 'Samuel' is to be understood as the real Samuel. This in no way validates necromancy but attests to the sovereign freedom of God to act in ways surprising not least to the necromancer herself.

In answer to Samuel's question *Why have you disturbed me . . . ?*, Saul explains his Philistine predicament and the failure of prophets or dreams to provide divine guidance.[116] *So I have called on you to tell me what to do* (v. 15). There is a sad irony in Saul's request, as it echoes the charge he received back in 10:8 at the time of his anointing: *I will surely come down to you*, Samuel had said, *but you must wait . . . until I come to you and tell you what you are to do*. Saul's failure to keep this charge (see at 13:8), compounded by further acts of faithlessness, now leaves him desperate for Samuel to tell him *what to do*, but it is too late (*now that the LORD has departed from you*, v. 16). All Saul receives is a reiteration of what he already knows (v. 17) and two final dire predictions of what will happen the next day (v. 19).

20–23. *Immediately Saul fell full length on the ground, filled with fear because of Samuel's words* (v. 20). Again, reference is made to Saul's stature, and to his fear. Earlier described as *a head taller than anyone else* (9:2), then as being brought from hiding behind the baggage and standing up before the people, *a head taller than any of the others* (10:23), he is now face down on the ground, impressive not because

---

116. Missing here from the list of oracular means in v. 6 is the Urim, perhaps because of Saul's 'guilty recollection of his massacre of the priests of Nob' (a possibility mooted by Alter 1999: 175).

of his height but because of his length. No more words are exchanged between Saul and Samuel.

The focus shifts to the woman, who *came to Saul and saw that he was greatly shaken* (v. 21). She appears not to have been present during the exchange between Samuel and Saul. Had she absented herself because of her own fright at the unexpected appearance of Samuel? Whatever the case, seeing Saul's distraught and depleted state, she reminds him that she *obeyed* him (šmʿ + bqwl) and *did what you told me to do* (šmʿ + dbr) (v. 21). In turn, she wants Saul to *listen* [šmʿ + bqwl] *to your servant and let me give you some food* (v. 22). *Some food* renders *pat-leḥem* ('a piece of bread'), a phrase occurring elsewhere only in the judgment speech of the 'man of God' to Eli (see 2:36). As with Eli on that earlier occasion, Saul's demise is imminent. How will he respond? Verse 23 states that *He refused and said, 'I will not eat.'* There is a faint glimmer of hopefulness in this. After all, Hannah's refusal to eat was in order that she might engage seriously with God (1:7–8). But this hope is immediately extinguished. Urged on by his men, who themselves were probably hungry, and by the medium, Saul *listened to them* (šmʿ + lqwl), *got up from the ground and sat on the couch* (v. 23). At the heart of Saul's failure is his propensity, when push comes to shove, to listen to the wrong voices (see, most pointedly, at 1 Sam. 15).

24–25. *The woman had a fattened calf at the house, which she slaughtered at once* (v. 24). Much more than a piece of bread, the woman prepares a meal fit for a king, even if it is to be his last. Though she 'hastens' (*wattĕmahēr*) to butcher the calf, just as Saul had 'hastened' (*wayĕmahēr*) to fall to the ground in verse 20, the process must still have taken several hours. Alter (1999: 178) muses:

> One must imagine Saul sitting in the house at En-dor, brooding or darkly baffled or perhaps a little catatonic. It is an odd and eerie juncture of the story. David has already twice been saved, from death and then from blood guilt, by women. Saul is now given sustaining nurture by a woman – but only to regain the strength needed to go out to the battlefield where he will die.

To this must be added the observation of just what kind of woman it is who serves up Saul's last meal. How much has changed since that auspicious occasion years before when Saul, in the presence of thirty witnesses and on the eve of Saul's anointing to be king, was served a meal prepared especially for him by the prophet Samuel (1 Sam. 9:22–24). His host now is the 'ghost-wife' and his witnesses but two men, for whom this will also be a final meal.

Meaning

The strange tale of chapter 28 is sad in almost every respect. As we have followed the career of Saul, we have noticed in him a declining commitment to hearing from God. We noted his failure to respond to his anointing by doing what lay at hand (10:7 and *passim*), we noticed his failure to wait long enough for Samuel to arrive and instruct him on the eve of the Philistine war recounted in chapters 13–14, we noticed his failure to follow through with the divine enquiry using the Urim and Thummim in 14:18–19 and we noticed his failure to listen to the voice of the Lord in chapter 15, though strongly urged by Samuel to do so (15:1). Saul was a man of great promise, at least with respect to his external qualities. But his consistent neglect of available avenues for hearing from the Lord, and his eventual outright rejection of the word of the Lord (15:23), eventually brought him to the crisis of the present chapter. Finally, now in a desperate situation, Saul wants to hear from the Lord, but it is too late. He is met with silence. Saul's consistent pattern of behaviour signals not so much a lack of good faith (at least in the early stages) as a lack of true faith. Yahweh did not carry full weight in Saul's thinking and acting. The Chronicler's summation is apt: 'Saul died because he was unfaithful to the LORD; he did not keep [*šmr*, 'give heed to'] the word of the LORD and even consulted a medium for guidance' (1 Chr. 10:13). One might suppose that the Chronicler's next statement that Saul 'did not enquire of the LORD' is a direct contradiction of 1 Samuel 28:6. But surely the Chronicler has in view Saul's general pattern of behaviour, and not the final act of desperation mentioned in 28:6. That Saul immediately turns to a medium confirms that his desire was not so much to hear from the Lord as to gain knowledge of his future, by which he might gain some control over it. Saul will figure in one more episode, but first we must return to David and the desperate situation in which he finds himself.

iii. David escapes a tight spot and rescues his own city of Ziklag (29:1 – 30:31)
Context

While chapter 28 focused largely on Saul, chapters 29 and 30 return to David, picking up where the narrative left off at 28:2. Much in chapter 29 recalls earlier episodes in the book of Samuel. As in chapter 4, the Philistines gather at Aphek, spoiling for a fight with Israel, though in the present chapter they move much farther north before engaging. In the former episode, the ark of God was captured and placed in the temple of the Philistine god, Dagon (ch. 5). Soon enough, the 'captive' ark proved too much for the pagan idol, which was repeatedly toppled and finally decapitated. In the present battle (which finds its conclusion in ch. 31), the armour of the slain Saul will be deposited in the *temple of the Ashtoreths*, and his decapitated body, along with the corpses of his sons, will end up hanging on the wall of Beth Shan (31:10). As Israel's defeat and loss of the ark in chapter 4 signalled the prophetically announced demise of the house of Eli, so the defeat of Saul in chapter 31 will mark the effective end of the house of Saul (cf. Bodner 2008: 304).

Further reminders of earlier episodes come in the angry words of the Philistine commanders addressed to Achish. Achish finds no fault in David and wishes to bring him and his men into the battle with the Israelites, but the other commanders are not so trusting. They have not forgotten David's military service under Saul, nor the manner in which his successes had been celebrated in chapter 18. The occasion of that earlier celebration was Israel's defeat of the Philistines in chapter 17, made possible by David's defeat and decapitation of Goliath. Though they don't mention that incident explicitly, their fear of David's regaining *his master's favour . . . by taking the heads of our own men* (v. 4) cannot but recall David's removal of Goliath's head. Nor can the attentive reader overlook the dramatic irony of Achish's having only recently promoted David to be 'keeper of my head' (see at 28:2).

That David is sent home by the Philistines turns out to be a 'God-send', as it means that David discovers the Amalekite raid on Ziklag soon enough to lead a successful rescue operation (ch. 30).

Comment

1. As they had done many years before in the time of Eli (see at 4:1), *The Philistines gathered all their forces at Aphek* (v. 1). This general muster was mentioned in virtually identical terms already in 28:1, though Aphek was not named. The hostile intent of the Philistines is made clear in 28:1. The gathering of *their forces* (lit. 'their camps') is in order to do battle with the Israelites, who we now learn in 29:1 have *camped by the spring in Jezreel*. The town of *Jezreel* has been identified with Tel Jezreel, and the spring in question is likely the 'spring of Harod' of Judges 7:1. It was at this spring that Gideon, at Yahweh's instructions, drastically reduced his troop numbers, lest they boast in their own strength (Judg. 7:2–8). Excavations at Tel Jezreel confirm occupation during the united monarchy period. Jezreel occupied a commanding position controlling the west–east road from Megiddo to Beth Shean and the north–south route from Shunem to the Dothan Valley.

The biblical description of troop deployments raises questions. What was the Philistine strategy? Perhaps the Philistines hoped 'to cut Saul off from the tribes further north' (Gordon 1986: 194), effectively dividing in order to conquer. But how could they have managed to enter the Jezreel Valley without being cut off at the pass (of Megiddo) by Saul, if Israelite troops were already deployed in Jezreel when the Philistines moved north? Perhaps Saul's troops were delayed in reaching Jezreel, as military strategists Herzog and Gichon (1997: 93–94) explain.

To summarize their view briefly: the Philistines, having been frustrated in attempts to overpower Israel from the west, moved north in order to attack from the Jezreel Valley, perhaps hoping to garner support from Canaanites in the Jezreel Valley before entering 'the central mountain massif' at present-day Jenin, and moving 'southwards along the plateau'. With the advantage of the interior lines, Saul 'waited to see in what direction the Philistines would move' and then 'moved his forces parallel to theirs' with the intent of taking up 'a blocking position' in 'the lower foothills of the Gilboa range'.

Herzog and Gichon speculate that Saul's failure to block Philistine passage may have resulted, first, from the Philistine muster at Aphek – which would have required the deployment of some of Saul's troops in that vicinity, lest the Philistines mount an attack from that direction – and, second, from an inadvertent 'diversionary movement' caused by the Philistine commanders' insistence (v. 4) that David and his troops not accompany them in their northwards march to Shunem but return south to Ziklag. As Herzog and Gichon explain, on his way home to Ziklag David would pass several 'obvious invasion routes into Judah', and this may have forced Saul to delay his march north until it was clear that 'no stab in the back was intended'. Only then could Saul 'rush to meet the northern threat'. This gave the Philistines time to set up in Shunem unmolested.

2–5. *As the Philistine rulers* (*sarnê pĕlištîm*) begin their march north, accompanied by *their units of hundreds and thousands* – standard military units – they notice *Hebrews* marching *at the rear with Achish* (v. 2). *The commanders of the Philistines* (*śārê pĕlištîm*)[117] are troubled by these Hebrews (did they regard them as Habiru?)[118] and query Achish about them. Achish's answer is straightforward: *Is this not David, who was an officer of Saul king of Israel?* (v. 3). If Achish's intent is to allay the fears of the commanders, his naming David is inept. Though Achish may be so thoroughly in thrall to David that he is willing to make David 'keeper of his head' (see at 28:2), the Philistines are not reassured by his statement that he has *found no fault in him* (v. 3). As the reader knows, this lack of discovery is a measure of Achish's gullibility, not of David's sincerity (recall 27:8–12). The commanders are well aware of the prowess of David, citing in verse 5 the women's praise of David in the aftermath of his defeat and decapitation of Goliath (see at 18:7; cf. 21:11). They recognize the danger of his turning on them in battle (cf. 14:21)

---

117. The term used in v. 2 is *seren*, generally used to describe the rulers/governors of the five chief cities of the Philistines (see Josh. 13:3; Judg. 3:3; etc.), while the term in v. 3 is *śar* and seems to refer to the military commanders themselves. If a distinction is to be drawn, then it is appropriate that the military commanders were most concerned with non-Philistines going into battle. But for the view that the two are not to be distinguished, see Tsumura (2007: 633).
118. See at 4:6 (and cf. Long 2009a: 289).

and collecting even more Philistine heads. Thus, they are *angry with Achish* and insist that David be sent home to *the place you assigned him* (v. 4).

6–11. To break the news to David, Achish calls him and reassures him of his own confidence in him, reinforcing his words with an oath in the name of Yahweh: *As surely as the LORD lives, you have been reliable, and I would be pleased* [lit. 'it would be good in my eyes'] *for you to serve with me in the army* (v. 6). The problem is that *the rulers don't approve of you* (lit. 'in the eyes of the rulers you are not good'). Achish's continuing references to his having found *no fault in you* from the day David arrived simply underscores that he is no match for the wily David. As hard as Achish seems to be trying not to upset David – *go in peace* – he is also concerned that David *do nothing to displease the Philistine rulers* (lit. 'do not do evil in the eyes of the Philistine rulers'; v. 7).

Without missing a beat, David continues his charade: *But what have I done?* (v. 8). David earlier posed the same question to Saul, and he meant it sincerely on that occasion (26:18). But here he is simply toying with Achish. The irony of David's question *What have you found against your servant . . . ?* is that Achish could have found much against him had he been less easily duped. David's final question is wonderfully ambiguous: *Why can't I go and fight against the enemies of my lord the king?* (v. 8). Achish doubtless hears *my lord the king* as referring to himself, but the reference is vague at best. Had David indeed accompanied Achish into battle, it may have become apparent that, when forced to choose, David still regarded Saul as his king. But fortunately for David, despite Achish's pronouncement that *you have been as pleasing in my eyes as an angel of God*,[119] the will of the Philistine commanders prevails (v. 9). That David is forced to return to Ziklag proves beneficial on several counts: he is not placed in the untenable situation of having to face Israel in battle; he is far from the scene of the battle in which the lives of Saul and his sons are lost and so he cannot be suspected of having a hand in their deaths; and his early return to Ziklag enables him

---

119. On the several references in Samuel to David as an *angel of God*, see at 2 Sam. 19:27.

to learn sooner rather than later of the Amalekite raid on Ziklag and to undertake a rescue operation (ch. 30).

30:1–2. *David and his men reached Ziklag on the third day* (v. 1). Given the distance from Aphek to Ziklag, some 50 or 60 miles (depending on the route taken), and given that armies on the march usually cover 15 or 20 miles a day,[120] this time notice makes good sense. David and his men have wasted no time in returning to Ziklag. David may well have been concerned for the safety of Ziklag in his absence, as it was from Ziklag that David had been launching raids against enemies in the Negev. Amongst these enemies were 'the Amalekites (27:8), the archetypal bandits of biblical tradition' (McCarter 1980: 434).

Before detailing what David and his men discovered when they reached Ziklag (v. 3), the narrator informs the reader that *the Amalekites had raided the Negev and Ziklag* (v. 1). Not only had they burned the city, but they had carried away its entire contents, material and human. Named in particular are *the women . . . both young and old* (v. 2); sons and daughters will also be mentioned in verse 3. Remarkable is the notice that the Amalekites *killed none of them, but carried them off* (v. 2). Before too quickly judging the Amalekites' behaviour favourably by contrast to David's annihilation of populations during his raiding exploits in the Negev (see 27:9 and comment), we must consider that the Amalekites spared women and children 'in order to exploit them as slaves' (Alter 1999: 183). Just how little regard the Amalekites apparently had for the lives of slaves will become clear later in the chapter (vv. 11–13). Already in verse 2 we get a hint of Amalekite cruelty, for the verb *nhg*, rendered *carried them off* near the end of that verse, is a 'rather brutal verb . . . typically used for driving animals' (Alter 1999: 184).[121]

---

120. See Eph'al (1983: 99); and especially Long (2009a: 384).
121. The verb occurs only five times in Samuel: in 23:5 it refers to driving livestock, as it does also in the present chapter at 30:20; in 30:22 it is used by 'worthless fellows' insisting that the exhausted two hundred men get nothing, but should just take their wives and children and drive (them) and leave; the final occurrence is in 2 Sam. 6:3, in reference to Uzzah and Ahio 'driving the new cart'.

3–6. Notice of the Amalekite raid having already been given to the reader (vv. 1–2), *David and his men* witness the devastation for themselves in verse 3. Hebrew *wĕhinnē*, though left untranslated in the NIV, means literally 'and behold' and signals that the reader is now 'seeing' what David and his men witnessed, as if through their own eyes: their city *destroyed by fire and their wives and sons and daughters taken captive* (v. 3). Little wonder that they wept until *they had no strength left* (v. 4). Verse 5 makes clear that David has not been spared; both his wives, *Ahinoam of Jezreel and Abigail, the widow of Nabal of Carmel*, are among the captives. This turn of events is tragically ironic if, as might be supposed, David's decision to flee to Philistine territory was motivated in part by concern for the safety of his and his men's families (see at 27:1–3).

David was greatly distressed because the men were talking of stoning him (v. 6). David has faced threats from enemies inside and outside Israel, but never from his own men. This might seem to be the end of the line for David, but he *found strength in the LORD his God* (v. 6). On an earlier occasion, when the chief threat to David had been Saul, Saul's son Jonathan had sought David out and *helped him to find strength in God* (23:16). Now David is alone, but having been encouraged by his friend on an earlier occasion of threat, David is able again to turn to Yahweh for strength. In the present context, this explicitly theological notice marks, as Firth (2009: 305) points out, 'an important turn' in the narrative. 'Overtly theological language has been lacking during David's Philistine period' (ibid.). Henceforth, though 'David remains the astute politician . . . he is again the politician who knows how much depends on his relationship to Yahweh' (ibid.: 306).

7–8. *Then David said to Abiathar the priest, the son of Ahimelek, 'Bring me the ephod'* (v. 7). On Abiathar and the circumstances by which he came to be in David's company, see at 22:20–23. On the ephod as an oracular instrument, see at 2:28.[122] For the first time since David fled to the Philistines – indeed, for the first time since 1 Samuel 23:4 – we read that *David enquired of the LORD* (v. 8). Having again

---

122. Recall also Saul's aborting the oracular enquiry in 14:18–19 and David's successful oracular use of the ephod in 23:9.

found strength in Yahweh (v. 6), he turns to him also for guidance as to whether he should *pursue this raiding party*, and he receives an affirmative answer.

9–10. *David and the six hundred men with him* have over the last few days covered 75 or 80 miles by the time they reach the *Besor Valley* (v. 9), 12 to 15 miles south of Ziklag.[123] It is little wonder that *two hundred* of the men are *too exhausted to cross the valley*. Leaving them behind, *David and the other four hundred continued the pursuit* (v. 10).

11–15. *They found an Egyptian in a field and brought him to David* (v. 11). In view of the recently proffered promise of success (v. 8) and the general sparsity in Hebrew narratives of incidental or insignificant details, this 'chance' discovery of a lone Egyptian is portentous. He is near-dead, having *not eaten any food or drunk any water for three days and three nights* (v. 12). Thus, he must be revived with food and water, and what better for such a purpose than *pressed figs* and *raisins*. Whether David's motivation for taking time to revive the Egyptian was to show kindness or to extract information, or both, is not stated. As Brueggemann (1990: 202) notes, 'David's company' was 'accustomed to recruiting hopeless, isolated outsiders'.

As soon as the man is revived, David plies him with questions and discovers that the man is an Egyptian slave of an Amalekite. Having suffered the misfortune of falling ill while on a raiding party, the slave had been abandoned three days earlier by his master (v. 13). That the slave had not eaten for three days when David's men discovered him means that he been abandoned entirely without food or water by his heartless Amalekite master. Given what will soon transpire in respect of the Amalekite raiders, the slave's 'misfortune' in falling ill will in fact prove to be very fortunate indeed.

Though David's express questions had not included 'What have you been up to?', the slave volunteers a report of the raids in *the Negev of the Kerethites, some territory belonging to Judah and the Negev of Caleb* (v. 14). The Kerethites, mentioned here for the first time in the Old Testament, appear to have come from Crete and to be

---

123. On the geographic details, see Long (2009a: 384).

associated with the Philistines (as in Ezek. 25:16; Zeph. 2:5; and elsewhere – 'Pelethites' is probably a linguistic variant of 'Philistines'). Thus, the Amalekite raids seem to have taken advantage of the Philistines' military adventures in the north to attack Philistine territories in the south. The slave's final notice is that *we burned Ziklag* (v. 14). Whether aware of David's association with Ziklag or not, this admission could have cost the slave his life. But David, an astute military man, is quick to see the advantage to be gained by keeping the slave alive: *Can you lead me down to this raiding party?* (v. 15). The slave is willing but, astute in his own right, only on the condition David swear *before God that you will not kill me or hand me over to my master* (v. 15).

16–20. Presumably having received from David a positive response to his request for protection (v. 15), the revived Egyptian slave leads David down to where the Amalekites can be found, *and there they were, scattered over the countryside* (v. 16). NIV's *and there they were* renders *wĕhinnê* ('and behold'), allowing the reader to see, as it were, through David's eyes (see above at v. 3). And what David sees is Amalekites *nĕṭušîm* ('cast about') 'all over the ground' (JPS), *eating, drinking and revelling* (or 'staggering' as when drunk; cf. *ḥgg* in Ps. 107:27). Whether *David fought them from dusk until the evening of the next day* (v. 17) or attacked at the crack of dawn the next day is not made clear in the text. The Hebrew *nešep* in verse 17 essentially means 'twilight' and can refer to the semi-darkness of either dusk or dawn. Logically, given the exhausted state of David's men, it seems likely that he would have staged the attack early the next morning, after his men had had some sleep and while the Amalekites were still sleeping off the previous day's revelry.

The victory is complete, apart from *four hundred young men who rode off on camels and fled* (v. 17). That this number matches the four hundred men under David's command suggests how much larger the original Amalekite force must have been. The victory was large, and it was David's victory – the text emphasizes this by making David the subject of most of the sentences: *David fought* (v. 17); *David recovered everything* (v. 18); *David brought everything back* (v. 19). Little wonder that his men driving home the *flocks and herds* declare, *This is David's plunder* (v. 20). Not only did David recover *everything the Amalekites had taken, including his two wives* (v. 18), but absolutely *[n]othing was missing: young or old, boy or girl, plunder or anything else they had taken* (v. 19). As so often in the book of Samuel, the hand of providence is evident, even if not explicitly mentioned.

Before leaving verse 20, a word is in order regarding what is often regarded as difficult Hebrew. English translations typically assume that the *flocks and herds* taken by David were driven either ahead of some *other livestock* (NIV; JPS; NRSV) or ahead of 'him' (i.e. David; ESV) or 'them' (Alter 1999: 187; Firth 2009: 302–303). The first assumption raises the question of what 'other livestock' might be in view if David indeed took 'all the flocks and herds'. The plausibility of the second requires that *lipnê* be emended to *lipnāyw* or to *lipnêhem* and would likely also need the addition of the accusative particle before *hammiqneh* (read as 'livestock'). A simpler solution, requiring no (consonantal) emendations, would be to read *hammiqneh* not as 'livestock' but as 'property' or 'possessions' (perhaps revocalizing as *hammiqnâ*). This would then refer to the possessions recovered in verse 19. Thus, the problematic clause in verse 20 could be read as follows: 'He took all the flocks and herds, and his men drove them ahead of the (recovered) property, saying, "This is David's plunder"' (LXX and Syr. may lend some support to this suggestion).

21–25. Coming to the *Besor Valley*, where the *two hundred men who had been too exhausted to follow him* were waiting, David confronts a problem. His enquiry into the welfare of the men is gracious (v. 21).[124] But among his followers are some *evil men and troublemakers* who take a dim view of David's magnanimity and don't hesitate to voice their own opinion: those who *did not go out with us* should get none of *the plunder we recovered* (v. 22). It must not be forgotten that some of the property recovered belonged originally to the two hundred who stayed behind. While it could rightly be called *plunder* when in Amalekite hands, now back in Israelite hands it should be regarded as recovered property. All that the troublemakers are

---

124. Perhaps surprisingly gracious, which may have influenced LXX, e.g., to imagine that it was the two hundred left behind who ask after David's welfare. MT can be retained (cf. Gordon 1986: 200).

willing to return to the two hundred are their wives and children, who are to be 'led away' (Heb. *nhg* is often used for the 'driving' of animals; see at v. 2 above).

David replied, 'No, my brothers, you must not do that with what the LORD *has given us'* (v. 23). David's conciliatory posture continues, even with the *evil men and troublemakers* of verse 22, whom he refers to as *my brothers*. He then proceeds to make the point that the goods with which they are returning are in fact gifts from Yahweh (and so in that sense neither plunder nor even recovered property). Yahweh receives credit for the happy outcome of what could have been devastating loss (v. 23). So *[w]ho will listen to what you say?* (v. 24). David's declaration that *All shall share alike* (v. 24) became *a statute and ordinance for Israel from that day to this* (v. 25). The phrase *from that day to this* offers a rare hint of the narrator's presence in a story where such frame-breaks are rare.

26–31. Adroit in navigating through disagreements among his men (see immediately above), David is also astute in his dealings with *his friends* beyond his immediate circle. Back in Ziklag, he sends *some of the plunder to the elders of Judah* (v. 26). Notably, and understandably, no gifts are sent to the Philistines, though their villages also had been plundered by the Amalekites (see v. 16; cf. at v. 14). Undoubtedly, the Amalekites will have plundered Judahite villages, and it seems likely that stolen property will have been returned, insofar as possible. David's mention of a *gift* (lit. 'blessing') would suggest more than just the recovery of what had been taken. Perhaps David's gifts involve a redistribution of goods taken from Philistine territory to his friends in Judah.[125]

The episode concludes with five verses listing the specific recipients of David's largesse (vv. 27–31).[126] The concluding reference to *all the other places where he and his men had roamed* (v. 31) suggests the motivation for David's actions, namely, gratitude for past kindnesses. That *Hebron* is named last is not insignificant, as this

---

125. For a more thorough discussion of Ancient Near Eastern attitudes towards the spoils of war, see Long (2009a: 386).
126. For detailed discussion, see Youngblood (2009: 285–286); Tsumura (2007: 646–649).

will be the place where the men of Judah will anoint David as their king (2 Sam. 2:4) and from which he will rule for seven and a half years before becoming king over all Israel (2 Sam. 2:11; 5:5). Everything is falling into place for David to ascend the throne in the south, even while everything is falling apart for Saul far in the north, battling the Philistines. It is to Saul on Mount Gilboa that the narrative turns in the next chapter.

Meaning
It is not easy to know how an ancient audience would have assessed David's performance during his time with Achish. On the one hand, the 'trickster' was at times admired by ancient audiences, and David was certainly a skilled trickster. On the other hand, to a theologically attuned audience, the fact that David's flight to Achish began with an anxious moment of doubt (27:1), and not in response to an explicit divine directive, may have cast a shadow over the whole episode. Rabbinic interpreters struggled with this episode, especially with what David might have done had he been forced to accompany the Philistines into battle against Israel. Gersonides (1288–1344), for instance, thought that David would simply have turned on the Philistines in battle. Abrabanel (1437–1508), however, reasoned that, rather than engaging in such a betrayal, David would have fulfilled his bodyguard responsibilities by protecting Achish while otherwise remaining neutral in the battle itself.[127] The fact that David escaped being in such a predicament was sometimes attributed to his having prayed, but the biblical text makes no mention of his praying. Whether sought by David or not, a providential rescue of David from potentially calamitous circumstances is hard to overlook; not only was David exempted from the battle between the Philistines and the Israelites, a battle in which the house of Saul essentially came to an end, but also his early return to Ziklag gave him a chance to mount a rescue operation for those whom the Amalekites had abducted in his absence.

In the course of the rescue operation in chapter 30, David demonstrates the qualities that made him great. First among

---

127. Cf. Rosenberg (1980: *ad loc.*).

these was his ability to find *strength in the LORD his God* (30:6). The importance of this point cannot be overstated: 'David, without strengthening himself in the Lord, would have been just one more minor ancient Near Eastern potentate' (Birch 1998: 1195). In contrast to Saul, for whom dire circumstances often meant a diminished attentiveness to the Lord, for David the opposite was the case – at least most of the time. Despite the urgency of the situation, David did not proceed without first enquiring of Yahweh (30:7–8). Having thus begun well, David's actions throughout chapter 30 show him 'already demonstrating qualities of the kingdom God is bringing to Israel' (Birch 1998: 1194). As Alter aptly remarks,

> In all respects, this episode is meant to demonstrate David's attributes as a leader: he finds strength in the face of disaster, consults God's oracle, intrepidly leads his troops in a counterattack, and . . . makes the most equitable arrangement for the division of spoils.

He also acts with political wisdom, 'shoring up support among the sundry leaders of his home tribe of Judah . . . and preparing for himself a base in Hebron . . . where he will soon be proclaimed king' (Alter 1999: 188).

iv. Saul takes his own life in a losing battle with the Philistines (31:1–13)
Context

With David re-established in Ziklag, the focus of the narrative returns to King Saul, where Saul already has his hands full (see v. 1 below). After the events of chapter 28, the ultimate outcome of the battle recorded in the present chapter is not in doubt. Details of Israel's defeat by the Philistines and of the deaths of Saul and his sons constitute a sombre ending to the reign of the rejected king who refused to step aside.

Comment

1–3. *Now the Philistines fought against Israel* (v. 1). The text uses a participle, 'were fighting', which captures the sense that at the same time that David was in the south defeating the Amalekites, Saul and his troops were in the north being engaged in battle by the

Philistines. Israel under Saul is not faring well, and *many fell dead [wayyippĕlû ḥălālîm] on Mount Gilboa* (v. 1). Use of the adjective *ḥālāl* (slain, defiled) anticipates the similar-sounding description of Saul's being terrified (from *ḥyl*) or wounded (from *ḥlḥ*) in verse 3 (see below). Apart from verse 1 and verse 8 of the present chapter, the adjective *ḥālāl* is used only in 1 Samuel 17:52, in celebration of Israel's crushing victory over the Philistines in the aftermath of David's defeat of Goliath. In the present context, under Saul, the tables are decidedly turned, and Israel is the loser.

The Philistines' *hot pursuit* [or 'overtaking'; root *dbq*] *of Saul and his sons* (v. 2) finds its counterparts fore and aft in the only other occurrences of *dbq* in Samuel. In 14:22 the verb describes Israel's hot pursuit of the Philistines following Jonathan's daring lead (as described in 14:1–15). In 2 Samuel 23:10, the verb is used to describe how Eleazar's hand *froze* [root *dbq*] *to the sword* after he had *stood his ground and struck down the Philistines till his hand grew tired*. Again, in the present verse, the tables are reversed, and it is the Philistines who are in hot pursuit of Saul and his sons (v. 2).

The fighting grew fierce around Saul (v. 3) is in Hebrew literally 'the battle was heavy [*wattikbad*] against Saul', thus invoking yet again the keyword *kbd* (weight, honour, glory) that has appeared so prominently at key moments in the book of Samuel so far (see, e.g., 2:29–30; 4:18, 21; 5:6, 11; 6:5–6; 9:6; 15:30; 22:14). Overtaken by the archers, Saul is terrified ('trembled greatly'), if we accept the MT vocalization (*wayyāḥel*). Or, if we follow LXX, he is severely wounded (assuming *wayyēḥal*).[128] LXX also uses the Greek verb *traumatizō*, from which the English words 'trauma' and 'traumatize' are derived. The Greek speaks of a physical wound, not psychological trauma, but it seems fair to assume that Saul experiences both. The narrator's use of a Hebrew expression that, depending on the vocalization, can suggest Saul's being traumatized both physically and psychologically seems fitting.[129]

---

128. MT presents a qal of the root *ḥyl* (writhe, tremble), while LXX assumes either a nipʻal or perhaps a hopʻal of *ḥlḥ* (to be seriously wounded).

129. LXX also reads MT's *hammôrîm* (the archers) as *hammotnayim* (belly, or more specifically hips and loins), thus specifying the location of Saul's injury.

4–7. Saul's reaction to his extreme predicament is as predictable as it is tragic. As on earlier occasions, Saul's first thought is not to turn to Yahweh. Rather, in the present crisis, he turns to his armour-bearer: *Draw your sword and run me through* [*wĕdoqrēnî*], *or these uncircumcised fellows will come and run me through* [*ûdĕqārunî*] *and abuse me* (v. 4). Familiar in these words are Saul's self-focus (recall, e.g., the personal pronouns in 1 Sam. 15:30) and his fear. On earlier occasions, both Jonathan and David, relying on Yahweh, spoke of the *uncircumcised* with derision – Jonathan in his bold proposal to his armour-bearer (14:6) and David in his dismissal of the threat of the Philistine giant who defied *the armies of the living God* (17:26, 36). Saul, in the only other use of the term 'uncircumcised' in 1 Samuel, is simply overcome with fear. Saul's behaviour most closely resembles that of the less than admirable Abimelek of Judges 9, whose armour-bearer obeyed Abimelek and 'thrust him through' (same root, *dqr*) to spare him the indignity, as Abimelek saw it, of dying by the hand of a woman (Judg. 9:52–54). Saul's armour-bearer is not so willing. The reader is again reminded of the several times Saul's servants refused to comply with his specific commands (e.g. 14:45; 22:17).

So Saul took his own sword and fell on it and died (vv. 4–5). What David repeatedly refused to do to Yahweh's anointed (24:6; 26:10–11), Saul now does to himself. Saul's decisive action is sometimes lauded as worthy of a tragic hero, but the biblical perspective is rather different in respect of suicide. Lauded, rather, are those who in times of greatest danger or duress turn to Yahweh for strength, as David does in 23:16; 30:6, and who like Jonathan submit themselves fully to the divine will (e.g. 18:4 and *passim*).

The defeat of Israel under Saul is resounding, whether or not MT's inclusion of the phrase *and all his men* is original or not. The phrase is lacking in LXX and in the parallel text in 1 Chronicles 10:6, which substitutes 'all his house'. The word *kōl*, 'all', does not always mean 'all' in an absolute or mathematical sense.[130] The sense here

---

130. Cf. Judg. 7:7, where it is stated that Gideon dismisses 'all the men', whereas three hundred are retained; see also the contextually qualified uses of 'all' in 1 Sam. 13:7 (*all the troops*); 15:8 (*all his people*, i.e. the

is that the house of Saul is effectively at its end, though we learn later that there remains at least one surviving son, Ish-Bosheth (2 Sam. 2:8), and also supporters of the *house of Saul* (2 Sam. 3:1, 6).

Beyond the immediate scene of battle, the defeat is sufficiently dramatic to frighten *the Israelites along the valley and those across the Jordan* into abandoning their towns into the hands of the Philistines, who *came and occupied them* (v. 7).

8–10. The Philistines' treatment of the bodies of *Saul and his three sons fallen on Mount Gilboa* (v. 8) proves that his fear of being abused by them was well founded. After removing Saul's head – 'a king's head was a prized trophy' in the Ancient Near East (Dalley 2000: 420) – and stripping off (root *pšṭ*)[131] his armour (v. 9), they deposit *his armour in the temple of the Ashtoreths* (cf. the deposit of Goliath's sword in the sanctuary at Nob, 21:9). They then attach his decapitated body *to the wall of Beth Shan* (v. 10), along with the bodies of his sons (v. 12). Only two other decapitations are mentioned in Samuel, namely, David's removal of Goliath's head in 17:51 and the removal of the head of the insurrectionist Sheba son of Bikri by the citizenry of Abel, acting on the advice of a wise woman (2 Sam. 20:22). On the Ashtoreths, see at 7:4, and on the practice of depositing captured 'deities' in one's own temple(s), see at 5:2.

Beth Shan (v. 10) was an important, strategically placed city controlling two major trade routes at the eastern end of the Jezreel Valley. Though it was allocated to the tribe of Manasseh in the time of Joshua (Josh. 17:11), the Manassites failed to drive out the people of Beth Shan, citing both Canaanite determination to remain in the land (Judg. 1:27) and Canaanite chariots (Josh. 17:16) – poor reasons from the theological perspectives of the books of Joshua and Judges. Sometimes under Egyptian and sometimes under

---

(note 130 *cont.*) Amalekites); later references make it clear that not 'all' the Amalekites in an absolute sense were destroyed (e.g. 27:8; 30:1, 18).

131. The first occurrence of this verb in Samuel describes Jonathan's stripping off of his royal regalia (see at 18:4), and the second describes Saul's stripping off of his garments in 19:24. Thereafter, the verb occurs frequently in reference to 'raiding' other lands (e.g. 23:27; 27:8, 10; 30:1, 14).

Philistine control, Beth Shan did not come under Israelite control until after the reign of Saul (cf. 1 Kgs 4:12 and context). Of particular interest to the present passage is the discovery by archaeologists excavating in Beth Shan of two public buildings believed by the excavators to be 'twin temples', which they tentatively identify with 'the House of Ashtoreth' (v. 10) and 'the house of Dagon' mentioned in 1 Chronicles 10:10 (Negev and Gibson 2003: 84). While specific identifications inevitably are speculative, the presence of such public buildings at Beth Shan in the time of Saul (eleventh century) correlates well with the biblical narrative.

11–13. Historic ties between the Jabesh Gileadites and the Benjaminites (Judg. 21), as well as Saul's rescue of the village in 1 Samuel 11, may suggest something of the motivation for the *people of Jabesh Gilead* (v. 11) to send *all their valiant men* on a 13-mile overnight march to retrieve *the bodies of Saul and his sons from the wall of Beth Shan* (v. 12). That their burning of the bones once retrieved (v. 12) is not to be read negatively is shown by the proper burial and seven-day fast described in verse 13.[132]

Meaning

The contrast between David's successes in chapter 30 and Saul's utter defeat and death in chapter 31 could not be more striking. David's recovery of all that the Amalekites had taken provided an occasion for David's declaration that the Lord was the one who *protected us and delivered into our hands the raiding party that came against us* (30:23). Saul, by contrast, is terrified by the prospect of falling into the hands of the Philistines. And instead of turning to Yahweh, whom Saul has too long ignored, he turns to his armour-bearer with the request that he assist his suicide. When the armour-bearer refuses, Saul falls on his own sword and dies. This action, when viewed in the full biblical context, cannot be regarded as heroic. Saul is not a tragic 'hero', though his life is certainly tragic. His calling was to deal the Philistines a decisive blow (9:16), but in the end he dies by his own hand in fear of what the Philistines might do to him.

---

132. On the burning of bodies in the ANE, see Long (2009a: 392).

5. GOD'S KING REIGNS (2 SAMUEL 1:1 – 5:5)

When it became necessary to divide the book of Samuel into two smaller books (see Introduction), it made sense to begin the second book *After the death of Saul* (1:1). Other Old Testament books open with the same basic formula – 'After the death of Moses' (Josh. 1:1) and 'After the death of Joshua' (Judg. 1:1). In both Joshua and Judges, the formula signals a turning point in Israel's history. The death of Moses signalled that the time had come for Israel, under Joshua, to enter the land of promise (Josh. 1:2). The death of Joshua signalled the onset of the period of the 'judges', a period of repeated apostasy by a generation who 'knew neither the LORD nor what he had done for Israel' (Judg. 2:10). The death of Saul signals another turning point. The career of the people's king has run its sad course to a bitter end, and the time has finally come for David, the man 'of God's own choosing' (see at 1 Sam. 13:14), to ascend the throne.

To this point in the story, David has been patient. The narration in 2 Samuel 1:1 – 5:5 of David's ascent, first over Judah in Hebron and then over all Israel, is told in such a way as to make it very clear that David was not complicit in the death of Saul's former general,

Abner, nor in the death of Saul's sole surviving son, Ish-Bosheth. Some commentators assume the opposite to be the case, noting that David benefits from these deaths (and from others that follow) and concluding that he must therefore somehow be responsible. But this assumption is not warranted, as I have argued more fully elsewhere (Provan, Long and Longman 2015: 288–293). First, David is not the only one to benefit from these and later deaths, if he benefited at all. And, second, to assume that one must have a hand in every event from which one benefits is to assume a much too mechanistic view of how the world works.

In terms of literary segmentation, the notice of Saul's death (1:1) provides an opening frame for the story of David's ascent to the throne, while the summary 'regnal formula' of 5:4–5 offers a closing frame. This regnal formula, which states David's age at the time of accession (thirty years old) and the length of his reign first in Hebron (seven and a half years) and then over all Israel and Judah (thirty-three years), does more than conclude the preceding section; it also anticipates the remainder of David's forty-year reign and thus the remainder of 2 Samuel.

A. David's reaction to news of Saul's death (1:1–27)

i. David's interrogation and execution of the Amalekite messenger (1:1–16)

Context

David was anointed as the man of God's choosing already back in 1 Samuel 16, but he has been patient. Relentlessly pursued by the rejected king Saul, David has refused to lift a hand against him, even when faced in 1 Samuel 24 and 26 with golden opportunities to rid the world of the one so keenly desirous of sending him to an early grave (e.g. 1 Sam. 19:1). The present episode shows that David takes no delight in the death of Saul and his sons.

Comment

1–2. These opening verses assume that the reader is aware of the contents of 1 Samuel, and especially of the true circumstances of the death of Saul (1 Sam. 31:4–6) and of David's very recent recovery of everyone and everything that Amalekite marauders had taken from Ziklag (1 Sam. 30; on how Ziklag became David's, see 1 Sam. 27:6). We learn in verse 1 that only two days have elapsed since David returned to Ziklag after rescuing family and fortune from the revelling Amalekites (1 Sam. 30:16–19). David was far from Mount Gilboa when Saul died, so he may well have been unaware of the defeat that Israel and the house of Saul suffered at the hands of the Philistines. The arrival of a man from the battlefield changes that. The man's appearance – torn clothes and dust on his head – is meant to suggest not that he has been in combat but, as an ancient audience would have understood, that he is in mourning.[1] Unlike the messenger in 1 Samuel 4:12, who is identified as a Benjaminite, the identity of the man who comes to David in this episode is not made known until verse 8, where he himself reveals that he is an Amalekite. The irony of an Amalekite making a beeline to David to prostrate himself before him is hard to miss.[2] But for the present, David does not know that the man is an Amalekite, and the Amalekite must not know that David has just returned from a miraculous victory (see 1 Sam. 30:18–19, 23) over other Amalekites.

3–4. Noting the man's appearance, and knowing that a mighty battle from which he was excluded (1 Sam. 29) must by now have been joined, David is anxious to hear whence the man has come and why, and what he has to report. So he begins to ply him with questions. The man begins with the basic facts: he has *escaped from the Israelite camp* (v. 3), Israel has suffered a great defeat and *Saul and his son Jonathan are dead* (v. 4). That only Jonathan is mentioned of

---

1. See the very similar expression in 1 Sam. 4:12; for discussion of conventional signs of mourning in the Ancient Near East, see Long (2009a: 290).
2. NRSV's 'fell to the ground and did obeisance' is preferable to NIV's *fell to the ground to pay him honour*, as the latter might lead the English reader to assume the presence of the keyword 'honour' that figures inter alia in the early chapters of 1 Samuel. The Hebrew word in the present context is *ḥwh*, meaning 'to bow before' or (when God is the object) 'to worship'. The keyword 'honour', on the other hand, reflects the Hebrew root *kbd*.

the three sons who died with Saul in battle (1 Sam. 31:2) suggests either that the man knows of David's close friendship with Jonathan or that he recognizes Jonathan as next in line after Saul and assumes that David will be happy to have both king and crown prince out of the way. Or it may simply be a first indication that the man reporting to David is unreliable.

5–10. To David's query how he can know all this, the *young man who brought him the report* (v. 5) offers a more detailed response. To this point in the narrative the messenger has been called simply *a man* (*'îš*). He is now called a *young* man (or possibly 'servant, attendant', Heb. *na'ar*) and is described as the one 'reporting to him' (*hammāgîd lô*; so NRSV). The reader already knows that the man is reporting to David, so the explicit reminder here and twice more in the chapter (vv. 6 and 13) may call 'attention to the act of telling and by underlining that act may make us wonder whether this is an authentic report or a fabrication' (Alter 1999: 195).

Encouraged by David's continued questioning, the young man unfolds (or contrives?) his story. Beginning with an emphatic Hebrew construction, *I [just] happened to be [niqrā' niqrêtî] on Mount Gilboa*, he describes how he came upon Saul *leaning on his spear, with the chariots and their drivers in hot pursuit* (v. 6). The Hebrew expression translated *drivers* is *ba'ălê happārāšîm* ('masters of the horses' or the like), and should be understood as 'charioteers'. The mention of chariots may offer a hint that the young man is fabricating his report. Chariots are not explicitly mentioned in the account of Saul's death in 1 Samuel 31 and, so it is sometimes argued, would have been of little use in mountainous terrain. But it is hard to understand why the young man would embellish with an implausible detail. On closer inspection, there may in fact be hints of chariotry in 1 Samuel 31. Malamat (1982: 28) and others have noted that chariots served various functions in combat: to protect infantry, to chase down fleeing enemies, to provide mobile firing platforms for archers and generally to terrorize the enemy. Perhaps the *archers* who *wounded* Saul *critically* in 1 Samuel 31:3 were operating from such mobile firing platforms. Moreover, given the variety of ways in which chariots were useful (including simply to frighten the enemy), Ancient Near Eastern powers would sometimes go to great lengths to get their chariots to the scene of battle. The

Assyrian king Tiglath-pileser I (1114–1076), for instance, boasts of hacking through a 'rough mountain range and difficult paths with copper picks' to make 'a good way for the passage of my chariots and troops' (*ARI* 2.13). He even claims to have loaded chariots on his soldiers' necks to traverse 'high mountains, which *cut* like the blade of a dagger and which were impassable for my chariots' (*ARI* 2.21).[3] So the young man's mention of chariots bearing down on Saul might well be accurate.

Other details raise greater suspicion. For instance, the young man's description of Saul's *leaning on his spear* (v. 6) is in tension with the statement of 1 Samuel 31:4 that Saul *took his own sword and fell on it*. To attempt to harmonize the two scenarios by assuming that Saul botched his own suicide attempt and then hoisted himself up on his sword seems a stretch and, in any case, does not take adequate account of the fact that Saul's armour-bearer took his own life only when he was convinced that Saul was dead (1 Sam. 31:5).

The supposed conversation between Saul and the young man reported in verses 7–9 is evidently a cleverly devised fabrication. It allows the young Amalekite (v. 8) to take credit for administering the *coup de grâce* to the dying king, but only at the request of Saul, who was going to die anyway: *I'm in the throes of death* (v. 9).[4] The irony of an Amalekite hoping to receive a reward from David, who has just been fighting Amalekites, is not lost on the reader, and perhaps not on David either. Still, the Amalekite (as we may now call him) plunges on, first describing how he came by Saul's crown and armlet and then presenting them to David, doubtless expecting a handsome reward.[5]

---

3. For fuller discussion of chariots in general and in Samuel, and for relevant literature, see Long (2009a: 327–328; 2009b: 414).

4. *Throes of death* renders the Hebrew *šābāṣ*, which occurs only here in the OT. The versions, ancient and modern, attempt to offer something contextually appropriate: e.g. 'terrible darkness' (LXX), 'trembling' (Targ.), 'agony' (JPS), 'convulsions' (NRSV).

5. On the kind of lightweight crown an ancient potentate might wear into battle, see Long (2009b: 414). Saul's crown is called a *nēzer*, or diadem, most likely a headband made of precious metal (cf. *HALOT* 684).

11–16. Now that David has the whole story, he responds – and in a way that may have made the Amalekite's blood run cold. Both David and all his men tear their clothes, mourn, weep and fast till evening. There is much to mourn; Israel has suffered a catastrophic defeat at the hands of its arch-enemy (1 Sam. 31:1, 7). Given that great defeat, the Amalekite may have taken the display of grief in his stride, assuming that any great national catastrophe should be mourned. And perhaps he assumed that the death of Saul would still be welcome news to David. The narrator, however, steers the reader away from such possibilities by listing Saul and Jonathan first among those whom David and his company mourned (v. 12).

In verse 13, David resumes his questioning of the Amalekite: *Where are you from?* Although the question may seem redundant, inasmuch as David already knows the man to be an Amalekite, it does have a point. The Amalekite's reply that he is a *son of a foreigner* (*ben-'îš gēr*, better rendered 'son of a resident alien') reveals to David that he has lived long enough within Israel's borders to be well familiar with its values, including the sacrosanct status of the LORD's *anointed* (v. 14). Having established the guilt of the reward-seeking Amalekite, David rewards him with his own death (v. 15), explaining that he is self-condemned (v. 16).

Meaning
Several related themes emerge in this scene recounting David's response to the news of the deaths of Saul and Jonathan. First, he has played no part in their demise. He was far from the scene of battle, engaged in a battle of his own. Second, he takes no delight in the news that Saul and Jonathan are dead, despite the fact that Saul's express wish was that David might go to an early grave, and despite the fact that these two deaths brought David closer to ascending the throne for which he had been destined ever since his anointing in 1 Samuel 16. Third, David's insistence on honouring the status of *the LORD's anointed* (lit. Yahweh's anointed) shows that David has not moved from where he was in 1 Samuel 24 and 26. After due enquiry, he visits justice upon the one who claimed to have raised a hand against Yahweh's anointed. It is possible, of course, to read David's protection of Yahweh's anointed as mere

self-protection, as he, too, is Yahweh's anointed – and now the sole surviving one. To read the text that way, however, would require a cynical reading of much of the narrative portrayal of David. David is not portrayed in Samuel as a plaster saint but as a fully human being, warts and all. But as a fully human being, David's desire to honour Yahweh's anointed grows out of his desire to honour Yahweh himself. By giving the Lord weight, allowing him to loom large in his vision, David was able to wait through years of danger and difficulty in the wilderness. He was able to wait for the Lord to open the way to the throne rather than take it by force. He was able to wait, in other words, for the Lord's timing. Such waiting is possible only for those endued with the Spirit of the Lord (cf. 1 Sam. 16:13). The time has now come, and David will soon find himself established and exalted as king over not just Judah but all Israel (5:12). But before that story continues, we hear David's lament over the fall of the mighty.

ii. David's lament over Saul and Jonathan (1:17–27)
Context
The first half of 2 Samuel 1 testifies to David's public and outward response to news of the death of Saul and Jonathan and of Israel's crushing defeat by the Philistines. He mourns the loss of life and then executes the Amalekite opportunist who claimed to have terminated the wounded Saul (vv. 1–16). In the second half of the chapter (vv. 17–27), we witness David's inner, emotional response, though there is still a public aspect. Since David's sorrow is expressed in the form of an elegy, or funerary dirge, others will have heard it and, indeed, according to David's instruction (v. 18), were to learn it. While David's skill as a stringed instrumentalist and perhaps singer has been evident from the beginning of his service in Saul's court (1 Sam. 16:18–23), this is the first evidence in Samuel of David's remarkable giftedness as a poet.

David's lament, a 'pearl of Hebrew poetry' (Fokkelman 1986: 2.649), is not to be confused in form with the 'psalms of lament'. The latter comprise various elements absent in David's lament, notably an address to God, expressions of trust in God, petitions and a vow to praise God when he has intervened. Lament psalms emerge in times of situational crisis and look forward to rescue. David's lament is more properly a funeral song, or dirge,[6] which looks back on the lives of those now departed.

A number of features tie David's lament together structurally and thematically. Most immediately evident is the refrain *How the mighty have fallen!* (vv. 19b, 25a, 27a). Further features suggest that verses 19–25 may exhibit a kind of structural integrity, with verses 26–27 adding a final, very personal expression of David's affection for Jonathan. For instance, verses 19a and 25b have the identical phrase *lies slain on your heights*; only the subjects of the respective lines are distinct. While many translations place verse 25b together with verses 26–27 (e.g. NRSV), if we keep verse 25b together with verse 25a, then the first major unit is framed fore and aft by virtually identical verses, with their lines in reverse order:

v. 19   A gazelle[7] lies slain on your heights, Israel.
          How the mighty have fallen!
. . .
v. 25   How the mighty have fallen in battle!
          Jonathan lies slain on your heights.

Immediately inside the frame of these two verses are references to *the daughters of the Philistines* (v. 20) and *Daughters of Israel* (v. 24). And inside these are lines involving flora (v. 21a) and fauna (v. 23b). At the heart of the poem (vv. 21b–23a) is a concentration of explicit references to Saul and Jonathan. If the first word of verse 19 can be understood as a veiled allusion to Jonathan (see comment below), then the names Jonathan and Saul form an alternating pattern that reverses in the middle so that the first major section begins and ends with Jonathan and places Saul in the middle: Jonathan (?), Saul, Jonathan, Saul, Saul, Jonathan, Saul, Jonathan.

---

6. Verse 17 uses Heb. *qînâ*, a term that never occurs in the Psalter.
7. Heb. has the definite article, thus 'the gazelle'. On this rendering, instead of the more common 'your glory' (so NRSV, ESV, JPS), see comment below on v. 19.

v. 19	The gazelle (=**Jonathan**?) <u>lies slain on your heights</u>, Israel.
	<u>How the mighty have fallen!</u>
v. 21b	shield of *Saul*
v. 22b	bow of **Jonathan**
	sword of *Saul*
v. 23a	*Saul* and
	Jonathan
v. 24a	weep for *Saul*
v. 25	<u>How the mighty have fallen</u> in battle!
	Jonathan <u>lies slain on your heights.</u>

The first major section complete, David turns in verse 26 to address his departed friend in the second person: *I grieve for you, Jonathan my brother.* Verse 27 concludes the entire lament with the familiar refrain.

Comment

17–18. *Lament of the bow* (v. 18) has traditionally been understood as a title by which David's lament was known, but not all are content with this explanation. Alter (1999: 198) departs from the traditional rendering and, following Fokkelman, revocalizes Hebrew *qešet* (*bow*) as *qāšôt* ('hard things'), yielding 'he said to teach hard things to the sons of Judah'.[8] As 'song of' is not present in the Hebrew text but simply assumed for the sake of sense, and as the Hebrew text would originally have lacked vowels, this reading is plausible. On the other hand, the LXX simply omits 'bow' entirely and is followed by RSV and various commentators (e.g. McCarter 1984: 67–68). NRSV wisely returns to the MT and includes 'bow'. In the end, the traditional understanding is probably best – namely, that 'bow' is a title by which David's lamentation came to be known.

Several points can be made in explanation of how this curious title came to be. First, in 2 Samuel 1:22, Jonathan's *bow* is explicitly mentioned. A bow was one of the weapons Jonathan transferred to David in 1 Samuel 18:4, and a bow was undoubtedly used in

---

8. Similarly, Firth (2009: 318): 'to be taught the harsh realities'.

Jonathan's early warning system involving shooting arrows (1 Sam. 20:18–22, 35–40). Second, biblical writers were adept in the use of metonymy, sometimes referring to prominent leaders not by their names or official titles but by some common object (often military) intended to represent them. Elijah and Elisha, for instance, are both called 'the chariots and horsemen of Israel' (2 Kgs 2:12; 13:14). The promised ruler of Zechariah 10:4 is variously described as 'the cornerstone', 'the tent peg' and 'the battle-bow'.[9] David's lamentation was, of course, for Saul as well as Jonathan, but in support of the particular prominence of Jonathan in the dirge, see the comment on verse 19 below. Third, while it may seem curious to refer to a poem simply as 'Bow', instances of texts being designated by a single word, either the first word or a particularly prominent word, are not lacking in the Hebrew tradition. The book of Genesis is sometimes designated simply as *bĕrē'šît*, 'in the beginning', the first word in the book; the book of Numbers is known as *bammidbār*, 'in the wilderness', a word occurring in the first verse of Numbers and then thirty-one more times throughout the book (far more occurrences than in any other biblical book). In Mark 12:26 (cf. Luke 20:37), Jesus refers to Exodus 3 – the account of Moses at the burning bush – simply as 'the bush' (Gordon 1986: 211). So, despite ingenious attempts to revocalize or remove 'bow' from 2 Samuel 1:18, it is probably best to regard it simply as the name by which the lament was known in *the Book of Jashar*.

The *Book of Jashar* (v. 18), mentioned elsewhere in the Old Testament only in Joshua 10:13, is no longer extant but appears to have been an anthology of early Israelite poetry. Its name may derive from Hebrew *yāšār* ('just, upright'), and its contents may have celebrated heroic exploits, individual, corporate or divine. An alternative explanation of the name relates it to the Hebrew word for 'song' or 'singing' (*ABD* 3: 646–47). Gordon (1986: 211) notes a possible link to 'Jeshurun', a name by which Israel is designated in Deuteronomy 32:15.

19. As noted earlier, verse 19a is twinned by the almost verbatim verse 25b. In the latter, it is Jonathan who *lies slain on your heights*. In

---

9. For further such examples, see Isa. 13:5; Jer. 50:23; 51:20; Hos. 1:5.

verse 19b, it is *haṣṣĕbî* that *lies slain on your heights*. Two homonymous nouns, both written *ṣĕbî*, exist in Hebrew, one meaning 'beauty, glory', or the like, and the other meaning 'gazelle'. Most English translations opt for the first meaning and assume that Saul and Jonathan are so designated, as the glory of Israel. *Gazelle* (so NIV) also works, however, as this is an apt metaphor for the adroit prowess of Jonathan and Saul (cf. the faunal imagery of v. 23: *swifter than eagles ... stronger than lions*). Perhaps we might entertain the possibility of a polyvalent usage, as both nouns would be apt in this context. Either way, it is Saul and Jonathan who are so described, or perhaps just Jonathan.[10] If the 'glory' or 'gazelle' in verse 19a is Jonathan, then the symmetry with verse 25b (*Jonathan*) is underscored, and the likelihood that the title *bow* in verse 18 refers to Jonathan is buttressed.

20. *Tell it not in Gath.* Though David spent some time among the Philistines, under the benefaction of the gullible Achish, king of Gath (1 Sam. 27), he has remained staunchly loyal to Israel. He has no desire that Israel's great loss should become the cause of rejoicing among the *daughters of the Philistines ... the uncircumcised* (on this term of opprobrium, see especially at 1 Sam. 14:6 and 31:4). *Ashkelon* was a prominent commercial seaport city in David's day,[11] and the thought of Philistines rejoicing over the spoils of war in its *streets*, or 'bazaars' (which the Hebrew *ḥûṣôt* supports), was repugnant to David. Gath and Ashkelon were two of the cities of the Philistine 'pentapolis', which included also Ashdod, Gaza and Ekron.

21. Exploiting the imagistic power of Hebrew poetry, David invokes a malediction on the very mountain where Saul and Jonathan were killed: *may you have neither dew nor rain*. Environmental devastation is to be a visible reminder of Israel's loss. Reference in verse 21b to *the shield of Saul – no longer rubbed* [lit. 'anointed', *māšîaḥ*] *with oil* makes sense from a physical standpoint, inasmuch as some shields in Saul's day were constructed of leather stretched over a wooden frame, and the leather needed to be conditioned with oil

---

10. See my brief comment on structure in the preceding 'Context' section.
11. As its name may reflect; see Walton (2009: 2.416).

(Yadin 1963: 83–84; Millard 1978: 70). But David may be lamenting more than the fact that Saul's military equipment will now fall into disuse and degrade. Saul, himself the Lord's 'anointed', is no more.

22–23a. In keeping with the tendency of elegies to involve eulogies, David turns a blind eye to the more sordid aspects of the relationship between Saul and Jonathan – the former had, after all, not only cursed his son but even tried to kill him (1 Sam. 20:30–33) – and celebrates only their virtues. In a martial culture, a *bow* and *sword* that did not *return unsatisfied* were to be celebrated. David's description of *Saul and Jonathan* as *loved and admired* falls square in the middle of his full composition and is a reflection more of David's attitude towards Saul than the reverse. And the fact that *in death they were not parted* speaks more of Jonathan's loyalty to his father than the reverse. Jonathan's loyalty to David (and to Yahweh) superseded his loyalty to his father, Saul, but insofar as Jonathan could remain a faithful son without betraying David, he did.[12]

23b–24. David's return to nature imagery (cf. v. 21a) in describing Saul and Jonathan as *swifter than eagles* and *stronger than lions* 'evokes the wide open spaces, powerful movement and formidable strength. Saul and Jonathan had been in a class apart' (Baldwin 1988: 193). His return to talk of *daughters* recalls his earlier express desire that the *daughters of the Philistines* be given no cause for rejoicing (v. 20). This time it is the *daughters of Israel*, and they are enjoined to *weep for Saul* and all the benefits that they will no longer receive from his hand (v. 24). Whether Saul did, in fact, enrich Israel with such luxuries (contrast the warnings of 1 Sam. 8) or whether David is simply continuing in the hyperbole permitted in eulogies is unclear.

25. *How the mighty have fallen* recalls the way the elegy began (v. 19b) and adds *in battle!* Most translators and commentators make a break at verse 25a and save verse 25b to begin the poem's next section. As suggested above, however (see 'Context'), structural symmetry commends our including verse 25b with the preceding main section of the elegy, so that the very first line (or opening frame) of the poem – *A gazelle lies slain on your heights, Israel* (v. 19a) – finds its

---

12. On the topic generally, see Rowe (2012).

match in the closing frame: *Jonathan lies slain on your heights* (v. 25b). And if the 'glory/gazelle' of verse 19a is meant to imply Jonathan, then both Saul and Jonathan are mentioned four times each in the elegy. The elegy now balanced and complete, David turns in a kind of postscript (v. 26) to speak very personally of (and even to) his friend Jonathan.

26–27. The shift to second-person address here is striking: *I grieve for you, Jonathan my brother.* David's sense of personal loss is great. *You were very dear to me. Your love for me was wonderful* (v. 26). In verse 23 David extols *both* Saul and Jonathan as *loved and admired*, using the same two Hebrew roots with which he here describes Jonathan. The root *'hb* underlies both *loved* in verse 23 and *your love* in the present verse, while the root *n'm* underlies *admired* in verse 23 and *very dear* in this verse. It is the last line of David's personal postscript to Jonathan that has attracted the most interest, particularly in recent decades: *more wonderful than that of women.* Alter (1999: 200) rightly describes the repeated modern attempts to 'read a homoerotic implication into these words' as 'unconvincing'. Not only could '[t]he bond between men in this warrior culture ... easily be stronger than the bond between men and women' (ibid.: 211), but it was a fact of Ancient Near Eastern culture that political loyalty was often expressed in 'love language'.[13] As an example, in the thirteenth-century BC so-called Hittite Bronze Tablet, the Hittite king Tudḫaliya IV uses love language to describe the mutual loyalty that existed between him and his cousin Kurunta, who ruled over a vassal kingdom:

> I Tudḫaliya, the Great King, before I became king,
> the god had already earlier brought me and Kurunta together in
>   friendship
> And already we were dear and beloved to each other.
> And we had an oath between us (saying): 'one shall be loyal to the other.'[14]

---

13. Cf. Moran (1963: 77–87).
14. Adapted from a longer selection in Taggar-Cohen (2005: 256); for the full text in translation, see H. A. Hoffner *COS* 2.18:100–106 (cited above is a portion of §13).

See further the discussion at 1 Samuel 18:1.

Having voiced his great sorrow over the loss of a friend and ally so loyal as Jonathan, David in verse 27 intones one last time,

> How the mighty have fallen!
> The weapons of war[15] have perished!

Meaning

Despite occasional lapses (see comment on 1 Sam. 27:1), David has generally honoured God by waiting patiently for the arrival of his promised future (1 Sam. 16). Amidst sometimes great trial and danger, David has given greater weight to God than to the press of circumstances. He has trusted the Lord to value his life and to *deliver me from all trouble* (1 Sam. 26:24). God has shown himself worthy of David's trust, and the way is now clear for David to begin moving towards the throne. Saul and Jonathan have died at the hands of the Philistines, and David has honoured them both in a moving elegy (1:17–27). That David is innocent of and, indeed, distressed by their deaths is demonstrated by the severe justice he visits upon the Amalekite who claims to have had a hand in Saul's demise (1:1–16). Waiting for God's timing, even in the midst of severe trial, is a key theme in the book of Samuel. Saul's failure to wait in 1 Samuel 13 was a failure to honour God, to give him weight. David's patience in the midst of danger and hardship while on the run from Saul, and his distress at the death of the Lord's anointed (notwithstanding Saul's murderous aggression towards him), give evidence of what, or, better, who, loomed largest in David's mind.

As is regularly pointed out, David's concern for the sacrosanct status of the Lord's anointed is not without significance for his own person, for he himself has for some time been the Lord's anointed. Piety and politics are not mutually exclusive categories in the complex person who is David.

---

15. I.e. Jonathan and Saul; see at vv. 17–18.

B. David becomes king over Judah, and the war between the houses of David and Saul continues (2:1 – 4:12)

Context

Now that the path is clear for David to begin his march to the throne, the first thing he does is pray (2:1). He learns that Hebron is to be the place where he is to begin his reign over the tribe of Judah (2:2–7). But what of the remaining tribes of Israel? Here the path is not so clear. Thanks to the actions of Saul's former general Abner, the ensuing war between the house of Saul and the house of David is destined to last *a long time* (3:1). Abner's first initiative is to set up the surviving son of Saul, Ish-Bosheth (who somehow managed to escape the catastrophic battle with the Philistines), as king in Mahanaim (2:8–9). When this proves not to be working very well, Abner seeks to form an alliance with David (3:9–21). David is receptive, and Abner's overture might have worked were it not for the treacherous intervention of Joab (3:22–39). Abner's murder is followed by the similarly treacherous murder of Ish-Bosheth by two opportunistic assassins from the tribe of Benjamin. Their hope of reward from David is disappointed, as their only reward is condemnation and execution (ch. 4).

Comment

1–4a. *In the course of time* [lit. 'after this'], *David enquired of the LORD.* David is a king who prays before acting – at least some of the time. And when he prays (cf. 1 Sam. 23:2, 4, 9–12; 30:7–8), his actions lead to success. When he doesn't, disaster sometimes follows, often for others (cf. the events of 1 Sam. 21 – 22 and 27). David's prayer here is two-fold: 'Shall I go up into any of the cities of Judah?' and 'To which . . . ?' The mode of David's enquiry is not specified, but if the Urim and Thummim were employed (see, e.g., at 1 Sam. 14:41; 28:6), then a binary question expecting a yes or no response was probably posed – something like, 'Shall I go up to Hebron . . . ?' (cf. Alter 1999: 202). Hebron was an obvious choice: a royal (Canaanite) city already in Joshua 10:3, with patriarchal associations (Gen. 13:18; 23:2, 19; 35:27), geographically favoured (high in elevation and watered by some twenty-five springs) and located on one of 'the most important crossroads in southern Judea' (Dorsey 1991: 121). To the people of Judah, David himself appears to have been an obvious choice; his anointing over the house of Judah is recorded (v. 4a) with no fanfare or further explanation, as if it were a matter of course.

On David's two wives, Ahinoam of Jezreel and Abigail, as well as his third, Michal, not mentioned here, see 1 Samuel 25:39–44.

4b–7. *When David was told* (v. 4b) is literally 'and they told David'. Who are 'they'? If the people of Judah, then we are invited to ask what lies behind the Judahites' interest in making David aware that *it was the men from Jabesh Gilead who had buried Saul*. Were they suggesting the kind of politically astute overture that David in fact makes in verses 5–7? Perhaps, but the Hebrew can also be read as simply expressing an indefinite subject, as in English expressions such as 'they say' or 'they are all doing it', where no particular people are in view (see GKC §144f.). In any case, David's overture to the citizens of Jabesh Gilead reveals both political savvy and an awareness that his kingdom is destined to extend beyond Judah. Commending the Jabesh Gileadites for their *kindness* (*ḥesed*) to Saul (v. 5), David invokes the Lord's blessing upon them and aligns himself with the Lord (v. 6): *May the LORD now show you kindness [ḥesed] and faithfulness, and I too will show you the same favour* (lit. 'do you this good'). Verses 6 and 7 both open with the formula *wĕʿattâ* (left untranslated in v. 6 and rendered *Now then* in v. 7). Amongst the various senses of this particle, it here is 'drawing [a] conclusion from [a] previous statement' (*DCH* s.v.). The *kindness* of the Jabesh Gileadites is to be rewarded by God and by David. The implication of David's message to the men of Jabesh Gilead – though he doesn't spell it out – is this: Now that Saul your master is dead and in view of the fact that the people of Judah (lit. 'house of Judah') have anointed me king over them (v. 7), the next logical step for you Jabesh Gileadites is to continue your laudable behaviour by transferring your loyalty to me.

8–11. An immediate impediment to David's design is the ambitious Abner, who has installed the rather malleable surviving son of Saul as king in Mahanaim, east of the Jordan River along the northern bank of the Jabbok River (v. 8).[16] Esh-Baal, as he is called in 1 Chronicles 8:33; 9:39, is renamed *Ish-Bosheth* ('man of shame') by the Samuel narrator(s), substituting Hebrew *bōšet* ('shame') for the element *ba'al*, which can simply mean 'lord' but was also the well-known name of the Canaanite storm and fertility god Baal. A similar substitution occurs in the name of Jonathan's son, Mephibosheth (see 2 Sam. 4:4 and comment on 1 Sam. 7:4 for further examples).[17]

The list of the territories over which Ish-Bosheth gained control (v. 9), beginning with *Gilead*, in which Mahanaim was located, and ending with *all Israel*, suggests a gradual expansion of Ish-Bosheth's effective control over time. This may explain how it is that Ish-Bosheth is credited with a mere two-year reign (v. 10) before his death: the reckoning did not begin until Ish-Bosheth was king over all Israel (v. 9). Ish-Bosheth's two years over all Israel would have come only near the end of David's seven and a half years as king in Hebron (v. 11; see 4:12 – 5:3). The northern provenance of Ish-Bosheth's rule is indicated by the list of his territories. Problematic in that list is the name *Ashuri* (v. 9), as no such people or territory are known.[18] Two options present themselves: either to follow some ancient versions in reading Geshur[19] or to read Asherites – namely, members of the tribe of Asher (cf. Judg. 1:32). The latter option seems the more likely. *Jezreel* must refer to the Jezreel Valley in the north and is not to be confused with Ahinoam's Jezreel (v. 2), a town in the south.

Though nothing is said in the text, it may be that the Philistines tolerated David's establishment of a kingdom in Hebron in the

---

16. Recent opinion is that Telul ed-Dhahab el-Garbi is the site of ancient Mahanaim (so Edelman, 'Mahanaim', *ABD* 4: 471–472).
17. On many such instances of pejorative punning in antiquity, see Rollston (2013). For a survey of opinion regarding the significance of the names Mephibosheth and Ish-Bosheth, see Avioz (2011: 11–20).
18. Assyria is called *aššûr* in the Hebrew Bible, but this yields an impossible sense in the present context.
19. So Syr., Vulg. and Targ.

hope that he would prove a thorn in the side of what remained of Saul's kingdom, whose headquarters had removed to Transjordan.

12–17. Conflict between the two kingdoms, David's and Ish-Bosheth's, comes soon enough. Generals Abner and Joab confront each other at the *pool of Gibeon*. Gibeon, a Benjaminite town identified as modern el-Jib, some 5 miles north of Jerusalem, offered a meeting place more or less midway between Mahanaim and Hebron.[20] The contest proposed by Abner, and agreed to by Joab, involves twelve young men from each side arising to *fight hand to hand in front of us* (vv. 14–15). While it has been a popular view that the young men were to engage in some kind of mock battle which then got out of hand,[21] it is more likely that they were to engage in 'representative combat' in which the fate of the few determined the fate of the many.[22] Of course, as the medieval practice of jousting suggests, the line between sport and battle can be rather thin. In the event, the contest ends in a draw – *each man grabbed his opponent by the head and thrust his dagger into his opponent's side* (v. 16). The result is that the twenty-four combatants *fell down together* at a *place in Gibeon ... called Helkath Hazzurim* (v. 16). Suggested understandings of *Helkath Hazzurim* include 'field of flint' – thus knives or daggers, which sometimes had flint blades – or 'field of hostilities' or, with a minor textual emendation, 'field of sides'.[23] As curious as the fighting posture of opponents grabbing each other by the head and thrusting a sword into the other's side sounds, it is attested in ancient iconography. A pre-ninth-century orthostat relief from Tell Halaf (an Aramean site in north-eastern Syria) shows two combatants each grabbing the

---

20. On the importance of Gibeon in the biblical period and on the possibility of identifying the pool of Gibeon with the large (12 m wide by 11 m deep) limestone carved pool or cistern discovered by Pritchard in his excavation of the site, see Long (2009b: 421–422).
21. The view finds some support in the verb used to describe their engaging in 'martial sport'. This verb (*śḥq*) is elsewhere used to describing playing, jesting, amusing, and the like.
22. Cf. the contest proposed by Goliath in 1 Sam. 17.
23. Cf. Gordon (1984: 16); McCarter (1984: 93); Youngblood (2009: 825).

other by the head and simultaneously thrusting a dagger into the other's side.[24]

As the contest produced no winner, all-out battle ensues and is *very fierce* that day (v. 17). In this full-on battle, *Abner and the Israelites were defeated by David's men* (v. 17).

18–23. In typical Hebrew narrative fashion, a brief summary statement of the outcome of the day (v. 17) is followed by a more detailed accounting (beginning in v. 18). To begin, we learn that in addition to Joab, two other sons of David's sister *Zeruiah* are present, *Abishai and Asahel*. *Abishai* we know already from 1 Samuel 26, where he is introduced as a son of Zeruiah (26:6) and the story is told of his accompanying David in the daring night-time escapade into the camp of Saul. Abishai urged David to take the opportunity to be rid of Saul once and for all, but David refused, citing Saul's status as Yahweh's anointed and contenting himself with taking Saul's spear and water jug from near the sleeping king's head. *Asahel* we meet for the first time in the present chapter. He is described as being *as fleet-footed as a wild gazelle* (v. 18). The Hebrew literally reads 'like one of the gazelles which is in field' (cf. JPS: 'like a gazelle in the open field'). The common rendering *wild gazelle* should not be taken to suggest that there were domesticated gazelles in the ancient world; animals that respond to fear by fleeing and are capable of doing so are seldom domesticated.

Asahel turns his athleticism to good advantage – or so it seemed to him – by chasing after Abner, *turning neither to the right nor to the left as he pursued him* (v. 19). Despite Abner's urging that he turn aside and *take on one of the young men and strip him of his weapons* (v. 21), Asahel is relentless. A second time Abner urges Asahel to abandon the pursuit: *Why should I strike you down?* (v. 22). Supremely confident in his ability to dispatch the less experienced Asahel if necessary, Abner is concerned with how this would complicate his relationship with Joab. As Alter (1999: 206) observes,

---

24. See photo in Yadin (1963: 362). For further discussion and bibliography, see Long (2009b: 423).

What is at stake here is not merely a question of diplomatic relations with the opposing commander but vendetta justice (Hebrew, *ge'ulat hadam*, 'redemption of the blood'): if Abner sheds the blood of Joab's brother, Joab will feel honor bound to shed the blood of the killer in return.

Abner may also have been concerned not to throw an obstacle in the path of an eventual detente with David (cf. 3:12 and context).

Despite Abner's repeated urging, *Asahel refused to give up the pursuit; so Abner thrust the butt of his spear into Asahel's stomach, and the spear came out through his back* (v. 23). Lest this seem an improbable story or lay too much stress on Abner's physical strength, it is worth noting that the butt end of a spear was typically encased with a metal fitting that was not sharp like the point of the spear but was sufficiently pointed to allow the butt end of the spear to be stuck in the ground (cf. 1 Sam. 26:7). Such casings are attested in wall paintings, and many have been uncovered by archaeologists (cf. Yadin 1963: 352).

24–28. Rather than being deterred by the death of Asahel, as some of Joab's men were (v. 23), Asahel's two surviving brothers, Joab and Abishai, are spurred on in their pursuit of Abner. *As the sun was setting, they came to the hill of Ammah, near Giah* (v. 24). Both sites are of unknown location, though Alter (1999: 206), noting that *Ammah* can mean 'conduit' and *Giah* 'gushing' (among various other meanings), offers the creative speculation that 'both may be related to an aqueduct system linked to the pool of Gibeon'. Abner and his largely Benjaminite troops take a stand *on top of a hill* (v. 25), where they see and call out to Joab. *Abner called out to Joab, 'Must the sword devour for ever?'* (v. 26). Joab will hear of the 'sword devouring' on a later occasion (11:25). On that occasion, the hypocrisy of David will be evident. On the present occasion, Abner is entirely earnest and enjoins Joab to call off his men: *How long before you order your men to stop pursuing their fellow Israelites?* (v. 26). NIV's *their fellow Israelites* renders *'ăḥêhem*, which literally means 'their brothers'. Perhaps sensing that the house of David is destined to replace the house of Saul, Abner assumes a familial tone in addressing Joab. For his part, Joab is willing to break off the pursuit, but not without first driving home the point that Abner was the first to raise the flag of truce, as it were: *if you had not spoken, the men would have continued pursuing them until morning* (v. 27). With that, *Joab blew the trumpet*, ending for the time being the pursuit of Abner and his men (v. 28). On trumpets as signalling devices for troops in the field, see at 1 Samuel 13:3.

29–32. Clearly the truce struck between Abner and Joab is a fragile one. Abner and his men beat a hasty retreat, marching *All that night ... through the Arabah*, crossing the Jordan and continuing *through the morning hours*[25] until they arrive safely at Mahanaim (v. 29). Joab abandons the pursuit of Abner, but before returning to Hebron he first assembles his army to discover casualties, which come to *nineteen of David's men* plus *Asahel* (v. 30). By contrast, *David's men had killed 360 Benjaminites* (v. 31), thus eighteen times the number lost in Joab's troops. Once *Asahel* is buried *in his father's tomb at Bethlehem*, Joab and his troops also put distance between themselves and Abner, marching all night and arriving at Hebron by daybreak (v. 32).

3:1–5. As 2 Samuel 3 opens, it is clear that the fragile truce of the preceding chapter has not held: *The war between the house of Saul and the house of David lasted a long time* (v. 1). Despite the protracted conflict, there is little doubt about which house will triumph. While *David grew stronger and stronger ... the house of Saul grew weaker and weaker* – Saul himself, of course, is dead (1 Sam. 31:4–6). The inclusion of a list of sons who *were born to David in Hebron* (vv. 2–5) serves as evidence of David's growing strength. This information is not without some foreboding elements, however.

First, the list adds to the two known wives of David – namely, *Ahinoam of Jezreel* and *Abigail the widow of Nabal of Carmel* – four more: *Maakah, Haggith, Abital* and *Eglah* (vv. 3–5). David had also been married to Saul's daughter Michal, but during David's fugitive period Saul had given her to another man (see comment at 1 Sam. 25:35–44). More wives and concubines taken by David after his assumption of power over all Israel will be mentioned in 2 Samuel 5:13–16. While it was business as usual in the Ancient Near East for

---

25. Heb. *bitrôn* may mean 'morning hours' [about half a day], or perhaps 'gorge', or it may be the name of a place near Mahanaim.

kings to acquire a harem comprising wives and concubines, the ideal Israelite king, according to Deuteronomy 17:17, 'must not take many wives' lest 'his heart ... be led astray'. Thus, David's consolidation of power in typical Ancient Near Eastern style raises concerns; the biblical narrator, as is often the case, withholds explicit comment.[26]

Second, of the four wives named here for the first time, only one is accompanied by information beyond the wife's name; *Maakah* is described as *daughter of Talmai king of Geshur* (v. 3). Biblical narratives do not generally include extraneous details, so the point of mentioning Maakah's royal lineage may be to suggest that David's marriages were motivated at least as much by politics as by affection (cf. Levenson and Halpern 1980). An alliance with the Aramean kingdom of Geshur, north of Ish-Bosheth's tenuous domain, would have been strategically useful.[27]

A third foreboding element in the list of David's sons born at Hebron is the names themselves. Three sons in particular anticipate very trying events in David's life – events in which David will not show himself to be at his best. *Amnon*, David's firstborn, will be the villain in the sordid tale of his rape of his half-sister Tamar (2 Sam. 13). As David's outrage does not lead to action, *Absalom*, Tamar's full brother, takes it upon himself to exact a vigilante justice by killing Amnon (13:28–29) and then is forced to flee to Geshur (13:37–38). Upon his return, Absalom finds little reconciliation with David (see comment at 14:33) and launches a revolt against him (2 Sam. 15). *Adonijah* will trouble the transfer of power from David to Solomon, and for his unwise actions will lose his life (1 Kgs 1 – 2).

6–11. While David is consolidating his rule in the south, someone else is seeking to strengthen his position in the north. Not Saul's son Ish-Bosheth but his cousin and former general *Abner had*

---

26. First Chronicles 3:1–9 lists nineteen sons of David 'besides his sons by his concubines'; one daughter is singled out for mention – Tamar – doubtless because of her significance in the story of David.

27. There is also an element of narrative foreshadowing, as Absalom will flee to Geshur after his murder of Amnon (2 Sam. 13:37–38).

been strengthening his own position in the house of Saul (v. 6). For the first time we learn that *Saul had had a concubine named Rizpah*[28] *daughter of Aiah.* Perhaps concerned by Abner's evident ambitions, Ish-Bosheth accuses Abner of having slept with *my father's concubine* (v. 7). Such an action would have been tantamount to 'a direct assault on the king's status and position' (cf. 16:21; 1 Kgs 2:22), as the royal harem reflected the king's prowess and prestige (cf. Long 2009b: 424). The narrator again leaves the reader in the dark with respect to the validity of Ish-Bosheth's charge; Abner's fiery response may suggest his innocence, but he may simply be enraged that Ish-Bosheth would dare to accuse him.

Am I a dog's head – on Judah's side? (v. 8). Dogs were not well regarded in the Ancient Near East, so to be a *dog's head*[29] was uncomplimentary in the extreme. Notably, Abner does not so much protest his innocence as express his anger at Ish-Bosheth's effrontery (v. 8). Whatever the truth of the matter, this altercation provides Abner with the opportunity to abandon – with an oath – all loyalty to Ish-Bosheth: *May God deal with Abner, be it ever so severely, if I do not do for David what the* LORD *promised him on oath* (v. 9). That Yahweh's promise to David[30] should only now seem to count with Abner suggests that his actions are driven more by personal aggravation than by theological conviction. Nevertheless, his intent going forward is to *transfer the kingdom from the house of Saul and establish David's throne over Israel and Judah from Dan to Beersheba* (v. 10), thus over the whole land from its far north to its far south. Faced with such a formidable personality, Ish-Bosheth does *not dare to say another word to Abner* (v. 11).

12–16. With Ish-Bosheth effectively cowed, Abner wastes no time in attempting to make good on his threat to transfer to David the former kingdom of Saul. The first recorded words of the messengers that Abner sends to David are *Whose land is it?* (v. 12). Whose

---

28. The name *rispâ* is spelled the same as a fem. noun meaning 'glowing coal'. She will figure again in 21:7–13.
29. An expression used only here in biblical and extant Ancient Near Eastern literature.
30. On which, see, e.g., 1 Sam. 13:14; 15:28; 16:13; 23:17; 24:20; 25:28; 2 Sam. 5:2.

indeed – David's by divine promise, or Abner's by dint of circumstances? The rhetorical question is sufficiently ambiguous to set up the proposition that Abner wishes to make to David: *Make an agreement* [lit. 'cut a covenant'] *with me, and I will help you* [lit. 'and look, my hand will be with you to'] *bring all Israel over to you* (v. 12). David is favourably inclined but only on the condition that his erstwhile wife *Michal daughter of Saul* be returned to him. Otherwise, Abner will not be granted even an audience with David (v. 13). David himself *sent messengers to Ish-Bosheth son of Saul*, stating his demands (v. 14).

David's desire to get Michal back seems prompted more by political ambition than by personal affection. The narrator includes two pieces of information that suggest this. First, David cites the bride-price Saul had set for Michal (v. 14, recalling 1 Sam. 18:25; David actually paid double, 1 Sam. 18:27).[31] By paying this bride-price, David secured his standing in the royal house. Re-establishing his link through Michal to the house of Saul will serve David's ambitions in the north. Ish-Bosheth, apparently powerless to resist David, orders that Michal be *taken away from her husband Paltiel son of Laish* (v. 15). The narrator's inclusion of a brief vignette of Paltiel, about whom we know nothing other than what is presented here, may offer a second hint that David's motivations are mainly political. David's personal feelings for Michal go unmentioned here (and, for that matter, anywhere in Samuel), while Paltiel's grief at losing Michal is palpable: he *went with her, weeping behind her all the way to Bahurim* (v. 16). Powerless, Paltiel has no choice but to go back home when ordered to do so by Abner.

By Ancient Near Eastern legal standards, David was within his rights to demand the return of Michal. He had not abandoned her voluntarily but had been forced to flee by Saul's aggressions. The involuntary nature of David's separation from Michal also means that the strictures of Deuteronomy 24:1–4 would not apply.[32]

---

31. On this gruesome mode of paying a bride-price, see comment at 1 Sam. 18:20–27.
32. For a short summary of Ancient Near Eastern stipulations regarding the return of wives separated by circumstances from their husbands, see Long (2009b: 425) and the bibliography cited there.

17–21. An astute power player, Abner methodically prepares to approach David personally. Having already forced compliance by Ish-Bosheth with David's one demand, namely, the return of Michal (vv. 13–16), Abner next confers *with the elders of Israel*, reminding them (or planting the idea) that they *For some time . . . have wanted to make David [their] king* (v. 17). He even cites a promise of Yahweh to David that he would be the one through whom *I [Yahweh] will rescue my people Israel from the hand of the Philistines* (v. 18). No such promise to David is explicitly recorded in Samuel, though the wording mirrors Yahweh's statement to Samuel in 1 Samuel 9:16 just before Samuel's encounter with and eventual anointing of Saul. The elders' response is not recorded, but they are apparently agreeable to the direction Abner is taking.

Abner next speaks *in person* (suggested by Heb. *gam-'abnēr*) to the Benjaminites (v. 19). Inasmuch as Saul was from the tribe of Benjamin, gaining their support for David was particularly important. Having covered all the bases, Abner *went to Hebron to tell David everything that Israel and the whole tribe of Benjamin wanted to do* (v. 19). Though David's reaction to Abner's proposal is not spelled out in the narrative, he is clearly favourable towards it, first preparing a *feast* (*mišteh*, 'banquet [with wine]') for Abner and the twenty men accompanying him (v. 20) and then sending Abner away *in peace* (*bĕšālôm*) (v. 21).

22–25. While Abner has been pursuing his diplomatic mission, Joab has been occupying himself militarily. *Just then*[33] – that is, just as Abner has departed in peace – Joab returns *from a raid* bearing *a great deal of plunder* (v. 22).[34] When Joab is informed that *Abner son of Ner had come to the king and that the king had sent him away . . . in peace* (v. 23), he is far from pleased, and he doesn't mince words! Indeed, his abrupt staccato sentences pile up rapidly. Beginning with a classic accusing question (often used by Israel's prophets in judgment speeches), *What have you done?*, Abner reproaches David:

---

33. Lit. *hinneh*, 'and behold' or 'look'!
34. The target of Joab's raid is not mentioned, but one is reminded of the raids that David himself had conducted from his base in Ziklag, back in 1 Sam. 27:8–9.

Look [hinneh], Abner came to you. Why [on earth][35] *did you let him go? Now he is gone!*[36] (v. 24). Still not done, Joab explicitly maligns Abner – *he came to deceive you* – and implicitly criticizes David for being duped (v. 25).[37] The three-fold repetition of the phrase *in peace* in verses 21, 22 and 23 emphasizes David's peaceable treatment of Abner and underscores how starkly Joab's attitude towards Abner differs.

26–27. Ever the man of action, Joab wastes no time in taking the matter of Abner into his own hands. He sends messengers who catch up with Abner at *the cistern at Sirah*, probably just a few miles north of Hebron.[38] David – as the narrator is careful to tell us – knew nothing of Joab's actions (v. 26). Joab, having just accused Abner of being a deceiver, proves himself to be a better deceiver still. Taking Abner aside *into an inner chamber* of the gate, *as if to speak with him privately*, Joab treacherously kills him by stabbing him *in the stomach* (v. 27). The combination of the verb *nkh* ('strike' or, in this context, 'stab') and *ḥōmeš* ('stomach') occurs only four times in Samuel. The first occurrence is when Abner, unable to deter Joab's relentless brother Asahel from pursuing him in battle, strikes him down with a backwards thrust of the butt end of his spear (see at 2:23). Joab's murder of Abner is ostensibly *to avenge the blood of his*

---

35. This sharpening is suggested by the Heb. syntax of appending an enclitic *zeh* to the interrogative *lāmmâ* (see R. J. Williams 2007: §118; Joüon and Muraoka 1996: §143g).
36. NIV's intitial *Now* and concluding exclamation point rightly capture the emphatic and exasperated tone of Joab's words, indicated by the Heb. use of an infinitive absolute (cf. R. J. Williams 2007: §205; Joüon and Muraoka 1996: §123 l.1).
37. Alter (1999: 213) suggests that Joab's words contain ironic echoes of Ish-Bosheth's earlier complaint against Abner – namely, that he 'slept with' (Heb. *ba' 'el*, lit. 'came to') Saul's concubine (v. 7). Abner has now come to (*ba' 'el*) David (v. 20; cf. v. 25) and 'deceive[d]' him (pi'el of *pth*-1), which can mean 'to seduce' as well as 'to persuade'.
38. While the site has not been positively identified, *'Ain 'Sārah* about a mile north of Hebron and *Ṣîret el-Bella* some 2.5 miles in the same direction have been suggested; see Driver (1960: 250); and McCarter (1984: 117), respectively.

brother Asahel (v. 27; cf. v. 30), but it is hard to suppress the suspicion that Joab's treachery is designed to do more, namely, to protect his own position in David's army from a potential rival. This suspicion is confirmed by the fourth occurrence of the combination 'strike' and 'stomach', where Joab dispatches another rival, Amasa (20:10). The third occurrence of the combination is in 4:6, where Ish-Bosheth is the hapless victim of treachery at the hands of Benjaminites Rekab and Baanah.

28–29. When David hears of Abner's murder, his first response is to declare himself innocent *for ever . . . before the* LORD *concerning the blood of Abner son of Ner* (v. 28). Failure to make it clear that he had no part in Abner's death would surely have jeopardized his hope of gaining the loyalty of Israelite tribes to the north. His second response is to pronounce a five-fold curse *on the head of Joab and on his whole family* (v. 29). The first two curses involve chronic diseases that would lead to social ostracization and would suggest to an ancient audience divine displeasure. The fourth and fifth involve violence and deprivation, respectively. The middle item is more debated. The traditional understanding is that it involves physical impairment requiring the use of a crutch. But as the Hebrew word *pelek*, here translated *crutch*, can also mean 'spindle' (cf. Prov. 31:19), some have suggested that David is invoking an effeminacy curse on Joab's house. Spinning was typically work done by women. Such effeminacy curses are attested in the Ancient Near East in respect of disloyal soldiers (see Holloway 1987: 370). The word can also mean 'work-duty' or 'tax in the form of conscripted labour', which has led to the further suggestion that the malediction is that Joab should never lack someone working on a 'chain gang' (so Holloway 1987; for fuller discussion and bibliography, see Long 2009b: 426–427).

30–39. Given David's more severe sanctions in other cases of lethal treachery (see, e.g., 4:9–11), his decision to forgo direct disciplinary action and simply utter a curse on Joab and his house raises questions. Perhaps, as the narratorial comment of verse 30 intimates, the decision reflected the fact that Abner was responsible for the death of Joab's brother Asahel. Joab may have rationalized his killing of Abner on the basis of being an 'avenger of blood' (*gōʾēl*), as described in Numbers 35:19. But the rationalization does not quite work, for the simple reason that Asahel died in the course of a battle and only after repeated warnings from Abner, even urgings, that Asahel not force his hand (see 2:18–23). David's leniency may stem in part also from the fact that Joab was his nephew and was, in some respects at least, useful to David. So a combination of factors may help to explain David's handling of Joab (for David's own view, see v. 39). Not until he is passing the sceptre to Solomon will David suggest taking a strong line with Joab (1 Kgs 2:5–6, 28–35).

That said, David does require Joab and his men to *put on sackcloth and walk in mourning in front of Abner*, while *King David*[39] *himself* walks *behind the bier* (v. 31). Moreover, though Abner was from Benjamin, David honours him with burial in Hebron, weeping aloud at his tomb (v. 32). These actions, along with the short but finely wrought elegy David delivers on the occasion (vv. 33–34), simultaneously honour Abner and humble Joab. The elegy, or *lament*, comprises four lines in an A-B-B-A pattern. The opening line asks *Should Abner have died as the lawless die? Lawless* renders the Hebrew word *nābāl*, thus recalling the churlish (and culpable) folly of Nabal in 1 Samuel 25 (cf. Rudman 2000a). Nabal died for his refusal to help David, whereas Abner was cut down by Joab while trying to help David. Thus, Joab (*and his brother Abishai*, who is also held responsible for the murder of Abner, v. 30) becomes *the wicked* in the short poem (v. 34). The two middle lines imply the deceptive treachery of Joab: Abner was not *bound* or *fettered*, but he was caught off guard by Joab's sucker punch.

David honours Abner's memory with more than words, refusing to eat anything until the sun sets and reinforcing this act of respect with an oath of self-malediction (v. 35). All David's words and actions are pleasing to *all the people* (v. 36). The reference is probably to Joab's own men, as the next verse distinguishes *all the people* from *all Israel*. In the end, everyone north and south *knew that the king had no part in the murder of Abner son of Ner* (v. 37).

---

39. As Brueggemann notes, though David is called 'king' elsewhere in Samuel, this is the first occurrence of the combination 'King David'. Brueggemann remarks: 'No one doubts David's governance in this moment of grief, honor, and rebuke' (1990: 230).

After proclaiming Abner's greatness one last time (v. 38), David remarks that *these sons of Zeruiah are too strong [qāšîm] for me* (v. 39). Hebrew *qāšeh* means to be 'hard' in the sense of being severe, stubborn, fierce, and the like. By contrast, David presents himself as *weak* (that is, tender or soft). In essence, David says that he is unable to handle these nephews and leaves the matter in Yahweh's hands: *May the LORD repay the evildoer according to his evil deeds!* (v. 39).

4:1–3. Abner is not the only named casualty of the war between the house of Saul and the house of David; Saul's surviving son Ish-Bosheth, no longer enjoying any protection from the murdered Abner, is soon to suffer the same fate. The MT of verse 1 does not actually name *Ish-Bosheth* but refers simply to the *son of Saul*. Curiously, both LXX and 4QSam[a] assume Mephibosheth to be the son in question, perhaps influenced by the mention of Mephibosheth in verse 4. But as the son of Saul in view has *leaders of raiding bands (śārê-gĕdûdîm)* in his service (v. 2), NIV is surely correct in supplying the name Ish-Bosheth in verse 1 (the first mention of Ish-Bosheth is in 2:8). The two leaders, named *Baanah* and *Rekab*, are described as *sons of Rimmon the Beerothite from the tribe of Benjamin* (v. 2). Beeroth was one of the four major cities in the Gibeonite enclave mentioned in Joshua 9:17 and has been tentatively identified with el-Burj, some 2 miles south of Gibeon. While the town of Beeroth would have been included in the Israelite treaty with the Gibeonites in Joshua 9, the town was also allocated to the tribe of Benjamin in Joshua 18:25. It is unclear, therefore, whether Baanah and Rekab were in fact Benjaminites occupying Beeroth, after *the people of Beeroth fled to Gittaim* (v. 3),[40] or whether they were themselves of Beerothite ancestry. In either case, the effect of their Benjaminite association – given that they will be responsible for the death of Saul's surviving son Ish-Bosheth – is to confirm that the house of Saul is indeed growing weaker and weaker even in Saul's own tribal territory (cf. 3:1). *Gittaim* ('Twin-Winepress'?) has been tentatively identified with Rall Ras Abu-Hamid, a site some 18 miles west of Beeroth (Negev and Gibson 2003: 204).

---

40. The flight of the original Beerothites may have been in response to Saul's aggression towards the Gibeonites, mentioned in 2 Sam. 21:1–2.

4. *(Jonathan son of Saul had a son who was lame in both feet . . . His name was Mephibosheth.)* NIV places this paragraph in parentheses to indicate that it is a narratorial aside (so also JPS, NLT). Mephibosheth will not figure prominently until 2 Samuel 9, but his introduction here is typical of Hebrew narrative style, whereby the reader receives an early alert to something or someone who will become significant as the narrative progresses. Coming as it does in an account of Ish-Bosheth's murder, the mention of a crippled descendant of Saul – and thus one deemed, by Ancient Near Eastern standards, as unlikely to rule – may further underscore the waning prospects of the house of Saul. *Mephibosheth* is called Merib-Baal in 1 Chronicles 8:34; 9:40. Chronicles attests two spellings of the name, Meri-Baal and Merib-Baal. The former sounds like 'hero of Baal', while the latter sounds like 'Baal contends' or 'contender with Baal'. Mephibosheth sounds like 'from the mouth of shame'; the situation is probably more complex than these simple observations suggest. On the substitution of 'shame' for 'Baal', see at 2:8.

5–8. After the brief aside to mention Mephibosheth, the narrative returns to *Rekab and Baanah, the sons of Rimmon the Beerothite* (v. 5). We already know from verse 2 that these two *were leaders of raiding bands* in Ish-Bosheth's retinue. Setting out for *the house of Ish-Bosheth*, they arrive *in the heat of the day while he was taking his noonday rest* (v. 5). What happens next is debated, as the Hebrew of verses 6 and 7 in MT seems difficult, and LXX offers an alternative account which is favoured by many commentators. According to LXX, verse 6 describes how a doorkeeper, who was engaged in cleaning wheat, became drowsy and fell asleep, allowing Rekab and Baanah to slip into the house unnoticed (cf. RSV, NLT).

Most English translations, however, attempt to make sense of MT. NIV's rendering of verses 6–7 is representative of others such as ESV, JPS, NASB and NRSV. One point at issue is the fact that MT seems to have the miscreants enter the house, stab Ish-Bosheth in the stomach and then slip away, all in verse 6, only to have them enter the house again in verse 7 to stab, kill and decapitate their victim. The suggestion that the two verses represent a compilation of distinct sources is unconvincing and, in view of Hebrew narrative style, unnecessary. A brief summary of an event is often followed by a more detailed accounting. That being the case, it is unnecessary to assume that the brothers entered the house twice; rather, their entry of the house (as well as their departure) is described twice (in vv. 6 and 7).[41]

Whatever the precise details of the murder, the account recalls aspects of earlier acts of treachery and/or opportunism involved in deaths within the house of Saul: opportunism in the Amalekite's attempt to gain a reward from the death of Saul (1:1–16) and treachery in Joab's murder of Abner (3:26–30).

9–12. If Rekab and Baanah hoped that their neatly (if hypocritically) theologized announcement of the death of Saul's son – supported by the material evidence of his severed head (v. 8) – would gain David's approval and earn some reward or advancement, they quickly learn otherwise. David's immediate answer to their report is that it is *the LORD*, not assassins, *who has delivered me out of every trouble* (v. 9). Referencing the very similar instance of the Amalekite in 2 Samuel 1 who thought to gain a reward by claiming some credit for the death of Saul, David states that the Amalekite's only reward was death by execution (v. 10). *How much more – when wicked men have killed an innocent man in his own house and on his own bed – should I not now demand his blood from your hand and rid the earth of you!* (v. 11).[42]

---

41. Some small difficulties remain in MT, however, which has prompted Mastéy (2011) to proffer an alternative reading that not only resolves the difficulties but also makes sense of the verbal sequences from a discourse perspective. Mastéy's reading involves a third party, namely, 'grain robbers' (Mastéy's understanding of the difficult *lōqĕḥê ḥiṭṭîm*, lit. 'takers of grain') in v. 6. On Mastéy's reading, Rekab and Baanah first go to Ish-Bosheth with the intent of taking advantage of the power vacuum brought about by Abner's demise, perhaps hoping for promotion by Ish-Bosheth. Upon their arrival, however, they discover a violent robbery in progress and flee (v. 6). Later, they return to find Ish-Bosheth either dead or mortally wounded and thus change their plan. Removing Ish-Bosheth's head, they take it to David (v. 7), hoping to curry favour with him (v. 8). For more detailed discussion of Mastéy's view and of the majority view, see Newkirk (2015: 102–103).

42. Though spelled slightly differently, the Hebrew verb *b'r* used in the phrase *rid the earth* contains a faint echo of the frequent description

How David knew the specific circumstances of Ish-Bosheth's demise is not disclosed. In view of the fact that Rekab and Baanah *travelled all night* to bring Ish-Bosheth's head to David at Hebron (vv. 7–8), it seems unlikely that the news could have reached David by a speedier messenger. More likely, the brothers must have given David a more detailed report than is recounted in the narrative. If we assume the standard reading of verses 6–7, the brothers were solely responsible. If Mastéy's suggested reading should be correct, then their claim would be much like that of the Amalekite in 2 Samuel 1, namely, that they found Ish-Bosheth already wounded and delivered the *coup de grâce*.[43] Either way, David has no time for such treachery and orders that the two be executed, after which his men *cut off their hands and feet* and hang *the bodies by the pool in Hebron* (v. 12). Such display, common enough in the Ancient Near East, is particularly appropriate in the present instance, as it removes the offending hands that wielded the weapon and the feet that travelled through the night to bring the head.

The chapter ends with the burial of Ish-Bosheth's head in the tomb of Abner in Hebron. Thus, the governing 'heads' in the north are now buried in the south, and the path is clear for a rapprochement between David and the tribes to the north. The civil war that began at the pool of Gibeon now ends at the pool of Hebron (cf. Bodner 2004: 49).

Meaning

As the saying goes, 'good things come to those who wait'. But, of course, this depends on for whom or for what one is waiting. David has known for years that he is destined to be king in Israel, but he repeatedly refuses to clear the path by taking the lives of those who

---

of the two assassins as from *be'erōt* (4:2, 3, 5, 9), particularly in its conjugated form here, *bi'artî*. Is there a hint of the two assassins getting their just deserts? Cf. Matzal 2012. The phrase 'rid the earth' is used elsewhere in the Old Testament for the removal of 'male-shrine prostitutes' (1 Kgs 22:46) and of 'Asherah poles' associated with false worship (2 Chr. 19:3).

43. Both scenarios are discussed above at vv. 6–7.

stand in his way. Nor is David pleased when others think they can ingratiate themselves with him by clearing the path for him. David did not look for the opportune moment to take matters into his own hands. He waited, rather, for the Lord. Psalm 27, a psalm ascribed to David, begins with the confident declaration 'The LORD is my light and my salvation' and concludes with the exhortation

> Wait for the LORD;
> > be strong and take heart
> > and wait for the LORD.

The theme of waiting for the Lord is pervasive in Scripture (cf. Pss 37:9; 130:5). It is the antidote to the desire for personal vengeance:

> Do not say, 'I'll pay you back for this wrong!'
> > Wait for the LORD, and he will avenge you.
> (Prov. 20:22)

Such confident waiting is possible only for those who, like David (1 Sam. 16:13), are endued with and empowered by the Spirit of God. The New Testament speaks of such patience as a mark of the fruit of the Spirit (Gal. 5:22). As would become true in a far grander sense in the life of the messianic Son of David to come, David's suffering ended in exaltation. The confidence of the believer is that there is hope on the far side of suffering:

> And the God of all grace, who called you to his eternal glory in Christ, after you have suffered a little while, will himself restore you and make you strong, firm and steadfast. To him be the power for ever and ever. Amen.
> (1 Pet. 5:10–11)

C. David becomes king over all Israel (5:1–5)

Context
Just as 2 Samuel 3 and 4 described how *the house of Saul grew weaker and weaker* (3:1), 2 Samuel 5 shows the house of David growing

stronger and stronger (3:1). David has been patient during the years of hardship since it first became clear that he was to succeed Saul. The first two stages in the three-stage accession process were fulfilled while David was still a young man: first, David's *designation* by Yahweh as *nāgîd*, 'king-designate' (cf. 1 Sam. 13:14; 16:1–13); and second, the *demonstration* of David's divine empowerment (1 Sam. 17:1 – 18:7). The third stage, David's *confirmation* by all the people, has been delayed, however, first by Saul's refusal to relinquish a throne no longer rightfully his, and then by Abner's initial attempt to set up Saul's surviving son, Ish-Bosheth, as king in Mahanaim. David has not been averse to diplomatic overtures (see at 2:4b–7), but even now when impediments to his rise are removed, he does not make the first move in approaching the northern tribes. The Israelite elders come to him at Hebron in the hope that he will become their shepherd and ruler.

Comment

1–2. *All the tribes of Israel came to David at Hebron* (v. 1) and present three reasons why he should become their ruler: first, they are blood related (*We are your own flesh and blood*); second, David has already proven his ability to lead, especially militarily (even *while Saul was king over us, you were the one who led Israel on their military campaigns*); and third, and most significantly, Yahweh himself has declared that David should *shepherd* Israel and become their *ruler* (*nāgîd*; vv. 1–2).

While David's early years involved actual shepherding of sheep, the term is here used metaphorically. Ancient Near Eastern rulers regularly assumed the title of shepherd of their subjects. In the Old Testament, it is pre-eminently God who is the shepherd of his people (e.g. Gen. 48:15; 49:24; Pss 23:1; 80:1; 95:7). But human leaders could also be thought of as shepherds of the people. On the plains of Moab, prior to Israel's entry into the land of promise, Moses implored Yahweh to 'appoint someone over this community . . . so that the LORD's people will not be like sheep without a shepherd' (Num. 27:15–17). In response, Yahweh designated 'Joshua son of Nun, a man in whom is the spirit of leadership' (Num. 27:18). Joshua was the answer to Moses' desire for a shepherd to lead the people, but David is the first of Israel's leaders explicitly to be called a 'shepherd'. In the biblical context, the title is enriched both by the image of a human shepherd as one who cares for, provides for and protects his sheep and by the fact that Yahweh himself sets the standard of what a good shepherd should be. Such expectations are met only partially in David but fully in David's greater son, Jesus, the 'good shepherd' (John 10:11, 14), the 'great Shepherd' (Heb. 13:20), the 'Chief Shepherd' (1 Pet. 5:4) and the shepherd who is also the lamb of God who was slain (Rev. 5:12; 7:17).

3. While verse 1 spoke of all the *tribes of Israel* coming to *David*, here it is *all the elders of Israel* who come to *the king*. Ancient Israel was a patriarchal, tribal society whose leadership was drawn from 'the fathers of the basic family units', namely, the fathers' houses (see Reviv 1989: 187; cf. King and Stager 2001: 36–39). The terminological shifts in verses 1–2 from *tribes* to *elders* and from *David* to *the king* are noteworthy, as these changes suggest the legal, constitutional nature of what transpires in the covenant-making of verse 3. The terms of the covenant are not given in the narrative, but doubtless they involved binding obligations on both sides meant to establish a rule that was 'conditional, limited, and negotiated' (Brueggemann 1990: 239).[44]

4–5. *Thirty years old* refers to David's age when he became king over Judah in Hebron. His *forty*-year reign is the sum of his *seven years and six months* in Hebron and his *thirty-three years* over *all Israel and Judah*. Regnal formulae are common in the Old Testament, signalling a king's age at accession and the length of his reign (e.g. 1 Sam. 13:1 for Saul; 2 Sam. 2:10 for Ish-Bosheth; 1 Kgs 14:21 for Rehoboam; 22:42 for Jehoshaphat; and so forth). Though David has already been ruling in Hebron, his regnal formula is appropriately placed here at the start of his rule over *all Israel*.

Meaning
After years of hardship, danger and patient waiting on Yahweh, David has finally become shepherd and ruler over all Israel, north

---

[44]. See comment at 1 Sam. 10:25 on the written document deposited by Samuel *before the* LORD, which described *the rights and duties of kingship* (the *mišpaṭ hammĕlûkâ*).

and south. He has arrived. The challenges will now become different from those when he was in the desert and on the run. How David responds to these challenges will be told in the story as it continues.

6. DAVID'S REIGN BLESSED BY GOD (2 SAMUEL 5:6 – 10:19)

In the course of the events described in 2 Samuel 5:6 to the end of chapter 10, David goes from strength to strength. The fundamental reason for David's successes is offered in 5:10: *he became more and more powerful, because the LORD God Almighty was with him* (cf. 1 Sam. 16:18; 17:37; 18:12, 14, 28; 20:13; 2 Sam. 7:3). Elsewhere in Samuel, such a statement of divine accompaniment is made only of the young Samuel (1 Sam. 3:19).[1]

David's successes are many: he establishes Jerusalem as his capital city (5:6–9), he defeats the ever-troublesome Philistines (5:17–25) and he eventually manages to bring the ark of God safely into Jerusalem (6:1–19). He is militarily successful (8:1–14) and able to begin building an administrative system designed to do what is *just and right for all his people* (8:15–18). He is magnanimous to Jonathan's son Mephibosheth (ch. 9). And his attempt to show kindness to Hanun, king of the Ammonites, when rebuffed, leads

---

1. On Saul, see commentary at 1 Sam. 20:13.

to further military victories over not just the Ammonites but also their erstwhile allies, the Arameans (ch. 10).

David proves to be a good leader, but hardly a perfect one, as we see, for instance, in his initial mishandling of the ark (6:6–8) and perhaps also in his animosity towards the Jebusite *blind and lame* (5:8), in his multiplication of wives and concubines (5:13) and in his altercation with Michal, daughter of Saul (6:20–23). Even David's desire to build a *house* for the Lord proves in the end to be misguided (ch. 7). It is the Lord, rather, who promises to build a *house* for David (7:11b–16). It is this divine promise that forms the bedrock assurance of David's place in the plan of God. This plan finds its climax in a future descendant of David. This future son of David shares none of David's weaknesses but, rather, establishes at great personal cost the everlasting kingdom that David was promised.

A. David secures his rule (5:6–25)

Context

This section describes two accomplishments that secure David's rule: the capture of Jerusalem as his capital city (5:6–16) and the resounding defeat of Israel's arch-enemies, the Philistines (5:17–25).

Comment
i. David conquers Jerusalem and makes it his capital (5:6–16)

6–8. *The king and his men marched to Jerusalem to attack the Jebusites, who lived there* (v. 6). The Jebusites (first mentioned in Gen. 10:16) seem to have been of non-Semitic origin, perhaps to be associated with Hurrians or Hittites.[2] Despite some brief reversals during the settlement period (Judg. 1:8, 21; cf. Josh. 15:63), the Jebusites occupied and controlled Jerusalem (called 'Jebusite city' in Josh. 15:8; cf. 1 Chr. 11:4) until the time of David. The motivations for and timing of David's attack on the Jebusites in Jerusalem are not explicitly stated. But the city's strategic location within the small tribal allotment of Benjamin near the northern border of Judah

---

2. Mazar (1993: 699). For other suggestions, see Reed (1992: 652–653).

doubtless made it attractive as a potential capital city, as it would not arouse intertribal jealousies (see comment at 1 Sam. 17:54).

For their part, the Jebusites are confident in the impregnability of their city: *You will not get in here; even the blind and the lame can ward you off* (v. 6). The Jebusites' taunting reference to the blind and lame has elicited various interpretations. Does it reflect supreme confidence (even the blind and lame can keep you out) or determination to fight to the last man (even to the physically impaired) or something more obscure, such as a hex or an otherwise unmentioned treaty existing between David and the Jebusites?[3] The first option seems the more likely. But whatever the precise meaning of the taunt, the Jebusites are quite mistaken in their assertion that *David cannot get in here*.

David captured the fortress of Zion – which is the City of David (v. 7). In typical Hebrew narrative style, a brief statement of the outcome of the confrontation is given, only to be followed by a spelling out of a few more details (see vv. 8–10). Both *Zion* and *City of David* occur here for the first time in the Old Testament. Jerusalem's designation as 'the City of David' will be repeated many times throughout Samuel, Kings and Chronicles, and in Nehemiah 3:15; 12:37; and Isaiah 22:9. The *fortress of Zion* probably refers to a stronghold atop the stepped-stone structure that has been excavated on the south-eastern hill of Jerusalem. The etymology of Zion (*ṣiyyôn*) is uncertain (see *HALOT* s.v.). Mare (1992: 1096) canvasses multiple possibilities before concluding that the 'Arabic etyma would suggest that Zion was a fortress located on a ridge.' Over time the designation 'Zion' was extended to stand in parallel to Jerusalem (e.g. 2 Kgs 19:21; Isa. 2:3) or even to the nation of Israel as such (e.g. Ps. 149:2; Isa. 46:13; Zeph. 3:14).

How David captured the fortress of Zion is intimated in verse 8, with David's statement that *Anyone who conquers* ['strikes'] *the Jebusites will have to use the water shaft*. We learn from 1 Chronicles 11:6 that Joab was the one who led the charge and by his success gained the command of David's troops. Just how he breached the Jebusite defences is not entirely clear. The traditional understanding that

---

3. Cf. Gordon (1986: 226); Cahill (2004: 26).

Joab entered via Warren's shaft (an approximately 50-ft vertical shaft discovered by Charles Warren in 1867 in the vicinity of the Gihon Spring) has been questioned in recent years, for two reasons. The first involves questions regarding the meaning of the word *ṣinnôr*, traditionally rendered *water shaft* but possibly meaning something like 'grappling hook' or 'throat' (Kleven 1994). The second has to do with archaeological explorations of Jerusalem's water systems, which call into question whether the entry to Warren's shaft could have been visible to locals much before the eighth century BC (Reich and Shukron 2004: 216). These uncertainties notwithstanding, on present evidence it seems likely that Joab 'entered through some kind of water shaft or water tunnel system … especially given the new support for the traditional reading of *ṣinnôr*' (see Long 2009b: 434–435 for more detailed discussion).

The exclusion of *those 'lame and blind' who are David's enemies* from *the palace* (lit. 'the house') may not betray a prejudice against physically impaired individuals (v. 8). Though one can only speculate, David may be turning back on the Jebusites their own words (cf. v. 6), calling them all the 'blind and lame' and barring them, the Jebusites, from entering the royal house.

9–12. David has finally arrived. He takes up *residence in the fortress* and calls it *the City of David*. He builds up *the area around it, from the terraces* [the Millo] *inwards* (v. 9).[4] David is becoming increasingly powerful (v. 10), and his neighbours take note. *Hiram king of Tyre* sends materials and skilled craftsmen to David, *and they built a palace* [lit. 'a house'] *for David* (v. 11).[5]

In the midst of these summary verses, two fundamentally important statements are made, one expressing the narrator's conviction regarding David's success – *because the* LORD *God Almighty was with him* (v. 10) – and the second revealing David's own perspective – *David knew that the* LORD *had established him as king over Israel and had exalted his kingdom for the sake of his people Israel* (v. 12). The final

---

4. For a convenient summary of the architecture and archaeology of Jerusalem in this period, see Long (2009b: 433).

5. On the difference between literary and chronological sequencing of events, especially in relation to Hiram, see Klement (2000a).

phrase is significant; David grasps that his success is not for the sake of his own gain but for the sake of God's people (see Frisch 2004).

13–16. *David took more concubines and wives in Jerusalem.* After the high points of the preceding verses, in which Yahweh is credited with David's success and David is described as understanding the *raison d'être* of his kingship, this familial notice is disconcerting. Mention of *concubines* and the acquisition of a harem calls to mind the royal politics of the Ancient Near East (see at 15:16) and flies in the face of the explicit statement in Deuteronomy that an Israelite king 'must not take many wives, or his heart will be led astray' (Deut. 17:17). With typical reticence, the narrator does not make the point explicitly, but the notice of David's growing harem gives the attentive reader pause. David's concubines will figure tragically in Absalom's revolt, one of the greatest familial and political crises of David's reign (see esp. 16:21–22). Many of the children listed in the present passage – Solomon, for instance – will be born sometime later. But as Brueggemann (1990: 246–247) remarks, 'The cast of characters for the upcoming royal story begins to develop: first Hiram, then Solomon.'

ii. David conquers Israel's arch-enemy, the Philistines (5:17–25)

17–21. News that *David had been anointed king over Israel* does not please the Philistines. They had tolerated his rule over Judah from Hebron, but this further strengthening of David's position required a response, so they *went up in full force* [lit. 'all the Philistines went up'] *to search for him.* When news of the Philistine advance reached David, he *went down to the stronghold* (*měṣûdâ* II; v. 17). In the present context, the apparent *stronghold* in question would be the *fortress* [same word, *měṣûdâ*] *of Zion,* which David had captured (v. 7) and occupied (v. 9).[6] Of note from an archaeological perspective is Eilat Mazar's excavation of a 'large-stone structure' on the narrow ridge rising northwards from the 'stepped-stone structure' atop which

---

6. For discussion of evidence supporting this identification, over against the view that the stronghold of Adullam is in view, see Long (2009b: 436–437).

the fortress of Zion probably stood (Mazar 2006; 2009; cf. also Provan, Long and Longman 2015: 303). Certainty of identification is elusive at this stage, but the 'large-stone structure' may represent David's palace (cf. at v. 11). If so, the statement that David went down (from the palace) to the stronghold makes good topographical sense.

The Philistines . . . spread out in the Valley of Rephaim (v. 18). This valley (often identified with the Wadi-el-Ward) begins a mile or so south of Jerusalem and descends in a westwards direction towards Philistine territory. Philistine troops deployed in this valley would have hindered Judahite reinforcements from reaching David. *So David enquired of the* LORD (v. 19), as he had often, though not always, done before (see comments at 1 Sam. 23:1–5; 30:7–8; 2 Sam. 2:1–4). Having received an affirmative answer from Yahweh, *David went to Baal Perazim* (site uncertain, but see Garsiel 2000: 159–160). Whether David gave the place the name Baal Perazim or, as seems more likely in this instance, simply found the pre-existing name to be fitting (cf. Garsiel 1991: 15), he exclaims, *As waters break out, the* LORD *has broken out against my enemies before me* (v. 20). *Break out* and *broken out* render the root *prṣ*, which is found also in the name Baal Perazim (*baʿal-pĕrāṣîm*). Alter (1999: 224) suggests that the image of breaking through may imply 'that David's forces succeeded in punching a hole in the Philistine lines rather than in producing a general rout'. Verse 22 will again find the Philistines arrayed against David.

The Philistines abandoned their idols there, and David and his men carried them off (v. 21). David thus inflicts on the Philistines the same indignity they had earlier inflicted on Israel by the capture of the ark of God (1 Sam. 4:11). On the treatment of defeated 'gods' (here *idols*), see at 1 Samuel 5:2. While polytheistic peoples sometimes placed captured 'gods' in the presence of their own chief god or gods, David would have been extremely unlikely to do this. The parallel passage in 1 Chronicles 14:12 states explicitly that 'David gave orders to burn them [i.e. the Philistine idols] in the fire', which is in keeping with the instructions of Deuteronomy 7:5, 25. Ancient Near Eastern victors also sometimes destroyed captured gods. For instance, the seventh-century BC Neo-Assyrian king Assurbanipal in one place boasts, 'I smashed their gods and thereby soothed the heart of the lord of lords' (quoted in Miller and Roberts 1977: 93).

22–25. Whether relentlessly persistent or unable to learn from earlier mistakes, *Once more the Philistines came up and spread out in the Valley of Rephaim* (v. 22). David responds as before by enquiring of Yahweh, and again an affirmative answer is received. But this time special instructions are given. David is to circle around behind the Philistines and listen for *the sound of marching in the tops of the poplar trees* (vv. 23–24). Whether the sound was meant to provide cover for the movements of David's own troops or to strike terror in the hearts of the Philistines,[7] or both, the key point that David is to grasp is that *the LORD has gone out in front of you to strike the Philistine army* (v. 24).[8] The notion that God or the gods would go before the troops to demoralize, confuse, trick or terrify the enemy was not unique to Israel; it was the God Israel worshipped who was regarded as unique. David's 'song of praise' in 2 Samuel 22:8–16 is replete with images of Yahweh as warrior and rescuer. The present passage combines two typical features of Israelite warfare: deceptive strategies capitalizing on the element of surprise (cf. Malamat 1982: 24–35) and Yahweh's marshalling of the natural (or supernatural) world to defeat the enemy.[9] *David did as the LORD commanded him*, and the victory extended *from Gibeon to Gezer* (v. 25). This rout of the Philistines was more extensive and decisive than the earlier victory initiated by Jonathan but vitiated by Saul in 1 Samuel 14 (on the extent of that earlier victory, see 14:31). Both Saul and David were commissioned to deliver the people *from the hand of the Philistines* (1 Sam. 9:16; 2 Sam. 3:18, respectively). Saul failed, but David succeeded (see further at 8:1), and his 'fame spread throughout every land, and the LORD made all the nations fear him' (1 Chr. 14:17).

---

7. Cf. 2 Kgs 7:5–7, where Yahweh causes the Arameans to hear 'the sound of chariots and horses and a great army' and to panic and flee.
8. On Yahweh as the divine warrior who goes before his people, see Exod. 15:3 and Exod. 14:14 respectively (and cf. Deut. 1:30).
9. The natural/supernatural distinction would have made little sense in OT times.

Meaning

In 2 Samuel 5, David defeats the Jebusites and takes Jerusalem to be his capital city (5:6–9). He deals a decisive blow to Israel's archenemies, the Philistines (5:17–25). David understands that Yahweh's abiding presence is the key to his successes (v. 10), and he also understands that his elevation to kingship is not for his own sake but *for the sake of his people Israel* (v. 12). With so much accomplished, the time seems right for David to bring the symbol of God's presence, the ark of God, to take its place in his capital city, Jerusalem. As correct as this notion seems, the transport of the ark to Jerusalem is not accomplished without mishap, as the next chapter makes clear.

B. David brings the ark to Jerusalem (6:1–23)

Context

That Yahweh was with David is stated not just in the preceding chapter but frequently in the book of Samuel (see at 1 Sam. 3:19). David was indeed *a man after his [the LORD's] own heart*, that is, 'a man of God's own choosing' (1 Sam. 13:14).[10] Another way to express God's abiding presence with David is to say that he was endued with the Spirit of the Lord on a continuing basis (see at 1 Sam. 16:13). Yahweh has been with David through all his trials and dangers. And now that David is established, it seems appropriate that God symbolically take up residence at the heart of David's kingdom in the midst of his newly acquired capital city. The last time the ark of God was mentioned, it was residing in Kiriath Jearim (1 Sam. 7:2).[11] In the present chapter, David undertakes to bring the ark to Jerusalem. The attentive reader will have become accustomed to noticing when David's actions are preceded by divine enquiry and when they are not. In the present instance, no mention is made of David's praying about how or whether to fetch the ark from Kiriath Jearim (here called Baalah in Judah). And

---

10. On this phrase, see the discussion at 1 Sam. 13:14.
11. In 1 Sam. 14:18, we should read 'ephod' instead of 'ark' (see comment there).

costly mistakes are made. As Alter (1999: 224) succinctly remarks: 'David has now completed the consolidation of his rule over all the land, and his real troubles are about to begin.'

Comment

1–5. Given the importance of what David intends to do in bringing to his new capital *the ark of God, which is called by the Name, the name of the LORD Almighty* (v. 2),[12] he gathers *all the able young men of Israel* (v. 1) before proceeding to *Baalah in Judah* to retrieve the ark. *Able young men* renders Hebrew *bāḥûr*, which describes a man who is chosen, or picked. The reference, then, is not literally to all the young men of Israel but to David's 'elite troops' (NLT), or 'chosen men' (NRSV, ESV, NASB) or 'picked men' (JPS). The same phrase is used in 1 Samuel 24:2 of Saul's three thousand elite troops, one-tenth the size of David's *thirty thousand* (v. 1). Thirty thousand is a large but not impossible number in the present context; but since *'elep* can sometimes refer to a 'unit', a smaller escort than thirty thousand might be in view.[13] Whatever the case, the notion of a 'large military escort for returning the ark is no more than we should expect, given its cultic importance and previous role in Israel's military history' (Gordon 1986: 231). Earlier in Samuel, Israel lost *thirty thousand foot soldiers* (or thirty units) when the Philistines captured the ark (1 Sam. 4:10). There is thus a certain symmetry in *thirty thousand* accompanying the ark in its journey to Jerusalem. The cultic significance of bringing the ark to Jerusalem is underscored in the parallel account in 1 Chronicles 13, where David gathers not just military personnel for the procession but priests and Levites as well (1 Chr. 13:1–4).

Baalah in Judah (v. 2) is an alternative name for Kiriath Jearim (see at 1 Sam. 6:21), where the ark rested for several decades, neglected in the days of Saul (1 Chr. 13:3). Baalah lies some 7 miles west of Jerusalem.

---

12. On the physical character of the ark and its religious significance, see at 1 Sam. 3:3.

13. Cf. Josh. 8:3, where Joshua sends 'thirty thousand' (thirty units?) to set an ambush.

The plot thickens in verse 3 with the notice that *They set the ark of God on a new cart and brought it from the house of Abinadab* (on Abinadab, see at 1 Sam. 7:1). It is perhaps excusable that the Philistines, back in 1 Samuel 6:7, returned the ark to Israel on a new cart; they will have known no better. But the proper way to transport the ark, according to Exodus 25:12–14 (cf. 37:5), was for priests to carry it with poles inserted through rings attached to its sides. The texts are replete with instances of this being done (e.g. Num. 7:9; Deut. 10:8; Josh. 3:8). The stated reason for this mode of transport was to ensure that no-one touched the holy things and died (Num. 4:15). Moreover, while a single cart could topple, multiple porters were unlikely to lose their footing all at the same time. As noted above, the lack of any reference to David praying before undertaking the transport of the ark is unsettling.

In the event, *Uzzah and Ahio, sons of Abinadab, were guiding the new cart*, Ahio in front and Uzzah walking beside or behind it (vv. 4–5). While attempts have been made to link one or the other of these sons with the Eleazar of 1 Samuel 7:1, it seems more likely that these two were brothers of Eleazar or perhaps grandsons of Abinadab (Heb. 'son' can also mean 'grandson' or simply 'descendant').

As the cart moves along, *David and all Israel were celebrating* [*mĕśaḥăqîm*][14] *with all their might before the* LORD. The general sense of verse 5 is evident, but there are questions in matters of detail. MT reads *bĕkōl ʿaṣê bĕrôšîm* ('with all kinds of juniper wood'). Some translations (e.g. JPS) take this to be a reference to wooden instruments of various kinds, which the text then lists. 4QSam^a, though fragmentary, attests *ʿz* ('might') in place of *ʿṣ* ('wood') and *bšyrym* ('with songs') in place of *brwšym* ('juniper'), yielding 'with all [their] might, with songs'. This same wording is found in the parallel verse in 1 Chronicles 13:8. LXX of the present verse seems to reflect both phrases: 'with tuned instruments, with strength and with songs' (NETS). NIV takes a middle ground, replacing 'wood' with *might*, but retaining 'juniper' as *castanets*, and making no

---

14. See note at v. 12 below.

mention of songs. Whatever uncertainties remain, the picture is of a vigorous celebration.[15]

6–8. In due course the procession reaches *the threshing-floor of Nakon* (v. 6), where the oxen stumble. Uzzah reaches out and takes hold of the ark and is struck down *because of his irreverent act* (v. 7). Before we consider the fundamental issue of Yahweh's severe justice, a comment on the name *Nakon* is merited. The parallel verse in 1 Chronicles 13:9 has 'Kidon', but neither Nakon nor Kidon is otherwise attested in the Old Testament. In form, Nakon is identical with a verbal adjective *nākôn* (nipʻal ptc. of *kûn*), which describes something that is firm, established, secure or – we might say – stable.[16] Hebrew ears may well have detected a fine irony in the oxen's stumbling just at the place of assumed 'stability'. *Nākôn* might also be related to the verb *nākâ*, 'to smite', leading Baldwin (1988: 222) to speculate that 'the name may have been coined to encapsulate memories of the disaster, witnessed by the great company of worshippers'.

The disaster in view is, of course, the death of Uzzah, brought about by *his irreverent act* (v. 7). Though there are some textual uncertainties regarding the precise reading,[17] the general sense is clear. Uzzah acts improperly in respect of the ark, Yahweh becomes angry and Uzzah pays the ultimate price. Uzzah may have been well intentioned in seeking to steady the ark, but his manner of approach betrays a lack of care and respect towards the primary symbol of the presence of God.

---

15. On the musical instruments named in v. 5, see Long (2009b: 438–440).
16. In its only other occurrences in Samuel, *nākôn* is translated in 1 Sam. 23:23 and 26:4 as *definite* and in 2 Sam. 7:16, 26 as *established*.
17. Heb. *šal* (here translated *irreverent act*) occurs but once in the OT and is perhaps the result of scribal error involving the omission of the final consonant of the verb *šālaḥ*, 'to stretch out'. The parallel verse in 1 Chr. 13:10 faults Uzzah because he 'stretched out his hand' (*šālaḥ yādô*) upon the ark. Though fragmentary, 4QSam[a] seems to have this same wording in 2 Sam. 6:7. Targ. speaks of Uzzah's being 'negligent' or 'in error'. The notion of an irreverent act may find some support from Akkadian cognates (see *HALOT* s.v.).

In response, David himself becomes angry, *because the* LORD's *wrath had broken out against Uzzah*, and he names the place *Perez Uzzah* ('outbreak against Uzzah'; v. 8). We are told the cause of David's anger but not its direction. Is his anger directed towards Yahweh for his apparent severity, or towards Uzzah for his recklessness, or perhaps towards himself and his assistants for their own cavalier handling of the ark? Perhaps we should think of a combination of factors, with an emphasis on the last (see 1 Chr. 15:13–15). The exuberant celebration of *David and all Israel . . . before the* LORD (v. 5) is evidence of their enthusiasm and sincerity, but enthusiasm and even sincerity are not enough when Yahweh's explicit instructions are neglected (see at v. 3).

9–11. *David was afraid of the* LORD *that day* (v. 9). Fear of Yahweh is one of the hallmarks of biblical wisdom (Job 28:28; Pss 34:11; 111:10; Prov. 1:7; 9:10; Isa. 33:6; and *passim*). Thus, Brueggemann's remark is apt: 'The death [of Uzzah] has its salutary effect; David becomes freshly afraid of Yahweh (v. 9). When people are no longer awed, respectful, or fearful of God's holiness, the community is put at risk' (1990: 249).

Having overstepped, and now fearful, David is *not willing to take the ark of the* LORD *to be with him in the City of David* but deposits it, rather, in *the house of Obed-Edom the Gittite* (v. 10). *Gittite* means a 'man of Gath', but the question is which Gath: the Philistine city or one of several Israelite cities that contain the name Gath (e.g. Gath Hepher; Gath Rimmon; or even Gittaim)?[18] Of the non-Philistine Gaths, only Gittaim is mentioned in Samuel (see at 2 Sam. 4:3), and a man from Gittaim would also be called a Gittite. On balance, Philistine Gath seems the likeliest possibility. It is mentioned frequently in Samuel (most famously in the ark narrative, in David's defeat of Goliath the Gittite, in David's two flights to Gath, and so forth), and *Obed-Edom* ('servant of Edom') may have been amongst *the six hundred Gittites who . . . accompanied him* [*David*] *from Gath* (2 Sam. 15:18). Obed-Edom obviously no longer lived in Gath (or, for that matter, in Gittaim) but, rather, lived somewhere along the route from Kiriath Jearim to Jerusalem,

---

18. On all these, see Youngblood (2009: 369).

where David could easily 'divert' the ark to his house (cf. JPS). In 1 Chronicles, Obed-Edom is included amongst the Levites, serving both as a 'gatekeeper' (1 Chr. 15:18), or 'doorkeeper for the ark' (1 Chr. 15:24), and as a musician (1 Chr. 15:21; 16:5).

> If this Obed-edom was a native of Gath, his case sheds light on the way in which foreigners could be co-opted into religious offices in the early days of the monarchy. Isaiah 56:3, 6f (and 66:21?) is fulfilled some centuries ahead of its time!
> (Gordon 1986: 233)

12–15. News that the sojourn of the ark in the house of Obed-Edom has brought blessing from Yahweh (see v. 11) prompts David to attempt again to *bring up the ark of God . . . to the City of David*, and he does so *with rejoicing* (v. 12). The *celebrating* (*měśaḥăqîm*) described in verse 5 may suggest elements of revelry, merrymaking or even jesting. Here the phrase *with rejoicing* renders *běśimḥâ*, employing a word often (though not invariably) used to express the joy experienced at sacred festivals or formal occasions such as the coronation of a king (see further at v. 21). Significantly, reference is made to *those who were carrying the ark* – not carting it this time! Proper protocol is being observed (see at v. 3). After those carrying the ark take their first *six steps*, sacrifices are offered: *a bull and a fattened calf* (v. 13).[19] First Chronicles 15:26 mentions more sacrificial animals ('seven bulls and seven rams') and explains that these were in response to the fact that 'God had helped the Levites who were carrying the ark of the covenant of the LORD'. For his part, David is *wearing a linen ephod* (v. 14), a priestly garment, fully in keeping with the role he is playing, as he lays aside his own kingly robe to welcome Yahweh as King into the city that would become known as 'the city of the Great King' (Ps. 48:2). Psalm 24, possibly composed for or in commemoration of David's bringing the ark to Jerusalem, five times in verses 7–10 refers to Yahweh as the 'King of glory' (*melek hakkābôd*).

16. *As the ark of the LORD was entering the City of David, Michal daughter of Saul watched from a window.* When last Michal was at a

---

19. Or 'a fattened bull'.

window, she was in the process of saving David's life (1 Sam. 19:11–13), but much has changed in her relationship with David since then: David has taken other wives (1 Sam. 25:42–43; 2 Sam. 3:2–5); Michal has been given by her father to another man (1 Sam. 25:44), only to be demanded back by David and forcibly returned (much to the sorrow of her husband Paltiel; her own reaction is not recorded, 2 Sam. 3:13–16); a bloody war has been fought between David and Michal's paternal house, with David emerging the stronger (2 Sam. 3:1); and David has now ascended the throne previously occupied by her father (2 Sam. 5:1–5). We know little of David and Michal's marital relationship. In fact, apart from Michal's urging of David to *run for your life* just prior to her lowering him through the window (1 Sam. 19:11–12), we have no recorded verbal exchanges between them at all, until the present chapter. Here Michal proves herself every bit a *daughter of Saul*, an epithet that will be repeated in verses 20 and 23, and *she despise[s] him in her heart*. The verb 'despise' (*bāzah*) is first introduced in the book of Samuel in the 'benchmark' pronouncement of 1 Samuel 2:30b – *Those who honour me I will honour, but those who despise me will be disdained*. As in its first occurrence, so also in the present context the verb is enmeshed in pronouncements about honour, or weight (*kābôd*), and who should receive it (see further at vv. 20–23).

17–19. *They brought the ark of the* LORD ... *and David sacrificed* (v. 17). The picture is of a very happy ending to an episode that began very badly. David, this time, has been careful not only in transporting the ark appropriately (see at v. 13) but also in housing it properly in its place inside the tent. David's *tent*, according to 2 Chronicles 1:2–6, is distinct from the tabernacle, which remained at the time at Gibeon (1 Chr. 16:39; 21:29). In priestly fashion, David *blessed the people in the name of the* LORD *Almighty* (v. 18). Gordon (1986: 234) notes the viewpoint that links David's priestly activities (sacrificing, blessing) with 'an older Jerusalemite priest-king tradition of which traces are preserved in Genesis 14:18–20 and Psalm 110'. Additionally, David's activities find analogies in 'ancient Near Eastern accounts of the introduction of a national god to a new royal city' (McCarter 1984: 181), where the basic pattern is as follows: the god enters the new royal city, sacrifices are offered and feasting ensues (cf. Long 2009b: 438, at 6:2). It is a joyous scene, as *the people* return to *their homes* (lit. each to 'his house'), but the mood changes quickly when David returns to 'his house' (v. 20).

20–23. To go out to meet a returning victor was standard practice in the ancient world, but when Michal daughter of Saul came out to meet David, who was returning to bless his house, she was in no mind to join in celebration of any sort. Instead, apparently before David can say anything and with sarcasm dripping from her lips, Michal exclaims, *How the king of Israel has distinguished himself today, going around half-naked in full view of the slave girls of his servants as any vulgar fellow would!* (v. 20). *Distinguished himself* renders *nikbad*, 'honoured himself', recalling all the honour/weight language that has threaded itself through the book of Samuel.

David is quick to retort that *It was before the* LORD (v. 21) – a point already confirmed by the narrator's comment in verse 16, to wit, Michal observed *King David leaping and dancing* **before the** LORD (emphasis added). This is the fact of the matter, but establishing the facts is seldom sufficient to quiet domestic disputes when tempers flare. And so David continues by reminding Michal that he, not her father nor any of her father's house, is the one whom the Lord *chose* (*bāḥar*) and *appointed* (or 'charged', *ṣiwwāh*) as *ruler* [*nāgîd*] *over the* LORD'*s people Israel*. David could have referred to himself as 'king' rather than 'ruler' (or 'designee'), but his chosen terms unmistakably echo Saul's rejection in 1 Samuel 13. Saul, introduced in 1 Samuel 9:2 as *bāḥûr* ('choice'), learned in Gilgal – after his failure to wait for Samuel – that his kingdom would not endure and that Yahweh had *appointed* ('charged') another as *ruler* (*nāgîd*) over his people. Yahweh did this because Saul had not done what he 'charged' him to do (1 Sam. 13:13–14, which see for further discussion).

David could have stopped speaking here, or even after establishing that his dancing was before Yahweh (beginning of v. 21), but he continues: *I will celebrate* [or 'revel']²⁰ *before the* LORD (end of v. 21). David's further insistence that he will become *even more undignified* ['lightly esteemed'] *than this* and will be *humiliated* ('low,

---

20. David uses the same word as in v. 5; see comment on v. 12.

abased') in his *own eyes* is appropriate (v. 22). Yahweh is true King, and David his vassal. Unlike Eli and his sons (see at 1 Sam. 2:29–30) and Saul (see at 1 Sam. 15:12, 30), David is willing to lower himself that Yahweh may receive the honour (weight) that is his due.

Again, David could have stopped speaking here, but he has one more thing to say. Though not apparent in NIV's translation, David takes up the very words of Michal's biting comment in verse 20 that he has *distinguished* (*kbd* nipʻal) himself before the *slave girls* (*'amhôt*) and throws them back in her face: *by these slave girls* [*'amhôt*] *you spoke of, I will be held in honour* [*kbd* nipʻal] (v. 22). The notion that the lowly slave girls may prove more worthy than Michal is in keeping with the general biblical truth that 'the lowly will be exalted and the exalted will be brought low' (Ezek. 21:26; cf. 1 Sam. 2:7–8; Matt. 23:12; Luke 14:10–11; 18:14). Perhaps that is all that is involved here. But perhaps David's words carry a sarcasm of their own, particularly in the light of the narrator's immediately following comment: *And Michal daughter of Saul had no children to the day of her death* (v. 23). The reader is left to wonder if this is a result of divine decision, or her own, or David's.

Meaning
The narrative recounted in 2 Samuel 6 is momentous in terms of its central event. By the end of the chapter, the ark of God is installed in Jerusalem, the newly established capital of the kingdom of Israel. But the chapter is framed in human misjudgment. Many things are not spelled out in the chapter. What precisely was the nature of Uzzah's fatal offence? And what precisely was David's responsibility for the loss? At whom was he angry? And what of his relationship with Michal? Was his part in the exchange that apparently ended their conjugality honourable, or did he lower himself in returning sarcasm for sarcasm? And what was the cause of Michal's childlessness to the day of her death? Many questions remain unanswered. Perhaps the intended effect of all this is to make the reader watchful as the narrative progresses. David's faith in and commitment to Yahweh are genuine, but as we have seen before, David is capable of serious lapses. The greatest lapse is yet to be told. But here we get ahead of ourselves.

C. The dynastic promise to David: on the building of houses (7:1–29)

Context
Second Samuel 7 is all about houses and building plans. Well settled in his own 'house' (palace), David wants to build a 'house' (temple) for Yahweh. But Yahweh has very different building plans.

After the action-packed adventures of the last several chapters, chapter 7 may seem like a lull. As Peterson (1999: 166) puts it: 'From the moment David is anointed king in Hebron (2:1–4), the story plunges from one dramatic episode to the next in breathless succession, a narrative equivalent to whitewater rafting. And then, suddenly, nothing. Still waters.' But still waters can run deep, and so it is with 2 Samuel 7.

Words dominate the chapter: David's words to Nathan and Nathan's response (vv. 1–3); the Lord's words to Nathan and through Nathan to David (vv. 4–17); and, finally, David's words of response to the Lord (vv. 18–29). Inexperienced readers may be tempted to underestimate the importance of a chapter with more words than actions. But readers conversant in Hebrew narrative style will know that climactic moments, and indeed climactic chapters, are often characterized by a slowing of narrative pace and a dominance of words over actions.

To say that 2 Samuel 7 is a climactic moment is to say too little. Brueggemann (1990: 253) describes 2 Samuel 7 as 'the dramatic and theological center of the entire Samuel corpus' and 'one of the most crucial texts in the Old Testament for evangelical faith'. Gordon (1986: 235) calls the divine promise to David in 2 Samuel 7 the 'ideological summit' of the entire Old Testament. What makes this promise special is, first, the way in which it recalls the 'patriarchal promise' (first uttered to Abraham in Gen. 12:2–3) and refocuses it on David and his descendants (see esp. vv. 5, 9, 10, 12) and, second, the way it sets the stage for the 'messianic expectation' that will become a dominant theme in the writings of the later monarchic and exilic periods (e.g. Isa. 11:1; Jer. 23:5–6; Ezek. 34:24; Hos. 3:5; Zech. 3:8; 6:12).

Comment

1–3. The events of this chapter take place *After the king was settled in his palace* (v. 1). The text does not indicate how much time has elapsed since the events of chapter 6, when David brought the ark of Yahweh to Jerusalem, installed it in a tent, blessed and dismissed the people, and returned home in a failed attempt to bless his own house (or *household*, 6:20). But as chapter 7 opens, we find David *settled* (lit. 'sitting') in his *palace* (lit. 'house') and beginning to think about providing a more permanent 'house' for the ark of God. Before the chapter is over, we shall find David sitting before Yahweh, astonished by what he has just heard (v. 18). The keyword 'house' (Hebrew *bāyit*) occurs fifteen times in chapter 7, referring variously to David's palace (vv. 1, 2), to a temple for the Lord (vv. 5, 6, 7, 13) or to a dynasty for David (vv. 11, 16, 18, 19, 25, 26, 27, 29 [2x]). The presence of this keyword is partially obscured in most English translations, which render *bāyit* as palace, temple, family, dynasty or house, according to context.

Yahweh *had given him rest from all his enemies around him* (v. 1). A second key theme introduced in verse 1 is that of rest. With the Lord having given the king rest from all his enemies around him (but see at v. 11), David has time to ponder the fact that his quarters are rather fine (*a house of cedar*, implying costly cedar panelling in a stone structure), while the ark *remains in a tent* (v. 2, the reference being to the tent of 6:17).[21]

---

21. The statement of MT v. 1 that Yahweh had given David rest round about from all his enemies is felt to be problematic on several counts. David's major battles are yet to be fought (see 2 Sam. 8), and v. 11 sees David's rest as lying in the future (*I will also give you rest from all your enemies*). Moreover, the Chronicles parallel (1 Chr. 17:1) does not contain the clause, while LXX speaks not of rest but of inheritance: 'the Lord had given him an inheritance round about from all his enemies who were round about him' (NETS). While LXX might seem to reflect a very different text, either reading could actually quite easily arise from the same consonantal Hebrew text, depending on where word division is assumed. LXX apparently reads the string *hnhylw* as one word, yielding

Nathan, introduced in verses 2–3 without further explanation, is destined to play an important prophetic role not just in the present episode, when David is at a high point, but also in 2 Samuel 12, when David is at his low point, and in 1 Kings 1, when David is physically failing (further references to Nathan include 1 Chr. 29:29; 2 Chr. 9:29; 29:25). Nathan's response to David's evident desire to build a house for *the ark of God* (v. 2) is affirmative: *Whatever you have in mind, go ahead and do it, for the* LORD *is with you* (v. 3). Nathan is correct that Yahweh is with David (see at 1 Sam. 16:18), but he is mistaken regarding Yahweh's will in the present circumstances, as we shall see below.

4–11a. *But that night the word of the* LORD *came to Nathan* (v. 4). Yahweh wastes no time in correcting his prophet and in telling him what he must say to David. *Go and tell my servant David* (v. 5). In the Old Testament, only select individuals receive the title 'servant of Yahweh' and then often only near the end of their lives: for example, Abraham (Gen. 26:24), Moses (Num. 12:7–8; Deut. 34:5), Caleb (Num. 14:24) and Joshua (Josh. 24:29). Thus, Yahweh's reference to David as *my servant* places him in very select company (cf. also 2 Sam. 3:18; Ps. 89:3).

The message for David begins with a (gentle?) rhetorical question expecting a negative answer: *are you the one to build me a house to dwell in?* (v. 5). The Chronicler turns the question into an indicative sentence: 'you are not the one to build me a house to dwell in' (1 Chr. 17:4; LXX of 2 Sam. 7:5 reflects this reading). Elsewhere in Chronicles, the reason given is that David is 'a warrior' who has 'shed blood' (1 Chr. 28:3; cf. 22:8; also 1 Kgs 5:3). In Samuel, Yahweh explains to David that *from the day* [*he*] *brought the Israelites up out of Egypt to this day* he has neither had nor required a house,[22] but has *been moving from place to place with a tent as my dwelling*

(note 21 *cont*.) 'he gave him an inheritance', while MT divides the string as *hnyḥ lw*, yielding 'he gave him rest' (cf. LEH 2 sub *kataklēronomeō*).

22. Worth noting is the contention by Oswald (2008) that, contrary to the ubiquitous pattern in the Ancient Near East of a link between temple-building and dynastic stability, Yahweh makes it clear that David's dynasty is assured by God and does not require that a temple be built.

(v. 6).²³ Another rhetorical question underscores the point: *did I ever say to any of their rulers* that they should build me a house (v. 7)?²⁴ Yahweh has in fact been on the move with his people, accompanying them at every stage – out of Egypt, through the wilderness, into the land, through the failed experiment of the people's king, Saul, and now in the establishment of Yahweh's chosen king, David (vv. 8–9). Pointedly, he says to David, *I have been with you wherever you have gone, and I have cut off all your enemies from before you* (v. 9). This does not mean that David no longer has any enemies (cf. v. 11) but, rather, that in every conflict so far, Yahweh has given David victory.

The declaration *Now I will make your name great* (v. 9) calls to mind the promise to Abraham of a great name through which 'all peoples on earth' would be blessed (Gen. 12:2–3). Further, the assurance *I will provide a place for my people Israel* (v. 10) echoes the Abrahamic promises of land (Gen. 12:1, 7; 15:18; 17:8), now being reiterated to David. The ensuing promise of a future in which the people will be planted in a *home of their own and no longer disturbed* by oppressors, and will be given rest (v. 11), hints at what in Hebrew idiom is called 'shalom', full and complete well-being, both circumstantial and relational. How this will come about is explained in what Yahweh says next.

11b–17. *The* LORD *declares to you that the* LORD *himself will establish a house for you* (v. 11b). The *house*, *bayit*, in this instance implies a dynasty, as the next verse confirms: *I will raise up your offspring* [*zarʿăkā*, 'your seed'] *to succeed you* (v. 12). While the grammatically

---

23. The Heb. reads *bĕʾōhel ûbĕmiškān*, thus, 'in a tent, namely, in a tabernacle' (assuming an explicative waw before tabernacle; R. J. Williams 2007: §434). Cf. Firth (2009: 381).
24. NIV's *rulers* either takes MT's *šibṭê yiśrāʾēl* as 'tribal leaders of Israel' or revocalizes the form as *šōbĕṭê* ('sceptre-holders') or adopts the Chronicler's *šōpĕṭê yiśrāʾēl*, 'judges/rulers of Israel' (1 Chr. 17:6). The differences between these readings is minimal, the first and second involving revocalizing the same consonantal text, and the third involving a *p* in place of the *b*. For fuller discussion and other options, see Youngblood (2009: 384).

singular *zeraʿ* (seed, offspring) is often used as a collective, here it denotes a particular offspring, *your own flesh and blood* (*'ăšer yēṣē' mimmēʿêkā*, lit. 'who comes forth from your own body'). Yet again, this recalls the promises made to Abraham, repeating verbatim Yahweh's promise to Abraham of an heir *'ăšer yēṣē' mimmēʿêkā* (Gen. 15:4).

With respect to David's offspring, Yahweh makes a string of remarkable pronouncements involving an established kingdom (v. 12), a throne for ever (*'ad-ʿôlām'*, v. 13), a father–son relationship that will include both discipline if needed (*floggings inflicted by human hands*, v. 14) and unremitting love (*my love will never be taken away from him*, v. 15). The significance of this father–son relationship is realized to a degree in the special relationship Yahweh establishes with the Davidic kings (cf. Pss 2:7; 89:18–37) but is fully realized only in Christ (cf. Mark 1:11; Acts 13:33; Heb. 1:5). Sandwiched between these pronouncements is the notice that David's offspring, Solomon as it turns out, *will build a house for my Name* (v. 13; see 1 Kgs 5:5, 17; 6:1 – 9:3).[25] The primary focus, though, is not on Yahweh's house, but David's. And the bottom line is this: *Your* [i.e. David's] *house and your kingdom will endure for ever before me; your throne shall be established for ever* (v. 16). At a profound level, however, the distinction between the two houses is minimal, if not non-existent. The Chronicler's parallel to verse 16 perceptively brings to full expression what is already implicit in the promise: 'I will set him over *my* house and *my* kingdom for ever; *his* throne will be established for ever' (1 Chr. 17:14; emphasis added). The throne of David, the Lord's 'anointed' (*māšîaḥ*, from which we get our word 'messiah'), is in a deep sense the throne of Yahweh himself. This throne was destined, in the fullness of time, to be the eternal throne of Yahweh's one true Son,

---

25. That there is a conditional element in respect of the enjoyment by Solomon or any subsequent Davidic kings of Yahweh's unconditional promises is evident from 1 Kgs 9 (especially vv. 4–9): 'As for you, if you walk before me faithfully with integrity of heart and uprightness . . . I will establish your royal throne' (vv. 4–5). Yahweh's promises are certain with respect to fulfilment but conditional with respect to agency.

the Messiah ('Christ' in Greek). But already long before the coming of the Messiah, the Davidic hope was understood in messianic terms (cf. Isa. 9:7; 11:1–5; Jer. 33:14–26; Mic. 5:1–5).

Nathan reported to David all the words of this entire revelation (v. 17). The *word of the LORD* (v. 4) is here described as a *ḥizzāyôn* (*revelation*, or 'vision'). The weight of this revelation from Yahweh is not lost on David, as his response shows.

18–24. *Then King David went in* [presumably into the tent mentioned in 6:17] *and sat before the LORD* (v. 18; probably before the ark of Yahweh).[26] The chapter began with David sitting in his palace, pondering what he should do for Yahweh. He now is sitting *before the LORD*, pondering and praying in amazement at what Yahweh has promised to do for him.

Who am I, Sovereign LORD . . . ? (v. 18b). David addresses Yahweh as *Sovereign LORD* (NIV's rendering of *'ădōnāy yĕhwih*)[27] seven times in his prayer (vv. 18, 19 [2x], 20, 22, 28, 29). This appellative appears nowhere else in Samuel but occurs often elsewhere, especially in prayers: by Abraham in Genesis 15:2, 8; by Moses in Deuteronomy 3:24; 9:26; by Joshua in Joshua 7:7; by Gideon in Judges 6:22; and by Samson in Judges 16:28. *What is my family* is literally 'what is my house [*bayit*]', thus touching on the central concern of Yahweh's promise to David, namely, the future of his house/dynasty. Like the appellative *Sovereign LORD*, the word *house* occurs seven times in David's prayer (vv. 18, 19, 25, 26, 27, 29 [2x]; cf. Youngblood 2009: 395). David is astonished by how far Yahweh has brought him, a man of humble beginnings.

---

26. On the ark as a physical symbol of Yahweh's presence, see Exod. 25:22; 30:6; Deut. 10:8; Josh. 6:8; 1 Sam. 6:20; 2 Sam. 6:16–17.
27. The consonants of the personal divine name YHWH are usually vocalized in the MT using the vowels of the word Adonai, with the intent that the reader not (mis)pronounce the divine name but pronounce the name as Adonai. However, in instances such as the present one where the word Adonai (Lord) precedes YHWH, the latter is read as Elohim, thus yielding 'Lord God', which is how many English translations render *'ădōnāy yĕhwih* here and in other places: e.g. JPS, NRSV, ESV.

Verse 19 has proven difficult for translators, as the variety evident in English translations suggests. *And as if this were not enough in your sight* (NIV) might more literally be rendered, 'And yet this was a small thing in your eyes' (NRSV). David's awe is inspired by the fact that Yahweh has *also spoken about the future of the house of your servant* (NIV here takes the compound expression *lĕmērāḥôq* temporally, as referring to that which lies far in the future). To assume a future reference makes good sense in the present context, although *lĕmērāḥôq* can also refer to that which lies far off in the past (e.g. 2 Kgs 19:25 = Isa. 37:26, 'Long ago I ordained it').[28] The most difficult phrase in verse 19 is the last one, a literal reading of which would yield 'and this is the torah (instruction, law, rule, custom?) of/for humankind'. Is David uttering a declarative statement ('this is instruction for mankind', ESV; cf. NASB), expressing a wish ('may that be a law for the people', JPS; cf. NRSV), asking a question ('is this the manner of man . . . ?', KJV; cf. NLT) or simply exclaiming (*and this decree . . . is for a mere human!*, NIV)? The parallel phrase in 1 Chronicles 17:17 does not help much, as it involves its own complexities and yields its own variety of translations, most having something to do with Yahweh's having 'looked on me [David] as though I were the most exalted of men', NIV (cf. JPS, NRSV, NLT), though ESV manages 'have shown me future generations'.

Whatever uncertainties remain in our reading of verse 19, the tenor of David's praise is clear. *What more can David say to you? For you know your servant* (v. 20). *You know* (*yāda'tā*) might also be rendered 'you chose' (cf. Amos 3:2). David is awed by the fact that in keeping with his *word* and *will*, Yahweh has not only done *this great thing* but has also *made it known to your servant* (v. 21).

David's praise for what Yahweh has done turns in verse 22 simply to who Yahweh is: *There is no one like you . . . no God but you, as we have heard with our own ears*. *As we have heard* (*bĕkōl 'ăšer-šāma'nû*) might possibly be read 'whatever we have heard', much as *bĕkōl 'ăšer* in the near context means *wherever* (so 7:7, 9; 8:6, 14; cf. also 1 Sam. 14:47; 18:5). The sense, then, would be that 'whatever' the

---

28. The compound can also have a spatial sense, as in Job 36:3; 39:29; 2 Chr. 26:15; Ezra 3:13.

polytheistic chatter we hear around us, we know that *there is no God but you* (v. 22). Having declared the uniqueness of Yahweh, David concludes his praise with a declaration of the uniqueness of the people redeemed by this God and with a brief summary of his mighty deeds in history on their behalf (vv. 23–24).

25–29. *And now,* LORD *God [yĕhwāh 'ĕlōhîm], keep for ever the promise you have made concerning your servant and his house* (v. 25). *And now* (*wĕ'attāh*) is a standard marker of a shift in a speech (or prayer, as here) from what has gone before to its logical consequence. In a prophetic judgment speech, for instance, this formula marks the transition from the 'accusation' to the 'announcement of judgment'. Here it marks the transition from David's rehearsal of what God has promised to David's confident prayer that God's promises be kept. It is on the basis of what God has *revealed . . . to your servant* (lit. 'you opened the ear of your servant') that David *has found courage* [lit. 'found his heart'] *to pray this prayer to you* (v. 27). Verse 28 lays out the logic of David's assurance: (1) *you are God!*; (2) *Your covenant is trustworthy* (lit. 'your words, they are truth'); and (3) *you have promised these good things* [lit. 'spoken this good'] *to your servant*. From this, only one conclusion can follow: the marvellous promise of an everlasting kingdom for the house of David cannot fail. If the outcome is so certain, why then does David pray? Perhaps his prayer functions as a kind of verbal processing by which he reminds himself of who God is and who he himself is, as the recipient of God's promise. Unlike his predecessor on the throne, David has a firm grasp on the nature of his relationship to Yahweh, referring to himself seven times in verses 25–29 as *your servant*. As noted above at verse 5, to be the 'servant of Yahweh' was a high calling. David is king, but not an autocrat. His primary responsibility as king is to remain the servant of the Great King. David's seven-fold assumption of the role of servant is matched by seven namings of God, five including the personal name Yahweh and three including God, and the middle naming being the most complete: LORD *Almighty, God of Israel* (v. 27).

Meaning

This chapter recounting Yahweh's promise to David of an enduring dynasty, followed by David's astonished response, is a pivot point in the sweep of redemptive history. The chapter began with David, in good Ancient Near Eastern style, desiring to build a 'house' for God in his newly established capital city. But Yahweh is utterly unlike the 'gods' worshipped by the nations, and David is to be a king unlike the kings of the surrounding nations. The latter undertook to serve their gods by housing and feeding them, and having done so, expected their gods to assist them in whatever they might initiate. Yahweh did not need to be housed and fed, and Israelite kings were not to be the initiators (see at 1 Sam. 8). The duty of Israelite kings, like the Israelites themselves, was to *follow the LORD your God* (1 Sam. 12:14 and *passim*).

We have noted in the story of David references to his praying, seeking the divine will. And we have noted on occasion the lack of such references. The present chapter lacks any reference to David praying to Yahweh before proposing to Nathan that he would like to build a house for Yahweh. Nathan gives the go-ahead to what seems a good idea, but the Lord quickly intervenes with a corrective and a promise. Though David may not build a house (temple) for the Lord, the Lord will build an enduring house (royal lineage) for David: *Your house and your kingdom shall endure for ever before me* (v. 16). Overwhelmed by the momentous and gracious character of this promise, David breaks into a prayer of praise. The divine counter-initiative lays David's initiative to rest. As Brueggemann (1990: 260) remarks, 'The bold prayer of David is a perfect match for the remarkable oracle. David and Yahweh have reached an understanding. They now know their proper roles vis-à-vis each other.'

This chapter which began with what David wanted to do for God ends with David's astonished response to what God promises to do for him. The promise to David becomes a recurrent motif in the remainder of the Old Testament, but it is not fulfilled until the coming of 'Jesus the Messiah the son of David, the son of Abraham' (Matt. 1:1). The New Testament, from beginning to end, is fixed upon this one, this Jesus, who says concerning himself, 'I am the Root and the Offspring of David, and the bright Morning Star' (Rev. 22:16).[29]

---

29. Cf. further Isa. 9:1–7; Luke 1:32–33, 69–70; Acts 2:30–31; 13:22–23; Rom. 1:1–4; 2 Tim. 2:8.

D. David's successes and his officials (8:1–18)

Context

After a chapter comprising mainly words – a profound promise and an astonished prayer of response – 2 Samuel 8 returns to a summary listing of actions – military victories, to be precise. This list appears to be structured more geographically than chronologically, and some of the victories may have been accomplished between the events of chapters 5 and 6. The victories move from west (v. 1) to east (v. 2), then from north (vv. 3–11) to south (vv. 13–14). David's successes can be viewed through both theological and political lenses: 'Twice it is affirmed that his rampant victories came from Yahweh (vv. 6, 14)', while it 'undoubtedly was a help that none of the great powers of the near east was able, or was disposed, to contest the areas in which David showed interest' (Gordon 1986: 242).

Comment

1. First to be mentioned in the summary listing of David's victories are the *Philistines*, Israel's arch-enemies throughout Samuel. The Philistines are mentioned more than 170 times in Samuel. (On Yahweh's desire that Israel be freed from Philistine oppression, see, e.g., 1 Sam. 9:16; 2 Sam. 3:18.) King Saul had enjoyed some limited success against the Philistines, though most of the credit would go either to David (e.g. 1 Sam. 17) or to Jonathan (1 Sam. 13:3; 14:1–14). Saul was not able to subdue them (1 Sam. 14:52). It was David who finally *subdued*, or 'humbled' (*knʿ* hipʿil), the Philistines (see at 5:17–25) and wrested from them (lit. 'took ... from the hand of the Philistines') *Metheg Ammah*. No site by this name is otherwise known,[30] and this has led to various speculations as to what might be in view. Most English translations settle for treating *meteg hāʾammāh* as a proper noun, but if we take the two nouns as common nouns, the meaning would be 'reins of the forearm'. Perhaps this is an expression similar to the English

---

30. A *hill of Ammah* is mentioned in 2:24, but see comment there.

expression 'reins of power'.³¹ For other possibilities, see McCarter (1984: 243).

2. *David also defeated the Moabites,* Israel's near-neighbours east of the Dead Sea.³² David's treatment of captured Moabite soldiers may strike modern readers as unconscionable. Having measured them off, David has *Every two lengths of them . . . put to death, and the third length was allowed to live.* This must be read, however, in the context of Ancient Near Eastern military practices, in which captive soldiers were often all executed, or all enslaved (whether retained or sold) and often blinded (see at 1 Sam. 11:2) or mutilated in some way so as to control them. Imprisonment of large numbers of captives was generally neither logistically possible nor practical. Against this backdrop, the sparing of a third of the Moabites to return unimpaired to their homes was not without mercy (cf. Bergen 1996: 347). Given the proximity of Moab to Israelite territory, simple repatriation of the defeated foes was not a good option. *So the Moabites became subject to David and brought him tribute.* The exacting of tribute from conquered foes was standard practice, both enriching the victor and depressing the economy of the vanquished land, thus lessening the likelihood of a resurgence.

3–4. Shifting its focus to the far north, the list next mentions David's defeat of *Hadadezer* ['(the god) Hadad is helper'] *son of Rehob* [apparently both a personal and place name; see 10:6], *king of Zobah* [an Aramean region north of Israel; see 1 Sam. 14:47], *when he went to restore his monument at the Euphrates River* (v. 3).³³ It is not clear whether *he,* that is, the one who went to 'restore control' or 'set up a monument' at 'the river' (NIV correctly supplies Euphrates), refers to David or to Hadadezer. If it was David who travelled north to

---

31. Non-English modern translations sometimes move in this direction (e.g. in German 'Zügel der Herrschaft' [Elberfelder] or 'Zügel der Regierung' [Schlachter]; in French 'les rênes de la capitale' [Segond Révisée]). Among ancient versions, perhaps cf. Vulgate's *frenum tributi*.
32. See Gen. 19:37 for the biblical account of their origin. And on David's familial connection through Ruth 'the Moabitess', see Ruth 4:13–17. See also 1 Sam. 22:3.
33. For further detail, see Long (2009b: 449–450).

the river, this would explain the circumstances of his encounter with Hadadezer, who was en route (cf. McCarter 1984: 247). If, on the other hand, it was Hadadezer who was focused on restoring control in the north, then David may have exploited this preoccupation to attack him from the south (cf. Malamat 1963: 3).

David's defeat of Hadadezer puts him in possession of a significant quantity of military machines and personnel (v. 4).[34] *He hamstrung all but a hundred of the chariot horses.* Some have posited military reasons for this action – for example, that David's chariot force, if he had one, was either so small or so well supplied that only a hundred horses were needed (cf. Yadin 1963: 285). But the biblical narrator would probably have us consider theological reasoning (e.g. the instruction of Deut. 17:16 that Israel's future kings were not to 'acquire great numbers of horses') and biblical precedent (the fact that Joshua, at Yahweh's command, had hamstrung horses and burned chariots captured during the northern campaign, Josh. 11:6, 9). Yahweh's warnings through Samuel in 1 Samuel 8:11 about royal chariots and horses will begin to be realized in the respective bids for the throne launched by Absalom (2 Sam. 15:1) and Adonijah (1 Kgs 1:5) and will be fully realized in Solomon's extensive chariot forces (1 Kgs 4:26–28; 9:22; 10:26–29).

5–6. David's defeat of *the Arameans of Damascus* who *came to help Hadadezer* (see vv. 3–4) and the setting up of *garrisons* [*nĕṣîbîm*] *in the Aramean kingdom of Damascus* reduces the Arameans to tributary status. Putting garrisons in conquered territory was both a sign and a means of domination. Compare the earlier garrisoning of Israel by the Philistines (see 1 Sam. 10:5; 13:3–4, where the same Hebrew word, *nĕṣîb*, is used but rendered *outpost* in NIV).

The LORD gave David victory wherever he went, literally 'Yahweh saved/delivered (*yš' hip'il*) David' (v. 6). This important theological claim is repeated in verse 14 and continues to develop the theme of Yahweh's being 'with David' (see at 1 Sam. 16:18; 18:12, 14, 28; 2 Sam. 7:9). Contrast Saul, whose summary list of military accomplishments concludes with a statement somewhat similar to

---

34. MT is textually difficult but can be reconstructed on the basis of LXX, 4QSam[a] and the parallel in 1 Chr. 18:4.

David's but with dramatically different import: *Wherever he turned, he inflicted punishment* (or 'made himself guilty'); see discussion at 1 Samuel 14:47. Assuming *yaršîaʿ* in that verse to be correct, two striking contrasts with David's summary are evident: (1) Yahweh is not the subject of the verb; and (2) the verb is not the expected *yôšîaʿ* (he saved) but *yaršîaʿ* (he made [himself] guilty). Even should the verb in Saul's summary be textually corrupt and in need of correction to 'he was saved', the avoidance of any mention of Yahweh would still be damaging to Saul's reputation.

7–14. Materials taken from defeated foes – *gold shields*[35] . . . *a great quantity of bronze* – were brought by David to Jerusalem (vv. 7–8), where he *dedicated* them *to the* LORD (vv. 11–12). Perhaps this was in anticipation of the temple that Yahweh had said one of his sons would build (7:12–13).[36]

Sandwiched between the notices of what David did with *the silver and gold from all the nations he had subdued* (v. 11) are two verses describing how *Tou king of Hamath* reacted when he *heard that David had defeated the entire army of Hadadezer* (v. 9). King Tou was probably of Hurrian extraction, as distinct from the Arameans to his south. His city, Hamath, lay along the Orontes River some 130 miles north of Damascus. From this city Tou governed a Neo-Hittite state stretching from the Euphrates River southwards to Zobah. Seeing the handwriting on the wall, so to speak, Tou positioned himself as a subject ally of David by sending his son *Joram*, laden with gifts, to congratulate David *on his victory in battle over Hadadezer, who had been at war with Tou* (v. 10).[37] Gordon (1986: 243) remarks on the fragile state of affairs that existed amongst the petty kingdoms

---

35. Probably to be understood as 'bow (and arrow) cases' (Long 2009b: 451).
36. The Chronicler has much more to say about David's material preparations for the building of the temple (1 Chr. 22:1–16; 29:1–9, 16–19). For a general discussion of the handling of spoils of war in the Bible and the ANE, see Elgavish (2002: 242–273).
37. That Tou's son had a Yahwistic name, 'Yahweh is exalted', is surprising. The parallel verse in 1 Chr. 18:10 has 'Hadoram' ('Hadad is exalted'). McCarter (1984: 250) follows Malamat in suggesting that Hadoram may have taken a second name, Joram, to indicate his 'fealty to David'.

north of Israel, what might be called the 'Aramean' bloc. Sometimes they banded together against a common foe (v. 5). Sometimes they fought one another (v. 10).

David became famous, literally 'David made a name (for himself)' (v. 13). On the one hand, we are reminded of Yahweh's promise of a great name for David in 7:9. On the other, though, we recall also Saul's setting up a monument for himself in 1 Samuel 15:12. Should the present event be read as Yahweh's fulfilling his promise or as David beginning to build up his own reputation? The defeat of *Edomites in the Valley of Salt* is referenced in several places in the Old Testament. In 1 Chronicles 18:12, the victory is ascribed to Abishai, brother of Joab and one of David's commanders (2 Sam. 18:2; see 1 Sam. 26:6–9 for Abishai's first mention), while the superscription to Psalm 60 credits Joab – if indeed the same battle is in view (only twelve 'thousand' enemy dead are mentioned in the superscription, while the Samuel and Chronicles notices mention eighteen 'thousand'). Such engagements would have involved David's commanders and troops, so the varying ascriptions are not necessarily problematic.

Like the other conquered territories, *the Edomites became subject to David*, and he ensured their continued subjection by placing *garrisons throughout Edom* (v. 14), as he had done to the Aramean kingdom of Damascus (v. 6). For a second time, the mention of *garrisons* is followed by the refrain *The LORD gave David victory wherever he went* (v. 14; see comment at v. 6).

15. Military victories mean little if the ensuing peace is not well administered. The declaration that *David reigned over all Israel* is formulaic (cf. 1 Kgs 4:1), but what follows is crucial: *doing what was just and right* [*mišpāṭ ûṣĕdāqâ*][38] *for all his people*. More is implied in this statement than that David effected a proper judicial system. Implied also is the effecting of 'social justice and equity, which is bound up with kindness and mercy' (Weinfeld 2000: 36). Such justice expresses itself in concern for the vulnerable in society, 'the stranger, widow and orphan' (ibid.: 43). The responsibility of kings to cultivate a just society is attested also in Ancient Near Eastern texts (see,

---

38. 'True justice' (JPS) is another valid rendering.

e.g., Lambert 1965: 1–11; for fuller discussion, see Long 2009b: 452–453). What is distinctive in respect of Israel's theocratic king is that he is to rule in the power of Yahweh's spirit (cf. 1 Sam. 16:13; cf. Ps. 72:1) and according to the pattern of Yahweh's own rule (on which, see Ps. 89:14; 99:4), a rule designed to bring blessing to 'all nations' (Ps. 72:17). In keeping with the constancy of Yahweh's just rule, the pattern of a just society remains constant through changing times, as the post-exilic prophecy of Zechariah illustrates: 'This is what the Lord Almighty said: "Administer true justice; show mercy and compassion to one another. Do not oppress the widow or the fatherless, the foreigner or the poor. Do not plot evil against each other"' (Zech. 7:8–10). As an earlier summary noted, 'David knew that the Lord had established him as king over Israel and had exalted his kingdom for the sake of his people Israel' (2 Sam. 5:12). David has made a good start, but there is trouble of his own making ahead (2 Sam. 11 and following). At the heart of Absalom's rebellion will be the issue of a failure of justice (15:1–6).

16–18. The general statement of David's good leadership (v. 15) is followed by a listing of his chief officials (vv. 16–18). Heading the list is *Joab*, who is *over the army* (v. 16). While it was customary in ANE 'cabinet' listings[39] to begin with the chief military commander, second only to the king, one cannot but be reminded of the dint of Joab's own personality, who, despite David's later attempts to replace him (e.g. with Amasa in 17:25; 19:13), will always manage to claw, or kill (20:8–10), his way back to the top.

Next is *Jehoshaphat*, the *recorder* (*mazkîr*; from the root 'to remember', thus 'remembrancer' ['herald'?]). The office of recorder is mentioned here for the first time in the Old Testament but frequently hereafter (20:24; 1 Kgs 4:3; 2 Kgs 18:18, 37; etc.). The recorder may have functioned both like a modern press secretary, 'handling the communications between the king and the country', and like a chief of protocol, orchestrating 'the ceremonial at the royal audiences' (Mettinger 1971: 61). Jehoshaphat continued as 'recorder' into the reign of Solomon (1 Kgs 4:3).

---

39. On which, see, e.g., Parpola (1995: 379–401); Mattila (2000: 161–168). For Israel in particular, see Mettinger (1971).

Next to be mentioned (v. 17) are two priests, *Zadok son of Ahitub* and *Ahimelek son of Abiathar* – or more likely the reverse, 'Abiathar son of Ahimelek', assuming a transcriptional error in the Hebrew text.[40] After all, it was Abiathar, a son of Ahimelek son of Ahitub, who survived the massacre at Nob and fled to David (1 Sam. 22:20); who carried the ephod for David (1 Sam. 23:6, 9; 30:7); who will, along with Zadok and the Levites, bear *the ark of the covenant of God* to David during his flight from Absalom (2 Sam. 15:24 and *passim*); who, again along with Zadok, will serve David covertly during Absalom's revolt (17:15) and overtly after Absalom's death (19:11); who will be listed along with Zadok in a later listing of David's administrative personnel (20:25); and who will ultimately be deposed for siding with Adonijah in his bid for David's throne (1 Kgs 1:7 and *passim*) and be replaced by Zadok (1 Kgs 2:35).

Zadok son of Ahitub, mentioned here for the first time in the Old Testament, also raises questions. Inasmuch as he is not mentioned as having survived the massacre at Nob, his priestly lineage must be other than through Eli. One suggestion is that he was serving as priest in Jerusalem before its capture by the Israelites and was retained in office, resulting in the 'integration of the old Jerusalemite cultus (cf. Gn. 14:18–20; Ps. 110:4) into the Israelite religion' (Gordon 1986: 246, who characterizes the view as a 'speculative' but nevertheless 'serious attempt to deal with a real problem'). The Chronicler includes Zadok in the line of Aaron via Eleazar (1 Chr. 6:3–8, 50–53). Given the flexibility in genealogical conventions in biblical times, the two approaches are not necessarily mutually exclusive.[41]

---

40. The emended reading is supported by the Syriac. For a summary of how the corruption may have occurred, see McCarter (1984: 253–254).
41. On the point generally, see Stager (1998: 150): 'Genealogies, it must be emphasized, are charters of sociopolitical organization, not necessarily actual family trees that detail blood relations.' On Chronicles in particular, Braun (1997: 96) writes that genealogies 'may reflect not only blood relationships, but geographical, social, economic, religious, and political realities as well' (see his full discussion, 1997: 92–105).

Seraiah was secretary (v. 17), a high-ranking official in charge of the secretariat where state documents were preserved. Variety in the spelling of his name – *šĕrāyâ* in the present passage; *šĕwā'* in 20:25; *šawšā'* in 1 Chronicles 18:16; and, if referring to the same person, *šîšā'* in 1 Kings 4:3 – may suggest that he is of foreign origin. If from Egypt, as has been suggested, then he would have been well versed in administrative and scribal practice.

Benaiah son of Jehoida was over the Kerethites and Pelethites (v. 18). *Benaiah*, mentioned here for the first time in the Old Testament, will distinguish himself as a 'valiant warrior' against man and beast in the colourful account of 23:20–22 and will continue in service under David and into the reign of Solomon, eventually (on Solomon's orders) dispatching and replacing Joab as commander of the army (1 Kgs 2:31–35). The *Kerethities* (likely of Cretan origin) are known already from 1 Samuel 30:14, and though the *Pelethites* are here mentioned for the first time, they are quite likely of Philistine origin, perhaps having joined David during his Philistine sojourn (1 Sam. 27 and following). The unusual spelling *pĕlētî* (Pelethite), in place of the more normal *pĕlištî* (Philistine), may represent either a dialectical variation or an assimilation to Kerethites, *kĕrētî* (Gordon 1986: 247). The Kerethites and Pelethites arrived in Palestine along with other 'Sea Peoples' around the beginning of the Iron Age (*c.*1200 BC). As foreigners lacking pre-existing local loyalties, they were well suited to serve as David's personal, professional troops.

The final notice, that *David's sons were priests*, has raised questions for several reasons: David was not in the levitical line; David's priests (Zadok and Abiathar) have already been named; versional support for the reading is mixed; and 1 Chronicles 18:17 designates David's sons as 'chief officials at the king's side' (*hāri'šōnîm lĕyad hammelek*). Several considerations favour retaining the Hebrew reading *priests*: David himself is presented as a priest-king in the tradition of Melchizedek, who was 'king of Salem' and 'priest of God Most High' (Gen. 14:18; cf. Ps. 110:4), and his sons may have shared this royal-priestly status; the Chronicler's terminology could apply to priests as well as other chief officials; and on text-critical grounds, *priests* represents the *lectio difficilior* (the more difficult reading), which means that it is easier to imagine 'priests' being replaced by a less controversial term than the reverse.[42]

Meaning

In reflecting on 2 Samuel 8, Birch (1998: 1267) asks whether 'David's success as an empire builder [is] a testimony to his own achievement or to the grace of God'. For the reader familiar with David's story as it continues into chapter 11, the lack of explicit reference to David's seeking of 'divine guidance in these conquests' (ibid.) may be disconcerting. But the narrative does not raise the issue directly, and twice it is explicitly stated that *The LORD gave David victory wherever he went* (vv. 6, 14). Furthermore, David understands that his elevation to kingship is not for purposes of self-aggrandizement but that he may do what is *just and right for all his people* (v. 15). Ideally, his successes internationally (vv. 1–14) and his development of a domestic royal infrastructure (vv. 16–18) should serve such purposes. But still Birch is correct to call attention to the fact that power, if autonomous, 'leads to injustice and violence' (ibid.). Even David, if careless, can fall into such abuses of power, as will become painfully clear in chapter 11.

E. David's kindness received by Mephibosheth (9:1–13)

Context

The preceding chapter recounted David's military victories and the beginnings of his royal administration. The focus was largely on matters of politics and power, both internationally and domestically. It dealt with groups of people, be they troublesome foes or friendly functionaries. The present chapter shifts the focus to a more personal concern. David had made promises both to Jonathan and to Saul that he would not eradicate their descendants. To Jonathan he had sworn an oath to show him *ḥesed*

---

42. McCarter (1984: 255). See also Armerding (1975), who favours retaining 'priests'. And for an opposing view, see Wenham (1975).

(1 Sam. 20:14–17; see at 2 Sam. 9:1, 3, 6–8).[43] The present chapter describes David's attempt to make good on his promises.

Between David's opening question regarding survivors in the line of Saul (v. 1) and the concluding notice that Jonathan's son Mephibosheth was brought to Jerusalem and treated like one of the king's sons (vv. 11b–13) there are three dialogues. The first and third are with Ziba, a servant in the household of Saul (vv. 2–4 and 9–11a), while the middle conversation takes place between David and Mephibosheth (vv. 5–8). Both Ziba and Mephibosheth will figure again in David's later reign (16:1–4; 19:17, 24–30).

Comment
   1. *David asked, 'Is there anyone still left of the house of Saul to whom I can show kindness [ḥesed] for Jonathan's sake?'* When last we heard David speaking, he was extolling the trustworthiness of Yahweh's promises and offering thanks for the blessing Yahweh had pronounced on David's house (7:27–29). Now, after the narrator's summary in chapter 8 of David's successes against his adversaries round about and of David's key officers, David again speaks. His own house having received kindness from a promise-keeping God, David wishes to keep his promise to his friend Jonathan (1 Sam. 20:14–17, 42; 23:18) and what remains of the house of Saul (1 Sam. 24:20–22). David's beneficence stands in marked contrast to the harsh treatment often meted out against former rivals, both in the Bible (e.g. Judg. 1:6–7; 1 Kgs 15:29) and in the Ancient Near East generally.[44]
   2–5. *Now there was a servant of Saul's household named Ziba* (v. 2). Ziba's character will be developed more fully in his encounters with David during Absalom's revolt (see 16:1–4; 19:17–30). But

---

43. *Ḥesed* is one of those Heb. words that is difficult to capture in a single English synonym, leading to various combinations such as 'lovingkindness', 'covenant loyalty', etc.
44. The later Assyrian king Assurbanipal (669–633) offers a particularly striking example. Speaking of those who opposed him, he boasts, 'I fed their corpses, cut into small pieces, to dogs, pigs, *zíbu*-birds, vultures, the birds of the sky and (also) to the fish of the ocean' (*ANET* 288d).

already in the present context, we detect hints that he may be a savvy operator. Though introduced as a *servant of Saul's household*, his response to David's question *Are you Ziba?* is simply 'Your servant', *'abdekā*. Translations often paraphrase 'Your servant' as *At your service* (NIV, NRSV) or simply 'Yes, sir' (JPS, NLT).

To David's enquiry about survivors from the house of Saul to whom he might show *God's kindness*, Ziba replies, *There is still a son of Jonathan; he is lame in both feet* (v. 3). David has not mentioned Jonathan to Ziba, but their friendship will have been well known. Ziba's singling out of a son of Jonathan gets to the heart of David's concern, while perhaps also accomplishing two things. It leaves unmentioned any others who may yet remain from the house of Saul (see at 21:1–14) and gives the impression that David has nothing to fear from the house of Saul; as someone with a disability, Jonathan's son Mephibosheth (introduced already in 4:4) would be an unlikely contender for the throne, at least by Ancient Near Eastern standards.

After enquiring further of Ziba concerning Mephibosheth's whereabouts (v. 4), *King David had him brought from Lo Debar, from the house of Makir son of Ammiel* (v. 5). The location of *Lo Debar* continues to be debated, but it is likely to be found in Gilead, perhaps not too far from Ish-Bosheth's capital at Mahanaim (see at 2:8).[45] Not to be confused with the Makir son of Manasseh mentioned in Joshua 17:1, *Makir son of Ammiel* appears to have been a man of means, capable not only of hosting Mephibosheth but also of coming to David's aid when he comes to Mahanaim in 2 Samuel 17:27.

6–8. Mephibosheth *came* [willingly?] *to David* (v. 6).[46] His first action is to bow down (lit. fall on his face) and *pay him honour*. Seeing the crippled Mephibosheth's falling face down may have alarmed David and evoked his exclamation *Mephibosheth!* Mephibosheth's reply is the same as Ziba's had been in verse 2, *At your service*, but

---

45. Anderson (1989: 141); cf. McCarter (1984: 256).
46. In v. 5, the initiative was David's; he 'sent' and 'took' (NIV combines the two verbs into *brought*). In v. 6, Mephibosheth *came* to David, which may suggest a certain willingness, or at least compliance with the inevitable.

with the addition of *hinnēh* ('behold'), thus literally 'Behold, your servant'. As a surviving member of the house of Saul, Mephibosheth has reason to fear for his life, but David is quick to reassure him: *Don't be afraid . . . for I will surely show you kindness for the sake of your father Jonathan* (v. 7). The fact that Mephibosheth was but five years old when his father Jonathan died on Mount Gilboa (4:4) and is now a grown man with a son of his own (see 9:12) indicates that years have elapsed since David became king. Thus, David may be faulted perhaps for taking so long in making good on his promises to Jonathan (1 Sam. 18:3–4; 20:14–17, 42; 23:18) and to his father Saul (1 Sam. 24:21–22), but the emphasis in the text is on David's *kindness*, or 'covenanted loyalty' (*ḥesed*), to Jonathan (cf. also at vv. 1 and 3).

David's kindness has two parts. First, as was the prerogative of kings in the Ancient Near East, he makes a land grant to Mephibosheth, restoring to him *the land that belonged to your grandfather Saul*,[47] and, second, he welcomes him to a place of honour at the royal table (v. 7; cf., from a much later period, 2 Kgs 25:29). Mephibosheth's presence in court will of course allow David to keep an eye on him, but for several reasons it seems unjustified to view David's generosity to Mephibosheth as merely self-serving. Mephibosheth himself, as someone with a disability, poses little threat to the throne. Mephibosheth's son, Mika (v. 12), might in due course mount a challenge, but David will have known from his own experience that bringing a potential rival to the royal court hardly lessens the danger – much better, in that case, to leave Mephibosheth and family in relative obscurity in Lo Debar. See further the description in verse 11 of Mephibosheth as eating *at David's table like one of the king's sons*.

Mephibosheth's response is appropriately deferential and self-effacing. Bowing (or still bowing; recall v. 6), he asks, *What is your servant, that you should notice a dead dog like me?* (v. 8). On the expression

---

47. On land grants in ancient Israel, see Ben-Barak (1981). Whether Saul's former lands had been expropriated by others (Ziba?) in the power vacuum following the deaths of Ish-Bosheth and Abner or had simply become the property of the reigning King David is not made clear.

dead dog, see at 1 Samuel 24:14 (David's rhetorical self-reference in his defence of his actions to Saul). Goliath mockingly asks if he is a *dog* when he mistakes the young David with his sling for a mere boy with a stick (1 Sam. 17:43). And Abner, in his heated exchange with Ish-Bosheth, asks if the latter thinks him a *dog's head – on Judah's side* (2 Sam. 3:8).[48]

9–11. Having said what he needed to say to Mephibosheth, *the king summoned Ziba* (v. 9). It is noteworthy that David is referred to as *the king* when in conversation with Ziba, but as *David* when talking to Mephibosheth. This may suggest David's more personal interest in Mephibosheth's welfare, as distinct from his purely formal interaction with Ziba. Ziba, with his *fifteen sons and twenty servants* (v. 10), appears to be a man of some means – had he perhaps taken control of some of Saul's properties? If so, the king reverses that situation by informing Ziba that *everything that belonged to Saul and his family* now belongs to Mephibosheth, *your master's grandson* (v. 9). Ziba's duty is to *farm the land for him and bring in the crops* (v. 10). Whether the crops were to be brought to David's court to supply Mephibosheth's needs (as the MT may suggest) or were meant to supply the household of Mephibosheth beyond the royal court (as the Lucianic recension of LXX intimates) is not entirely clear.[49] In either case, Ziba and his sons and servants are clearly to serve the interests of Mephibosheth and his family. Ziba is in no position to contest the king's decision and submits, but without any show of enthusiasm: *Your servant will do whatever my lord the king commands his servant to do* (v. 11). Later episodes will reveal more about Ziba's attitude towards Mephibosheth (see at 16:1–4; cf. 19:24–30).

So Mephibosheth ate at David's table like one of the king's sons (v. 11). This description suggests a kindly and paternal attitude of David towards Mephibosheth. Only later will the descriptor *like one of the king's sons* lose its lustre, in the light of the behaviours of Amnon, Absalom and Adonijah.

12–13. Only now does the narrator state that *Mephibosheth had a young son named Mika* (v. 12). As noted in the commentary above, this

---

48. For discussion, see Long (2009b: 424).
49. Cf. McCarter (1984: 262), who regards the LXX reading as superior.

young Saulide could in principle pose a danger to David, not least given the fact that *all the members of Ziba's household were servants of Mika's father Mephibosheth*. Perhaps it is to allay such fears that the narrator concludes the story with a reminder of the otherwise redundant notice that *Mephibosheth lived in Jerusalem*, eating always *at the king's table*, and *was lame in both feet* (v. 13). As it happens, Mika will not be mentioned again in Samuel. The house of Saul is essentially finished.[50] As Alter (1999: 243) colourfully remarks: 'King David came into Jerusalem whirling and dancing before the LORD; the surviving Saulide limps into Jerusalem, crippled in both legs.'

Meaning

In this story of the invitation of Mephibosheth to David's court and to his table, we see David seeking to keep his promise to Jonathan (and to Saul) by showing kindness to Jonathan's surviving son. Whether bringing a survivor of the house of Saul into his court was a savvy political move – along the lines of keeping one's enemies close – does not appear to have been of interest to the biblical narrator. Rather, the point seems to be that David's *kindness* (*ḥesed*) to Jonathan's son is an appropriate response to the *kindness* he had experienced from Jonathan and indeed from God (v. 3). Good and generous behaviour and the keeping of promises, emanating from a genuine trust in Yahweh, are in themselves good things. That such behaviours are often rewarded does not justify reading them cynically. There is no suggestion in the text that David's main concern is his own personal welfare; rather, it is that of Mephibosheth. For his part, Mephibosheth receives David's benevolence gratefully. On a political level and in terms of the story of David as it continues to unfold, Halpern (2010: 76 n. 1) maintains that

> the point of 2 Samuel 9 is not only that the Saulide coalition has been smashed, the family eliminated, [and] organized competition for power

---

50. It should be noted that 1 Chr. 8:34–35 (par. 9:40–41) lists four sons born to Mika. So the house of Jonathan and thus also of Saul does survive due to David's kindness to Merib-Baal (Mephibosheth), but as a political power the house of Saul is finished.

in the highlands destroyed, but that the uprising to follow had nothing to do with an attempt at a restoration of a non-Davidic kingship in Israel.

F. David's kindness rebuffed by Hanun (10:1–19)

Context

While David's extension of *kindness* (*ḥesed*) to Mephibosheth in the preceding chapter was gratefully received, his attempt in the present chapter to show the same to Hanun, the new king of the Ammonites, upon the death of his father Nahash is rebuffed in strikingly offensive fashion. The 'vague temporal formula' that introduces the chapter leaves the chronology of the events uncertain (Alter 1999: 244). In terms of literary structuring, the return to the Ammonite war at the end of chapter 12 will serve to frame the story of David's great lapse in chapter 11 and his eventual repentance in chapter 12. The framing Ammonite war, where David's *kindness* is displayed to a neighbouring people, contrasts markedly with his abuse of his own people in the Bathsheba–Uriah episode. As Birch (1998: 1279) remarks: 'There is a sad and ironic contrast between David's willingness to go to war to defend an insult to his *ḥesed* (ch. 10) and his subsequent willingness to abandon *ḥesed* to his subjects by committing adultery and murder.'

Comment

1–5. *In the course of time, the king of the Ammonites died* (v. 1). The Ammonites and their general location and lineage were discussed briefly at 1 Samuel 11:1. There, the aggression of their king Nahash provided an opportunity for Saul to prove himself on the eve of his kingship. Once defeated by Saul, King Nahash apparently established more friendly relations with David, as evidenced by David's proposal to *show kindness to Hanun son of Nahash, just as his father showed kindness to me* (v. 2). Perhaps Nahash had shown kindness to David during the latter's years on the run from Saul; a common adversary can occasion unlikely alliances.[51] Whether there was a

---

51. Alternatively, Brueggemann (1990: 269) contends that following Saul's victory 'the Ammonites must have been subservient to Israel' and that

formal (covenantal) relationship between David and Nahash is not certain, though the *kindness* (*ḥesed*) language may be suggestive of a formalized relationship. As already noted, reference to David's desire to show *ḥesed* links this episode to the preceding one, where he had shown *ḥesed* to Mephibosheth (9:1, 3, 7).

However laudable David's motives may have been in sending a delegation to Hanun, *the Ammonite commanders* take a cynical view (v. 3), and Hanun responds by humiliating David's envoys. He *shaved off half of each man's beard, cut off their garments at the buttocks, and sent them away* (v. 4). In the iconography of the Ancient Near East, Israelite men are typically shown with beards (Gruber 2000: 643). That Hanun should shave off half the beards of the envoys in a grotesque fashion (probably vertically) was an insult to their manhood. Moreover, as beards were sometimes voluntarily shaved to express mourning (Isa. 15:2; Jer. 41:4–5; 48:37), Hanun's removal of but half the beard mocks the sincerity of David's stated intention to *express . . . sympathy* by sending emissaries. As if that were not enough, Hanun has the envoys' diplomatic robes[52] cut in half (whether vertically or horizontally is unclear) exposing the buttocks, a form of symbolic emasculation sometimes suffered by prisoners of war (Isa. 20:4).

Sensitive to the humiliation of his envoys, David instructs them to *Stay at Jericho till your beards have grown, and then come back* (v. 5). Jericho would have been one of the first sites that the returning envoys would encounter and would have been sparsely populated,[53] thus limiting the number of people observing the envoys' humiliation.

(note 51 *cont.*) David's initiative in sending envoys was to 'reaffirm his dominance of Ammon' after the death of Nahash.

52. NIV's *their garments* renders Heb. *madwêhem* (root *mad* I; so *DCH*), which is not the common word for 'garments' (*bĕgādîm*). Alter (1999: 245) suggests that some kind of official 'garb' is in view both here and in 1 Sam. 17:38 (where the reference is to Saul's battle garb).

53. According to Josh. 6:20–24, Jericho was destroyed in the time of Joshua and not substantially rebuilt until the reign of King Ahab, when Hiel's attempt to rebuild the city fulfilled the curse Joshua had pronounced on the site (1 Kgs 16:34; cf. Josh. 6:26).

6–14. The Ammonites' shameful treatment of David's envoys was tantamount to a declaration of war, and they quickly realized *that they had become obnoxious to David* (v. 6), just as on an earlier occasion Israel had *become obnoxious to the Philistines* by virtue of Jonathan's attack on the Philistine outpost at Geba (1 Sam. 13:3–4). The root *b'š* ('be odious, make oneself odious') is used four times in Samuel. In addition to the two occurrences just mentioned, it is used in 1 Samuel 27:12, where Achish trusts David because he believes him to have made himself obnoxious (or odious) to the people of Israel, and in 2 Samuel 16:21, where Ahithophel urges Absalom to sleep with David's concubines and thereby make himself *obnoxious to your father*. The sense in all four cases involves an irrevocable act of defiance.

The Ammonites quickly realize that their defiance of David will not be ignored, so they set about hiring reinforcements from their northern neighbours in Transjordan. The Bible makes frequent reference to such coalitions, which were common in the Ancient Near East. Some were based on a common threat, while others, as here, involved payment. The territories in verse 6 are listed from the more northerly to the more southerly: *Beth Rehob* and *Zobah* lay far to the north in what would today be Lebanon; *Maakah* lay south of Mount Hermon; and *Tob* lay nearest to Ammon itself.[54]

The battle formations described in verses 7–8 find Joab and David's *fighting men* caught between two hostile forces. The Ammonites are *in battle formation at the entrance of their city gate* (the city is assumedly Rabbah, modern Amman), the mercenaries of Aram, Tob and Maakah are *in the open country*, and Israel is in between. To be forced to fight on two fronts is never ideal (Herzog and Gichon 1997: 107). Whether or not Joab was guilty of a tactical error in allowing himself to be caught in this position, as suggested by Yadin (1955: 347–350), he quickly devises a strategic response to fight on both fronts (vv. 9–11): Abishai is to engage the Ammonites, while Joab will face the probably more daunting Aramean mercenaries. Should either Abishai or Joab find himself in trouble,

---

54. On these territories, see 8:3, 5 and notes. For more detail, see McCarter (1984: 271–272).

the other is to come to his aid. The strategy is risky but, in the end, successful (vv. 13–14).

More remarkable than this brief description of battle strategy and outcome is Joab's explicitly theological exhortation in verse 12. Joab is known mostly for his ruthless political pragmatism, so this glimpse of an element of faith in Joab is worth noting. Baldwin's description of Joab as 'a believer' (1988: 246) goes beyond what we can ascertain from the text. But Joab's acknowledgment that *The LORD will do what is good in his sight* is not to be discounted. It echoes Eli's submissive utterance in 1 Samuel 3:18, which we interpreted as a sign of spiritual reawakening in Eli. Overall, as Firth (2009: 410) remarks, 'Such expressions are more typical of David than Joab', but 'this is part of a process of character reversals running through chs. 10–12, where David becomes a murderer, Joab expresses piety and a Hittite is the most faithful Yahwist of all'.

Joab succeeds in putting the Arameans to flight (v. 13), which in turn contributes to Abishai's success against the Ammonites, who scurry *inside the city* (v. 14). That Joab *returned from fighting the Ammonites and came to Jerusalem*, but apparently without actually capturing Rabbah, leaves that task for another occasion (see 11:1; 12:26–29).

15–19. The Arameans live to fight another day, and that is precisely what they do in verse 15, regrouping under the leadership of *Hadadezer* (see at 8:3). Hadadezer gathers more Arameans *from beyond the River Euphrates* (v. 16). That no solicitation by Hadadezer is mentioned suggests that the Arameans beyond the river were at the time subject to him, a fact confirmed in verse 19. *Shobak* (Shophak in the parallel in 1 Chr. 19:18) served as *the commander of Hadadezer's army*, just as Joab served as commander of David's army. The gathered Aramean forces *went to Helam*, a Transjordanian town or region north of Ammonite territory (Thompson 1992: 116–117).

When David was told of this, he himself *gathered all Israel, crossed the Jordan and went to Helam* (v. 17). David's personal leadership in this instance anticipates a contrast with 11:1, where David sends Joab while remaining at leisure in Jerusalem. The Arameans suffer heavy losses at David's hands: *David killed seven hundred of their charioteers* (Heb. *rekeb* can mean 'chariot' or 'charioteer') and *forty thousand*[55] *of their foot soldiers* (MT reads *pārāšîm*, 'horsemen'; NIV follows the Lucianic recension of LXX in reading *foot soldiers* [attested also in MT 1 Chr. 19:18, *'îš raglî*]). David's resounding victory over Hadadezer's forces triggers a political realignment, and the former *vassals of Hadadezer* become subject to David and the Israelites. The Ammonites will no longer be able to look to the Arameans for help (v. 19). David's multi-tiered kingdom – comprising heartland, conquered territories and subject allies – continues to expand (see Long 2009b: 457).

Meaning
On the one hand, the present chapter shows how David's kingdom continued to gain strength against neighbouring peoples, even though David's actions were not in the first instance aggressive. His initial actions were meant to be conciliatory and consoling to Hanun on the occasion of his father's death. Only Hanun's rebuff of David's kindness and his hiring of reinforcements from his Aramean neighbours led to David's taking the field against him. On the other hand, however, the chapter serves another function in its current literary context. In the present chapter, Joab shows himself to be an astute military strategist. Therefore, Joab's loss of men in the next chapter (ch. 11), pointedly including Uriah, cannot be attributed to a strategic blunder, as the narrative makes painfully clear. For David's part, in the present chapter he shows initiative in gathering forces and leading them to victory in battle (vv. 17–18). In the light of his proactivity in chapter 10, his laxity in chapter 11, staying behind in Jerusalem and sending others out to fight his battles, is disconcerting.[56]

---

55. On large numbers in the OT, see at 1 Sam. 4:2.
56. Alter (1999: 246) notes Polzin's puzzlement at all the dividing of things in the chapter (beards, garb, troops on both sides) and himself wonders if 'this narrative dynamic of mitosis ... might be a thematic introduction to all the inner divisions in court and nation, the fractures in the house of David, that take up the rest of the narrative'. If there is anything to be said for this very subtle suggestion, one should add that the most serious dividedness of all will show itself in David's own actions.

7. DAVID'S SIN AND ITS CONSEQUENCES (11:1 – 20:26)

David's sin and abuse of power in 2 Samuel 11 mark a major turning point in his narrative portrayal and, indeed, in his life. While it may not be quite right to describe David after chapter 11 as David under God's curse (so Carlson 1964), there can be little doubt that his sins of adultery, murder and attempted cover-up leave him stunned and stumbling for a time – a long time. Even before this turning point, David is not presented as a flawless hero. He is a man of many failures, but still a man of deep faith. The sobering story recounted in chapter 11 of David's abusive treatment of Bathsheba and Uriah (and even to some extent of Joab) and the stories that follow this abuse offer a window into the scarring effects of moral failure and the abuse of power. But these stories also offer a window into the nature of true repentance and of the profound grace of God.

A. Sin and reconciliation (11:1 – 12:31)

i. *David's sin (11:1–27)*
Context
To this point in the narrative, things have gone reasonably well for David. His house has waxed stronger and stronger, as Saul's has

waned (3:1). His kingdom is now firmly established (5:12; ch. 7), while Saul's is no more. David has arrived. He has had challenges along the way, not least during his years on the run from a rejected monarch bent on ensuring that David not succeed him. But, through it all Yahweh has been 'with David'. For his part, David has sometimes faltered. His deceptive audience with Ahimelek (if that is what it was) proved very costly to the priests at Nob (1 Sam. 21; cf. 22:22). His desire to kill not just Nabal but all the males of his family was forestalled only by the timely intervention of Abigail (1 Sam. 25). His despondency in 1 Samuel 27:1 landed him in Philistine territory where he callously duped his Philistine benefactor and conducted (apparently unsanctioned) pillaging raids on non-Israelite populations in and to the south of the territory of Israel, leaving no survivors (men or women) to report his actions (1 Sam. 27:10–12). Behaviours such as these suggest that David on occasion failed to give due weight to Yahweh and, instead, took matters into his own hands. But, by and large, David's life to this point has been characterized by trust and loyalty towards Yahweh. Such trust enabled him to defeat the Philistine champion Goliath (1 Sam. 17) and to resist killing Saul even when given opportunities to do so (1 Sam. 24:6–7; 26:9–11).

So, despite the ups and downs, David's life has been blessed, and his heart for God evident. But this is about to change. After an opening exposition that sets the stage (v. 1), 2 Samuel 11 follows an orderly narration of David's disorderly conduct: his adultery with Bathsheba (vv. 1–5), his two attempts to manipulate her husband Uriah so as to cover up his misdeeds (vv. 6–11 and 12–13), his use of Joab to eliminate the uncooperative Uriah (vv. 14–21) and his callous response to the report that Uriah is dead (vv. 22–25). The final verses recount Bathsheba's period of mourning, David's taking her as wife and the Lord's response to all that has transpired (vv. 26–27).

Comment

1. *In the spring, at the time when kings go off to war, David sent Joab*, but he himself *remained in Jerusalem.* The opening verse seems straightforward enough, setting the stage for David's dramatic fall in the episode to follow. While Joab and *the whole Israelite army* take the

field against the Ammonites, David inexplicably and contrary to his custom (e.g. 5:2; 10:17) remains behind. As straightforward as the opening verse may seem, it does involve textual complexities that have given rise to different readings. First, while most translations assume the correct reading to be *kings* (*mĕlākîm*), the Hebrew text actually has 'the messengers' (*hammal'akîm*). Second, *In the spring* reads literally 'at the (re)turn of the year' (cf. JPS). These two features have led some (e.g. Fokkelman 1981: 1.50–51) to suggest that the verse is speaking of the first anniversary of David's sending messengers to express his condolences to the Ammonite king Hanun, on which occasion they were shamefully treated (10:2–4).[1] In favour of the more traditional understanding, however, is the fact that springtime was the typical time for military initiatives in the ANE (cf. 1 Kgs 20:22, 26, where the same Heb. expression, 'turn of the year', is used for 'spring')[2] and was viewed as the beginning of the new year (see Long 2009b: 457–458). Perhaps MT's 'the messengers' is simply a textual corruption (the extant versions and the parallel verse in 1 Chr. 20:1 attest 'kings'). But it is also possible that the narrator wishes a kind of double entendre: instead of fulfilling his duties by doing what 'kings' are supposed to do, David remains in Jerusalem, taking his ease and sending 'messengers' to do his bidding (e.g. see v. 4).[3] David will, in fact, do a lot of sending in chapter 11.[4]

---

1. Garsiel (1993: 251–252) maintains that the reference is most likely to the kings of the Syrian alliance that had failed in its attempt to help the Ammonites (10:15–19).
2. Gordon (1986: 252) notes that the month of March, which in our calendar marks the beginning of spring, is named after Mars, the Roman god of war.
3. Cf. Alter (1999: 249–250): 'What some see here as a scribal error may well be a deliberate orthographic pun.'
4. The Heb. verb *šlḥ* ('send') occurs more frequently in ch. 11 (i.e. 12x) than anywhere else in the OT. The verb also occurs with some frequency in ch. 10 (8x; perhaps preparing the reader for ch. 11) and again significantly in ch. 12, where the Lord (2x) and Joab (1x) do the sending.

Verse 1 ends by contrasting the activity of Joab and *the whole Israelite army* (lit. 'all Israel') with the passivity of David. Having *destroyed the Ammonites*, Joab and company *besieged* their capital city, *Rabbah* (mod. Amman), which lies some 24 miles east of the Jordan River a little north of the latitude of Jericho. David, by contrast, simply *remained* [lit. 'was sitting'] *in Jerusalem*.

2–5. The impression that David is simply idling in Jerusalem is confirmed in verse 2: *One evening David got up from his bed*. Earlier, in 2 Samuel 4:5, Ish-Bosheth was described as taking a *noonday rest* (lit. 'bed of noonday', *miškab haṣṣohŏrayim*). Ish-Bosheth's bed was mentioned twice more: in 4:7 in the account of his murder and in 4:11 in David's incensed response. Now we find David arising from his bed in the evening (!) to succumb to temptations that will infringe upon another man's bed and result in the man's murder. The next explicit mention of bed (*miškab*) comes in 11:13, where Uriah refuses David's urging to refresh himself with his wife and, instead, goes out *to sleep on his mat* [*miškab*] *among his master's servants*.

Having arisen in the evening, David *walked around on the roof* (the hitpa'el of *hlk* can suggest a kind of to-ing and fro-ing). A roof was mentioned once before, in 1 Samuel 9:25–26, but apart from that and the present context, the word *gag* ('roof') occurs elsewhere in Samuel only in 2 Samuel 16:22 (where Absalom violates David's concubines) and in 18:24, where David's sentinel (watchman) espies *a man running alone*, bringing news of Absalom's death.

From the roof he saw a woman washing. The phrase *From the roof* is omitted in the Syriac translation and is perhaps an unnecessary notice, as the reader already knows that David is on the roof of his house/palace. Hebrew syntax also allows the sentence to be read 'he saw a woman washing on the roof' (that is, on the roof of her house; cf. R. J. Williams 2007: §323a). The striking beauty of the woman attracts David's attention, and he sends (verb *šlḥ*) *someone to find out about her*. Undeterred by the discovery that *She is Bathsheba, the daughter of Eliam*[5] *and the wife of Uriah the Hittite*'(v. 3), David *sent* [verb *šlḥ*] *messengers to get her* (lit. 'and he took her') (v. 4). What

---

5. Eliam is elsewhere mentioned only at 2 Sam. 23:34, as the son of Ahithophel the Gilonite. The notice here is significant.

follows is rapidly reported, with no exploration of the feelings involved: she came, he lay with her, and she went home, discovered that she was pregnant and notified David (lit. 'she sent [verb *šlḥ*] and told David'). In the midst of this chain of events is a parenthetical notice (indicated by the word order in Hebrew) explaining that *she was purifying herself from her monthly uncleanness*. If, as seems likely, the reference is to a post-menstruation purification ritual such as is described in Leviticus 15:19–24, this notice leaves no doubt about the paternity of the child conceived. David, nevertheless, immediately sets about trying to obscure that very issue.[6]

6–11. *So David sent this word to Joab: 'Send me Uriah the Hittite'* (v. 6). When Uriah arrives, David makes several general enquiries regarding the state of the soldiers and of the war (v. 7), and then he gets to the point: *Go down to your house and wash your feet* (v. 8). Whether or not *wash your feet* involves a double entendre suggesting not simply the customary refreshment of washing after a journey but also the sexual enjoyment of one's wife,[7] Uriah's remark in verse 11 will show that he understands what is implied. In this first encounter with David, however, Uriah utters no reply but simply 'goes out' from the *palace* (lit. 'house of the king'), while *a gift from the king* 'goes out' *after him* (v. 8; the verb is *yṣ'* in both clauses).

The notion of a gift 'going out' after someone is a bit odd, and the suggestion has been made that *maś'at hammelek* (usually rendered 'gift of the king') should in fact be rendered 'spy of the king'.[8] Evidence for reading *maś'at* as 'spy' is modest at best. With its relation

---

6. The narrator reveals nothing of the inner thoughts of David or Bathsheba, leaving some to speculate regarding Bathsheba's potential complicity in the affair. Garsiel (1993: 253–256), however, notes textual and historical considerations that support the idea that Bathsheba is but 'a tragic figure involuntarily caught up in events' (256). Garsiel's observations, though speculative, carry some force.
7. Cf. Yee (1988: 245); for discussion and bibliography, see Gordon (1986: 254); Youngblood (2009: 434); Vannoy (2009: 338–339).
8. Kim and Nyengele (2003: 107) cite Bailey (1990: 97–98) as making this argument.

to the verb *nś'*, 'to lift', the noun *maś'ēt* can refer to something lifted up, like a gift or offering, or perhaps to someone who lifts (or raises) an alarm, like a spy. Both the verb and the noun occur together in Jeremiah 6:1, in a context where the sense must mean something like 'raise a signal'.[9] The purpose of a spy going out after Uriah, if that is what happened, may have been to discover whether Uriah did in fact go home, or perhaps even to catch him in a military-cultic infraction[10] and thereby to find grounds for eliminating him (cf. Firth 2008: 325). In the present context, 'gift' seems to be the more likely surface meaning (cf. Gen. 43:34, where the term occurs three times in the sense of 'gift' or 'portion'), but the narrator's curious word choices may suggest yet another double entendre – whether it was a 'gift' or a 'spy' that 'went out' after Uriah, David's sole concern is to cover up his crime, whatever the cost to Uriah.[11]

When David discovers that *Uriah did not go home*, he presses the issue: *Haven't you just come from a military campaign? Why didn't you go home?* (v. 10). NIV's *military campaign* is an overtranslation of the Hebrew word *derek*, which literally means 'way' or 'journey'. David would likely wish to avoid explicitly military terms, lest these bring to mind the strictures regarding soldiers keeping themselves from women during military campaigns. It is better to follow most translations in reading 'journey' here.

Uriah's response to David's urging is unequivocal: so long as the ark and the armies of Israel and Judah are with Joab in the field, it

---

9. Extra-biblically, the noun appears on one of the Lachish ostraca (*KAI* 194: 10) with the meaning 'signal fire' (*NIDOTTE* 2: 1105).
10. First Sam. 21:5 (cf. Exod. 19:15; Deut. 23:9–10) supports the notion that soldiers on active duty were to abstain from sexual activity.
11. Cole (2015) suggests that the gift (which he regards as rich fare from the king's table) is personified in the text as a seductress seeking to prove Uriah's undoing. My student Mike Evanson moots the possibility that a gift 'going out after' Uriah could have involved a procession that would attract public attention and thus confirm Uriah's home visit; such a scheme would have backfired, however, as in the event Uriah did not go home.

would be reprehensible to *go to my house to eat and drink and make love to my wife* (v. 11). We are left in the dark as to whether Uriah had heard of David's activities in his absence,[12] but whether wittingly or unwittingly, Uriah's loyalty to his covenant duty exposes David's own deplorable behaviour.

12–13. David's first attempt to use Uriah to cover his own sin failed, so David tries a less subtle approach. He convinces Uriah to remain another day in Jerusalem (v. 12), then plies him with wine until he *made him drunk* (v. 13). But even inebriated, Uriah *did not go home*. David's sole concern is that Uriah go and 'lie with' (*škb*) his wife. Twice, immediately following David's urgings, the verb *škb* ('to lie with') is used with Uriah as subject. In verse 13b, we even read that he went out in the evening 'to sleep in his own bed [*liškab běmiškābô*] with . . .' The reader might be forgiven for thinking that David's plan is about to succeed; surely the next words will be 'his wife'. But in both verse 9 and verse 13 we quickly discover that Uriah *did not go down to his house*. Instead, he bedded down with *his master's servants* (v. 13b). As Ackroyd (1977: 102) pithily remarks, 'Uriah drunk is more pious than David sober.'

14–21. With his two attempts to manipulate Uriah having failed, David takes a more direct approach. *In the morning David wrote a letter to Joab and sent it with Uriah* (v. 14). A callous and cynical act, it was nevertheless cunning. Even should Uriah suspect that the contents of the letter (disclosed to the reader in v. 15) would prove his undoing, there was nothing he could do. If he opened the letter (which would likely have been bound with string and sealed with wax bearing the impression of the king's own seal), this would surely be discovered, and his life would be forfeit. Alternatively, if he tried to desert his duties by fleeing, the result would be the same as soon as he was caught.

The hardened Joab (see at 3:38–39) wastes no time in putting Uriah *at a place where he knew the strongest* [Ammonite] *defenders were*

---

12. Given the messengers involved in David's 'taking' of Bathsheba and her reporting back of her pregnancy, it is not unlikely that Uriah heard some palace 'whisperings' (cf. 12:19).

(v. 16). This was part of David's instruction, namely, to put Uriah *out in front where the fighting is fiercest* (v. 15). The second part of David's command, namely, that you (plural) *withdraw from [Uriah] so that he will be struck down and die* (v. 15), appears not to have been followed by Joab. He will likely have realized that to withdraw suddenly from Uriah would arouse suspicion (cf. Alter 1999: 254). No matter: Joab's modified plan works, though at the cost of more lives than just Uriah's (v. 17). Nothing is said of Joab's feelings about any of this, but then the whole episode says next to nothing about anyone's feelings, whether David's, Bathsheba's, Uriah's or those of any of the other agents caught up in David's machinations.

Aware that David may take exception to the collateral damage suffered in ensuring that Uriah's death not look suspicious, Joab carefully instructs his *messenger* about what to say should his *full account of the battle* arouse David's anger. He is simply to say, *Moreover* [Heb. *gam*, 'also'], *your servant Uriah the Hittite is dead* (v. 21). In the course of his instruction (vv. 20–21), Joab also demonstrates his detailed knowledge of the story of *Abimelek son of Jerub-Besheth* (Gideon)[13] and thus of the dangers of drawing too close to defended city walls (see Judg. 9:50–53). Is Joab concerned that his reputation as a military strategist not be besmirched by the losses recently suffered?

22–25. *The messenger set out* and dutifully reported to David *everything Joab had sent him to say* (v. 22). He appears also to have embellished Joab's words, perhaps unaware of the fact that mentioning Uriah's demise would suffice to answer any objection David might have to the conduct of the battle. After joining battle in the open, Israel drove their foes *back to the entrance of the city gate* (v. 23). This leads to the notice that *some* [unspecified number] *of the king's*

---

13. Note mongrelization to *Jerub-Besheth* (LXX attests Jerub-ba'al). The name of the judge Gideon is changed to Jerub-Baal ('let Baal contend'?) in MT of Judg. 6:32, and that name is used for Gideon frequently in the remainder of the book of Judges. It appears again in Samuel's speech in 1 Sam. 12:11, while here in 2 Sam. 11:21 'shame' is substituted for 'Baal'.

men died. The point of it all, whether the messenger sensed it or not, is that David's *servant Uriah the Hittite is dead* (v. 24).[14] Unless we adopt LXX's longer reading of verse 22 or the lengthy expansion of Josephus (*Ant.* 7.142–143), there is nothing to suggest that David reacted negatively to the message, as Joab had feared that he might. Instead, David tells the messenger to encourage Joab with the words *Don't let this upset you* (lit. 'don't let this matter be evil in your eyes'), adding that *the sword devours one as well as another* (v. 25). Given the circumstances, David's assertion that the casualties of war are random is outrageously hypocritical. *Press the attack against the city and destroy it* (v. 25). Now that David's private business has been taken care of, Joab can return to the military business at hand.

26–27. *When Uriah's wife heard that her husband* [*'îšāh*, 'her man/husband'] *was dead, she mourned for him* (*baʿlāh*, 'her husband/master'). The Hebrew uses two different nouns for Bathsheba's spouse in this sentence. Some English translations (e.g. ESV, JPS, NKJV, NASB) translate both as 'husband', creating a stylistic redundancy, while others (e.g. NIV, NLT, NRSV) reduce the second noun to the pronoun 'him'. In the Hebrew, the multiplication of spousal terms makes David's crossing of marital boundaries excruciatingly clear, as does the reference to Bathsheba simply as *Uriah's wife*. It is noteworthy that after her initial identification in verse 3 as *Bathsheba, the daughter of Eliam and the wife of Uriah the Hittite*, the name Bathsheba is not mentioned again until 12:24. In the interim, she is described simply as the woman, or the wife of Uriah, or by the feminine pronoun. The narrator's choice and ordering of designations for Bathsheba underscore David's transgressions which pervade the section (cf. Petter 2004).

While Bathsheba's feelings for Uriah are not stated, she does mourn for him, assumedly the customary seven days (cf. Gen.

---

14. Two apparent Heb. misspellings in v. 24 (both involving an unexpected aleph: *wayyōʾrû* [they shot arrows] and *hammōrĕʾîm* [the archers]) may be suggestive of a rustic dialect spoken by the messenger (cf. Zahavi-Ely 2012), or may echo the name of Uriah (*ʾûriyyâ*), or both.

50:10; 1 Sam. 31:13).[15] *After the time of mourning was over, David had her brought to his house* (the latter clause is literally, 'David sent and collected her to his house'). No longer Uriah's wife, *she became his wife* [though not his first; see at 3:2–5] *and bore him a son* (v. 27).

Throughout the chapter, Yahweh has not been mentioned once, but he gets the last word: *But the thing David had done displeased the LORD* (lit. 'was evil in the eyes of Yahweh').[16] David may have encouraged Joab not to let *this* (i.e. the deaths of Uriah and others) 'be evil in your eyes' (v. 25), but it is Yahweh's appraisal that counts. David has broken at least four of the Ten Commandments (Exod. 20:2–17; Deut. 5:6–21): the sixth, murder; the seventh, adultery; the ninth, false testimony; and the tenth, coveting one's neighbour's wife. And, of course, underlying all these abuses of his fellow human beings is contempt for Yahweh and his word (see 12:9).

Meaning

The tragic episode recounted in 2 Samuel 11 illustrates two fundamental verities. First, success poses dangers. As Friedrich Nietzsche famously observed, 'We seldom break our leg so long as life continues a toilsome upward climb. The danger comes when we begin to take things easily and choose the convenient paths.' David seems to have been at his best when he was in the wilderness and in danger. Once settled in his palace, David appears to have begun 'tak[ing] things easily'. His very success placed him in greater danger than he could have suspected. Second, then, David's experience teaches that prayerful vigilance is needed, especially for those who 'have arrived'. No-one is immune from the temptation to do

---

15. Persons of particular prominence were sometimes mourned for longer periods – Aaron and Moses each for thirty days (Num. 20:29; Deut. 34:8, respectively) and Jacob for seventy (Gen. 50:3).
16. For a nuanced discussion of the ambiguities involved in identifying precisely what *the thing* (*haddabar*) is that Yahweh finds evil, see Firth (2008). He concludes that it was David's two-pronged attack on Uriah involving, first, David's adultery with Uriah's wife and, second, his murder of Uriah.

evil. Sin crouches at the door (cf. Gen. 4:7), even (or perhaps especially) at the door of a palace.

ii. *David's repentance (12:1–31)*
Context

David's sins of the preceding chapter cannot be overlooked, least of all by a holy God of justice. But this same God is rich in mercy, and so he devises ways to be both just and the justifier of those who turn to him in repentance and trust (cf. Rom. 3:26). In the present chapter, the Lord sends a prophet, Nathan, to bring David to his senses. God might simply have thundered condemnation for David and forced him to his knees. But instead he sends a prophet to tell a tale of two men, one rich and one poor. There is great mercy in this indirect approach. As we shall see, it enables David not simply to understand but to feel the gravity of his own sin. Such remorse is a gift.

Like the preceding chapter, this one tells a coherent and (probably) sequential story. It begins with the Lord's sending Nathan to entrap David with a parable and to elicit from him an outraged response (vv. 1–6). Then comes the surprise revelation, a surprise at least for David: *You are the man!* (vv. 7–12). David's response is genuine repentance (vv. 13–14) followed by his intercession for the child dying as a result of David's selfish actions (vv. 15–23). As the chapter nears its close, the Lord blesses David and Bathsheba with another child (vv. 24–25), and David returns to his royal duties (vv. 26–31).

Comment

1–6. *The LORD sent Nathan to David* (v. 1). If David did most of the sending in the preceding chapter, it is now Yahweh himself who does the sending. Both Bathsheba and Uriah had 'come to David' at David's bidding. Now Nathan 'comes to David' at God's bidding to tell the tale of two very different men, one rich and powerful, the other poor and vulnerable. Nathan tells David of a poor man who had but one little ewe lamb that *grew up with him and his children . . . shared his food, drank from his cup and even slept in his arms.* This little lamb was *like a daughter to him* (v. 3). The activities of eating, drinking and sleeping in someone's arms recall Uriah's refusal in the preceding chapter to do precisely these things with his wife (11:11). Furthermore, the Hebrew word *daughter* (Heb. *bat*) echoes the first element in the name Bathsheba. Somehow David misses these and other hints that Nathan's story is not a straightforward judicial case. Perhaps, as Alter (1999: 257) suggests, David's judgment is clouded by a kind of 'compensatory zeal' to do the right thing, since he has done such very wrong things in the recent past.

The prophet Nathan was first introduced in chapter 7. There he was Yahweh's prophetic spokesman in proclaiming the good news that David's house and throne would endure for ever. But prophets were not always bearers of good news. As intermediaries between Yahweh and Israel's kings (see at 1 Sam. 10:1; 15:1), prophets sometimes had to speak words of rebuke and judgment. Such was Nathan's sober duty in the present circumstance. There is mercy in Yahweh's sending Nathan, however. Nathan's words put an end to David's cover-up attempts. And they are delivered in such a way as to evoke an emotional response from David. *David burned with anger against the man.* So incensed is David that he first pronounces *the [rich] man* worthy of death: *the man who did this must die!* (v. 5). Perhaps this first expostulation was the ancient equivalent of 'that man ought to be shot!' For David immediately reduces the sentence: *He must pay for that lamb four times over* (v. 6).[17] This was the penalty for sheep theft stated in the law (see Exod. 22:1).

7–12. The mercy in all this is that David's visceral reaction to the crime of the rich man positions him emotionally also to 'feel' the heinousness of his own crimes when Nathan's courageous indictment is finally spoken (v. 7a). Just two words in Hebrew (*'attâ hā'îš*), Nathan's *You are the man!* is followed by words of elaboration that bear all the hallmarks of a prophetic judgment speech.[18] The so-called 'messenger formula', *This is what the* LORD, *the God of Israel, says,* is followed by a description of Yahweh's beneficence towards David: he chose him to be king – *I anointed you* – and protected him

---

17. On early speculations that David himself suffered four-fold retribution in the violent fate of four of his own children, see note below on v. 14.
18. For the formal features of a judgment speech, see 'Context' section at 1 Sam. 2:27–36.

on his way to becoming king – *I delivered you from the hand of Saul* (v. 7b). Moreover, *I gave . . . your master's wives into your arms* (v. 8).

We must pause briefly over the comment about wives in verse 8, as it seems troubling to modern sensibilities. Is the Lord approving and enabling polygamy? The short answer is 'no'. Rather, 'this statement (indeed all of ch. 12) should be read in the context of power – its use and abuse – and not as a comment on the (im)propriety of polygamy' (Long 2009b: 460). In ANE polities, diplomatic relations were often sealed by marriages with foreign princesses. To take over a former king's house meant to take responsibility for its persons, including sometimes the king's wives – or widows, as in the case of Saul. The Samuel narrative mentions but one wife of Saul, Ahinoam (1 Sam. 14:50), and one concubine, Rizpah (2 Sam. 3:7), though he may have had more.[19]

The point at issue in the present passage is not polygamy but power and its abuse. But isn't the statement that Yahweh *would have given you even more* (v. 8) tantamount to an endorsement of polygamy? Again, the answer is 'no'. This acknowledgment of Yahweh's sovereignty in human affairs no more expresses endorsement than does the use of the same phrase in verse 11 in respect of Absalom's predicted violation of David's concubines: *Before your very eyes I will take your wives and give them to one who is close to you, and he will sleep with your wives in broad daylight* (fulfilled in 16:21–22). As Davidson (2007: 205) notes, this is 'a case of divine accommodation in the use of language, to describe God's permissive will, in which God is said to do what he allows'.[20] Polygamy is never presented in the Old Testament as desirable.

---

19. On the distinction between Saul's wife Ahinoam and David's wife of the same name, see comment at 1 Sam. 25:43. Rizpah will figure prominently in 2 Sam. 21.
20. On pp. 177–212, Davidson offers a thorough discussion of monogamy versus polygamy in the OT. After canvassing the thirty-three cases of polygamy in the OT – a relatively modest number of instances in view of the 'approximately three thousand men mentioned in the scriptural record' (210) – Davidson concludes that the narratives describing polygamous situations invariably include 'tacit condemnation of these

The point in the present passage is that Yahweh had provided David with everything he could possibly need to rule well, so that it was a great wickedness indeed for David to defraud and destroy those whom he was to shepherd. It can be argued that David's greatest sin in the current episode, even more than adultery and murder, was his usurping of the Lord's rightful place in providing for David's needs (cf. Janzen 2012). *Why did you despise the word of the LORD by doing what is evil in his eyes?* (v. 9). *Despise* (*bzh*) recalls the programmatic word of judgment spoken against the house of Eli: *Those who honour me I will honour, but those who despise* [*bzh*] *me will be disdained* (1 Sam. 2:30). David's actions entail a serious 'underweighting' (dishonouring) of Yahweh, and create a dilemma. How will Yahweh maintain his promises to David (ch. 7) while at the same time proving himself just and protecting his own honour?[21]

The 'accusation' section of the judgment speech now complete, the 'announcement of judgment' is introduced with the standard formula *we'attâ* (rendered *Now, therefore* in NIV). David's house will be plagued with violence – *the sword shall never depart from your house* (v. 10) – and sexual sin (v. 11) for all to see (v. 12).

13–14. *I have sinned against the LORD* (v. 13). David's confession is immediate, succinct and precise in its focus. David is of course aware of his sins against Bathsheba and Uriah, but he understands that all such abuse of people begins with a decision to defy their Maker (cf. Prov. 14:31; 17:5). David's genuine repentance[22] is met with divine forgiveness: *The LORD has taken away your sin. You are not going to die* (v. 13). As both the preceding and the following verses make clear, however, even forgiven sin can have devastating ripple

---

practices... Thus, although the OT shows the departure from the Edenic model of sexuality in actual practice, this departure is not approved by God, with both narrative and legislation condemning practices that violate the monogamous Edenic norm' (211).

21. I am indebted to my student Jared Power for highlighting the promise versus honour dilemma of ch. 12
22. Contrast Saul's confessions in 1 Sam. 15:24–25, 30. According to its superscription, Psalm 51 offers a fuller picture of David's contrition in the present circumstance.

effects. David's life is spared, but the calamity he has brought on his house will unfold tragically as the narrative continues, beginning with the death of the son conceived in his illicit liaison with Bathsheba (v. 14). That three more of David's children die violent deaths has led to a very old speculation that the four deaths constitute David's own four-fold repayment for his crimes (see v. 6).[23] At the heart of David's sin, as suggested already, was his showing *utter contempt for the LORD* (v. 14).[24]

15–23. The first consequence of David's sin is that, as prophesied in verse 14, *the child that Uriah's wife had borne to David . . . became ill*. This child's illness is attributed to the fact that Yahweh *struck the child* (v. 15). David's response is to plead with God for the child's life. Like Hannah before him (see 1 Sam. 2:6), David understands that authority to grant life or to take it belongs to God. David's servants interpret his sackcloth, his weeping and his refusal of food – even when urged to eat by the *elders of his household* (v. 17) – as devastation over the child's condition, and so naturally assume that the child's death might drive David to *do something desperate* (v. 18). Noticing their *whispering among themselves*, David deduces that the child is dead. When this is confirmed (v. 19), he rises, washes, changes his clothes and goes to *the house of the LORD* (the tent of 6:17?) to worship. He then returns to his own house and, much to the astonishment of his servants, requests something to eat (v. 20).

---

23. One Targum manuscript (Sperber's Ms c) lists, in addition to the child who died, Amnon, Absalom and Adonijah, all of whom died violent deaths (as noted by Gordon 1986: 359 n. 120). The Talmud (*Yoma 22B*) omits Adonijah, whose death is recorded in the book of Kings, and adds David's daughter Tamar, who suffered a violent fate at the hands Amnon (2 Sam. 13).

24. MT has 'contempt for the enemies of the LORD', and this is reflected in renderings such as NASB's 'you have given occasion to the enemies of the LORD to blaspheme'. NIV, with most modern translations, rightly regards 'enemies of' as a euphemism used in order to avoid directly conjoining 'show contempt' and 'Yahweh'. 4QSam[a] avoids the problem by inserting 'the word of' before 'Yahweh'. For defences of MT, see Firth (2009: 424–425); Youngblood (2009: 452).

In answer to his attendants' question *Why are you acting in this way?* (v. 21), David explains that his actions had been driven not by desperation but by his hope in the graciousness of Yahweh: *Who knows? The LORD may be gracious to me and let the child live* (v. 22). Now that Yahweh's will is known, to go on fasting would be futile: *I will go to him, but he will not return to me*, meaning, 'I will join him in the grave' (v. 23). David's resilience in the face of loss reflects both his healthy acknowledgment of his guilt and his confidence in a God who can be trusted (cf. Bosworth 2011).

24–25. *Then David comforted his wife Bathsheba.* For the first time since 11:3, when she was introduced as *the daughter of Eliam and the wife of Uriah the Hittite*, Bathsheba is called by her personal name. We are not told just how David *comforted* Bathsheba. Perhaps he told her of his repentance and of God's forgiveness. David's sin was worthy of death, but by God's grace he was spared, though another had to die. In due course, and as a further sign of grace, Yahweh enables David and Bathsheba to have another child, *and they named him Solomon* (v. 24).[25] First Chronicles 22:9 links the name Solomon (*šĕlōmōh*) with 'peace' (*šālôm*), and credits Yahweh himself with the name. Peace will later characterize Solomon's reign. Alternatively, or additionally, the name may contain a hint of Hebrew *šillēm*, 'replacement', suggesting that Solomon replaces, or compensates for, the child who died (cf. McCarter 1984: 303).

The opening scene of chapter 12 began under the shadow of Yahweh's displeasure (11:27) and with Yahweh sending Nathan to pronounce judgment. The current scene ends in the light of Yahweh's grace, with Yahweh again sending Nathan, this time to bring assurances that Yahweh's favour rests on the newborn Solomon.

---

25. MT has 'he named him' and is followed by, e.g., ESV, NASB, NLT, NRSV. Mothers were often the ones to name their newborns, and there is some textual support for reading 'she named him' (so JPS; evidence includes the Qere in MT, as well as Syr. and Targ.). Both Hannah (1 Sam. 1:20) and the dying widow of Phinehas (1 Sam. 4:21) named their newborns. NIV sidesteps the question by reading *they named him* (*they* could imply both parents or could be functioning as an impersonal subject; on the latter, see GKC §144f.).

Through Nathan, Yahweh renames the child *Jedidiah* (v. 25), which means 'beloved of Yahweh'. In the Hebrew text, the final lines of the scene begin and end with Yahweh: 'And Yahweh loved him ... because of [*ba'ăbûr*] Yahweh.' The last phrase has been clarified by cognate usages in the Phoenician Karatepe inscriptions where, as McCarter (1984: 304) notes, the expression *b'br* followed by a divine name (DN) seems to mean something like 'by the grace of DN'. NIV's *The LORD loved him; and because the LORD loved him, he sent ... Nathan* (vv. 24b–25a) captures something of the emphatic sense of the Hebrew, even if the word order of the final lines is rearranged.

26–31. Having traced the story of David's great fall into sin (actually a string of sins) and of David's repentance and initial restoration, the narrative returns to the matter with which the whole story began: the siege of the Ammonite city of Rabbah (11:1). The story began with the notice that, at the time of year when *kings* (Heb. has 'messengers') go forth, David sent Joab to fight the king's battle.[26] Now on the cusp of vanquishing the Ammonites, Joab sends *messengers* to tell David that he must come and *besiege the city and capture it*. Otherwise, worries Joab, the city will be taken and will be *named after me* (v. 28). With *its water supply* taken (v. 27), Joab knows that the city cannot hold out much longer. Joab's insistence that David personally take the city may have been prompted by one or more of the following: concern for David's reputation; the fact that a name could connote ownership (cf. 5:7–9); and the fact that David should be the one to receive the captive crown. Whatever the case, the narrative effect of the final verses of chapter 12 is to show David reassuming – after a period of laxity and lapse – his leadership responsibilities.

Having been rudely awakened from his complacency by his own sin and its consequences, David heeds Joab's messengers, takes to the field and, in due course, takes the city of Rabbah (v. 29). *David took a great quantity of plunder from the city* (v. 30). Meriting special mention is the 'crown of their king' ('*ăṭeret-malkām*), which weighed just under 75 lb (i.e. *a talent of gold*).[27] Many find it doubtful that a

---

26. See comment at 11:1.
27. It is worth noting in passing that Ammonite statuary provides many examples of individuals (whether gods or kings) wearing large crowns.

human king would have worn such a heavy crown, and it may be that Hebrew *malkām* (*their king*) should be revocalized as *milkōm* (Milkom, the national god of the Ammonites).[28] The crown, then, would have adorned a statue of Milkom. Alternatively, the crown may have been merely ceremonial and worn only for short periods by the Ammonite king.[29] With respect to David, the text says no more than that the crown (?) *was placed on his own head* (v. 30), with no indication of how long it remained. In fact, it may not have been the crown itself that was placed on David's head. A 'precious stone' (singular) adorned the crown, and it may have been only the stone that David wore.[30]

In addition to the plunder from Rabbah, David *brought out the people who were there* (v. 31). What he then did to them is a matter of dispute. Given his treatment of the Moabites in 8:2 (and with possible encouragement from 1 Chr. 20:3), some older commentators assume that David rather cruelly executed the Ammonite captives (Keil and Delitzsch 1996: *ad loc*. 2 Sam. 12:31).[31] The milder interpretation reflected in most modern translations – namely, that David subjected *all the Ammonite towns* to forced labour – seems the more likely (cf. Gordon 1986: 261).

---

28. For versional support and discussion, see McCarter (1984: 311, 312–313). Milkom is regularly called Molek in the OT (e.g. Lev. 18:21); on the intentional corruption of foreign deity names in the OT, see at 1 Sam. 7:4 and 2 Sam. 2:8.
29. For a defence of retaining MT's 'their king', see Firth (2009: 425); Youngblood (2009: 953).
30. NIV obscures this possibility by changing the word order of the Hebrew and pluralizing 'stone'; NRSV adheres more closely to the Hebrew: 'and in it was a precious stone; and it was placed on David's head'.
31. The Chronicles parallel has *wayyāśar*, 'he sawed' them (JPS has 'he hacked them'). But this differs by only one consonant from the reading of the Samuel text, namely, *wayyāśem*, 'he set' them (or 'consigned' them). Most modern translations assume consignment to hard labour, not hacking to pieces, in both Samuel and Chronicles.

Meaning

As grievous as David's sins were in chapter 11, the present chapter shows that sin and failure need not be the last word. In response to the direct indictment *You are the man!*, David proves capable of deep and genuine repentance. He grasps the fundamental truth that before wronging a fellow human being one first shakes one's fist in the face of one's Maker (cf. Prov. 14:31; 17:5). In acknowledging that truth and repenting, David receives forgiveness. Nevertheless, as the narrative continues, we see that sin, even forgiven sin, can be a cause of disorientation and impairment. Much of the remaining story of David will feature his attempt to regain his balance in the aftermath of the great fall of chapter 11.

B. Sin and incomplete reconciliation (13:1 – 14:33)

i. Sexual abuse and murder within the household of David (13:1–39)
Context
It doesn't take long for the word of Yahweh pronounced by Nathan in 12:11 – *Out of your own household I am going to bring calamity on you* – to show initial signs of fulfilment. The problem begins with David's firstborn, *Amnon the son of Ahinoam of Jezreel* (3:2). The first of David's sons to be mentioned in chapter 13, however, if we observe the Hebrew word order, is Absalom (see at v. 1). It will be through Absalom that David will experience the greatest calamity of his life, both familially and politically, in the long narrative that culminates in chapter 19. Central to the present chapter is Absalom's beautiful sister Tamar. And facilitating the action will be cousin Jonadab, described as Amnon's friend, or advisor.

All persons mentioned in the Old Testament must have had names, but their names are not always noted. So when names are specifically mentioned in the biblical narrative, it is worth asking whether they are significant in some way, beyond simply being a label. So, briefly and for what it's worth, the name Absalom combines 'father' and 'peace or well-being', while Amnon reflects the root *'mn* (from which our 'amen' is derived) and means something like 'faithful'. Given the events about to unfold, the irony of both names is hard to miss. Tamar means 'date palm' and, according to Noth (cited in *HALOT*), 'suggests not only the idea of the stature of the date-palm but also the sweetness of its fruit' (Song 7:7 compares the bride to a date palm [*tāmār*]). Several meanings have been suggested for Jonadab, including 'Yahweh is noble', 'Yahweh is liberal/generous' and 'Yahweh has impelled' (cf. BDB). The last of the three is tempting in terms of the divine pronouncement of calamity that is to arise out of the house of David. The second is also tempting, as it might suggest at the outset of the narrative that, given the generosity of Yahweh, it is heinous that Amnon should be scheming to gain what Yahweh would never grant.[32] That said, the safest (and perhaps correct) course is simply to acknowledge the name of Amnon's cousin as Jonadab and seek no further significance in it.[33]

With respect to its structure, the chapter can be analysed as a large chiasm, centred around Amnon's rape of Tamar and his abrupt change from lust to hatred (Ridout 1974: 75).

Comment

1–6. *In the course of time, Amnon son of David fell in love with Tamar, the beautiful sister of Absalom son of David* (v. 1). As is often the case in biblical narratives, the main characters for the ensuing episode are mentioned at the outset. Supporting actors such as Jonadab will be introduced as needed. While there is some syntactical justification for NIV's ordering the opening sentence as it does, in the Hebrew text the first individual mentioned after the opening temporal clause is *Absalom son of David*, signalling the important role he will play in the ensuing narrative. ESV captures well the sense of the Hebrew: 'Now Absalom, David's son, had a beautiful sister, whose name was Tamar. And after a time Amnon, David's son, loved her.' Familial terms mark the opening sentence (son, sister) and will continue throughout the chapter. Against the backdrop of the divine announcement in 12:11 that *calamity* will befall David from

---

32. The name carries the same components as Nedabiah (1 Chr. 3:18), which Noth glosses with 'Yahweh is generous' (*HALOT*).
33. The name is attested as a personal name on an ancient Hebrew seal (*ABD* 3: 936).

his own household, this opening is foreboding, as is the notice that Amnon is *in love* with his half-sister.

The character of Amnon's *love* becomes increasingly clear as the events unfold. For now, we learn that Amnon is *so obsessed* [root *ṣrr*] *with his sister Tamar that he made himself ill* (v. 2). More than obsessed, Amnon is 'tormented' (NRSV, ESV)[34] by the fact that Tamar is out of reach: *it seemed impossible for him to do anything to her.* The stated reason for her inaccessibility is that *She was a virgin.* There is no explicit mention here of the legal sanctions against incest (e.g. Lev. 18:9, 11; 20:17; Deut. 27:22), though these probably hover in the background (see further at v. 13 below).[35]

The plot thickens with the introduction of Amnon's cousin and *adviser* (lit. 'friend'),[36] *Jonadab son of Shimeah, David's brother* (v. 3). In addition to his identification as a nephew of David, Jonadab is described as *a very shrewd man* (lit. 'a very wise man').[37] Amnon's torment is showing in his *haggard* (or dejected, sullen) appearance, and Jonadab wants to know why (v. 4). Amnon's answer again focuses on Tamar and her inaccessibility. But this time he mentions not her virginity but the fact that she is the sister of his brother Absalom (the Heb. word order in v. 4b places emphasis on this fact).

---

34. Heb. *ṣrr* can describe someone as being 'bound' or, as we might say, 'tied up in knots'.
35. See the section on 'Brother–Sister Marriages in the Ancient World' in Long (2009b: 462).
36. On suggestions that 'friend' here may connote something like best man, matchmaker or adviser, see the cautious discussion in McCarter (1984: 321).
37. This description, along with the fact that Jonadab seems assured in 13:32 that Absalom will have killed only Amnon among the king's sons, has led to the suggestion that Jonadab may have conspired with Absalom to eliminate Amnon from the line of succession to the throne (e.g. Hill 1987). Difficulties with this proposal include the fact that Jonadab is described as Amnon's friend and, more significantly, that it would require that Absalom heartlessly exploit his own sister.

Whether official advisor or simply friend, Jonadab has an idea: *Go to bed and pretend to be ill* (v. 5). Feigning illness should be easy for Amnon, as his obsession with Tamar has already tormented him to the point of illness (v. 2, where the same verb as here, hitpaʻel of *ḥlh*, is used) and left him looking haggard (v. 4). Amnon's apparent malaise will secure a visit from David, and Jonadab suggests what Amnon should say to David about Tamar: *Let her prepare the food in my sight so that I may watch her and then eat it from her hand* (v. 5). The request sounds vaguely voyeuristic, notwithstanding the fact that in Egyptian love poetry the sight of the beloved is described as having health benefits.[38] Amnon agrees to the scheme, and when David makes his sick call, Amnon adds to the script the request that Tamar come *and make [ûtĕlabbēb] some special bread [lĕbibôt] in my sight* (v. 6). The double occurrence of words containing the consonants *lbb*, also attested in Hebrew *lēbab* ('heart'), suggests that some kind of heart-shaped pastry or dumpling, or perhaps a particularly nourishing ('hearty') food, may be in view. At the same time, Amnon's choice of words may carry a subtly amorous connotation.[39] David seems to miss any innuendo in Amnon's request, as his subsequent actions demonstrate.

7-14. *David sent word to Tamar at the palace* (v. 7). Evidently oblivious to Amnon's true condition and intentions, David sends for Tamar. After the disasters that flowed from David's 'sendings' in chapter 11, the notice that he is sending again, this time for Tamar, is unsettling. *Go . . . and prepare some food for him.* David does not repeat Amnon's words verbatim but speaks simply of Tamar's

---

38. Cf. McCarter (1984: 320-321); Hill (1987: 389) cites a particularly close analogue in a New Kingdom Egyptian love poem, where the young man feigns illness to gain a visit from neighbours including 'my girl', who will then put out the others and remain alone with him; missing from this analogue is any sense of resistance on the part of the girl.

39. Cf. Song 4:9, where the phrase 'stolen my heart' translates the same form of the verb here rendered 'make', or 'bake' (enflame?). The only certain occurrences of piʻel verbal forms of *lbb* are in these two contexts.

preparing *food*, possibly a kind of food for the ill.[40] Had David repeated Amnon's explicit words, Tamar might have had misgivings about going. The fact that, upon her arrival, Tamar sets about preparing *the bread* (*hallĕbibôt*, i.e. the *special bread* mentioned by Amnon in v. 6) suggests either that David had said more to her than is recorded, or that Amnon requested this bread upon her arrival, or that the presence of the ingredients alone was sufficient to indicate what she was to bake. The process of her kneading and baking the bread *in his sight* is described in unusual detail (*took . . . kneaded . . . made . . . baked . . . took the pan . . . served*), as if following Amnon's gaze (vv. 8–9). The phrase *served him the bread* is literally 'poured out (the pan) before him'. There is no hint that she had been told to feed him from her hand.

Amnon, *who was lying down* when she arrived (v. 8) and remained so throughout the process, at first *refused to eat* what she prepared (v. 9). He orders the room emptied of everyone other than Tamar, then asks Tamar to *Bring the food here into my bedroom so that I may eat from your hand*. Still unaware of Amnon's true design, she complies (v. 10). *But when she took it to him to eat, he grabbed her and said, 'Come to bed with me, my sister'* (v. 11).[41] Suddenly aware that Amnon's sickness is not physical, Tamar resists his advance with every argument she can muster: *Don't force me!* (v. 12a);[42] *Don't do this wicked thing* (v. 12b). Where wicked folly, or outrageous behaviour (*nĕbālâ*), is referenced in the Bible, it usually involves sexual sin and invariably results in

---

40. The word is *biryâ*, a word that occurs only in this chapter and is rendered 'patient's diet' by *HALOT*. It seems to echo the word for 'fat' or 'healthy'. The related verb, *bārâ*, occurs twice elsewhere, each time in reference to David's refusal to take nourishment (in 3:35 after the assassination of Abner and in 12:17 after the death of the baby he fathered by Bathsheba).

41. Bar-Efrat (1989: 259–260) remarks that Amnon's rhyming appeal, *bôʾî šikbî ʿimmî ʾăḥôtî*, lit. 'come, lie with me, my sister', establishes a close connection between Tamar and Amnon, which Amnon desires and attempts to realize.

42. The Heb. verb *ʿnh* II, piʿel, means to 'humiliate (a woman sexually)', whether by 'rape or unlawful intercourse' or 'enforced marriage' (*DCH*).

death (e.g. Deut. 22:21; Judg. 20:6; Jer. 29:23). She points to the distinctive moral standards of Israel: *Such a thing should not be done in Israel!* (v. 12). She appeals to simple human decency and compassion: *Where could I get rid of my disgrace?* (v. 13a). She even appeals to Amnon's own self-interests: *You would be like one of the wicked fools in Israel*. Desperate to buy time, Tamar pulls out all the stops. It is probably in this light that her final words are to be understood: *Please speak to the king; he will not keep me from being married to you*; the Hebrew says simply 'he will not withhold me from you' (v. 13b). Amnon heard her pleas but gave them no heed, *and since he was stronger than she, he raped her* (v. 14).[43]

15–19. Having given his lust full sway and having spent himself, *Amnon hated her with intense hatred* (v. 15). As Tacitus remarks, 'It is a principle of human nature to hate those whom you have injured' (*Agricola* 42).[44] This principle is not absolute, however, as the story of Shechem and Dinah in Genesis 34 illustrates. In the aftermath of his violation of Dinah, Shechem's 'heart was drawn to Dinah daughter of Jacob; he loved the young woman and spoke tenderly to her' and wanted to marry her (Gen. 34:2–4). By contrast, not a hint of compassion or affection is detected in Amnon. He will not again call her *my sister* (v. 11), nor will the name Tamar cross his lips. Rather, he dismisses her with a mere two words in Hebrew, *qûmî lēkî* (approximately, 'Up, out!'). His dismissal is a mocking reversal of his proposal in verse 11b (see note there).

Tamar protests that being sent away would be an even greater wrong than she has already suffered.[45] But, as before (v. 14), her

---

43. The rape is described with two verbs in the Heb. text. The first is *'nh* II ('humiliate sexually', see note at v. 12a). The second is *škb* followed by the accusative particle *'t*, which combination occurs often in instances of illicit sexual intercourse (e.g. Gen. 19:33–34; 34:2, 7; 35:22; Lev. 19:20; 20:11; 1 Sam. 2:22; to name a few). The more common Hebrew usage for sexual intercourse is *škb* followed by *'m* ('lie with'), as in David's lying with Bathsheba in 11:4.
44. Cited by Kirkpatrick (1886: 136).
45. As Alter (1999: 269) notes, '"Sending away" is an idiom that also has the sense of "divorce" – precisely what the rapist of a virgin is not

words fall on deaf ears: *he refused to listen to her* (v. 16). There is no record of his saying anything to her at all in response. Rather, he summons his *personal servant* and says, *Get this woman out of my sight and bolt the door after her* (v. 17). *Woman* is supplied in translation, but Amnon's words could as easily be read 'get this (thing) away from me'. As there were no witnesses to Amnon's crime, his polite request to his servant[46] and his objectifying description of Tamar could give the impression that the offending behaviour had been hers.

Cast out, locked out (v. 18), Tamar is devastated, and she makes no attempt to hide what has happened. Quite visibly adopting signs of mourning (cf. King and Stager 2001: 372–373), she *went away, weeping aloud* [lit. 'crying out' (*zʿq*)] *as she went* (v. 19). Rending of robes was a sign of mourning. But beyond that, Tamar's rending of her *ornate robe*[47] proclaimed that she could no longer be counted among *the virgin daughters of the king* (v. 18).

20–22. At this point, Absalom re-enters the story. He asks Tamar, *Has that Amnon, your brother, been with you?* (v. 20). Absalom employs euphemisms in deference to his sister's dignity (*been with you*; *this thing*), but his meaning is clear. Absalom's pronunciation of the name Amnon as Aminon is unique to the Old Testament and,

---

(note 45 *cont.*) allowed to do in biblical law.' See Exod. 22:16; Deut. 22:13–29. Whether Tamar is thinking of such legal matters or not, she is surely 'alluding to the psychological and social suffering that will be her lot as a result of the rape because Amnon is sending her away' (Bar-Efrat 1989: 267).

46. The Hebrew particle of entreaty, *nāʾ* (please), is included.

47. The combination *kĕtōnet passîm* occurs elsewhere only in the description of Joseph's special robe in Gen. 37:3. The precise nature of these robes is disputed, as evidenced already in the ancient versions. LXX suggests a long garment reaching to the wrists (and ankles), thus perhaps protecting the modesty of the wearers. Vulg. seems to presuppose a multi-coloured garment. Whatever its precise appearance, the garment carried symbolic significance. On various links between the Tamar and Joseph stories, see Alter (1991: 114–117, 164–165).

if not simply a transmissional error, may represent a disparaging diminutive (cf. Driver 1960: 300). His guidance to Tamar may at first blush seem callous: *Be quiet for now, my sister; he is your brother. Don't take this thing to heart* (v. 20). But subsequent events will make clear that Absalom himself very much takes *this thing* to heart and devises a plan to deal with Amnon in due course.[48] The offence is within the family and shall be dealt with within the family. Bar-Efrat (1989: 272) draws attention to the symmetry in verse 20, where *my sister* (Tamar) is surrounded by *your brother* (Amnon), who in turn is surrounded by *her brother* (Absalom). Tamar was unable to escape Amnon. Amnon will be unable to escape Absalom.

When news of *all this* gets to David – by what means we are not told – *he was furious* (v. 21). In MT, that's all we get from David. NRSV follows LXX and 4QSam[a] (partial) in adding 'but he would not punish his son Amnon, because he loved him, for he was his firstborn'. Whether this additional material is original or not,[49] it does touch upon a weakness in David's handling of his sons that is seen elsewhere. Witness his handling of Absalom in 14:24, 33 and of Adonijah in 1 Kings 1:6. As *King David* (our verse uses the full title), David had a familial and a state duty to do *what was just and right for all his people* (8:15). Perhaps David felt morally crippled by his own recent adultery and homicide. Be that as it may, his passivity in respect of Amnon's violation of Tamar will lead to the greatest domestic and political crisis of his life, Absalom's revolt. Aggrieved over the issue of justice (cf. 15:4–6), Absalom will launch a coup meant to take David's kingdom and his life.

As for Amnon, *Absalom never said a word* to him, *either good or bad* (v. 22). This stony silence cannot be read as indifference, for the text states explicitly that Absalom was motivated by hatred for Amnon, *because he had disgraced* ['violated'] *his sister Tamar.*

---

48. At the risk of over-interpreting, we might observe that the Heb. rendered 'be quiet' is a hip'il of *ḥrš* II, which is homonymous with *ḥrš* I. In 1 Sam. 23:9, the latter occurs in the hip'il to describe Saul's *plotting against* David. Is there a faint hint, already in his words to Tamar, that Absalom is plotting to avenge his sister?

49. It looks like an expansion seeking to account for David's silence.

23–29. Two years later, Absalom uses the occasion of sheep-shearing (often a time of feasting and celebration) to invite the king's sons as well as the king and his attendants to join the party at Baal Hazor (probably Jebel 'Aṣûr), some 14 miles north of Jerusalem. David declines the invitation and seeks to dismiss Absalom with a blessing (v. 25; cf. JPS's 'he said good-bye to him'). Absalom persists, however, expressly requesting that Amnon come (v. 26a). The explicit mention of Amnon is daring. As eldest son and crown prince, Amnon could serve as David's representative and so, under normal circumstances, the request might not raise suspicion. But these are not normal circumstances, and David's follow-up question suggests at least a hint of apprehension (v. 26b). Absalom offers no answer to the question *Why should he go with you?* and David does not press it; did he fear what Absalom might say regarding the king's duties in the matter of Tamar's violation? At Absalom's urging, David simply agrees to send all the king's sons (v. 27), perhaps hoping that there will be safety in numbers.[50]

As it turns out, there is no safety in numbers, especially when *Amnon is in high spirits from drinking wine* (v. 28). Absalom's men respond on cue, Amnon is killed and all the other *king's sons got up, mounted their mules and fled* (v. 29). In one stroke, Absalom avenges the wrong done to his sister and moves himself a step closer to the throne (cf. 3:3; 15:1–6). The words of judgment pronounced by Nathan in 12:10–12 continue their relentless forward march – first sexual violence and now murder.

30–33. With the king's surviving sons now in full flight, the scene changes to David, back in Jerusalem. He receives the report that *Absalom has struck down all the king's sons; not one of them is left* (v. 30). In order for the report to precede the sons' flight, the one bearing the report must have fled Absalom's camp just as the violence began. This may explain the report's inaccuracy. King and court immediately tear their garments as mourners do (v. 31), but Jonadab (mentioned for the first time since verses 3–5 and now

---

50. An additional sentence, included in LXX (and suggested also by the fragmentary 4QSam[a]), is accepted by NRSV and NLT, the latter reading: 'So Absalom prepared a feast fit for a king.'

keeping company with David) quickly assures the king that *only Amnon is dead* (v. 32). Lest David (or the reader) mistake Absalom's fundamental motivation, Jonadab spells out that the death of Amnon *has been Absalom's express intention ever since the day that Amnon raped his sister Tamar* (v. 32). Very much the same thing is said a second time in verse 33. The only surprise is that David has not surmised as much, given the evident animosity between Absalom and Amnon.

The place of Jonadab in Absalom's actions is uncertain. One theory is that Jonadab and Absalom conspired from the beginning to remove Amnon from the royal succession and clear the way for Absalom. As noted earlier, however, this requires us to assume that Absalom willingly put his sister in harm's way, in order to achieve his political goals. This seems unlikely, as evidenced, for example, by the fact that he named his own daughter Tamar (14:27), hardly something he would do had he victimized his own sister Tamar. As for Jonadab, it is unclear whether he had any notion that Amnon would actually harm Tamar; he may simply have thought he was arranging a rendezvous, not a rape. In the present scene, Jonadab, as a 'wise' man, is able to connect the dots, better than David.

34–39. *Meanwhile, Absalom had fled* (v. 34). Absalom is now a fugitive. More detail will be given in verses 37–38, but first the approach and arrival of the king's sons is described: *The watchman went and told the king, 'I see men in the direction of Horonaim, on the side of the hill'* (v. 34). This rendering follows LXX. MT has 'from the road behind him by the side of the mountain'. In Hebrew, 'Horonaim' and 'behind him' sound somewhat alike. Deciding between the two is difficult, as variance in the ancient and modern versions attests. But the general sense is clear. The king's surviving sons are coming. As they approach, Jonadab, ever the 'wise' man (v. 3), takes the opportunity to point out the accuracy of his words to the king (v. 35). The king's sons arrive *wailing loudly* and are soon joined by the king and his court, who *wept very bitterly*, literally 'wept a very great weeping' (v. 36).

In verse 37, the focus shifts briefly to Absalom, who has fled to his maternal grandfather *Talmai son of Ammihud, the king of Geshur* (see comment on 3:3). Forced to flee one king, Absalom finds refuge with another. Absalom will remain in Geshur for *three years*

(v. 38). Interlaced with these notices about Absalom are remarks about David. In verse 37b we read that *King David mourned many days for his son*. The likeliest referent is Amnon, but Absalom cannot be excluded.

The concluding verse of the chapter, as it stands, is as troubled and uncertain as David's fatherly emotions must have been, with one son dead and another, his killer, banished. Several features of verse 39 in MT contribute to its uncertainty: first, the initial verb, a feminine singular form of *klh*, cannot take 'David' (masc. sg.) as its grammatical subject; second, the verb *klh* is patient of at least two translations in this context, 'ceased from' or 'longed to'; third, the preposition before 'Absalom' can be rendered either 'to' or 'against'; fourth, the verb *niḥam* in the concluding causal clause can be rendered either 'was consoled' or 'was grieved'. The feature that earns the verdict 'untranslatable' from Driver (1960: 305) is the first one, which he then resolves by noting that LXX (Lucianic recension) attests 'spirit' (Heb. *rûaḥ*, which is fem. sg.) instead of 'David' – in consonantal Hebrew the words 'David' and 'spirit' look fairly similar. The last letter of *rûaḥ*, 'spirit', also appears in 4QSam[a]. Taking all these features into account, four renderings of the verse are possible:

1. The spirit (heart) of the king longed to go out to Absalom, because he was comforted about Amnon, because he was dead. (Cf. ESV, NIV and many English translations.)
2. The spirit (heart) of the king ceased to go out to Absalom, because he was grieved about Amnon...
3. The spirit (anger) of the king longed to go out against Absalom, because he was grieved about Amnon...
    (Similarly, R. G. Smith 2009: 161.)
4. The spirit (anger) of the king ceased to go out against Absalom, because he was comforted about Amnon...
    (Similarly, McCarter 1984: 335, 344.)

On balance, though all are possible, options 1 and 4 seem to fit best with what comes next, namely, Joab's ruse to trick David into allowing Absalom to return. Firth (2009: 441) nicely captures some of the ambiguity of the statement in his rendering: 'King David's spirit ceased to go out after Absalom because he was consoled over Amnon since he was dead.'

Meaning
Sexual violence within his household and fratricide are just the beginnings of the repercussions that will flow from David's own sins in chapter 11. As chapter 13 ends, Tamar is desolate, Amnon is dead and Absalom is in exile. David has been deeply shaken by these events, infuriated, distraught, bereaved, but he has remained largely passive. He has taken no actions to right wrongs. Furthermore, he has seemed somewhat imperceptive and incautious (e.g. in unwittingly putting Tamar in harm's way). Are these signs that David is still reeling after his own great fall? Even forgiven sin can have crippling effects. As Birch (1998: 1307) remarks:

> In this story, it is David who might have broken the chain of violence he himself had begun. But, though angered, he does nothing, and his refusal to act continues the chain... David's example should teach us that anger is not enough. Tolerance and inaction in the face of violence fosters further violence.

ii. *The return of Absalom to Jerusalem (14:1–33)*
Context
As is so often the case in the story of David, Joab in this chapter assumes the role of fixer. David, in his apparent disorientation following recent events, seems incapable of decisive action. And so Joab devises a scheme by which David can be convinced to bring Absalom out of exile and back to Jerusalem. Joab's scheme involves the rhetorical and acting skills of a *wise woman* from Tekoa. She proves successful in moving David to action (vv. 1–20). The young man Absalom is brought back from Geshur to Jerusalem, but if Joab hopes for an easy reconciliation within the royal household, he is to be disappointed (vv. 21–33).

Comment
1–3. *Joab . . . knew that the king's heart longed for Absalom* (v. 1). Despite the clarity of NIV's rendering, David's attitude towards

Absalom remains as unclear in the Hebrew here as in the final verse of the preceding chapter. The Hebrew of verse 1 reads more literally, 'the king's *lēb* (heart/mind) was *'al* (on, concerned with, against) Absalom'. Most ancient versions and modern translations assume that David's attitude was positive, and the Syriac version uses a verb that can express being 'reconciled' with someone (J. P. Smith 1903: 545). It is best, however, to retain the ambiguity of the Hebrew, as in both JPS and NRSV: 'the king's mind was on Absalom' – whether for good or for ill is not specified.

Joab, likely as concerned for the future of the Davidic house as for the state of David's affections, contrives a plan to bring Absalom back to Jerusalem. To effect his plan he needs the services of a *wise woman* whom he collects from *Tekoa*, a town some 10 miles south of Jerusalem and the later birthplace of the prophet Amos (Amos 1:1). As the 'wise' Jonadab in the preceding chapter had instructed Amnon to feign illness, Joab now instructs the 'wise' woman to feign mourning, all in the interests of turning David in the desired direction (v. 2). To appearance must be added a story, so *Joab put the words in her mouth* (v. 3).

4–7. The Tekoan woman plays her part effectively, both gaining David's attention and then telling a moving story. She begins her answer to David's question in verse 5 with 'Alas' (*'ăbāl*), *I am a widow*.[51] In ancient society, a widow was vulnerable, although sons provided some protection. Due to a fight in a field that ended in fratricide (reminiscent of the Cain and Abel story), the widow now has but one surviving son. Worse still, *Now the whole clan* [or 'family', *mišpāḥâ*] *has risen up against your servant* (v. 7). Their intent is to exercise blood revenge by putting the second son to death *for the life of his brother whom he killed*. The duty to avenge unlawful killing apparently overrides the clan's concern to keep alive the name of one of their number who has died. Their motivation for favouring one side of these competing duties is suggested by

---

51. Unlike most English translations, NIV leaves *'ăbāl* untranslated here. In Hebrew, the interjection *'bl* nicely echoes Joab's instructions in v. 2, which three times use the lexeme *'bl* in describing *mourning, mourning clothes* and *grieving*/'mourning'.

words that the woman puts in their mouths, though they would have been unlikely to say them out loud: *then we will get rid of the heir as well* (v. 7).

8–20. David responds favourably, but vaguely, to the woman's plight: *I will issue an order on your behalf* (v. 8). The woman's next words indicate that she wants something more specific. Because she knows that her more specific request will contravene the king's duty to avenge wrongful deaths, she begins by taking the guilt upon herself and her family (v. 9). NIV's *Let my lord the king pardon me and my family* renders Hebrew that more literally reads 'upon me, O king, is [or be] the iniquity and upon the house of my father'. She continues, *and let the king and his throne be without guilt*. The woman's most likely surface meaning is that she accepts responsibility for any breach of the normal protocols of (ancient) justice, while the king and his throne are exempt from any blame. But given the whole point of the exercise, there may also be a hint of accusation in her words: I and mine are to blame, while the king and his throne are not?

David continues to respond affirmatively to the woman (v. 10), so in verse 11 she plainly states her petition: *Then let the king invoke the LORD his God to prevent the avenger of blood from adding to the destruction, so that my son shall not be destroyed*. Again, David responds affirmatively, this time with an oath: *As surely as the LORD lives . . . not one hair of your son's head will fall to the ground* (v. 11).

The trap has been cleverly set, and David has stepped into it. The ever-wise woman still moves cautiously, requesting permission to *speak a word* (v. 12) before springing the trap shut. Having been told to speak, she utters her equivalent of Nathan's *You are the man!* (12:7): *does he not convict himself, for the king has not brought back his banished son?* (v. 13). She continues, explaining that death is inevitable and, *Like water spilled on the ground*, unrecoverable. Her allusion is to the death of Amnon. But God devises ways to mitigate the damage; *he devises ways so that a banished person* [Absalom] *does not remain banished from him* (v. 14).[52]

---

[52]. JPS offers an alternative reading: 'God will not take away the life of one who makes plans so that no one may be kept banished.' On Ewald's suggested minor emendation of the Heb. text to achieve this sense,

Having dared to be so direct with the king about his own situation, the woman retreats quickly back to her own story. Fear of the people pushed her to approach the king in the hope that he would *deliver his servant ('ămātô)* from those *trying to cut off both me and my son from God's inheritance* (v. 16). NIV's rendering of verse 17 suggests a final appeal by the woman: *And now your servant says*. However, the very same Hebrew phrase (*wattō'mer šiphātĕkā*) appears in verse 15, where NIV reads *Your servant thought*. It is possible that the woman is still recounting the putative thought process that led her to present her case to the king in the first place, that he might *secure my inheritance* (or, as with many English translations, that he might 'set me at rest', or 'give me comfort').

Her comment that *my lord the king is like an angel of God in discerning good and evil* may reflect an understanding of the king's duty to speak for God in dispensing justice. But it is hard to ignore a sense of irony in her words, 'a gesture of deference to the king that is ironically contradicted by fact' (Alter 1999: xx). Two other times in Samuel David is compared to an angel of God – by the Philistine Achish in 1 Samuel 29:9 and later by Mephibosheth in 2 Samuel 19:27. In neither circumstance does David appear in a very good light: a deceiver in the first and a rather befuddled judge in the second, unable to divine between the competing narratives of the servant Ziba and his master Mephibosheth (cf. Provan 2000: 167–169). Nor is David's wisdom much in evidence in the present episode. Only very slowly does David come to a true appraisal of what is actually happening, as his next words show.

While heretofore it has been the woman taking the initiative in guiding the conversation and asking to speak (v. 12), in verse 18 the king charges her not to *keep from me the answer to what I am going to ask you* and is encouraged to speak by the woman. What triggers David's suspicion that the hand of Joab is in all this (v. 19) is not stated. It may simply be the outcome of the conversation with respect to Absalom's return. But it may also be that the woman's flattery and concluding invocation in verse 17 (*May the LORD your God be with you*) sound a bit too much like talking points such as

---

see McCarter (1984: 341).

Joab might have supplied. The irony continues in the woman's response to David's direct enquiry about Joab's involvement: *no one can turn to the right or to the left from anything my lord the king says*. In the end, she admits that it was *your servant Joab . . . who put all these words into the mouth of your servant* (v. 19). She even discloses Joab's motive, which was either 'to conceal the real purpose of the matter' (JPS) or *to change the present situation* (NIV and, similarly, most English translations), or both. McCarter's rendering (1984: 336) closely approximates the Hebrew wording and captures something of the ambiguity of the comment: 'It was in order to put another face on the matter that Joab devised this stratagem.' For her last words, the woman returns to the flattery of verse 17, comparing the king to *an angel of God* and adding that *he knows everything that happens in the land* (v. 20).

21–24. *The king said to Joab, 'Very well, I will do it. Go, bring back the young man Absalom'* (v. 21). Joab's sudden appearance on the scene is not explained. Perhaps he has been there all along, witnessing the wise woman's performance, or perhaps the narrative simply gets to the point quickly, omitting extraneous information about how Joab found himself in David's presence. Joab is duly grateful and deferential upon receiving the king's permission to bring Absalom home (v. 22), and he wastes no time in travelling to Geshur to do just that (v. 23). The king's next words, however, indicate that Absalom is not exactly coming home to David, his father: *He must go to his own house; he must not see my face* (v. 24). Why David should set this condition is not explained, leaving the reader to wonder. Judging by later events, David seems to have felt deep affection for Absalom, or at least deep regret when he is gone (18:33 – 19:4).[53] So why did David wish not to see Absalom face to face? We are never told directly, but perhaps, given his own sense of failure, he feared the hard conversation that would be required to effect reconciliation with Absalom (see at v. 33).

25–27. David may not have wished to see Absalom, but others were certainly seeing him, and praising him. In fact, *In all Israel there*

---

53. Brueggemann (1990: 298) cites 14:1 as further evidence of David's affection for Absalom, but this verse is in fact ambiguous, as we have noted.

was not a man so highly praised for his handsome appearance as Absalom. Absalom apparently returned from exile in Geshur unblemished *From the top of his head to the sole of his feet* (v. 25). Of particular note is his imposing head of hair, carefully weighed after each annual cutting, and coming in at around 5 lb *by the royal standard* (lit. 'by the stone/weight of the king'; v. 26).[54] A commanding appearance was certainly advantageous for one in line for the throne. But this description of Absalom is unsettling, on two scores. First, its exclusive focus on outward appearance recalls both the initial description of the failed King Saul (see 1 Sam. 9:1–2 and comment) and Yahweh's reminder to Samuel in 1 Samuel 16:7 that, while outward appearance impresses people, Yahweh looks at the heart. Second, and ironically, it will be precisely Absalom's famed head of hair that will prove his undoing (see at 18:9).

The familial notice of verse 27 accomplishes two things. It suggests Absalom's virility: *Three sons and a daughter were born to Absalom* (on the tension with 18:18, see discussion there). Only the name of his daughter is given, and it is Tamar, the namesake of Absalom's sister whose violation by Amnon set in motion the events that have led to the present situation. This reminder of the wrong done to Absalom's sister Tamar is apt at this point in the narrative, as it remains an unresolved issue between Absalom and David.

28–33. *Absalom lived for two years in Jerusalem without seeing the king's face* (v. 28). Absalom finds this situation intolerable and sends for Joab, the man who had brought him back from Geshur and who was in the best position to gain Absalom an audience. Joab, however, pays no heed to a first summons, nor even to a second (v. 29). No reason is given for Joab's reticence to set up a meeting

---

54. Having been sensitized to the significance of semantic range and usage of the root *kbd* (weight, glory, etc.), which appears at significant points in the book of Samuel (see, e.g., 1 Sam. 2:29–30 and comment), the attentive reader may find the description of Absalom's hair as 'heavy upon him' (*kābēd ʿālāyw*) unsettling. Eli's weightiness contributed to his death in 1 Sam. 4:18. And Absalom's weighty head of hair will contribute to his death in 2 Sam. 18:9. (I am indebted to seminar student Brent Siemens for drawing my attention to the potential significance of *kbd* in 14:26.)

between David and Absalom. One might speculate that he feared the fireworks that such a meeting might ignite. In any case, his reticence leads to fireworks of a different sort. Determining that dramatic action is necessary, Absalom takes a page out of Samson's playbook (Judg. 15:4–8) and has his servants set fire to Joab's field, which happens to abut Absalom's own property (v. 30). The notice that there was barley (*śĕ'ōrâ*; one of the 'hairiest' of the food grains) growing in the field may seem extraneous, but perhaps its inclusion is a playful reminder of references to 'hair' earlier in the chapter (v. 11 *śa'ărâ*; v. 26 *śē'ār*).[55]

Absalom's stratagem succeeds in getting Joab's attention (v. 31). All Absalom wanted from Joab was that he carry a message to the king: *Why have I come from Geshur? It would be better for me if I were still there!* To Joab, Absalom adds, *I want to see the king's face, and if I am guilty of anything, let him put me to death* (v. 32). There is even a hint of judicial language in Absalom's words: accusing questions followed by *wĕ'attâ* (*Now then*), the interjection that typically introduced an announcement of judgment. Absalom's mention of guilt and his willingness to die should it be demonstrated, whether seriously meant or not, indicates that he feels very aggrieved by the current state of affairs and the events that have led up to it. He is, in effect, asking that his actions be put on trial, which, by implication, suggests that David's, too, should come under scrutiny. The establishment of Absalom's guilt or innocence can only be accomplished by serious conversation and sober consideration of actions taken, or not taken, by Absalom and by David himself.

Joab makes no protest but goes directly to the king and tells him what Absalom has said (v. 33). For his part, the king also makes no protest but simply summons Absalom. Upon arriving, Absalom bows down *with his face to the ground before the king*. After three years in exile and two years in isolation from David, surely father and son have much to talk about. All we read, though, is that *the king kissed Absalom*. And thus, the narrative comes rather abruptly to an end. Some commentators refer to this kiss as a 'kiss of reconciliation',

---

55. Elsewhere in Samuel, 'hair' is mentioned in 1 Sam. 14:45 and 'barley' in 2 Sam. 17:28 and 21:9.

but it is doubtful that any meaningful reconciliation took place. Certainly, subsequent events would suggest otherwise. It is worth noting, moreover, that familial language is absent in the encounter. Neither 'father' nor 'son', nor even the name 'David', is mentioned in verse 33 – just *the king* and his kiss. It will not be long before Absalom himself will be doling out kisses and stealing the hearts of the people, convincing them that a proper judge is needed in Israel and that he should be it (15:4–6).[56]

Meaning
Reconciliation between estranged parties does not come easily. And it does not come without honest communication. Grievances can be suppressed or ignored, but they do not go away. And there is ever the danger that they will resurface in particularly ugly ways. The chain of events set in motion, in the first instance not by Amnon's offence but by David's, could have been arrested at a number of points along the way. The return of Absalom to Jerusalem, made possible by the initiative of Joab and the skilled performance of the wise woman of Tekoa, offered one such opportunity. But judging from the events that follow, it was an opportunity lost. David allowed Absalom to return to Jerusalem, but he kept him at arm's length. When finally, after three years of exile and two years in Jerusalem without an audience with David, Absalom forces one, the story has little to report. Absalom clearly anticipated a conversation, even a trial – *if I am guilty of anything, let him put me to death* (v. 32) – but all the text reports is a kiss from the king. Whether there was anything fatherly in the royal kiss is not stated. Nor are we expressly told whether the kiss was too little or simply too late. All we know – and this we know from what comes next – is that no true reconciliation takes place been David and Absalom.

---

56. For a differing, but in my view unconvincing, reading of v. 33, see Brueggemann (1990: 298).

C. Absalom's revolt and death (15:1 – 19:43)

i. Absalom's revolt, David's flight (15:1 – 16:14)
Context
The consequences of David's sins of adultery and murder have been grave. A daughter has been raped by her half-brother, and a son, Absalom, has avenged his sister's violation by orchestrating the murder of his half-brother, Amnon. David, guilty of killing Uriah *with the sword of the Ammonites* (12:9), has had to witness the 'sword' decimating his own house, as the Lord through Nathan had said that it would (12:10). Throughout the sordid and devastating chain of events, David, though *furious* (13:21), has remained largely passive. But that is about to change, for Absalom's revolt will be directed at David himself. Passivity in such a situation could cost David his life.

Absalom is clearly at fault in launching a conspiracy, but he is not the only one at fault. His are the sins of commission, but sins of omission can arguably be charged to David. As we have seen, the 'kiss' of 14:33 – absent of any hard-but-healing conversation – effected no true reconciliation between *the king* and Absalom. Absalom remains as incensed as ever over David's failure to administer 'justice' in respect of his sister Tamar and, we may assume, in respect of his own situation (recall 14:32). It is no surprise, then, that whatever else may have motivated Absalom's bid for the throne, *justice* is at the core of his appeal to the people, whom he seeks to win over with a *kiss* (15:5).

Comment
1–6. *In the course of time*, or perhaps better 'after this' (that is, after his unsatisfactory audience with David), *Absalom provided himself with a chariot and horses and with fifty men to run ahead of him* (v. 1). Already recognized for his impressive personal appearance (14:25–26), Absalom now adds the trappings of power. Not only in the Bible but also in the ANE generally, persons of high rank, particularly kings, would sometimes appear in chariots accompanied by an

impressive honour-guard.[57] Before Absalom can challenge his father directly (if that is what he has in mind), he must win a public following, and this he does quite effectively. Rising early, Absalom positions himself *by the side of the road leading to the city gate*, in order to intercept complainants coming to Jerusalem with a judicial case (*rîb*) to present before the king (v. 2). In ancient Israel, city gates were the place where elders would gather and where judicial decisions were often rendered. The response given to Absalom's enquiry about each traveller's home town – *Your servant is from one of the tribes of Israel* (v. 2) – might sound like an evasion, but *one of the tribes of Israel* is simply the narrator's place-holder, which in each actual occurrence would contain specific information (one person might say 'from Ephraim', another 'from Judah', etc.). That Absalom responds to each complainant with *your claims are valid and proper* (v. 3) reveals that his intent is not to render a true judgment – as not all claims are likely to have been *valid and proper* – but, rather, to win the support of the people. His basic ploy is to plant the idea that *there is no representative of the king to hear you* (v. 3), which may or may not have been true, and to put himself forward as one from whom the people could expect to get justice, if only he *were appointed judge* (v. 4). To his show of concern and his promise of justice, Absalom adds finally (and ironically) a *kiss* (v. 5). And *so he stole the hearts of the people of Israel* (v. 6). Winning the people's *hearts* indicates more than gaining their affection, as the 'heart' (*lēb*) in Hebrew signifies the core of one's being, including one's intellectual faculties. The people found him and his proposal convincing.

7–12. To this point in the narrative, Absalom has not directly challenged his father, the king, and it might be thought that his initial goal even now is judicial reform, not a coup.[58] Be that as it may, Absalom's ultimate aim eventually becomes clear. *At the end of*

---

57. See, e.g., Long (2009a: 309–310, commenting on 1 Sam. 8:11–17); Malul (2010); Wagner (2013).

58. Malul (2010) draws attention to the preponderance of juridical terminology in the passage before us, as well as to the association of chariots accompanied by runners with judicial process. Wagner (2013) suggests that Absalom's judicial focus may lessen his culpability.

four years (v. 7), Absalom launches a conspiracy aimed at toppling his father and taking the throne. Why David allows Absalom to leave Jerusalem ostensibly in order to *fulfil a vow* made years before during Absalom's exile in *Geshur in Aram* and to *worship the* LORD *in Hebron* is mystifying (vv. 7–8). Surely David cannot be unaware of Absalom's public relations campaign (vv. 1–6). Nor does Absalom's long delay in getting round to fulfilling his vow speak well of his sincerity (Deut. 23:21 stresses the importance of fulfilling vows quickly). But since David's great lapse into sin in chapter 11, he has often shown lapses of judgment as well (misreading Nathan's parable in ch. 12; missing clues that might have forewarned him of Amnon's true designs on Tamar or, indeed, Absalom's designs on Amnon in ch. 13; misreading the true nature of the woman of Tekoa's 'case' in ch. 14). Even with his judgment impaired, David must sense something amiss in Absalom's request to go to Hebron, the site where David's own reign was first established (2:4). Perhaps there is a hint of apprehensiveness in David's injunction to Absalom to *Go in peace* (v. 9), which may in this context represent more than just a formulaic granting of permission.

David's words will have no effect, however, for Absalom's sole intent is to put himself and the people in a position to say *Absalom is king in Hebron* (v. 10). Two hundred men accompany him quite innocently, unaware of what is afoot (v. 11), but Absalom's summoning of *Ahithophel the Gilonite* may be a different story, inasmuch as with Ahithophel's arrival *the conspiracy gained strength* (v. 12).[59] Psalm 3, whose superscription associates the psalm with David's flight from Absalom, begins appropriately:

> LORD, how many are my foes!
>   How many rise up against me!

13–18. David first learns of his dire predicament through an 'informant' who comes to him in verse 13.[60] The informant tells

---

59. On what may have motivated Ahithophel to join in Absalom's attempt to overthrow David, see comment on 23:34.
60. 'Informant' captures the sense of the Heb. word used here, *maggîd*.

David that *The hearts of the people of Israel are with Absalom* (v. 13). In contrast to his previous passivity, David in verse 14 takes action quickly. He informs his *officials who were with him in Jerusalem* that *We must flee*. His concern is not merely for his own safety but for the city itself, lest Absalom *put the city to the sword*. Even in the midst of crisis, David appears to remember that *the* LORD *... had exalted his kingdom for the sake of his people Israel* (5:12).

Curiously, while taking *his entire household* with him in his escape, David leaves behind *ten concubines to take care of the palace* (v. 16). Is this yet further evidence of David's impaired judgment following his great lapse in chapter 11? Perhaps, but there may be more to the story. Hill (2006: 130–131) has argued, first, that at least some of the concubines taken '*from* Jerusalem' (5:13)[61] must have been Jebusites and, second, that David's 'treaty marriages' would have been intended to form political alliances with the Jebusite elite still living in Jerusalem after David's capture of the city. In keeping with Egyptian policy regarding diplomatic marriages – and it is widely agreed that Egyptian influence continued in Canaan in the time of David – 'Jebusite members of the royal harem' would have been prohibited from 'leaving the environs of the city' (Hill 2006: 138). In view of these considerations, the older conjecture that 15:16 is a secondary redactional insertion designed to anticipate Absalom's taking of David's concubines in 16:21–22 is unnecessary. The Hebrew phrase rendered *to take care of the palace* (v. 16) is *lišmōr habbāyit*, which can also be translated 'to keep/guard the house/dynasty'. Does David hope that leaving concubines behind might guard his 'house', maintain his claim to the city and encourage

---

Messenger (so NIV and many English translations) does not work as well here, as it would imply that someone had dispatched the messenger and, in any case, the normal Heb. word for messenger is *mal'āk*.

61. This rendering, rather than the more common '*in* Jerusalem' (so NIV), is supported by the basic sense of the preposition *min* ('from') in 5:13, by LXX's *ex Ierousalēm* ('from Jerusalem) in its rendering of 5:13 and by the Heb. narrator's use of *bĕ* in 15:14, where '*in* Jerusalem' is intended.

loyalty from his Jebusite allies? If so, the continuation of the story will prove this to be a vain hope.

Reaching *the edge of the city* (Heb. *bêt hammerḥāq*, lit. 'the distant house' – probably a landmark), David stops (v. 17) while his supporters pass in review (v. 18). Landy (2010: 20–21) highlights the drama of this brief scene, which 'is in slow motion: one sees the troops passing by, while David stands still, and their passage corresponds to the passing of his life, and the memories they bring with them'.[62] On the *Kerethites and Pelethites*, see at 1 Samuel 30:14 and 2 Samuel 8:18. Mention of *six hundred Gittites* recalls not only David's sojourn amongst Philistines in Gath, the city of King Achish (see 1 Sam. 27:1–12), but also his wilderness period in which he was on the run from another man wishing him dead, King Saul, and was accompanied by six hundred men (e.g. 1 Sam. 23:13; 25:13; 27:2; 30:9–10).[63] David's stopping to let his troops pass before him is significant. Were his concern only for his own safety, he would surely have continued his flight at the head of his people, rather than allowing them to march past him (v. 18).

19–23. To this point in the narrative of David's escape from Jerusalem, groups of people have been mentioned: his officials, his mercenary troops (Kerethites and Pelethites) and the six hundred Gittite supporters David had gained while in Philistine territory. As the story continues, David begins to encounter individuals, the first of whom is *Ittai the Gittite* (v. 19). In Hebrew, the name *Ittai* sounds something like 'with me' (*'ittî*), and in typical fashion the narrator exploits this fact to play on similar-sounding words in the dialogue between David and Ittai. David's first question is *Why should you* [Heb. *'attâ*] *come along with us* [*'ittānû*]*?* David reminds Ittai that he is a *foreigner*, an *exile* (v. 19), who *came only yesterday* (a hyperbolic expression?), and exhorts him not to follow David (now

---

62. On the 'many ways in which characters cross over ('ābar) boundaries' in this and subsequent chapters, and on the 'eyewitness flavor of this portion of the story', see Polzin (1993: 153).

63. *Six hundred* may suggest a standard military unit, since it occurs often in military contexts (e.g. Judg. 3:31; 18:11; 20:47; 1 Sam. 13:15).

himself an exile) on an uncertain path but, rather, to *Go back* (v. 20). In a scene reminiscent of the exchange between Ruth and Naomi in Ruth 1:16–17, Ittai assures David that he has every intention of staying with the true king (v. 21). Earlier David had referred to *King Absalom* (v. 19), but the three-fold repetition of *king* as David's rightful title in verse 21 shows that both the biblical narrator and Ittai know who the true king is. The theological cast of David's blessing on Ittai, *May the* LORD *show you kindness and faithfulness* (v. 20),[64] and of Ittai's oath of allegiance to David, *As surely as the* LORD *lives* (v. 21), suggests the possibility that Ittai is 'with' David not only in politics but also in faith.[65] Faced with such loyalty, David encourages Ittai to *Go ahead, march on*, and Ittai does so, accompanied not only by his *men* but also by their *families* (Heb. *ṭāp*, 'children, infants', which would imply families). This notice underscores the extremity of the situation and perhaps raises again questions about the wisdom of David's leaving concubines behind in Jerusalem.

This scene of individual encounter draws to its close in verse 23 with a notice regarding the state of the people more generally – *The whole countryside wept aloud as all the people passed by* – and with a notice regarding the king's itinerary – *The king also crossed the Kidron Valley, and all the people moved on towards the wilderness*. In crossing the Kidron Valley, which runs north to south to the east of Jerusalem, David has officially left the city; the next itinerary notice will find David ascending the Mount of Olives (v. 30).

---

64. The MT does not include 'May the LORD show you', prompting Bodner (2004: 148) to wonder if 'the king [is] moved by emotion' and utters an incomplete sentence; the words are included in the LXX, however, and could have been lost in MT due to homoioteleuton (see Driver 1960: 314).
65. Cf. Peterson (1999: 209): 'David started out killing Philistines; he ends up converting them!' It is worth noting that, although NIV and many modern versions have David mention Yahweh in v. 20 (perhaps following LXX), in MT David only invokes mercy and truth upon Ittai. Thus, in MT, Ittai (a Gittite) is the first to speak of Yahweh (v. 21). This forms an intriguing reversal of 1 Sam. 17, where David was the first to speak of Yahweh in the face of the Gittite giant (I am indebted to David Firth for this insight).

24–31. David's next encounter is with the priests *Zadok* and *Abiathar*, and their levitical entourage. The *ark of the covenant of God* is with them, and Abiathar, after carefully setting the ark in place, offers *sacrifices until all the people* have *finished leaving the city* (v. 24).[66] Apparently, the priests thought it only proper that the ark accompany David, but he tells them to *Take the ark of God back into the city*, reasoning that his future depends on the Lord's favour (*If I find favour in the* LORD's *eyes*) and not, as the people had wrongly assumed much earlier (1 Sam. 4), on the physical presence of the ark (v. 25). Understanding that his current misfortune is, in some measure at least, a result of his own sins and their prophesied consequences (12:10–11), David surrenders control of his future to God: *I am ready; let him do to me whatever seems good to him* (v. 26). Gunn (1978: 101) speaks of David's 'passivity' here. But one must observe that if passivity is an appropriate description, it is not the kind of passivity we saw earlier in David's failures to deal effectively with Amnon and Absalom. A better approach might be to speak of David's 'active' trust in the God to whom he has committed his life, despite (or perhaps even because of) his own very evident failings. David's *whatever seems good to him* recalls Eli's similarly phrased submission to the divine judgment in 1 Samuel 3:18 (*He is the* LORD; *let him do what is good in his eyes*). In Hebrew the two responses are virtually identical. Both Eli and David recognized the importance of actively honouring God by submitting to his will, even should that will involve punishment or removal from office.

That 'passivity' is not quite the right word to describe David's posture is indicated also by what happens next. In verses 27–28 David proposes to Zadok a strategy whereby he and his fellow priest Abiathar, and their respective sons, Ahimaaz and Jonathan, can gather and communicate intelligence to David, who will wait to hear from them at the fords (of the Jordan) in the wilderness (v. 28). David's opening words to Zadok in verse 27 invite two

---

66. The combination of the ark, attending priests, and people leaving (lit. crossing over; *'ābar*) recalls Israel's crossing over into the land under the leadership of Joshua (Josh. 3 – 4). Here the direction of movement is reversed.

possible renderings: *Do you understand?* (as in NIV) or 'Aren't you a seer?' (as in NIV 1984). The Hebrew, *hărô'eh 'attâ*, can be read 'are you seeing?' or 'are you a seer?' LXX's simple 'Look!' (followed, e.g., by NRSV, NLT) makes sense in context and avoids the difficulty arising from the fact that 'seer' is a term for prophets, not priests.[67] But perhaps there is a place for reading David's words both ways: 'Don't you see, you can be a seer' (or spy) for me in Jerusalem.

This episode, like the preceding one, concludes with notices regarding David's itinerary and *All the people with him*. Having crossed the Kidron Valley, David continues *up the Mount of Olives* (v. 30). The repetition of *weeping as he went . . . weeping as they went* captures the mournful state of both king and people. While most translations describe David as having his head covered and his feet uncovered, there is linguistic and cultural evidence to suggest that both head and feet may have been uncovered. Gordon (1986: 275) cites evidence of 'a second root *ḥāpâ* meaning "to uncover", hence NEV "bare-headed"', and draws attention to Ezekiel 24:17, 23 (where the prophet is forbidden to perform these mourning acts). Whether *David had* already *been told* of Ahithophel's defection to Absalom (so NIV) and the narrator has withheld this information to this point in the narrative for dramatic effect, or David only learns of this betrayal as he ascends the Mount of Olives (so NRSV and most English translations), the loss of this reputed advisor (see 16:23) is devastating. In response, David prays (lit. 'says'), L ORD, *turn Ahithophel's counsel into foolishness* (v. 31).[68] References to David speaking to Yahweh have been notably absent throughout the sorry tale of Amnon's and Absalom's misdeeds, following upon David's own. The next recorded instance of David seeking the Lord will be in 21:1.

32–37. David does not have to wait long for an answer to his prayer to begin to take shape. Arriving at the summit of the Mount of Olives *where people used to worship God* – an auspicious notice[69]

---

67. For more, see Gordon (1986: 275).
68. The 'meaning' of Ahithophel's name is uncertain, but it sounds like 'my brother is folly' (BDB) or 'brother of folly'.
69. On whether the priestly city of Nob might be in view here, see

– David encounters *Hushai the Arkite* (v. 32). The name *Hushai* may be a shorted form of Hashabiah (see *HALOT*, s.v. *ḥûšay*), which in turn may mean something like 'Yahweh has esteemed' (*HALOT*) or 'Yahweh has taken account' (BDB). Alternatively, or perhaps additionally, the name sounds like the verb *ḥûš* ('hurry, hasten, rush', etc.), prompting Garsiel (1991: 105) to draw attention to the pairing of the name Hushai with a synonym *mhr* ('hasten') in 17:15–16, 'send *quickly* [*mhrh*]'. As is typical in biblical narratives, the writer seems to get some mileage out of the sound of Hushai's name. Might the same be true of *Arkite*? At one level, the word is a gentilic (a designation of affiliation with a people or place) linking Hushai to a clan residing not far from Bethel (cf. Josh. 16:2). But the fourfold repetition of *the Arkite* in the account of David's flight from Absalom (15:32; 16:16; 17:5, 14) just might contain a hint of Hushai's eventually successful mission. Arkite contains the Hebrew root *'rk*, which in its various forms can suggest length, being long or prolonging (cf. *HALOT*; BDB), or, we might say, delaying. In the face of Ahithophel's advice that Absalom should make haste and track David down 'tonight', Hushai the Arkite (aka 'Speedy the Prolonger') will in due course succeed in delaying Absalom's response (cf. 17:14). In the present scene, David spells out what he wants Hushai, his *confidant*, or 'friend' (v. 37), to do. He wants him to return to Jerusalem to *frustrat[e] Ahithophel's advice* (v. 34) and to feed *anything you hear in the king's palace* to Zadok and Abiathar, who will then get the information to David via their two sons (vv. 35–36). David even spells out what he wants Hushai to say (v. 34), though in the event Hushai improves on David's words (see on 16:15 – 17:14). Hushai certainly proves to be David's 'friend' in the mundane sense, but it may also be that the term 'friend' indicated a formal office, a 'special confidant' of some sort (cf. Gordon 1986: 276; McCarter 1984: 372). Worth noting, however, is the fact that Absalom, in 16:17, twice refers to David as Hushai's *friend*, which can only be understood in the mundane sense.

16:1–4. With Hushai and Absalom both having arrived in Jerusalem (15:37), the narrative returns its focus to David and his flight.

McCarter (1984: 371 at v. 32).

No sooner has he *gone a short distance beyond the summit* of the Mount of Olives (cf. 15:30, 32) than 'behold!',[70] he meets *Ziba, the steward* [Heb. *na'ar*] *of Mephibosheth* (v. 1). Both Ziba and Mephibosheth have appeared before in 2 Samuel (9:1–12), and both will appear again (19:17–18, 24–30). Unaccompanied by Mephibosheth, Ziba meets David with an impressive supply of logistical support, including not just food and drink but *a string* [Heb. *ṣemed*][71] *of donkeys* as well (v. 1). The answer to David's first question, *Why have you brought these?*, would seem obvious, but David's asking affords Ziba the opportunity to underscore his allegiance to David as the rightful king: *The donkeys are for the king's household to ride on* (v. 2). The answer to David's second question, *Where is your master's grandson?*, is less obvious, but David's asking allows Ziba to put Mephibosheth in a bad light (v. 3). Whether there is any truth in Ziba's claim that Mephibosheth is hoping to regain his grandfather's throne remains unclear at this stage in the narrative, though it is difficult to imagine how Absalom's rebellion could have furthered Mephibosheth's interests. Whatever the explanation of Mephibosheth's absence (on which, see 19:24–28), Ziba succeeds in eliciting from David the pronouncement that *All that belonged to Mephibosheth is now yours* (v. 4). David had formerly restored all of Saul's property to Mephibosheth (9:7). On that earlier occasion, Ziba had submitted to David's wishes, but with no particular show of enthusiasm: *Your servant will do whatever my lord the king commands his servant to do* (9:11). Now his response is much more enthusiastic: *I humbly bow . . . May I find favour in your eyes, my lord the king* (v. 4). This will not be the end of the matter, however, as David will encounter both Ziba and Mephibosheth again in chapter 19.

---

70. Each of David's encounters with individuals during his flight is introduced with Hebrew *hinnēh*, 'behold' (15:24, Zadok; 15:32, Hushai; 16:1, Ziba; 16:5, Shimei). The effect is to invite the reader to experience the encounter as if through the eyes of David.

71. This Hebrew word is often rendered 'yoke' or 'a couple of', but it can simply mean a 'team' of animals. In the present context, more than two donkeys seem to be implied by the explanation Ziba gives for the saddled donkeys in v. 2.

5–14. If Ziba's protestations of loyalty to David are of uncertain value (see above), there can be no doubt that the next man David encounters, *a man from the same clan as Saul's family* (v. 5), is very much opposed to David. As David approaches the town of *Bahurim*, about 1.5 miles east of Jerusalem (see at 3:16), *Shimei son of Gera* comes out cursing and *pelt*[*ing*] *David and all the king's officials with stones* (v. 6). This is audacious behaviour, especially as *all the troops and the special guard were on David's right and left* (v. 6). We learn from verse 13 that Shimei *was going along the hillside opposite* David, but he couldn't have been more than a literal 'stone's throw' away.[72] Abishai's request that he be allowed to *go over and cut off his head* (v. 9) indicates that Shimei was not at an entirely safe distance, so his rage towards David must have overcome his instinct for self-preservation.

Get out, get out, you murderer [lit. 'man of blood'], *you scoundrel!* (v. 7). Shimei's grievance against David, no doubt shared by many Saulide partisans, is that David has murdered his way to the throne. McCarter's (1984: 373) rendering of Shimei's scathing epithet as 'you bloodstained fiend of hell' is striking, and gains some support from the paralleling of Hebrew *bĕlîya'al* (NIV's *scoundrel*) with 'death' and 'Sheol' in 22:5–6 (thus 'hell' in McCarter's view). But such a rendering doesn't work very well in most other occurrences of the word (e.g. Abigail refers to her husband Nabal as *bĕlîya'al* in 1 Sam. 25:25, where the charge is that he is a fool, not a 'hell-fiend'). Shimei's words may be emboldened by his apparent belief that the Lord is repaying David *for all the blood you shed in the household of Saul* (v. 8). He may have in mind not simply that David ascended the throne vacated by Saul at his death, but that Saulide supporters such as Abner and Ish-Bosheth died violent deaths (3:27 and 4:5–6, respectively) and that David permitted the Gibeonites to execute seven of Saul's descendants in 21:1–14, an event which, despite the textual arrangement, likely preceded David's kindness to Mephibosheth (9:1–3). As a citizen of Bahurim, Shimei may also have witnessed the bitter scene in which Paltiel, second husband of

---

72. On the likely route of the road from Jerusalem to the fords of the Jordan, via Jericho, see Dorsey (1991: 204–205).

Michal daughter of Saul, was forced to turn back in tears, as Michal was being reclaimed by David (see 3:13–16). The biblical account maintains David's innocence in the cases of Abner and Ish-Bosheth (see 3:21–28, 37; 4:9–12), and it is quite forthright in instances of David's guilt, such as the death of Uriah (2 Sam. 12). So there is little reason for modern readers to share Shimei's mistaken view.

David does agree with part of what Shimei is saying, namely, that the Lord is involved in what is happening to him: *Leave him alone; let him curse, for the* LORD *has told him to* (v. 11). Shimei is wrong about the cause(s) of David's plight, but David must be keenly aware of how his own sins against Bathsheba and Uriah set in train the *calamity* (12:11) that is now befalling him and his house. Punning on Shimei's gloating remark in verse 8 that Yahweh is 'repaying' (Heb. *hēšîb*) David, David hopes in verse 12 that Yahweh will indeed 'repay' him, but in a very different sense: *It may be that the* LORD *will look upon my misery and restore* [Heb. *hēšîb*] *to me his covenant blessing instead of his curse today.* Abishai and the other *sons of Zeruiah* (v. 10) serve as foils to David's patient endurance of the Lord's chastisement.

The scene closes with yet another travel notice, David and his men continuing *along the road*, while Shimei continues his cursing and stone-throwing from *the hillside opposite him* (v. 13), until finally *The king and all the people* arrive *at their destination* [likely the Jordan River][73] *exhausted, where David refreshed himself* (v. 14).[74]

Meaning
Where true reconciliation is lacking, things can only get worse. Chapter 14 ended with the notice that *the king kissed Absalom* (14:33). The narrator's avoidance of the personal name 'David' in favour

---

73. Cf. 17:16, 22 and the remarks *ad loc.* by Driver (1960) and McCarter (1984).
74. Perhaps the focus on David's refreshing himself (and not all the people's refreshing themselves) is explicable simply by the fact that he is the principal character in the story. But there may also be a hint that his refreshment involved more than just food and rest (cf. David's 'strengthening himself in the LORD his God' in 1 Sam. 30:6).

of the official title, *the king*, signalled trouble. No words were exchanged, at least as far as the narrative reports, and this also signalled trouble. As noted above, Absalom wanted justice (14:32), and an appraisal of his guilt or innocence required words. He must have left the audience with *the king* in chapter 14 as disaffected as ever. In chapter 15, Absalom's disaffection turns to sedition and eventually outright rebellion. David is forced to flee Jerusalem, along with all his house, save for ten concubines left behind to guard the house. While in flight David encounters both friends and foes, most notable among them his friend Hushai, whose timely appearance just after David prays (see at v. 31) betokens the vital role he will play in the story as it continues. For his part, David is humbled. Chased off the throne by his own son, he patiently endures cursings, reasoning that God may be speaking words he needs to hear, even through such a one as Shimei (16:10–12). He refuses to use God by manipulating the ark, as Israel had done so long ago in 1 Samuel 4. Instead he insists that it be returned to Jerusalem, and he entrusts his fate fully to Yahweh (15:25–26). David is beginning to reorient towards Yahweh, but as subsequent events will demonstrate, he still has not fully regained his balance.

ii. Absalom's folly, David's escape (16:15 – 17:29)
Context
As this section opens, the focus shifts from David at the Jordan to Absalom in Jerusalem. We encounter immediately the two figures who, along with Absalom, will dominate the new scene. Ahithophel and Hushai each present their case to Absalom, but in the end it is Yahweh who determines the outcome (17:14).

Comment
15–19. *Ahithophel* [known already from 15:12, 31] *was with him* (v. 15), as was *Hushai the Arkite, David's confidant* (lit. 'friend', v. 16). The account of Hushai's earlier encounter with David (15:32–37) ended with the notice that Hushai arrived *at Jerusalem as Absalom was entering the city*. The current scene picks up where the earlier one left off. Hushai is the first to speak: *Long live the king! Long live the king!* Hushai's repeated exclamation is doubtless meant to appeal to Absalom's vanity, but the reader can appreciate the clever ambiguity

of Hushai's choice of words. Which 'king' does Hushai have in mind? Absalom assumes the reference to be to himself, thus taking the bait (v. 17), and he wonders aloud at Hushai's apparent disloyalty to David, twice referring to David as Hushai's *friend*. In verses 18 and 19 Hushai continues his subterfuge, at once duping Absalom and delighting the reader. His loyalty will remain with *the one chosen by the* LORD, *by these people and by all the men of Israel.* Absalom again thinks of himself, but Hushai is several steps ahead, using words that more properly point to David. Hushai's own answer to his rhetorical question in verse 19, *whom should I serve?*, is the ultimate evidence of his clever deception. His words can easily be taken by Absalom as expressing Hushai's commitment to shift his loyalty from the father to the son, but Hushai's exact phrasing leaves room for a very different construal. The sense of the Hebrew (obscured in many English translations) is essentially as follows (in paraphrase): 'Whom shall I serve? Should not my service in the presence of the son be the same as in the presence of the father (i.e. to David in both instances!)? That's how I will be in your presence (i.e. still serving David!).'

20–23. Apparently clueless to the several double entendres in Hushai's words, Absalom seems satisfied with Hushai's responses and turns to Ahithophel to hear his advice first. Ahithophel's first piece of advice is that Absalom *Sleep with* (lit. 'go in to') the concubines of David, who had been left behind in Jerusalem *to take care of the palace* (see 15:16 and comment). Ahithophel's stated motivation for this reprehensible action is to make it abundantly clear to all Israel that Absalom's break with his father is irrevocable and that their break with David must be as well (v. 21). Absalom follows Ahithophel's advice without hesitation, taking his father's concubines on the very rooftop of the palace from which David had first succumbed to the temptation to take another man's wife (11:2). Thus are the dire words spoken by Nathan in 12:11–12 fulfilled. Before moving to Ahithophel's next piece of advice, the narrator pauses in verse 23 to describe the very high esteem in which Ahithophel's counsel was held by both David and Absalom. The challenge for Hushai – to counter the advice of one whose words were considered almost divinely inspired – will be great indeed.

17:1–4. Having advised Absalom about how to make his break with David definitive and obvious to all (16:21), Ahithophel now advises Absalom as to how he should deal with David himself: *I would choose twelve thousand men and set out tonight in pursuit of David* (v. 1). NIV gives the impression that Ahithophel is suggesting to Absalom what he would do were he in Absalom's place. In fact, however, according to the Hebrew text Ahithophel is expressing his desire to carry out the mission himself: 'Let me now choose twelve thousand men . . .' (cf. NRSV, ESV, JPS, NASB, NLT and most other English translations). The grievance that may have prompted Ahithophel to join Absalom's revolt (see at 15:12; 23:34) seems to be driving him still. A string of Hebrew cohortative verbs puts Ahithophel in the middle of the proposed attack on David: 'Let me choose . . . and I will arise . . . and I will pursue' (v. 1). Ahithophel's plan involves speed (*tonight*, v. 1) and focus (*I* [*will*] *strike down only the king*, v. 2), leaving the rest of the people unharmed, so that Ahithophel can return *all the people back to you* (v. 3). The Hebrew of verse 3b is difficult, and it is possible that a longer reading, reflected in LXX, has dropped out of the Hebrew text through haplography (for details see Driver 1960: 320–321). The longer reading is reflected in NRSV of verse 3: 'and I will bring all the people back to you as a bride comes home to her husband'. This simile is surprising in the mouth of the practical and to-the-point Ahithophel (later in the passage, it will be Hushai who proves himself the master of metaphor and simile).[75] But perhaps Ahithophel's single metaphorical usage, which refers to a 'bride' and 'her husband', hints at his festering resentment towards David for his disruption and ultimate destruction of the marriage of Bathsheba, Ahithophel's granddaughter.[76] Ahithophel's counsel that Absalom lie with David's concubines (16:21) may have been similarly motivated.

5–6. *Summon also Hushai the Arkite.* Apparently Hushai was not present while Ahithophel was giving his advice, as he must now be

---

75. For detailed discussions of Hushai's rhetorical skill, see Fokkelman (1981: 1.203–223); Bar-Efrat (1989: 223–237); Park (2009).
76. I am indebted to senior seminar student Amy Anderson for suggesting this possibility.

summoned (v. 5) and come to Absalom (v. 6). *This advice* (lit. 'this word, matter') of verse 6 is meant to imply that Absalom imparted to Hushai the details of Ahithophel's counsel. Now it is Hushai's turn: *give us your opinion* (v. 6; lit. 'You speak!').

7–10. Hushai begins his response emphatically, placing *not good* in first position (v. 7). His reference to *this time* suggests agreement with the general high regard for Ahithophel's advice – just not 'this time'! But of course, 'this time' is all that matters at present, if Hushai's task of buying time for David is to succeed. Hushai next explains why Ahithophel's advice should be ignored. David and his men are fierce warriors, especially when embittered, and they are savvy – David will not be found in the camp with his soldiers (v. 8). Furthermore, given that he is doubtless already in hiding, David might be in a position to deliver the first blow (v. 9) and thereby demoralize *even the bravest soldier* in Absalom's retinue (v. 10). Hushai's passing references to *bear* (v. 8) and *lion* (v. 10) subliminally recall the exploits of the young David (1 Sam. 17:34–36) – and, in turn, David's defeat of Goliath. By these references, Hushai effectively supports his claim that *your father is a fighter* (v. 10).

11–14. *Let all Israel . . . be gathered to you.* In contrast to Ahithophel's advocacy of a quick tactical strike, led by Ahithophel himself and focused exclusively on killing the king, Hushai advises a massive assault, led personally by Absalom and as irresistible (and indeed as effortless) as *dew* settling *on the ground*. Even if David *withdraws into a city*, there shall be no escape for him or his supporters, all of whom must die. Irresistible force shall prevail. Hushai's proposal meets with the approval of both Absalom and his men. Hushai's clever rhetoric played its part, but the key reason, as the narrator is careful to point out, is that *the* LORD *had determined to frustrate the good advice of Ahithophel* – a clear answer to David's prayer of 15:31.

15–16. Having ended his audience with Absalom, Hushai speaks (in private, we must assume) to the priests Zadok and Abiathar. Hushai's words are presented as direct address in Hebrew, and English translations are correct to place his words within quotation marks. As is typical in Hebrew parlance, however, standards of direct quotation are not the same as in English. In the present instance, Hushai reports that Ahithophel advised Absalom *to do such and such, but I have advised him to do so and so*; both *such and such* and *so and so* render the Hebrew phrase *kāzō't wekāzō't* ('like this and like this'). The reader is to understand that Hushai mentioned the actual specifics of the two proposals. *Now send a message at once and tell David* (v. 16). That Hushai's message for David is that he should not spend the night at the fords of the Jordan but, rather, should make speed to get across the river indicates that he is not yet sure that Absalom will in fact follow his and not Ahithophel's advice.

17–20. Despite a carefully planned messenger system, the sons of Zadok and Ahimaaz are spotted, and their location at En Rogel (a spring in the Kidron Valley outside the walls of Jerusalem and south of the Gihon Spring) is reported to Absalom (v. 18). They flee to Bahurim, less than 2 miles to the north-east, and find refuge there – David apparently has allies in this Saulide village as well as enemies (recall Shimei's cursings of 16:5). With the help of the woman of the house to which they fled, the two hide themselves in a well; wells were numerous in this semi-arid region and typically consisted of vertical shafts sunk to the water table and lined with field stones to prevent collapse. The openings of the wells, some 5 or 6 ft in diameter, were normally flush with the ground and thus could be covered and disguised (v. 19). When the servants of Absalom arrive searching, the woman 'covers' for the men also verbally (v. 20).[77]

The combination rendered *brook* in the woman's statement that *They crossed over the brook* (v. 20) is Hebrew *mîkal hammāyim*. This combination occurs nowhere else in the Hebrew Bible, and its meaning is unclear, as variance in the English translations suggests. McCarter (1984: 383) suspects a textual corruption and suggests reading *miyyĕbal hammāyim*, 'in the direction of the watercourse' (for other suggestions, see Driver 1960: 325, who notes that the versions offer no help). Whatever the intended literal meaning of the statement, the appearance of the word *mîkal* draws attention, as it occurs often in the David story as the name of one of his wives, Saul's daughter Michal. Interestingly, it was at the site of the present

---

77. One is reminded of the similar actions of Rahab in protecting the Israelite spies in Jericho, both hiding them and diverting their pursuers (Josh. 2).

scene (Bahurim) that Michal, at David's insistence, was forcibly separated from Paltiel, the husband to whom she had been given by Saul during David's wilderness years (3:15–16). If the appearance of *mîkal* in the present context is not simply the result of a copyist's error, perhaps the narrator used the word to subtly recall David's mistreatment of women (Michal? Bathsheba!). The use of messengers both here and in chapter 11 reinforces this impression. Reminders of David's earlier experiences have surfaced before, as in Hushai's reference in verses 7–10 to both bear and lion.

21–22. Having escaped detection, the two men deliver their message to David, noting that *Ahithophel has advised such and such against you*. *Such and such* is again a filler for what was actually said (see note on vv. 15–16). David responds with dispatch and *By daybreak, no one was left who had not crossed the Jordan* (v. 22). This notice indicates that getting across the Jordan was an all-night affair, which in turn indicates that had Ahithophel's advice been followed – namely, to attack that very night (17:1–2) – David would not have escaped. Thus, as Firth (2009: 469) observes, 'this chronological note hints again at Yahweh's involvement' in sparing David.

23. His advice ignored, Ahithophel takes matters into his own hands, puts *his house*[hold] *in order*[78] and takes his own life. In this desperate action, Ahithophel is in some senses anticipated by the suicide of Saul (1 Sam. 31:4–6). To rebel against the Lord is to set oneself on a path that ends in destruction.[79]

24–26. After the brief notice about Ahithophel, the narrative returns to David (now relocated in Mahanaim, Ish-Bosheth's old capital, 2:8) and to Absalom, who has *crossed the Jordan* (v. 24) and *camped in the land of Gilead* (v. 26). Given Joab's loyalty to David, Absalom has *appointed Amasa over the army* in his place (v. 25). *Amasa was the son of Jether* [or 'Ithra'], *an Ishmaelite* [see NIV text note] *who had married* [lit. 'had gone to'; marriage may not be implied] *Abigail*

---

78. Or perhaps 'gives final instructions to his house' (cf. *HALOT, ṣwh* pi'el, 4.ii). Might these instructions have included reference to the grievance of the house of Ahithophel respecting the Bathsheba affair?
79. In the Bible and the biblical world, suicide is not regarded as heroic in any sense (see Long 2009a: 388–389; 2009b: 467–468).

[different from David's wife], *the daughter of Nahash and sister of Zeruiah the mother of Joab* (v. 25). MT is clearly difficult as it stands (McCarter 1984: 391–392; Alter 1999: 301), but when all is said and done (and taking 1 Chr. 2:13–17 into account), it appears that Abigail was at least a half-sister of David, thus making Amasa David's nephew (cf. Firth 2009: 463–464). At a later point in the narrative, David himself will seek to replace Joab with Amasa (see at 19:13). But Joab doesn't brook rivals, so Amasa's tenure is brief (20:9–10).

27–29. David is met in Mahanaim by several supporters. *Shobi son of* the Ammonite king *Nahash* 'may even have been David's appointee in Rabbah following the Israelites' capture of the city (cf. 12:26–31)' (Gordon 1986: 283). *Makir* is from *Lo Debar* (a site of uncertain location, but likely near Mahanaim and the Jabbok River). Makir had taken in Jonathan's son Mephibosheth after the death of Saul (9:5–6). Perhaps Makir is here repaying David for the kindness he had shown Mephibosheth. Finally, *Barzillai the Gileadite* (who will appear prominently in 19:31–39) joins the others in provisioning David and his exhausted men not only with food and drink but with bedding as well (vv. 28–29).

Meaning

Various factors may have influenced Absalom's decision to follow Hushai's advice rather than the advice of the highly reputed Ahithophel. The latter's desire to take care of things himself may have left Absalom feeling marginalized. Hushai's advice, by contrast, puts Absalom squarely in the centre of things and also seems to offer the less risky approach. Hushai's clever, if evasive, rhetoric may have flattered Absalom's ego. In the end, though, it is Yahweh's frustration of *the good advice of Ahithophel* (17:14b) – an answer to David's prayer of 15:31 – that spells Absalom's doom.

iii. Absalom's death, David's grief and Joab's ultimatum (18:1 – 19:43)
Context

As 2 Samuel 18 opens, we find David both giving orders (three commanders over three companies) and taking orders (*I will do whatever seems best to you*, v. 4). The latter means that David will not be on the field of battle when Absalom is killed. Youngblood (2009: *ad loc.*) notes several similarities between David's actions in the face of Absalom's threat and his earlier actions when faced with the curses of Shimei (16:5–8). On both occasions David insists that the adversary be spared. And on both occasions the sons of Zeruiah are disinclined to be so mild. In the earlier incident, Joab's brother Abishai offered to separate Shimei's head from his body (16:9), but David prevented him. In the present instance, however, David will not be on the battlefield to prevent Joab from taking Absalom's life, despite David's direct orders to Joab and his men to *Be gentle with the young man Absalom for my sake* (18:5). The story of Absalom's death (18:1–18), of David's near-inconsolable grief over the loss of his 'son' who is no longer simply called the 'young man' (18:19 – 19:8a) and of Joab's rough words to bring David back to his senses and ultimately back to Jerusalem (19:8b–43) paints a wrenching picture. Though various characters in the story make reference to God or the Lord, the Lord himself is never consulted and he is not presented as initiating any actions. It is as if the consequences of unreconciled wrongdoing simply unfold as a matter of course.

Comment
a. Absalom's death (18:1–18)
1–5. Apparently refreshed by the ministrations at the end of chapter 17, David begins to act, mustering *the men who were with him and [appointing] over them commanders of thousands and commanders of hundreds* (v. 1). *Thousands* and *hundreds* (sometimes along with fifties and tens) were the standard measures by which the people were subdivided, whether for military purposes (Exod. 18:21; Num. 31:14; and *passim*) or for judicial oversight (see Deut. 1:15 in context). The *commanders* (*śārîm*) of military units were themselves under a superior commander, often called the *śar-ṣĕbā'*, 'commander of the army' or 'general' (e.g. Abner in 1 Sam. 14:50) or simply 'head' (1 Chr. 11:6). In the present context, David divides the troops into three divisions, each under a commander. The first is Joab, mentioned in 1 Samuel 26:6 but whose first actions are recorded in 2 Samuel 2:12–32. The second is Joab's brother Abishai, first met in 1 Samuel 26:6–12 as David's daring accomplice in the night visit

to Saul's camp. And the third is Ittai from Gath, whose loyalty to David was demonstrated in 15:19–22.

Once David has mustered his troops and established how they are to be deployed, *the king* states emphatically, *I myself will surely march out with you* (v. 2).[80] The people, however, have a different idea and object strongly, perhaps fearing that David's advancing age (cf. 21:15–17) or his attachment to Absalom (v. 5; 18:33 – 19:8) might make him a liability in the field. The reason they give, however, is that their lives are insignificant compared with the life of the king, who is *worth ten thousand of us. Even if half of us die, they won't care* (v. 3). Who *they* are is unspecified. Are David's men concerned that Absalom's supporters will not rest until David is dead, or that David's own supporters will not lose heart so long as David is alive, no matter how many others die? Either way, David's men press him to stay behind and *give us support from the city* (v. 3).[81] And *the king* acquiesces.

So the king stood beside the gate in Mahanaim (see 17:24, 27) *while all his men marched out* (v. 4). These actions, or inactions, of David are sensible enough in some respects, but the attentive reader may feel some unease, as an earlier occasion when David sent out troops while staying behind did not turn out well (ch. 11). Moreover, as noted already, David was quite emphatic in verse 2 about his intention to accompany the troops (the Hebrew construction involves not only an intensifying infinitive absolute but also the unnecessary *gam-'ănî* ['even I'], together yielding 'I myself will surely . . .'). David's willingness to change his mind in response to the people's resistance is, in one sense, commendable, as stubbornness is not a virtue. But his reversal is nevertheless mildly disconcerting, hinting perhaps at the disorientation that has plagued David since his tragic lapse in 2 Samuel 11. As the troops march out, David charges (*ṣwh*) his three commanders with but one order: *Be gentle with the young man Absalom for my sake* (v. 5). The notice that *all the troops heard the king* prepares for events later in the chapter

---

80. The shift from *David* to *the king* reflects the perspective of *the troops* and the fact that the crisis is political and not merely familial.
81. The Targum assumes that the *support* in view will be David's prayers.

when Joab determines to be anything but gentle with Absalom (vv. 10–14).

6–8. Battle is joined in the *forest of Ephraim* (v. 6), likely located somewhere in the vicinity of Mahanaim. We know from 17:24–26 that Absalom and his troops are already on the east side of the Jordan in Gilead. Since Ephraim's tribal territory is to the west of the Jordan, the presence of a forest bearing Ephraim's name east of the Jordan is surprising. But it may simply reflect the known history of conflict across tribal boundaries (see, e.g., Judg. 12:1–6). Noth (1983: 60–61, 201) suggests locating the 'wood of Ephraim' in the 'well-wooded mountain country' on both sides of the Jabbok River, which in the tribal period 'had hardly been opened up at all'. In this wild environment, *the forest swallowed up more men that day than the sword* (v. 8). Whether the loss of soldiers was through desertion, made all the more tempting by the thick cover, or through injuries suffered in the treacherous terrain is not stated. Some support for the latter notion may come from verse 17's mention of *a big pit in the forest* (cf. Gordon 1986: 284); and one cannot forget that a tree will prove Absalom's undoing (vv. 9–15). The Old Testament is replete with examples of nature being enlisted to fight on behalf of those with divine approval (e.g. Josh. 10:11–14; Judg. 5:20–21; 1 Sam. 2:10; 7:10; 12:17–18; 14:15; 2 Sam. 5:24; 22:8–16).

9. *Now Absalom happened to meet David's men.* The Hebrew combination (*qr'*–II followed by *lipnê*) supports the notion of a chance encounter (cf. the only other occurrence of the phrase, in Deut. 22:6: 'If you come across a bird's nest'), but the biblical view is that nothing happens purely by chance, least of all Absalom's encounter with *the thick branches of a large oak* which left him *hanging in mid-air*[82] and helpless. While the text makes no mention of Absalom's prized head of hair (14:25–26), it is hard to escape a sense of dramatic irony in Absalom's predicament. It is also hard to escape the sense that Absalom is under divine sanction: 'for a

---

82. Lit. 'between heaven and earth', suggesting to some Absalom's liminal state; cf. Fokkelman (1981: 1.242), for whom Absalom has become 'a nowhere man'.

hanged man is cursed by God' (Deut. 21:23, ESV).⁸³ Adding to the sense of irony is the notice that he was left hanging while *the mule [pered] he was riding kept on going*. While donkeys make regular appearances in Samuel, mules are mentioned in only one other context, namely, when the king's sons make their escape from the site of Absalom's orchestrated murder of his brother Amnon – each on his mule (*pered*; 13:29). As some have noted, the fact that the royal steed continues its flight without Absalom is a fitting picture of the kingdom departing from Absalom.

10–13. *One of the men* (lit. 'a certain man'; cf. 1 Sam. 1:1) spots Absalom and reports to Joab, *I have just seen* (lit. 'and behold I saw', *wĕhinnê rā'îtî*) *Absalom hanging in an oak tree* (v. 10). In response to this news, Joab chides the man in words that are at once mocking and ambiguous: *What! You saw him?* [lit. 'and behold you saw', *wĕhinnê rā'îtā*]. *Why didn't you strike him to the ground right there?* (v. 11). Does *strike him to the ground* mean kill him, or simply dislodge him from the tree? Joab avoids saying 'kill him', but this is his likely meaning (cf. Abner's use of 'strike to the ground' in 2:22, and Abishai's in 1 Sam. 26:8). When Joab mentions a sizeable reward that he would have owed the man had he dealt with Absalom (v. 11), the man responds by insisting that no amount of reward would bring him to disobey the king's explicit command, which he rephrases as *Protect the young man Absalom for my sake* (v. 12).⁸⁴ To disobey the king

---

83. While MT uses a qal passive of the verb *ntn* to describe Absalom's hanging, Qumran and the ancient versions attest the verb *tlh* in v. 9, which is the verb found in Deut. 21:23 and also in v. 10 of the present passage.

84. *Protect . . . for my sake* renders *šimrû-mî*, which is an unusual expression in Hebrew, occurring only here in the MT. Suspecting a copyist's error, some emend *mî* ('who') to *lî* ('for me'), citing versional support. Others retain *mî* and read 'whoever you may be'. On these two options, see McCarter (1984: 401), who himself prefers to treat *mî* as reflecting an 'enclitic mem' (a feature well known from other Semitic languages such as Ugaritic but vestigial in biblical Hebrew). On the possible import of an enclitic mem, such as to add emphasis, see Waltke and O'Connor (1990: §9.8).

would be folly, as *nothing is hidden from the king*, and, furthermore, had he struck Absalom down, *you [Joab] would have kept your distance* (v. 13). The unnamed man is savvy with respect to Joab's character and has the temerity to say so.

14–15. Impatient of being drawn into a debate over what should be done, and perhaps recognizing the difficulty of refuting the man's argument, Joab takes matters into his own hands: *So he took three javelins in his hand and plunged them into Absalom's heart while Absalom was still alive in the oak tree* (v. 14). Three factors suggest that Joab struck Absalom with rods rather than plunging javelins into his heart: (1) three javelins in the heart would hardly have left it necessary for ten armour-bearers in verse 15 to surround Absalom and finish him off; (2) the basic meaning of the Hebrew word used here, *šēbeṭ*, is 'rod, staff' and in no other context means 'spear' or 'javelin';[85] (3) the Hebrew text repeats 'in the heart' (*bēlēb*) both in reference to where Absalom was struck and in reference to where he was hanging when struck, namely, 'in the heart' of the tree. The best rendering for 'in the heart', then, should be something like in the 'middle' or, one might say, in the 'trunk' (torso). Once dislodged from the tree, Absalom is dispatched by *ten of Joab's armour-bearers* who *struck him and killed him* (v. 15).

16–18. Having struck three blows to Absalom's midsection in verse 14, Joab now in verse 16 strikes another blow, this time on the shofar (*trumpet*),[86] thus halting the pursuit. Ironically, Joab's action mirrors what Ahithophel had urged upon Absalom in 17:2 – kill the principal, and the rest of the people can be spared to return to you. A final irony in the account of Absalom's demise is effected by the juxtaposition of verses 17 and 18. Having met his end, Absalom in verse 17 is 'taken' and cast into a pit and buried under a very large pile of stones (a form of burial reserved for defeated enemies or criminals; cf. Josh. 7:25–26; 8:29). Verse 18 then notes that Absalom had earlier 'taken' and erected for himself a stone

---

85. In 23:21, Benaiah's *šēbeṭ* is contrasted with the *ḥănît* (spear) of his Egyptian foe; Benaiah wins the contest by wresting the spear from the Egyptian and killing him with his own weapon.
86. The same Hebrew verb (*tq'*) is used for both actions.

memorial (*maṣṣebet*),[87] lest his lack of a son cause his name to be forgotten. Second Samuel 14:27 mentions three (unnamed) sons born to Absalom as well as a beautiful daughter, Tamar, no doubt named for his sister Tamar who was violated by his half-brother Amnon (ch. 13). Perhaps Absalom's memorial was erected prior to his siring these children or (as seems more likely, since no sons of Absalom are mentioned in the ensuing narrative) the sons died before the memorial was built. A third possibility is that 'one or more of his sons were unwilling (for whatever reason) to perpetuate their father's memory' (Youngblood 2009: 526).

b. David's grief (18:19 – 19:8a)

19–23. With Absalom now dead and the rebellion quashed, the time has come to send word to David, and *Ahimaaz son of Zadok* is quick to volunteer to run and take the news. After all, he has a track record as a messenger to the king, beginning already at the start of Absalom's rebellion (15:27–28; 17:15–21); who better to bring the news of its definitive end? The message Ahimaaz wants to bring *to the king* is that *the* LORD *has vindicated him by delivering him from the hand of his enemies* (v. 19).[88] Joab resists sending Ahimaaz: *You are not the one to take the news today* (lit. 'you are not a man of *bĕśôrâ* today'; *bĕśôrâ* can connote either good news or the reward for bringing good news. On the link between good news and reward, see 4:10). Another day would be fine, but not today (v. 20), so Joab dispatches *a Cushite* (a Nubian or Ethiopian) to *tell the king what you have seen* (v. 21). Still Ahimaaz persists, pleading that he be allowed to run *behind the Cushite*, and still Joab resists: *You don't have any news that will bring you a reward* (v. 22). But Ahimaaz is not to be denied: *Come what may, I want to run* (v. 23). *Come what may* renders a single Hebrew word, *mâ* ('what'), and functions here like English 'whatever (the case)'. Finally, Joab relents, and in the event, though Ahimaaz

---

87. Not to be confused with the Hellenistic-period so-called Tomb of Absalom still found in the Kidron Valley.

88. NIV's *vindicated . . . by delivering* renders the single verb *špṭ*, whose base meaning is 'to judge'. In the actual delivery of the message, Ahimaaz will use a different verb (see v. 28), while the Cushite will use *špṭ* (v. 31).

begins *behind the Cushite*, he soon overtakes him by running *by way of the plain* (of the Jordan; v. 23). Ahimaaz's route from the field of battle in the *forest of Ephraim* (v. 6) down into the Jordan Valley and then back up to Mahanaim would have been longer than the mountainous route likely taken by the Cushite, but it would have been less strenuous and thus faster. Ahimaaz may also have been known for his running ability (cf. the lookout's comment in v. 27).

24–27. Meanwhile, David is in Mahanaim, *sitting between the inner and outer gates* (v. 24). When a *watchman* atop *the roof of the gateway by the wall* spies a runner coming in their direction, David remarks hopefully, *If he is alone, he must have good news* (v. 25). A defeat would have led to the flight of many troops, not just one, so David naturally assumes that a lone runner is bringing good news. Then a second lone runner is spotted, and David applies the same logic as before, assuming that the second man also is bringing good news (v. 26). When the lookout observes that the runner in front *runs like Ahimaaz son of Zadok*, David's confidence is bolstered, because *He's a good man* and must be bringing *good news* (v. 27). This may have been precisely the impression that Joab wanted to avoid by preventing Ahimaaz from bringing the message. Joab will have understood that his less than 'gentle' treatment of Absalom will not be welcomed as 'good' news by David, and he probably didn't want David to think that he himself thought it 'good' either, even if necessary.

28–33.[89] Ahimaaz arrives with a shout of *All is well!* (lit. *šālôm*), but the message he delivers is not quite so strongly worded as he had proposed in verse 19. Avoiding the verb *špṭ*,[90] he states only that the Lord has 'handed over' (*sgr* pi'el) *those who lifted their hands against my lord the King* (v. 28).[91] In answer to David's direct question about

---

89. MT places its chapter division after 18:32, so that v. 33 becomes 19:1. This means that the verse numbers in ch. 19 are one greater in Hebrew than in English: e.g. 19:1 in English is 19:2 in Hebrew. We cite the English verse numbers in this commentary.

90. See note on v. 19.

91. NIV obscures the terminological distinction by rendering both *špṭ*

the welfare (*šālôm*) of *the young man Absalom*, Ahimaaz becomes even more guarded: *I saw great confusion … but I don't know what it was* (v. 29). So David tells Ahimaaz to step aside and wait (v. 30). At that moment (lit. 'and behold', *wĕhinnē*), the Cushite arrives, flush with what he believes to be *good news* (v. 31). David's first question is again *Is the young man Absalom safe?*, in answer to which the Cushite makes clear that Absalom is dead (v. 32). This news trumps any other news the messengers might bring, and David asks no further questions. He is deeply *shaken* (v. 33); the Hebrew verb *rgz* can mean to 'quake' or 'tremble', to be 'shaken' emotionally. And he immediately goes up *to the room over the gateway* where he can be relatively alone, and he weeps. No longer referring to Absalom simply as *the young man* (*na'ar*, 18:5), David sobs, *O my son Absalom! My son, my son Absalom! If only I had died instead of you – O Absalom, my son, my son!* Fatherly feelings, so absent (or at least invisible) in David's last recorded face-to-face meeting with Absalom (14:33), now come tumbling out, but Absalom will not hear them.

19:1–8a.[92] News of David's inconsolable *mourning for Absalom* (v. 1) turns the *victory that day … into mourning* for the victorious troops (v. 2a), who instead of returning in glory steal *into the city … as men steal in who are ashamed when they flee from battle* (v. 3). The focus structurally as well as thematically is squarely on the fact – as the troops hear – that *The king is grieving for his son* (v. 2b). It may be no more than coincidence, but this statement (including its formulaic introduction *lē'mōr*, 'saying') is dead centre in the section bounded by David's framing lament, *O my son Absalom! O Absalom, my son, my son!* (first uttered in 18:33 and repeated in 19:4). To be precise, the statement of verse 2b is separated fore and aft from the framing laments by twenty Hebrew words. Moreover, in the span of five verses (18:33 – 9:4) we are returned four times to David's grieving for Absalom, either in description (vv. 1 and 2) or in demonstration (18:33 and 9:4).

That the king should be consumed with grief is entirely unacceptable to Joab, who wastes no time in getting to David and

---

(vv. 19, 31) and *sgr* (v. 28) as 'deliver (up)'.
92. On verse numbers in ch. 19, see footnote on 18:28–33 above.

issuing a stinging rebuke: *Today you have humiliated all your men . . . You love those who hate you and hate those who love you* (vv. 5–6). Joab's insistence that the troops have saved not only David's life but the lives of David's entire house, *sons and daughters . . . wives and concubines* (v. 5), is no exaggeration, if the behaviour of later royal usurpers be any indication (see 1 Kgs 15:29; 16:11–12; 2 Kgs 10:6–7, 17). As one of David's three appointed *commanders* (v. 6; cf. 18:1–2), Joab includes himself among those aggrieved by David's behaviour and couches his complaint in either/or terms: *you would be pleased if Absalom were alive today and all of us were dead* (v. 6).

Joab concludes his upbraiding of David with an ultimatum: encourage your men or *not a man will be left with you by nightfall*, a calamity the likes of which you have not experienced *from your youth till now* (v. 7). David complies without a word, taking *his seat in the gateway* (v. 8). It was at this same gateway in Mahanaim that David had ordered Joab and the other commanders to *Be gentle* [*lĕ'aṭ*] *with the young man Absalom* (18:5), and it was in the room over the gateway that he had most recently *covered* [*lā'aṭ*] *his face* and wept (v. 4). The sonorous affinity of *lĕ'aṭ* and *lā'aṭ* draws together the two moments – plea and loss. Further features tie the present scene together with what started it all: Absalom standing near the 'gate' of Jerusalem, 'stealing' (*gnb* pi'el) the 'hearts' of the people (15:2, 6); now David's troops are 'stealing' (*gnb* hitpa'el) into the city,[93] and he must take his place in the 'gate' and 'speak to the hearts' of the people (19:7; NIV renders Hebrew 'speak to the heart' as *encourage*).[94]

c. *David's return to Jerusalem (19:8b–43)*

8b–15a. If Joab's rough words had not succeeded in redirecting David's attention away from family to matters of state, political circumstances certainly would have. His own men returned to him in verse 8a, but his opponents, the Israelites, *had fled to their homes* (v. 8b), where they began debating what they should do next. Having backed Absalom (now dead), they are in an awkward

---

93. Elsewhere in Samuel, the root *gnb* occurs only in 2 Sam. 19:41 (Heb. v. 42) and 21:12.

94. On these lexical links, see Alter (1999: 312), referencing M. Garsiel.

position. Recalling how David had delivered them from the Philistines in the past, the northern tribes begin to blame one another for the current predicament: *So why do you say nothing about bringing the king back?* (vv. 9–10). Meanwhile, David, having heard what the northern tribes of Israel are saying, sends a message to the priests Zadok and Abiathar (who were his covert agents in Jerusalem throughout the rebellion of Absalom), instructing them to do two things. First, they are to press the elders of Judah with the question why they, as David's kinsmen, have not sought to bring him back to Jerusalem (vv. 11–12). Second, they are to announce to Amasa, who had sided with Absalom, that he is to replace Joab as commander over David's army (v. 13). This is an astute political move, extending an olive branch towards the northern tribes and applying a rod of discipline to Joab (lest David seem impotent in the face of the fact that Joab had brazenly ignored his orders by killing Absalom). In reality, of course, being appointed to replace Joab was tantamount to a death sentence.[95] David's efforts are successful (v. 14), and he begins his return to Jerusalem, getting *as far as the Jordan* (v. 15a).

15b–18a. Rivalry between Israel and Judah will feature again at the end of the chapter (vv. 40–43), but in the interim the focus shifts to David's encounters with individuals, most of whom he had already encountered while fleeing Jerusalem. The *men of Judah* get as far as Gilgal, in the Jordan Valley(v. 15b), and with them is the infamous Benjaminite *Shimei* of Bahurim (v. 16; recall his cursing episode in 16:5–14). Shimei is accompanied by *a thousand Benjaminites* (v. 17). The purpose of this entourage is unspecified. Is it to show the king that Shimei has manpower to offer him? Or is it to afford protection for Shimei, should his attempt to make amends fail? Or is it simply the case that many Benjaminites in addition to Shimei are keen to side with David, now that the attempted coup has failed? The situation is ambiguous, as is the case of another Benjaminite, *Ziba, the steward of Saul's household* (v. 17). During David's flight from Jerusalem, Ziba had curried favour with David and

---

95. See 3:27 with respect to Abner and 20:4–10 for the end of the story of Amasa.

incriminated his master, Saul's grandson Mephibosheth (16:1–4). Naturally desperate to make amends, Shimei and his men, along with Ziba, *crossed at the ford to take the king's household over* (v. 18).

18b–23. Shimei's are the first words to the returning king to be recorded, and how different they are from his earlier cursings, now that the tables are turned. No longer is it *you murderer, you scoundrel!* (16:7) but, rather, *I have sinned* (v. 20a). Pleading for his life, Shimei stresses that he is *the first from the tribes of Joseph to come down and meet my lord the king* (v. 20b). Who gets to approach David first has been an issue already in the dispute between the tribes of Israel and Judah (vv. 8b–15), and Shimei is desperate to marshal any reasons he can to gain clemency from David. Disinclined to show mercy, *Abishai son of Zeruiah* suggests for a second time (see 16:9) that Shimei should die (v. 21), and for a second time David rebukes one of the *sons of Zeruiah*; on the first occasion David expressed his submission to the divine will (16:10) and now on the second occasion he cites his vindication: *Don't I know that today I am king over Israel?* (v. 22). Then the king swears an oath to Shimei: *You shall not die* (v. 23). In due course, Shimei is in fact put to death by a king – not by David but by his son Solomon (1 Kgs 2:36–46). In his charge to Solomon at the time of Solomon's accession, David recalls both Shimei's violent cursings of David and also David's oath to Shimei at the Jordan. David's rephrasing of the oath, however, 'I will not put you to death by the sword' (1 Kgs 2:8), leaves open the possibility that someone else might, and David does not mince words with Solomon: 'Bring his grey head down to the grave in blood' (2:9).[96]

24–30. Next to speak with David is *Mephibosheth, Saul's grandson*. His neglect of personal hygiene, confirmed by the narrator as having begun *from the day the king left [Jerusalem] until the day he returned safely* (v. 24), provides tangible evidence to support his answer to David's query, *Why didn't you go with me, Mephibosheth?* (v. 25). Mephibosheth's answer incriminates Ziba (v. 26), who had *betrayed* Mephibosheth by telling a very different story (16:1–4), and

---

96. The Shimei of 1 Kgs 1:8, who refused to join Adonijah's attempted coup, is likely a different Shimei, perhaps the son of Ela mentioned in 1 Kgs 4:18 as one of Solomon's district governors.

Mephibosheth expresses confidence that David, as perceptive as *an angel of God*, will do the right thing (v. 27). Only three other times does the phrase *angel of God* appear in Samuel: once in the context of David's duping the Philistine king Achish (1 Sam. 29:9) and twice in the context of David's being duped by Joab's agent, the wise woman of Tekoa (2 Sam. 14:17, 20). That Mephibosheth refers to him here as *like an angel of God*, therefore, does not in fact bolster confidence that David will know the right thing to do. David's decision to split the Saulide holdings (earlier promised to Ziba; 16:1–4) between Mephibosheth and Ziba (v. 29), rather than devising means to get to the bottom of the vying claims, is not explained by the narrative. It may suggest a desire to make peace through compromise, or it may reflect David's exhaustion and a degree of continuing disorientation. Mephibosheth's *Let him take everything* (v. 30) may be sincerely meant, or it may reflect an awareness that little more can be expected of David in his current state, or it may be a bargaining manoeuvre (cf. Hertzberg 1964: 367). Though David seems unsure whom to believe, the evidence supports Mephibosheth's version of events (e.g. his physical appearance; the narrator's confirmation that personal grooming had ceased the day David left Jerusalem; the improbability that Mephibosheth, as a cripple, should have seen David's distress as an opening for his own ascendancy; and thus Mephibosheth's lack of motive, in contrast to Ziba's opportunism).

31–39. David's final encounter is with *Barzillai the Gileadite* (v. 31), who along with Shobi and Makir had provided physical support for David in Mahanaim in Transjodan (see 17:27–29). It is not clear from the Hebrew text of verse 31 (v. 32 in Heb.) whether or not Barzillai actually crosses the Jordan with David, but it seems unlikely that he does. He is, after all, eighty years old, and he is quite clear about his diminished capacities.[97] His statement in verse 36 (Heb. 37), *kim'at ya'ăbōr 'abdĕkā 'et-hayyardēn 'et-hamelek* – rendered by NIV as *Your servant will cross over the Jordan with the king for a short*

---

97. The prime physical condition of another octogenarian, Caleb, is remarked upon in Josh. 14:10–11 precisely because it was remarkable, not the rule.

distance – should probably read as something like 'Your servant is hardly able to cross the Jordan with the king' (similarly, JPS). Most likely, then, Barzillai simply came to the Jordan to 'give [David] a good send-off' (MSG).

Barzillai was a man of means (v. 32),[98] and he had *provided [kilkal] for the king during his stay in Mahanaim* (v. 32). Now David wants to return the favour: *Cross over with me . . . and I will provide [wĕkilkaltî] for you* (v. 33). Barzillai demurs, however, explaining that he is too old to enjoy the sights, sounds and tastes of life in David's court (vv. 34–35). But having declined to accompany David personally, Barzillai suggests a younger substitute, *your servant Kimham* (v. 37), probably his own son (made explicit in some LXX manuscripts). The name 'Geruth Kimham' ('Kimham's holding') in Jeremiah 41:17 may suggest that David gave Kimham land in the vicinity of Bethlehem (cf. Gordon 1986: 292). Barzillai's wish is that he himself return to his *own town*, that is, Rogelim (v. 31; cf. 17:27), and that David do for Kimham *whatever you wish* (v. 37). David agrees, insisting that he will do for Kimham *whatever you [Barzillai] wish* (v. 38).

So all the people crossed the Jordan, and then the king crossed over (v. 39). That this notice immediately precedes David's kissing Barzillai and bidding him farewell does not indicate that Barzillai crossed the Jordan. Hebrew usage allows a brief summary of an event (in this instance, that king and people crossed) to precede a more detailed accounting of the event in its various stages (David kissed Barzillai before crossing; note that the king crosses with Kimham in v. 40).[99]

40–43. Now that David's encounters with key individuals have been reported, the focus returns to the rivalries between the northern tribes of Israel and Judah. That *All the troops of Judah* but

---

98. An '*îš gādôl mě'ôd* (Heb. v. 33). Cf. 1 Sam 25:2, where the same description is used to describe the obviously wealthy, if brutish, Nabal.

99. Alternatively (or additionally), there may be a transcriptional error involving the substitution of the verb '*ābar* (yielding 'the king crossed') for an original '*āmad* (which would read the king 'stood' or 'stayed behind'); the latter reading may be suggested by the Greek *histēkei* ('had stood') of some manuscripts of the LXX (cf. McCarter 1984: 418).

only *half*[100] *the troops of Israel* bring David across the Jordan (v. 40) signals continued reservation in the north. But *Soon all the men of Israel* are *coming to the king*, complaining that their *brothers, the men of Judah . . . together with all his* [Hebrew has *David's*] *men*, have treated them unfairly by *steal[ing] the king away and bring[ing] him . . . across the Jordan* (v. 41). The men of Israel make no mention of their recent allegiance to a different would-be king, but seek to tie themselves to the winning side, referring to the men of Judah as *our brothers*. The men of Judah are quick to respond to the northerners' complaint, stressing that *the king is closely related to us* and insisting that they, nevertheless, have taken no material advantage from that fact (v. 42). The men of Israel retort that they have *ten shares in the king*, referencing the number of northern tribes (cf. the prophet Ahijah's symbolic action in 1 Kgs 11:30–31, 'Take ten pieces . . . ten tribes') or, less likely in this context, simply using a 10–1 numeric convention (cf. 1 Sam. 18:7, *Saul has slain his thousands, / and David his tens of thousands*). The men of Judah respond harshly (v. 43), and the stage is set for those claiming ten shares in David to disavow (in the next chapter) having any share in David at all. Noteworthy in all this is the fact that, though the men of Israel *were coming to the king*, as verse 41 explicitly states, the king apparently says nothing to keep the situation from unravelling as it did.

Meaning
For a good long time, David has been destabilized by the ripple effects of his own sin. His loss of his son Absalom only makes matters worse. Absalom's death eventually returns David to his kingdom but not immediately to his senses. His disorientation is evident even in his victorious recrossing of the Jordan on his way to Jerusalem. But David is not alone in his confusion. Those, especially the northern tribes, who had sided with Absalom are red-faced and scrambling to make amends. Even David's supporters are disoriented by his inconsolable grief over the death of Absalom, the very one who had sought David's death and whose defeat was achieved at the risk of their own lives. Joab, ever the man of action,

---

100. Or 'part of' (so JPS; cf. *NIDOTTE*, s.v. ḥāṣâ).

intervenes to get David back on track. He issues an ultimatum, and David complies. In their behaviours, both Joab and David are partly right, but only partly. Joab escalates his challenges to either/or categories. David yields to Joab's demands and saves the political situation, for the time being at least. But he seems weak in his dealings with several individuals, not least with Joab himself, who simply brushes aside David's attempt to replace him with Amasa. The justly frightened Shimei manages to secure an oath from David that he will not die, but the oath does not ultimately hold (1 Kgs 2). Ziba, who betrayed Mephibosheth, goes unpunished, while Mephibosheth's loyalty to David, suggested by the narrator's reference to Mephibosheth's cessation of personal hygiene during David's exile, goes unacknowledged by a king lacking the will or the wisdom to get to the bottom of the situation. David simply divides the property between Ziba and Mephibosheth, and leaves questions of guilt or innocence unanswered. David's encounter with Barzillai, a friend, is less fraught, and David readily follows Barzillai's every suggestion about how, and with whom, they should return each to his own domain. Finally, the brewing dispute between north and south heats up, and, though *all the men of Israel* come *to the king*, there is no record of his saying or doing anything to calm the situation. Instead, the overheated exchanges between the tribal leaders continue into the next chapter, where they boil over into yet another political crisis for David.

D. Sheba's revolt and death (20:1–26)

Context
Though Absalom's revolt has been successfully put down, David's troubles are not yet at an end. The growing tensions between north and south are such that it only takes a scoundrel, a trumpet and a shout to plunge the Davidic kingdom into another crisis. This crisis, launched by a Benjaminite who just happened to be on the scene, is relatively short-lived, but it nevertheless has its share of treachery, bloodshed and death. Were it not for the intervention of the wise woman of Abel Beth Maakah, the losses would surely have been much greater. Chapter 20 ends with four verses detailing the royal bureaucracy developing under David's

rule. Apart from the ominous introduction of a reference to *forced labour*, this section mirrors the earlier list of 8:15–18. 'Thus the narrative of David's family is framed in 8:15–18 and 20:23–26 by two inventories of bureaucratic organization' (Brueggemann 1990: 332).

Comment
1–2. Such are the tensions between north and south that developed in the last chapter that it only takes *a troublemaker named Sheba son of Bikri* to induce the northern tribes to abandon their claim to *ten shares in the king* (19:43) and follow Sheba in his insurrectionist manifesto:

We have no share in David,
  no part in Jesse's son!
(v. 1)

As a *Benjaminite*, and possibly a relative of Saul,[101] Sheba seems more than happy to draw followers away from David, and he does so very effectively: *So all the men of Israel deserted David to follow Sheba son of Bikri* (v. 2).

3. Upon re-entering *his palace in Jerusalem*, David's first action is to deal with *the ten concubines he had left to take care of the palace* (see 15:16 and comment). Ironically, those left 'to guard/watch over the house' (*lišmōr habbayit*) are now put in *a house under guard* (*bêt mišmeret*). Presumably this action is necessary because of Absalom's violation of the concubines during David's absence from Jerusalem (16:22). Beyond this basic point, opinions vary regarding David's motivations for cloistering the concubines. Peterson (1999: 236–238) senses a chastened David who refuses to *use* the concubines to aggrandize his royal status; we might contrast his insistence on the return of his wife Michal in 3:13–16, after she had been given to another man. Brueggemann (1990: 330) moots the possibility that David's putting away of the concubines may have been done in

---

101. Bright (2000: 210) links *Bikri* with the *Bekorath* of Saul's genealogy in 1 Sam. 9:1.

deference to the appropriate scruples of the more traditional northern tribes, signalling a desire on David's part to move away 'from the royal ideology [of the Near East] in the direction of the old requirements of the covenant'. Birch (1998: 1351) suggests that David may simply be concerned with preserving his own honour by 'refusing to restore to his household the women Absalom has defiled'. Whatever the reason for David's treatment of the concubines, they pay a high price for the misdeeds of others – violation, then lifelong confinement and 'interrupted conjugality', as Alter puts it (1999: 322). David does provide for their basic subsistence, as was expected in the Ancient Near East when a wife became unfit for wifely duties (Long 2009b: 472, citing *ANET* 172§148: 'continue to support her as long as she lives'), but relational–familial needs must have been a different story.

4–7. Whether David's sequestering of the concubines (v. 3) was in any sense a response to the desertion of the northern tribes, some kind of response was certainly called for, and David orders Amasa, recently appointed to replace Joab as commander of David's army (19:13), to *Summon the men of Judah* and report back personally *within three days* (v. 4).[102] As it happens, Amasa does not keep to the time frame (v. 5). We are not told whether Amasa's tardiness was wilful – after all, he had earlier been part of Absalom's rebellion (17:25) – or logistical, but David wastes no time in turning to Abishai to take charge. David's concern is that *Sheba son of Bikri will do us more harm than Absalom did*. David is particularly worried that Sheba may *find fortified cities and escape from us* (v. 6). Speed is of the essence, and so Abishai is to *Take your master's men and pursue him* (v. 6). Is Abishai's *master* David or, as seems more likely given the reference to *Joab's men* in verse 7, Joab himself? Whatever the case, Joab's men and David's personal troops, *the Kerethites and Pelethites* (see at 1 Sam. 30:14 and 2 Sam. 8:18), along with *all the mighty warriors*, depart from Jerusalem *under the command of Abishai* and in pursuit of Sheba (v. 7). As the narrative unfolds, it becomes increasingly clear who the real commander is. While Abishai is putatively in charge

---

102. Three days was a short, though not impossible, amount of time for Amasa to carry out his orders; see comment on 1 Sam. 11:4.

in verse 7, by verse 10 we find both *Joab and his brother Abishai pursuing Sheba*, and by verse 13 we read that *everyone went on with Joab to pursue Sheba son of Bikri*. Joab was never one to give way to rivals, as the very next section illustrates.

8–10. When Abishai and Joab get to *the great rock in Gibeon*,[103] some 6 miles north of Jerusalem, *Amasa came to meet them* (v. 8). To encounter Amasa in Benjaminite territory is disconcerting (Gordon 1986: 294), given that his orders were to gather the men of Judah (v. 4) in the south. The bulk of verse 8 is taken up with a description of Joab's attire and arms. As biblical narrative is typically sparing in such details, this description draws the reader's attention. Unfortunately, the Hebrew of the verse is obscure, but whatever its precise meaning – for example, whether Joab had one sword (*ḥereb*)[104] or two – the point of the description is that he was able to catch Amasa off guard. The text tells us that as Joab *stepped forward, it* [the sword/dagger] *fell*, or *dropped*; NIV adds *out of its sheath* (v. 8). Several scenarios are possible. Perhaps the sword fell into a fold of Joab's tunic and was thus concealed. Or the sword fell to the ground and was left lying there, giving Amasa the impression that Joab was unarmed, when in fact he had a second, concealed weapon. Or, as seems most likely, Joab retrieved the one fallen sword with his left hand but did not take it by his fighting hand, and so, when *Joab took Amasa by the beard with his right hand to kiss him* [v. 9], *Amasa was not on his guard against* the weapon in Joab's left hand (v. 10). One blow is all it took to inflict a mortal wound. Joab is well practised in delivering unexpected mortal blows (e.g. to Abner in 3:27). Having dispatched Amasa, *Joab and his brother Abishai* continue the pursuit of *Sheba son of Bikri* (v. 10).[105]

11–13. While Joab and Abishai show no inclination to linger over spilt blood, not so the troops. *One of Joab's men stood beside*

---

103. Possibly a local landmark; for other possible examples, see 1 Sam. 19:22; 20:19; 2 Sam. 15:17.
104. This is the normal word for 'sword', though it can possibly mean 'dagger'.
105. Again, we note how Joab progressively reverses his demotion by David (see comment on v. 7).

Amasa, who *lay wallowing in his blood in the middle of the road* (vv. 11–12), in order to challenge passers-by. We may assume that not all those on the road would have been the troops who had left Jerusalem under Abishai's (now Joab's) command. Some may have been men of Judah whom Amasa, at David's behest, had summoned (see vv. 4–5). The challenge issued by Joab's man (Heb. *naʿar*, so possibly one of Joab's personal servants) was this: *Whoever favours Joab, and whoever is for David, let him follow Joab!* (v. 11). That the challenge begins and ends with Joab is suggestive of the power politics at work – and, unsurprisingly, Abishai gets no mention at all. Henceforth, Joab is firmly in charge. The sight of Amasa *in the middle of the road* does not spur the troops on but brings them *to a halt*, and so Joab's man finds it necessary to drag Amasa's dead body *into a field* and throw *a garment over him* (v. 12). The road cleared of Amasa's bloody corpse, *everyone went on [ʿābar] with [or 'after'] Joab to pursue Sheba son of Bikri* (v. 13).

14–15. The scene changes to focus on *Sheba*, who *passed through all the tribes of Israel to Abel Beth Maakah and through the entire region of the Bikrites* (v. 14).[106] *Passed through* renders the Hebrew verb *ʿābar*, the same verb rendered *went on* in verse 13. As Alter (1999: 325) notes, 'the repetition of [a] verb in a slightly different meaning' is 'in accordance with an established technique of biblical narrative' by which a new scene is linked to the preceding: the soldiers 'pass' by the corpse, while Sheba 'passes' through the northern territories.[107] *Abel Beth Maakah* is perhaps to be identified with Tell Abil el-Qamh, which lies in the very far north, some 12 miles north of Lake Hulah and 4 miles west of Dan.[108] On the kingdom of *Maakah*, see on 10:6.

---

106. MT has 'Berites' in place of 'Bikrites', but 'Berites' is otherwise unattested, and 'Bikrites' is to be preferred (supported by LXX's *pantes en Xarri*, which retroverts to Heb. *kol-habbikrîm*, 'all the Bikrites'); see Driver (1960: 345).
107. The underlying Heb. verb, *ʿābar* ('cross over'), occurs some fifteen times in the preceding chapter. In the present chapter, a similar linking function is achieved by the Heb. verb *bôʾ* ('come') in vv. 14–15.
108. On the archaeology of the site, see Yahalom-Mack, Panitz-Cohen and Mullins (2018).

Abel was a city of some importance, attracting the attention of the Aramean king Ben-Hadad in 1 Kings 15:20 and of the Assyrian king Tiglath-pileser in 2 Kings 15:29. Sheba gains followers, particularly among the *Bikrites* (his family, clan or sympathizers), and they gathered and 'entered [the city] following after him'; this seems a more accurate rendering of verse 14's final clause, *wayyābō'û 'ap-'aḥărāyw*, than NIV's *and followed him*, as the verb *bô'* suggests coming to or entering (the city).

Joab and his troops also come (verb *bô'*) to Abel, where they *buil[d] a siege ramp up to the city*, against its *outer fortifications* (v. 15). NIV's *built* renders the Hebrew verb *šāpak* (to pour [out]), the same word used to describe the 'spilling out' of Amasa's intestines onto the ground in verse 10. Here the sense is that the earthen siege ramp is 'poured out' of containers used to transport the dirt. Not only do Joab's troops seek to surmount the city wall, they batter (Heb. *šāḥat* hipʻil), or 'savage' (so Alter), the wall, in order *to bring it down*. And well they might have done, had it not been for the intervention of a wise woman.

16–22. *Listen! Listen!* are the wise woman's first words.[109] And she is savvy enough to know that Joab is the man in charge (v. 16), though she has not before encountered him (note *Are you Joab?* in v. 17). Having gained a hearing – '*Listen to what your servant has to say.*' '*I'm listening*' – the wise woman presents her case, and it has to do with asking. Abel has a long-standing reputation; people would say, '*Get your answer at Abel,' and that settled it* (v. 18). NIV's rendering of *šā'ōl yĕšā'ălû bĕ'ābēl* suggests that the wise woman is pointing to the renowned wisdom of the city of Abel (an understanding commonly assumed and reflected in most translations). A more literal translation would be 'they would just[110] ask'. *And that settled it*, or 'ended the matter' (v.18).[111] The wise woman's emphasis, then, may be not so much on Abel's wisdom as on its peaceableness, reinforced by

---

109. For another wise woman who plays a key role, see 2 Sam. 14.
110. Meant to capture the intensifying function of the qal infinitive absolute *šā'ōl*.
111. *HALOT* (*tmm*, hipʻil–6) renders the final clause of v. 18 as 'then it is brought to a proper conclusion'.

her next words: *We are the peaceful and faithful in Israel* (v. 19). Her point is that the crisis need not come to blows; Joab need only ask (state his grievance), and a solution can be found. *Far be it from me to swallow up or destroy!* responds Joab (v. 20) – the dramatic irony of Joab's self-description will be evident to those who have followed his story to this point. In the present instance, though, Joab is wisely restrained and requests only that the *one man* be handed over. In response, the woman promises that the requisite head will shortly be delivered over the wall (v. 21). As persuasive with her own people as with Joab, the wise woman soon delivers on her promise. Sheba is dead, Joab sounds the trumpet, the city is spared and Joab returns to Jerusalem, David's crisis averted (v. 22). The crisis that began with a trumpet blast and the call for the men of Israel to abandon David and return *Every man to his tent* ends with another trumpet blast and Joab's men *each returning to his home* (or 'tent', v. 22; the phrases are identical in Hebrew, *'îš lĕ'ōhālāyw*).

23–26. The summary listing of David's chief officials is appropriately placed, now that both Absalom's and Sheba's revolts have been quelled and David's throne is secure. This summary mirrors the earlier listing, which was also appropriately placed in 8:15–18 at the point when David's rule was established over both Judah and Israel and when, even with respect to neighbouring territories, *The LORD gave David victory wherever he went* (8:14). When these two lists are compared, however, notable differences in the second appear, involving both omissions and additions. Many of the officials are the same in the second list. *Joab*, despite David's attempt to replace him (19:13), remains *over Israel's entire army*; *Benaiah* continues to command David's personal bodyguard, *the Kerethites and Pelethites* (v. 23); *Jehoshaphat* is still *recorder* (v. 24); *Sheva* (spelled *Seraiah* in the earlier list) is still *secretary*; and *Zadok and Abiathar* are still *priests* (v. 25). On all these, see discussion of the list in 8:15–18. That the ordering of the second list differs from the first – Benaiah being elevated to second position after Joab, the priests Zadok and Abiathar being lowered to next to last position – may or may not be significant. (Are military matters given primacy over the priestly?)

Clearly significant is the addition of *Adoniram* who *was in charge of forced labour* (v. 24). *Forced labour* (Heb. *mas*) was part of Israel's experience from the days of their slavery in Egypt (Exod. 1:11). The labour force in view in the present passage may comprise subjugated non-Israelites (cf. Josh. 16:10; 17:13; etc.), but by Solomon's day labourers are 'conscripted' also 'from all Israel' (1 Kgs 5:13) as well as from 'the descendants of all these peoples remaining in the land – whom the Israelites could not exterminate' (1 Kgs 9:21) and are put to work on Solomon's building projects (1 Kgs 9:15). Adoniram remained in charge of forced labour even into the reign of Solomon's son Rehoboam, when he met a violent end (1 Kgs 12:18). David's introduction of a forced labour force may suggest his interest in developing the physical infrastructure of his kingdom: roadways, administrative buildings, fortresses, and so on.

Also potentially significant is the addition of *Ira the Jairite* as *David's priest* (v. 26). The earlier list had David's sons in this role, but of course much has changed with respect to David's sons. Of *Ira the Jairite* little is known with certainty. Perhaps he is to be identified with *Ira son of Ikkesh* (23:26), one of David's 'thirty' mighty men (23:24–39), or perhaps more likely with *Ira the Ithrite* (23:38), another of David's 'thirty'. *Jairite* is equally uncertain; does it refer to the levitical city of 'Jattir' (Josh. 21:14), to 'Jair, a descendant of Manasseh' (Num. 32:41; Deut. 3:14), to 'Jair of Gilead' (Judg. 10:3), or to none of the above?

Most notable by its absence in the second list is the statement that had introduced the earlier listing of David's court: *David reigned over all Israel, doing what was just and right for all his people* (8:15). Much has changed in the character of David's rule since his tragic fall in the Bathsheba–Uriah affair of 2 Samuel 11. The results in both family and kingdom have been tragic. And it is now much more difficult to state with confidence that David has done *what was just and right for all his people*.

Meaning
David's return to Jerusalem in chapter 19 proved explosive in terms of north–south rivalries, and there is no indication in the text that David intervened in any way to lessen the tensions. His apparent passivity, or incapacity to speak words of reconciliation, led to yet another political crisis. The situation became so heated that the Benjaminite Sheba – with but a trumpet blast and a few

insurrectionist lines – was able to spark a full-blown desertion of David by the north. Back in Jerusalem, David had internal affairs to deal with. The heaviest price was again paid by his concubines, once violated and now isolated. Amasa, too, failing in his duties, paid with his life for David's attempt to promote him over Joab. Joab, on the other hand, despite David's attempts to demote him, reasserted his command and ultimately quelled Sheba's rebellion. The words of a wise woman in Abel Beth Maakah defused what might otherwise have become a very violent confrontation.

And so through all this, David's kingdom was saved and, if Joab's command *over Israel's entire army* (v. 23) be any indication, its unity preserved. But the saving of David's kingdom was accomplished not so much by what he did or said, as by what others (Joab, the wise woman of Abel) did and said. Remarkable by its absence is any mention of Yahweh, or of prayer for guidance, throughout the entire episode.

8. CONCLUSION: LAST WORDS ABOUT DAVID AND HIS REIGN (2 SAMUEL 21:1 – 24:25)

In the account of events in David's family and kingdom following his fall into adultery, murder and cover-up, the portrayal of David has been mixed. Though his continued trust in Yahweh has shone through on occasion (e.g. 15:25–26; 16:11–12), David has appeared at times still to be struggling to find his feet after his great fall. But this period of disorientation is not the final word on David. The book of Samuel ends with a well-ordered epilogue, or conclusion, that paints a more rounded picture of David as a flawed but profoundly God-fearing man, and a man to whom God has made enduring promises. As Childs opined many decades ago, 'the final four chapters, far from being a clumsy appendix, offer a highly reflective, theological interpretation of David's whole career' (1979: 275).[1]

---

1. Notions that the final chapters of 2 Samuel are mere appendices containing material for which no place was found earlier in the book seriously underestimate the coherence and significance of 2 Samuel's final four chapters (cf., e.g., Klement 2000b: 241–246 and *passim*).

The symmetrical arrangement of the Samuel conclusion, now regularly highlighted by commentators, may be represented as follows:

- A. Royal sin and its resolution (21:1–14)
  - B. Short list of David's champions (21:15–22)
    - C. Long poetic composition: David's song of praise (22:1–51)
    - C.' Short poetic composition: David's last words (23:1–7)
  - B.' Long list of David's champions (23:8–39)
- A.' Royal sin and its resolution (24:1–25)

The symmetrical arrangement of these concluding sections is aesthetically pleasing (and not atypical of numerous such arrangements in the OT). But it also seems to carry thematic and theological significance, as shall become apparent below.

A. Royal sin and its resolution (21:1–14)

Context
Following immediately upon the long and sad tale of David's sin and its consequences (2 Sam. 11 – 20), the first element in the symmetrically structured conclusion to the book of Samuel returns to an earlier period in David's reign and to a crisis brought about not by his own sin but by the sin of his predecessor, Saul. The crisis was a severe famine in the land that persisted for three years. To discover the cause of the famine, David prays (lit. *sought the face of the LORD*, v. 1). Having discovered the sin, David asks the sinned-against, the Gibeonites, to suggest the solution. This leads to further complications, and it is not until David takes further action that *God answered prayer on behalf of the land* (v. 14).

Comment
1. *During the reign of David* [lit. 'in the days of David'], *there was a famine*. The time reference is vague, but the famine quite likely occurred before Absalom's revolt; Shimei's cursing David in 16:8 for *all the blood you shed in the household of Saul* seems to presuppose the

killing of seven descendants of Saul recounted in the present chapter. And it probably occurred after David's induction of Jonathan's son Mephibosheth into his court in 2 Samuel 9, as 21:7 mentions this event. The severity of the famine is emphasized in the Hebrew; *three successive years* is literally 'three years, year after year'. Famines were regular occurrences in the Levant where fertility of the land depended on rainfall, and references to them are frequent (Gen. 12:10; 26:1; Ruth 1:1; 1 Kgs 18:2; 2 Kgs 4:38; etc.). Whatever the meteorological forces at play, famines were seen as signs of divine displeasure (Deut. 32:24; 2 Sam. 24:13; 1 Kgs 17:1; 2 Kgs 8:1; Ps. 105:16; Isa. 14:30; Jer. 11:22; Ezek. 14:21). In keeping with this perspective, *David sought the face of the LORD*,[2] and was told that the famine was *on account of Saul and his blood-stained house . . . because he put the Gibeonites to death*. Why this was a grave offence is made clear as the story continues.

2–3. Having sought the Lord and determined the problem, David's next action is to summon the Gibeonites and ask, *What shall I do for you?* (v. 3). Though the narrator does not comment, one wonders if David's question about what to do should have been addressed to Yahweh, at least in the first instance, especially in view of the fact that David had sworn an oath to Saul not to *kill off* his descendants (1 Sam. 24:21–22). To fail to enquire further of Yahweh is particularly ironic in the present context, inasmuch as the Gibeonites' protected status goes back to their ruse in Joshua 9, where the people of Israel were duped due to their own failure to 'enquire of the LORD' (Josh. 9:14). Once *the Israelites had sworn to spare them*, as the narrator reminds us in the frame-break of verse 2, the oath was to be honoured. Saul's offence was that *in his zeal for Israel and Judah [he] had tried to annihilate them*. Saul's nationalistic zeal and political pragmatism[3] may have been stoked by the fact that the

---

2. Though this is the only reference in Samuel to 'seeking the face of' someone (*biqqēš 'et-pĕnê* + name), the expression is well attested elsewhere in the OT (2 Chr. 7:14; Pss 24:6; 27:8; 105:4 [= 1 Chr. 16:11]; Hos. 5:15). More common in Samuel is 'enquiring of' someone (*šā'al bĕ* + name); for David as subject, see 1 Sam. 23:2, 4; 30:8; 2 Sam. 2:1; 5:19, 23.

3. On which, see Malamat (1955: 10–11); Long (2009b: 474).

Gibeonites lived quite close to his own home in Gibeah (Gibeon, e.g., lay about 4 miles west of Gibeah).[4]

4–9. The Gibeonites' disavowal in verse 4 of the right to demand compensatory damages (*silver or gold from Saul or his family*) or punitive damages (*put anyone in Israel to death*) may be their way of getting these items on the table. In answer to David's follow-up question, they do have punitive action in mind against the one who *destroyed*[5] *us and plotted against us so that we have been decimated and have no place anywhere in Israel* (v. 5). Most modern translations read the final clause as referring to what the Gibeonites suffered at Saul's hand, whereas LXX understands the Gibeonites to be suggesting what should be done to surviving Saulides: 'let us do away with him [Saul, i.e. his descendants], so he has no stand within any boundary of Israel' (NETS). Either way, reducing the numbers of their Saulide neighbours would likely free up some land holdings and thus add compensatory damages to the punitive damages.

Precisely how all this is to be done, and where, is uncertain, for several reasons. First, the Gibeonites request that *seven of his* [*Saul's*] *male descendants be given to us* (v. 6), and seven are given: two offspring of *Rizpah, whom she had borne to Saul*,[6] and *five sons of Saul's daughter Merab* (v. 8).[7] The number seven in the Hebrew mind signifies completeness (cf. 1 Sam. 2:5), so a more extensive extirpation of Saulides could be implied. The mode of execution is also unclear, as the verb used (*yqʻ*) is relatively rare in the Hebrew Bible and seems

---

4. 1 Chr. 8:29–33 even suggests a link between Gibeon and Saul's ancestors.
5. Heb. *klh* (in the piʻel) has the sense of 'finished (off)'; cf. LXX, 'brought an end upon us'.
6. On Rizpah, see at v. 10. Her son Mephibosheth is not to be confused with the son of Jonathan.
7. MT has Michal instead of Merab, but some MSS in Hebrew and Greek attest Merab, as do the Syriac and the Aramaic. First Sam. 18:19 makes it clear that the wife of *Adriel . . . the Meholathite* was Merab. Adriel's father, *Barzillai*, is not to be confused with the Gileadite Barzillai of 17:27; 19:31; and 1 Kgs 2:7.

to mean to 'dislocate' or to 'alienate'. In reference to execution, as here and in Numbers 25:4, the meanings 'impale', 'hang' or 'expose' have all been suggested and are reflected in the versions, both ancient and modern. NIV renders the one Hebrew verb with two in English: 'kill' and 'expose'. Whatever the precise mode, the executions are to take place, according to MT, *before the* LORD *at Gibeah of Saul – the* LORD's *chosen one* (v. 6). It seems odd that the Gibeonites should refer to Saul as the *chosen one* of Yahweh – unless in bitter sarcasm – and this oddity, along with verse 9's notice that the bodies of the slain were *exposed . . . on a hill before the* LORD, has led to the suggestion that 'chosen one' (*běḥîr*) should be emended to 'on the hill' (*běhār*) of Yahweh. Adopting this emendation, and following LXX's attestation of Gibeon in place of Gibeah, NRSV renders the disputed phrase as 'impale them before the LORD at Gibeon on the mountain of the LORD'. Most versions, ancient and modern, stick closer to MT. That David keeps his oath before the Lord by sparing Mephibosheth son of Jonathan (v. 7; see 1 Sam. 20:14–17, 42) contrasts with Saul's disregard for the oath with the Gibeonites. The less fortunate seven *All . . . fell together* (v. 9) – a verbal reprise of an earlier event (2:16) in the *war between the house of Saul and the house of David* (3:1).

If mode and location of the executions remain uncertain, the time of year does not: *they were put to death . . . just as the barley harvest was beginning* (v. 9). The barley harvest, mentioned not only in Ruth 1:22 but also in the famous tenth-century agricultural calendar discovered at Gezer in 1908, would have begun in April.

10–14. *Rizpah . . . took sackcloth* (v. 10). Rizpah's life has not been easy. After Saul's death, she found herself in the middle of a bitter dispute between Abner and Saul's surviving son Ish-Bosheth (3:7–11). Now her two sons not only have been executed but have been left exposed to the elements and to scavengers, which in the ancient world was a disgrace and a sign of curse.[8] The verb used to describe

---

8. Cf. Deut. 28:26; 1 Sam. 17:44, 46; Isa. 18:6; Ps. 79:2; Jer. 7:33; 16:4; and from a vassal treaty of Esarhaddon: 'May Ninurta, leader of the gods . . . fill the plain with your corpses, give your flesh to eagles and vultures to feed upon' (*ANET* 538).

Rizpah's spreading the sackcloth *for herself on a rock* (v. 10) is the same verb typically used for pitching a tent,[9] so it is possible that she constructed a simple shelter of sackcloth to provide some shade and cover as she protected the corpses from *birds . . . by day* and *wild animals by night* (cf. Alter 1999: 332). She continued in this arduous service from *the beginning of the harvest till the rain poured down from the heavens on the bodies* (v. 10). Whether the rain in view was an unseasonable shower or the autumn rains (cf. Deut. 11:14; Jer. 5:24) arriving months later, beginning in October, is not made clear in the text.

News of Rizpah's vigil (v. 11) stirs David to action. After collecting the remains of Saul and Jonathan from Jabesh Gilead (v. 12) and gathering also *the bones of those who had been killed and exposed* (v. 13), he has them buried *in the tomb of Saul's father Kish* in Benjamin. Only the bones of Saul and Jonathan are explicitly mentioned in the burial, but presumably those of the seven were included; cf. LXX's inclusion of 'those who were hung in the sun'. Significantly, it is not after the executions required by the Gibeonites that *God answered prayer on behalf of the land* (v. 14), but only after David has done his duty in providing proper burial for the slain. Once again, one is prompted to wonder whether David's taking direction from the Gibeonites, rather than from the Lord, was appropriate (see above on v. 2).

Meaning
While the three-year famine is described as *on account of Saul and his blood-stained house*, the narrative describing its resolution is more complex. As we have seen, David himself may not be above reproach in the present section. He does right in 'seeking the face' of the Lord, in order to discover the cause of Israel's distress. But then, instead of continuing to seek the face of the Lord, he turns to the Gibeonites to discover how the matter should be adjudicated. Violence follows, and the famine continues. Only after Rizpah's actions provoke David to provide proper burial for the slain does

---

9. I.e. *nṭh*, here in the hipʻil, used also in 2 Sam. 16:22 of the tent pitched for Absalom on the roof of the palace.

the Lord answer *prayer on behalf of the land* (v. 14). The accounts of David's years on the run from Saul and of his early years consolidating the kingdom contain fairly regular references to David's praying (1 Sam. 23:2, 4; 30:8; 2 Sam. 2:1; 5:19, 23; plus the description of David's prayer in 7:27). But after 2 Samuel 7, notices that David prayed are virtually absent (the expostulation of 15:31 marking the one potential exception). This is not to say that David didn't pray – indeed, David's poetic compositions at the centre of the Samuel conclusion cast David as a man of prayer (22:1 – 23:7). But the narrative does not foreground David's dependence on Yahweh in the latter (more troubled) part of his reign in the same way that it does in David's earlier years.

B. Short list of David's champions (21:15–22)

Context
The sin of Saul was front and centre in the opening frame of the Samuel conclusion (21:1–14). David's sin will be highlighted in the closing frame in chapter 24. Inside these framing accounts are summary lists of David's valiant followers (21:15–22 and 23:8–39). These lists underscore the fact that David both earned and needed the support of others. And at the heart of the Samuel conclusion are two poems of David expressive of his fundamental dependence on Yahweh (22:1–51 and 23:1–7). In the passage currently before us, the focus is on the heroes at David's side.

Comment
15–17. The notice that *Once again there was a battle between the Philistines and Israel* introduces a new section (vv. 15–22) in which four heroic exploits of David, or, more precisely, of David's men, are recorded. In the first encounter, David *became exhausted* (v. 15), which suggests that these exploits probably took place in the middle or latter years of David's reign, as he was beginning to feel the physical diminishment of ageing.[10]

---

10. Contrast Josephus, who attributes David's endangerment to his 'courage and boldness' in battle (*Ant.* 7.300).

David's challenger, a certain Ishbi-Benob (v. 16) – a curious and otherwise unattested personal name, if that is how the Hebrew should be read[11] – is presented as a big man, *one of the descendants of Rapha*. Despite some uncertainties (see McCarter 1984: 449–450), *Rapha* is probably to be associated with oversized, pre-Israelite inhabitants of Canaan, among whom were counted such peoples as the Emites, Zamzummites and Anakites.[12] Joshua largely succeeded in eradicating these gigantic foes from the land; 'only in Gaza, Gath and Ashdod did any survive' (Josh. 11:21–22). All three sites are associated with the Philistines.

David's Raphaite challenger was not only big but also heavily armed, wielding a spear whose *bronze spearhead weighed three hundred shekels* (v. 16; about 7.5 lb), half the weight of Goliath's (1 Sam. 17:7) but heavy enough to merit a comment. Whether he also sported a new sword is uncertain, as *sword* (*ḥereb*) is not in the text, just the statement that he was 'girded' with something 'new'; LXX fits him out with a 'club' or 'mace' (Gk *korúnē*).

Abishai son of Zeruiah, well known by now and ever ready to draw his sword (cf. 1 Sam. 26:6–9; 2 Sam. 3:30; 16:9; 19:21), is the one who comes to *David's rescue* (v. 17). Having witnessed a close call, *David's men* swear to him that he must no longer accompany them in battle, *so that the lamp of Israel will not be extinguished* (v. 17). In the Ancient Near East, kings were sometimes described as bringing light to their lands (well-being, hope, justice, etc.); see 23:3–4. References to David or his dynasty as Israel's *lamp* are frequent (e.g. 1 Kgs 11:36; 15:4; 2 Kgs 8:19; 2 Chr. 21:7), the point being that Israel's hope is tied in a unique way to David and the promises made to him by

---

11. For attempts to emend 'Benob' to 'in Gob' (*běgōb*) and repoint 'and Ishbi' to read 'and they camped' (*wayyēšěbû*), see Na'aman (2008: 5; online numeration). If correct, these changes would result in a typical 3/4 pattern – three battles in Gob (vv. 15–19) and a fourth in Gath (v. 20) – and a very general suggestion of westwards advance. As attractive as these emendations might be, they do not square well syntactically with the rest of the verse.

12. E.g. Gen. 14:5; Deut. 2:10–11, 20–21. For discussion and further references, see Long (2009b: 475–476).

Yahweh (2 Sam. 7), of whom David himself declares, *You, LORD, are my lamp; / the LORD turns my darkness into light* (22:29).[13]

18–22. *In the course of time*, further battles with the Philistines are engaged, and three are mentioned in the remainder of this section, two at *Gob* (vv. 18 and 19) and one at *Gath* (v. 20). The site of *Gob* is unknown, as its only mentions are in the present context.[14] *Gath* is modern Tel Zafit (*tell es-safi*) and is one of the cities of the Philistine pentapolis (see on 1 Sam. 5:8). The account of the second of the four battles sticks to the barest details (v. 18), while the fourth (v. 20) is more intriguing by virtue of the fact that the unnamed Philistine is not only a *huge man* sporting an extra digit at the end of all four limbs[15] but is bested by a *son of Shimeah, David's brother* (v. 21).

Elhanan son of Jair the Bethlehemite killed the brother of Goliath. NIV's rendering of the central statement of 2 Samuel 21:19 masks a famous *crux interpretum*, widely regarded as 'one of the most famous contradictions in the Book of Samuel' (Alter 1999: 334). Translated literally, the Hebrew text of 21:19 reads as follows: 'Elhanan son of Jaare-Oregim the Bethlehemite killed Goliath the Gittite.' The difficulty is apparent. Did David kill Goliath, as 1 Samuel 17 insists, or did Elhanan? Various responses to the problem have been offered: (1) there must have been more than one 'Goliath' in Gath (Kirkpatrick 1919: 197); (2) Goliath should be understood more as a descriptor than a personal name (Hertzberg 1964: 387); (3) Elhanan and David are the same person, Elhanan being a personal name and David a throne name (Baldwin 1988: 305–306)[16] – after

---

13. For more on the metaphorical uses of *lamp*, see on 1 Sam. 3:3 (cf. 2 Sam. 14:7).
14. Na'aman (2008) contends that the recently excavated site of Khirbet Qeiyafa is Gob, but his arguments are largely unconvincing; see Adams (2010).
15. Such features, masked in many modern societies by surgical treatment, were of interest to the ancients; see Barnett (1990: 46–51).
16. A view proposed by Honeyman (1948). Targ. simply replaces Elhanan with 'David, son of Jesse' and makes the latter a weaver of the curtain of the sanctuary, while Josephus (*Ant.* 7.302) tells a different story that

all, various biblical characters bear more than one name (e.g. the baby named Solomon in 12:24 receives also the name Jedidiah in 12:25). There are weaknesses in each of these approaches, leaving a majority of modern scholars to draw the conclusion that (4) the deed of Elhanan has simply been reassigned to enhance the reputation of the much more famous David (Alter 1999: 334). The parallel verse in 1 Chronicles 20:5, however, suggests a fifth possibility, which is worthy of consideration.

The Chronicles text reads: 'Elhanan son of Jair killed Lahmi the brother of Goliath.' While many scholars dismiss the Chronicler's reading as a harmonizing attempt to avoid an obvious difficulty (i.e. disagreement over who killed Goliath), it cannot be denied that the Chronicles text is superior to the Samuel text in at least some respects: for example, 'son of Jair' is to be preferred to Samuel's 'son of Jaare-Oregim', as 'oregim' is an evident duplication of 'oregim' (*weaver's*) at the end of the verse. Might 1 Chronicles 20:5 be superior in other respects as well? We note, in favour of this possibility, that the direct object of the sentence in Chronicles – *'et laḥmî* (=untranslatable direct object marker plus 'Lahmi') could easily have been misread (or misheard) in Samuel as a gentilic attached to Elhanan – *bêt laḥmî* ('Bethlehemite'), perhaps under the influence of a famous Bethlehemite named Elhanan mentioned in 2 Samuel 23:24. This misreading of the original direct object as a gentilic would then have necessitated the discovery of a different direct object in the Samuel text, and so the Chronicler's *'aḥî golyāt* ('brother of Goliath') could have been misread (or misheard) as *'et golyāt* (=direct object marker plus 'Goliath'). In sum, 1 Chronicles 20:5 may preserve the superior text, or at least point to it, while the differences in 2 Samuel 21:19 are explicable as corruptions.[17] NIV's rendering of verse 19 is similar to the solution here presented and is viable, though it must assume that the Chronicler's 'Lahmi' is a

---

(note 16 *cont.*) mentions by name neither Goliath, David nor Elhanan (unless the last is represented somehow in 'Ephan').

17. On this proposed solution, see Provan, Long and Longman (2015: 296–297; first ed. appeared 2003); Long (2009b: 477); now also Adams (2010).

misreading. It is also possible that the original text included both 'Bethlehemite' and 'Lahmi', one or the other being lost because they look and sound so much alike in Hebrew.

Mention of *David and his men* in verse 22 recalls the introductory verse 15 and nicely frames the short listing of heroic exploits.

Meaning

The exploits described in this section convey two truths about David as a leader. First, he was able to earn the loyalty of others, and second, he needed their support. Though there were times when he acted solo, counting on Yahweh's help alone, as in his defeat of Goliath (1 Sam. 17), David generally worked in concert with those whose confidence he had gained. The lengths to which David's men were willing to go in his service are indicated not only in this listing of Philistine engagements but also in the daring exploit described in 23:15–16.

C. Long poetic composition: David's song of praise (22:1–51)

Context

David's lengthy song of thanksgiving recorded in 2 Samuel 22 corresponds in a number of ways to Hannah's briefer song of thanksgiving in 1 Samuel 2:1–10, and together these two poems form a fitting thematic frame around the book of Samuel as a whole. Both emphasize Yahweh's faithfulness to deliver those who trust fully in him. Both call Yahweh the *Rock* (Heb. *ṣûr*, 1 Sam. 2:2; 2 Sam. 22:3, 32, 47), a title suggestive of stability, immovability and security.[18] Both speak of Yahweh's abasing the proud and elevating the humble (e.g. 1 Sam. 2:7; 2 Sam. 22:28 and *passim*). And both conclude with references to Yahweh's *king*, his *anointed* one (1 Sam. 2:10; 2 Sam. 22:51).

It would be wrong to suggest that these themes and others like them occur exclusively in the poetic songs that frame the book; the narratives that form the book of Samuel put flesh on these thematic

---

18. Yahweh is also called *my rock* in 2 Sam. 22:2, but there a different word is used (Heb. *selaʿ*).

bones. It is true, though, that *Rock* as divine title occurs only in these framing poems in the book of Samuel, the final occurrence coming in the 'oracle of David' in 2 Samuel 23:3. It is also true that nowhere else are *king* and *anointed* mentioned in the same breath in quite the same way as here, with the emphasis falling on Yahweh as the king's source of strength and victory. Hannah anticipates divine favour for the coming king; David experiences it and, having taken to heart the assurances of 2 Samuel 7, anticipates the continuance of Yahweh's 'steadfast love' to him and his descendants for ever.

As with several other Scripture passages, David's song of thanksgiving earns more than one placement in the biblical canon.[19] With minor variations and additions, it constitutes Psalm 18, the third-longest psalm in the Psalter.[20] Despite aspects that may surprise and perplex modern readers (more on these below), David's song of thanksgiving – together with his shorter poetic composition in 23:1–7 – forms a magnificent poetical centrepiece to the epilogue with which the book of Samuel closes. The two compositions will be discussed together in the 'Meaning' section following the commentary on 23:1–7.

Comment

1. Apart from its narrative setting, the opening verse of 2 Samuel 22 is repeated almost verbatim in the superscription of Psalm 18. The summary reference to Yahweh's delivering David *from the hand of all his enemies and from the hand of Saul* defies attempts to locate a particular point in time. In one sense David's final deliverance from Saul came when the latter took his own life on Mount Gilboa (1 Sam. 31:4), but already in David's fugitive years Yahweh repeatedly delivered David from the hand of Saul. One might suppose that David was not freed from *all his enemies* until he was crowned king over all Israel, north as well as south (see 2 Sam. 5).

---

19. E.g. Pss 14 and 53 are essentially the same, apart from the substitution of 'God' (*ĕlōhîm*) in the latter for 'Yahweh' (*yhwh*) in the former.
20. Only Ps. 119, with 176 verses, and Ps. 78, with seventy-two verses, surpass the fifty-one verses of 2 Sam. 22/Ps. 18.

But even after that key event enemies had to be bested, as the listing of David's victories in 2 Samuel 8 attests. And still David's path was plagued by pro-Saulides such as Shimei (2 Sam. 16) and Sheba (2 Sam. 20), and even by 'enemies' from his own house (2 Sam. 15 – 19). Perhaps this notice covers all the king's victories.

2–4. Unlike its twin in Psalm 18, David's song of thanksgiving in 2 Samuel 22 does not begin with an explicit expression of his love for Yahweh,[21] but his piling up of nine metaphors in praise of Yahweh leaves little doubt of his passionate love for his *rock* (*selaʽ*), *fortress*, *deliverer*, *rock* (*ṣûr*),[22] *shield*, *horn* (cf. on 1 Sam. 2:1), *stronghold*, *refuge* and *saviour* (vv. 2–3). That the metaphors cluster around issues of security, defence and salvation reflects David's life. David's early years saw threats from savage beasts (lion and bear; 1 Sam. 17:34), from Goliath and eventually from Israel's first king, Saul, whose jealous animosity towards David began early and continued 'all his days' (1 Sam. 18:29). Once established as king, threats continued to come, from without – hostile neighbours and foreign powers (cf. 2 Sam. 8:1–14) – and even from within – his own moral lapses in 2 Samuel 11 and their terrible ripple effects within his family and kingdom (2 Sam. 13 – 20). David knew danger, but he also knew deliverance: *I called to the LORD, who is worthy of praise, / and have been saved from my enemies* (v. 4).

5–6. David's description of mortal danger is rich with poetic imagery. There is nothing in his story that would suggest he ever faced the threat of drowning, but in speaking of (over)whelming waters and ensnaring cords, David is drawing on standard dramatic images in his culture. Even today one sometimes speaks of 'drowning' in sorrow or being 'tied up in knots'. Threatening waters, as

---

21. David's 'I love you, LORD, my strength' (Ps. 18:1) is unusual in its use of the Hebrew word *rāḥam* for 'love' instead of the more familiar *'āhēb*. The former term is often used of God's passionate love for his people. Perhaps David's preference for this evocative term reflects his 'visceral sense of well-being and renewal' as a result of Yahweh's having delivered him through many years both as fugitive and warrior (cf. Terrien 2003: 197).

22. On *Rock* as divine title, see discussion at 1 Sam. 2:2.

forces of destruction and death, figure regularly in Israel's poetry, perhaps most famously in Isaiah 43:2: 'When you pass through the waters, / I will be with you.'[23] *Cords* can bind one metaphorically to many things: to the grave, as here; to sin (Prov. 5:22); to affliction (Job 36:8); to deceit (Isa. 5:18); and, more positively, to human kindness (Hos. 11:4).

7. David's life was marked by peril, or *distress*, as most English translations have it. The Hebrew (*ṣrr*) connotes being in a narrow, restricted or confining space – in dire straits, we might say. Because the 'single most characteristic thing about David is his relationship to God' (Peterson 1999: 248), his instinctual reaction in a tight spot is to pray; he calls to the Lord, and the Lord, from his (heavenly) *temple*, hears and responds.[24] In a life of peril, every hardship became for David – when he prayed – an opportunity to deepen his conviction that *The* Lord *lives!* (22:47). Even 'one specific answer to prayer can bring home the fact that the Lord lives' (Baldwin 1988: 310), and David experienced many such answers.

8–16. No sooner does David's cry reach his *ears* (v. 7) than Yahweh is roused to respond – and what a response it is, both powerful and personal! Verses 8–16 describe the cosmic convulsions wrought by the Lord's righteous anger: *The earth trembled and quaked . . . because he was angry* (v. 8). In biblical Hebrew, anger is picturesquely described as a burning nose/face (thus, to be 'long of nose' is to be slow to anger; in English parlance we speak of someone having a 'long fuse' or, conversely, 'a short fuse'). Yahweh is often described as 'long of nose', and his patience is exhibited in countless places in Scripture. But in response to David's prayer, *Smoke rose from [Yahweh's] nostrils*, and *consuming fire came from his mouth* (v. 9). To modern ears this sounds like a dragon, but ancient ears would have been well familiar with such figurative language for anger (cf. Hilber 2009: 332–333). Bent on rescuing his servant, Yahweh 'bends'[25] the sky and comes down, riding (as in a chariot)

---

23. Cf. also Pss 30:1; 32:6; 69:1–2, 14; 144:7; Jon. 2:5 [Heb. v. 6]).
24. On Yahweh's heavenly temple, see, e.g., Ps. 11:4; Isa. 6:1.
25. Or 'bows down', 'stretches out' or 'parts' (as in NIV); the Hebrew verb here can bear such meanings (*HALOT* 2: 693, s.v. *nṭh*).

a 'cherub'.[26] He *soared*[27] on the *wings of the wind*. Darkness, brightness, water, fire, thunder (Yahweh's voice), lightning (Yahweh's arrows) – image piles upon image as Yahweh's rebuke (*the blast . . . from his nostrils*) lays bare the very *foundations of the earth* (v. 16). And all because David prayed!

17–20. Yahweh's response to David's prayer involved more than powerful cataclysm, it also involved personal condescension: *He reached down from on high and took hold of me, he drew me out of deep waters* (v. 17). When David was sorely overmatched by his *powerful enemy* (Saul?), by foes *too strong for me* (v. 18), Yahweh pulled him out. When he was in dire straits, a 'tight' spot (recall v. 7), Yahweh brought him out *into a spacious place* (v. 20). Why? Simply *because he delighted in me* (v. 20). But is this divine delight God's gracious gift to David or David's just deserts? At first glance, the verses that follow might seem to suggest the latter. But we must take a closer look.

21–25. *The LORD has dealt with me according to my righteousness . . . / I have kept the ways of the LORD . . . / I have been blameless before him / and have kept myself from sin. / The LORD has rewarded me according to my righteousness, / according to my cleanness in his sight.* Is David serious? Surely no-one can make these kinds of claims, if taken in an absolute sense. Surely only the Son of David to come, the Messiah, will be able to make such claims. For all others, such declarations mark the height of hypocrisy – if taken absolutely – and for David, perhaps, most of all: adulterer, murderer, deceiver, and more. What are we to make of this?

---

26. NIV has *cherubim* (plural of MT's singular 'cherub'). Cherubim are mentioned some ninety times in the Bible and seem to suggest winged, composite 'heavenly' creatures, such as appear in Ancient Near Eastern iconography. Cherubim guarded the entrance to Eden (Gen. 3:24), rested atop the ark of the covenant (Exod. 25:18–22), appeared in Ezekiel's visions, etc.
27. The Hebrew text of 22:11 reads 'was seen' (*wyr'*), but the parallel verse in Ps. 18 attests the contextually more appropriate *soared* (*wyd'*); the confusion of two very similar Heb. consonants (*resh* for *dalet*) could account for the difference.

It seems unlikely that we are to understand David's words as self-righteous false boasting. If that were the case, surely he could hardly escape being classed among *the haughty* of verse 28, upon whom the Lord had his *eyes . . . to bring them low*?

Might chronology help resolve the mystery? Perhaps David first sang this song at the pinnacle of his career before his tragic fall into adultery with Bathsheba and his orchestrated murder of her husband Uriah (2 Sam. 11). But even so, the biblical narrator includes this song at the summative centre of the Samuel conclusion and seems to intend it to capture the essence of David's life before God. So chronology is not an adequate answer.

Perhaps the way forward is to take David's words *not* in an absolute sense, but in a properly contextualized sense (cf. Firth 2009: 519). When a defendant in court enters a plea of 'innocent', no-one thinks to retort with charges of hypocrisy and self-righteousness. All understand that the claim is to be 'innocent' of the charges laid, not innocent in any grander or absolute sense. Chief among the charges laid against David was that he had murdered his way to the throne, that he was, as Shimei protested in 2 Samuel 16:7, a *murderer* (lit. 'man of blood') and a *scoundrel* (lit. 'man of belial'; 2 Sam. 16:5–8). But such is not the verdict of the biblical narrator.[28] For the biblical narrator, David continued, despite his quite evident moral lapses, to 'please' God. To understand how this can be, we need to look more closely at the basis of God's pleasure in David.

At the time of David's flight from Jerusalem during Absalom's attempted coup, the priest Zadok brought the ark of the covenant to David. But David had it returned to Jerusalem, stating, *If I find favour in the* LORD'*s eyes, he will bring me back . . . But if he says, 'I am not pleased with you,' then I am ready; let him do to me whatever seems good to him* (15:25–26). David's words on that occasion echo Eli's earlier words of submission to the divine will: 'He is the LORD. Let him do what seems good to him' (1 Sam. 3:18, my translation). It is often remarked that, if David was a great sinner, he was also a great

---

28. Despite the tendency of some modern writers to continue to present David from the perspective of his enemies (e.g. Halpern 2001; McKenzie 2000).

repenter. Despite his occasional and serious lapses, David, as we meet him in Scripture, lives his life with God at the centre. He

> believes in God, thinks about God, imagines God, addresses God, and prays to God. He also forgets God, disobeys God, sins against God, and ignores God. But God is the reality that accounts for and defines all that David does and says. The largest part of David's existence is not David, it is God.
> (Peterson 1999: 248)

In short, David is to be classed among the 'righteous', not the 'wicked'. Like Job, he is *blameless* – which is to say, his relationship with God has *integrity* – though he is far from sinless.[29] In the Psalter, the book of Proverbs and pervasively in Scripture, 'the righteous' are those who live in *active dependence* on God, as opposed to 'the wicked' who 'consider themselves autonomous' (McCann 1994: 38) and display 'an attitude and behaviour in which Israel's God and his will are ignored'.[30] 'The way of the wicked leads to destruction,' Psalm 1:6b assures us, but Yahweh 'watches over [knows, cares for] the way of the righteous' (Ps. 1:6a). With 'the righteous' God is 'pleased', despite their sinful lapses.

Does this mean that behaviour doesn't matter? David's own biography puts the lie to such a notion. His lapses cost him dearly, in his family and in his realm. Active dependence that issues in active obedience always proves best in David's life, as it puts him in the path of God's blessing. To put this another way, David's behaviour influences how God's unchanging love for him is expressed, whether in discipline or affirmation. God's character is stable and his interactions with people predictable, in a qualified sense at least, as the next section indicates.

26–37. *To the faithful you show yourself faithful, / to the blameless . . . blameless, / to the pure . . . pure* (vv. 26–27). The first three of the four

---

29. On integrity of relationship as lying at the heart of what it means to be 'blameless', cf. Job 1:1, 8; 2:3, 9; and *passim*.
30. Kwakkel (2002: 298–299); cited by Vannoy (2009: 410); which see for an insightful discussion.

poetic lines in verses 26–27 show a nice parallelism, a balance between human character and the character of divine response. One is reminded of the programmatic statement of the man of God to Eli near the beginning of the book of Samuel: 'to those who give me weight, I will give weight, but those who undervalue me will be small' (1 Sam. 2:30, my translation). But what of the fourth line: *but to the devious you show yourself shrewd*, or, as NRSV has it, 'with the crooked you show yourself perverse' (v. 27b)? The *devious* or 'crooked' (*'iqqēš*) are 'twisted, false' and in that sense 'perverse'. Is Yahweh similarly 'perverse', as NRSV's rendering might seem to suggest? No; the underlying Hebrew word suggests that which shows itself 'tortuous', or perhaps 'astute'.[31] When David himself strayed into the crooked way in the Bathsheba–Uriah affair, he certainly found God to be both astute and tortuous in his relentless pursuit of David and his dismantling of David's attempted cover-up.

Might we imagine that David sees himself in *each* line of the four lines of verses 26–27? Perhaps. He can count himself among the *humble* (afflicted) of verse 28, and he knows *darkness* (v. 29); he knows what it means to be 'saved' by God (v. 28) and can confess Yahweh as *my lamp* (v. 29). He knows himself capable of great deeds, but only with God's help (v. 30). David has experienced much, and God has always shown himself true to his character and to the conditions of David's life. Like a good parent, Yahweh has wrestled well with David, when that was what love required. All this underscores how little we should read of self-congratulation in David's claim to *righteousness* in verses 21–25.

In verse 31 it is God whose way is *perfect*, or 'blameless' (*tāmîm*), the same Hebrew word as in verse 26b. And it is God who is credited in verse 33 with making David's way *secure*, literally

---

31. Cf. *HALOT* 3: 990, s.v. *ptl*, which is the verb attested in the parallel verse in Ps. 18:26. The Hebrew of 2 Sam. 22:27 reverses two consonants, attesting *tpl*, which is probably a copyist's error. But if not, *tpl* might still work, as the meaning of the hitpa'el form could mean to exhibit what appears to the crooked as 'stupid behaviour' (cf. *HALOT* 4: 1775, s.v. I-*tpl*) – thus, foolishness to those who are perishing?

'perfect', or 'blameless' (also *tāmîm*).³² All credit goes to *the Rock* (v. 32, recalling how David's song began). In the heat of battle, David's shield (v. 31), his trainer (v. 35), his strengthener and enabler (vv. 33–34), *You* – David shifts in verse 36 to address God directly – *your help has made me great* (v. 36). Both this reference to personal condescension in verse 36 and the use of the root *rḥb* (broad, spacious) in verse 37 – *You provide a broad path for my feet* – neatly recall the earlier description of David's rescue in verses 17–20.

38–46. If David's claims of 'righteousness', 'cleanness' and 'blamelessness' in verses 21–25 seemed wrong on a first reading but came to be seen in a different light once literary, cultural and theological contexts were considered, might the same prove true for this next problematic section? Admittedly, David's unabashed exuberance in his description of how he crushed his enemies (vv. 38–39), beating them *as fine as the dust of the earth*, trampling them *like mud in the streets* (v. 43), certainly strikes modern ears as wrong. The fact that in the centre of this section Yahweh is credited with making all this possible (vv. 40–41), refusing even to answer David's foes, though they cried out explicitly to Yahweh (v. 42), only seems to make things worse.³³ What are we to make of all this?

First, we must keep in mind both the literary and the cultural context in which these words were penned. We are dealing with Hebrew poetry, part of the genius of which is to employ parallel lines and graphic imagery to pound home a point. Furthermore, we are dealing with a cultural context in which effective rule typically required the subjugation of opposing forces, enemies within and without. One need only consult Ancient Near Eastern iconography to see how pervasive is the image of the victorious king striking down his foes, sometimes in multiples at once! So David was in one sense simply accommodating himself to prevailing cultural conditions and modes of expression. Life is always lived out within particular conditions, as Peterson, in an

---

32. NIV and some other English translations obscure the word repetition.
33. But on the silence of God in respect of those in rebellion against him, see 1 Sam. 8:18.

insightful discussion (1999: 253–255), points out. Referencing Charles Williams (1939: 4), he notes that even Jesus lived out his life under conditions of 'Roman power, Greek culture, and human sin'. Indeed, the work of God always takes place under conditions: 'there are virtually no conditions that preclude the Spirit's work, and the Spirit never works apart from conditions' (Peterson 1999: 254). And the conditions in David's day 'were made up in large part of Philistine culture and Canaanite morality – which is to say, violence and sex' (ibid.) – not very different from today.

Ancient Near Eastern imagery, Ancient Near Eastern conditions – these thoughts are helpful, as far as they go, but are they the whole story? Is not something much larger involved in the establishment of David's reign? Broadening the perspective to include the whole of Samuel, we recall, first, the remarkable promises that were made to David and his descendants in 2 Samuel 7 of a *house and . . . kingdom* that would *endure for ever before me* [*the* LORD], promises of a *throne* that would *be established for ever* (2 Sam. 7:16). In the parallel passage in 1 Chronicles 17, we learn that David's house and kingdom are in truth 'my [God's] house and my [God's] kingdom' (v. 14). Broadening the perspective beyond Samuel, we discover, second, in Psalm 2 that Yahweh's anointed king (v. 6), also called 'my son' (v. 7), will not only receive 'the nations' as his 'inheritance' and 'the ends of the earth' as his 'possession' (v. 8), but will also 'break them with a rod of iron' and 'dash them to pieces like pottery' (v. 9). The imagery denotes sovereign judgment upon those who 'conspire' and 'plot' 'against the Lord and against his anointed' (vv. 1–2). It is in the greater son of David, Jesus the Lord's anointed (messiah), that the promises of Psalm 2 – and indeed of 2 Samuel 7 – find their ultimate fulfilment (cf. the multiple NT citations of Ps. 2 in reference to Jesus: e.g. at his baptism [Matt. 3:17; Luke 3:22] and in respect of the coming judgment [Rev. 19:15; cf. Rev. 2:26–28; 12:5]). On this broader canvas, the dramatic imagery of the destruction of the king's sworn enemies finds its truest sense and most fitting fulfilment. 'At the name of Jesus, every knee [shall] bow' (Phil. 2:10).

47–51. The closing stanza of David's psalm recapitulates the themes and much of the vocabulary of its opening lines: *my God, the Rock, my Saviour* (v. 47; cf. v. 3). The psalm echoes in numerous ways Hannah's prayer in 1 Samuel 2:1–10 but with even greater assurance, now in the light of the dynastic promise of 2 Samuel 7:5–16. The Lord's *king* and *anointed*, for whom Hannah prayed (1 Sam. 2:10), is now known and exalted in *David and his descendants for ever*, the greatest of whom will, in the course of time, be the Christ (messiah).

D. Short poetic composition: David's last words (23:1–7)

Context

The structure of this short poem can be analysed according to various criteria, yielding various, complementary results. Attending to who is speaking, one arrives at a chiasm with the direct speech of God himself at the centre (vv. 3b–4). This centre is framed by David speaking in the first person of what he has received from God (his inspiring Spirit, v. 2, and his everlasting covenant, v. 5). And the whole is framed by third-person descriptions of who David is in God's economy (v. 1b) and what will become of evil men (vv. 6–7). Another approach to structure sees three sections (cf. the layout in NIV): the introduction in verse 1 of David's elevated, anointed (messianic) status; a description in verses 2–4 of his vocation to righteous rule in the fear of God; and a celebration in verses 5–7 of the everlasting divine covenant that guarantees a good outcome.

Comment

1. The last words of a worthy person are of special significance, and *the last words of David* (v. 1) are particularly so. David will have more to say in the form of instructions – to Solomon in 1 Kings 2:1–10 and to the Levites, according to 1 Chronicles 23:27 – but this *inspired utterance* of David (v. 2) constitutes his last recorded poem in the books of Samuel and in a significant sense the 'last word' on what made David great.

As to human parentage, David is *son of Jesse*, but what makes him special is that he is *the man exalted by the Most High*. The Hebrew of this phrase, *haggeber huqam 'āl*, is cryptic, and many translations read 'the man who was raised on high' (ESV; cf. NASB, JPS). A divine reference is supported, however, by key ancient witnesses. LXX speaks of the 'faithful man, whom the Lord (*kyrios*) raised up'. 4QSam^a has *'l* ('God') where MT has *'l* ('above', though MT could represent a shortening or a synonym of a divine title like *'elyôn*, 'most high').³⁴ The further description of David as *the man anointed [mĕšîaḥ] by the God of Jacob* is rich with associations, recalling both the patriarchal promise of blessing and the divine wrestling with these human recipients of promise. As the Lord's 'messiah' (anointed one), David, who himself has wrestled with God, is now the one through whom blessing shall come (see on 2 Sam. 7).

The final line in verse 1 is traditionally rendered 'the sweet psalmist of Israel', or similar, in both ancient and modern versions. Although this is an apt description of David, a convincing case has been made on the basis of cognate literature that the Hebrew phrase should be rendered as in NRSV, 'the favorite of the Strong One of Israel', or, as in a seminal essay by H. N. Richardson, 'the beloved of the Guardian of Israel' (1971: 259, with explanation on 261–262).³⁵

Exalted, anointed, protected, David is great because God has made him so, and the *inspired utterance* (*nĕ'um*) that constitutes his last word on the subject leaves this in no doubt. 'Following the proportions of the text, David's identity is made up of one part Jesse to three parts God' (Peterson 1999: 256). As a technical term, *nĕ'um* ('utterance, oracle') is associated with prophetic announcements (e.g. Num. 24:3–4; 2 Kgs 9:25–26), and David's inspiration is confirmed in the next verse.³⁶

2–4. The ability to say *The Spirit of the LORD spoke through me* (v. 2) marks the *sine qua non* of true prophecy. Having been endued with the Spirit at the time of his anointing (1 Sam. 16:13), David's

---

34. The former proposal goes back at least to Dhorme (1910); see Richardson (1971: 260 n. 16), who suggests also the latter possibility on 261.
35. In addition to the full discussion in Richardson, see *HALOT*, *zmr**III; *DCH*, *zimrâ**III ('refuge') and *zimrâ**IV ('warrior'). Similar terminology is involved in Exod. 15:2; Ps. 118:14; Isa. 12:2, where NIV renders 'my strength and my defence' (cf. JPS, NET, NRSV) instead of the more traditional 'my strength and my song' (ESV; cf. NASB, NKJV, etc.).
36. Cf. also David's reputation as a prophet in 2 Chron. 29:25; Acts 2:30.

speaking by the Spirit is noted in both Testaments (e.g. 1 Chr. 28:11–12; Matt. 22:43; Mark 12:36; Acts 1:16; 4:25). The parallelistic character of Hebrew poetry allows the poet to name God in several different ways, as LORD (i.e. YHWH, the personal covenantal name), as *God of Israel* and as *Rock* [*ṣûr*] *of Israel*, reprising a key appellative from Hannah's song (1 Sam. 2:2) and from David's song of praise in 2 Samuel 22 (vv. 2, 32, 47).

Central to the entire poem/psalm is the direct speech of God himself (vv. 3b–4), which describes the essential character of the ideal theocratic ruler: he is one who *rules over people in righteousness*, that is, who rules *in the fear of God* (on what it means to fear God, see on 1 Sam. 12:14). The benefits that flow from this righteous rule are symbolized in terms of light – *sunrise . . . cloudless morning . . . brightness after rain* (v. 4; see comment on 21:17). Such rule brings encouragement, as light drives out the darkness, and it also brings fruitfulness, as sun breaking out after rainfall *brings grass from the earth* (v. 4). How this righteous rule, empowered by God himself, brings well-being to God's people is beautifully described in Psalm 72 and finds its ultimate fulfilment in the righteous rule of the true Messiah and greater son of David.

5–7. NIV's rendering of the start of verse 5 – *If my house were not right with God, / surely he would not have made with me an everlasting covenant* – suggests an inappropriate conditionality in God's gracious covenant with David and is an overtranslation of the Hebrew (which makes no mention of 'right' nor of a conditional covenant). The Targum's 'More than this is my house before God' also goes beyond the Hebrew. Better is a translation like NRSV's 'Is not my house like this with God?' or, better still, JPS's 'Is not my House established before God?' The ground of David's confidence is that God 'has made with me an everlasting covenant [*bĕrît 'ôlām*], ordered in all things and secure' (v. 5, NRSV). The last phrase is suggestive of legal terminology (cf. JPS, 'Drawn up in full and secured').[37] The reference is fundamentally to the promise to David

---

37. Cf. Gordon (1986: 311), who notes other instances where the verb *'ārak* (here in its past participle form and rendered 'ordered', 'drawn up' or, as in NIV, *arranged*) bears a legal sense (Job 13:18; 23:4; Ps. 50:21).

in 2 Samuel 7 (see esp. 7:11–16).³⁸ Because the covenant with David is a 'done deal', David is confident that God will *bring to fruition* [lit. *yaṣmîaḥ*, 'will cause to sprout' or 'blossom'] *my salvation* and *my every desire* (v. 5). As in Psalm 1's fruitful tree versus chaff metaphors, botanical imagery is used here to contrast the fate of the righteous with that of the wicked (vv. 4, 6–7).

In contrast to the 'fruition' of the Davidic king, *evil men* [*bĕliyyaʿal*]³⁹ *are all to be cast aside like thorns* [*kĕqôṣ*].⁴⁰ The ancient versions indicate uncertainties in rendering the final verses of David's last words. LXX renders the final line of verse 5 as an imprecation against the wicked: 'my whole salvation and total will is that the lawless shall not sprout' (NETS), though 'lawless' (*paranomos*) is not represented in MT. The Targum takes the opportunity of verses 6–7 to provide an extended warning about allowing 'thorns' (sins) to remain; as tender shoots they are easily plucked, but left to grow they overwhelm like clothing of iron that can be eradicated only by fire at the judgment of the world. One might think of the similar warnings about choking thorns in the parable of the sower (Matt. 13:7; Mark 4:7), but the Targum's moral reflection goes beyond the sense of 2 Samuel 23:6–7. The basic point is that the wicked, like thorns, cannot be *gathered with the hand* or, as we might say, 'taken in hand' (NASB). The only way to deal with thorns (the wicked) is with *iron or the shaft of a spear* or 'with fire to burn them completely on the spot' (my literal rendering of the final line of v. 7). LXX's 'they shall be burned by their shame' apparently reads *bbšt* ('in shame') instead of MT's *bšbt* ('in place').

Meaning
The two central poetic compositions by David anchor the Samuel conclusion and, along with the song of Hannah (1 Sam. 2:1–10), provide a theological-thematic frame for the entire book of Samuel.

---

38. Cf. also 2 Chr. 13:5; 21:7; Pss 89:3–4, 28–29; 132:11–12; Isa. 55:3; Ezek. 37:25–26.
39. See on 1 Sam. 2:12.
40. Psalm 1 contrasts the righteous one, who is 'like a tree' (*kĕʿēṣ*; 1:3), with the wicked, who are 'like chaff' (*kammōṣ*; 1:4).

The longer of David's compositions (22:2–51) celebrates Yahweh's deliverance and preservation of David, while the second, shorter composition (23:1–7) celebrates the 'everlasting covenant' with David and his descendants, which David – on the basis of the dynastic promise of 2 Samuel 7 – knows to be *arranged and secured in every part* (23:5). This shorter composition also acknowledges that there is more behind David's words than poetic genius: *The Spirit of the* LORD *spoke through me; / his word was on my tongue* (23:2). Only in the divinely anointed son of David, the Messiah, would the ideals of just rule and an everlasting kingdom be fully realized.

E. Long list of David's champions (23:8–39)

Context

As part of the structural arrangement of the Samuel conclusion in 2 Samuel 21 – 24, the central section comprising David's two poetic compositions is framed by two lists of those whose support had helped him succeed. The shorter listing of heroes in 1 Samuel 21:15–22 now finds its counterpart in a much longer listing of *David's mighty warriors* (*haggibbōrîm 'ăšer lĕdāwid*, v. 8). Not surprisingly, this long list of personal names and affiliations has sparked scholarly interest and debate.[41] The discussion here will focus on the character and ordering of the groupings (e.g. *the Three* and *the Thirty*) and on details of exegetical or theological interest. The parallel list in 1 Chronicles 11:10–47 includes more than fifteen additional names.

Comment

8–12. *These are the names of David's mighty warriors* (v. 8). In fact, more than just the names are sometimes given. For instance, the first to be named, *Josheb-Basshebeth*, is characterized as *chief of the Three* and is credited with killing *eight hundred men* [1 Chr. 11:11 has 'three hundred'] . . . *in one encounter* (v. 8). *Eleazar*, the second *of the three mighty warriors . . . was with David when they taunted the Philistines*

---

41. See, e.g., the relevant commentary sections in Gordon (1986); McCarter (1984); Youngblood (2009); and the article by Garsiel (2011).

(v. 9). This close association in battle implies that *the Three* were elite soldiers in David's immediate service, not just members of David's regular army. Eleazar refused to give ground when Israel retreated, and he *struck down the Philistines till his hand grew tired and froze to the sword*. As heroic as this sounds, the narrator is quick to underscore the real cause of Israel's success: *The LORD brought about a great victory that day* (v. 10). The third of the three, *Shammah*, defended a *field full of lentils* from Philistine encroachment (vv. 11–12). Mention of this odd-seeming detail makes sense in an ancient context, where troops in the field were dependent on foraging and where destroying their enemies' crops was a common strategy (cf. Judg. 6:3–6, 11). Again, Yahweh is credited with bringing about the *great victory* that day (v. 12).[42]

13–17. This section recounts an act of daring by *three of the thirty chief warriors* (v. 13; on *the thirty*, see v. 24 below). They are not named but are apparently to be distinguished from the three mentioned in verses 8–12. The setting is *harvest time* (*qāṣîr*), though 1 Chronicles 11:15 sets the scene at 'the rock' (*ḥaṣṣur*); the two words sound similar in Hebrew. If the former is correct, then the timing of enemy incursion would be similar in motivation to that described above at verses 11–12, namely, to steal or destroy the harvest. David is at the *cave of Adullam*, some 12 miles west of Bethlehem (see on 1 Sam. 22:1), while the Philistines are *encamped in the Valley of Rephaim*, near Bethlehem (see on 2 Sam. 5:18). Bethlehem itself was the site of a *Philistine garrison* (v. 14), and this vexatious situation may have prompted David's wistful comment, *Oh, that someone would get me a drink of water from the well near the gate of Bethlehem!* (v. 15). That the three undertook to do just that is a testimony to their devotion to David; that David, moreover, upon their successful return with Bethlehem water, *refused to drink it* but *instead ... poured it out before the LORD* (v. 16) is a mark of his respect for his men and the sanctity of their lives (v. 17). The end of verse 17 reads literally 'these things did the three warriors [*gibbōrîm*]' and probably refers to the events of verses 13–17 (cf. NRSV, JPS, ESV, etc.) rather than to the events described in the next section (vv. 18–23).

---

42. On the theme of divine victory, see also 1 Sam. 14:15, 23; 19:5; 2 Sam. 8:6, 14.

18–23. *Abishai the brother of Joab* has a long association with David, from the daring night raid into Saul's camp (1 Sam. 26:6–11) to Abishai's rescue of the weary (ageing?) David from the frightening Philistine 'giant' Ishbi-Benob (2 Sam. 21:15–17).[43] The exploit described here may have occurred during David's fugitive years in the wilderness, as Abishai was still in the process of becoming *as famous as the Three* and indeed *chief* over them (*rōʾš* 'head' in v. 18 and *śar* 'prince, chief' in v. 19). There is some question, however, over whether Abishai was *chief of the Three* (NIV) or of the 'Thirty' (NRSV). While the latter is only modestly supported in the ancient witnesses, the immediate context suggests that it may be the better understanding (see below on v. 24).

Benaiah son of Jehoida (v. 20) is known already from 8:18 and 20:23. His memorable exploits noted here – besting *Moab's two mightiest warriors* (NIV) or '[sons] of Ariel of Moab' (JPS), killing a lion (mightiest of beasts and the animal that tested the mettle of kings; see Long [2009a: 350–351; 2009b: 479–480]) and doing so in a pit and on a snowy day (v. 20), and killing a *huge Egyptian* by disarming him and killing him *with his own spear* (v. 21) – rightly earned him as great fame as *the three mighty warriors* (v. 22) and *greater honour than any of the Thirty* (v. 23). *David put him in charge of his bodyguard* (comprising the Kerethites and Pelethites; see 8:18).

24–39a. *Among the Thirty* (v. 24) is not in the Hebrew as a heading, but it is implied in the first entry, which reads literally *Asahel the brother of Joab* was 'among the thirty'. The Chronicles parallel heads the listing with 'The mighty warriors were: Asahel . . .' (1 Chr. 11:26). By one reckoning, the Samuel list actually contains thirty-one men (see below on v. 39b). The *Thirty*, similar to the *Three*, seems to designate an elite force distinguished from and perhaps in charge over David's regular army. In terms of the structure of verses 8–39, the pattern seems to be to begin with those closest to David, *the Three* (vv. 8–12), followed by an account of a daring exploit and exemplary loyalty among *three of the thirty* (vv. 13–17), followed by key officers, Abishai brother of Joab, who

---

43. For Abishai, see also 2 Sam. 2:18, 24; 3:30; 10:10, 14; 16:9, 11; 18:2, 5; 19:21; 20:6, 10.

at times replaced Joab as commander over the army, and Benaiah who was in charge of David's bodyguard (vv. 18–23), followed finally by *the Thirty* (vv. 24–39a).

To comment on each in the list of thirty is beyond the scope of this commentary. But the following brief observations are in order. *Asahel the brother of Joab* heads the list followed by a certain *Elhanan son of Dodo from Bethlehem* (v. 24). On possible confusion of the Elhanan of 21:19 with this Elhanan, see discussion of 21:19. *Eliam son of Ahithophel the Gilonite* (v. 34) recalls the only other mention of an *Eliam* in Samuel, namely, the father of Bathsheba, the wife of Uriah the Hittite (11:3). If these refer to the same individual, then a sense of personal, familial grievance may have contributed to Ahithophel's turning against David during Absalom's rebellion (15:12; see on 11:3; 16:20–23; and 17:1–4). Mention of *Ithai son of Ribai from Gibeah of Benjamin* (v. 29) indicates that David's supporters extended even to citizens of Saul's home town (1 Sam. 10:26; 11:4). Lest all these mighty warriors in support of David seem to lift him to undeserved heights, the last to be named, *Uriah the Hittite* (v. 39a), brings him back down: David was a deeply flawed man much in need of grace and forgiveness. This brief notice prepares for the David we encounter in the last episode (ch. 24) of the Samuel conclusion. But before turning to that, we must do some arithmetic.

39b. *There were thirty-seven in all.* The longer listing of David's mighty men in 1 Chronicles 11 does not include a final summation. Numerous text-critical issues make certainty impossible, but the following is at least one way to arrive at the sum of thirty-seven for the warriors listed in 2 Samuel 23:8–39. First, there are *the Three* named in verses 8–12 and referred to, for example, in verses 18–19, 23. The three of verses 13–17 are counted among *the thirty* (v. 13), so should not be added to the sum. Abishai and Benaiah (vv. 18–23) make two more, bringing us to five so far. In the listing of verses 24–39, a couple of curiosities present themselves in the NIV rendering. Verse 32 refers to *the sons of Jashen* and verse 36 to *the son of Hagri*, but the names of these individuals appear to be lacking. Elsewhere in the list, proper names are always given. Beginning with verse 36, we may note that the Hebrew of MT, *bānî haggādî*, is not vocalized as 'son of' (*ben/bin*) nor 'sons of' (*bĕnê*), nor does it read 'Hagri' but, rather, *haggādî* ('the Gadite').[44] As it stands, verse 36 can be read as 'Bani the Gadite', as indeed it is read in most translations, ancient and modern ('Bani' is a well-attested name: 1 Chr. 6:46; 9:4; Ezra 2:10; Neh. 9:4–5; etc.). This removes one of the two anomalies, where a personal name seemed lacking.

Moving to verse 32, we note, first, that *sons of [bny] Jashen* may involve a dittograph of the last three letters of the immediately preceding *Shaalbonite (šʿlbny)*. We note, second, that the parallel verse in 1 Chronicles 11:34 adds 'the Gizonite' after the proper name. Possibly, then, 2 Samuel 23:32b should not read *sons of Jashen* but, rather, 'Jashen the Gizonite'.[45] If we can assume a proper name in verse 32b ('Jashen the Gizonite')[46] and in verse 36b ('Bani the Gadite'), we arrive at thirty-one named warriors in verses 24–39. Together with *the Three* plus Abishai and Benaiah, this brings the total to thirty-six.

Notably missing from the list is Joab, who despite David's attempts to replace him, always managed to regain top position in the list of David's commanders (20:23). Though not singled out in 23:8–39, Joab does show up in descriptions of *Abishai the brother of Joab son of Zeruiah* (v. 18); of *Asahel the brother of Joab* (v. 24), who heads the list of the Thirty; and of *the armour-bearer of Joab son of Zeruiah* (v. 37). Moreover, Joab will be the first person David addresses in the next chapter (24:2–3). That Joab is not on the lists in 2 Samuel 23 may reflect the fact that his pre-eminence over all David's mighty men is simply assumed or, alternatively, there may be a hint of censure in respect of some of his methods and his occasional defiance of David's orders (e.g. in the deaths of Abner and Absalom). There can be no doubt, though, that Joab was the most

---

44. NIV appears to follow 1 Chr. 11:38 in reading 'Hagri'; the consonants of the two words vary only in terms of two easily confused letters in Hebrew, the *dalet* of the Samuel text appearing as a *resh* in the Chronicles text.

45. Some LXX manuscripts, including the Lucianic recension, attest a gentilic bearing some resemblance to Gizonite (i.e. *gōuni* or *gounei*).

46. On issues surrounding Gizonite (Gunite?) and suggested locations, see *ABD* s.v. 'Gizonite'; McCarter (1984: 492–493).

powerful of David's military officers. Adding Joab to the thirty-six named warriors in verses 8–39 brings the total to thirty-seven.[47]

Meaning
As noted already in the 'Meaning' section to the shorter listing of David's champions in 21:15–22, David very much needed the support of others and was able to earn it. The lengths to which David's men were willing to go for him attest to the character of his leadership and his concern for those under his command. The mutual loyalty of his men to David and of David to his men is evidenced, for instance, in the high-risk adventure described in 23:13–17. Undergirding, or, perhaps better, arching over David's successes was the providential action of Yahweh himself (see, e.g., vv. 10, 12).

F. Royal sin and its resolution (24:1–25)

Context
The final chapter in Samuel fittingly corresponds to the opening episode of the Samuel conclusion (2 Sam. 21 – 24). Both chapters 21 and 24 describe an instance of public suffering brought about by the sinful actions of a king. The royal sinner on the first occasion was Saul (though David may not have been entirely above reproach in his handling of the crisis; see 21:2 and comment). In the present instance, David is by his own admission the king at fault (24:10, 17). It must be noted, however, that 24:1 opens with the statement that *the anger of the LORD burned against Israel*. In this light, the census-taking to which David is incited results, it seems, in a form of discipline for the people whose unspecified actions angered the Lord. The chapter can be divided into three scenes: the taking of the census (vv. 1–9); David's remorse in the context of divine judgment (vv. 10–17); and David's building of an altar as directed by Yahweh and the ending of the plague (vv. 18–25).

---

47. Given the complexity of the textual data, both in Samuel and in Chronicles, various other solutions can be proposed, and, as noted, certainty is elusive; see, e.g., Firth (2009: 532–533).

Comment

1. *Again the anger of the LORD burned against Israel.* This may refer back to the episode of calamity (famine) resulting from *Saul and his blood-stained house* (21:1). Why *the anger of the LORD burned against Israel* in the present circumstance is not stated, but perhaps it involved some act(s) of irreverence; the only other place in Samuel where the precise phrase 'the LORD's anger [*'ap yhwh*] burned against [*ḥrh*]' someone is in 6:7, where Uzzah is struck down for committing an 'irreverent act'[48] in touching the ark. In the light of David's words in verse 17, however, it is possible that Yahweh's anger towards 'Israel' is not so much anger towards the people as towards David himself, though the people certainly pay a price.

Whatever the cause of the Lord's anger, *he incited David against them, saying, 'Go and take a census of Israel and Judah'* (v. 1). This bald statement is perplexing, not least because David is later *conscience-stricken* for taking the census, admits to having *sinned greatly* (v. 10; cf. v. 17) and is punished along with the *people from Dan to Beersheba* (v. 15). If the God of the Bible is himself holy and not one to tempt anyone to sin (cf. Jas 1:13–15), how are we to understand the present passage? While the most natural grammatical antecedent of 'he' in this verse is the Lord, the Chronicler makes Satan the one who 'rose up against Israel and incited David to take a census' (1 Chr. 21:1). Is there a way to make sense of all this?

To begin, we must acknowledge that the presence of evil in the world is beyond full human understanding. That said, various biblical passages may shed some light. First, there are passages that indicate that wilful hardness of heart can be punished with more of the same (Exod. 4:21; Josh. 11:20; 1 Sam. 2:25). False prophets receive lying spirits (1 Kgs 22:20–23); idolatrous prophets will be enticed by the Lord himself and destroyed (Ezek. 14:7–10). Second, divine action takes place against a backdrop of human (mis)behaviour. The story of Balaam tells of a man who asks God for permission to go on a lucrative mission and is refused (Num. 22:10–12). When Balaam persists, however, God eventually says 'go' (v. 20), but then is 'very angry when he went' (v. 22). One is

---

48. If that is how the Hebrew hapax legomenon *šal* is to be rendered.

reminded of the Lord's concession to the people's demand for a king like those of other nations (1 Sam. 8). Third, God sometimes uses an individual or nation as his instrument of judgment and then subsequently punishes them for their own sinful behaviour (e.g. Jer. 25:8–14). Fourth, in view of the Chronicler's attribution of the incitement of David to Satan, the complex picture painted by the book of Job is pertinent; the sovereign God allows the accuser (*haśśāṭān*) to test Job (Job 1:12; 2:6) but is nevertheless displeased with the accuser for doing so (2:3). In both Old and New Testaments, there is a mysterious sense in which the sovereign God accomplishes his will in spite of and even through the unforced sinful acts of people (Prov. 16:4; Acts 4:27–28), even through what Paul refers to as 'a messenger of Satan' (2 Cor. 12:7). This brief survey only begins to scratch the surface, but it suggests that the Samuel and Chronicles descriptions of how David was incited and by whom are not conceptually incompatible.

2–4. In verse 2, David spells out what he wants Joab to do: *Go throughout the tribes of Israel from Dan to Beersheba and enrol the fighting men, so that I may know how many there are*. The reason why David desires this knowledge is not stated, though NIV's mention of 'enroll[ing] the fighting men'[49] suggests that David may wish either to pride himself on his troop strength or to put them to work conquering more territory (cf. Dillard 1985).

Whatever may have been David's motivation,[50] Joab politely objects (v. 3) but is overruled by the king's word (v. 4). That David offers Joab no justification for his insistence may suggest that his motives were questionable. The taking of a census was not unusual

---

49. Most English translations speak of 'counting the people', and this is a fair rendering of the Hebrew. NIV's rendering is also possible, however, as Heb. *'am*, 'people', can connote 'army' or 'troops' (cf. Judg. 20:10; 1 Sam. 14:17; 2 Sam. 2:26; 10:10), while *pāqad* qal can mean 'muster' or 'enrol' (cf. Josh. 8:10; 1 Sam. 11:8; 13:15; 15:4).

50. On this much-debated question, see Greenwood (2010), who surveys various theories before offering his own, namely, that David was prematurely preparing for the building of the temple, which according to 2 Sam. 7 he was not to build.

in the Ancient Near East (Long 2009b: 480). But the purpose of censuses was not, as in modern societies, to establish long-term trends. Rather, the purpose typically involved a specific and immediate need, such as land allocation, taxation, and so on. Thus, censuses were not necessarily welcomed by local populations, which may explain David's including *the army commanders* in the mission (v. 2). Still, neither in the ANE nor in the Bible was the mere taking of a census wrong in itself (cf. Num. 1:1–2; 4:1–2; 26:1–4; but cf. Exod. 30:11–12). So the motivation behind David's census must be the point at issue. Here we might recall the elders' request for a king in 1 Samuel 8, where we argued that the idea of Israel having a king was not the problem but, rather, the elders' desire to have a king of the sort that other nations had.

5–9. The route taken by the census-takers runs in an anti-clockwise direction, beginning on the east side of the Jordan and mentioning especially towns on the outer edges of David's territories (vv. 5–6). Mention of *all the towns of the Hivites and Canaanites* (v. 7), as well as the instruction to go throughout all the tribes of Israel *from Dan to Beersheba* (v. 2), indicates that the census was nevertheless to include *the entire land* (v. 8; cf. Birch 1998: 1380). The journey itself could have been accomplished in a matter of weeks, but the actual taking of the census required much longer. Thus, Joab and his men *came back to Jerusalem at the end of nine months and twenty days* (v. 8).

Joab reported the number of the fighting men . . . In Israel . . . eight hundred thousand . . . and in Judah five hundred thousand (v. 9). As Gordon (1986: 319) remarks, these numbers would imply a total population of some five million. As we have noted on various occasions in our reading of Samuel, how best to read large numbers in the Old Testament is a difficult question (see, e.g., at 1 Sam. 4:2). Sometimes the Hebrew rendered 'thousand' may simply refer to a 'clan' or a 'unit' of much smaller number. Perhaps military figures were sometimes augmented by a factor of ten.[51]

---

51. For a succinct survey of options, and for bibliography, see Long (2009a: 288–289).

10–17. *David was conscience-stricken* (v. 10), as he had been on an earlier occasion (1 Sam. 24:5–6). The precise Hebrew expression for a stricken conscience is used only on these two occasions in the book of Samuel. On both occasions David has taken an action that might seem to be a grasping after more than was rightfully his at the time. Moreover, David's admission of having *done a very foolish thing* (v. 10b) recalls Samuel's earlier charge to Saul that he had *done a foolish thing* (1 Sam. 13:13).[52] Unlike Saul, however, David does not seek to explain or excuse his folly. David's repentance is genuine. As we have noted before, however, even genuine repentance does not sweep away all possible consequences of folly or sin (cf. 12:13–14).

As David arises *the next morning* (v. 11), a prophet named Gad is already on his way to present David with a difficult choice (v. 12). For his folly, David is presented with three possible consequences: *three years of famine, three months of fleeing from your enemies* or *three days of plague in your land* (v. 13). That the Lord allows David to choose but one of the three suggests an element of mercy, as famine, sword and plague are often all three threatened (cf. Lev. 26:23–26; Deut. 28:21–26; 32:24–25; 1 Kgs 8:37; 2 Chr. 20:9; Isa. 51:19; Ezek. 6:11–12). In *deep distress*, David's response to Gad is, *Let us fall into the hands of the LORD, for his mercy is great* (v. 14). David has gained experience in both the cruelty of human enemies and the mercy of the Lord.[53] His choice eliminates the sword option, but leaves famine and plague both as possibilities. The Lord sends the shorter, three-day option, *and seventy thousand of the people from Dan to Beersheba* die (v. 15). Verses 16 and 17 show something of the heart of God and of the man after God's own heart. Before the angel/agent (*malʾāk*) of the Lord[54] lays his hand on Jerusalem, the Lord says,

---

52. Two other times in Samuel the verb *skl* is used, once in Saul's admission to David that in seeking to harm him he had *acted like a fool* (1 Sam. 26:21) and also in David's request that the Lord *turn Ahithophel's counsel into foolishness* (2 Sam. 15:31).
53. See v. 16. On divine mercy generally, see Exod. 34:6–7; Neh. 9:17; Pss 30:5; 86:14–16; 103:8–10; Isa. 54:7–8; 60:10; Hos. 11:8–9; Joel 2:13.
54. On God's angels as agents of judgment, see Exod. 33:2; Pss 35:5–6; 78:49; Matt. 13:41; Acts 12:23.

Enough! Withdraw your hand (v. 16). Apparently the three days have not yet elapsed when the Lord's mercy intervenes. In verse 17 David again confesses his sin (cf. v. 10) and, unaware that the Lord has already stayed his hand, pleads that he may be allowed to take the blow in the place of the people. Like God himself, David is grieved by his people's suffering and asks that judgment fall not on them but *on me and my family* (lit. 'and on the house of my father').

18–25. As was noted in passing in verse 16, the hand of judgment was stayed at the threshing floor of a Jebusite named Araunah. Now at this point in the narrative Gad, the prophet through whom the Lord had announced judgment in verses 11–13, reappears with a message from the Lord: David is to *build an altar to the L*ORD *on the threshing floor of Araunah the Jebusite* (v. 18). So David goes up in obedience to the Lord (v. 19). Seeing king and officials approaching, Araunah adopts the appropriate posture and asks why the king has come. David responds that he wishes to buy the threshing floor and build an altar, *that the plague on the people may be stopped* (v. 21). Araunah offers to give all that David needs, adding, *May the L*ORD *your God accept you* (vv. 22–23), but David is insistent: *I will not sacrifice to the L*ORD *my God burnt offerings that cost me nothing* (v. 24). David seems to understand that while grace and forgiveness are free to the truly repentant, true repentance leads to worship, and worship is never to be cheap or careless (cf. Mal. 1:6–14; 2 Cor. 8:1–5). So David buys, builds and worships. *Then the L*ORD *answered his prayer on behalf of the land, and the plague on Israel was stopped* (v. 25).

Meaning
While the significance of the threshing floor of Araunah as the future site of Solomon's temple may have contributed to the decision to conclude the book of Samuel with this episode, the significance of these events goes far deeper.[55] In this final chapter of the Samuel conclusion, we see David as he truly was, a flawed sinner, but a sinner who knew how to repent deeply (cf. 12:13; Ps. 51). David's repentance led to worship and a restored relationship with his God.

---

55. Nothing in Samuel actually connects this story to the site of the future temple.

In this respect, David was quite unlike his predecessor Saul (see 1 Sam. 15:24–31 and *passim*). David was not immune to lust and the abuse of power. But David in the end was a man who gave weight to God. His relationship with Yahweh, though at times troubled, was genuine. David loved God (cf. Ps. 18:1). And he cared for the people of God. As their shepherd-king, he asked that the hand of judgment fall not on them but on him (v. 17). In David's willingness to suffer in the place of his 'sheep', we catch a glimpse of the greater shepherd-king to come (Matt. 2:6; 25:32–34), who would lay down his life for his sheep.[56]

---

56. John 10:11; Rom. 5:8; 6:23; 1 Cor. 15:3; Phil. 2:8; Heb. 9:15; 12:2; 1 Pet. 3:18.